Microsoft® Office 2008 for Mac

ILLUSTRATED

BRIEF

Kelley P. Shaffer
Marjorie Hunt

Australia • Brazil • Japan • Korea • Mexico • Singapore • Spain • United Kingdom • United States

COURSE TECHNOLOGY
CENGAGE Learning

**Microsoft® Office 2008 for Mac—
Illustrated Brief**
Kelley P. Shaffer/Marjorie Hunt

Executive Editor: Marjorie Hunt

Senior Product Manager: Karen Stevens

Associate Acquisitions Editor: Brandi Shailer

Associate Product Manager: Michelle Camisa

Editorial Assistant: Kim Klasner

Director of Marketing: Cheryl Costantini

Marketing Manager: Ryan DeGrote

Marketing Coordinator: Kristen Panciocco

Developmental Editor: Jeanne Herring

Senior Content Project Manager: Jill Braiewa

Associate Content Project Manager: Lisa Weidenfeld

Art Director: Jill Ort

Print Buyer: Fola Orekoya

Text Designer: Joseph Lee, Black Fish Design

Copyeditor: Mary Kemper

Proofreader: Wendy Benedetto

Indexer: Liz Cunningham

QA Reviewers: Jeff Schwartz, Marianne Snow,
   Susan Whalen

Cover Artist: Mark Hunt

Compositor: GEX Publishing Services

For product information and technology assistance, contact us at
Cengage Learning Customer & Sales Support, 1-800-354-9706
For permission to use material from this text or product, submit all requests online at **www.cengage.com/permissions**
Further permissions questions can be emailed to
permissionrequest@cengage.com

Library of Congress Control Number: 2009929878

ISBN-13: 978-1-4390-4047-8

ISBN-10: 1-4390-4047-8

Course Technology
20 Channel Center Street
Boston, MA 02210
USA

Apple product screen shot(s) courtesy of Apple Incorporated.

Intel product image(s) reprinted with permission from Intel Corporation.

Adventuretravel.com Web site image(s) used with permission from Adventuretravel.com.

Figures A-8A, A-18, and B-3C courtesy of Kelly Coursey-Gray.

Cengage Learning is a leading provider of customized learning solutions with office locations around the globe, including Singapore, the United Kingdom, Australia, Mexico, Brazil, and Japan. Locate your local office at:
www.cengage.com/global

Cengage Learning products are represented in Canada by Nelson Education, Ltd.

To learn more about Course Technology, visit **www.cengage.com/coursetechnology**

Purchase any of our products at your local college store or at our preferred online store **www.ichapters.com**

Printed in the United States of America
1 2 3 4 5 6 7 15 14 13 12 11 10 09

About This Book

Welcome to *Microsoft® Office 2008 for Mac—Illustrated Brief*! Since the first book in the Illustrated Series was published in 1994, millions of students have used various texts in the Illustrated series to master software skills and computer concepts. We are proud to bring you this new Illustrated book on Microsoft Office 2008 for Mac, the best-selling office suite for the Mac operating system.

This textbook is designed to introduce you to the Mac operating system v.10.5, also known as Leopard, and to help you become productive with Office 2008 for Mac. Leopard has many new features that compliment the power and flexibility that are inherent in every Mac. With new view options and an updated sidebar, the functionality of Finder has increased dramatically.

Office 2008 for Mac embraces the unique features of the Mac in new and exciting ways. Prior to this version of the Office Suite, Microsoft has produced editions for the Mac and PC that were very similar. The concepts and many of the operating commands were universal. This is no longer the case. Microsoft has redesigned the interface by adding an Elements Gallery, combining the Toolbox and Formatting Palette from the 2004 edition, and drastically expanding the flexibility and functionality of the software.

The Word, Excel, PowerPoint, and Integration units in this book are adapted from our Windows-based text *Microsoft Office 2007 Illustrated Brief* (1-4390-3789-2). So, if you need to teach Office to a mix of students using both Macs and PCs, using these two books together is a good solution.

The unique design of this book, which presents each skill on two facing pages, makes it easy for novices to absorb and understand new skills, and also makes it easy for more experienced computer users to progress through the lessons quickly, with minimal reading required. We hope you enjoy exploring the features of Office 2008 for Mac as you work through this book!

Author Acknowledgments

This book has taken me on an incredible journey. I have a new respect for the authoring process and have come to realize and appreciate the manpower involved to transform classroom lessons and ideas into print. Words cannot truly express the gratitude I feel for all the people that have devoted their time and effort into producing this book. I couldn't have asked for a better team of professionals to guide, edit, and mentor me through this process. Course Technology has provided incredible resources and personnel that have shown unwavering faith in this book. Thanks to Karen Stevens for keeping me on task, Mary Kemper for editing a novice, and especially Jeanne Herring for all her guidance during this process and especially her patience. I'd also like to thank the remaining team members for their expertise on this project.

Finally, to Matt, Jordan, and Sami, thanks for being so supportive and making sacrifices while I turned this idea into a reality.

Kelley Shaffer

Preface

Welcome to *Microsoft® Office 2008 for Mac— Illustrated Brief.* The unique page design of the book makes it a great learning tool for both new and experienced users. Each skill is presented on two facing pages so that you don't have to turn the page to find a screen shot or finish a paragraph. See the illustration on the right to learn more about the pedagogical and design elements of a typical lesson.

This book is an ideal learning tool for a wide range of learners—the "rookies" will find the clean design easy to follow and focused with only essential information presented, and the "hot shots" will appreciate being able to move quickly through the lessons to find the information they need without reading a lot of text. The design also makes this a great reference after the course is over!

About This Book

This all-new text covers everything students need to create documents, spreadsheets, and presentations with the Mac. Here are some highlights of what's included:

- **Learn important Office skills**—Coverage includes creating and formatting documents in Word, working with functions and charts in Excel, and creating polished presentations with PowerPoint.

- **Discover the Office for Mac interface**— Includes an interactive Elements Gallery, Standard toolbar buttons identified by name, and expanded Help. The Toolbox and Formatting Palette have been combined into one interactive tool and offer contextual groups that appear only when needed.

- **Teach both Mac and PC skills**—This text was designed to make teaching in a dual-platform lab easier. Office units correspond to similar units in *Microsoft Office 2007—Illustrated Brief* (1-4390-3789-2).

Each two-page spread focuses on a single skill.

Concise text introduces the basic principles in the lesson and integrates a real-world case study.

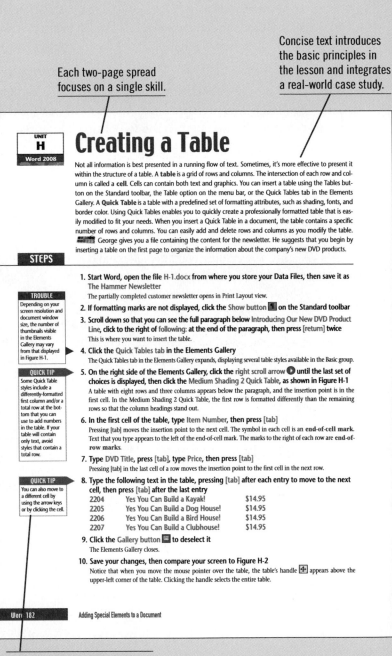

Hints as well as troubleshooting advice appear right where you need them—next to the step itself.

Every lesson features large, full-color representations of what the screen should look like as students complete the numbered steps.

Application tabs indicate which section of the book you are in.

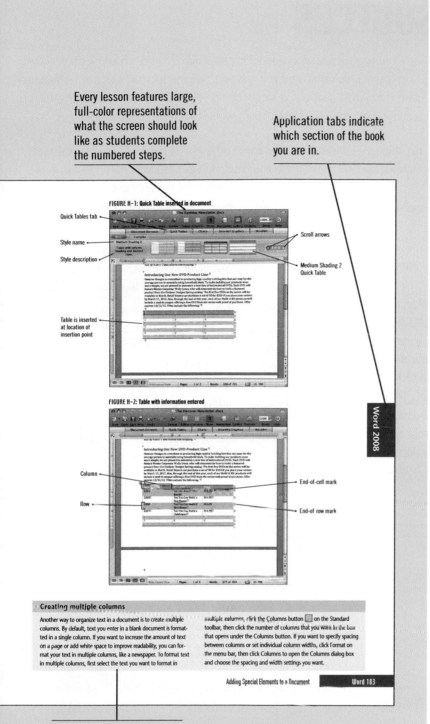

Clues to Use boxes provide concise information that expands on the lesson skill or describes a related task.

• **Explore new features in Leopard**— Preview page one and a detailed list of files with Cover Flow, or use Quick Look to view the contents of a file without actually opening it.

• **Stay up-to-date with Safari 4**—View previously visited Web sites in the book-marks library using Cover Flow view, or review thumbnails of favorite Web sites using Top Sites.

Assignments

The lessons use Quest Specialty Travel, a fictional adventure travel agency, and Outdoor Designs, a fictional recreational product company, as the case studies. The assignments on the light purple pages at the end of each unit increase in difficulty. Additional case studies provide a variety of interesting and relevant exercises for students to practice skills.

Assignments include:

• **Concepts Reviews** consist of multiple choice, matching, and screen identification questions.

• **Skills Reviews** provide additional hands-on, step-by-step reinforcement.

• **Independent Challenges** are case projects requiring critical thinking and application of the unit skills.

• **Real Life Independent Challenges** are practical exercises to help students create documents to assist them with their everyday lives.

• **Visual Workshops** are practical, self-graded capstone projects that help develop independent problem solving skills.

Instructor Resources

The Instructor Resources CD is Course Technology's way of putting the resources and information needed to teach and learn effectively into your hands. With an integrated array of teaching and learning tools that offer you and your students a broad range of technology-based instructional options, we believe this CD represents the highest quality and most cutting edge resources available to instructors today. Many of these resources are available at *www.cengage.com/coursetechnology*. The resources available with this book are:

• **Instructor's Manual**—Available as an electronic file, the Instructor's Manual includes detailed lecture topics with teaching tips for each unit.

• **Sample Syllabus**—Prepare and customize your course easily using this sample course outline.

• **PowerPoint Presentations**—Each unit has a corresponding PowerPoint presentation that you can use in lecture, distribute to your students, or customize to suit your course.

• **Figure Files**—The figures in the text are provided on the Instructor Resources CD to help you illustrate key topics or concepts. You can create traditional overhead transparencies by printing the figure files. Or you can create electronic slide shows by using the figures in a presentation program such as PowerPoint.

• **Solutions to Exercises**—Solutions to Exercises contains files students are asked to create or modify in the lessons and end-of-unit material. Also provided in this section is a document outlining the solutions for the end-of-unit Concepts Review, Skills Review, and Independent Challenges.

• **Data Files for Students**—To complete many of the units in this book, your students will need Data Files. You can post the Data Files on a file server for students to copy, or instruct students to follow the steps on page xvi to download the data files from the book's Web page.

Instruct students to use the Data Files List included on the Review Pack and the Instructor Resources CD. This list gives instructions on copying and organizing files.

• **ExamView**—ExamView is a powerful testing software package that allows you to create and administer printed and computer (LAN-based) exams. ExamView includes hundreds of questions that correspond to the topics covered in this text, enabling students to generate detailed study guides that include page references for further review. The computer-based testing components allow students to take exams at their computers, and also saves you time by grading each exam automatically.

CourseCasts – Learning on the Go. Always Available...Always Relevant.

Our fast-paced world is driven by technology. You know because you are an active participant—always on the go, always keeping up with technological trends, and always learning new ways to embrace technology to power your life.

Let CourseCasts, hosted by Ken Baldauf of Florida State University, be your guide into weekly updates in this ever-changing space. These timely, relevant podcasts are produced weekly and are available for download at *http://coursecasts.course.com* or directly from iTunes (search by CourseCasts).

CourseCasts are a perfect solution to getting students (and even instructors) to learn on the go!

Brief Contents

Preface   iv

CONCEPTS   **Unit A: Understanding Essential Computer Concepts**   1

MAC OS X   **Unit B: Getting Started with Mac OS X Leopard**   33

MAC OS X   **Unit C: Understanding File Management**   57

INTERNET   **Unit D: Getting Started with Safari**   81

OFFICE 2008   **Unit E: Getting Started with Microsoft Office 2008 for Mac**   105

WORD 2008   **Unit F: Creating a Document**   131

WORD 2008   **Unit G: Enhancing a Document**   157

WORD 2008   **Unit H: Adding Special Elements to a Document**   181

EXCEL 2008   **Unit I: Creating and Enhancing a Worksheet**   207

EXCEL 2008   **Unit J: Using Complex Formulas and Functions**   235

EXCEL 2008   **Unit K: Working with Charts**   259

POWERPOINT 2008   **Unit L: Creating a Presentation**   285

POWERPOINT 2008   **Unit M: Polishing and Running a Presentation**   309

INTEGRATION   **Unit N: Integrating Office 2008 Programs**   335

Appendix A: Setting System Preferences   **Appendix 1**

Glossary   **Glossary 1**

Index   **Index 1**

Contents

Preface iv

| CONCEPTS |

Unit A: Understanding Essential Computer Concepts   1

Investigating Types of Computers...2
    Understanding terminals

Examining Computer Systems...4
    Comparing microprocessor speeds

Examining Input Devices...6
    Using assistive devices

Examining Output Devices...8

Investigating Data Processing...10

Understanding Memory..12
    Upgrading RAM

Understanding Storage Media...14
    Erasing and rewriting on CDs and DVDs

Exploring Data Communications..16

Learning about Networks...18
    Understanding telecommunications

Learning about Security Threats...20
    Protecting information with passwords

Understanding System Software...22

Understanding Application Software 24
    Understanding object linking and embedding (OLE)

Concepts Review...26

Independent Challenges...29

| MAC OS X |

Unit B: Getting Started with Mac OS X Leopard   33

Starting Mac OS X Leopard 34

Using a Pointing Device..36

Starting a Program..38
    Starting a program not found on the dock

Moving and Resizing Windows..40

Using Menus 42
    Keyboard shortcuts

Using Dialog Boxes...44

Getting Mac Help 46
    Opening Help for programs

Ending a Leopard Session 48

Concepts Review 50

Skills Review 52

Independent Challenges 53

Visual Workshop 56

MAC OS X   **Unit C: Understanding File Management**   **57**

Understanding File Management 58
> Organizing your folders and files efficiently

Opening the Finder Window 60
> The home folder and its contents

Changing Views 62

Creating and Saving Documents 64

Opening, Editing, and Printing Files 66

Copying, Renaming, and Moving Files 68
> Using drag and drop to copy and move files

Searching for Files 70
> Working with stacks

Deleting and Restoring Files 72
> Emptying the Trash

Concepts Review 74

Skills Review 76

Independent Challenges 78

Visual Workshop 80

INTERNET   **Unit D: Getting Started with Safari**   **81**

Understanding Web Browsers 82
> The Internet, computer networks, and intranets

Starting and Exploring Safari 84
> Understanding URLs

Viewing and Navigating Web Pages 86
> Setting the home page

Using Tabbed Browsing 88
> Quitting Safari when you have multiple tabs open

Bookmarking Web Pages 90
> Creating and organizing bookmarks

Printing a Web Page 92
> Copying information from a Web page

Searching for Information 94
> Handling pop-ups

Getting Help and Exiting Safari...96
    Saving or mailing a Web page
Concepts Review..98
Skills Review...99
Independent Challenges..101
Visual Workshop..104

OFFICE 2008   **Unit E: Getting Started with Microsoft Office 2008 for Mac**   **105**

Understanding Office 2008 for Mac..106
Starting an Office Program..108
Using Menus and the Standard Toolbar..................................110
Exploring the Toolbox..112
Viewing the Elements Gallery...114
Saving and Closing a File..116
    Saving files and understanding the Microsoft Office file formats
Creating a New File with a Template......................................118
Getting Help and Quitting an Office Program..........................120
Concepts Review..122
Skills Review...123
Independent Challenges..126
Visual Workshop..130

WORD 2008   **Unit F: Creating a Document**   **131**

Creating a New Document from an Existing File.......................132
Entering Text in a Document...134
    Using AutoCorrect
Selecting and Editing Text...136
    Using Click and Type
Copying Text...138
    Copying and pasting items with the Scrapbook
Moving Text..140
Finding and Replacing Text...142
    Using the Reference Tools in the Toolbox
Formatting Text Using the Formatting Palette.........................144
Checking Spelling and Grammar..146
    Translating words or documents into other languages
Previewing and Printing a Document......................................148
Concepts Review..150
Skills Review...151
Independent Challenges..153
Visual Workshop..156

WORD 2008

Unit G: Enhancing a Document 157

Changing Font and Font Size 158
Changing Font Color, Font Style, and Font Effects 160
Changing Alignment and Line Spacing 162
Changing Margin Settings 164
Setting Tabs...166
Setting Indents 168
Adding Bulleted and Numbered Lists...170
Applying Styles 172
Concepts Review...174
Skills Review 175
Independent Challenges..177
Visual Workshop...180

WORD 2008

Unit H: Adding Special Elements to a Document 181

Creating a Table 182
    Creating multiple columns
Inserting and Deleting Table Columns and Rows 184
    Creating a table with the Draw Table command
Formatting a Table 186
    Adding SmartArt
Adding Clip Art..188
Inserting Footnotes and Citations 190
Inserting a Header or Footer..192
Adding Borders and Shading...194
    Inserting manual page breaks
Working with Themes 196
Concepts Review..198
Skills Review 199
Independent Challenges..201
Visual Workshop...206

EXCEL 2008

Unit I: Creating and Enhancing a Worksheet 207

Navigating a Workbook 208
Entering Values and Labels..210
    Using data entry keys
Changing Column Width and Row Height 212
Using Formulas..214
    Using absolute cell references
Editing a Worksheet 216
    Copying, moving, and pasting cells

Changing Alignment and Number Format 218
    Changing the number format
Changing Fonts, Borders, and Shading 220
Adding Headers and Footers..222
Printing a Worksheet 224
    Alternatives to printing
Concepts Review...226
Skills Review 227
Independent Challenges..230
Visual Workshop...234

EXCEL 2008

Unit J: Using Complex Formulas and Functions   **235**

Creating Complex Formulas..236
Understanding Functions..238
Using AutoSum 240
    Using ledger sheets
Using Date and Time Functions 242
    Understanding how dates are calculated using serial values
Using Statistical Functions 244
Applying Conditional Formatting 246
Sorting Rows in a Worksheet 248
    Adding subtotals and grand totals to a worksheet
Filtering Data..250
Concepts Review...252
Skills Review 253
Independent Challenges..255
Visual Workshop...258

EXCEL 2008

Unit K: Working with Charts   **259**

Understanding and Planning a Chart 260
Creating a Chart 262
Moving and Resizing a Chart and Chart Objects...264
Adding Chart Objects and Applying Styles 266
Customizing Chart Objects..268
    Fine-tune your formatting
Enhancing a Chart 270
    Using WordArt in a chart
Creating a Pie Chart 272
Adding Text and Printing Charts 274
    Guidelines for enhancing a chart
Concepts Review...276

Skills Review 277

Independent Challenges..280

Visual Workshop...284

POWERPOINT 2008 | **Unit L: Creating a Presentation** | **285**

Viewing a Presentation 286

Moving among slides in a slide show

Using a Theme 288

Entering Text on a Slide 290

Formatting Text 292

Adding a Text Box..294

Creating a custom theme

Creating SmartArt...296

Adding a Header and Footer..298

Editing the slide master

Printing Handouts 300

Converting a presentation to a PDF file

Concepts Review...302

Skills Review 303

Independent Challenges...305

Visual Workshop...308

POWERPOINT 2008 | **Unit M: Polishing and Running a Presentation** | **309**

Adding a Shape..310

Resizing and modifying images

Adding Clip Art...312

Downloading clip art from Microsoft Office Online

Working with Pictures 314

Adding Video and Sound 316

Inserting media files

Customizing a Slide Show 318

Setting Slide Timing and Transitions 320

Animating Slide Objects...322

Creating Speaker Notes..324

Concepts Review..326

Skills Review 327

Independent Challenges...329

Visual Workshop...334

Inserting an Excel Chart onto a PowerPoint Slide 336

Creating PowerPoint Slides from a Word Document...338
> Creating an outline in Word for use in a PowerPoint presentation

Saving a PowerPoint Presentation for the Web 340
> Customizing the presentation for the Web

Inserting Text from a Word File into an Open Document.......................................342

Linking Excel Data to a Word Document..344
> The differences between embedding and linking data

Updating Linked Excel Data in a Word Document 346

Inserting Data Source Placeholders in a Word Document.....................................348

Performing a Mail Merge 350
> Using Word to create a data source

Concepts Review..352

Skills Review 353

Independent Challenges..355

Visual Workshop..360

Appendix A: Setting System Preferences   **Appendix 1**

Glossary   **Glossary 1**

Index   **Index 1**

Read This Before You Begin

Frequently Asked Questions

What are Data Files?

A Data File is a partially completed Word document, Excel workbook, PowerPoint presentation, or another type of file that you use to complete the steps in the units and exercises to create the final document that you submit to your instructor. The Data Files that you need for each unit are listed on the opening page of each unit.

Where are the Data Files?

Your instructor will provide the Data Files to you or direct you to a location on a network drive from which you can download them. Alternatively, you can follow the instructions on page xvi to download the Data Files from this book's Web page. As you download the files, select where to store them, such as a hard drive, a network server, or a USB storage device. The instructions in the lessons refer to "the location where you store your Data Files" when referring to the Data Files for the book.

What software was used to write and test this book?

This book was written and tested on a computer with a typical installation of Mac OS X Leopard (OS X v10.5) and Office 2008 for Mac, Home and Student edition. The browser used for any steps that require a browser is Safari 4.

In this book, Macintosh commands instruct users to press the [return] key to enter information. On some newer Macintosh keyboards, this key may be named [enter] or the keyboard may include both [return] and [enter].

Do I need to be connected to the Internet to complete the steps and exercises in this book?

Some of the exercises in this book assume that your computer is connected to the Internet. If you are not connected to the Internet, see your instructor for information on how to complete the exercises.

What do I do if my screen is different from the figures shown in this book?

This book was written and tested on computers with monitors set at a resolution of 1024 x 768. If your screen shows more or less information than the figures in the book, your monitor is probably set at a higher or lower resolution. If you don't see something on your screen, you might have to scroll down or up to see the object identified in the figures. In some cases, the figures will not match your screen because the program windows have been resized or moved in an effort to make the figures as easy to read as possible. Be aware that the tops of dialog boxes and windows may appear to slip beneath the menu bar when you drag them near the top of the screen.

Downloading Data Files for This Book

In order to complete many of the lesson steps and exercises in this book, you are asked to open and save Data Files. A **Data File** is a partially completed Word document, Excel workbook, PowerPoint presentation, or another type of file that you use as a starting point to complete the steps in the units and exercises. The benefit of using a Data File is that it saves you the time and effort needed to create a file; you can simply open a Data File, save it with a new name (so the original file remains intact), then make changes to it to complete lesson steps or an exercise. Your instructor will provide the Data Files to you or direct you to a location on a network drive from which you can download them. Alternatively, you can follow the instructions in this lesson to download the Data Files from this book's Web page.

1. Start your browser, type www.cengage.com/coursetechnology in the address bar, then press [return]

2. Click in the Enter ISBN Search text box, type 9781439040478, then click Search

3. When the page opens for this textbook, click the About this Product link for the Student, point to Student Downloads to expand the menu, and then click the Data Files for Students link (an empty browser window may open)

4. Close your browser and then open your Downloads folder

5. Double-click the file 9781439040478_Data.hqx in the Downloads folder, then navigate to the 9781439040478_Data folder containing the Data Files

   You are now ready to open the required files.

Understanding Essential Computer Concepts

Files You Will Need:

No files needed.

Computers are essential tools in almost all kinds of activity in virtually every type of business. In this unit, you will learn about computers and their components. You will learn about input and output, how a computer processes data and stores information, how information is transmitted, and ways to secure that information. Finally, you will learn about system and application software.  Quest Specialty Travel is expanding its North American offices and just purchased Sheehan Tours, an established travel agency in Boston, Massachusetts. Sheehan Tours has been in business for over 40 years and has a large customer base. Unfortunately, its computer system is tremendously outdated. Its office contains a hodgepodge of computer equipment, most of which has been purchased used. The office staff still carries data between computers on floppy disks, and only one computer is connected to the Internet. Kevin O'Brien, the manager of the New York office, has been sent to the new Boston office to help them switch to Quest's business practices. He has already ordered and installed new computer equipment. His next task is to teach the staff how to use the new equipment.

OBJECTIVES

Investigate types of computers

Examine computer systems

Examine input devices

Examine output devices

Investigate data processing

Understand memory

Understand storage media

Explore data communications

Learn about networks

Learn about security threats

Understand system software

Understand application software

Investigating Types of Computers

A **computer** is an electronic device that accepts information and instructions from a user, manipulates the information according to the instructions, displays the information in some way, and stores the information for retrieval later. Computers are classified by their size, speed, and capabilities. Most of the staff at Sheehan Tours do not know anything about computers except for the ones that sit on their desks, so Kevin decides to start with a basic explanation of the types of computers available.

DETAILS

The following list describes various types of computers:

QUICK TIP

Machines dedicated primarily to playing games, such as the Xbox and PlayStation, are also computers.

- **Personal computers** are computers typically used by a single user, for use in the home or office. Personal computers are used for general computing tasks such as word processing, manipulating numbers, working with photographs or graphics, exchanging e-mail, and accessing the Internet.

- A personal computer is available as a **desktop computer**, which is designed to sit compactly on a desk; as a **notebook computer** (also referred to as a **laptop computer**), which is small, lightweight, and designed for portability; or as a **tablet PC**, which is also designed for portability, but includes the capability of recognizing ordinary handwriting on the screen. Figure A-1 shows a MacBook, one of Apple's notebook computers. Desktop personal computers can be purchased for as little as $300, but high-end notebooks can cost more than $3500. A notebook computer with similar capability is usually more expensive than a desktop computer, and tablet PCs are generally more expensive than notebook computers. Many computer users spend between $800 and $1500 when purchasing a new personal computer.

- **Hand-held computers** are small computers that fit in the palm of your hand. Hand-held computers have more limited capabilities than personal computers.

  - **PDAs** (**personal digital assistants**) are generally used to maintain an electronic appointment book, address book, calculator, and notepad. See Figure A-2. High-end PDAs are all-in-one devices that can send and receive e-mails and make phone calls.
  - **MP3 players** are hand-held computers that are primarily used to store and play music, although some models can also be used to play digital movies or television shows.
  - Cell phones are another type of hand-held computer. In addition to being used to make telephone calls, cell phones store contact information. Many cell phones can take and store digital photos and video and play and store music. Most cell phones have additional capabilities such as built-in calculator programs. High-end cell phones can also perform many of the same functions as a PDA.

- **Mainframe computers** are used by larger businesses and government agencies to provide centralized storage, processing, and management for large amounts of data. The price of a mainframe computer varies widely, from several hundred thousand dollars to several million dollars.

- The largest and fastest computers, called **supercomputers**, are used by large corporations and government agencies when the tremendous volume of data would seriously delay processing on a mainframe computer. A supercomputer, like the one shown in Figure A-3, can cost tens of millions of dollars.

Understanding terminals

When an organization uses mainframes or supercomputers, each user inputs processing requests and views output through a **terminal** or a **terminal emulator**. A terminal has a keyboard for input and a monitor for output, but processes little or no data on its own. A terminal emulator is a personal computer, workstation, or server that uses special software to imitate a terminal so that the PC can communicate with the mainframe or supercomputer for complex data processing.

FIGURE A-1: Apple's MacBook

FIGURE A-2: Apple's iPhone

FIGURE A-3: Supercomputer

Examining Computer Systems

A **computer system** includes computer hardware and software. **Hardware** refers to the physical components of a computer. **Software** refers to the intangible components of a computer system, particularly the **programs**, or lists of instructions, that the computer needs to perform a specific task. Kevin explains how computers work and points out the main components of a computer system.

The following list provides an overview of computer system components and how they work:

* The design and construction of a computer is referred to as its **architecture** or **configuration**. The technical details about each hardware component are called **specifications**. For example, a computer system might be configured to include a printer; a specification for that printer might be a print speed of eight pages per minute or the capacity to print in color.

* The hardware and the software of a computer system work together to process data. **Data** refers to the words, numbers, figures, sounds, and graphics that describe people, events, things, and ideas. Modifying data is referred to as **processing**.

* In a computer, processing tasks occur on the **motherboard**, which is located inside the computer and is the main electronic component of the computer. The motherboard is a **circuit board**, which is a rigid piece of insulating material with **circuits**, electrical paths, on it that control specific functions. See Figure A-4. The motherboard contains the following processing hardware:

    * The **microprocessor**, also called the **processor** or the **central processing unit** (**CPU**), consists of transistors and electronic circuits on a silicon **chip** (an integrated circuit embedded in semiconductor material). See Figure A-5. The processor is mounted on the motherboard and is responsible for executing instructions to process information.
    * **Cards** are removable **circuit boards** that are inserted into slots in the motherboard to expand the capabilities of the motherboard. For example, a sound card translates the digital audio information from the computer into analog sounds that the human ear can hear.

* The data or instructions you type into the computer are called **input**. The result of the computer processing input is referred to as **output**. The computer itself takes care of the processing functions, but it needs additional components, called **peripheral devices**, to accomplish the input, output, and storage functions.

    * You use an **input device**, such as a keyboard or a mouse, to enter data and issue commands. **Commands** are input instructions that tell the computer how to process data. For example, you might want to center the title and double-space the text of a report. You use the appropriate commands in the word processing program that instruct the computer to modify the data you have input so the report text is double-spaced and the report title is centered.
    * Output can be in many different forms, including reports, documents, graphs, sounds, and pictures. Computers produce output using **output devices**, such as a monitor or printer.
    * The output you create using a computer can be stored either inside the computer itself or on an external storage device, such as a DVD. You will learn more about storage devices later in this unit.

FIGURE A-4: Motherboard

FIGURE A-5: Microprocessor

Comparing microprocessor speeds

How fast a computer can process instructions depends partially on the speed of the microprocessor, which is determined by its clock speed, word size, and cache size, and whether it is single or dual core. **Clock speed** is measured in **megahertz (MHz)**, millions of cycles per second, or in **gigahertz (GHz)**, billions of cycles per second. **Word size** refers to the amount of data that is processed at one time. Finally, a **dual-core processor**, one that has two processors on a single chip, can process information up to twice as fast as a **single-core processor**, one with one processor on the chip.

Examining Input Devices

Before a computer can produce useful information, people must get data into the computer. This is accomplished by using input devices. In a typical personal computer system, you input data and commands by using an input device such as a keyboard or a mouse. Computers can also receive input from a storage device. You will learn about storage devices later in this unit. As Kevin explains peripheral devices to the Sheehan Tours staff, they ask several questions about input devices. For example, one person doesn't understand the difference between a mouse and a trackball. Kevin continues his explanation with a discussion of various input devices.

DETAILS

There are many types of input devices, as described below:

QUICK TIP

Another way to avoid repetitive motion injuries is to take frequent breaks when working at a computer and stretch your hands and wrists.

- One of the most frequently used input devices is a **keyboard**. The top keyboard in Figure A-6 is a standard Mac keyboard. The bottom keyboard in Figure A-6 is **ergonomic**, which means that it has been designed to fit the natural placement of your hands and should reduce the risk of repetitive-motion injuries. It also has several additional keys programmed as shortcut keys to commonly used functions.

- Another common input device is a **pointing device**, which controls the **pointer**, a small arrow or other symbol on the screen. Pointing devices are used to select commands and manipulate text or graphics on the screen.

  - The most popular pointing device for a desktop computer is a **mouse**, such as the one shown on the left side in Figure A-7. An ordinary mouse has a rolling ball on its underside, and an optical mouse has a tiny camera on its underside that takes pictures as the mouse is moved. You control the pointer by moving the entire mouse. A mouse usually has two or more buttons for clicking commands. A mouse might also have a **scroll wheel** that you roll to scroll the page on the screen and that may function as one of the buttons.
  - The **trackball**, such as the one shown on the right side in Figure A-7, is similar to a mouse except that the rolling ball is on the top side and you control the movement of the pointer by moving only the ball.
  - Notebook computers are usually equipped with a trackpad or a pointing stick. See Figure A-8. A **trackpad** is a touch-sensitive device that you drag your finger over to control the pointer. The buttons or button are located in front of the trackpad. Some Mac notebook computers are equipped with a Multi-Touch trackpad, which does not have any buttons in front of it; the trackpad itself is the button. A **pointing stick** is a small, eraser-like device embedded among the typing keys that you push up, left, right, or down to move the pointer. Two buttons equivalent to mouse buttons are located in front of the spacebar.

- A **scanner** is a device that transfers the content on a piece of paper into memory. To do this, you place a piece of paper on the glass, a beam of light moves across the glass similar to a photocopier, and stores the image or words on the paper as digital information. You can scan a document or a photo and save it as an image file, or you can scan a document and have the text "read" by the scanner and saved in a document file for editing later.

- Microphones are another type of input device. You can use them to record sound for certain types of files, or, if you have the voice-recognition software, you can use them to input data and commands.

- Input devices can be connected to the computer with cables or wirelessly. Wireless input devices connect to the computer using infrared or radio frequency technology, similar to a remote control for a television.

Using assistive devices

People with physical impairments or disabilities can use computers because of advances in making computers accessible to everyone. For example, people who cannot use their arms or hands instead can use foot, head, or eye movements to control the pointer. People with poor vision can use keyboards with large keys for input, screen enlargers to enlarge the type and images on the monitor, or screen readers to read the content of the screen aloud. Computers are being developed that can be controlled by a person's thoughts, that is, the brain's electromagnetic waves.

FIGURE A-6: Keyboards

Function keys

Main keyboard

Editing keypad

Numeric keypad

Ergonomic keyboard

FIGURE A-7: Personal computer pointing devices

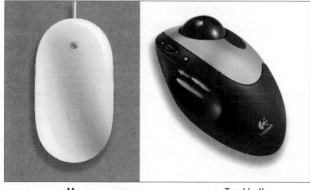

Mouse   Trackball

FIGURE A-8: Notebook pointing devices

Trackpad   Multi-Touch trackpad   Pointing Stick

Examining Output Devices

As stated earlier, output is the result of processing data; output devices show you those results. The most commonly used output devices are monitors and printers. Kevin continues his discussion of peripheral devices with an explanation of output devices.

Output devices are described below:

- The **monitor** displays the output from a computer.

  - The monitor shown on the left in Figure A-9 is a **flat panel monitor**, a lightweight monitor that takes up very little room on the desktop. Most flat panel monitors use **LCD (liquid crystal display)** technology, which creates the image you see on the screen by manipulating light within a layer of liquid crystal. A **CRT (cathode ray tube) monitor**, shown on the right in Figure A-9, uses gun-like devices that direct beams of electrons toward the screen to activate dots of color to form the image you see on the screen. CRT monitors require much more desk space than flat-panel display monitors. Apple's iMac combines the LCD monitor and the internal components of the computer into one unit, as shown in Figure A-10.

  - Monitor **screen size** is the diagonal measurement from one corner of the screen to the other. In general, monitors on desktop computers range in size from 15" to 30", whereas monitors on notebook computers range in size from 12" to 20".

  - Most monitors have a **graphics display**, which divides the screen into a matrix of small dots called **pixels**. **Resolution** is the number of pixels the monitor displays. Standard resolutions range from 640 × 480 to 1600 × 1200, although some Macs have a higher resolution. If your screen is small, a 1600 × 1200 resolution will make the objects on the screen too small to see clearly. **Dot pitch (dp)** measures the distance between pixels, so a smaller dot pitch means a sharper image. A .28 or .26 dot pitch is typical for today's monitors.

  - To display graphics, a computer must have a **graphics card**, also called a **video display adapter** or **video card**. The graphics card is installed on the motherboard, and controls the signals the computer sends to the monitor.

- A **printer** produces a paper copy, often called **hard copy**, of the text or graphics processed by the computer. There are three popular categories of printers: laser printers, inkjet printers, and dot matrix printers.

  - **Laser printers**, like the one shown on the left in Figure A-11, are popular for business use because they produce high-quality output quickly and efficiently. In a laser printer, a temporary laser image is transferred onto paper with a powdery substance called **toner**.

  - **Inkjet printers**, such as the one shown on the right in Figure A-11, are popular printers for home use. These printers spray ink onto paper and produce output whose quality is comparable to that of a laser printer.

  - **Dot matrix printers** transfer ink to the paper by striking a ribbon with pins. A 24-pin dot matrix printer produces better quality print than a 9-pin. Dot matrix printers are most often used when a large number of pages need to be printed fairly quickly or when a business needs to print multi-page continuous forms.

- Speakers, like speakers on a sound system, allow you to hear sounds from the computer. Speakers can be separate peripheral devices attached to the computer, or they can be built in to the monitor.

- Like input devices, output devices can be connected to a computer using cables or a wireless connection.

FIGURE A-9: Monitors

Flat panel monitor

CRT monitor

FIGURE A-10: Apple's iMac

FIGURE A-11: Printers

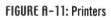

Laser printer

Inkjet printer

Investigating Data Processing

In order to understand how data is processed in a computer, you first need to learn how the computer represents and stores data. All data and programs are stored as files. A computer **file** is a named collection of stored data. An **executable file** contains the instructions that tell a computer how to perform a specific task; for instance, the files that are used while the computer starts are executable. A **data file** is created by a user, usually with software. For instance, a report that you write with a word processing program is data, and must be saved as a data file if you want to access it later. ▓▓▓▓ Kevin gives a basic description of how information is represented inside a computer.

DETAILS

The following information will help you understand data processing:

- The characters used in human language are meaningless to a computer. Like a light bulb, the computer must interpret every signal as either "on" or "off." A computer represents data as distinct or separate numbers. Specifically, it represents "on" with a 1 and "off" with a 0. These numbers are referred to as **binary digits**, or **bits**.

- A series of eight bits is called a **byte**. As Figure A-12 shows, the byte that represents the integer value 0 is 00000000, with all eight bits "off" or set to 0. The byte that represents the integer value 1 is 00000001, and the byte that represents 255 is 11111111.

- A **kilobyte** (**KB** or simply **K**) is 1024 bytes, or approximately one thousand bytes. A **megabyte** (**MB**) is 1,048,576 bytes, or about one million bytes. A **gigabyte** (**GB**) is 1,073,741,824 bytes, or about one billion bytes. A **terabyte** (**TB**) is 1,024 GB, or approximately one trillion bytes.

- Personal computers commonly use the ASCII system to represent character data. **ASCII** (pronounced "ASK-ee") stands for **American Standard Code for Information Interchange**. Each ASCII number represents an English character. Computers translate ASCII into binary data so that they can process it.

  - The original ASCII system used 7 bits to represent the numbers 0 (0000000) through 127 (1111111) to stand for 128 common characters and nonprinting control characters. Because bits are usually arranged in bytes, the eighth bit is reserved for error checking.

  - Extended ASCII uses eight bits and includes the numbers 128 (10000000) through 255 (11111111) to represent additional characters and symbols. Extended ASCII was developed to add codes for punctuation marks, symbols, such as $ and ©, and additional characters, such as é and ü, that were not included in the original 128 codes.

  - Most computers use the original ASCII definitions, but not all computers use the same definitions for Extended ASCII. Computers that run the Leopard operating system use the set of Extended ASCII definitions defined by the American National Standards Institute (ANSI). Figure A-13 shows sample ASCII code with ANSI standard Extended ASCII characters.

FIGURE A-12: Binary representation of numbers

Number	Binary representation
0	00000000
1	00000001
2	00000010
3	00000011
4	00000100
5	00000101
6	00000110
7	00000111
8	00001000
⋮	⋮
253	11111101
254	11111110
255	11111111

FIGURE A-13: Sample ASCII code representing letters and symbols

Character	ASCII Code	Binary Number
(space)	32	00100000
$	36	00100100
A	65	01000001
B	66	01000010
a	97	01100001
b	98	01100010
?	129	10000001
£	163	10100011
®	217	11011001
é	233	11101001

Understanding Memory

In addition to the microprocessor, another important component of personal computer hardware is the **memory**, which stores instructions and data. Memory is different from permanent storage in a computer. Your computer has five types of memory: random access memory, cache memory, virtual memory, read-only memory, and complementary metal oxide semiconductor memory. Kevin realizes that most of the Sheehan Tours staff don't understand the difference between memory types, so he explains the different types of memory.

Types of memory include the following:

When the computer is off, RAM is empty.

- **Random access memory** (**RAM**) temporarily holds programs and data while the computer is on and allows the computer to access that information randomly; in other words, RAM doesn't need to access data in the same sequence in which it was stored. For example, if you are writing a report, the microprocessor temporarily copies the word processing program you are using into RAM so the microprocessor can quickly access the instructions that you will need as you type and format your report. The characters you type are also stored in RAM, along with the fonts, graphics, and other objects that you might use. RAM consists of chips on cards that plug into the motherboard.

    - Most personal computers use some type of **synchronous dynamic random access memory** (**SDRAM**), which is synchronized with the processor to allow faster access to its contents.
    - RAM is sometimes referred to as **volatile memory** or **temporary memory** because it is constantly changing as long as the computer is on and is cleared when the computer is turned off.
    - **Memory capacity**, sometimes referred to as **storage capacity**, is the amount of data that the computer can handle at any given time and is measured in megabytes or gigabytes. For example, a computer that has 512 MB of RAM has the capacity to temporarily store more than 512 million bits of data at one time.

- **Cache memory**, sometimes called **RAM cache** or **CPU cache**, is a special, high-speed memory chip on the motherboard or CPU itself that stores frequently accessed and recently accessed data and commands.

You can often add more RAM to a computer by installing additional memory cards on the motherboard. You cannot add ROM; it is permanently installed on the motherboard.

- **Virtual memory** is space on the computer's storage devices that simulates additional RAM. It enables programs to run as if your computer had more RAM by moving data and commands from RAM to the hard drive and swapping in the new data and commands. See Figure A-14. Virtual memory, however, is much slower than RAM.

- **Read-only memory** (**ROM**) is a chip on the motherboard that has been prerecorded with data. ROM permanently stores the set of instructions that the computer uses to check the computer system's components to make sure they are working and to activate the essential software that controls the processing function when you turn the computer on.

The act of turning on the computer is sometimes called **booting up**.

    - ROM contains a set of instructions called the **BIOS** (**basic input/output system**), which tells the computer to initialize the motherboard, how to recognize the peripherals, and to start the boot process. The **boot process** is the set of events that occurs between the moment you turn on the computer and the moment you can begin to use the computer. The set of instructions for executing the boot process is stored in ROM.
    - ROM never changes and it remains intact when the computer is turned off; therefore, it is called **nonvolatile memory** or **permanent memory**.

- **Complementary metal oxide semiconductor** (**CMOS**, pronounced "SEE-moss") **memory** is a chip installed on the motherboard that is activated during the boot process and identifies where essential software is stored.

    - A small rechargeable battery powers CMOS so its contents are saved when the computer is turned off. CMOS changes every time you add or remove hardware on your computer system.
    - CMOS, often referred to as **semipermanent memory**, changes when hardware is added or removed, but doesn't empty when the computer is shut off.
    - Because CMOS retains its contents when the computer is turned off, the date and time are stored there.

FIGURE A-14: How virtual memory works

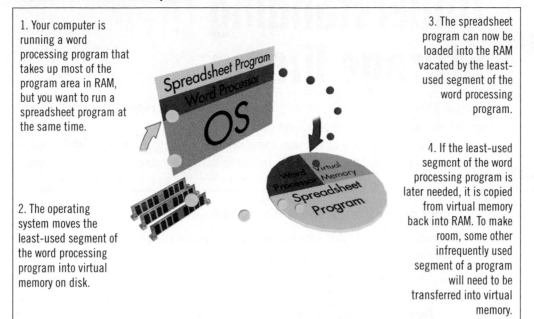

1. Your computer is running a word processing program that takes up most of the program area in RAM, but you want to run a spreadsheet program at the same time.

2. The operating system moves the least-used segment of the word processing program into virtual memory on disk.

3. The spreadsheet program can now be loaded into the RAM vacated by the least-used segment of the word processing program.

4. If the least-used segment of the word processing program is later needed, it is copied from virtual memory back into RAM. To make room, some other infrequently used segment of a program will need to be transferred into virtual memory.

Upgrading RAM

One of the easiest ways to make a computer run faster is to add more RAM. This enables the computer to access instructions and data stored in RAM very quickly. The more RAM a computer has, the more instructions and data can be stored there. Currently, you can buy from 64 MB to 1 GB RAM cards, and usually, you can add more than one card. You need to check your computer's specifications to see what size RAM cards the slots on your motherboard will accept.

Understanding Storage Media

Because RAM retains data only while the power is on, your computer must have a more permanent storage option. As Figure A-15 shows, a storage device receives data from RAM and writes it on a storage medium, such as a CD. Later the data can be read and sent back to RAM to use again. ▰▰▰ Kevin explains the types of storage media available. He starts with magnetic storage because almost all computers have a hard disk.

DETAILS

The types of storage media are discussed below:

- **Magnetic storage devices** store data as magnetized particles on mylar, a plastic, which is then coated on both sides with a magnetic oxide coating. Common magnetic storage devices are hard disks, tape, and floppy disks.
  - A **hard disk** is the most common type of magnetic storage media. It contains several magnetic oxide-covered metal platters that are usually sealed in a case inside the computer.
  - **Tape** is another type of magnetic storage media. Tape storage is much too slow to be used for day-to-day computer tasks; therefore, tapes are used to make backup copies of data stored on hard disks. Tape provides inexpensive, though slow, archival storage for large companies who need to back up large quantities of data.
  - A **floppy disk** is a flat circle of magnetic oxide-coated mylar enclosed in a hard plastic case; a floppy disk can store 1.44 MB of data. Floppy disks are sometimes called 3½" disks because of the size of the hard plastic case. The floppy disk has almost become obsolete, and most personal computers are now manufactured without a floppy disk drive.

QUICK TIP

Optical storage devices, such as CDs and DVDs, are much more durable than magnetic storage media.

- **Optical storage devices** are polycarbonate discs coated with a reflective metal on which data is recorded using laser technology as a trail of tiny pits or dark spots in the surface of the disc. The data that these pits or spots represent can then be "read" with a beam of laser light.
  - The first standard optical storage device available for personal computers was the **CD** (**compact disc**). One CD can store 700 MB of data.
  - A **DVD**, though the same size as a CD, currently stores between 4.7 and 15.9 GB of data, depending on whether data is stored on one or two sides of the disc, and how many layers of data each side contains. The term *DVD* is no longer an acronym, although it was originally an acronym for *digital video disc* and later was sometimes updated to *digital versatile disc*.
  - New formats of optical storage include Blu-ray Discs and HD-DVD, which are capable of storing between 15 and 50 GB of data. They are used for storing high-definition video. Different companies support each format and it remains to be seen if one dominates the market.

- **Flash memory** is similar to ROM except that it can be written to more than once. **Flash memory cards** are small, portable cards encased in hard plastic to which data can be written and rewritten. They are used in digital cameras, handheld computers, video game controllers, and other devices.

- A popular type of flash memory is a **USB flash storage device**, also called a **USB drive** or a **flash drive**. See Figure A-16.

QUICK TIP

There is only one way to insert a flash drive, so if you're having problems inserting the drive into the slot, turn the drive around and try again.

  - USB drives for personal computers are available in a wide range of sizes; they currently range from drives capable of holding 32 MB of data to drives capable of holding 16 GB of data. They are becoming more popular for use as a secondary or backup storage device for data typically stored on a hard disk drive.
  - USB drives plug directly into the USB port of a personal computer; the computer recognizes the device as another disk drive. The location and letter designation of USB ports varies with the brand and model of computer you are using, but the physical port may be on the front, back, or side of a computer.
  - USB flash storage devices are about the size of a pack of gum and often have a ring that you can attach to your key chain.

FIGURE A-15: Storage devices and RAM

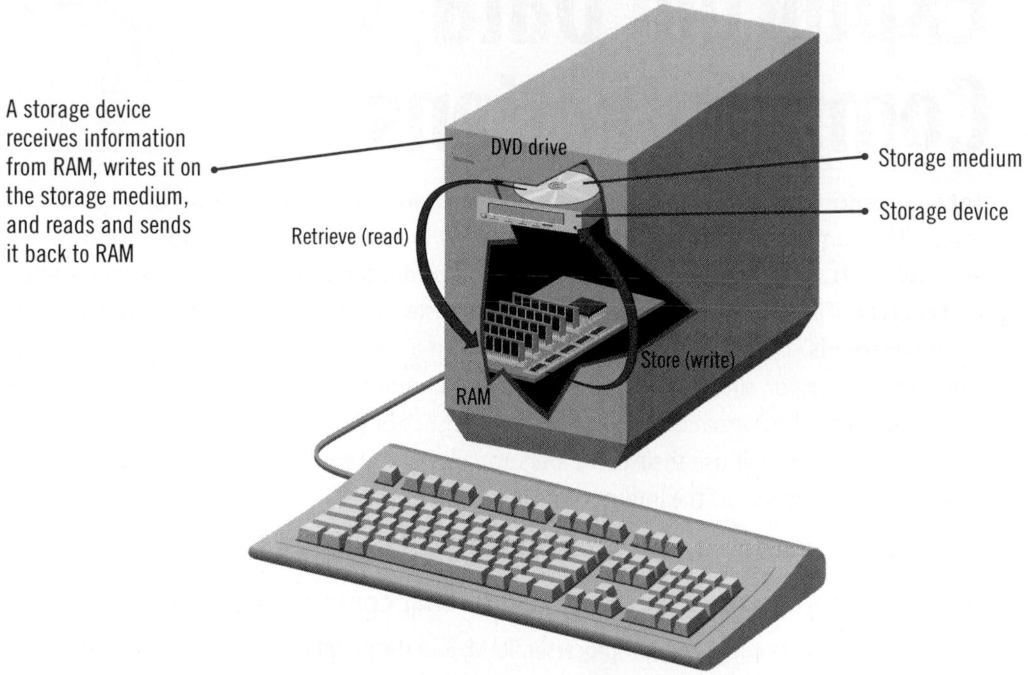

A storage device receives information from RAM, writes it on the storage medium, and reads and sends it back to RAM

DVD drive

Retrieve (read)

RAM

Store (write)

Storage medium

Storage device

FIGURE A-16: Flash storage device

Erasing and rewriting on CDs and DVDs

CD-ROM stands for **compact disc read-only memory**. CDs that you buy with software or music already on them are CD-ROMs—you can read from them, but you cannot record additional data onto them. In order to record data on a CD, you need a **CD-R (compact disc recordable)** or **CD-RW (compact disc rewritable)** drive and a CD-R or CD-RW disk. On CD-ROMs, data is stored in pits made on the surface of the disk; when you record data on a CD-R or -RW, a laser changes the reflectivity of a dye layer on a blank disk, creating dark spots on the disk's surface that represent the data. On a CD-R, once the data is recorded, you cannot erase or modify it, but you can add new data to the disk, as long as the disk has not been finalized. In contrast, you can re-record a CD-RW. CD-R disks can be read by a standard CD-ROM drive or a DVD drive; CD-RW disks can be read only by CD-RW drives or CD-ROM drives labeled "multi-read." Recordable DVD drives are also available. As with CDs, you can buy a DVD to which you can record only once, or a rewritable DVD to which you can record and then re-record data. Recordable and rewriteable DVDs come in several formats; for example, recordable DVDs are available as DVD-R and DVD+R. Make sure you know which type of DVD your DVD drive uses. Newer DVD drives are capable of reading from and writing to both -RW and +RW DVDs and CDs, as well as DVDs with two layers.

Exploring Data Communications

Data communications is the transmission of data from one computer to another or to a peripheral device. The computer that originates the message is the **sender**. The message is sent over some type of **channel**, such as a telephone or coaxial cable. The computer or peripheral at the message's destination is the **receiver**. The rules that establish an orderly transfer of data between the sender and the receiver are called **protocols**. The transmission protocol between a computer and its peripheral devices is handled by a **device driver**, or simply **driver**, which is a computer program that can establish communication because it contains information about the characteristics of your computer and of the device. The Sheehan Tours staff will use their computers to connect to the computers at the Quest headquarters in California as well as to surf the Internet, so Kevin next explains how computers communicate.

DETAILS

The following describes some of the ways that computers communicate:

- The data path between the microprocessor, RAM, and the peripherals along which communication travels is called the **data bus**. Figure A-17 illustrates the data bus that connects a printer to a computer.

- An external peripheral device must have a corresponding **port** and **cable** that connect it to the computer. Inside the computer, each port connects to a **controller card**, sometimes called an **expansion card** or **interface card**. These cards plug into electrical connectors on the motherboard called **expansion slots** or **slots**. Personal computers can have several types of ports, including parallel, serial, SCSI, USB, MIDI, and Ethernet. Figure A-18 shows the ports on a Windows desktop personal computer and on the back of an iMac (your port configuration may differ).

QUICK TIP

Typically, a printer that is near the computer is connected to a parallel port, and the mouse, keyboard, and modem are connected to serial ports.

  - A **parallel port** transmits data eight bits at a time. Parallel transmissions are relatively fast, but they have an increased risk for interference. A **serial port** transmits data one bit at a time.
  - One **SCSI** (**small computer system interface**, pronounced "scuzzy") **port** provides an interface for one or more peripheral devices at the same port. The first is connected directly to the computer through the port, and the second device is plugged into a similar port on the first device.

QUICK TIP

FireWire is another standard for transferring information between digital devices similar to USB.

  - A **USB** (**Universal Serial Bus**) **port** is a high-speed serial port which allows multiple connections at the same port. The device you install must have a **USB connector**, a small rectangular plug, as shown in Figure A-19. When you plug the USB connector into the USB port, the computer recognizes the device and allows you to use it immediately. You can connect multiple devices to a single USB port by "daisy chaining" them or by using a hub. USB flash storage devices plug into USB ports. For most USB devices, power is supplied via the port, so there is no need for extra power cables.
  - The port for a sound card usually includes jacks for speakers and a microphone, which are designed to work with a **MIDI** (**Musical Instrument Digital Interface**, pronounced "middy") **card**.
  - You can connect to another computer, a LAN, a modem, or sometimes directly to the Internet using an **Ethernet port**. Ethernet ports allow data to be transmitted at high speeds.

- An internal peripheral device such as a hard disk drive may plug directly into the motherboard, or it may have an attached controller card.

- Notebook computers may also include a **portable computer card** (**PC Card**). PC Cards are credit card-sized cards that plug directly into the PC Card slot and can contain additional RAM, a fax modem, or a hard disk drive (similar to a USB flash storage device).

FIGURE A-17: Components needed to connect a printer to a computer

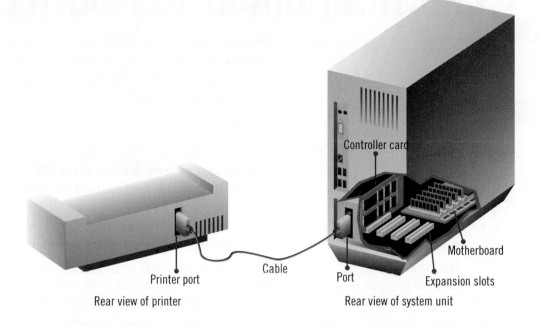

Controller card

Motherboard

Printer port

Cable

Port

Expansion slots

Rear view of printer

Rear view of system unit

FIGURE A-18: Computer ports and connections

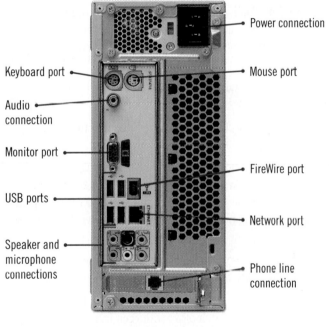

Keyboard port

Audio connection

Monitor port

USB ports

Speaker and microphone connections

Power connection

Mouse port

FireWire port

Network port

Phone line connection

Windows PC

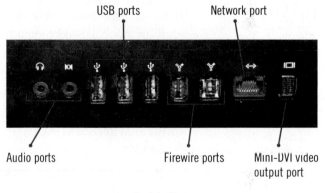

USB ports

Network port

Audio ports

Firewire ports

Mini-DVI video output port

Apple's iMac

FIGURE A-19: USB connector

Learning about Networks

A **network** connects one computer to other computers and peripheral devices, enabling you to share data and resources with others. There are a variety of network configurations; however, any type of network has some basic characteristics and requirements that you should know. Kevin continues his discussion of how computers communicate with an explanation of networking.

Types of networks are described below:

- Each computer that is part of the network must have a **network interface card** (**NIC**) installed. This card creates a communications channel between the computer and the network. A cable is used to connect the NIC port to the network.

- **Network software** is also essential, establishing the communications protocols that will be observed on the network and controlling the "traffic flow" as data travels throughout the network.

- Some networks have one or more computers, called **servers**, that act as the central storage location for programs and provide mass storage for most of the data used on the network. A network with a server and computers dependent on the server is called a **client/server network**. The dependent computers are the **clients**.

- When a network does not have a server, all the computers essentially are equal, and programs and data are distributed among them. This is called a **peer-to-peer network**.

- A personal computer that is not connected to a network is called a **standalone computer**. When it is connected to the network, it becomes a **workstation**. You have already learned that a terminal has a keyboard and monitor used for input and output, but it is not capable of processing on its own. A terminal is connected to a network that uses mainframes as servers. Any device connected to the network is called a **node**. Figure A-20 illustrates a typical network configuration.

- In a **local area network** (**LAN**), computers and peripheral devices are located relatively close to each other, generally in the same building.

- A **wide area network** (**WAN**) is more than one LAN connected together. The Internet is the largest example of a WAN.

- In a **wireless local area network** (**WLAN**), computers and peripherals use high-frequency radio waves instead of wires to communicate and connect in a network. **Wi-Fi** (short for **wireless fidelity**) is the term created by the nonprofit Wi-Fi Alliance to describe networks connected using a standard radio frequency established by the Institute of Electrical and Electronics Engineers (IEEE). Wi-Fi is used over short distances to connect computers to a LAN.

- A **personal area network** (**PAN**) is a network that allows two or more devices located close to each other to communicate or to connect a device to the Internet. In a PAN, devices are connected with cables or wireless.

  - **Infrared technology** uses infrared light waves to beam data from one device to another. The devices must be compatible, and they must be positioned close to each other with their infrared ports pointed at each other for this to work. This is the technology used in TV remote controls.

  - **Bluetooth** uses short range radio waves to connect a device wirelessly to another device or to the Internet. The devices must each have a Bluetooth transmitter, but unlike infrared connections, they can communicate around corners or through walls.

- **WiMAX** (short for **Worldwide Interoperability for Microwave Access**), another standard defined by the IEEE, allows computer users to connect over many miles to a LAN. A WiMAX tower sends signals to a WiMAX receiver built or plugged into a computer. WiMAX towers can communicate with each other or with an Internet service provider.

FIGURE A-20: Network configuration

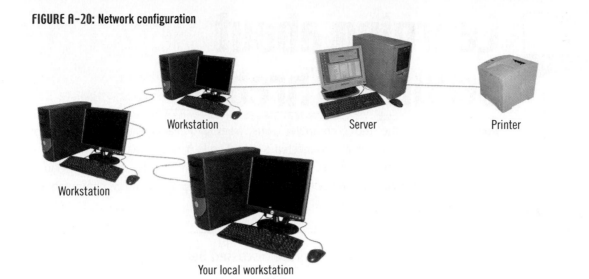

Workstation

Server

Printer

Workstation

Your local workstation

Understanding telecommunications

Telecommunications means communicating over a comparatively long distance using a phone line or some other data conduit. When it is not possible to connect users on one network, telecommunications allows you to send and receive data over the telephone lines. To make this connection, you must use a communications device called a modem. A **modem**, which stands for *modulator-demodulator*, is a device that connects your computer to a standard telephone jack. The modem converts the **digital**, or stop-start, **signals** your computer outputs into **analog**, or continuous wave, **signals** (sound waves) that can traverse ordinary phone lines. Figure A-21 shows the telecommunications process, in which a modem converts

digital signals to analog signals at the sending site (modulates) and a second modem converts the analog signals back into digital signals at the receiving site (demodulates). Most computers today come with a built-in 56 K modem and/or NIC (network interface card). 56 K represents the modem's capability to send and receive about 56,000 **bits per second (bps)**. Actual speed may be reduced by factors such as distance, technical interference, and other issues. People who want to use a high-speed connection either over phone lines, such as a **DSL (digital subscriber line)**, or over a cable connection, usually need to purchase an external DSL or cable modem separately.

FIGURE A-21: Using modems to send and receive data

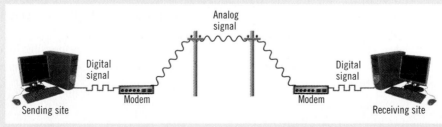

Learning about Security Threats

Security refers to the steps a computer owner takes to prevent unauthorized use of or damage to the computer. Once a computer is connected to a network, it is essential that the computer be protected against possible threats from people intent on stealing information or causing malicious damage. Kevin explains how important it is to be vigilant about keeping the office computers secure and reviews ways to do this.

DETAILS

Several types of security threats are discussed below:

- **Malware** is a broad term that describes any program that is intended to cause harm or convey information to others without the owner's permission.

  - Unscrupulous programmers deliberately construct harmful programs, called **viruses**, which instruct your computer to perform destructive activities, such as erasing a disk drive. Some viruses are more annoying than destructive, but some can be harmful, erasing data or causing your hard disk to require reformatting. **Antivirus software**, sometimes referred to as **virus protection software**, searches executable files for the sequences of characters that may cause harm and disinfects the files by erasing or disabling those commands. Figure A-22 shows the screen that appears after AVG Anti-Virus Free Edition finished scanning a computer.

  - Some software programs contain other programs called **spyware** that track a computer user's Internet usage and send this data back to the company or person that created it. Most often, this is done without the computer user's permission or knowledge. **Anti-spyware software** can detect these programs and delete them.

- A **firewall** is like a locked door on a computer. It prevents other computers on the Internet from accessing a computer and prevents programs on a computer from accessing the Internet without the computer user's permission. A firewall can be hardware, software, or a combination of both.

  - A hardware firewall provides strong protection against incoming threats. A **router**, a device that controls traffic between network components, usually has a built-in firewall.

  - Software firewalls track all incoming and outgoing traffic. If a program that never accessed the Internet before attempts to do so, the user is notified and can choose to forbid access. There are several free software firewall packages available. Figure A-23 shows an alert from Zone Alarm, a software firewall.

- Criminals are getting more aggressive as they try to figure out new ways to access computer users' personal information and passwords.

  - A Web site set up to look exactly like another Web site, such as a bank's Web site, but which does not actually belong to the organization portrayed in the site, is a **spoofed** site. The site developer creates a **URL** (address on the Web) that looks similar to a URL from the legitimate site. Usually, spoofed sites are set up to try to convince customers of the real site to enter personal information, such as credit card numbers, Social Security numbers, and passwords, so that the thief collecting the information can use it to steal the customer's money or identity.

  - **Phishing** refers to the practice of sending e-mails to customers or potential customers of a legitimate Web site asking them to click a link in the e-mail. The link leads to a spoofed site where the user is asked to verify or enter personal information.

  - Sometimes a criminal can break into a **DNS server** (a computer responsible for directing Internet traffic) and redirect any attempts to access a particular Web site to the criminal's spoofed site. This is called **pharming**.

FIGURE A-22: Completed antivirus scan

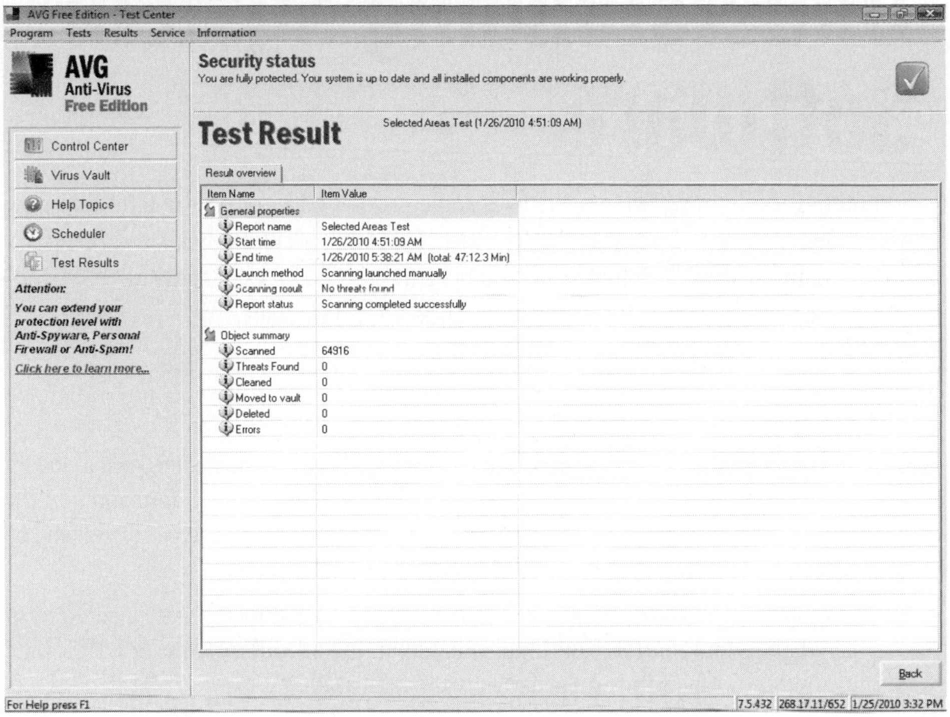

FIGURE A-23: Security alert from a software firewall

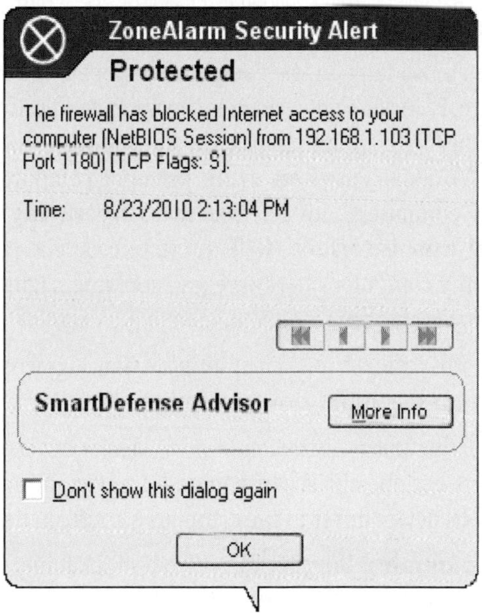

Protecting information with passwords

You can protect data on your computer by using passwords. You can set up accounts on your computer for multiple users and require that all users sign in with a user name and password before they can use the computer. This is known as **logging in**. You can also protect individual files on your computer so that people who try to open or alter a file need to type the password before they are allowed access to the file. Many Web sites require a user name and password in order to access the information stored on it. To prevent anyone from guessing your password, you should always create and use strong passwords. A **strong password** is at least eight characters of upper and lowercase letters and numbers. Avoid using common personal information, such as birthdays and addresses.

Understanding System Software

Sometimes the term software refers to a single program, but often the term refers to a collection of programs and data that are packaged together. **System software** helps the computer carry out its basic operating tasks. Before Kevin describes the various types of software that people use to accomplish things like writing memos, he needs to describe system software.

DETAILS

The components of system software are described below:

- System software manages the fundamental operations of your computer, such as loading programs and data into memory, executing programs, saving data to disks, displaying information on the monitor, and transmitting data through a port to a peripheral device. There are four types of system software: operating systems, utilities, device drivers, and programming languages.

- An **operating system** allocates system resources, manages storage space, maintains security, detects equipment failure, and controls basic input and output. **Input and output**, or **I/O**, is the flow of data from the microprocessor to memory to peripherals and back again.

  - The operating system allocates system resources so programs run properly. A **system resource** is any part of the computer system, including memory, storage devices, and the microprocessor, that can be used by a computer program.
  - The operating system is also responsible for managing the files on your storage devices. Not only does it open and save files, but it also keeps track of every part of every file for you and lets you know if any part is missing.
  - While you are working on the computer, the operating system is constantly guarding against equipment failure. Each electronic circuit is checked periodically, and the moment a problem is detected, the user is notified with a warning message on the screen.
  - Microsoft Windows, used on many personal computers, and the Mac OS, used exclusively on Macintosh computers, are referred to as **operating environments** because they provide a **graphical user interface** (**GUI**, pronounced "goo-ey") that acts as a liaison between the user and all of the computer's hardware and software. Figure A-24 shows the starting screen on a Mac using Leopard (Mac OS X v10.5.6).

- **Utilities** are another category of system software that augment the operating system by taking over some of its responsibility for allocating hardware resources.

- As you learned earlier in the discussion of ports, device drivers handle the transmission protocol between a computer and its peripherals. When you add a device to an existing computer, part of its installation includes adding its device driver to the computer's configuration.

- Computer **programming languages**, which a programmer uses to write computer instructions, are also part of the system software. The instructions are translated into electrical signals that the computer can manipulate and process.

> **QUICK TIP**
>
> The operating system's responsibility to maintain security may include requiring a username and password or checking the computer for virus infection.

> **QUICK TIP**
>
> Some examples of popular programming languages are BASIC, Visual Basic, C, C++, C#, Java, and Delphi.

FIGURE A-24: Mac OS X Leopard starting screen

Menu bar

Icon (you might see additional icons on your screen)

Dock

Understanding Application Software

Application software enables you to perform specific computer tasks. Some examples of tasks that are accomplished with application software are document production, spreadsheet calculations, database management, and giving presentations. Now that the Sheehan Tours staff understands operating systems, Kevin describes some common application software.

DETAILS

Typical application software includes the following:

QUICK TIP

Most document production software allows you to perform **copy-and-paste** and **cut-and-paste operations**, which allow you to duplicate or move words around.

- **Document production software** includes word processing software, desktop publishing software, e-mail editors, and Web authoring software. All of these production tools have a variety of features that assist you in writing and formatting documents, including changing the **font** (the style of type). Most offer **spell checking** to help you avoid typographical and spelling errors, as shown in Figure A-25.

- **Spreadsheet software** is a numerical analysis tool. Spreadsheet software creates a **worksheet**, composed of a grid of columns and rows. You can type data into the cells, and then enter mathematical formulas into other cells that reference the data. Figure A-26 shows a typical worksheet that includes a simple calculation and the data in the spreadsheet represented as a simple graph.

- **Database management software** lets you collect and manage data. A **database** is a collection of information stored on one or more computers organized in a uniform format of records and fields. A **record** is a collection of data items in a database. A **field** is one piece of information in the record. An example of a database is the online catalog of books at a library; the catalog contains one record for each book in the library, and each record contains fields that identify the title, the author, and the subjects under which the book can be classified.

- **Graphics** and **presentation software** allow you to create illustrations, diagrams, graphs, and charts that can be projected before a group, printed out for quick reference, or transmitted to remote computers. You can also use **clip art**, simple drawings that are included as collections with many software packages.

- **Photo editing software** allows you to manipulate digital photos. You can make the images brighter, add special effects to the photo, add additional images to a photo, or crop the photo to include only relevant parts of the image.

- **Multimedia authoring software** allows you to record digital sound files, video files, and animations that can be included in presentations and other documents.

QUICK TIP

Some information management software allows you to synchronize information between a PDA and a desktop or notebook computer.

- **Information management software** keeps track of schedules, appointments, contacts, and "to-do" lists. Most e-mail software allows users to add all the information about contacts to the list of e-mail addresses. In addition, some software, such as Microsoft Entourage, combines a contact list with information management components, such as a calendar and to-do list. The main screen of Microsoft Entourage is shown in Figure A-27.

- **Web site creation and management software** allows you to create and manage Web sites. They allow you to see what the Web pages will look like as you create them.

Understanding object linking and embedding (OLE)

Many programs allow users to use data created in one application in a document created by another application. **Object linking and embedding (OLE)** refers to the ability to use data from another file, called the **source**. **Embedding** occurs when you copy and paste the source data in the new file. **Linking** allows you to create a connection between the source data and the copy in the new file. The link updates the copy every time a change is made to the source data. The seamless nature of OLE among some applications is referred to as **integration**.

FIGURE A-25: Spell checking a document

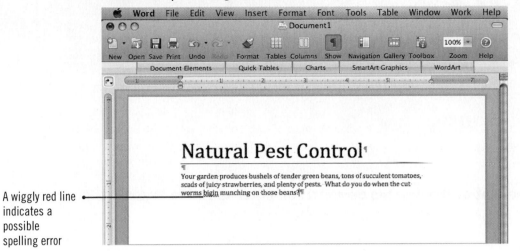

A wiggly red line indicates a possible spelling error

FIGURE A-26: Typical worksheet with numerical data and a chart

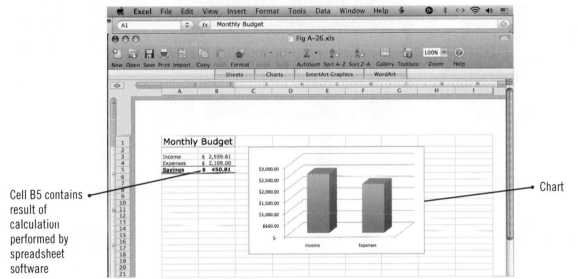

Cell B5 contains result of calculation performed by spreadsheet software

Chart

FIGURE A-27: Information management software

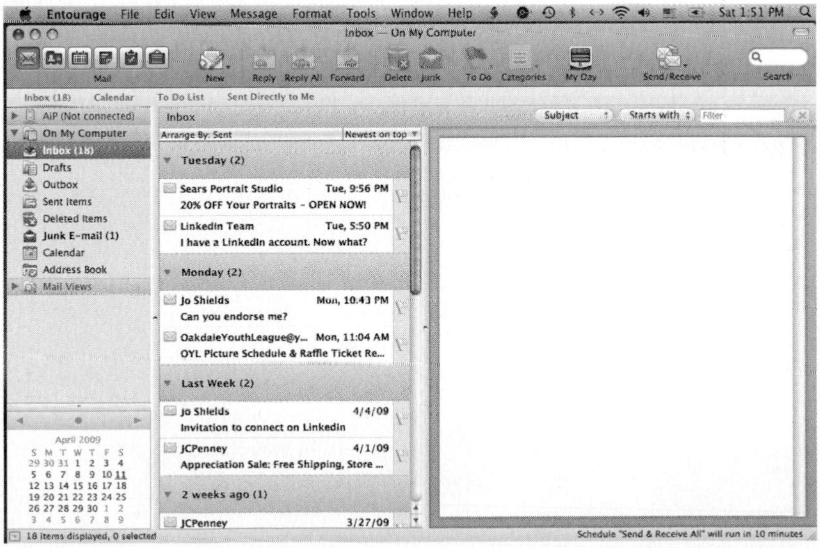

Practice

Label each component of the desktop personal computer shown in Figure A-28.

FIGURE A-28

1. Which component do you use to point to items on the screen?
2. Which component displays output?
3. Which component is used to enter text?
4. Which component processes data?
5. Which component transmits audio output?

Match each term with the statement that best describes it.

6. **configuration**
7. **byte**
8. **RAM**
9. **hard disk**
10. **expansion slot**
11. **server**
12. **spyware**
13. **operating system**
14. **font**

a. Software that allocates resources, manages storage space, maintains security, and controls I/O
b. The style of type
c. The design and construction of a computer
d. Magnetic storage media that is usually sealed in a case inside the computer
e. Series of eight bits
f. A computer on a network that acts as the central storage location for programs and data used on the network
g. A program that tracks a user's Internet usage without the user's permission
h. A slot on the motherboard into which a controller card for a peripheral device is inserted
i. Temporarily holds data and programs while the computer is on

▼ SKILLS REVIEW

Select the best answer from the list of choices.

15. Which one of the following would not be considered a personal computer?
    a. Desktop
    b. Notebook
    c. Mainframe
    d. Tablet PC

16. The intangible components of a computer system, including the programs, are called _____.
    a. software
    b. hardware
    c. price
    d. peripherals

17. What part of the computer is responsible for executing instructions to process information?
    a. Card
    b. Processor
    c. Motherboard
    d. Peripheral device

18. What are the technical details about each hardware component called?
    a. Configuration
    b. Circuits
    c. Specifications
    d. Cards

19. Keyboards, monitors, and printers are all examples of which of the following?
    a. Input devices
    b. Output devices
    c. Software
    d. Peripheral devices

20. Which of the following is a pointing device that allows you to control the pointer by moving the entire device around on a desk?
    a. Mouse
    b. Trackball
    c. Trackpad
    d. Pointing stick

21. In order to display graphics, a computer needs a monitor and a _____.

    a. parallel port

    b. network card

    c. graphics card

    d. sound card

22. What do you call each 1 or 0 used in the representation of computer data?

    a. A bit

    b. A byte

    c. An ASCII

    d. A pixel

23. Another way to refer to 1024 bytes is a _____.

    a. byte

    b. kilobyte

    c. megabyte

    d. binary

24. Which of the following is a chip installed on the motherboard that is activated during the boot process and identifies where essential software is stored?

    a. RAM

    b. CMOS

    c. CPU cache

    d. ROM

25. Which of the following is space on the computer's storage devices that simulates additional RAM?

    a. Cache memory

    b. Virtual memory

    c. Read-only memory

    d. Volatile memory

26. Which of the following permanently stores the set of instructions that the computer uses to activate the software that controls the processing function when you turn the computer on?

    a. RAM

    b. CMOS

    c. CPU cache

    d. ROM

27. Which of the following storage media is not a magnetic storage device?

    a. Hard disk

    b. Floppy disk

    c. DVD

    d. Tape

28. The transmission protocol between a computer and its peripheral devices is handled by a _____.

    a. channel

    b. data bus

    c. driver

    d. controller card

29. Which of the following is the data path between the microprocessor, RAM, and the peripherals?

    a. Data bus

    b. Data channel

    c. Data port

    d. Cable

▼ SKILLS REVIEW (CONTINUED)

30. The computer that originates a message to send to another computer is called the _____.
   a. channel
   b. sender
   c. receiver
   d. driver

31. A personal computer that is connected to a network is called a _____.
   a. desktop
   b. workstation
   c. terminal
   d. PDA

32. Which of the following acts as a locked door on a computer?
   a. Antivirus software
   b. Firewall
   c. DNS server
   d. Spyware

33. A _____ consists of connected computers and peripheral devices that are located relatively close to each other.
   a. LAN
   b. WAN
   c. WLAN
   d. PAN

34. The term that describes networks connected using a standard radio frequency established by the IEEE is _____.
   a. WiMAX
   b. WAN
   c. WLAN
   d. Wi-Fi

35. A Web site set up to look exactly like another Web site, such as a bank's Web site, but which does not actually belong to the organization portrayed in the site, is a _____ site.
   a. malware
   b. phished
   c. spoofed
   d. served

▼ INDEPENDENT CHALLENGE 1

This Independent Challenge requires an Internet connection. In order to run the newest software, many people need to upgrade their existing computer system or buy a brand new one. What do you do with your old computer when you purchase a new one? Most municipalities have enacted laws regulating the disposal of electronics. Research these laws in your city and state and write a brief report describing them.

   a. Start your browser, go to your favorite search engine, then search for information about laws regarding the disposal of electronics in your city and state. Try finding your city's Web site and searching it for the information, or use **electronics disposal laws** followed by your city name as a search term and then repeat that search with your state's name in place of your city's name.
   b. Open each Web site that you find in a separate tab or browser window.
   c. Read the information on each Web site. Can some components be thrown away? Are there laws that apply only to monitors?

Advanced Challenge Exercise

- Search for organizations to which you can donate your computer.
- How do these organizations promise to protect your privacy?
- Can you take a deduction on your federal income tax for your donation?

d. Write a short report describing your findings. Include the URLs for all relevant Web sites. (*Hint*: If you are using a word processor to write your report, you can copy the URLs from your browser and paste them into the document. Drag to select the entire URL in the Address or Location bar in your browser. Right-click the selected text, then click Copy on the shortcut menu. Position the insertion point in the document where you want the URL to appear, then press [⌘][V].)

▼ INDEPENDENT CHALLENGE 2

This Independent Challenge requires an Internet connection. New viruses are discovered on an almost daily basis. If you surf the Internet or exchange e-mail, it is important to use updated anti-virus software. Research the most current virus threats and create a table listing the threats and details about them.

a. Start your browser, go to Symantec's Web site at **www.symantec.com**, click the Viruses & Risks link, then click the link to Threat Explorer. (If you don't see that link, type **threat explorer** in the Search box on the page, then click appropriate links to get to the Threat Explorer page.) On the Threat Explorer page, click the Latest tab if necessary.

b. Click links to the first five latest threats.

c. Open a new word processing document and create a table listing each virus threat, a description of what each virus does, how widely it is distributed (the Wild value), and how damaging it is (the Damage Level value).

d. In your browser, go to the Security Advisor on CA's Web site at **www3.ca.com/securityadvisor**, and then click the Virus Information Center link. If any of the first five latest virus threats are different from the ones on the Symantec site, add them to your table. (*Hint*: After you click a virus name, check the "Also known as" list.)

e. For any viruses that are already in your table because they were on the Symantec site, read the CA description to see if there is any additional information describing how the virus could damage your system. Add this information to your table.

f. Save the word processing document as **Latest Threats** to the drive and folder where you store your Data Files.

▼ INDEPENDENT CHALLENGE 3

This Independent Challenge requires an Internet connection. One of the keyboards shown in this unit is an ergonomic keyboard. Ergonomics is the study of the design of a workspace so that the worker can work efficiently and avoid injury. The U.S. Occupational Safety and Health Administration (OSHA) has developed guidelines that describe a healthy computer work environment. Research these guidelines and evaluate your workspace.

a. Start your browser, and then go to **www.osha.gov/SLTC/etools/computerworkstations/index.html**.

b. Read the information on the main page. Follow links to descriptions of the best arrangement for equipment you use when working on a computer. (*Hint*: Look for the Workstation Components link, and point to it to open a submenu of links.)

c. Locate and print the checklist for evaluating your workspace. (*Hint*: Click the Checklist link, then click the View/Print the Evaluation Checklist PDF link. A new tab or window opens and the checklist opens in Adobe Acrobat Reader, a program that displays PDF files. If a dialog box opens telling you that you need to install Acrobat Reader to continue, ask your instructor or technical support person for help.)

d. Using the checklist, evaluate each of the conditions listed. If a condition does not apply to you, write N/A (not applicable) in the Yes column.

▼ INDEPENDENT CHALLENGE 3 (CONTINUED)

Advanced Challenge Exercise

ACE

- Use the OSHA Web site or a search engine to research repetitive motion injuries to which computer users are susceptible.
- Evaluate your risk for at least three common injuries.
- On the OSHA checklist, note what injury or injuries each applicable item or behavior will help prevent.

▼ REAL LIFE INDEPENDENT CHALLENGE

You are buying a new Mac for home use, but you're having trouble deciding between a desktop or a notebook. You know that the computer you buy will need to run Leopard and Office 2008 for Mac and have enough hard disk space for all your files, and you want to make sure you are protected against security threats. You'll also need a printer.

a. To help you make a decision and organize the information to make it easy to compare, create the table shown in Figure A-29.

FIGURE A-29

Name: Your Name

	Your Requirements	Notebook		Desktop	
		Tehnical Specs.	Price	Tehnical Specs.	Price
Model (and starting Price):		MacBook		iMac	
Hardware:	Processor (brand and speed)				
	RAM (amount)				
	Video RAM (amount)				
	Hard disk (size)				
	Printer (type and speed)				
	External speakers				
Maintenance Plan:	Apple Care				
Software:	Leopard (Mac OS X v10.5.6 or higher)				
	Office 2008				
	Antivirus Software				
Total Price:					

Information Source(s): _____

b. You'll need to determine which edition of Office 2008 you should get (Standard Edition, Home and Student Edition, or Special Media Edition). Use the Internet to research the different editions to determine which one will best suit your needs. Enter the cost for the edition in the appropriate cells in the table.

c. Research the hardware requirements for running the edition of Office 2008 that you selected. Enter the technical specifications required in the appropriate cells in the table.

d. Research the cost of a new iMac that has Mac OS X Leopard as its operating system and that meets the system requirements needed to run Office 2008. Next, research the cost of a new MacBook or MacBook Pro with the same or similar configuration. To begin, visit *www.apple.com* to review the technical information to ensure that you are comparing models with similar hardware characteristics. Enter the starting costs for each model in the appropriate cells in the table. (*Hint*: The Apple store at *www.apple.com* can help you configure your computer and provide you with the cost of the Apple Care maintenance plan.)

e. Search the Web to find an inexpensive inket printer that will work with your Mac. Enter the cost in the appropriate cells in the table.

f. Search the Web to find external speakers that will work with your Mac. Enter the cost in the appropriate cells in the table.

g. Search the Web to find antivirus software for your Mac. Enter the cost in the appropriate cells in the table.

h. Review the items to make sure you have entered information in all the rows. Total the costs you entered in the table for the various items.

i. Based on the information you found, determine whether the better purchase would be the notebook (MacBook or MacBook Pro) or the iMac. Write a brief summary justifying your decision.

j. Submit the completed table and your summary to your instructor.

Getting Started with Mac OS X Leopard

Files You Will Need:

No files needed

Mac OS X v10.5, or **Leopard**, is an **operating system**—software that manages the complete operation of your computer and keeps all the hardware and software working together properly. When you start your Mac, Leopard starts automatically, activates **Finder**, which provides access to files and programs on your computer, and then displays the **desktop**—a graphical user interface (GUI) that you use to interact with Leopard and the other software on your computer. Finder helps you organize **files** (collections of stored electronic data, such as text, pictures, video, music, and programs) in **folders** (containers for files) so that you can easily find them later. When you open a file or program, Leopard displays the file or program in a rectangular-shaped work area known as a **window**. As a new Oceania tour guide for Quest Specialty Travel (QST), you need to develop basic Leopard skills to keep track of all the tour files on your company's Mac computer.

OBJECTIVES

Start Mac OS X Leopard

Use a pointing device

Start a program

Move and resize windows

Use menus

Use dialog boxes

Get Mac Help

End a Leopard session

Starting Mac OS X Leopard

When you start your Mac, Leopard steps through a process called **booting** to get the computer up and running. During this time, you might need to enter your user account name and password, which identifies you to Leopard as an authorized user of the computer. As part of the boot process, Leopard activates Finder and displays the Mac desktop. The desktop is a way for you to interact with your Mac and to access its tools. The desktop appears with preset, or **default**, settings; however, you can change these settings to suit your needs. When your computer starts, the desktop contains the Finder menu bar, the Macintosh HD (hard drive) icon, and the dock. The **Macintosh HD icon**, located in the upper-right corner of your computer screen, gives you quick access to all items stored on your computer. Your supervisor, Nancy McDonald, Oceania's tour developer, asks you to become familiar with Leopard and its features before your upcoming tour.

STEPS

1. **If your computer and monitor are turned off, press the** Power button

   Depending on the Mac model you have, the power button may be located in the middle of your tower, on the back of your iMac, or near the monitor of your laptop. After your computer starts, you'll either be prompted to enter a user name and password (if your Mac is part of a network, or if it is set up for multiple users), or you'll see the desktop. If you're prompted for a user name and password, continue with Step 2 and compare your computer screen to Figure B-1. If not, skip to Step 4.

> **QUICK TIP**

If you don't know your user name or password, ask your instructor or technical support person.

2. **In the Name box, type your** user name

3. **In the Password box, type your** password, **then press** [return] **or click** Log In

   After Leopard verifies your user name and password, you see the desktop.

4. **Compare your computer screen to Figure B-2**

   Your desktop may look slightly different.

FIGURE B-1: Mac login screen

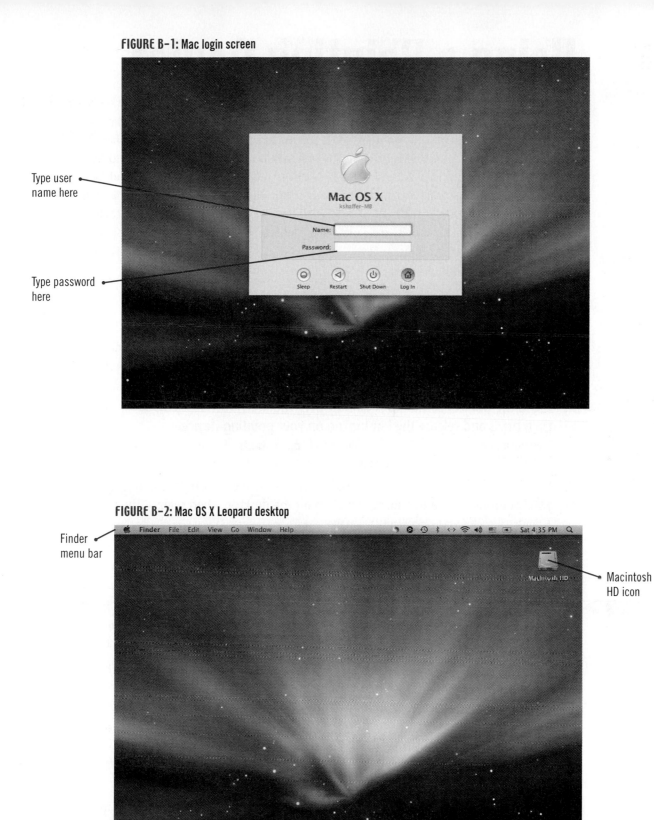

Type user name here

Type password here

FIGURE B-2: Mac OS X Leopard desktop

Finder menu bar

Macintosh HD icon

Dock

Mac OS X

Using a Pointing Device

The most common way to interact with your Mac and the software you are using is with a **pointing device**, such as a mouse or a trackpad, as shown in Figure B-3. As you move your pointing device, a small arrow (or other symbol), called a **pointer**, moves on the screen in the same direction. Table B-1 illustrates common pointer shapes and their functions. You press a button on the pointing device to select and move objects (such as icons and desktop windows); open programs, windows, folders, and files; and select options for performing specific tasks, such as saving your work. Table B-2 lists the basic ways in which you can use a pointing device. Pointing devices can work with your computer through a cable or through a wireless connection that transmits data using radio waves. ▨▨▨ You'll practice using your pointing device so you can work more efficiently.

STEPS

QUICK TIP

If your pointing device is a trackpad, move your finger across the trackpad to control the pointer.

1. **Locate the pointer on the desktop, then move your pointing device**

   The pointer moves across the desktop in the same direction as you move your pointing device.

2. **Move the pointer so the tip is directly over the Finder icon ▨ on the dock**

   Positioning the pointer over an item and hovering is called **pointing**. As you point to an item, a **ScreenTip** appears with the name of the item.

QUICK TIP

To single-click with a Mighty Mouse, press the left side of its touch-sensitive button; with a trackpad that has a separate button, click the button; with a Multi-Touch trackpad, press down on the trackpad with one finger.

3. **Move the pointer so the tip is directly over the Macintosh HD icon ▨ on the desktop, then press and release the left button on your pointing device**

   Pressing and releasing the left button, called **clicking** or **single-clicking**, selects an icon on the desktop or in a window, and selects options and objects within a program.

4. **With ▨ still selected, press and hold down the left button on your pointing device, move your pointing device to another location on the desktop, then release the left button**

   A dimmed icon of the Macintosh HD icon moves with the pointer. When you release the left button on your pointing device, the Macintosh HD icon is placed on the desktop at a different location. You use this technique, called **dragging**, to move icons and windows.

5. **Drag ▨ back to its original desktop location**

QUICK TIP

To right-click with a Mighty Mouse, press the right side of its touch-sensitive button; with a trackpad with a separate button, press and hold [control] while pressing the button; with a Multi-Touch trackpad, press down on the trackpad with two fingers.

6. **Position the pointer over ▨, then press and release the right button on your pointing device**

   This action, called **right-clicking**, opens a shortcut menu, as shown in Figure B-4. A **shortcut menu** lists common commands for the object that is right-clicked. A **command** is an instruction to perform a task, such as renaming an object. If a command is dimmed, it is not currently available.

7. **Click the desktop background**

   The shortcut menu closes and the Macintosh HD icon remains selected.

8. **Point to ▨, then quickly press the left button on your pointing device twice and release it**

   Quickly clicking the left button twice is called **double-clicking**, which opens a window or a program. In this case, the Finder window opens to display the contents of the Macintosh hard drive.

9. **Click the Close button ▨ in the upper-left corner of the Finder window**

   The Finder window closes. Every window has a Close button; clicking it is the fastest way to close a window.

TABLE B-1: Common pointer shapes

shape	name	description
▸	Normal Select	Points to an object and selects a command
▨ or ▨	Busy	Indicates that Leopard or another program is busy and you must wait before continuing
I	Text Select (also called I-Beam)	Identifies where you can type, select, insert, or edit text
▨	Link Select	Identifies a link you can click to jump to another location, such as a Help topic or a Web site

FIGURE B-3: Common Mac pointing devices

Mighty Mouse

Wireless Mighty Mouse

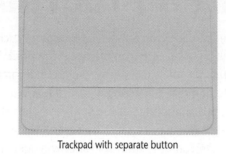

Trackpad with separate button

Multi-Touch trackpad

FIGURE B-4: Shortcut menu

Shortcut menu for the Macintosh hard drive

Open

Get Info
Duplicate
Make Alias

Copy "Macintosh HD"

Clean Up Selection

Label:
× ▪ ▪ ▪ ▪ ▪ ▪

More ▶

TABLE B-2: Basic pointing device techniques

technique	function	operation
Pointing	Points to an item; may also display a ScreenTip about the item	Move the pointing device to position the tip of the onscreen pointer over an object, and then hover
Clicking	Selects an item, such as a file or folder, or opens an item that resides on the dock	Point to an object, then quickly press and release the left button once
Double-clicking	Opens an item or resource, such as a file, folder, or software program (not residing on the dock)	Point to an object, then press the left button twice in quick succession
Right-clicking	Opens a shortcut menu	Point to an object, then quickly press and release the right button once
[control]-clicking	Opens a shortcut menu; functions as a right-click for a single-button pointing device	Point to an object, press and hold [control], then press the button once
Drag	Moves an object to a new location	Point to an object, press and hold the left button, move the object to a new location, then release the left button

Starting a Program

In addition to Finder, Leopard includes a variety of programs, such as Mail, Safari, iChat, iCal, iTunes, and iMovie, which by default are all available on the dock. The **dock** is a glossy ribbon at the bottom of your screen that contains **icons**, or small images that represent programs, folders and files, and the Trash. The purpose of the dock is to give you quick, easy access to the most frequently-used items on your computer. By default, the dock is open and located at the bottom of your computer screen, but it can be moved or hidden. The dock is divided into two areas by a vertical dashed line; programs appear on the left side of the dashed line, and folders, files, and the Trash appear on the right. To open a program, simply click the program's icon on the dock. Once you open a program, you can adjust your view of the program window using the scroll bars located on the right side and/or bottom of the window. Because you need to schedule events for your upcoming tour, you want to try working with the iCal program. Once you open the program, you scroll through the program window to get a look at the workspace.

STEPS

QUICK TIP

To hide or show the dock, click the Apple icon on the menu bar, point to Dock, then click Turn Hiding On or Off.

TROUBLE

Your iCal window may differ from Figure B-6. If it contains a left pane, click View on the menu bar, then click Hide Calendar List to close the left pane.

1. **Locate the dock on your computer screen**

   If the dock is not visible, move the onscreen pointer to the bottom of your screen and the dock will slide into view.

2. **Point to the iCal icon 📅 on the dock**

   As shown in Figure B-5, the word "iCal" appears in a ScreenTip above the icon on the dock.

3. **Click 📅 on the dock**

   As shown in Figure B-6, the iCal program opens in a window on the desktop. Programs that are currently running have a blue light beneath their program icons on the dock. The blue light identifies an open program. Since Finder is always available on the desktop, a blue light always appears beneath its icon on the dock. On the right side of the iCal window, a vertical scroll bar appears that you can use to adjust your view.

4. **Click the down scroll arrow ▼ below the vertical scroll bar**

   The window scrolls down to show another part of the calendar, and part of the calendar has now scrolled out of view.

5. **Drag the vertical scroll box slowly down the window to the bottom of the vertical scroll bar**

   The window view changes in larger increments, and the bottom part of the calendar is visible at the bottom of the window.

6. **Click in the vertical scroll bar just above the vertical scroll box**

   The view moves up approximately the height of one window.

7. **Leave the iCal window open for the next lesson**

FIGURE B-5: The dock

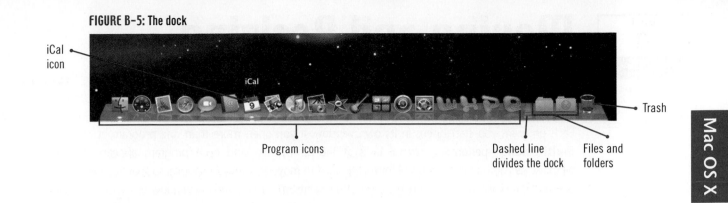

iCal icon

Trash

Program icons

Dashed line divides the dock

Files and folders

FIGURE B-6: iCal program open on desktop

iCal menu bar

iCal window

Blue lights identify open programs

Vertical scroll bar

Vertical scroll box

Scroll arrows

Mac OS X

Starting a program not found on the dock

If you'd like to use a program that is loaded on your computer but is not on the dock, click the Finder icon 🟦 on the dock to open the Finder window. Click Applications in the Sidebar (the left side of the Finder window), locate the program you'd like to use on the right side of the Finder window, then double-click the program to open it.

To save time in the future, you can add the program to the dock by dragging the program icon from the Finder window to the location on the dock where you'd like the icon to appear. Icons already on the dock will move to make room for the new icon.

Moving and Resizing Windows

Each program you start opens in its own window. If you open more than one program at once, you are **multitasking**—performing several tasks at the same time—and each program appears in a different window. As you multitask, you will invariably need to move and resize windows so that you can see more of one window or view two or more windows at the same time. To minimize a window to the dock or to increase a window to full size, you use the **window control buttons**—Minimize and Zoom —in the upper-left corner of the window. To adjust a widow's height or width (or both), you drag the size control located on the lower-right corner of the window. To move a window, you drag its **title bar**—the area across the top of the window that displays the window name or program name. The **active window** is the window you are currently using. An **inactive window** is another open window that you are not currently using. As you work on the schedule for your upcoming tour, you need to move and resize the iCal window.

STEPS

1. **Click the Zoom button in the upper-left corner of the iCal window**

   The iCal window expands to full-size, filling the screen, as shown in Figure B-7. If the window is already the fullest size available, clicking the Zoom button decreases the window size.

2. **Click again**

   The iCal window is restored to the size it was when you first opened it.

QUICK TIP

You can also minimize a window by double-clicking its title bar.

3. **Click the Minimize button in the upper-left corner of the iCal window**

   The iCal window is still open, just not visible. A **minimized window** collapses to an icon on the right side of the dock, as shown in Figure B-8. You can use this feature to hide a window that you are not currently using, but may use later.

4. **Click the minimized iCal window icon on the dock**

   The iCal window returns to its original size and position on the desktop.

5. **Drag the title bar on the iCal window to the upper-left corner of the desktop**

   The iCal window is repositioned on the desktop.

6. **Position the pointer on the size control on the lower-right corner of the iCal window, then drag down and to the right**

   Both the height and width of the window change, as shown in Figure B-9.

FIGURE B-7: iCal window expanded to full-size

Close button

Minimize button

Zoom button

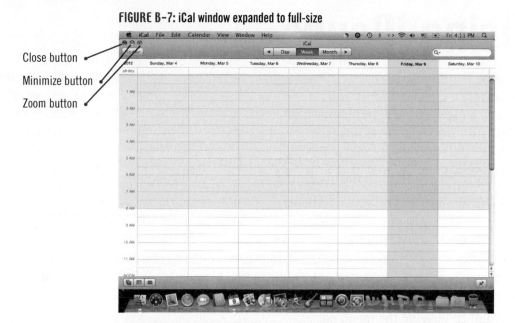

FIGURE B-8: Minimized window

iCal window minimized to the dock

FIGURE B-9: Resized window

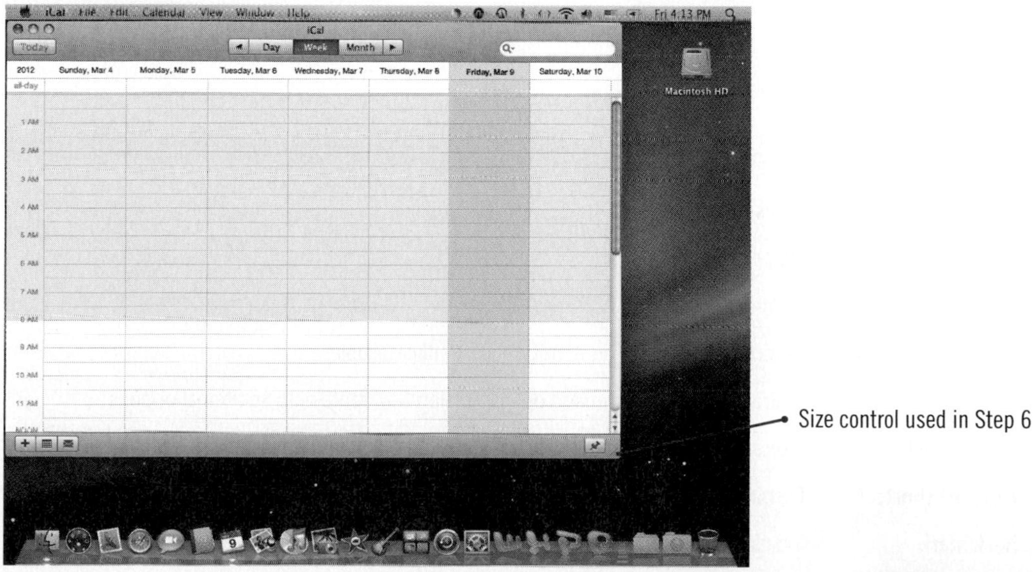

Size control used in Step 6

Mac OS X

Using Menus

A **menu** displays a list of commands that you use to accomplish a task. On your Mac, a silver bar called the **menu bar** appears across the top of the desktop, which contains menus for the active program. When no programs are open, the menu bar contains options for working with Finder. When you open a new program, the menu bar changes to accommodate the menu options for that program. Clicking a menu name on the menu bar opens a menu of available options. Table B-3 contains a list of items on a typical Mac menu. ▓▓▓▓▓ You decide to become familiar with the available commands for iCal by exploring the menu bar options.

STEPS

1. **Click iCal on the menu bar**

   The iCal menu opens, as shown in Figure B-10. You can use the commands on this menu to find out more information about iCal, change the iCal's default preference settings, access iCal services, hide iCal or other programs, and quit iCal.

2. **Point to View on the menu bar**

   The View menu opens. This menu contains commands for changing the view shown in the iCal window.

3. **Click by Month**

   The view of the calendar in the iCal window changes to by month, as shown in Figure B-11.

4. **Click View on the menu bar**

   As shown in Figure B-12, the by Month command is checked on the menu, indicating that the current view shown in iCal is by Month.

5. **Click by Week**

   The iCal window shows the current calendar week.

6. **Click the Close button ⬤ in the upper-left corner of the iCal window**

   The iCal window closes. However, because the Close button affects the iCal window only and not the iCal program, the iCal program is still open and running as indicated by the available iCal menu bar and by the blue light beneath the iCal icon on the dock.

TABLE B-3: Typical menu items

item	description
Bold command	Command or operation that can be executed
Dimmed command	Command or operation that is not currently available
Ellipsis (...)	Indicates that the command opens a dialog box containing additional options
Disclosure triangle	Indicates that a submenu is available containing an additional list of commands
Keyboard shortcut	Pressing the indicated keys will execute the command listed next to the keyboard shortcut
Check mark	Indicates the command is currently selected or active

FIGURE B-10: iCal menu

Available commands are bold

Unavailable command is dimmed

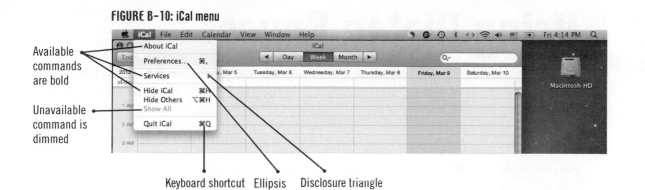

Keyboard shortcut   Ellipsis   Disclosure triangle

FIGURE B-11: iCal viewed by month

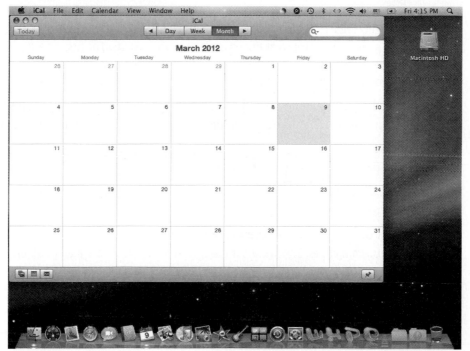

FIGURE B-12: iCal View menu

Check mark indicates current selected view

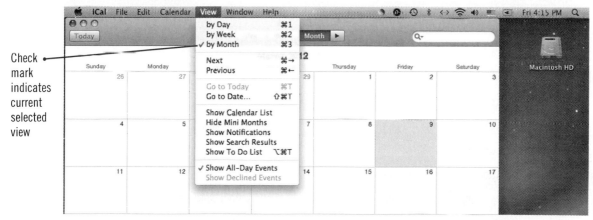

Keyboard shortcuts

You can execute a command without opening a menu by using a **keyboard shortcut**, which is a combination of keyboard keys that you press to perform a command. Available keyboard shortcut keys are listed to the right of a menu item. The **modifier key** (usually ⌘) can be pressed and held while you press the other key(s).

Using Dialog Boxes

If a program needs more information to complete an operation, it may open a **dialog box**, which enables you to select options or provide the information needed to complete the operation. Dialog boxes look similar to windows, but do not contain the window control buttons and usually cannot be resized. Table B-4 provides a list of typical elements found in a dialog box, and Figure B-13 shows many of these elements in a Print dialog box. ▰▰▰ You want to review the iCal default settings to determine whether they meet your needs while you work.

STEPS

1. **Click iCal on the menu bar, then click** Preferences

   The iCal Preferences dialog box opens, with the General preferences displayed, as shown in Figure B-14. The iCal Preferences dialog box provides access to the default iCal settings, such as days per calendar week, what day starts each week, and at what time each day's calendar starts. The first six settings in the dialog box are **pop-up menu arrows** that you click to open a pop-up menu that shows one or more options to choose. **Check boxes** at the bottom of the dialog box turn an option on when checked and off when unchecked.

2. **Click the** Day starts at arrows, **then review the options on the pop-up menu**

   The pop-up menu enables you to select the time of day that each day will start in iCal, as shown in Figure B-15.

3. **Press [esc]**

   The pop-up menu closes without any change to the selected day.

4. **Click the** Close button 🔘 **in the upper-left corner of the iCal Preferences dialog box**

   The iCal Preferences dialog box closes.

5. **Click** iCal **on the menu bar, then click** Quit iCal

   The iCal program closes. The menu bar changes to show the Finder menu options and the blue light no longer appears under iCal on the dock.

TABLE B-4: Typical elements found in a dialog box

item	description
Check box	A box that turns an option on when checked and off when unchecked
Collapse/Expand button	A button that shrinks or expands a portion of a dialog box to hide or unhide some settings
Command button	A button that completes or cancels an operation
Pop-up menu arrows	Arrows that, when clicked, display a pop-up menu of options from which you can choose
Option button	A small circle you click to select only one of two or more related options
Spin box	A text box with up and down arrows; you can type a setting in the text box or click the arrows to increase or decrease a setting
Text box	A box in which you type text (such as a password)
Tab	A clickable item at the top of a dialog box that switches to a different set of dialog box options; tabs are not available in all dialog boxes

Getting Started with Mac OS X Leopard

FIGURE B-13: Print dialog box

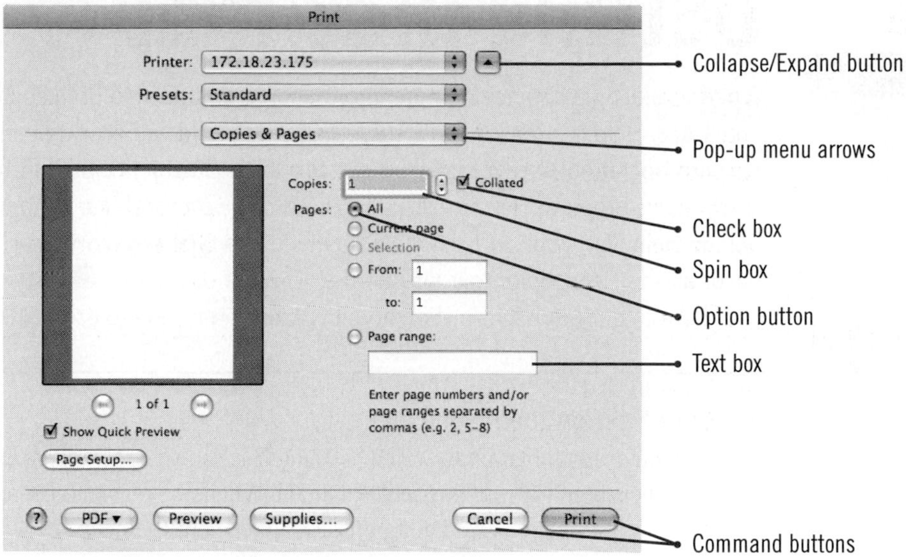

Print

Printer: 172.18.23.175 ● ● → Collapse/Expand button

Presets: Standard ●

Copies & Pages ● → Pop-up menu arrows

Copies: 1 ● ☑ Collated → Check box

Pages: ● All → Spin box
○ Current page
○ Selection → Option button
○ From: 1
to: 1

○ Page range:
→ Text box

Enter page numbers and/or
page ranges separated by
commas (e.g. 2, 5–8)

1 of 1
☑ Show Quick Preview
(Page Setup...)

(?) (PDF ▼) (Preview) (Supplies...)   (Cancel) (Print) → Command buttons

FIGURE B-14: iCal Preferences dialog box

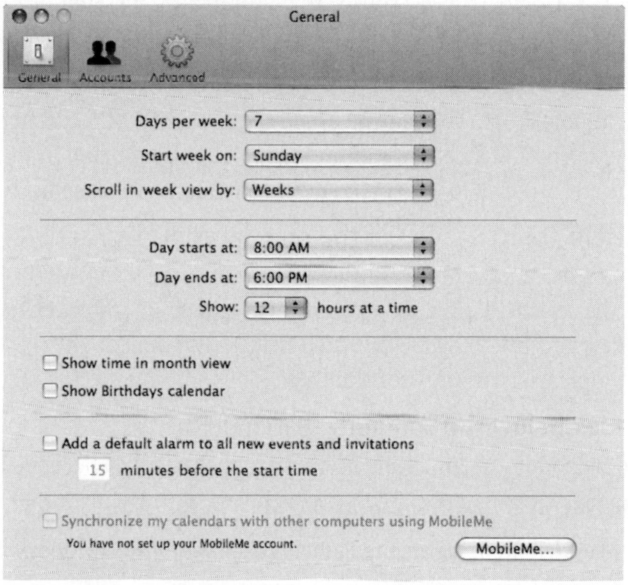

General

General Accounts Advanced

Days per week: 7 ●

Start week on: Sunday ●

Scroll in week view by: Weeks ●

Day starts at: 8:00 AM ●

Day ends at: 6:00 PM ●

Show: 12 ● hours at a time

☐ Show time in month view
☐ Show Birthdays calendar

☐ Add a default alarm to all new events and invitations
15 minutes before the start time

☐ Synchronize my calendars with other computers using MobileMe
You have not set up your MobileMe account.   (MobileMe...)

FIGURE B-15: Pop-up menu

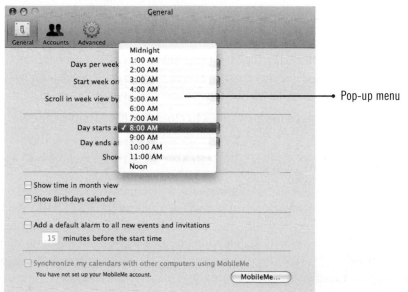

General

General Accounts Advanced

Midnight
1:00 AM
2:00 AM
Days per week   3:00 AM
4:00 AM
Start week on   5:00 AM → Pop-up menu
Scroll in week view by   6:00 AM
7:00 AM
Day starts a ✓ 8:00 AM
9:00 AM
Day ends a   10:00 AM
Show   11:00 AM
Noon

☐ Show time in month view
☐ Show Birthdays calendar

☐ Add a default alarm to all new events and invitations
15 minutes before the start time

☐ Synchronize my calendars with other computers using MobileMe
You have not set up your MobileMe account.   (MobileMe...)

Getting Mac Help

When you need assistance or more information about how to use Leopard, help is available right at your finger tips. Help is always an option on the menu bar, whether you need help with a program or with the Leopard operating system itself. You can search the interactive built-in Help files for Leopard or your currently active program. You can also go to *www.apple.com* and search Apple's Support section. To search the built-in Help files, you can open the Help menu and type **keywords** such as "Organizing files" to obtain a list of all the Help topics that include the keyword or phrase. Because you are a new Mac user, you'd like to get more information about Finder. You decide to use Help.

STEPS

1. **Click Help on the menu bar**

   A menu opens containing a Search box and Mac Help as a menu option. The Help menu provides access to Help files about the currently active program. When no program is open, the Help menu provides Mac Help, which is information about using the Leopard operating system.

2. **In the Search box, type Finder**

   As soon as you start typing, Leopard begins searching the built-in Help files to narrow down the search results. As shown in Figure B-16, the results are divided into two sections: Menu Items and Help Topics.

3. **Point to About Finder at the top of the search results**

   When you point to an item in the Menu Items section of the search results, the menu containing that command opens and an arrow indicates the selected command. In this case, the Finder menu opens and a large blue arrow points to the About Finder command on the menu, as shown in Figure B-17.

4. **In the Help Topics section of the search results list, click About the Finder**

   When you select a topic in the Help Topics section of the search results list, the Mac Help window opens and displays the selected Help topic, as shown in Figure B-18. After you've reviewed the topic shown, you can enter a keyword in the Spotlight search field in the upper-right corner of the window to find help on a different topic. You can also access the Mac Help index by clicking Index below the Spotlight search field.

5. **Click Index below the Spotlight search field**

   The Mac Help index opens, listing keywords alphabetically. See Figure B-19.

6. **Click the letter F, scroll down to locate Finder, then click Finder**

   A list of Mac Help topics related to Finder is displayed in the window.

7. **Click on a topic listed and read the information presented**

   The chosen topic appears in the Mac Help window.

8. **Click Home above the topic title**

   The Mac Help home page opens in the Mac Help window. From here, you can click a listed topic to get more information, click the More topics link to find other topics of interest, click Index to access the Mac Help index again, or click the *www.apple.com* link under Index to open the Safari browser and go to Apple's Web site. You can find additional help about Mac products by clicking the Support link on Apple's home page.

9. **Click the Close button ● to close the Mac Help window**

Opening Help for programs

Your Mac has extensive Help features available. Help is always an option on your menu bar, regardless of what program is open and running. When you click Help on the menu bar with a program open such as iCal or Microsoft Word, you can click a help command (such as "iCal Help" or "Word Help") to open Help that is specific to the currently active program. You'll also find additional access to Help features within programs themselves. For example, each Microsoft Office 2008 for Mac program has a Help button ⊙ on its Standard toolbar. Clicking the Help button opens Help for that program, which provides thorough information on the program and includes a link to go to the software manufacturer's Web site for additional assistance.

FIGURE B-16: Help search results

Search results list

FIGURE B-17: Menu item containing keyword

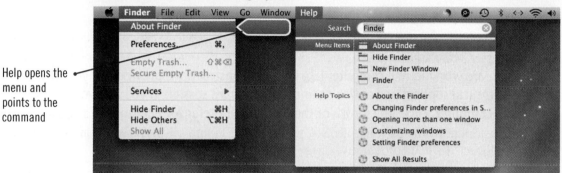

Help opens the menu and points to the command

FIGURE B-18: Mac Help window

Click to go to the Mac Help home page

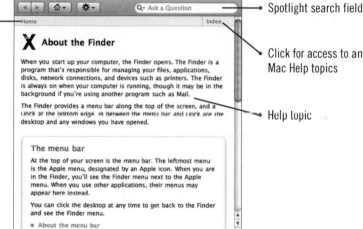

Spotlight search field

Click for access to an index of Mac Help topics

Help topic

FIGURE B-19: Mac Help index

Ending a Leopard Session

When you finish working on your Mac, you should save and close any open files, close any open programs, close any open windows, and shut down the operating system. As shown in Table B-5, there are four options for ending your Leopard sessions. Whichever option you choose, it's important to shut down your computer in an orderly manner. If you turn off the computer while Leopard is running, you could lose data or damage Leopard and your computer. If you are working in a computer lab, follow your instructor's directions and your lab's policies and guidelines for ending your Leopard session. You have examined the basic ways in which you can use Leopard, so you are ready to end your Leopard session.

1. **Click the Apple icon 🍎 on the menu bar**

   The Apple menu has four options for ending a Leopard session—Sleep, Restart, Shut Down, and Log Out, as shown in Figure B-20.

2. **If you are working in a computer lab, follow the instructions provided by your instructor or technical support person for ending your Leopard session; if you are working on your own computer, click Shut Down or the option you prefer for ending your Leopard session**

   After you shut down your computer, you may also need to turn off your monitor and other hardware devices, such as a printer, to conserve energy.

TABLE B-5: Options for ending a Leopard session

option	description
Sleep	Puts your Mac in a low power state to conserve energy while not in use. All drives are disengaged to protect your drives and data. Press any key on the keyboard to resume use.
Restart	All open files and programs are closed. All drives are disengaged and memory is cleared. Your Mac safely shuts down, and then restarts automatically.
Shut Down	All open files and programs are closed. All drives are disengaged and memory is cleared. Your Mac then safely shuts down and turns off.
Log Out	All open files and programs are closed. All drives are disengaged and memory is cleared. Your Mac then logs out the current user, but continues running so the next user can log in and begin using the computer immediately, without waiting for the computer to boot up.

Getting Started with Mac OS X Leopard

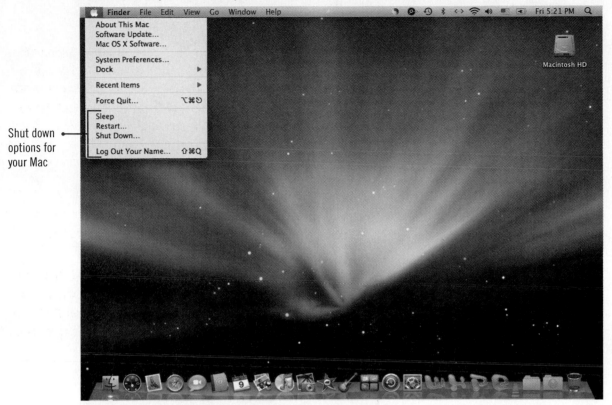

Shut down
options for
your Mac

Practice

▼ CONCEPTS REVIEW

Identify each of the items labeled in Figure B-21.

FIGURE B-21

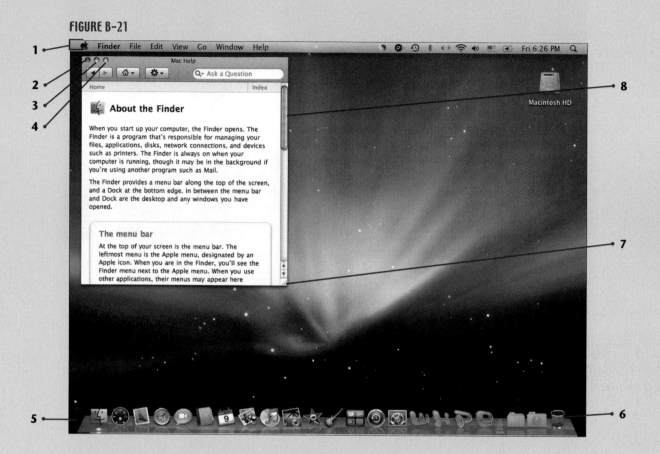

Match each statement with the term it describes.

9. The part of Leopard that is always active on the Leopard desktop and dock

10. A glossy ribbon at the bottom of your computer screen that contains icons

11. A silver bar across the top of the desktop that gives you easy access to operational commands

12. Small images that represent programs, folders and files, and the Trash

13. A type of window that opens after you select a menu command so you can specify settings for completing the operation

a. Dialog box
b. Menu bar
c. Dock
d. Icons
e. Finder

Select the best answer from the list of choices.

14. **Leopard is an operating system that:**
    a. Interferes with your use of a computer.
    b. Manages the operation of a computer.
    c. Performs a single task, such as connecting to the Internet.
    d. Creates documents, such as a resume.

15. **When you right-click with a pointing device such as a mouse, Leopard:**
    a. opens a Windows tool or program.
    b. moves an object, such as a desktop icon.
    c. opens a shortcut menu.
    d. deletes the object.

16. **Default settings are:**
    a. preset settings that cannot be changed.
    b. preset settings that can be changed.
    c. viewable on the dock.
    d. permanent settings for the menu bar.

17. **To open a menu:**
    a. click the title or word on the menu bar.
    b. click the item on the dock.
    c. click the folder on the dock.
    d. click the Trash.

18. **Which operation opens an item on the dock?**
    a. Point
    b. Click
    c. Double-click
    d. Right-click

19. **When you set your Mac to Sleep to end a Leopard session, Leopard:**
    a. Completely shuts down the computer.
    b. Provides an option for switching users.
    c. Restarts your computer.
    d. Puts your Mac in a low power state and allows you to resume use quickly.

20. **Which of the following options for ending your Leopard session safely turns your Mac off?**
    a. Sleep
    b. Restart
    c. Shut down
    d. Log Out

▼ SKILLS REVIEW

1. Start Mac OS X Leopard.
  a. Turn on your computer, then enter your user name and password (if necessary).
  b. Identify the Finder menu bar, the dock, and the Macintosh HD icon on the desktop without referring to the lessons.
  c. Compare your results to Figure B-2 to make sure that you have identified all the desktop items correctly.

2. Use a pointing device.
  a. Point to the Trash icon and display its ScreenTip.
  b. Drag the Macintosh HD icon to a new location on the desktop.
  c. Double-click the Macintosh HD icon to open the Finder window.
  d. Close the Finder window.
  e. Drag the Macintosh HD icon back to its original location.

3. Start a program.
  a. Using the ScreenTips, locate the Microsoft Word icon on the dock, then click it.
  b. In the Microsoft Word window, click the down scroll arrow below the vertical scroll bar.
  c. Drag the vertical scroll box slowly down the window to the bottom of the vertical scroll bar.
  d. Click above the vertical scroll box in the vertical scroll bar to move the view of the window up.

4. Move and resize windows.
  a. Click the Zoom button to expand the Microsoft Word window to full-size. (*Hint*: The size of the window may not change dramatically.)
  b. Click the Minimize button to minimize the Microsoft Word window.
  c. Click the minimized Word window on the dock to restore it to its original size and position on the desktop.
  d. Drag the Word window to the right on the desktop.
  e. Drag the Word window back to its original position.
  f. Click and drag the size control to change the window width and height.
  g. Close the Word window.

5. Use menus.
  a. Click Word on the menu bar, then click Quit Word.
  b. Click Finder on the menu bar, then click About Finder.
  c. Click Window on the menu bar, then view the options on the menu.
  d. Click away from the Window menu to close it.
  e. Close the About Finder window.

6. Use dialog boxes.
  a. Click the Apple icon on the menu bar, then click System Preferences.
  b. In the System Preferences window, click the Speech icon under System.
  c. Click the Text to Speech tab at the top of the Speech dialog box, if it is not already selected.
  d. Click the arrows next to System Voice, click the male or female voice of your choice, then click the Play command button to hear the voice play. (*Hint*: You may need to press [F12] or use the volume option on the right side of the menu bar to turn up the speaker volume.)
  e. Click to select the check box next to Announce when alerts are displayed.
  f. Click the Set Alert Options command button.
  g. Click the Play command button to hear the announcement.
  h. Click OK.
  i. Click to deselect the check box next to Announce when alerts are displayed.
  j. Close the Speech dialog box.

7. **Get Mac Help.**
   a. Click Help on the menu bar.
   b. In the Search box, type **dock**.
   c. In the list next to Help Topics, click **If you can't see the Dock**.
   d. In the Mac Help window, read the instructions in the box titled "To make the Dock reappear:".
   e. Go to the Mac Help index.
   f. Click "D" in the Mac Help index, then scroll down and click Dock.
   g. Click the About the Dock Help topic, then read the topic.
   h. Close the Mac Help window.
8. **End a Leopard session.**
   a. If you are working in a computer lab, follow the instructions provided by your instructor for using the Apple menu to put the computer to sleep, restart the computer, shut down the computer completely, or log out of the computer. If you are working on your own Mac, use the Apple menu to choose the shut-down option you prefer.

▼ INDEPENDENT CHALLENGE 1

You work as a teacher for ABC Computer Mentors. You need to prepare a set of handouts that provide an overview of some of the desktop features in Leopard for individuals enrolled in an upcoming class on Mac Survival Skills.

   a. Click Help on the menu bar.
   b. Type **About the menu bar** in the Search box, then click About the menu bar.
   c. Use the vertical scroll bar to read the information presented, click one of the links under Related Topics at the end, then read that information as well.
   d. Prepare a handwritten list of 5 features that you learned about using menus and the menu bar. Use the following title for your list: **Interesting Information about Using Menus**.
   e. Close the Mac Help window, write your name on your list, and submit it to your instructor.

▼ INDEPENDENT CHALLENGE 2

A friend of yours has just purchased an iMac to use at home. She recently read an interesting article about the Preview program that comes with all new Macs and would like your help to find out more about this program.

   a. Click Help on the menu bar, then type **Preview** in the search box.
   b. From the list of search results, open the About Preview topic and read the information presented.
   c. After reading the information in the About Preview topic, use the Help menu to find and read the Previewing a document before you print Help topic.
   d. Prepare a handwritten summary of 2-3 paragraphs with the title **What is Preview?** listing some of the information you found about this topic.
   e. Close the Mac Help window, write your name on your summary, and submit it to your instructor.

▼ INDEPENDENT CHALLENGE 3

The Dashboard is a feature of Mac OS X that displays information such as the weather, time, and date when the Dashboard icon is clicked on the dock. As a marketing analyst for Expert AI Systems in Philadelphia, Pennsylvania, you contact and collaborate with employees at an Australian branch of the company. Because your colleagues live in a different time zone, you want to add another clock to the Dashboard and customize it to show the time in Sydney, Australia. This way, you can quickly determine when to reach these employees at a convenient time during their workday hours.

a. Use the Help menu to search for information on **Customizing Dashboard widgets**.

b. Use this Help information to change the settings on the Dashboard's World Clock to apply to your city (or the closest big city to you in your time zone). If your Dashboard does not contain a World Clock, use the Help option to search for **Displaying Dashboard widgets** and follow the instructions to add the World Clock to the Dashboard.

c. Search for the **Adding widgets to the dashboard** Help topic, read the topic, then add a second World Clock to the Dashboard and set the time for Sydney, Australia.

Advanced Challenge Exercise

- Add a Unit Converter to the Dashboard.
- In the Unit Converter, change the Convert option to **Temperature**.
- Type **70** in the Fahrenheit box.

d. Search for a Help topic about removing Dashboard widgets, and then remove all widgets that you added to the Dashboard in this exercise.

e. Close the Dashboard.

f. Prepare a handwritten summary entitled **Using Widgets** that describes what settings you examined and how you might use them in your daily life.

g. Write your name on your summary and submit it to your instructor.

▼ REAL LIFE INDEPENDENT CHALLENGE

As a New Year's resolution, you have decided to automate more of your life and depend less on paper files. You've investigated the features of the Mac and found that your Mac has an application called Address Book where you can store the contact information for family, friends, and business associates. This is a great step towards meeting your resolution, so you decide to use this application.

a. Using ScreenTips, locate the Address Book icon on the dock and open it.

b. Click All on the left side of the Address Book window to select the All Group.

c. Below the Name column in the Address Book window, click the Create a new card button. (*Hint*: The button has a plus sign on it.)

d. In the right pane, add your first and last name in the spaces provided and complete the Company, work Phone, and work Email entries with fictional information.

e. When you're finished entering information, click the Edit button at the bottom of the right pane to add your information to the Address Book.

f. Add fictitious contact information for four additional people.

Advanced Challenge Exercise

- Click the All group to select it.
- Click File on the menu bar, then click Print.
- In the Print dialog box, click the Expand button to the right of the Printer arrows if necessary to expand the dialog box.
- Click the Style arrows, then click Lists.
- Click Print.
- Circle your name on the printed list and submit it to your instructor.

g. Close the Address Book window.

h. Click Address Book on the menu bar, then click Quit Address Book.

▼ VISUAL WORKSHOP

Now that you've been introduced to the Mac, you'd like to learn how to use the Grab program to take a picture of your screen. Use the skills you learned in this unit to print a screen shot like that shown in Figure B-22:

- Search Mac Help for information about Grab, then open the Help topic shown in Figure B-22.
- Click Open Grab within the Help topic to open the Grab program on the desktop (as shown in Figure B-22, the Grab menu bar appears but a Grab window does not).
- Following the instructions in the Help topic, click Capture on the Grab menu bar, then click Screen to capture a picture of the computer screen. Follow the instructions in the dialog box that opens. The screen shot will appear in a new window.
- Close the Mac Help window, click File on the Grab menu bar, click Print to open the Print dialog box, then click Print to print the screen shot. Write your name on the printed screen shot, and submit it to your instructor.
- Close the screen shot window, then quit Grab.

FIGURE B-22

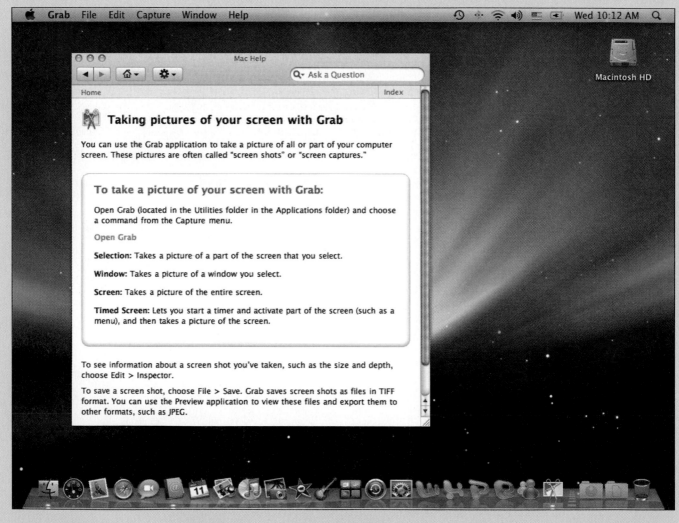

Understanding File Management

Finder is a program on the Leopard operating system that you use to access the folders and files in your various storage devices. Each **storage device**, or **drive**, is a physical location for storing files. Most people store their files on the computer's hard disk and keep duplicate copies on other storage devices, such as a USB flash drive or a CD. The **hard disk** is a built-in, high-capacity, high-speed storage device for all the software, folders, and files on a computer. When you work with a program, you save the results in a **file**, which consists of stored electronic data such as text, a picture, a video, or music. Each file is stored in a **folder**, which is a container for a group of related files, allowing you to group them into categories such as reports, correspondence, or e-mail contacts. As a tour guide for Quest Specialty Travel (QST), you want to better understand how you can use Finder to manage the files you need for proposing, planning, organizing, and documenting QST tours.

OBJECTIVES

Understand file management

Open the Finder window

Change views

Create and save documents

Open, edit, and print files

Copy, rename, and move files

Search for files

Delete and restore files

Understanding File Management

Most of the work you do on a computer involves using programs to create files, which you then store in folders. Over time, you create many folders and files and save them on different storage devices. The process of finding your folders and files can become a challenge. **File management** is a strategy for organizing your files and folders so you can find your data quickly and easily. Finder is the primary tool you'll use for file management.  As a QST tour guide for destinations in the South Pacific, you work with many types of files. You want to review how Finder can help you organize your files so you can find them when you need them.

DETAILS

You can use Finder to:

- **Create folders for storing and organizing files**

  Folders provide a location for your files and a way to organize them into groups of related files so that you can easily locate a file later. Leopard provides a **home folder** for each user that contains several subfolders in which you can save your files on the hard drive. The name of the user's home folder is the user's name. Most programs automatically open and use the Documents folder, a subfolder of your home folder, when you save or open files. You can also create additional folders or subfolders. You give each folder you create a unique, descriptive **folder name** that identifies the files you intend to place in the folder. A folder can also contain other folders, called **subfolders**, to organize files into smaller groups. This structure for organizing folders and files is called a **file hierarchy** because it describes the logic and layout of the folder structure on a disk. Figure C-1 illustrates how you might organize your tour folders and files within the Documents folder. In addition to the Documents folder, Leopard also provides folders in your home folder that are dedicated to specific types of files, such as the Pictures folder for image files, the Music folder for music or sound files, and the Downloads folder for content that you download from the Internet. Figure C-2 shows the standard folders that Leopard creates for each user in the home folder.

- **Rename, copy, and move folders and files**

  If you want to change the name of a folder or file, you can rename it. For example, you might change the name of the "French Polynesia Tour Proposal" file to "French Polynesia Tour" after your supervisor approves the tour. If you need a duplicate of a file, you can copy it. You can also move a folder or file to another folder or device.

- **Delete and restore folders and files**

  Deleting folders and files you no longer need frees up storage space on your devices and helps keep your files organized. Folders and files you delete are moved to a folder called the Trash. If you accidentally delete an important folder or file, or if you change your mind and want to restore a deleted folder or file, you can retrieve it from the Trash. If you're sure your Trash has nothing in it you might want to restore, you can empty it, which permanently removes the files or folders.

- **Locate folders and files quickly**

  Finder's search options help you quickly locate a folder or file if you forget where you stored it. If you know the date you last used the file or the type of the file, use the Search For group in the sidebar in the Finder window to find the file. If you can provide part of the folder or filename, or some text that appears in the file, use the Search field in the Finder window to easily locate it.

- **Use aliases to access frequently used files and folders**

  As your file structure becomes more complex, a file or folder you use often might be located several levels down the file hierarchy and require multiple steps to open. To save time, you can create aliases on your desktop to the files and folders you use frequently. An **alias** is a link that gives you quick access to an item, whether it's a folder, file, or program. Each icon on the dock is an alias for a program, folder, or file stored elsewhere on your computer.

FIGURE C-1: Sample folder and file hierarchy

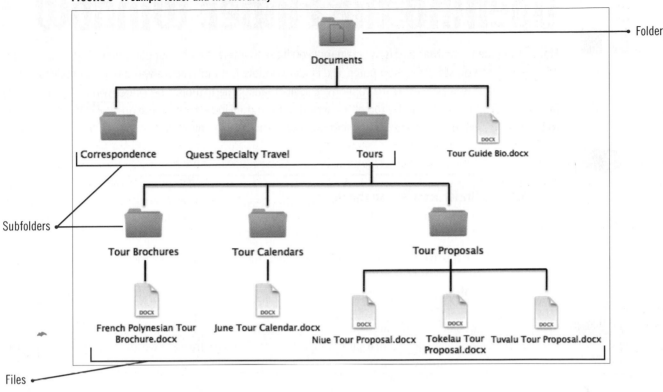

FIGURE C-2: Default user folders

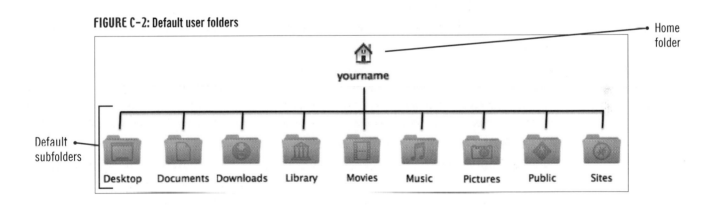

Organizing your folders and files efficiently

Good planning is essential for effective file management. First, identify the types of files you work with, such as images, music, reports, and so on, and then determine a logical system for organizing your files. The Pictures and Music folders are good places to store images and music. The Documents folder is the most common place to store all of your other files. Within each folder, use subfolders to organize the files into smaller groups. For example, use subfolders in the Pictures folder to separate family photos from vacation photos, or to group them by year. In the Documents folder, you might group personal files in one subfolder and business files in another subfolder, and then create additional subfolders to further distinguish sets of files. For example, your personal files might include subfolders for resumes, letters, and income tax returns, to name a few. Your business files might include subfolders for clients, projects, and invoices. You should periodically reevaluate your folder structure to ensure that it continues to meet your needs.

Opening the Finder Window

Finder is unique to the Mac and is the main tool you'll use to interact with your computer. Finder starts automatically when you start your computer. The Finder window is an interactive window that provides access to your storage devices, files, search options, and file management tools. The Finder window is accessible from the default menu bar at the top of the screen or from the Finder icon on the dock.  You decide to become acquainted with the Finder window so you can quickly and easily locate the files you'll need for QST tours.

STEPS

1. **Click the Finder icon** 📷 **on the dock**

    The Finder window opens with the home folder selected and the home folder's contents displayed in the right pane. Refer to Figure C-3 to identify the elements of the Finder window described below:

    - The **title bar** contains the name of the resource, such as a folder or a device, whose contents are displayed in the right pane of the Finder window.
    - The **toolbar** appears directly below the title bar and contains tools that aid with navigation, views, and file management. Table C-1 describes the tools on the Finder toolbar.
    - The light blue area that makes up the left pane of the Finder window is called the **sidebar**. The sidebar is a navigation tool that provides quick access to many frequently-used resources on your Mac. When an item is selected in the sidebar, the item's contents are displayed in the right pane of the Finder window. The sidebar is divided into three or four groups:
        - The **Devices** group provides quick access to all of the storage devices available to your Mac, such as the hard disk and any external drives.
        - The **Shared** group is only shown if your Mac is connected to a network or to other computers. It lists all shared computers and servers to which the user has access.
        - The **Places** group provides quick access to the Desktop folder, your home folder, the Applications folder, and your Documents folder.
        - The **Search For** group helps you find a file quickly by viewing files you've used recently or by viewing only a certain type of file.
    - The **toolbar control** in the upper-right corner of the window hides the toolbar and sidebar when clicked. Once the toolbar and sidebar are hidden, click the toolbar control again to show them.
    - The **size control** at the bottom-right corner of the window enables you to resize the Finder window.
    - The **status bar** lists the number of items in the selected folder or storage device. It also lists the available space on the selected storage device.

QUICK TIP

You can close or open a group in the sidebar by clicking the disclosure triangle next to it. When the triangle points to the right, the contents of the group are hidden; when the triangle points down, the contents appear below the group name.

TABLE C-1: Tools on the Finder toolbar

tool	used to
Back and Forward buttons	Display the previous or next file location in the window
View buttons	Change the arrangement and view of the files and folders in the window
Quick Look button	Display the contents of a selected file as a large preview without opening the file
Action button	Perform file management commands such as creating a new folder, opening a file, or copying a file or folder
Search field	Search for files by filename or file content

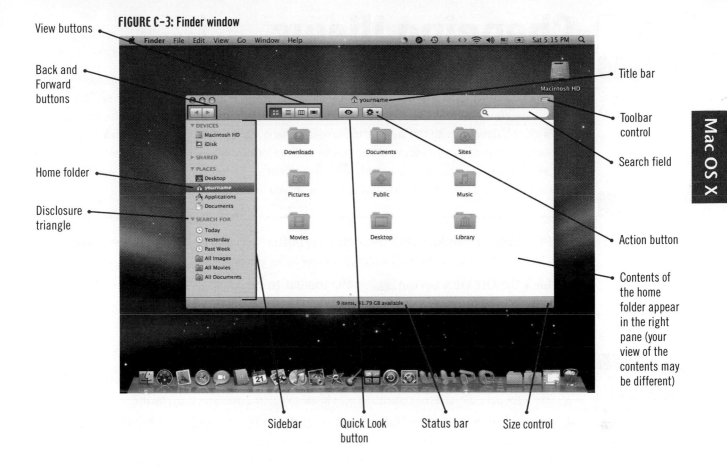

FIGURE C-3: Finder window

View buttons

Back and Forward buttons

Home folder

Disclosure triangle

Title bar

Toolbar control

Search field

Action button

Contents of the home folder appear in the right pane (your view of the contents may be different)

Sidebar   Quick Look button   Status bar   Size control

The home folder and its contents

The user's home folder is the location designated by Leopard to store all of the files created by the user. By default, each time you click the Finder icon on the dock, the Finder window opens with the home folder selected. Inside the home folder are the Documents folder and eight additional folders, each for different kinds of files. The Desktop folder contains all items on the user's desktop, except for external storage devices such as USB flash drives. The Downloads folder is the default location for all files downloaded from the Internet. The Library folder is the designated location for preferences files and user data and is maintained by Leopard. The Movies, Music, and Picture folders are the designated locations for all movies, music, and picture files, respectively. These folders open by default when you import video from a digital camera, download music from iTunes, or import digital photo files. The Public folder is the designated folder to place any files you'd like to share with other users of your Mac. The Sites folder is the location for your Web pages. Used in conjunction with the Apache Web server software, you can host a Web site on your computer. With the exception of the Public and Sites folder, all folders in the home folder are private and available only to the user.

Changing Views

Leopard provides several ways of displaying your files and folders in the Finder window. Each display, or **view**, presents the items shown in the main area of the Finder window in a different way. The four main views, **icon view**, **list view**, **columns view**, and **Cover Flow**, can be selected using the View buttons in the Finder window or using the View option on the Finder menu bar. The fifth view, **Quick Look**, is accessible only from the Finder window. When you open the Finder window, the current view is the view that was selected when Finder was last used. ░░░░ You decide to look at the different views in Finder to determine the view that you would most like to use as you work.

STEPS

1. **In the Finder window, click the Icon View button ▦ on the toolbar if necessary**
   The right pane displays the contents of your home folder as icons, as shown in Figure C-4.

2. **Click the List View button ▤ on the toolbar to switch to list view**
   As shown in Figure C-5, the right pane displays the contents of your home folder in an alphabetical list with additional details about each file and folder provided, such as Name, Date Modified, Size, and Kind. The Size column shows the sizes of files but does not list sizes for folders. The Kind column lists the file type or the program that created the file.

QUICK TIP

If you don't have an iChat icons subfolder in your Pictures folder, click the Library folder in the first column of the right pane, then scroll down in the second column and click the Safari subfolder. In steps 6 and 7, use the Safari subfolder and the History.plist file in place of the Planets subfolder and Jupiter.gif file.

3. **Click the Columns View button ▥ on the toolbar to switch to columns view**
   The right pane displays the contents of your home folder in a multicolumn format.

4. **In the right pane of the Finder window, click the Pictures folder in the first column**
   The contents of the Pictures folder are displayed in the column to the right.

5. **In the second column, click the iChat icons subfolder, then click the Planets subfolder in the third column**
   The Planets subfolder contains the planet icons available for use in the iChat program that comes with Leopard. Compare your computer screen to Figure C-6.

6. **With the Planets subfolder selected, click the Cover Flow button ▦ on the toolbar**
   The right pane of the Finder window is divided in two. In the top section of the pane, a preview of the first file in the Planets subfolder appears with a horizontal scroll bar beneath it. The bottom section of the right pane displays the selected subfolder's contents as a detailed list. Compare your screen to Figure C-7.

QUICK TIP

You can also activate Quick Look by selecting a file, then pressing [spacebar], or by clicking File on the menu bar, then clicking Quick Look "[filename]".

7. **Click the Jupiter.gif file in the bottom section of the right pane, then click the Quick Look button ◉ on the toolbar**
   When you initially click the file in the bottom section of the pane, a preview of the file appears in the top section of the pane. When you click the Quick Look button, a larger preview of the file is displayed in front of the Finder window, as shown in Figure C-8. Quick Look is a new feature of the Leopard operating system that allows you to preview the contents of a file without actually opening it. You can click the Full Screen button at the bottom of the Quick Look window to enlarge the Quick Look preview to full-screen size.

8. **Close the Quick Look window, then click ▥ on the toolbar**
   The Finder window changes to columns view again. A preview of the selected Jupiter.gif file appears in the furthest right column.

9. **Close the Finder window**

Understanding File Management

FIGURE C-4: Icon view

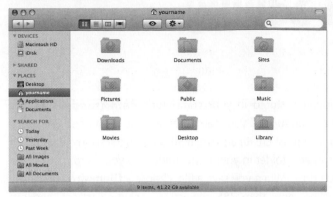

FIGURE C-5: List view

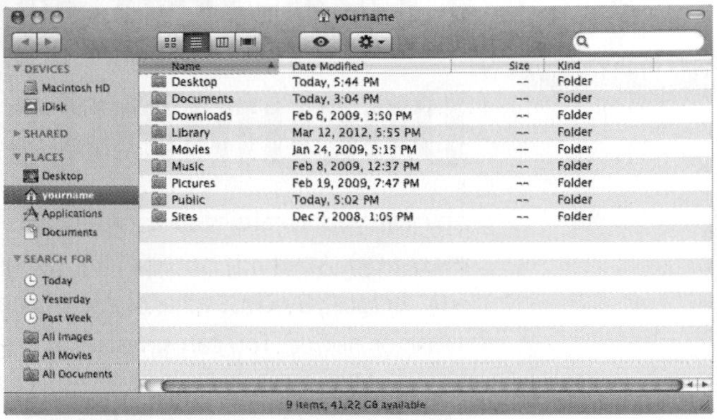

FIGURE C-6: Planets subfolder selected in columns view

FIGURE C-7: Cover Flow

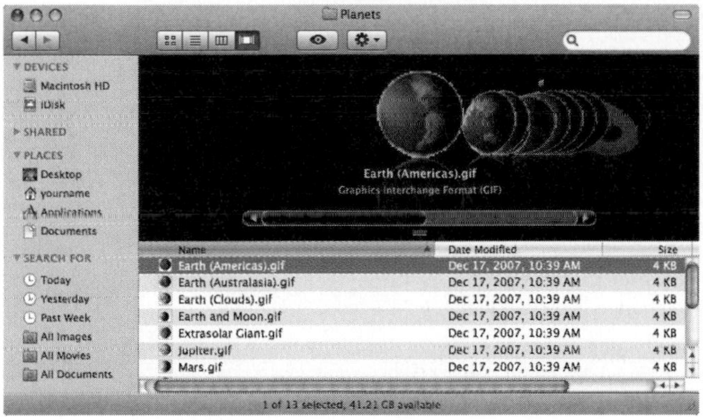

FIGURE C-8: Quick Look

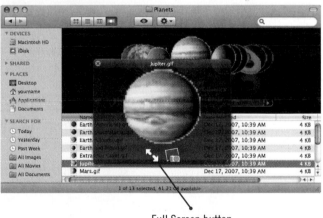

Full Screen button

Creating and Saving Documents

Any file you create with a program is temporarily stored in your computer's **RAM (random access memory)**. Anything stored in RAM is lost when you turn off your computer or if the power fails unexpectedly. Before you close a file or exit a program, you must create a permanent copy of the file by saving it on a disk or device. You can save files in the Documents folder in your home folder, on your hard drive, or on a removable storage device such as a USB flash drive. When you save a file, choose a **filename** that clearly identifies the file contents. Filenames can be no more than 255 characters, including spaces, and can include letters, numbers, and certain symbols. You want to use Microsoft Word to create a to-do list for your next tour, and you plan to save the file to the Documents folder.

1. **Click the Microsoft Word icon 🔳 on the dock**

   Microsoft Word 2008 opens and a new, blank document window appears on the desktop. In the document window, a blinking cursor identifies the insertion point, which is where any text you type will appear.

   If you make a typing mistake, press [delete] on the keyboard to delete the character to the left of the insertion point.

2. **Type To-Do List on the first line, then press [return] three times**

   Each time you press [return], Word inserts a new blank line and places the insertion point at the beginning of the line.

3. **Type the text shown in Figure C-9, pressing [return] at the end of each line**

   If the Save As dialog box is already expanded, click the Collapse button 🔳 to the right of the Save As text box to collapse the dialog box.

4. **Click File on the menu bar, then click Save As**

   The Save As dialog box opens with the Documents folder selected as the Where location in which to save the file, as shown in Figure C-10. By default, Word 2008 creates a temporary filename of To.docx in the Save As text box, with the word To highlighted in blue. You'll need to type a more descriptive filename.

5. **In the Save As text box, replace To with To-Do List, then click the Expand button 🔳 to the right of the Save As text box if necessary**

   The Save As dialog box expands to show the contents of the Documents folder, as shown in Figure C-11.

   If a Confirm Save As dialog box asks if you want to replace a file with the same name, click Yes.

6. **Click Save in the Save As dialog box**

   Word saves the document in a file named "To-Do List" in the Documents folder and closes the Save As dialog box. The title bar of the Word window now displays "To-Do List.docx"—the filename you entered, followed by the file extension .docx. A **file extension** identifies the type of file. Each program assigns a file extension to files you create, so you only need to enter a name for the file. Depending on how Leopard is set up on your computer, you may not see the file extensions.

7. **Click Word on the menu bar, then click Quit Word**

   The Word file and the program close.

FIGURE C-9: Word 2008 document

Program name

Insertion point

Standard toolbar

Document window

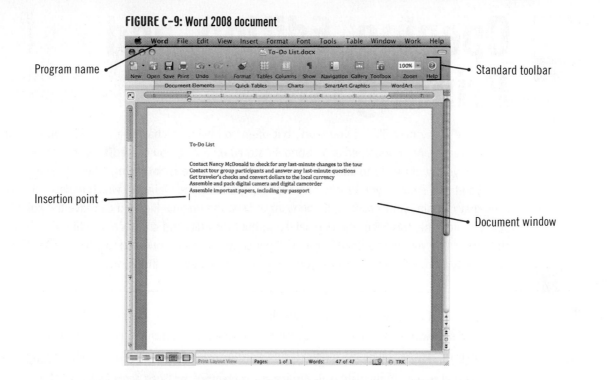

FIGURE C-10: Save As dialog box

Temporary filename

Expand button

Documents folder

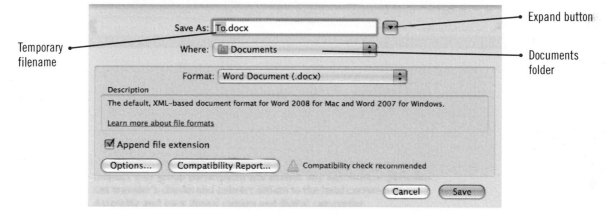

FIGURE C-11: Expanded Save As dialog box

New filename

Contents of the Documents folder (yours will differ)

File type

Save button

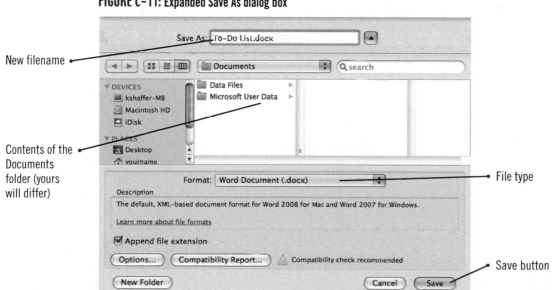

Opening, Editing, and Printing Files

You create many new files as you work, but often you want to change a file that you or someone else already created. After you open an existing file stored on a disk, you can **edit**, or make changes, to it. For example, you might want to add or delete text, or change the **formatting** (the appearance) of the text. After you finish editing, you usually save the file with the same filename, which replaces the file with the copy that contains your changes. If you want to keep the original file, you can save the edited file with a different filename; this keeps the original file without the edits and creates a new file with the most recent changes. When you want a **hard copy**, or paper copy, of the file, you need to print it. You need to add two items to your To-Do List, so you want to open and edit it, then print it.

STEPS

1. **Click the Finder icon 🖼 on the dock**
   The Finder window opens with the contents of the home folder displayed in columns view.

2. **Click the Documents folder in the first column of the right pane of the Finder window**
   A second column in the right pane displays the contents of the Documents folder, as shown in Figure C-12.

3. **Double-click To-Do list.docx in the second column**
   The program that created the file, Word, loads and opens the selected file, To-Do List.docx, in the Word window.

4. **Click at the beginning of the last blank line in the To-Do List, then type the two additional lines shown in Figure C-13, pressing [return] after each line**

5. **Click the Save button 💾 on the Standard toolbar**
   The original To-Do List.docx file is replaced by the edited To-Do List.docx file in the Documents folder.

6. **Click File on the menu bar, then click Print Preview**
   Print Preview displays a full-page view of your document, as shown in Figure C-14, so you can check its layout before you print. If you need to make additional edits, click the Close button on the Print Preview toolbar (not the title bar), make your changes, and then use Print Preview to check the document again before printing.

7. **Click the Print button 🖨 on the Print Preview toolbar, then retrieve your printed copy from the printer**
   Print Preview closes and returns to the Word window, and your document is printed.

8. **Click Word on the menu bar, then click Quit Word**
   Word closes.

FIGURE C-12: Documents folder in Finder window

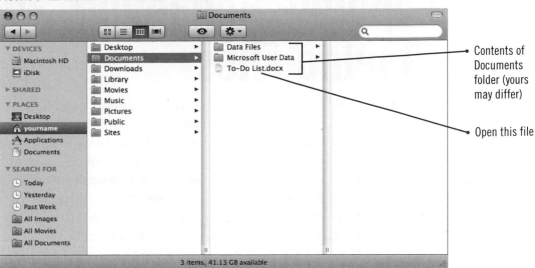

Contents of
Documents
folder (yours
may differ)

Open this file

FIGURE C-13: Edited To-Do List file

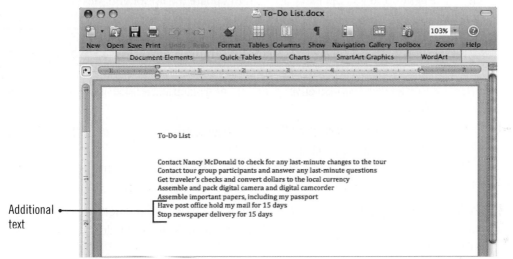

Additional
text

FIGURE C-14: Print Preview

Print button

Closes
Print
Preview,
but not the
document

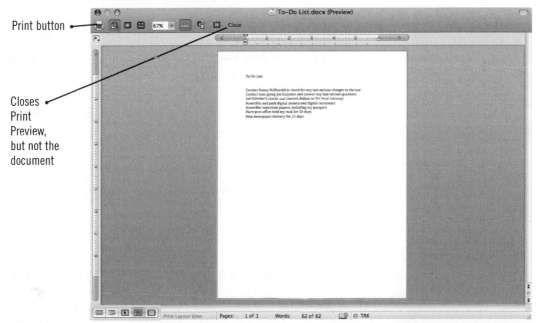

Copying, Renaming, and Moving Files

Periodically, you might need to copy, rename, or move a file to keep your files organized and easy to find. You can copy or move a file, a group of files, or a folder from one storage device to another or from one folder to another. When you **copy** a file, the original file stays in its current location and a duplicate of the file is created in another location. This feature lets you make a backup of your important files. A **backup** is a copy of a file that is stored in another location. If you lose the original file, you can make a new working copy from your backup. When you **move** a file, the original file is stored in a different location and no longer remains in the original location. One of the fastest ways to move a file is with **drag and drop** (which uses a pointing device to drag a file or folder to a new location). You might also need to rename a file, giving it a name that more clearly describes the file's contents and how you intend to use the file. So that you can work with your To-Do List.docx file when you travel, you plan to copy the file to a new folder on your USB flash drive and then rename it. You also want to move the original file to the desktop so you can easily access it to update the list for your next tour.

STEPS

QUICK TIP

If you are using a different storage device, insert the appropriate disk and substitute that device whenever you see USB flash drive in the steps.

1. **Attach your USB flash drive to your computer and wait for its icon to appear on the desktop**

   When the icon for your USB flash drive appears on the desktop and is listed under Devices in the Finder window, it is ready to use.

2. **In the Finder window, click the USB flash drive under Devices, click the Action button [⚙▾] on the toolbar, then click New Folder**

   A new folder, temporarily named "untitled folder", is added to your USB flash drive, as shown in Figure C-16. The folder name is highlighted so you can type a more descriptive name.

3. **Type French Polynesia Tour as the name of the new folder, then press [return]**

   The name of the folder changes and the folder is selected in the Finder window. Because the folder is empty, there are no contents to display in the next column.

QUICK TIP

A file can also be copied using the Finder Edit menu. Select the file, click Edit on the menu bar, click Copy "[filename]", navigate to the folder in the Finder window to which you want to copy the file, click Edit on the menu bar, then click Paste Item.

4. **Click Documents under Places in the sidebar, click and drag the To-Do List.docx file from the Documents folder on top of the USB flash drive under Devices until a rounded rectangle appears around the name of your USB flash drive and the contents of the drive appear in the right pane of the Finder window (do not release the mouse button)**

5. **Drag the file on top of the French Polynesia Tour folder in the right pane of the Finder window until the folder is highlighted blue, then release the mouse button**

   As shown in Figure C-17, the To-Do List.docx file has been copied to the French Polynesia Tour folder on your USB flash drive. This method of copying files is called drag and drop. The **spring-loaded folders** feature of Leopard, in which dragging the file on top of a folder causes the folder to "spring" open and display its contents in the Finder window, enables you to drag and drop files between different locations without having to open additional Finder windows. There are now two copies of the To-Do List.docx file stored in two different locations.

QUICK TIP

To rename a folder, select the folder, press [return] to highlight the folder name, then type the new folder name.

6. **Click the To-Do List.docx file in the second column, then press [return]**

   The first part of the filename is highlighted and can be edited.

7. **Type Tour Preparation, then press [return]**

   The file's name changes to Tour Preparation.docx.

8. **Click Documents in the sidebar, then click and drag the original To-Do list.docx file to the desktop**

   The file moves from the Documents folder to the desktop, as shown in Figure C-18.

Understanding File Management

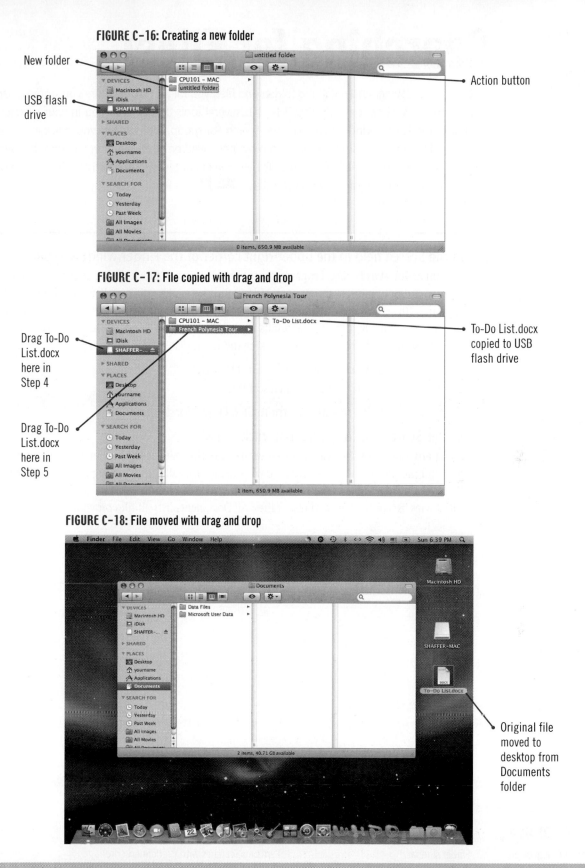

FIGURE C-16: Creating a new folder

New folder

USB flash drive

Action button

FIGURE C-17: File copied with drag and drop

Drag To-Do List.docx here in Step 4

Drag To-Do List.docx here in Step 5

To-Do List.docx copied to USB flash drive

FIGURE C-18: File moved with drag and drop

Original file moved to desktop from Documents folder

Using drag and drop to copy and move files

If you drag and drop a file to a folder on the same storage device, the file is moved into that folder. However, if you drag and drop a file to a folder on another device, the file is copied instead. If you want to move a file to another drive, press and hold down [⌘] while you drag and drop. If you want to copy a file to another folder on the same drive, press and hold down [option] while you drag and drop.

Searching for Files

After creating, saving, and renaming folders and files, you might forget where you stored a particular folder or file, forget its name, or both. Your Mac has several tools that can aid you in your search for a file. The sidebar in the Finder window contains the Search For group, which gives you quick access to predefined subsets of files on your computer organized by date saved or by file type. In addition, the **Search field** of your Finder window can help you find a file by name or content. Table C-2 lists the available search options that come with the Leopard operating system.  You want to quickly locate the copy of the To-Do List for your next tour.

STEPS

QUICK TIP
Searches are not case sensitive, so you can use uppercase or lowercase letters when you type search criteria.

1. **In the Search field in the upper-right corner of the Finder window, type To-**

   As soon as you start typing, Leopard goes to work. When you finish typing your entry, the search results are listed in the right pane of the Finder window, as shown in Figure C-19. Your search results will differ; however, all of the search results will have the characters "To-" somewhere either in the name of the item or in the file's contents. By default, the results are listed in order of the date each file was Last Opened, but can easily be sorted by Name or Kind by clicking the appropriate column heading.

2. **In the right pane, double-click To-Do List.docx**

   The To-Do List.docx file opens in Microsoft Word.

3. **Click Word on the menu bar, then click Quit Word**

4. **Under Search For in the sidebar, click Today**

   Using any option in the Search For group narrows the search based on predefined criteria. Today lists all files and programs opened or saved today. Yesterday lists all files and programs opened or saved yesterday. Past Week lists all files and programs opened or saved within the last week. All Images lists only image files; All Movies lists only video and movie files; All Documents lists all files on your computer.

TABLE C-2: Search options available with Leopard

search option	location	description
Search For group	Finder sidebar	Performs searches with predefined criteria
Search field	Finder toolbar	Performs searches based on filename and content
Spotlight search field	Accessible by clicking the magnifying glass icon on right side of the menu bar (available in all programs)	Performs searches on your entire computer and displays the results in several categories such as Top Hit, Definition, Documents, and Folders
Find command	Finder File menu	Performs the same search operation as Finder's Search field

FIGURE C-19: Search results

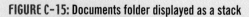

Search field

Search results (yours will differ)

Today search

232 items

Working with stacks

By default, the Documents and Downloads folders appear both in the Finder window and on the dock (to the right of the dashed line and next to the Trash). When you click a folder on the dock, it doesn't open in a separate window; instead, the folder springs open in an arc or grid to reveal its contents, as shown in Figure C-15. This method of displaying the contents of the folder is called a **stack**. Once a stack is open, click an item in the stack, such as a file or folder, to open it on the desktop.

FIGURE C-15: Documents folder displayed as a stack

UNIT
C
Mac OS X

Deleting and Restoring Files

If you no longer need a folder or file, you can **delete** (or remove) it from your computer. If you delete a folder, Leopard removes the folder as well as everything stored in it. Leopard places folders and files you delete in the **Trash**. If you later discover that you need a deleted file or folder, you can drag it out of the Trash as long as you have not yet emptied the Trash. Emptying the Trash removes the deleted folders and files from your computer. By deleting files and folders you no longer need and periodically emptying the Trash, you free up valuable storage space on your devices and keep your computer uncluttered. ▰▰▰▰ You have the updated copy of the Tour Preparation.docx file stored on your USB flash drive, so you want to delete the To-Do List.docx from the desktop.

STEPS

1. **Click Desktop in the sidebar in the Finder window**

QUICK TIP
You can also right-click a file or folder, then select Move to Trash to delete the file or folder.

2. **Drag the To-Do List file from the Desktop folder in the Finder window to the Trash icon ▦ on the dock**

   The To-Do List file is deleted from the desktop and the Desktop folder, as shown in Figure C-20. If your Trash icon on the dock appeared empty before this step, it will now appear to contain crumpled paper. This indicates that it contains deleted files or folders.

3. **Click ▦ on the dock**

   A new Finder window opens displaying the contents of the Trash, as shown in Figure C-21. Your Trash's contents may differ.

QUICK TIP
You can also delete a folder by moving it to the Trash. Keep in mind that all files in the folder are also moved to the Trash.

4. **Click and drag the To-Do List.docx file from the right pane over Documents in the sidebar until a rounded rectangle appears around Documents, then release the mouse button**

   When you release the mouse button, the file is **restored**, or moved from the Trash to a new location on your computer (in this case, the Documents folder).

5. **Click Documents in the sidebar if necessary, then drag the To-Do List.docx file from the Documents folder to ▦ on the dock**

QUICK TIP
You can also empty the trash by clicking the Empty button in the upper-right area of the Trash Finder Window, or by right-clicking the Trash icon, then clicking Empty Trash.

6. **Click Finder on the menu bar, click Empty Trash, then click OK in the dialog box that appears**

   The trash is emptied, and the Trash icon on the dock no longer has crumpled paper in it.

7. **Close all open Finder windows**

FIGURE C-20: Empty Desktop folder

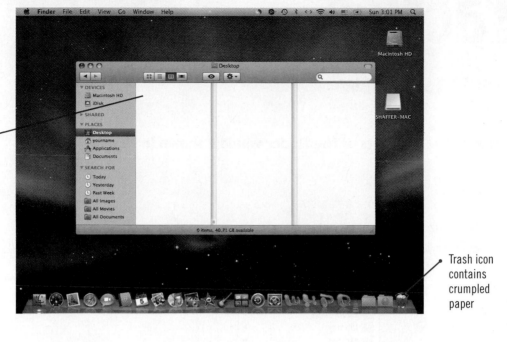

Desktop folder is empty

Trash icon contains crumpled paper

FIGURE C-21: Trash contents in Finder window

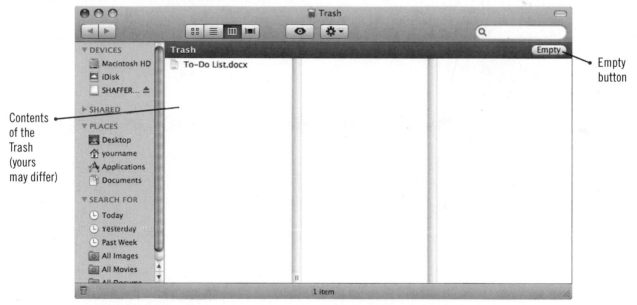

Contents of the Trash (yours may differ)

Empty button

Emptying the Trash

When you empty the Trash, Leopard marks the physical location of the files and folders in the Trash for reuse. Disk reading utilities can recover these files until the space has been reused. If you want to delete files that contain sensitive information and prevent them from being recovered, click Finder on the menu bar, then click Secure Empty Trash. Secure Empty Trash overwrites the space previously occupied by the deleted files and folders.

Practice

▼ CONCEPTS REVIEW

Label each of the elements of the Finder window shown in Figure C-22.

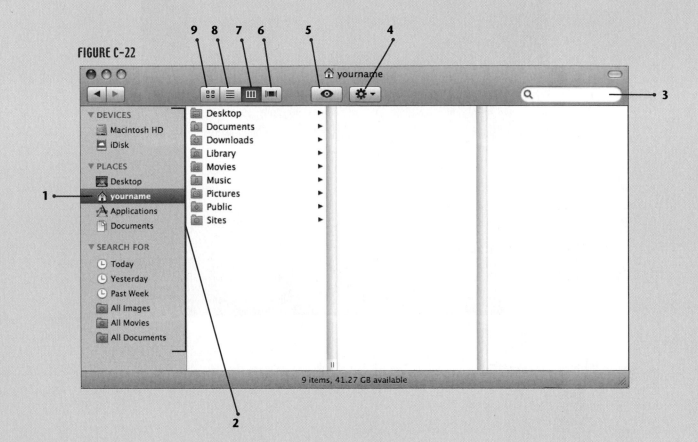

FIGURE C-22

Match each statement with the term it best describes.

10. file management
11. filename
12. folder
13. storage device
14. alias

a. A container for related files
b. A link that provides quick access to a folder, file, or program
c. A physical location for storing files and folders
d. Organizing and managing folders and files
e. The name that you assign to a file to identify its contents

Understanding File Management

Select the best answer from the list of choices.

15. The _____ is a built-in, high-capacity, high-speed storage medium for all the software, folders, and files on a computer.
    a. hard disk
    b. home folder
    c. sidebar
    d. USB flash drive

16. A _____ is a unit of stored, electronic data.
    a. device
    b. file
    c. folder
    d. search

17. _____ is a strategy for organizing your files and folders.
    a. The desktop
    b. The hard disk
    c. File hierarchy
    d. File management

18. _____ view displays the contents of the current folder as an alphabetical list with additional details about each file and folder provided.
    a. Icon
    b. List
    c. Columns
    d. Cover Flow

19. _____ view allows you to preview the contents of files within a folder and to see the folder's contents as a list.
    a. Icon
    b. List
    c. Columns
    d. Cover Flow

20. After you copy a file, you have:
    a. only one copy of the file.
    b. a duplicate copy of the file in a different location.
    c. moved the original file to a new location.
    d. deleted the file.

21. When you delete a file from your hard disk drive, Leopard:
    a. puts the deleted file in the Trash.
    b. permanently deletes the file from the hard disk drive.
    c. stores a duplicate copy of the file in the Trash.
    d. moves the file to a removable disk.

▼ SKILLS REVIEW

1. Understand file management.

    a. Assume you manage a small travel agency. How would you organize your business files using a hierarchical file structure?

    b. What aliases would you place on your desktop for easier access to your business files?

2. Open the Finder window.

    a. List and describe the functions of as many components of the Finder window as you can without referring to the lessons.

    b. Compare your results to Figure C-3 to make sure that you have identified all the elements.

3. Change views.

    a. Double-click the Macintosh HD icon on the desktop to open its contents in the Finder window.

    b. If necessary, change the view to icon view.

    c. Change the view to list view.

    d. Change the view to columns view.

    e. Click the Applications folder in the first column of the right pane to view its contents in the next column.

    f. Scroll down, locate the Utilities folder, then click the Utilities folder to view its contents in the next column.

    g. Change the view of the Utilities folder to Cover Flow to preview the icon images that represent the utilities.

    h. Scroll through the bottom section of the right pane until you find Disk Utility, click Disk Utility, then view Disk Utility in the Quick Look window.

    i. Close the Quick Look window.

    j. Change the view to columns view.

4. Create and save documents.

    a. Open Microsoft Word using the dock.

    b. Type Oceania Tours on the first line of the document, followed by one blank line.

    c. Type your name, followed by two blank lines.

    d. Use Word to create the following list of current Oceania tours. (*Hint*: After you type the first numbered line, the rest of the lines will be automatically numbered.)

        Current Tours:

        1. French Polynesia

        2. Fiji Islands

        3. Pitcairn Islands

        4. Tonga

        5. Niue

        6. Tokelau

    e. Save the Word file with the filename Oceania Tours in the Documents folder. (If you are prompted that "Oceania Tours already exists. Do you want to replace it?", click Replace.)

    f. View the filename in the Word title bar, then quit Word.

5. Open, edit, and print files.

    a. Use the Finder window to open the file named Oceania Tours.docx from the Documents folder.

    b. Click at the end of the line containing the last current tour (Tokelau), press [return], then add the names of two more tours on two separate lines: Palau and Tuvalu.

    c. Save the edited Word file.

    d. Use Print Preview to display a full-page view of the document.

    e. Print the Oceania Tours.docx document, retrieve your printed copy from the printer, then quit Word.

6. **Copy, rename, and move files.**
   a. Attach your USB flash drive to your computer.
   b. When your USB flash drive has been recognized by your Mac, open the drive and create a folder on it with the name **Oceania Tours**.
   c. Copy the Oceania Tours.docx file from your Documents folder to the Oceania Tours folder on your USB flash drive.
   d. Rename the Oceania Tours.docx file on your USB drive to be **Current Oceania Tours.docx**.
   e. Move the original Oceania Tours.docx file from your Documents folder to the Desktop folder.

7. **Search for files.**
   a. In the Finder window Search field, type **Oceania**.
   b. Examine the Search results, then open the original Oceania Tours.docx file.
   c. Quit Word.
   d. Using the Search For group on the sidebar, click Past Week to list all the programs and files open and saved within the last week.

8. **Delete and restore files.**
   a. Click and drag the original Word file with the name Oceania Tours.docx from the desktop (or the Desktop folder in the Finder window) to the Trash.
   b. Open the Trash to view its contents.
   c. Drag the file named Oceania Tours.docx to the Documents folder.
   d. Select the Oceania Tours.docx file in the Documents folder, move it to the Trash again, then close all open Finder windows.
   e. Empty the Trash.
   f. Submit the printed copy of your revised Word document and your answers to Step 1 to your instructor.

▼ INDEPENDENT CHALLENGE 1

To meet the needs of high-tech workers in your town, you have opened an Internet café named Internet To-Go where your customers can enjoy a cup of fresh-brewed coffee and bakery goods while they work online. To promote your new business, you want to develop a newspaper ad, flyers, and breakfast and lunch menus.

a. Connect your USB flash drive to your computer, if necessary.

b. Create a new folder named **Internet To-Go** on your USB flash drive.

c. In the Internet To-Go folder, create three subfolders named **Advertising**, **Flyers**, and **Menus**.

d. Use Word to create a short ad for your local newspaper that describes your business:

- Use the name of the business as the title for your document.
- Write a short paragraph about the business. Include a fictitious location, street address, and phone number.
- After the paragraph, type your name.

e. Save the Word document with the filename **Newspaper Ad** in the Advertising folder.

f. Preview and then print your Word document, then quit Word.

▼ INDEPENDENT CHALLENGE 2

As a freelance writer for several national magazines, you depend on your computer to meet critical deadlines. Whenever you encounter a computer problem, you contact a computer consultant who helps you resolve the problem. This consultant asked you to document, or keep records of, your computer's current settings.

a. Connect your USB flash drive to your computer, if necessary.

b. Open the Finder window so that you can view information on your drives and other installed hardware.

c. Open Word and create a document with the title My Computer Documentation and your name on separate lines.

d. List the names of the devices connected to your computer.

e. List the folders and files in your Documents folder (if there are more than five, list only the first five).

f. List the folders and files on your desktop (if there are more than five, list only the first five).

g. Save the Word document with the filename **My Computer Documentation** on your USB flash drive.

h. Preview your document, print it, then quit Word.

▼ INDEPENDENT CHALLENGE 3

As an adjunct, or part-time, instructor at Everhart College, you teach special summer classes for kids on how to use and create computer games, compose digital art, work with digital photographs, and compose digital music. You want to create a folder structure on your USB flash drive to store the files for each class.

a. Connect your USB flash drive to your computer, then open it.

b. Create a folder named **Computer Games**.

c. In the Computer Games folder, create a subfolder named **Class 1**.

Advanced Challenge Exercise

- In the Class 1 folder, create subfolders named **Class Outline** and **Hands-On Lab**.
- Rename the Class Outline folder to **Class Handouts**.
- Create a new folder named **Interactive Presentations** in the Class 1 folder.

d. Use Word to create a document with the title **Photocopying** and your name on separate lines, and the following list of items that you need to photocopy for the first class:

Class 1:

Class 1 Topics & Resources

Hands-On Lab Assignment

On Your Own Exercise

Interactive Presentation Slides

e. Save the Word document with the filename **Photocopying** in the Class 1 folder. (*Hint*: After you switch to your USB flash drive in the Save As dialog box, open the Computer Games folder, then select the Class 1 folder before saving the file.)

f. Preview and print the Photocopying.docx file, then quit Word.

g. Draw a diagram of your new folder structure on the printed copy of your Word document.

▼ REAL LIFE INDEPENDENT CHALLENGE

This Real Life Independent Challenge requires an Internet connection. You want to open a small specialty shop for pottery, stained glass, handcrafts, and other consignments from local artists and craftspeople. First, you need to search for information on the Internet about preparing a business plan so that you can obtain financing from your local bank for the business.

a. Search the Internet for information on **Preparing a Business Plan**. Locate a Web site that contains information on how to write a business plan.

b. Start Word and create a document in which you summarize in your own words the basic process for preparing a business plan. Include a title and your name in the document. At the bottom of your document, list the URL of the Web site or sites from which you prepared your Word document. (*Note*: Because many organizations copyright the content on their Web sites, you should not copy the exact content of a Web site, but instead summarize your findings in your own words. If you want to determine what content at a Web site is copyrighted and the conditions for using that content, scroll to the bottom of the Web site and click the link that covers copyright use and restrictions.)

c. Save the file on your USB flash drive with the filename **Preparing a Business Plan**.

d. Preview and print your Word document, then quit Word.

▼ VISUAL WORKSHOP

As a technical support specialist at Advanced Robotic Systems, Ltd., in Great Britain, you need to respond to employee queries quickly and thoroughly. You decide that it is time to evaluate and reorganize the folder structure on your computer so you can quickly access the resources required for your job. Create the folder structure shown in Figure C-23 on your USB flash drive. As you work, use Word to prepare a simple outline of the steps you followed to create the folder structure. Include your name in the document and save it as **Reorganizing My Folder Structure** on your USB drive. Preview and print the document, then submit it to your instructor.

FIGURE C-23

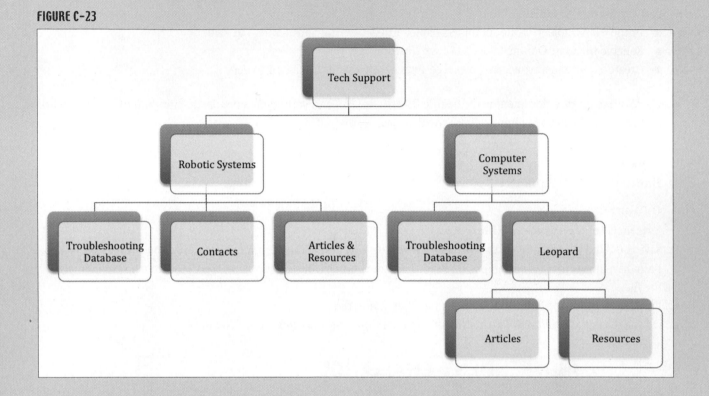

Getting Started with Safari

In this unit, you learn how to use the Safari browser to find information on the World Wide Web (WWW or the Web). You will learn how to navigate from one Web page to another and how to search for information on the Web. You will also learn how to print Web pages and how to get helpful information about using Safari. You need to connect to the Internet to complete this unit. At Quest Specialty Travel (QST), the tour developers for each region provide laptop computers with mobile Internet technology to all tour guides. Guides can then use the Internet to get the latest information on local weather, events, and news while traveling with the groups. Each computer has Safari installed as the browser. Your job is to teach the guides to use the Safari browser so they can use the Internet during their tours.

OBJECTIVES

Understand Web browsers

Start and explore Safari

View and navigate Web pages

Use tabbed browsing

Bookmark Web pages

Print a Web page

Search for information

Get Help and quit Safari

UNIT
D

Internet

Understanding Web Browsers

The **World Wide Web** (also called the **Web** or **WWW**) is the part of the Internet that contains linked Web pages. **Web pages** are documents that can contain text, graphics, sound, and video. **Web browsers** (also called **browsers**) are software programs used to access and display Web pages. You must have a computing device, an Internet connection, and a browser to view Web pages. Browsers such as Safari, Internet Explorer, Opera, and Firefox, make navigating the Web easy. When you view Web pages with a browser, you click words, phrases, or graphics called **hyperlinks**, or simply **links**, to connect to and view other Web pages. Links can also open graphics files or play sound or video files. This unit features **Safari**, a popular browser from Apple. Figure D-1 shows how the Safari browser displays a Web page from the U.S. government's White House Web site. ▄▄▟▟ The tour developers have asked you to become familiar with Safari and the Web so you can teach the guides how to find information for their tours. You discuss the features and benefits of using Safari.

DETAILS

Using Safari, you can:

• **Display Web pages**

   You can access Web sites from all over the world with a Web browser. A **Web site** is a group of Web pages focused on a particular subject. Web sites exist for individuals, businesses, museums, governments, charitable organizations, and educational institutions. There are Web sites for the arts, music, politics, education, sports, and commerce—for any topic, interest, or endeavor in the world. The QST tour guides can use the Web to get up-to-date information about the places they are touring.

• **Use links to move from one Web page to another**

   You can click the hyperlinks on a Web page to get more information about a business, city, or organization. For example, if a museum is on the tour, a guide can visit the museum's Web site and click links to Web pages that describe current exhibits, visiting hours, or special tours.

• **Play audio and video clips**

   A Web browser can play audio and video clips if it has been configured to do so and if your computer has the appropriate hardware, such as speakers. In their research, tour guides might find Web pages that include video clips of historic buildings, shopping trips, local stories and customs, or other information about a region.

• **Search the Web for information**

   A **search engine** is a special Web site that quickly searches the Internet for Web sites based on words or phrases that you enter. Tour guides can take advantage of search engines to look for Web sites that focus on a country, government, region of travel, or on a specific topic of interest.

• **Bookmark Web pages**

   You can bookmark Web pages that you might need to visit again, such as a page for a specific museum, city, or map. Safari makes it easy to bookmark your favorite Web sites so they are easily accessible when you want to view them later. Tour guides can save pages for historic sites or museums for each city they visit.

• **Print or save the text and graphics on Web pages**

   If you want to keep a hard copy of the information or images you find on the Web, you can simply print the Web page, including any graphics. You can also save the text or graphics on a Web page or copy the information temporarily to the Clipboard, where it is available for pasting into other programs. Tour guides can print maps or informational paragraphs from the Web to hand out to the groups.

• **E-mail Web pages**

   If you want to share a Web page with a colleague, you can e-mail a link to the page or e-mail the page itself directly from the browser window. The person receives the page or the link as part of an e-mail message.

Getting Started with Safari

FIGURE D-1: A sample Web page

The Internet, computer networks, and intranets

A **computer network** is the hardware and software that makes it possible for two or more computers to share information and resources. An **intranet** is a computer network that connects computers in a local area only, such as computers in a company's office. Users can connect to intranets from remote locations to share company information and resources. The **Internet** is a network of connected computers and computer networks located around the world. The Internet is an international community; Web pages exist from nearly every country in the world. There are over 200 million users worldwide currently connected to the Internet through telephone lines, cables, satellites, and other telecommunications media. Through the Internet, these computers can share many types of information, including text, graphics, sound, video, and computer programs. Anyone who has access to a computer and a connection to the Internet through a computer network or modem can use this rich information source.

The Internet has its roots in the U.S. Department of Defense Advanced Research Projects Agency Network (ARPANET), which began in 1969. In 1986 the National Science Foundation formed NSFNET, which replaced ARPANET. NSFNET expanded the foundation of the U.S. portion of the Internet with high-speed, long-distance lines. By the end of the 1980s, corporations began to use the Internet to communicate with each other and with their customers. In 1991, the U.S. Congress further expanded the Internet's capacity and speed and opened it to commercial use. The World Wide Web was created in Switzerland in 1991 to allow links between documents on the Internet. The first graphical Web browser, Mosaic, was introduced at the University of Illinois in 1993, leading to the development of browsers such as Netscape Navigator and Internet Explorer. With the boom in the personal computer industry and the expanding availability of inexpensive desktop machines and powerful, network-ready servers, many companies were able to join the Internet for the first time in the early 1990s. The Web is now an integral component of corporate culture, educational institutions, and individuals' personal lives. The Web is used daily for commerce, education, and entertainment by millions of people around the world.

Starting and Exploring Safari

To use the Internet, you need a computing device, an Internet connection, and a Web browser. Safari, Apple's Web browser, reads and displays Web pages, enabling you to view, print, and search for information on the Web. Typically, after Safari is installed, its icon appears on the dock. Before you teach the tour guides how to view Web pages and navigate from one page to another, you show them how to start the browser and explain the components of the Safari browser window.

STEPS

TROUBLE

If the Safari icon is not on your dock, click the Finder icon on the dock, then click Applications in the sidebar. In the right pane, scroll down until you locate Safari, then double-click Safari.

1. **Locate the Safari icon on the dock, as shown in Figure D-2, then click**

   Safari opens and displays your home page. A **home page** is the first Web page that opens every time you start a browser. The term "home page" also applies to the main page of a Web site. Figure D-3 shows the Apple home page. The home page for your browser may be different. Look at the home page on your screen and compare the elements described, using Figure D-3 as a guide.

The elements of the Safari window include the following:

- The **menu bar** provides access to most of the browser's features through a series of menus.
- The **toolbar** contains the following tools to help you browse Web pages with Safari:
  - **Back and Forward buttons** allow you to access the Web pages that you have viewed since opening the browser.
  - The **Add a bookmark button** opens a dialog box that you use to name a bookmark and add it to the bookmarks bar or the Bookmarks menu.
  - The **address field** displays the address of the Web page that's open in the active tab. The Web page's address, called the **Uniform Resource Locator (URL)**, appears in the address field after you open (or load) the page. A button for reloading the current page appears on the right side of the address field.
  - The **search field** uses the Google search engine to help you search the Internet for Web sites about a particular topic. You can enter a keyword or words in the search field, then press [return] to produce a Google Web page displaying relevant search results. To view your recent searches, you can click the magnifying glass button on the left side of the search field.
- The **bookmarks bar** contains buttons you can use to go directly to Web pages you have bookmarked, to the bookmark library, to a page showing your Top Sites, and to several popular Web sites whose bookmarks are built into the bookmarks bar.
- The **browser window** is the area where the current Web page appears.
- The **status bar** displays information about the page that is loading. It also displays the Web address of a link when you hold your mouse pointer over one.
- The **vertical scroll bar** appears along the right side of a page if the page is longer than the window's viewable area. The **horizontal scroll bar** appears along the bottom of a page if the page is wider than the window's viewable area. The **scroll box** within each scroll bar indicates your relative position within the Web page.

TROUBLE

By default, the status bar is hidden. To display it, click View on the menu bar, then click Show Status Bar.

FIGURE D-2: Starting Safari

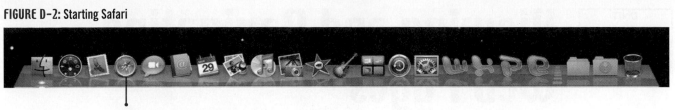

Safari icon

FIGURE D-3: Elements of the Safari window

Menu bar

Toolbar

Back button

Forward button

Add a bookmark button

Bookmarks bar

Status bar

Search field

Reload the current page button

Address field

Vertical scroll bar

Browser window

Scroll box

Horizontal scroll bar

Understanding URLs

Every Web page has a unique address on the Web, also known as the **URL** (Uniform Resource Locator) for the page. Browser software locates a Web page based on its address. All Web page addresses begin with "http," which stands for Hypertext Transfer Protocol, the set of rules for exchanging files on the Web. This is followed by a colon and two forward slashes. Most pages begin with "www" (which indicates that the page is on the World Wide Web), followed by a dot, or period, and then the Web site's name, known as the **domain name**. Following the domain name is another dot and the **top-level domain**, which tells you the type of site you are visiting. Examples of top-level domains are com (for commercial sites), edu (for educational institutions), and org (for organizations). After the top-level domain, another slash and one or more folder names and a filename might appear.

Viewing and Navigating Web Pages

Moving among Web pages is simple with hyperlinks. When you click a **hyperlink**, you navigate to, or open, another location on the same Web page or jump to an entirely different Web page. You can follow a link to obtain more information about a topic by clicking a linked word or phrase. In addition to links on Web pages themselves, you can use the navigation tools in Safari to move around the Web. You can navigate from page to page using the Forward and Back buttons, and you can use the History menu to return to your home page or to view a list of previously viewed Web pages. ▰▰▰▰ You look at the Library of Congress Web site for information for a tour traveling to Washington, D.C.

STEPS

1. **Triple-click anywhere in the address field**

   Clicking the address field once activates the address field; double-clicking the address field highlights a word or part of the Web site address; and triple-clicking the address field highlights the entire Web site address. Any text you type when the entire address is highlighted replaces the address.

> **QUICK TIP**
>
> If you previously entered an address in the address field beginning with the same set of letters, the AutoFill feature suggests the remaining characters of the Web site address. Press [return] to accept the address Safari suggests in the Address field.

2. **Type www.loc.gov, then press [return]**

   After you press [return], Safari automatically adds the "http://" (protocol) to the beginning of the address you type. As the page loads, the status bar displays the current status of the Web site; when the page is completely loaded, the status bar is blank. After a moment, the home page for the Library of Congress opens in the browser window, as shown in Figure D-4. The name of the Web page appears above the toolbar at the top of the window. A Web page icon matching the Library of Congress logo appears to the left of the Web page name in the address field. Web pages change frequently, so the Web page in your window may look different from that shown in the figure. The page contains both pictures and text, some of which are hyperlinks.

3. **Place your mouse pointer over the Visitors link in the Resources for section**

   When you place the pointer over a hyperlink, the pointer changes to 👆 and the URL for the hyperlink appears after the words "Go to" on the status bar. A ScreenTip may also appear, giving you more information about the linked page.

> **QUICK TIP**
>
> Click the Reload the current page button 🔄 on the toolbar to update a page that may have changed since it was last loaded in the browser window.

4. **Click the Visitors link**

   The Visitors page opens in your Web browser window, as shown in Figure D-5.

5. **Click the Back button ◀ on the toolbar**

   The Web page that you last viewed, the Library of Congress home page, opens in the browser window.

6. **Click the Forward button ▶ on the toolbar**

   The Forward button opens the Visitors page in the browser window again.

7. **Click History on the menu bar, then click Home on the History menu**

   The home page for your installation of Safari appears in the browser window.

8. **Click History on the menu bar, then click Show All History**

   As shown in Figure D-6, the view changes to Cover Flow and the bookmarks library opens in the browser window. The **bookmarks library** contains collections of links to sites you have visited or want to visit frequently. In the sidebar, the History collection is selected in the Collections group. The right side of the window shows the contents of your History: the bottom section contains a list of the Web pages you have most recently visited, and the top section provides a preview of the Web page selected in the list.

> **QUICK TIP**
>
> You can also return to the Library of Congress home page by double-clicking Library of Congress Home from the list in the bottom section of the window.

9. **In the top section of the window, drag the scroll bar to the left until you see the preview for Library of Congress Home, then click the Library of Congress Home preview**

   The home page of the Library of Congress Web site opens in the browser window.

Getting Started with Safari

FIGURE D-4: Home page for the Library of Congress

Web page icon

Web page name

FIGURE D-5: Visitors Web page at the Library of Congress Web site

FIGURE D-6: History collection in bookmarks library

History collection selected

Collections group

Web page previews

Scroll bar

Previously visited
Web pages

Setting the home page

Each time you start Safari and each time you click Home on the History menu, the page that appears in the browser window is your home page. If you want to change the home page, open the Web page that you want to be your new home page, click Safari on the menu bar, click Preferences, then click General (if necessary). The URL of the current home page is highlighted in the Home page text box. Click the Set to Current Page button to change the URL in the Home Page text box to the URL for the Web page currently open in the browser. Close the General dialog box.

Using Tabbed Browsing

When you open multiple Web pages on separate tabs within the same browser window, you are using **tabbed browsing**. This method for organizing Web pages while browsing makes navigation between Web pages fast and simple, and minimizes the number of windows you need to open as you browse the Web. You want to show the tour guides how tabbed browsing will allow them to more easily compare events in a location by viewing the Web pages in one browser window.

STEPS

1. **Triple-click the address field, type www.usa.gov, then press [return]**
   The Web page for the U.S. government opens.

QUICK TIP

To open Top Sites in the current window rather than on a new tab, click the Show Top Sites button ⊞ on the bookmarks bar.

2. **Click File on the menu bar, then click New Tab**
   By default, the Top Sites page opens in the browser window in a new tab, and the tab bar is displayed below the bookmarks bar. See Figure D-7. The **tab bar** shows the tabs currently open in the Web browser. The tab that appears on top in the tab bar is the tab currently active in the browser window. You can click the **Create a new tab button** on the far right side of the tab bar to open a new tab. The **Top Sites** page displays your 12 most frequently visited Web sites as thumbnail images; to go to one of the sites, you simply click its thumbnail.

3. **Click any thumbnail on the Top Sites page**
   The selected Web page opens in the browser window and the tab on the tab bar changes to display the name of the Web page, as shown in Figure D-8. Your Web page may differ.

4. **Click the Back button ◄ on the toolbar**
   The browser window collapses into a thumbnail image on the Top Sites page.

QUICK TIP

To display the tab bar without opening a second tab, click View on the menu bar, then click Show Tab Bar.

5. **Point to the Top Sites tab, then click the Close tab button ⊠ on the Top Sites tab in the tab bar**
   The Close tab button is hidden until you point to a tab. When it is clicked, the tab closes. With the Top Sites tab closed, the tab bar is no longer visible and the USA.gov Web page is now in the browser window.

6. **Right-click the Site Index link on the USA.gov Web page to open the shortcut menu shown in Figure D-9, click Open Link in New Tab on the shortcut menu, then click the Site Index of USA.gov tab on the tab bar to display the Web page**

7. **Right-click any link on the Site Index of USA.gov Web page, click Open Link in New Tab, then click the new tab on the tab bar**
   Using tabbed browsing, you now have three Web pages open in one browser window.

QUICK TIP

To close all tabs except one, press and hold [option], then click ⊠ on the tab for the Web page you want to keep open. All other tabs will close, the tab bar will be hidden, and the Web page you selected will appear in the browser window.

8. **Position the mouse pointer over each tab to display the ScreenTip for each**
   Each ScreenTip tells you the full name of the Web page on the tab.

9. **Click ⊠ for the second and third tabs**
   The Site Index Web page and the Web page for the link you selected on the Site Index page close and the tab bar is hidden. The USA.gov home page is open in the window.

Quitting Safari when you have multiple tabs open

When you finish looking at Web pages using Safari, you may find that you have several tabs open. When you quit Safari and you have more than one tab open, a dialog box appears noting how many tabs are open and asking you if you're sure you want to quit Safari.

If you want to quit Safari, click Quit. If you want to keep Safari open, click Cancel, then click the Close tab button on each Web page tab that you want to close.

FIGURE D-7: Top Sites page

Show Top Sites button

Tabs

Create a new tab button

New tab

Top Sites

FIGURE D-8: New page in a second tab

Name of Web page

FIGURE D-9: Link menu

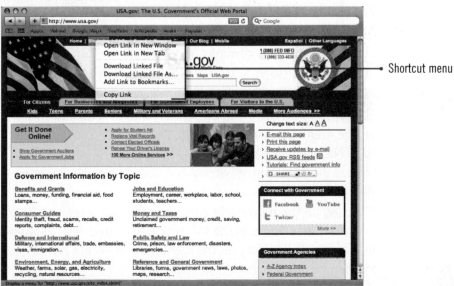

Shortcut menu

Internet

Bookmarking Web Pages

When you find a Web page that you know you will want to revisit, you can bookmark it. When you **bookmark** a Web page, you add it to the bookmarks bar or Bookmarks menu, where you can easily access the page in the future without having to enter the URL for the Web page in the address field. ▰▰▰ The tour guides want to be able to revisit some travel site Web pages multiple times without having to type the URLs in the address field each time, so you show them how to bookmark sites they revisit frequently.

1. **Triple-click the address field, type www.nps.gov/brca, then press [return]**
   The home page for Bryce Canyon National Park opens, providing information about the park. You decide to bookmark this page.

2. **Click the Add a bookmark button ⊞ on the toolbar**
   The Add a bookmark dialog box opens, as shown in Figure D-10. The Add a bookmark dialog box contains a text box for the name of the bookmarked page and a pop-up menu for selecting the location for the book-mark. By default, the full name of the Web page appears in the text box and Bookmarks Bar is selected as the location. You decide to shorten the name so it will be completely visible on a small tab on the bookmarks bar.

QUICK TIP
To add a bookmark to the Bookmarks menu, select Bookmarks Menu as the location in the Add a bookmark dialog box.

3. **Type Bryce Canyon Park in the text box, click the arrows next to the location box, click Bookmarks Bar if necessary, then click Add**
   Bryce Canyon Park is added as a button to the bookmarks bar. You decide that instead of adding it to the bookmarks bar, you'd prefer to create a folder called National Parks that appears on the Bookmarks menu and add the Bryce Canyon Park page as a bookmark to the folder. First, you need to remove the button from the bookmarks bar.

QUICK TIP
If you point to a but-ton on the book-marks bar, a ScreenTip appears with the URL of the Web page.

4. **Click and drag the Bryce Canyon Park button off the bookmarks bar and over the browser window, then release the mouse button**
   A small puff of smoke appears on your computer screen where you release the mouse button, and the button is removed from the bookmarks bar.

5. **Click the Show all bookmarks button 📖 on the bookmarks bar**
   The bookmarks library is displayed in the browser window.

QUICK TIP
To add a folder to the bookmarks bar, click the Bookmarks Bar collection in the bookmarks library, then click the Create a bookmarks folder button ⊞ below the right pane. To open a bookmarked Web page from a folder on the book-marks bar, click the folder name on the bookmarks bar, then click a bookmark on the list that opens.

6. **Click Bookmarks Menu under Collections in the sidebar, then click the Create a bookmarks folder button ⊞ under the right pane**
   As shown in Figure D-11, an untitled folder appears in the list of bookmarks in the Bookmarks Menu collection.

7. **Type National Parks, then press [return]**
   The untitled folder is renamed National Parks.

8. **Click the Show all bookmarks button 📖 to return to the Bryce Canyon Park page, click ⊞, click the arrows next to Bookmarks Bar, click the National Parks folder under Bookmarks Menu, then click Add**

9. **Click History on the menu bar, click Home to return to your home page, click Bookmarks on the menu bar, point to National Parks, then click Bryce Canyon National Park (U.S. National Park Service)**
   Clicking the Bryce Canyon National Park bookmark on the Bookmarks menu opens the Bryce Canyon National Park Web page.

10. **Click 📖 on the bookmarks bar, compare your screen to Figure D-12, right-click the National Parks folder in the list, click Delete to delete the folder and the bookmark in the folder, click History on the menu bar, then click Home**
    Your browser window returns to your home page.

Getting Started with Safari

FIGURE D-10: Add a bookmark dialog box

Add a bookmark button

Text box for Web page name

Location for new bookmark

Add button

FIGURE D-11: New folder added to Bookmarks Menu collection

Collections

You may have additional bookmarks listed

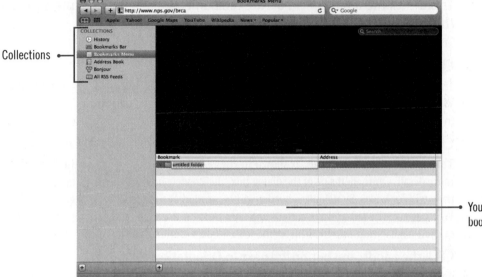

FIGURE D-12: Bookmark added to National Parks folder in Bookmarks Menu collection

Bookmark added to folder

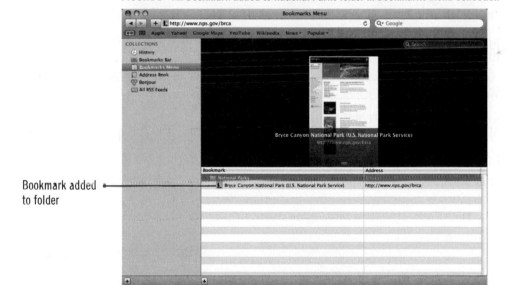

Creating and organizing bookmarks

Once you bookmark a Web page, returning to that page is much easier. To keep your bookmarks manageable, add only pages that you expect to visit frequently. You can organize bookmarks by placing them into folders by category. For example, you may want to create bookmark folders according to your interests, such as sports, cooking, and travel. You may want to create folders in which each member of a household can place his or her own favorites. Bookmarks can be listed individually or placed in folders on the bookmarks bar or on the Bookmarks menu.

Internet

Printing a Web Page

When you print a Web page, its text and any graphics appear on the printed page. You can use the Print dialog box to change the number of copies, number of pages, paper size, and orientation of the Web page before printing. In addition, a preview of the printed Web page appears in the Print dialog box; this is helpful because some Web pages are lengthy and you may only want to print the pages that have the information relevant to your task. You show the tour guides how to print a copy of a Web page so they can provide the information as handouts to the tour guests.

STEPS

QUICK TIP

If your print dialog box contains more options than those shown in Figure D-13, click the Collapse button ▲ to collapse the dialog box.

QUICK TIP

To print a Web page without previewing it or changing any settings, click the Print button in the Print dialog box when it first opens.

QUICK TIP

To print a range of pages other than the first page, click the From option button, enter the starting page number in the range in the first text box, then enter the ending page number in the second text box. To print a Web page no matter how many pages, click the All option button.

TROUBLE

If your computer is not connected to a printer or if an error message appears, ask your technical support person for assistance.

1. **Triple-click the address field on the toolbar, type www.nps.gov, press [return], then click the HISTORY & CULTURE link**
   The History & Culture page for the National Park Service opens.

2. **Click File on the menu bar, then click Print**
   The Print dialog box opens, as shown in Figure D-13. From this dialog box, you can select a printer, print the Web page, save the Web page as a Portable Document File (PDF) document, or view the Web page as a PDF in the Preview program. More print options are available when the Print dialog box is expanded.

3. **Click the Expand button ▼ to the right of the Printer arrows if necessary**
   The Print dialog box expands, as shown in Figure D-14. Table D-1 explains the Print dialog box options in more detail. On the left side of the dialog box, the Preview box shows what the first page of the printed Web page will look like. By default, a header will be printed at the top of each page containing the name of the Web page on the left and the current date and time on the right, and a footer will be printed at the bottom of each page containing the URL on the left and page number on the right.

4. **Click the Landscape button 🖼 next to Orientation**
   The Preview box shows the Web page in landscape orientation.

5. **Click the Next page button ▶ under the Preview box**
   The contents of page 2 of the printed document appear in the Preview box.

6. **Click the Previous page button ◀ under the Preview box, then click the Portrait button 🖼 next to Orientation**
   You prefer portrait orientation for the handout, and you'd like to print the first page only of the two-page Web page.

7. **Click the From option button next to Pages**
   With the range of pages to be printed set to From 1 to 1, only the first page of the Web page will be printed.

8. **Make sure 1 appears in the Copies text box, then click Print**
   The Print dialog box closes, and one copy of the first page of the current Web page prints.

Copying information from a Web page

You can select text on a Web page and use the Copy and Paste commands to insert the information into a file made with another program, such as Microsoft Word. You can also save a graphic image from a Web page by dragging it to the desktop or by right-clicking the image, clicking Save Image As on the shortcut menu, then specifying where to save the image. To copy an image to the Clipboard so that you can paste the copy in a new location, click the Copy Image command on the shortcut menu. Keep in mind that the same laws that protect printed works generally protect information and graphics published on a Web page. Do not use material from a Web page without citing its source and checking the site carefully for any usage restrictions.

FIGURE D-13: Print dialog box

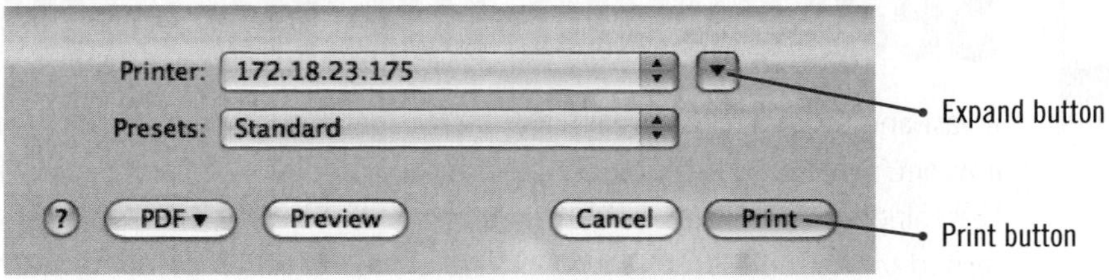

Expand button

Print button

FIGURE D-14: Expanded Print dialog box

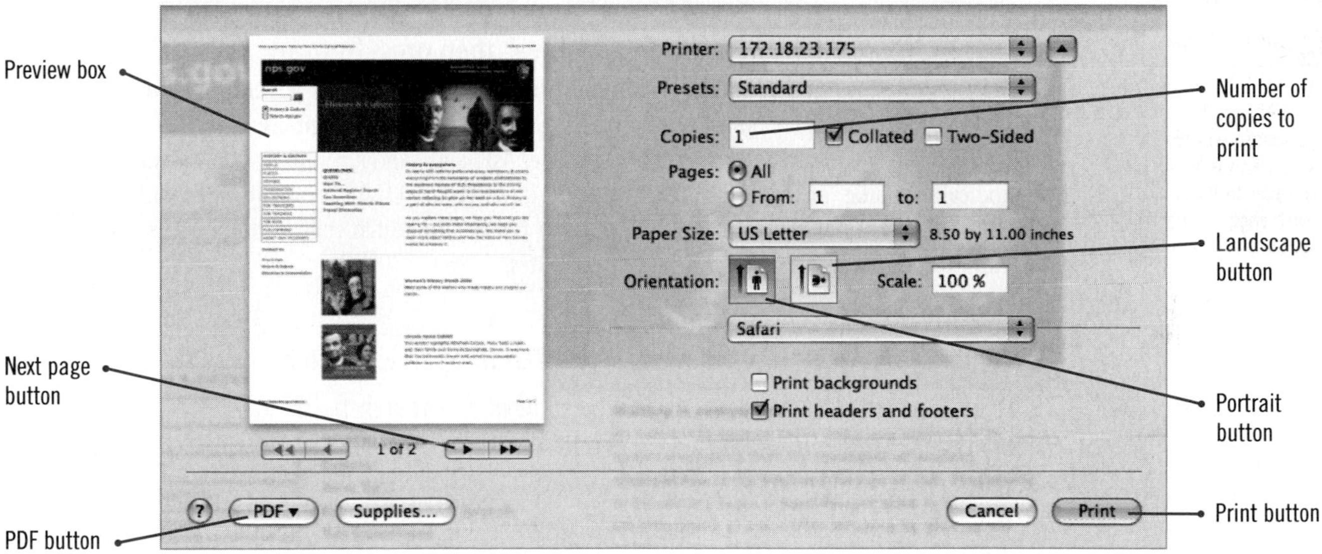

Preview box

Number of copies to print

Landscape button

Next page button

Portrait button

PDF button

Print button

TABLE D-1: Print dialog box options

option	use to
Printer	Select the printer to use; click the arrows to change or see a list of available printers for your computer
Copies	Indicate the number of copies of each page to print
Pages	Indicate whether all pages or a page range should be printed
Paper Size	Select the paper size; click the arrows to change or see a list of available paper sizes for your printer
Orientation	Select portrait or landscape orientation for the printed page
Scale	Increase or decrease the size of the item on the printed page
Print backgrounds check box	Indicate (when checked) that the background colors on a Web page are to be printed
Print headers and footers check box	Indicate (when checked) that the headers and footers on each page are to be printed
PDF button	Preview, save, or mail the Web page as a PDF (Portable Document Format) document

UNIT D
Internet

Searching for Information

A vast and ever-increasing number of Web pages and other information sources are available through the Internet. To find information on the Web on a specific topic, you can use Safari's built-in **search field**. Searching for relevant Web sites using the search field is based on criteria or **keywords**, which are words related to the topic for which you are searching. To search using the search field, you enter a keyword or words in the field, then press [return]. The search field uses the Google search engine to find relevant sites on the Web based on your keywords and opens a Google Web page containing your **search results**, a list of links called **hits**. You can click one of the links in the list to go to a Web site. If you prefer to use a search engine other than Google to locate information on the Web, such as Live Search, Ask, or Yahoo!, you can go directly to one of these sites rather than use the Safari search field. ▰▰▰ You decide to show the tour guides how to look for adventure travel information by searching with the browser.

STEPS

QUICK TIP

The sites listed at the top of the results in the Sponsored Links box have usually paid a fee to the search engine to be listed first when certain keywords are used for a search.

1. **Click in the search field, type** adventure travel, **then press [return]**

   The browser window changes to show a list of Google search results for adventure travel, as shown in Figure D-15. Each result provides a link to a Web site, a short description containing your keywords, and the URL of the Web site. Search engines such as Google, Ask, and Yahoo! routinely use software programs to methodically catalog, or crawl, through the entire Internet and create huge databases with links to Web pages and their URLs. When you enter a keyword or phrase, the search engine examines its database index for relevant information and displays a list of Web sites.

2. **Click** any link **to view a Web page**

3. **Click** File **on the menu bar, then click** New Tab **to open a new tab**

QUICK TIP

You can also use the Back button ◀ to return to previously viewed Web pages.

4. **Click the** magnifying glass ⌕⌄ **on the left side of the search field**

   A drop-down list of Recent Searches opens, as shown in Figure D-16. Your list may differ. You want to access the search results for adventure travel again.

5. **Under Recent Searches, click** adventure travel

   The browser window on the new tab displays the search results from Google about adventure travel.

6. **Click a** link **different than the one used in Step 2**

7. **Click the** SnapBack button ⊙ **on the right side of the search field**

   The most recent Google search results are displayed on the current tab.

8. **Right-click another** Web site link **on the Google search results page, click** Open Link in New Tab, **then select that** tab

   You now have three Web sites open, each on a different tab in the same browser window, as shown in Figure D-17. An advantage of using tabbed browsing when searching for information is that it allows you to compare information from different Web sites in the same window.

9. **Close all open tabs except the first tab, click** History **on the menu bar, then click** Home

   Your home page appears in the browser window.

Handling pop-ups

Pop-ups are windows that open on your screen as you visit Web sites, generally to advertise products you may or may not want. Most people find them annoying, so Safari blocks pop-ups by default. If you want to enable pop-ups to appear, click Safari on the menu bar, click Preferences, then click Security at the top of the dialog box. Click the check box for Block pop-up windows to deselect it, then close the dialog box.

Getting Started with Safari

FIGURE D-15: Google search results

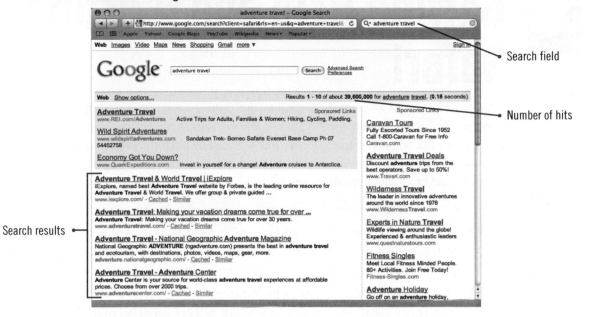

Search field

Number of hits

Search results

FIGURE D-16: List of recent searches

Click in
Step 5

FIGURE D-17: Multiple tabs open based on your search

3 open tabs

Getting Help and Quitting Safari

Safari provides a Help system with information and instructions on various features and commands in the browser. While demonstrating Safari, you were asked about how to protect private information such as Web site passwords on computers that are used by other people. Private browsing is a feature of Safari that protects users' private information. You decide to demonstrate the Help system to the tour guides by finding out more about private browsing.

STEPS

1. **Click Help on the menu bar, then type private in the Search box**

   As you type, potential matches to your keywords are immediately provided. As shown in Figure D-18, Private Browsing appears under Menu Items, and Browsing privately appears under Help Topics.

2. **Click Browsing privately under Help Topics**

   The Safari Help window opens, displaying information about private browsing and how to turn it on. See Figure D-19.

3. **Read the information presented, then click the Close button 🔘 to close the window**

   The Help window closes. You are now ready to quit Safari.

TROUBLE

Clicking the Close button on the Safari window closes only the window. Safari continues to run until you quit Safari.

4. **Click Safari on the menu bar, then click Quit Safari**

5. **If you connected to the Internet by telephone line, follow your normal procedure to close your connection**

Saving or mailing a Web page

Before quitting Safari, you may want to save a copy of the current Web page or send someone a copy of the page. To save the current Web page, click File on the menu bar, click Save As, then select a location in which to save the complete Web page, including any graphics, as a Web Archive file. If you want to e-mail the Web page to someone, click File on the menu bar, click Mail Contents of This Page, then use your e-mail program to address and send the message containing the Web page. If you want to e-mail only a link to the page, not the whole page, click File on the menu bar, click Mail Link to This Page, then address and send the message containing the link.

FIGURE D-18: Safari Help menu search results

Click to view menu item

Click to view Safari Help topic

FIGURE D-19: Topic in Safari Help window

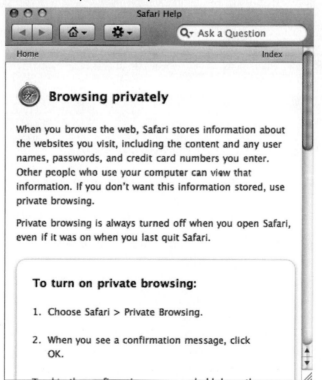

Practice

▼ CONCEPTS REVIEW

Label each element of the Safari browser window shown in Figure D-20.

FIGURE D-20

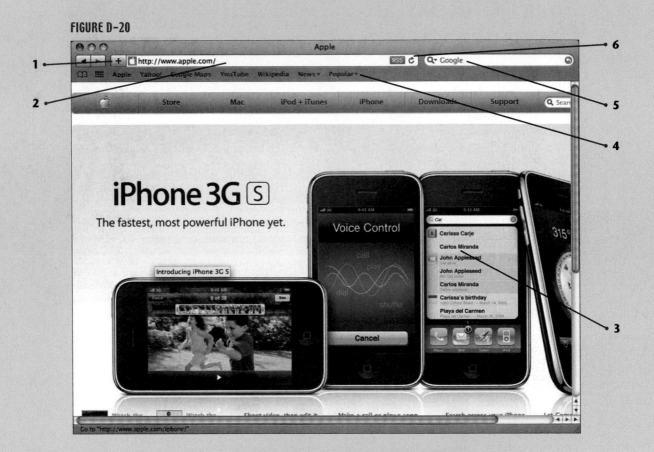

Match each term with the statement that best describes it.

7. **Hyperlink**
8. **Top Sites**
9. **Bookmarks menu**
10. **Address field**
11. **Uniform Resource Locator (URL)**

a. Click to view a new Web page
b. Displays the URL for the currently displayed page
c. Displays your most frequently visited Web pages as thumbnails
d. Displays a list of saved Web pages
e. A Web page's address

Select the best answer from the list of choices.

12. Software programs such as Safari and Firefox are called _____ .
    a. Web companions
    b. Web browsers
    c. Web documents
    d. Web windows

13. A(n) _____ is the hardware and software that makes it possible to share information and resources.
    a. computer network
    b. extranet
    c. Internet
    d. intranet

14. The page that opens every time you start a browser is called the:
    a. first page
    b. home page
    c. title page
    d. Web page

15. _____ browsing allows you to open more than one Web page at a time in a browser window.
    a. Favorites
    b. Linked
    c. Tabbed
    d. Web

16. The letters following the dot after the domain name are called the _____ domain and indicate the type of site you are visiting.
    a. top-level
    b. home-level
    c. dot-com
    d. main-level

17. Which button on the toolbar should you click if you want to view the previous Web page on your computer?
    a. Home
    b. Last
    c. Back
    d. Link

18. The toolbar that contains bookmarked Web sites is called the:
    a. Top Sites
    b. toolbar
    c. search field
    d. bookmarks bar

19. Safari's search field uses the _____ search engine.
    a. Ask
    b. Live Search
    c. Yahoo!
    d. Google

▼ SKILLS REVIEW

1. **Start and explore Safari.**
   a. Make sure your computer is connected to the Internet.
   b. Start Safari.
   c. Identify and list as many components of the Safari window as you can without referring to the lessons.
   d. Compare your results to Figure D-3 to ensure that you have identified all the essential components.
   e. Identify the complete URL of the current Web page.

2. **View and navigate Web pages.**
   a. Open the Web page www.nasa.gov using the address field, then compare your screen to Figure D-21. (The contents of your screen may differ.)
   b. Click the For Students link on the Web page.
   c. Return to the home page for your browser.
   d. Click the Back button.
   e. Follow another link to investigate the content.
   f. Click History on the menu bar, click Show All History, then click the NASA - Home preview in the top section of the History collection in the bookmarks library to open the NASA home page in the browser window.
   g. Return to the home page for your browser.

FIGURE D-21

3. **Use tabbed browsing.**

   a. Open the Web page **www.nytimes.com** using the address field.

   b. Right-click a link on the Web page to open an article in a new tab.

   c. Create a third tab in the browser window, then open **www.cnn.com** in the new tab.

   d. Create a fourth tab in the browser window, then click the first thumbnail on the Top Sites page. Your browser window should resemble that shown in Figure D-22.

   e. Close all tabs except the New York Times tab.

4. **Bookmark Web pages.**

   a. Open the Web page **www.nasa.gov** in the browser window again.

   b. Open the bookmarks library, then add a folder to the Bookmarks menu called **Science Sites**.

   c. Close the bookmarks library, then add the NASA Web page to the Science Sites folder on the Bookmarks menu.

   d. Return to the default home page for your browser.

   e. Using the Bookmarks menu, return to the NASA home page.

   f. Open the bookmarks library, delete the Science Sites folder from your Bookmarks menu, then close the bookmarks library. (*Hint*: Right-click the Science Sites folder, then click Delete.)

FIGURE D-22

5. **Print a Web page.**

   a. Click any link on the NASA home page that is interesting to you.

   b. Open the Print dialog box, then view all of the Web page's printed pages in the Preview box.

   c. Change the orientation of the printed page to landscape.

   d. Print one copy of the first page of the Web page only.

6. **Search for information.**

   a. Click the search field on the toolbar. (*Hint*: If the search field already contains text, triple-click the text in the field to select it so it can be replaced in the next step.)

   b. Type any keyword or phrase for which you would like to find information, then execute the search and review the results.

   c. Click any link in the Search results page and read the Web page.

   d. Click an additional link found on the Web page and read the new Web page.

   e. Use the SnapBack button to return to your search results.

   f. Explore some of the other hyperlinks you found.

7. **Get Help and quit Safari.**

   a. Using the Help menu, search Safari Help for a topic of interest to you.

   b. Click any link for the topic you want to learn more about.

   c. Read the results.

   d. Close the Safari Help window.

   e. Quit Safari.

▼ INDEPENDENT CHALLENGE 1

You are an aspiring journalist interested in understanding how different journalists approach the same story. You decide to use the Web to find some articles for comparison.

a. Start Safari.

b. Read and compare the coverage of a current international news story using two of the following sites:

- CNN   www.cnn.com
- MSNBC News   www.msnbc.com
- ABC News   www.abcnews.com
- CBS News   www.cbsnews.com

c. Open each news story in its own tab in the browser window.

d. Print one page of the same story from both sites that you chose.

Advanced Challenge Exercise

■ You should be able to find many English-language versions of non-U.S. papers. Use the search field or your favorite search engine to locate an online news media source from a country other than the United States. You can search on keywords such as "**Asian newspapers**" or "**European newspapers**."

■ See if you can find the news story you researched in Step b.

■ Read the article.

■ Print one page of the article from the site that you chose.

e. Close all but one of the tabs, then quit Safari.

f. Write your name on your printed pages and hand them in to your instructor.

▼ INDEPENDENT CHALLENGE 2

You have been asked by your local community college to teach a short course on classic films from the 1940s and 1950s. The class will meet four times; each class will begin with a screening and will be followed by a discussion. You decide to use the Web to research the material.

a. Start Safari.

b. Using the search field, find a Web site that contains information about films made in the 1940s.

c. Find two films from the 1940s that you want to show as part of the course. View the information about each film in a separate tab in the browser window.

d. Click several links on the film site and review the online resources.

e. Search the film site to find two films from the 1950s. View the information about each film in a separate tab in the browser window.

f. Using the bookmarks library, create a folder on the Bookmarks menu. Name the folder with your name.

g. Bookmark each film's Web page and put it in your folder on the Bookmarks menu.

h. Use the Bookmarks menu to open each film Web page in the browser window, and print the first page from each film Web page.

▼ INDEPENDENT CHALLENGE 2 (CONTINUED)

Advanced Challenge Exercise

- ■ Find one Web page that includes a link for media such as audio or video about a 1940s or 1950s film.
- ■ Click the link and listen to the audio or play the video.
- ■ After listening to or viewing the media file, close the window.
- ■ Bookmark this Web page in your Bookmarks menu folder.

i. Open the bookmarks library, then delete your folder from the Bookmarks menu.

j. Quit Safari.

▼ INDEPENDENT CHALLENGE 3

As a student of American political history, you want to learn about your representatives in the U.S. government. You decide to use the Web to get information about this topic.

a. Start Safari, then access the following government Web site: www.thomas.gov.

b. Explore the site to find information about members of Congress. Print one page from this site.

c. In a new tab, open the Web site www.senate.gov.

d. Click the Senators link, then find a link to a Web site for a senator who represents the state that you would most like to visit. Click the link, then print one page from this site.

e. Explore three links on the senator's Web site to learn more about those topics, opening each page in a new tab.

f. Print one page from each of these links.

g. Quit Safari.

h. Write your name on the printed pages and hand them in to your instructor.

▼ REAL LIFE INDEPENDENT CHALLENGE

You decide to compare several search engines to determine if there are differences in appearance or the number of hits you receive when you use them to search the Web.

a. Start Safari. Using two of the search engines listed below, type **nobel prize winners** in the Search text box, and then search for the topic.

- Yahoo!   www.yahoo.com
- Live Search   www.live.com
- Google   www.google.com
- Ask   www.ask.com

b. Print the first page of the results from each search. Circle the name of the search engine and the number of hits, or results it produced.

c. Compare and contrast the appearance and number of hits you received from each site. Also include which search engine you think is better and include a few reasons for your preference.

Advanced Challenge Exercise

ACE

- In the bookmarks library, create a folder in the Bookmarks Bar collection called **Search Results**.
- Bookmark the home page for your favorite search engine in the Search Results bookmark folder.
- Return to your home page, then use the Search Results folder on the bookmarks bar to go to the search engine home page.
- Delete the Search Results bookmark folder from the bookmarks bar. (*Hint*: Drag the bookmark folder off of the bookmarks bar, then click Delete Folder in the dialog box that opens.)

d. Quit Safari.

▼ VISUAL WORKSHOP

Graphics you find as you view pages on the Web can be static images, video, or animated graphics. Find two Web sites that include a video. You may be given the option to watch the video using a player such as Quicktime. Other viewing options may include other players or viewing the video in a viewing window on the Web page. Keep in mind that Windows Media Player files will not play on your Mac. View at least one video on a news site and one video on a topic-specific Web site such as an organization or tourism site. An example is shown in Figure D-23. Write a brief summary of the videos you watched. Identify the Web sites on which the videos were located.

FIGURE D-23

Getting Started with Microsoft Office 2008 for Mac

Microsoft Office 2008 for Mac, often referred to as "Office," is a collection (or **suite**) of programs that you can use to produce a wide variety of documents, including letters, income statements, mailing lists, presentations, Web pages, and comprehensive reports that combine many different elements. Office comes in several versions, or product combinations. Microsoft Office 2008 for Mac includes Word, Excel, PowerPoint, and Entourage. You have just joined the staff at Outdoor Designs, a company that sells do-it-yourself kits for building outdoor recreational products. In your new position, you will use Microsoft Office 2008 for Mac to create business documents.

OBJECTIVES

Understand Microsoft Office 2008 for Mac

Start an Office program

Use menus and the Standard toolbar

Explore the Toolbox

View the Elements Gallery

Save and close a file

Create a new file with a template

Get Help and quit an Office program

Understanding Office 2008 for Mac

Microsoft Office 2008 for Mac comes with a variety of **programs** (sometimes called **applications**) and tools you can use to create documents, analyze data, and complete many business tasks. In this book, you will learn how to use Word, Excel, and PowerPoint. All are powerful stand-alone programs, but what makes the Office suite so useful is that the programs share many common features. Once you are familiar with one Office program's **user interface** (the way commands and features are organized on screen), you can use the same knowledge in another Office program. Other common features allow you to transfer data between programs and to work more easily with others on a single project.  You decide to familiarize yourself with the programs and tools in Office 2008 for Mac before creating a new document.

Microsoft Office 2008 for Mac contains the following programs:

- **Microsoft Word** is a **word-processing program** you can use to create text-based documents, such as letters, memos, newsletters, and reports. You can also add pictures, drawings, tables, and other graphical elements to your Word documents. At Outdoor Designs, you'll use Word to create memos, letters, flyers, and newsletters to communicate with staff, customers, and distributors. Figure E-1 shows an Outdoor Designs newsletter created using Word.

- **Microsoft Excel** is a **spreadsheet program** you can use to manipulate, analyze, and chart quantitative data; it is often used to calculate financial information. In your work at Outdoor Designs, you'll use Excel to create product order worksheets, invoices, sales reports, and charts like the one shown in Figure E-2 to help the Sales and Marketing departments track sales and make informed business decisions.

- **Microsoft PowerPoint** is a **presentation graphics program** you can use to develop materials for presentations, including slide shows, computer-based presentations, speaker's notes, and audience handouts. The staff at Outdoor Designs is preparing for the spring selling season, so you'll use PowerPoint to create a presentation for the sales representatives that describes the new products they will sell. Figure E-3 shows one of the slides from this presentation.

In addition to the three programs you learn about in this book, Microsoft Office 2008 for Mac also includes the following program:

- **Microsoft Entourage** is an e-mail and information manager you use to send and receive e-mail, schedule appointments, maintain task lists, and store names, addresses, and other contact information.

Office 2008

Starting an Office Program

When you start an Office program, your computer reads the program stored on your computer's hard disk and displays it on the screen for you to use. This is called **launching** or **opening** a program. There are several ways you can start an Office program. The easiest way is to click the Office program icon on the **dock**, the row of icons at the bottom of your screen. You decide to explore Office by starting Microsoft Word and getting acquainted with the user interface.

QUICK TIP

If the dock is not visible on the desktop, it may be hidden. To show the dock, click the Apple icon on the menu bar, point to Dock, then click Turn Hiding Off, or move your mouse pointer to the bottom of your computer screen and the dock will slide into view.

1. **Locate the dock at the bottom of your screen**

   The dock, as shown in Figure E-4, contains icons representing programs, folders, documents, and other items.

2. **Click the Word icon 🔳 on the dock**

   Clicking a program icon on the dock launches the program. (*Note*: If the Word icon is not on the dock, click the Finder icon 🔳 on the dock, click Applications in the Finder window, locate and click Microsoft Office 2008, then double-click Microsoft Word.) Word starts and the program window opens, displaying a blank document on the screen. (Your screen might look a little different, depending on your settings.) Refer to Figure E-5 to identify the elements of the program window, described below:

   - The **menu bar** appears at the top of the screen and includes the names of all the Word menus. Menus are lists of commands you can click to perform tasks. Clicking a menu name on the menu bar opens its menu.
   - The **title bar** is at the top of the program window. It contains the name of the document (currently the temporary name "Document1"). At the left end of the title bar are the **Close**, **Minimize**, and **Zoom buttons**, which you use to close the current document, minimize the document to the dock, and maximize the window size.
   - All Office 2008 programs have toolbars. A **toolbar** is a customizable set of buttons that provide rapid one-click access to the most commonly used commands in a program. Buttons on a toolbar are often easier to remember than their menu counterparts because they display a picture illustrating their function, and the name of the button that depicts the function. The **Standard toolbar**, located directly below the title bar, contains buttons that perform the most common tasks in a program, such as creating a new document, opening, saving, and printing a document.
   - The **Elements Gallery** is a new feature for Office 2008. Its purpose is to make it easier to insert objects, such as charts and SmartArt graphics, into your office documents. The Elements Gallery is made up of tabs that, when clicked, expand the gallery and give you quick, easy access to commonly-used, preformatted elements.
   - The **document window** is the work area within the program window. This is where you type text in your document and format it to look the way you want. The work area looks slightly different in each Office program based on the type of document you are creating; in Excel, for example, you'll see a worksheet. The **insertion point** is a flashing vertical line in the document window that indicates where text will be inserted when you type.
   - The **status bar** at the bottom of the screen displays key information, such as the current view, current page, and the number of total words in the document. At the far left of the status bar are shortcuts for changing your view of the document. In Word, you can choose among five view buttons on the status bar and an additional view available as an option on the View menu.

FIGURE E-4: Mac desktop

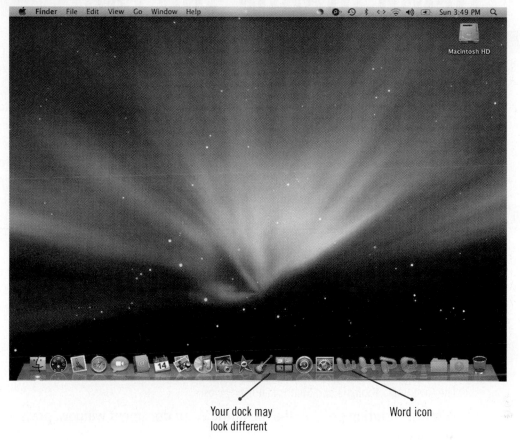

Your dock may
look different

Word icon

FIGURE E-5: Word program window

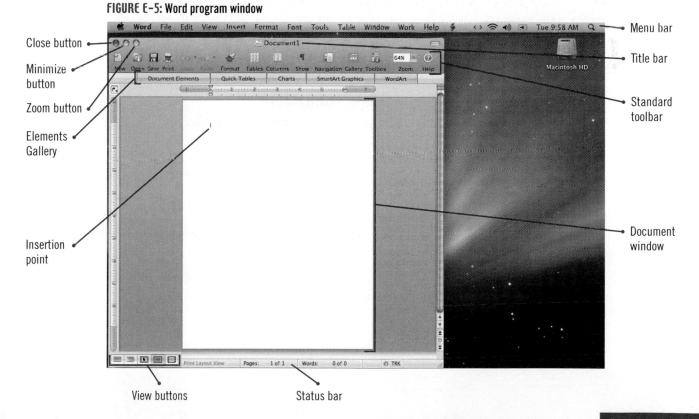

Close button

Minimize
button

Zoom button

Elements
Gallery

Insertion
point

View buttons

Status bar

Menu bar

Title bar

Standard
toolbar

Document
window

Using Menus and the Standard Toolbar

All Office 2008 programs share similar tools that help you complete tasks. Menus and toolbar buttons appear in all Office 2008 programs and contain buttons or commands that you select to perform a task. If Office needs more information in order to carry out a particular command from a menu or toolbar, it displays a **dialog box** that presents options you can select to complete the task. Once you learn how to use these tools to select commands in Word, you will be able to use them in any Office program. You decide to use Word to create a simple to-do list for yourself.

STEPS

1. Click View on the menu bar
The View menu opens, as shown in Figure E-6. As you click the items listed on the menu bar, drop-down menus appear giving you access to all the options available in this program.

2. Click Customize Toolbars and Menus on the View menu
The Customize Toolbars and Menus dialog box opens, as shown in Figure E-7. This dialog box lets you set the toolbars and menu commands that are shown onscreen.

3. Click OK
The Customize Toolbars and Menus dialog box closes.

4. With the insertion point at the top of the Word document window, press [return] four times
The insertion point moves down four lines.

5. Type To Do List, then press [return] twice
The insertion point moves down two lines below the text you typed.

6. Click the Undo button 🔄 on the Standard toolbar
The words you typed, "To Do List," are deleted, and the insertion point moves back up to the top of the page. The Undo button reverses your last action.

7. Click the Redo button 🔄 on the Standard toolbar
The Redo button restores your document to the state it was in before you clicked the Undo button.

8. Click the Zoom list arrow on the Standard toolbar
A list appears containing options for **zooming**, or changing the magnification level of the screen. You can zoom in to get a closer view of certain content, or zoom out to get a wider view so you can see more content at a reduced size. You can select an option on the menu to choose a predefined view of the document, such as 200%, or enter a specific percentage (up to 500%) by typing in the Zoom field. Zooming affects only your view of the content in a file, not the content itself.

9. Click 100%
The document magnification level changes to 100%, the actual size of the document as it would look printed.

10. Type Write letter for Paulette Chen, press [return], type Order new business cards, press [return], then type Schedule meeting with Dean Holmes
Compare your screen to Figure E-8.

> **QUICK TIP**
>
> When you place the mouse pointer over a button or tab, a ScreenTip appears that provides a brief description about the function of the button or tab.

FIGURE E-6: View menu

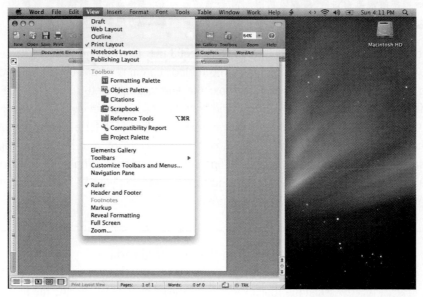

FIGURE E-7: Customize Toolbars and Menus dialog box

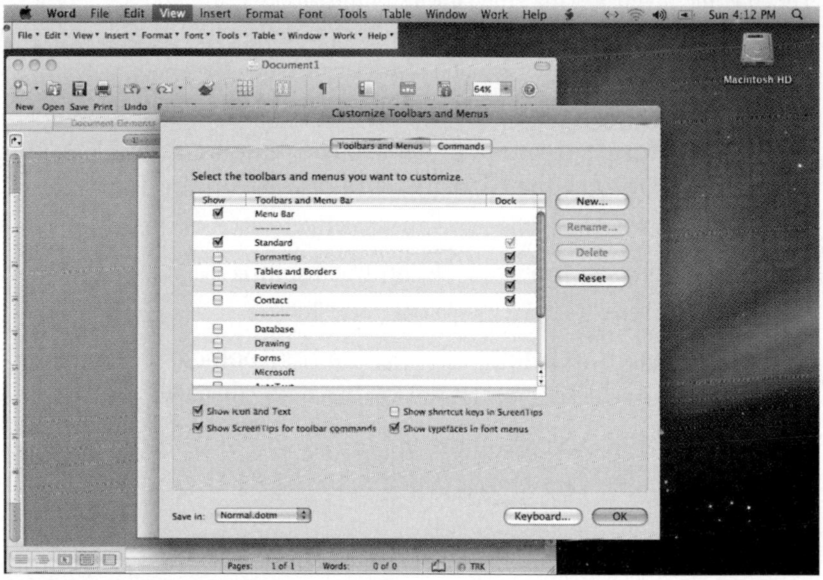

FIGURE E-8: Completed To Do List document

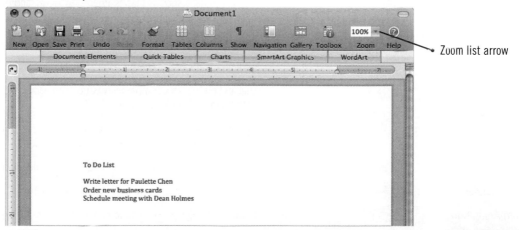

Zoom list arrow

Exploring the Toolbox

The **Toolbox** is an updated feature in Office 2008 that provides quick access to several tools you can use as you work within an Office program. The Toolbox contains six palettes of tools you can activate by clicking the appropriate tab on the Toolbox: the Formatting Palette, the Object Palette, the Scrapbook, Reference Tools, Compatibility Report, and Projects. In addition, in each Office program you'll find palettes in the Toolbox that are specific to that program. See Table E-1 for a description of each Toolbox palette. When activated, the Toolbox appears floating to the right of your document, but you can move it. By default, the Toolbox is closed when you open Word. To open the Toolbox, click the Toolbox button on the Standard toolbar. ████████ You are thinking about enhancing your To Do List document, so you review the tools in the Toolbox that are at your disposal.

STEPS

QUICK TIP

To reposition the Toolbox, click and drag its title bar.

1. **Click the Toolbox button ▦ on the Standard toolbar**

   The Toolbox opens to the right of the document window, as shown in Figure E-9. By default, the Formatting Palette is active when the Toolbox is opened. The Formatting Palette and the Toolbox were separate items in Office 2004 for Mac, but they have been combined and expanded in Office 2008 for Mac.

2. **Click the Alignment and Spacing group on the Formatting Palette**

   The Alignment and Spacing group opens. In this group, you'll find tools for text alignment, line and paragraph spacing, and indentation. The **disclosure triangle** next to a group's name indicates that the group has additional subcategories or options available. When the triangle points to the right, the additional options are hidden. When the triangle points down, the group is open and all of its options are visible.

3. **Click the disclosure triangle ▼ next to the Alignment and Spacing group again to close the group, then click the Object Palette tab ▦ on the Toolbox**

   The Object Palette becomes the active palette in the Toolbox, as shown in Figure E-10.

4. **Click the Reference Tools tab ▦ on the Toolbox**

   Reference Tools becomes the active palette in the Toolbox.

QUICK TIP

You can also close the Toolbox by clicking the Toolbox button on the Standard toolbar to deselect it.

5. **Click the Formatting Palette tab ▦ on the Toolbox**

   The Formatting Palette becomes the active palette in the Toolbox again.

6. **Click the Close button ● in the upper-left corner of the Toolbox**

   The Toolbox closes and the Toolbox button on the Standard toolbar is no longer selected.

TABLE E-1: Toolbox palettes

palette	tab	description
Formatting Palette	▦	Provides the most commonly used formatting options for your document
Object Palette	▦	Contains objects such as shapes, images, symbols, and photos, which you can insert into your document
Scrapbook	▦	Enables you to copy and paste multiple items to and from documents
Reference Tools	▦	Contains dictionary, thesaurus, and translation tools
Compatibility Report	▦	Enables you to check compatibility issues with earlier versions of Office, including both Windows and Mac versions
Projects	▦	An Entourage tool that allows you to group different elements (including Office documents, e-mail, and calendar events) into projects
Citations	▦	Word only: enables you to insert citations and build a bibliography
Formula Builder	fx	Excel only: helps you create mathematical calculations
Custom Animation	▦★	PowerPoint only: enables you to create animations for presentation slides

FIGURE E-9: Toolbox

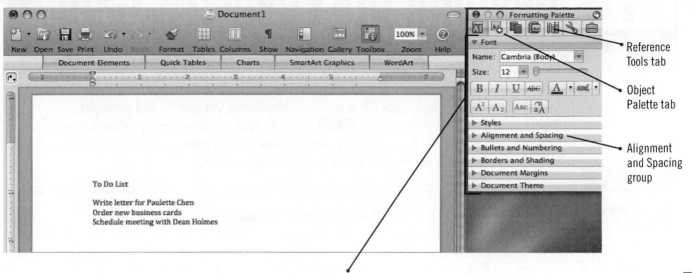

Reference Tools tab

Object Palette tab

Alignment and Spacing group

Formatting Palette

FIGURE E-10: Object Palette

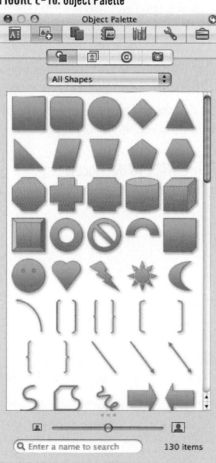

Viewing the Elements Gallery

In all Office programs for Mac, you have access to the Elements Gallery, a new feature in Office 2008. The Elements Gallery is a tool to help you insert professionally designed and formatted objects, such as charts, SmartArt graphics, and tables, into any Office 2008 document. The Elements Gallery is organized by tabs. Some of the tabs appear in each Office program, while others are specific to a particular program. See Table E-2 for a description of the tabs.  You learned at your new employee orientation meeting at Outdoor Designs that the Elements Gallery can help you create professional-looking documents quickly, so you decide to gain a better understanding of this important tool.

STEPS

> **QUICK TIP**
> You can also expand the Elements Gallery by clicking any Elements Gallery tab.

1. **Click the Gallery button ⊞ on the Standard toolbar**

   The Document Elements tab in the Elements Gallery for Word expands, as shown in Figure E-11. Just beneath the Document Elements tab, you can select from several groups of elements you can use in your document. The Cover Page group is currently displayed on the Document Elements tab. The right pane of the Cover Page group displays several cover page styles. The left pane of the group displays information about inserting a cover page.

2. **Click the Quick Tables tab in the Elements Gallery**

   The Quick Tables tab opens, displaying several table styles that can be used in the document.

3. **Click the Complex group on the Quick Tables tab**

   The Complex group opens on the Quick Tables tab. Several complex table styles are displayed in the right pane of the group.

4. **Move the pointer over the first table style in the right pane of the Quick Tables tab**

   As you move the pointer over a style in the right pane of the gallery, the name of the style and a description of the style appear in the left pane. See Figure E-12.

5. **Click the SmartArt Graphics tab in the Elements Gallery**

   The SmartArt Graphics tab opens, displaying several SmartArt Graphic styles that can be used in the document.

> **QUICK TIP**
> You can also close the Elements Gallery by clicking the currently expanded tab.

6. **Click the Gallery button ⊞ to deselect it**

   The Elements Gallery closes so that only the Elements Gallery tabs are visible in the document window.

TABLE E-2: Elements Gallery tabs in Office 2008

tab	appears in	contains
Charts	Word, Excel, PowerPoint	Preformatted charts
SmartArt Graphics	Word, Excel, PowerPoint	Graphic representations of text (new in Office 2008)
WordArt	Word, Excel, PowerPoint	Stylized text with sophisticated text formatting features
Document Elements	Word	Elements used in professional and educational documents, such as cover pages, headers, and bibliographies
Quick Tables	Word	Preformatted tables
Sheets	Excel	Common spreadsheet styles, such as budgets, invoices, and reports
Slide Themes; Slide Layouts; Transitions; and Table Styles	PowerPoint	Common elements used to build presentations

FIGURE E-11: Elements Gallery (Word)

Document Elements tab

Gallery button

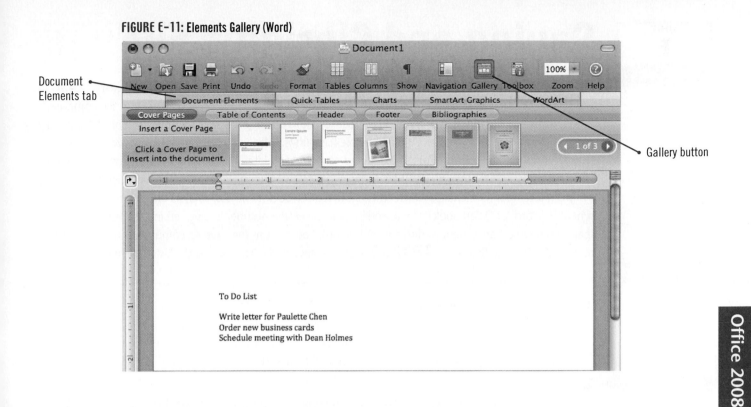

FIGURE E-12: Complex group on Quick Tables tab

Quick Tables tab

Complex group

Style name and description

Mouse pointer over first table style

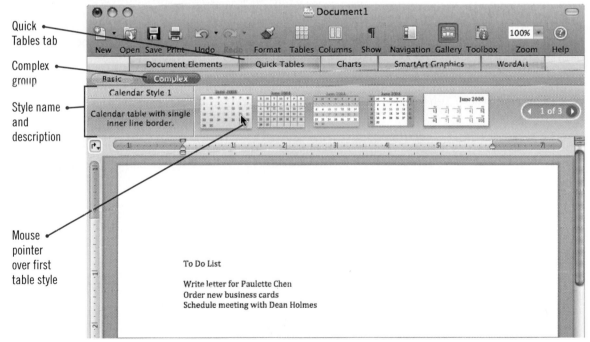

Office 2008

Saving and Closing a File

When you enter data into a computer, it is stored in the computer's **random access memory (RAM)**, a temporary storage location, until you turn off your computer, which erases the contents of the computer's RAM. To store your work permanently, you must save it as a **file** (an electronic collection of data), usually on your computer's hard disk or on a removable flash drive. When you save a document, you must assign it a unique **filename**, a name for the file so you can identify it later. You must also specify where you want to save the document (on which drive and in what folder, if any). Before you save a document, Office assigns it a temporary filename which reflects the type of document it is, such as "Document1" for a document in Word, or "Workbook1" for a workbook in Excel (the number is assigned in case you create more than one unsaved document during a work session). You can use the Save As command on the File menu to save a file for the first time. You decide to save and close your To Do List document.

STEPS

1. **Click File on the menu bar**

   The File menu opens. The menu contains a Save command and a Save As command, as shown in Figure E-13. You use the Save As command when you need to save a file for the first time, and the Save command when you want to save any changes made to an existing file since the last time you saved.

QUICK TIP

If you click the Save command before you save a file for the first time, the Save As dialog box opens, so that you can assign the file a name and folder location.

2. **Click Save As**

   The Save As dialog box opens, displaying the current folder. At the top of the dialog box is the Save As text box, where you enter the name you want for the file.

3. **Verify that To Do List.docx appears in the Save As text box**

   By default, the first words in your document, "To Do List", appear highlighted in the Save As text box as a suggested file name. The ".docx" at the end of the filename is the default file extension for this document. When you save a file, the program automatically assigns it a **file extension** to identify the program that created it. Documents created in Word 2008 have the file extension .docx; whereas documents created in older versions of Word have the file extension .doc. Your computer may not be set to display file extensions, in which case you won't see this information in the Save As text box or in the title bar of the program. This is not a problem; the information is still saved with the file.

4. **Navigate to the drive and folder where you store your Data Files**

   Compare your screen to Figure E-14.

5. **Click Save**

   The Save As dialog box closes and your To Do List document is saved in the drive and folder you specified. Notice that the title bar now displays the new filename.

6. **Click File on the menu bar, then click Close**

   The To Do List document and the Word window close. Word remains open, but only the menu bar is visible on your screen.

FIGURE E-13: Word File menu

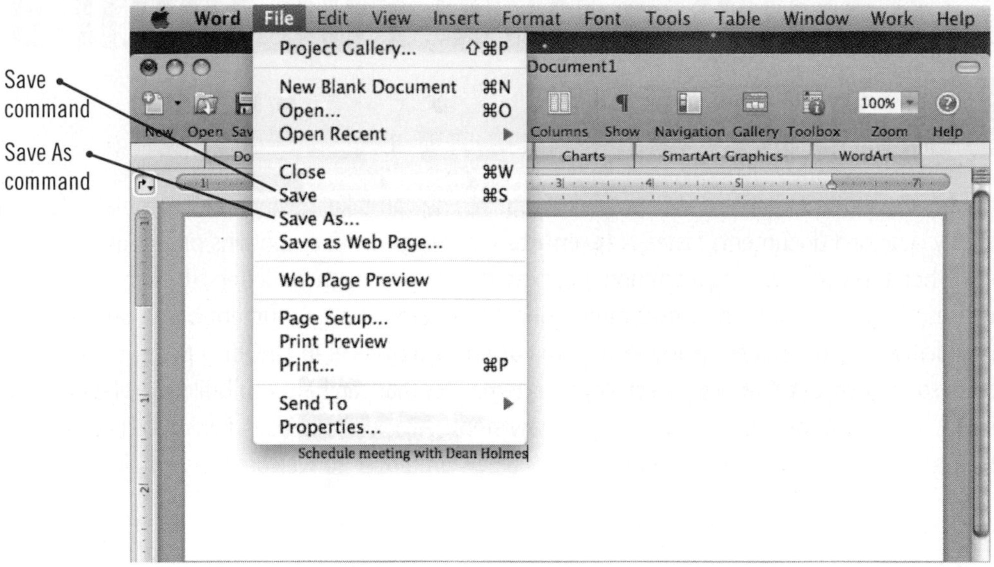

Save command

Save As command

FIGURE E-14: Save As dialog box

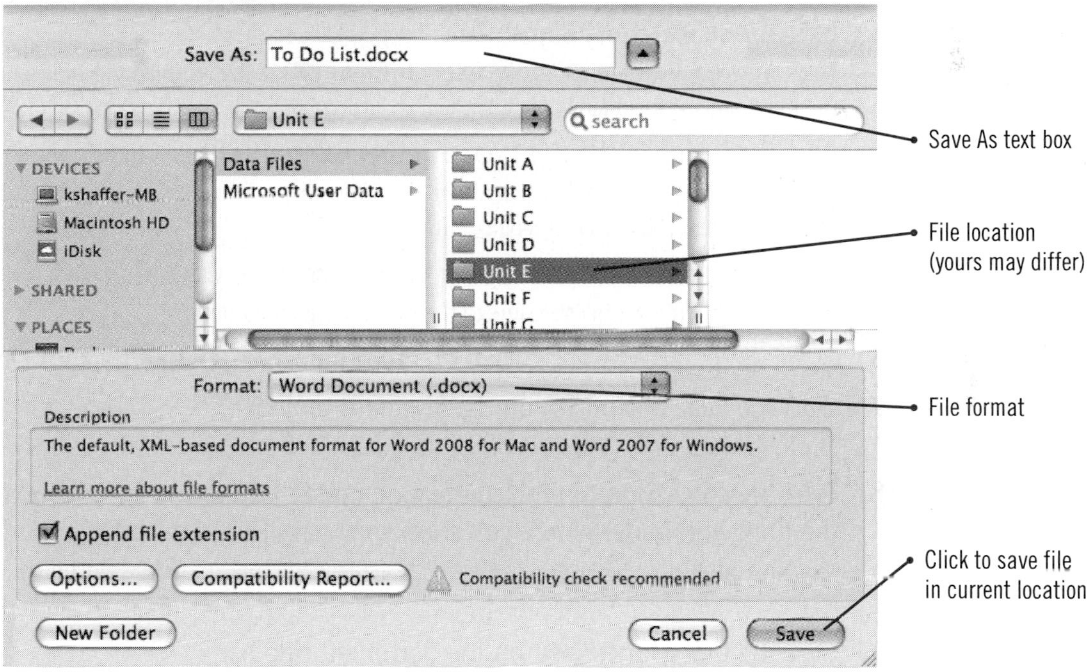

Save As text box

File location (yours may differ)

File format

Click to save file in current location

Saving files and understanding the Microsoft Office file formats

All files saved in Microsoft Office 2008 for Mac have the new Office XML format; that's why you see an 'x' in the file extension of most Office 2008 files. XML is a markup language that has many benefits, including better privacy controls, the ability to automatically compress files to a much smaller size, and the ability to repair damaged files. However, because previous versions of Microsoft Office saved files in a different binary format, files saved in Office 2008 cannot be viewed in previous versions of Office. Therefore, if you want to share a document with someone using Microsoft Office 2004, you need to save it in an earlier Office format. To do this, click the Format text box in the Save As dialog box, click the appropriate file format, such as Word 97–2004 Document (.doc), then click Save.

UNIT
E

Office 2008

Creating a New File with a Template

Though it's easy to create a document from scratch, you can take advantage of templates to create professionally designed documents faster. A **template** is a special file that contains predesigned formatting, text, and other tools for creating common business documents, such as letters, business presentations, and invoices. When you start a new document using a template, a new document based on the template opens immediately on your screen, ready for you to customize and save. In all Office programs for Mac, you have access to the **Project Gallery**, which contains templates that can help you build a professional looking document, worksheet, or presentation in a few easy steps. Your boss, Paulette Chen, has asked you to put together a sign to post outside the office of a new employee to welcome the employee to the company.

STEPS

1. **Click** File **on the menu bar, then click** Project Gallery

   The Project Gallery opens, as shown in Figure E-15.

2. **In the Category list in the left pane of the Project Gallery, click the** disclosure triangle ▶ **next to Marketing**

   A list of marketing document types appears under Marketing in the Category list.

3. **Click the subcategory** Signs

   When you click Signs, miniature images or **thumbnails** of the templates in the Signs subcategory appear in the right pane of the dialog box, as shown in Figure E-16.

4. **Click** Party Sign **in the right pane of the dialog box, then click** Open

   A new document based on the Party Sign template opens. The document contains an image and blocks of placeholder text that you can replace with your own text.

5. **Click** Welcome to the Party!, **then type** Welcome to the Company!

   The new text replaces the Welcome to the Party! placeholder text.

6. **Scroll down if necessary, click** (Lorem Ipsum Dolor), **then type** Your Name

7. **Click the** Save button 🖫 **on the Standard toolbar**

   The Save As dialog box opens, because you have not previously saved the current document.

8. **Type** Welcome Sign **to replace the highlighted text in the Save As text box, navigate to the drive and folder where you store your Data Files if necessary, then click** Save

   The Save As dialog box closes, and the new filename appears in the document title bar, as shown in Figure E-17.

9. **Click the** Close button 🔘 **on the document title bar**

   The Welcome Sign document closes.

Getting Started with Microsoft Office 2008 for Mac

FIGURE E-15: Project Gallery

Category list

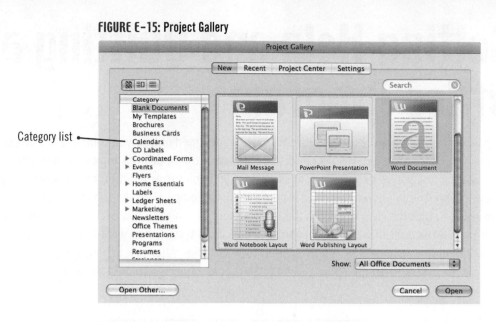

FIGURE E-16: Signs subcategory selected in Project Gallery

Template thumbnails

Signs subcategory

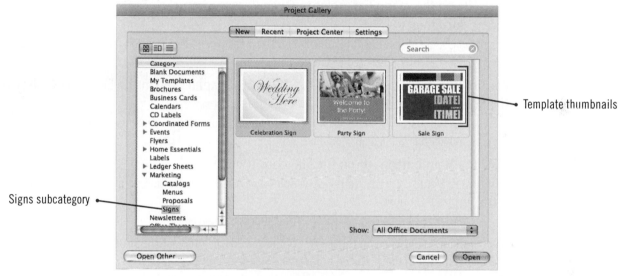

FIGURE E-17: Completed Welcome Sign document

Office 2008

Getting Help and Quitting an Office Program

Office 2008 for Mac has a context-sensitive Help system designed to help you complete any task or use any feature in an Office program. Help is **context-sensitive** in that it displays topics and instructions geared to the specific task you're performing. For example, if you point to any button or tab, a ScreenTip opens, displaying a brief description of what the feature is used for. To open Help for the Office 2008 program you are working in, click the Help button on the Standard toolbar. ▥▥▥ You decide to find out more about one of the new features of Word 2008 by using Word's Help system. You want to explore features related to working with a document, so first you need to open a file. After researching the new feature, you'll print your document, then quit Word. *Note*: You must be connected to the Internet to perform the steps in this lesson.

STEPS

1. **Click File on the menu bar, point to Open Recent, then click To Do List.docx in the list of recent documents**

   The To Do List document opens in the window. Using the Open Recent option on the File menu is a fast way to open a document you've used recently.

2. **Position the mouse pointer over the SmartArt Graphics tab in the Elements Gallery until the ScreenTip appears**

   See Figure E-18. The ScreenTip displays a brief description of the elements available on the SmartArt Graphics tab ("Process diagrams, graphical lists, and organizational charts").

> **QUICK TIP**
> You can also open the Word Help window by clicking Help on the menu bar, then clicking Word Help.

3. **Click the Help button ⊚ on the Standard toolbar**

   As shown in Figure E-19, the Word Help window opens with the insertion point blinking in the search field at the top of the window.

4. **Type SmartArt in the search field, then press [return]**

   A new window slides open on the left side of the Word Help window. The Search tab in the new window is selected, and a list of topics related to the term "SmartArt" appears on the tab.

5. **Click Add or edit a SmartArt graphic in the topic list**

   The Word Help window changes to show the Add or edit a SmartArt graphic topic, which contains options to choose to learn how to perform a specific task with a SmartArt graphic.

> **QUICK TIP**
> The Help button may not be visible on the Standard toolbar when using Publishing Layout view, depending on your computer's screen resolution. If it is not visible in Publishing Layout view, click the More Buttons button on the right end of the Standard toolbar, then click the Help button to open Help.

6. **Click the disclosure triangle ▶ next to Add a SmartArt graphic in the Word Help window**

   As shown in Figure E-20, the steps for adding a SmartArt graphic to a document appear in the window.

7. **Read the topic in the Word Help window, then click the Close button ⊗ on the Word Help window**

   The Help window closes and returns to the To Do List document.

8. **Click the Print button 🖶 on the Standard toolbar**

   A copy of the document prints on the default printer.

9. **Click Word on the menu bar, then click Quit Word**

   Both the To Do List document and the Word program close. If you had made changes to the document since you saved it, a dialog box would have opened, prompting you to save the changes before quitting Word. You can save changes to a document at any time by clicking the Save button on the Standard toolbar.

FIGURE E-18: Example of a ScreenTip

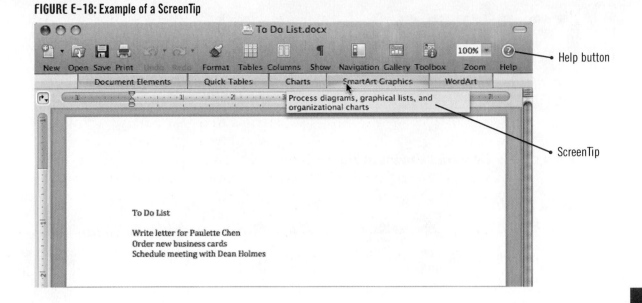

Help button

ScreenTip

FIGURE E-19: Word Help window

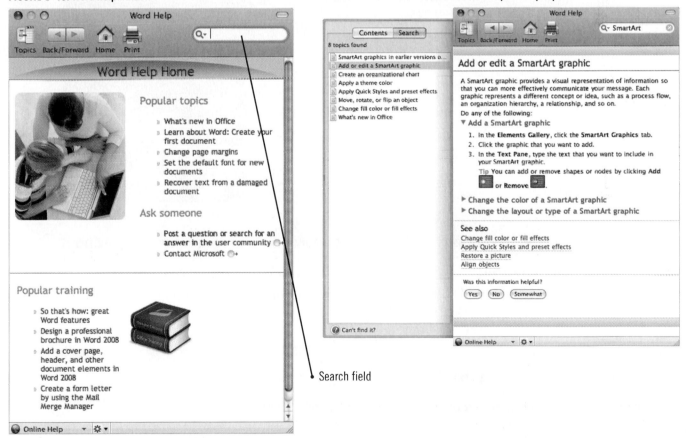

Search field

FIGURE E-20: Add or edit a SmartArt Graphic Help topic

Practice

▼ CONCEPTS REVIEW

Label each of the elements shown in Figure E-21.

FIGURE E-21

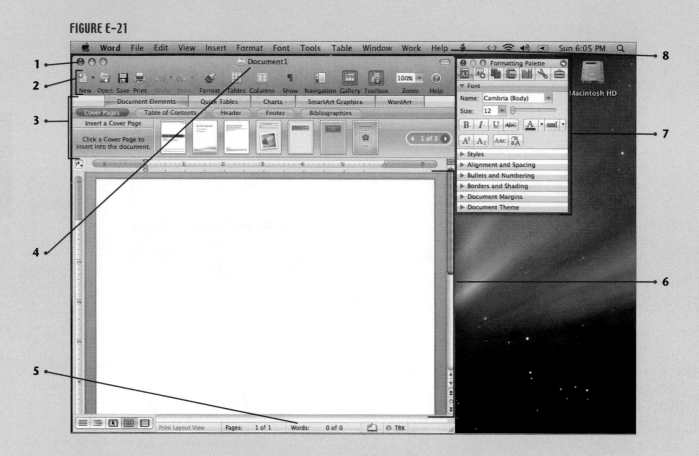

Match each of the following tasks with the most appropriate program for completing it.

9. Create an income statement
10. Create a newsletter containing graphics
11. Create slides for a sales meeting presentation
12. Store contact information and send e-mail

    a. Microsoft Entourage
    b. Microsoft Excel
    c. Microsoft Word
    d. Microsoft PowerPoint

Select the best answer from the list of choices.

13. The Project Gallery is accessed by what option on the menu bar?
    a.
    b. File
    c. Edit
    d. View

14. A file that contains predesigned formatting, text, and tools for creating common business documents is called a:

   a. Thumbnail.

   b. Template.

   c. Report.

   d. Wizard.

15. Which of the following options should you use when you save a document for the first time?

   a. Save

   b. Save As

   c. Open

   d. Project Gallery

16. To open the Toolbox or Elements Gallery in an Office program, you can use commands on the:

   a. Standard toolbar.

   b. Project Gallery.

   c. Title bar.

   d. Status bar.

17. Which of the following is the default file extension for documents saved using Word 2008?

   a. .docx

   b. .doc

   c. .word

   d. .xlsx

▼ SKILLS REVIEW

1. Understand Office 2008 for Mac.

   a. Name the programs that are included in Microsoft Office 2008 for Mac.

   b. Which Office program would you use to create a letter?

   c. Which Office program would you use to create a slide presentation?

   d. Which Office program would you use to create an invoice containing multiple calculations?

   e. Which Office program would you use to keep track of your calendar?

2. Start an Office program.

   a. Start Microsoft Word.

   b. View the program window and identify the following screen elements without referring to the lesson material: menu bar, Standard toolbar, title bar, status bar, document window, insertion point, and Elements Gallery.

3. Use the menus and the Standard toolbar.

   a. With Document1 open in the document window, type Meeting Agenda, then press [return].

   b. Type Product Line Presentation, then press [return] twice.

   c. Type the following agenda, pressing [return] at the end of each line (including the last line):

     Introductions (9:00)

     Present our new exercise video product line (9:10)

     Answer questions (9:45)

   d. Click and drag to select Answer questions (9:45).

   e. Press [delete].

   f. Click the Undo button on the Standard toolbar to undo the sentence deletion.

   g. Click View on the menu bar, then click Web Layout.

   h. Click to place the insertion point after Answer questions (9:45), press [return], then type Wrap up (9:55).

   i. Press [return] twice, then type your name.

   j. Click View on the menu bar, then click Print Layout.

4. Explore the Toolbox.

   a. Click the Toolbox button on the Standard toolbar to open the Toolbox.

   b. Click the disclosure triangle next to the Styles group on the Formatting Palette.

   c. Close the Styles group on the Formatting Palette.

   d. Click the Scrapbook tab on the Toolbox.

   e. Click the Object Palette tab on the Toolbox.

   f. Click the Formatting Palette tab on the Toolbox, then close the Toolbox.

5. View the Elements Gallery.

   a. Click the Gallery button on the Standard toolbar.

   b. Click the Charts tab in the Elements Gallery.

   c. Click the Bar group on the Charts tab.

   d. View the name of the first chart type in the right pane of the Charts tab.

   e. Click the WordArt tab in the Elements Gallery.

   f. Close the Elements Gallery so that only the Elements Gallery tabs are visible.

6. Save and close a file.

   a. Open the Save As dialog box.

   b. Save the document as **Meeting Agenda** where you save your Data Files.

   c. Close the Meeting Agenda document.

7. Create a new file with a template.

   a. Open the Project Gallery.

   b. Click Calendars in the Category list.

   c. Click Horizontal Calendar in the right pane of the Project Gallery, then click Open.

   d. Replace the Month placeholder text with **January**.

FIGURE E-22

   e. Replace the Year placeholder text with **2012**.

   f. On the dark gray bar, replace the left text placeholder with **Important Date:**.

   g. Replace the right text placeholder with **433 Eros, a large asteroid, will pass by Earth on 1/31/12**. Compare your screen to Figure E-22.

   h. Save the document as **January 2012 Calendar** where you save your Data Files.

   i. Close the January 2012 Calendar document.

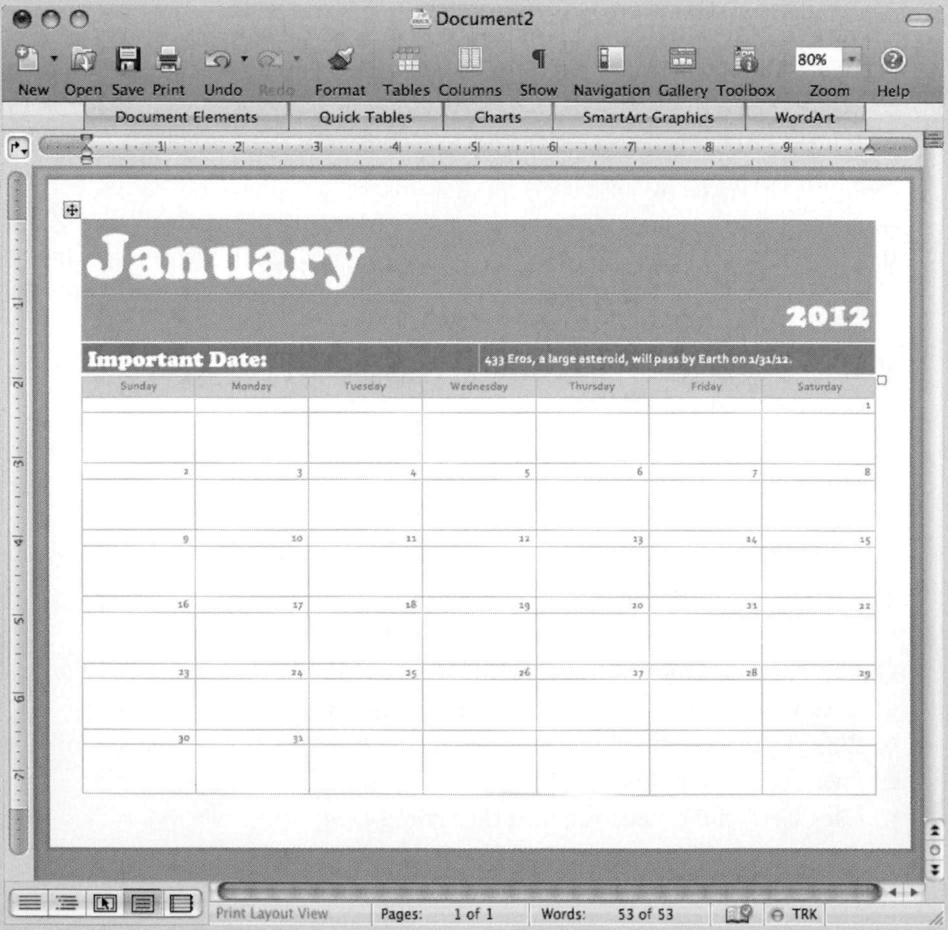

8. Get Help and quit an Office program.

a. Click File on the menu bar, then click Meeting Agenda on the list of recent documents to open it.

b. Display the ScreenTip for each button on the Standard toolbar.

c. Click the Help button on the Standard toolbar.

d. In the search field, type **save in a different format**, then press [return].

e. Locate the "Save a document in a different format" topic in the search results list.

f. Read the topic in the Word Help window to learn more about different formats.

g. Close the Word Help window.

h. Click the Print button on the Standard toolbar. Compare your printed document to Figure E-23.

i. Close the **Meeting Agenda** document.

j. Quit Word.

FIGURE E-23

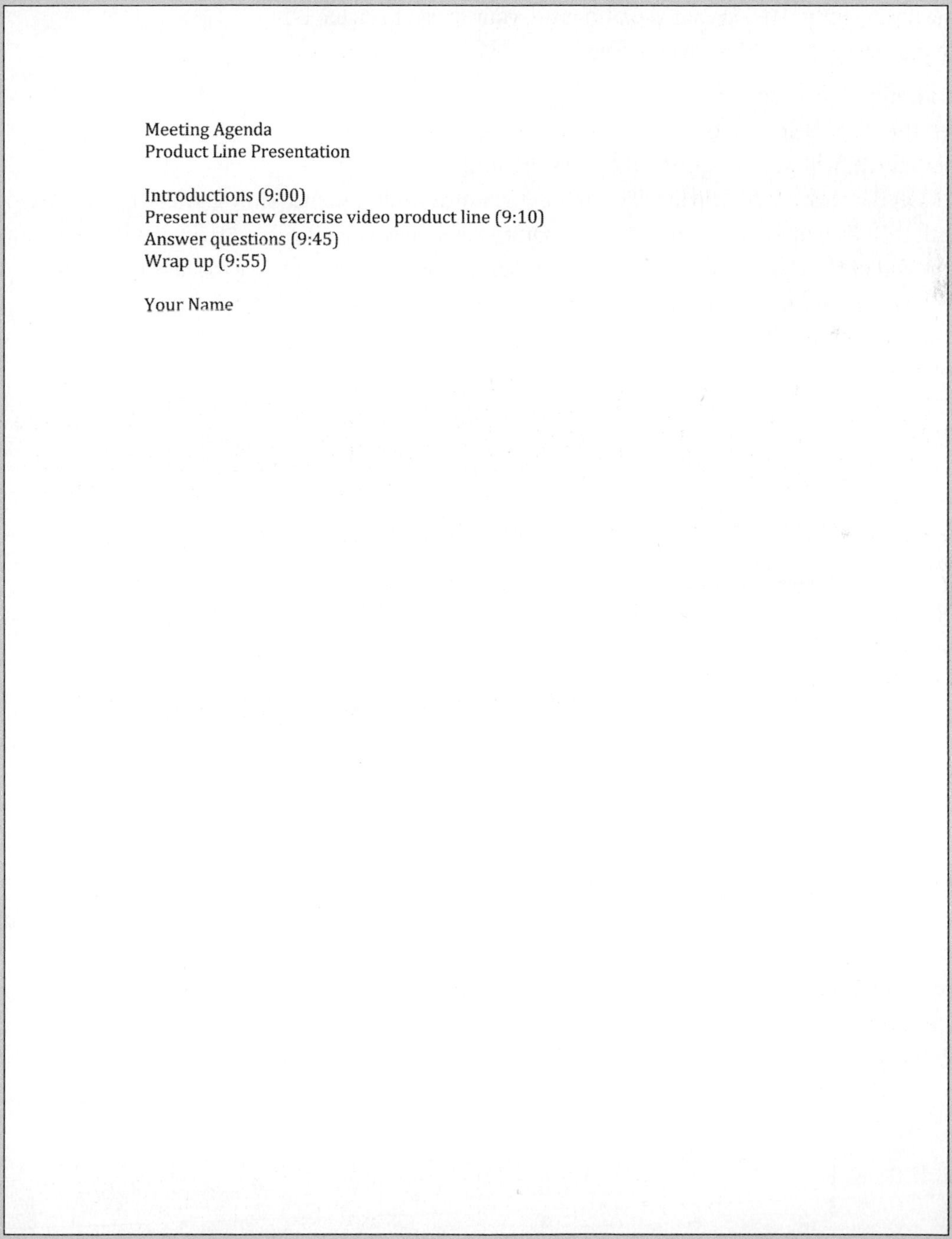

Meeting Agenda
Product Line Presentation

Introductions (9:00)
Present our new exercise video product line (9:10)
Answer questions (9:45)
Wrap up (9:55)

Your Name

Office 2008

▼ INDEPENDENT CHALLENGE 1

You provide administrative support to Carlos Garcia, the general manager at GetFit Fitness Center. Carlos has asked you to create a schedule for the gym to provide to members and post on the Web site.

   a. Start Microsoft Word. (*Hint*: If Word is already open and you need to create a new document, click New Blank Document on the File menu.)

   b. Type **Gym Summer Schedule** in the first line of the blank document, then press [return] twice.

   c. Type the following text, pressing [return] after each line:

      9:00 Jazzercise
      2:00 Youth basketball
      5:00 Pilates
      7:00 Yoga

   d. Type your name two lines below the last line of text.

   e. Save the document as **Gym Summer Schedule** where you save your Data Files.

   f. View the document in Web Layout view. Compare your screen to Figure E-24.

   g. Change the view back to Print Layout view.

Advanced Challenge Exercise

- ■ Open the Word Help window.
- ■ In the search field, type **help**, and then press [return].
- ■ Click Get the most out of Help in Office 2008 in the search results list, then click Start Video in the Word Help window.
- ■ Watch the video to learn how to get help in Office 2008, then close the Word Help window.
- ■ At the end of the Gym Summer Schedule document, type one new fact you learned about using Help.
- ■ Save your changes to the document.

   h. Print, save, and close the document.

   i. Quit Word.

FIGURE E-24

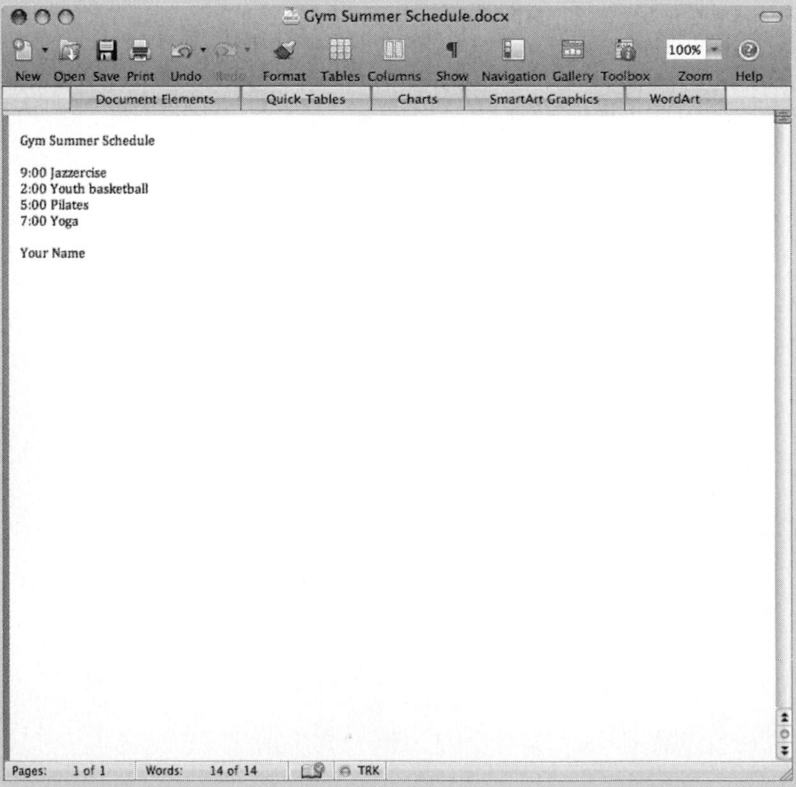

![Gym Summer Schedule document shown in Word window with menu bar items: New Open Save Print Undo Redo Format Tables Columns Show Navigation Gallery Toolbox Zoom Help; tabs: Document Elements, Quick Tables, Charts, SmartArt Graphics, WordArt. Document text reads: Gym Summer Schedule / 9:00 Jazzercise / 2:00 Youth basketball / 5:00 Pilates / 7:00 Yoga / Your Name. Status bar shows Pages: 1 of 1, Words: 14 of 14, TRK.]

▼ INDEPENDENT CHALLENGE 2

Throughout this unit, you used Microsoft Word to learn about many features that are common to all Office 2008 programs, including screen elements such as the menus, Standard toolbar, Toolbox, and Elements Gallery. Use what you have learned to explore another Office program and see the similarities for yourself.

a. Start Microsoft Excel. (*Hint*: Click the Excel icon on the dock. If the icon isn't on the dock, click the Finder icon on the dock, click Applications in the Finder window, locate and click Microsoft Office 2008, then double-click Microsoft Excel.)

b. Compare the Excel program window with what you know of the Word program window. The grid-like structure of the Excel worksheet window is different from the blank document window of Word, but many of the screen elements, such as the menu bar, Standard toolbar, Elements Gallery, and Toolbox are similar (except for differences specific to the program).

c. Experiment with entering text in the Excel worksheet by typing your name, then pressing [return].

d. Below your name, type the following numbers, one entry per cell. (*Hint*: A cell is formed by the intersection of a row and a column in a worksheet. To store data in a cell and move to the cell below, you press [return].)
100
2269
47
660

e. Use the File menu to open the Save As dialog box, then save the workbook as **Excel Practice** where you save your Data Files. Compare your screen with Figure E-25.

f. Print the worksheet.

g. Quit Excel.

FIGURE E-25

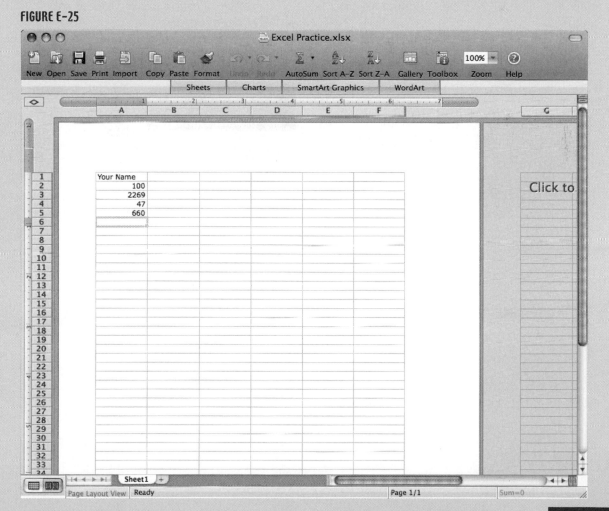

▼ INDEPENDENT CHALLENGE 3

You are a marketing intern for Jamal Johnson, the marketing director at Fancy Shoes, an Internet-based shoe company that caters to women and girls. Jamal has asked you to write a letter to the company's top customers, thanking them for their recent orders and enclosing a coupon to motivate them to buy again. You decide to create the letter using a template.

a. Start Word.

b. Open the Project Gallery.

c. Scroll down and click Stationery in the Category list.

d. Scroll down the list of templates, click the Plaza Letter template, then click Open.

e. Double-click the header area at the top of the document to open the header, click the [Company Name] placeholder, type **Fancy Shoes**, then click the Close tab under the header to close the header. (*Hint*: If the header area already contained a company or school name when the document opened, change it to **Fancy Shoes**.)

f. Use the table to the right as a guide to create the content of the letter.

g. If your name is not automatically used as the name under the salutation "Sincerely," replace the text with your name.

h. Save the memo as **Thank You Letter** where you save your Data Files, print it, compare your printout to Figure E-26, then close the document and quit Word.

Placeholder text	Replace with this text
[Insert Date]	Today's date
[Recipient]	Carol Chambers
[Title]	Buyer
[Company]	Domino Shoe Company
[Address 1]	44 Pond Acres Way
[Address 2]	Suite 101
[Address 3]	Jackson, MS 39201
[Recipient]	Carol
Placeholder text that begins with "Fusce neque mi..."	Thank you for all your orders at Fancy Shoes this year! We appreciate your business. As a token of our thanks, please use the enclosed coupon on your next order.
[Your Title]	Marketing Director

FIGURE E-26

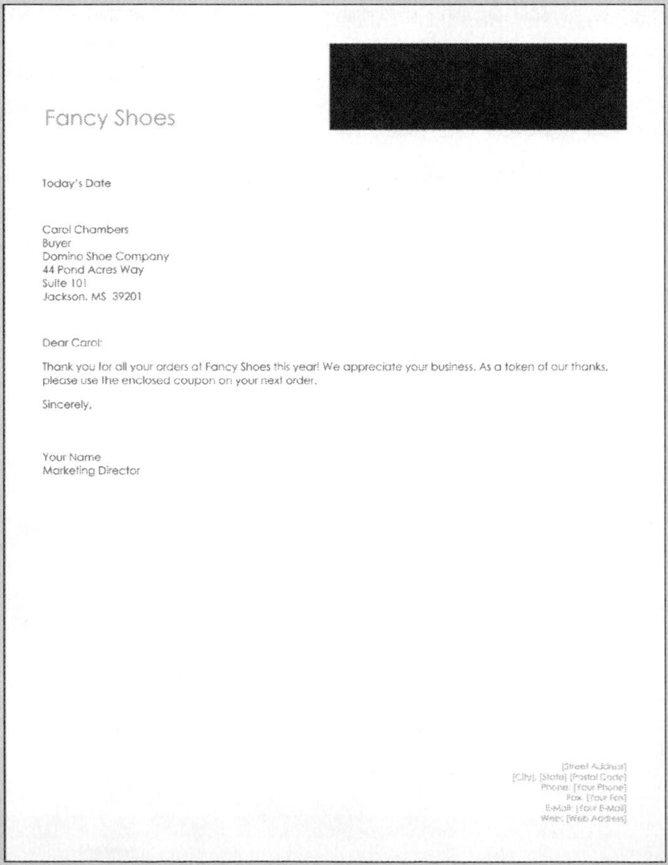

Getting Started with Microsoft Office 2008 for Mac

▼ REAL LIFE INDEPENDENT CHALLENGE

To get a good job—or even get an interview for a good job—it's important that you have a professional looking resume that describes you and your skills, accomplishments, and career goals. Starting a resume from scratch can be a daunting task! Thankfully, Microsoft Word comes with templates to help you write a resume. Creating a resume using one of these templates as a starting point can save time and help you create a resume that looks great. In this Real Life Independent Challenge, you will create your own resume using a template. If you need tips to help you write your resume, log on to the Internet and search for sites that help you find a job, such as Monster.com.

a. Start Microsoft Word.

b. Open the Project Gallery, click Resumes in the Category list, click Simple Resume, then click Open.

c. Double-click the name placeholder in the header at the top of the document to select the placeholder and open the header.

d. If necessary, replace the name placeholder in the header with your full name.

e. Replace the additional placeholders in the header with your address, telephone number, fax number, and e-mail address. If you don't have a fax number, you can delete this placeholder and text.

f. Click the Close tab under the header to close the header.

g. Under Objective, click the placeholder (Latin) text, then type one or two sentences that clearly describe the type of job you want. If you don't have a particular job goal, then for the purpose of this exercise, type **To get an entry-level sales position in the pharmaceutical industry**.

h. Under Experience, replace the placeholders (Latin text) with appropriate information, typing the name of the company where you last worked, and the start date and end date. Replace the bulleted items with two or three descriptions of responsibilities that you had while employed in this job and press [return] after each job responsibility except for the last one.

i. Under Education, replace the placeholders (Latin text) with information about your educational experience, listing each school name, completion date, and the degrees and awards that you earned at the school. If you have not yet earned a degree, then list the date you expect to complete your degree.

j. Under Skills, replace the placeholder (Latin text) with two or three job-related skills that you have. These skills could be computer related (such as "Proficient in Microsoft Office 2008 for Mac") or could relate to other types of proficiencies (such as "Fluent in Spanish"). Press [return] after each skill that you enter.

k. Save the document as **Resume** where you keep your Data Files, print it, then close it.

Advanced Challenge Exercise

- Open the Project Gallery, select Business Cards from the Category list, click the Light Business Card template, then click Open.
- Replace **[Lorem Ipsum]** in the top left card with a company name of your choosing.
- Replace **[Dolor Sit Amet]** in the top left card with your name.
- Replace the other placeholder text on the first card with fictional information that you make up. Make changes to the other cards so that they match the top left card.
- Save the document as **Business Cards ACE** where you keep your Data Files, then close it.

l. Quit Word.

▼ VISUAL WORKSHOP

Use the skills you learned in this unit to create the document shown in Figure E-27. (*Hint*: The document was created using a template called Revolution Fax, in the Faxes subcategory of the Coordinated Forms category.) Enter the Company name and information in the appropriate placeholders in the header. Add the information under "fax" as shown in the figure. After you create the document, enter the comments shown. Save the document as **Fax Sheet** where you store your Data Files, then print it. When you are finished, close the document, then quit Word.

FIGURE E-27

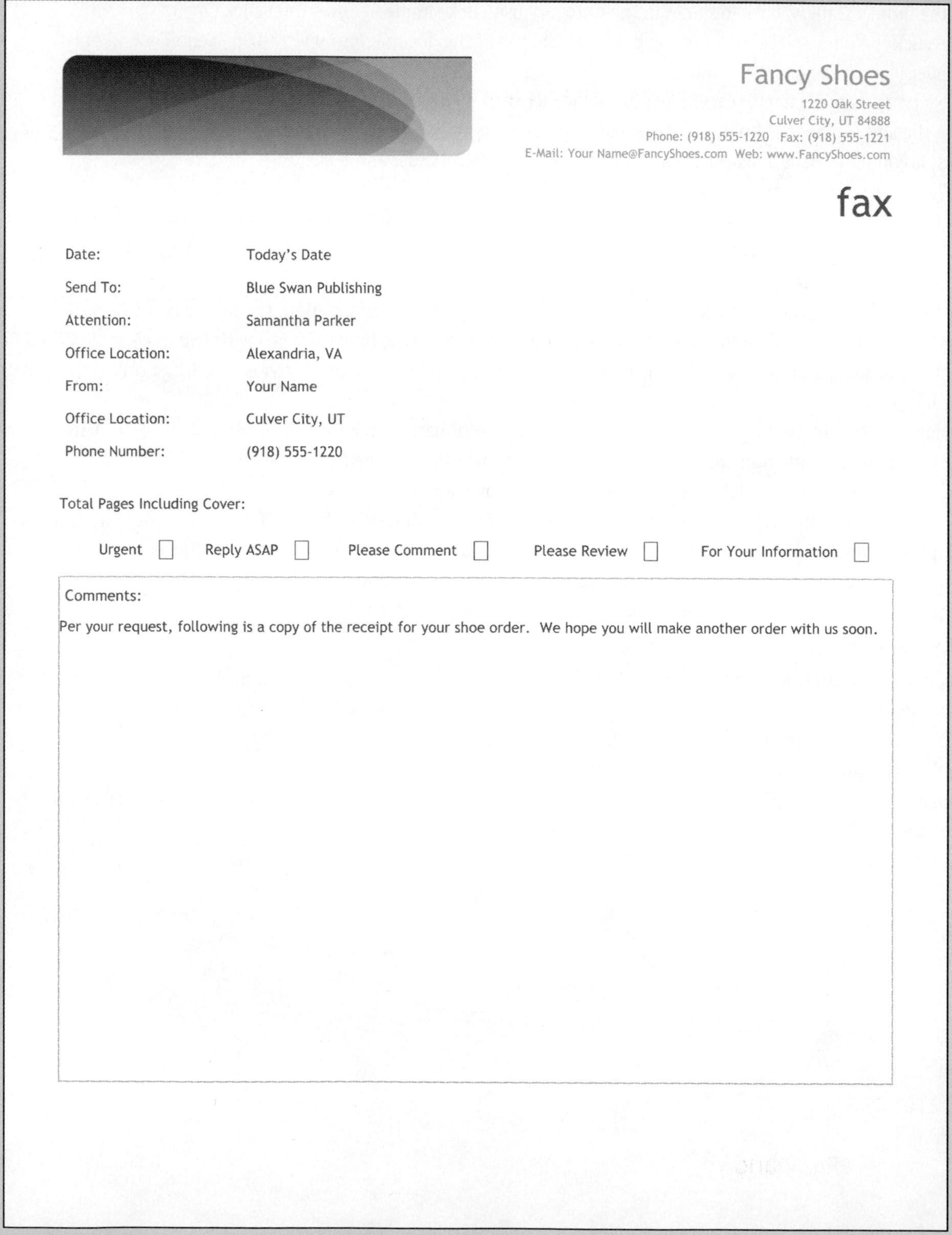

Fancy Shoes

1220 Oak Street
Culver City, UT 84888
Phone: (918) 555-1220   Fax: (918) 555-1221
E-Mail: Your Name@FancyShoes.com Web: www.FancyShoes.com

fax

Date:	Today's Date
Send To:	Blue Swan Publishing
Attention:	Samantha Parker
Office Location:	Alexandria, VA
From:	Your Name
Office Location:	Culver City, UT
Phone Number:	(918) 555-1220

Total Pages Including Cover:

Urgent ☐   Reply ASAP ☐   Please Comment ☐   Please Review ☐   For Your Information ☐

Comments:

Per your request, following is a copy of the receipt for your shoe order. We hope you will make another order with us soon.

Creating a Document

You can create professional looking documents using Microsoft Word 2008, the word processing program that comes with Microsoft Office 2008 for Mac. In this unit, you will learn some basic skills to help you create, edit, and print a document. You'll also learn how to copy and move text, find and replace text, enhance the appearance of text, and check your spelling and grammar. George Gonzalez, the marketing director for Outdoor Designs, asks you to finish a memo to the sales representatives that he started earlier. The memo announces a new product line of instructional DVDs. You will add new text that describes the new product features and benefits, and you'll edit, rearrange, and proof the text so it communicates your points more effectively.

OBJECTIVES

Create a new document from an
    existing file
Enter text in a document
Select and edit text
Copy text
Move text
Find and replace text
Format text using the Formatting
    Palette
Check spelling and grammar
Preview and print a document

Creating a New Document from an Existing File

In the course of working on various documents, you often need to open an existing file that you have already saved. To open an existing document, you use the Open dialog box. You can also use the Open dialog box to create a new document based on an existing file. This is useful when you want to create a new document that uses content from an existing document. For instance, suppose you need to write a new memo that will pick up most of the content from a memo you already wrote. In this case, you can use the Open dialog box to open the existing memo. Then, before making any changes to the opened memo, you can use the Save As command to save a copy of it with a new name. This keeps the original file intact in case you want to use it again, while saving you the trouble of creating the new memo from scratch. George gives you his partially completed memo, which lists the upcoming titles in the new DVD product line and provides other information. You want to open his document and save it with a different name, to keep George's original draft intact.

STEPS

QUICK TIP

If the Word icon is not on the dock, click the Finder icon on the dock, click Applications in the Finder window, locate and click Microsoft Office 2008, then double-click Microsoft Word.

1. **Click the Microsoft Word icon 🔲 on the dock**

   The Word program window opens with a new untitled document in the document window.

2. **Click the Open button 🔲 on the Standard toolbar**

   The Open dialog box opens and displays the folders and files in the current folder. (You can also click File on the menu bar, then click Open to open the Open dialog box.) Table F-1 describes some of the most commonly used features and buttons in the Open dialog box and the Save As dialog box.

3. **Navigate to where you store your Data Files**

   See Figure F-1.

4. **Click F-1.docx, then click Open**

   George's unfinished memo opens in the document window.

5. **Click File on the menu bar, then click Save As**

   The Save As dialog box opens, as shown in Figure F-2. You use the Save As dialog box to create a copy of the document with a new name. Notice that the name in the Save As text box is also **selected**, or highlighted. Because the text is selected, any words you type replace the selected text in the Save As text box.

6. **Type New Product Memo**

   The Save As text box now contains the new filename you typed.

7. **Navigate to where you store your Data Files, then click Save**

   Word saves the New Product Memo file on the selected storage device in the drive and folder you specified. The title bar changes to reflect the new name, as shown in Figure F-3. The file F-1 closes and remains intact.

TABLE F-1: Features in Open and Save As dialog boxes

feature name	purpose
Sidebar	Lists locations from which you can open files or to which you can save files
View buttons	Click to view files in the current folder as icons, in a list with details, or as columns
Where pop-up menu	Displays the currently selected folder or drive
Spotlight search field	Enables you to search for files or folders
Back button	Click to display the previous folder in the file management hierarchy
Forward button	Click to display the next folder location

FIGURE F-1: Open dialog box

View buttons •

Back button •

Forward button •

Sidebar •

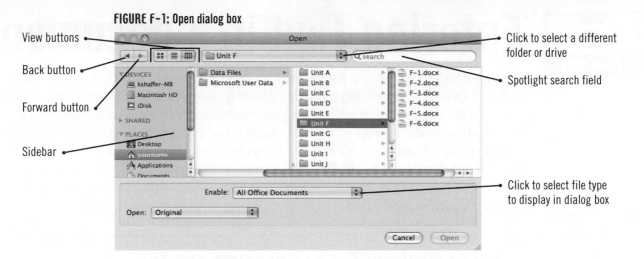

• Click to select a different folder or drive

• Spotlight search field

• Click to select file type to display in dialog box

FIGURE F-2: Save As dialog box

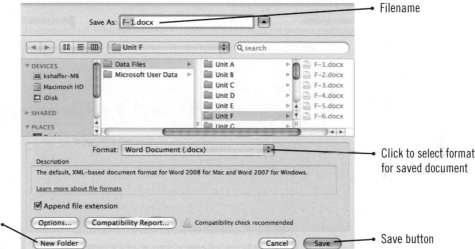

• Filename

• Click to select format for saved document

Click to create a new folder in the current folder •

• Save button

FIGURE F-3: Word program window with New Product Memo file open

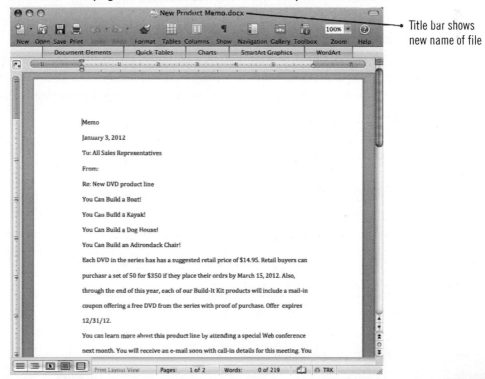

• Title bar shows new name of file

Word 2008

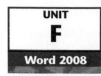

Entering Text in a Document

To add text to a document, you first need to click where you want to insert text, and then start typing. Typing text is also called **entering** text. Before you start typing, you should check that you are viewing the document in a way that's suitable for entering and editing text. **Draft** view is best for entering and editing text because several of the page elements are hidden so that you can focus on writing and editing. It's also a good idea to turn on formatting marks when you enter text in a document so that you can see blank spaces and paragraph marks. George's memo already contains some text describing the new product line. You need to add sentences above his text to announce the new product line and give some general information about the line.

STEPS

QUICK TIP

The Show button is a toggle button: clicking it once turns it on to show formatting marks; clicking it again turns it off to hide formatting marks.

1. **Click the Show button ¶ on the Standard toolbar**

   Your screen now displays formatting marks. Dots between words represent spaces, and a ¶ (paragraph mark) represents a paragraph return that Word inserts when you press [return]. Showing formatting marks when you write and edit makes it easier to see extra spaces, paragraph returns, and punctuation errors.

2. **Click the Draft View button ☰ on the left end of the status bar**

   The document now appears in Draft view, which is a better view for focusing on editing text. You can also switch to Draft view by clicking View on the menu bar, then clicking Draft.

3. **Click to the right of the word line in the Re: line of the memo (the fifth line of text)**

   Clicking in this location sets the **insertion point**, the blinking vertical line on the screen that controls where text will be inserted when you type.

4. **Press [return]**

   Pressing [return] inserted two blank lines and moved the insertion point down two lines to the left margin. Although you pressed [return] only once, two blank lines were inserted because the default style in this document is to double-space text. **Styles** are settings that control how text and paragraphs are formatted. Each document has its own set of styles, which you can easily change. You will work with styles in another unit.

QUICK TIP

As you type, the word count indicator on the status bar displays the number of words your document contains. For more specific word count information, click the indicator.

5. **Type I am pleased to announce a new line of Outdoor Designs instructional DVDs.**

   The insertion point moved to the right as you typed each word. Compare your screen to Figure F-4.

6. **Press [spacebar], then type the following text, but do *not* press [return] when you reach the right edge of your document: Each DVD will feature Master Carpenter Wally Jones, who will demonstrate how to build a featured product from the Spring catalog.**

   At some point as you typed the words "DVD will feature", the word you were typing moved down, or **wrapped**, to the next line. This is known as **word wrap**, a feature that automatically pushes text to the next line when the insertion point meets the right margin.

7. **Press [spacebar], type teh, then press [spacebar]**

   Notice that even though you typed "teh", Word assumed that you meant to type "The" and automatically corrected it. This automatic correction capability is called **AutoCorrect**.

8. **Type the following text exactly as shown (including errors): first five DVDs in the series will will be available in March and will include the follong titles:**

   You should see red, wavy lines under the second instance of "will" and the word "follong." These red lines indicate that the spelling checker automatically identified these as either misspelled or duplicate words. See Figure F-5. Green, wavy lines indicate possible grammatical errors.

9. **Click the Save button 🖫 on the Standard toolbar**

   Your changes are saved to the file.

Creating a Document

FIGURE F-4: Entering text in a Word document

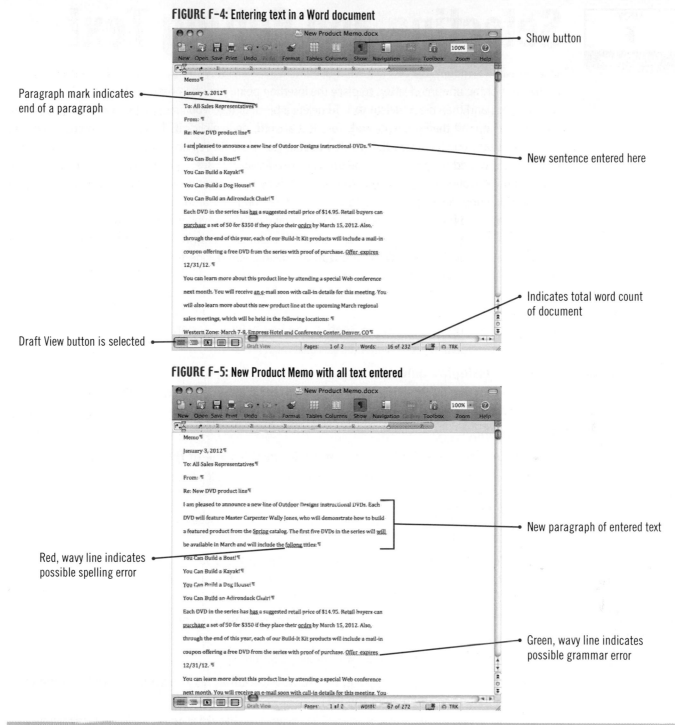

Show button

Paragraph mark indicates end of a paragraph

New sentence entered here

Indicates total word count of document

Draft View button is selected

FIGURE F-5: New Product Memo with all text entered

New paragraph of entered text

Red, wavy line indicates possible spelling error

Green, wavy line indicates possible grammar error

Using AutoCorrect

Like the spelling checker in Word, **AutoCorrect** is a feature that works automatically to proof your typing, making corrections to certain words as you type. For example, if you type "comapny" instead of "company", Word corrects the misspelling as soon as you press [spacebar]. After Word makes the correction, you can point to the word to make a small blue bar appear under the corrected text. If you place the mouse pointer over this bar, the AutoCorrect Options button appears. Click the AutoCorrect Options button to display a menu of options, as shown in Figure F-6, then click an option.

You can change AutoCorrect settings in the AutoCorrect dialog box. To open this dialog box, click Control AutoFormat Options in

the AutoCorrect Options menu, or click Word on the menu bar, click Preferences, then click AutoCorrect in the Authoring and Proofing Tools group in the Word Preferences dialog box.

FIGURE F-6: AutoCorrect Options menu

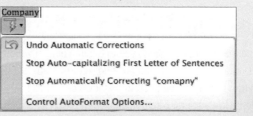

Word 2008

Selecting and Editing Text

You can **edit**, or modify, the text in a Word document in several ways. To delete individual letters, first click to the right of the unwanted letters to place the insertion point, and then press [delete]. Or click to the left of the letters, and then press [delete ⌫]. To delete a block of text, you first must **select**, or highlight, the unwanted text, and then press [delete]. To select a word, double-click it. To select a sentence, click and drag the I-beam pointer across the words you want to select. To replace unwanted text with new text, select the unwanted text, and then type the new text. As you can see, to edit text, you need to move the insertion point around the document. You can do this by pointing and clicking or by using the keyboard. Table F-2 describes keys you can use to move the insertion point around the document. (Note that the [home], [end], and [delete ⌫] keys appear on the standard Mac keyboard but do not appear on Mac laptop keyboards.) If you make a mistake as you edit, you can use the Undo button on the Standard toolbar to undo your last action. As you read the memo, you decide to make some changes to correct errors and improve the wording.

STEPS

1. **Click to the right of the word Boat! in the line below the paragraph you typed**
   The insertion point blinks just after the exclamation point.

2. **Press [delete] five times**
   When you pressed [delete] five times, "Boat!" was deleted. Pressing [delete] deletes the character to the left of the insertion point.

3. **Type Canoe!**

4. **Double-click the second instance of will in the third line of the first paragraph**
   The word "will" is now selected. Double-clicking a word selects the entire word. See Figure F-7.

5. **Press [delete]**
   The second instance of the word "will" is removed from the document. The text after the deleted word wraps back to fill the empty space.

6. **Double-click follong in the last line of the paragraph you typed, then type following**
   The selected word "follong" is replaced with "following". Notice that the red, wavy line no longer appears under the new word, indicating that it is spelled correctly.

7. **Double-click titles at the end of the first paragraph to select it, press [delete], then type products**
   The word "products" is now the last word of the paragraph.

8. **Click the Undo list arrow 🔄 on the Standard toolbar, as shown in Figure F-8, then click Typing (the second entry in the list)**
   The word "titles" reappears exactly where it was before you changed it. You can select as many actions from the Undo list as you want; the most recent action is listed first. Notice that the ScreenTip name for the Undo button changes, depending on your most recent action.

9. **Click the Save button 💾 on the Standard toolbar**

Using Click and Type

Click and Type is a feature that allows you to begin typing in almost any blank area of a document without pressing [return], [tab], or [spacebar] to move the insertion point to that location. Instead, you simply double-click where you want to begin typing. Click and Type is available only in Print Layout view, Notebook Layout view, and Web Layout view and only in areas that do not contain a bulleted or numbered list, a left or right indent, a picture with text wrapping, or multiple columns.

FIGURE F-7: Selecting a word

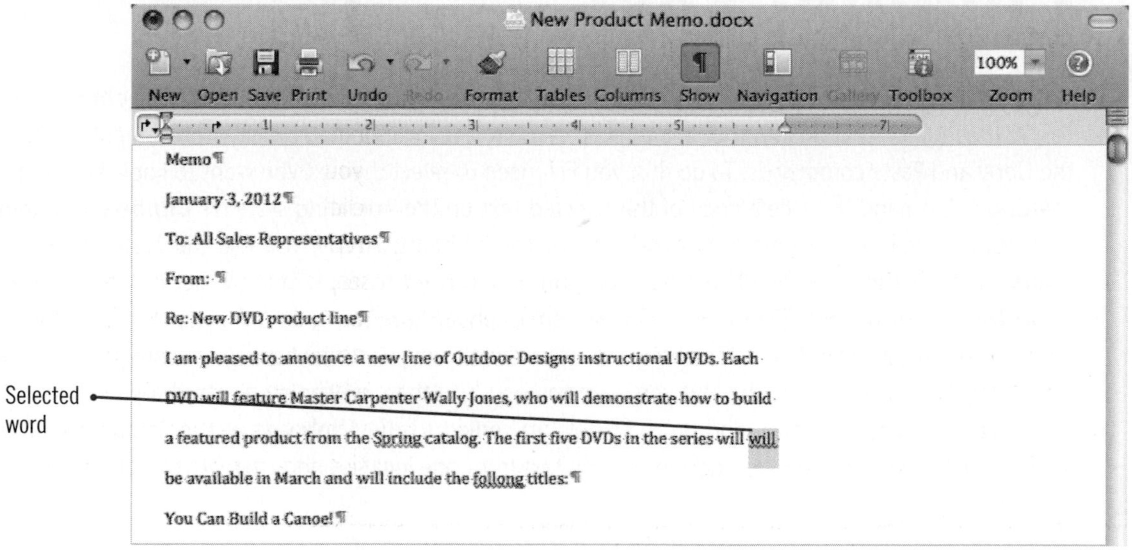

Selected
word

(Screenshot of "New Product Memo.docx" in Word 2008 with toolbar showing New, Open, Save, Print, Undo, Redo, Format, Tables, Columns, Show, Navigation, Gallery, Toolbox, 100%, Zoom, Help. Document text:)

Memo¶

January 3, 2012¶

To: All Sales Representatives¶

From: ¶

Re: New DVD product line¶

I am pleased to announce a new line of Outdoor Designs instructional DVDs. Each

DVD will feature Master Carpenter Wally Jones, who will demonstrate how to build

a featured product from the Spring catalog. The first five DVDs in the series will will

be available in March and will include the follong titles: ¶

You Can Build a Canoe! ¶

FIGURE F-8: Undo list

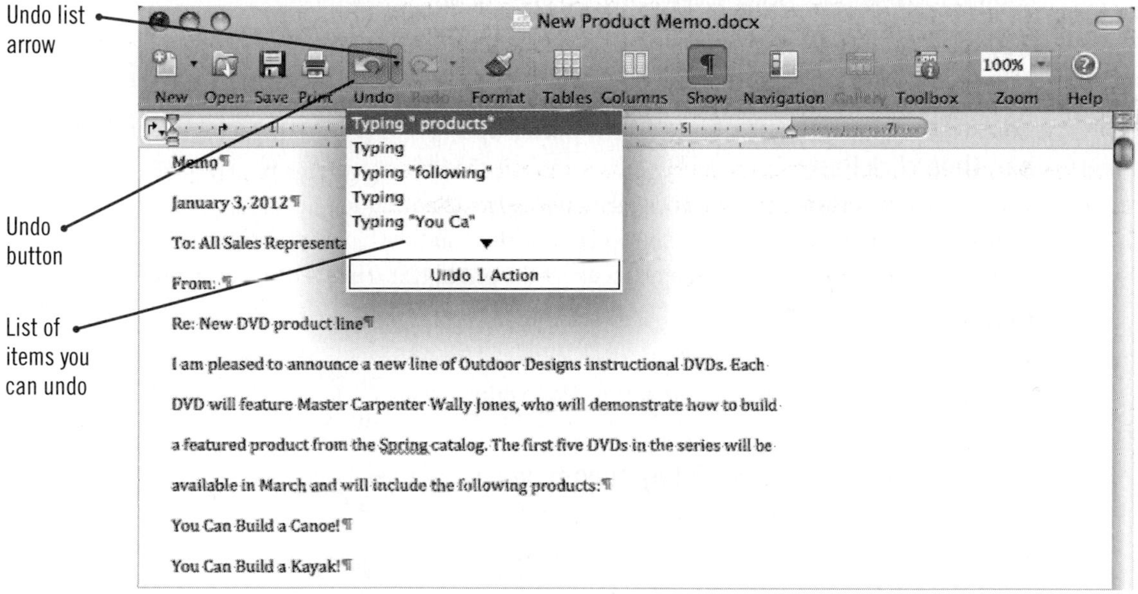

Undo list
arrow

Undo
button

List of
items you
can undo

(Screenshot of "New Product Memo.docx" with Undo list dropdown showing:)

Typing " products"
Typing
Typing "following"
Typing
Typing "You Ca"
▼

Undo 1 Action

Memo¶

January 3, 2012 ¶

To: All Sales Representa

From: ¶

Re: New DVD product line¶

I am pleased to announce a new line of Outdoor Designs instructional DVDs. Each

DVD will feature Master Carpenter Wally Jones, who will demonstrate how to build

a featured product from the Spring catalog. The first five DVDs in the series will be

available in March and will include the following products:¶

You Can Build a Canoe! ¶

You Can Build a Kayak! ¶

TABLE F-2: Useful keys for moving the insertion point around a document

keyboard key	moves insertion point
[↑][↓]	Up or down one line
[←][→]	One character to the left or right
[option] [←], [option] [→]	One word to the left or right
[home]	To the beginning of the line
[end]	To the end of the line
[⌘][home]	To the beginning of the document
[⌘][end]	To the end of the document

Copying Text

When editing a document, you often need to copy text from one place to another. **Copying** leaves the text in its original location and moves a duplicate of it to the location you specify. You can copy text using the Copy and Paste commands. To do this, you first need to select the text you want to copy. Next, you use the Copy command to place a copy of the selected text on the operating system's **Clipboard**, a temporary storage area in your computer's memory for copied items. Finally, you use the Paste command to **paste** or insert the copied text to a new location. If you need to copy multiple items, you can use the **Scrapbook**, which works like the operating system Clipboard but stores an unlimited number of items at a time and is available only in Office programs. You can also duplicate text using a technique called **drag and drop**, where you select the text you want to copy, and then use the mouse to drag a copy of it to a new location. Items you drag and drop do not get copied to the Clipboard or the Scrapbook. While checking your memo, you decide to copy text from one location and paste it to another.

STEPS

1. **Click to the left of the** Y **in** You Can Build a Canoe! **to set the insertion point, press and hold** [Option] **and** [Shift]**, then press** → **four times**

   The words "You Can Build a" are now selected. Holding [Option] and [Shift] together while pressing an arrow key lets you select sequential words using the keyboard.

2. **Click** Edit **on the menu bar, then click** Copy

   The selected text is copied to the operating system Clipboard.

QUICK TIP
You can use the keyboard to copy selected text to the Clipboard by pressing [⌘][C]. To paste text from the Clipboard, press [⌘][V].

3. **Click to the right of** Chair! **in the fifth paragraph, press** [return]**, click** Edit **on the menu bar, then click** Paste

   The copied text is pasted into the document and also remains on the Clipboard, where you can paste it as many more times as you like (until you replace the item on the Clipboard with another copied item). See Figure F-9. Notice the icon that appears under the pasted text. This is the Paste Options smart tag.

4. **Click the** smart tag

   The smart tag menu opens and displays several options for applying formatting to the pasted text. By default, the pasted text maintains its original formatting, which in this situation is fine, since it matches the text.

5. **Press** [esc] **to close the smart tag, then type** Bird House!

   The memo now lists a total of five new DVD titles.

6. **Select** Outdoor Designs **in the first line of the first paragraph**

7. **Press and hold** [option]**, drag the selected text to the left of** Spring **in the third line of the paragraph, then release** [option] **and the mouse button**

   As you drag, the pointer changes to ⊕ and a transparent image of the selection moves with the pointer. As shown in Figure F-10, "Outdoor Designs" is copied to the new location to the left of "Spring". When you copy text by dragging it while pressing [option], the text does not get copied to the Clipboard.

8. **Click the** Save button **on the Standard toolbar**

Creating a Document

FIGURE F-9: Text pasted from the Clipboard

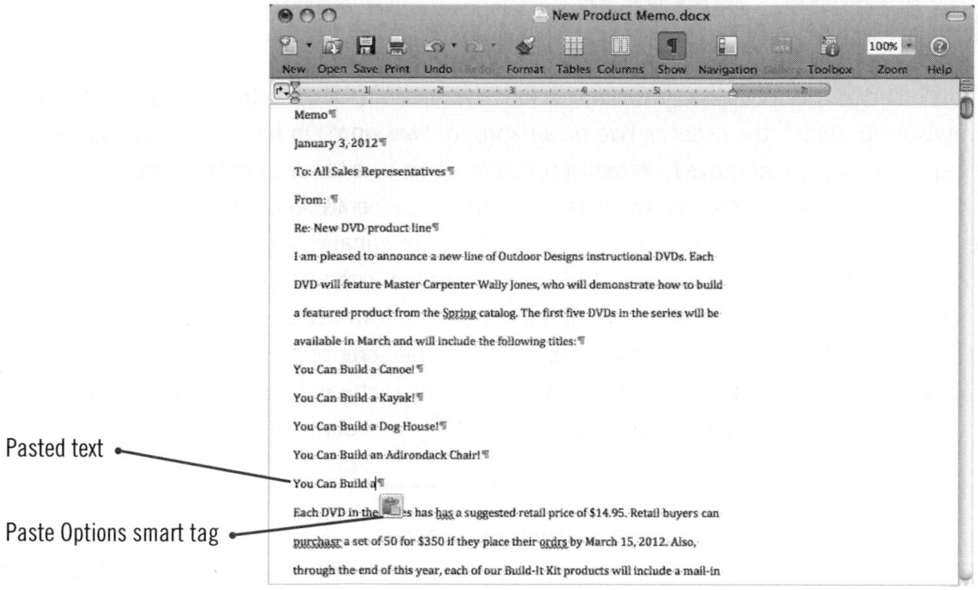

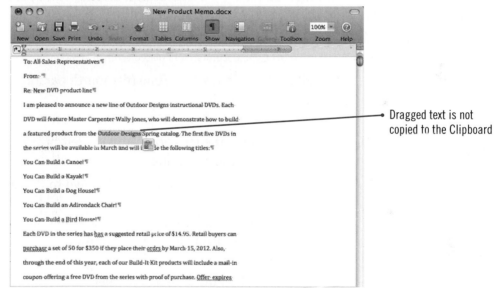

Pasted text

Paste Options smart tag

FIGURE F-10: Dragged and copied text

Dragged text is not copied to the Clipboard

Copying and pasting items with the Scrapbook

If you need to copy multiple items, you can open the Scrapbook in the Toolbox. To open the Scrapbook, click the Toolbox button on the Standard toolbar to open the Toolbox, then click the Scrapbook tab at the top of the Toolbox. To add an item to the Scrapbook, select it, then click the Add button on the Scrapbook. Repeat the process for any additional items you want to add to the Scrapbook. See Figure F-11. An item added to the Scrapbook is called a **clip**. To paste a clip into a document, first place the insertion point where you'd like the item to be pasted, select the clip on the Scrapbook, then click the Paste button on the Scrapbook. The Scrapbook stores unlimited items only if the Scrapbook is active (open on the Toolbox). If the Scrapbook is not active, you can copy only one item at a time using the operating system Clipboard. Items placed in the Scrapbook remain there until deleted, even after you quit Word.

FIGURE F-11: Scrapbook containing multiple items

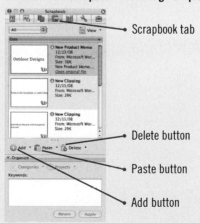

Scrapbook tab

Delete button

Paste button

Add button

Moving Text

In the process of editing a document, you may decide that certain text works better in a different location. Perhaps you want to switch the order of two paragraphs, or two words in a sentence. Instead of deleting and retyping the text, you can move it. **Moving** text removes it from its original location and places it in a new location that you specify. You can move text to a new location using the Cut and Paste commands. Using the Cut command removes selected text from your document and places it on the operating system Clipboard. To place the cut text in another location, you use the Paste option on the Edit menu. You can also move text by selecting it and then dragging it to a new location. Items that you move using the drag-and-drop method do not get copied to the Clipboard or to the Scrapbook. ▓▓▓▓ While checking your memo, you decide that you want to rearrange the paragraphs that list the sales meeting dates and locations so that they appear in chronological order.

STEPS

1. **Scroll down until the bottom of the document is in view, position the mouse pointer to the left of Northern Zone (the fifth line from the bottom) until it changes to ✦, then click**

   The entire line, including the paragraph mark, is selected. See Figure F-12. The area to the left of the left margin is the **selection bar**, which you use to select entire lines. When you place the mouse pointer in the selection bar, it changes to ✦.

   > **QUICK TIP**
   > To cut selected text to the Clipboard using the keyboard, press [⌘][X].

2. **Click Edit on the menu bar, then click Cut**

   The text is removed from the document and placed on the Clipboard.

3. **Click to the left of the W in Western Zone (the fourth paragraph from the bottom), click Edit on the menu bar, then click Paste**

   The text is pasted from the Clipboard to the new location.

4. **Place the mouse pointer in the selection bar to the left of Western Zone until it changes to ✦, then click to select the entire line**

5. **Move the pointer over the selected text, drag it down to the left of Please let me know if their is..., then release the mouse button**

   As you drag, the selection becomes transparent and moves with the pointer ▶. Also, an indicator line shows you where the text will be placed. Now the sales meeting dates are listed in the order that they will take place. See Figure F-13.

6. **Click the Save button ▤ on the Standard toolbar**

FIGURE F-12: Selecting a line of text

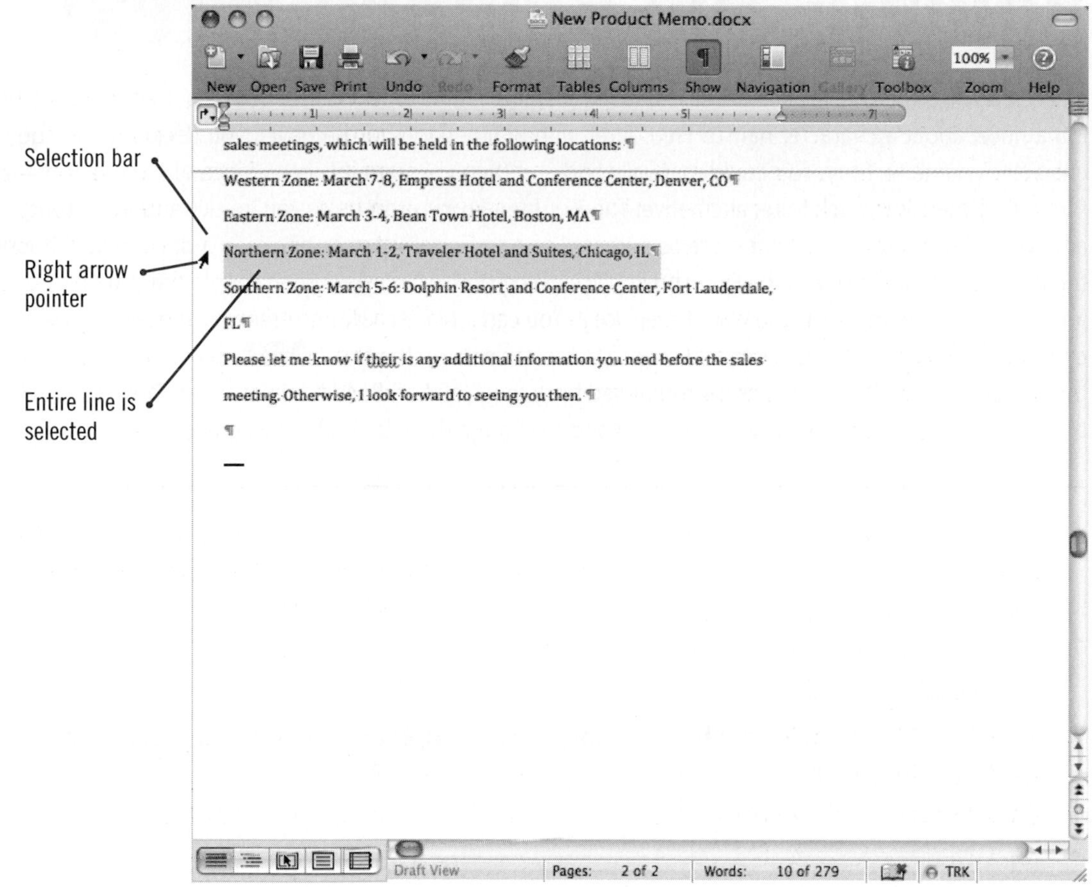

Selection bar →

Right arrow pointer →

Entire line is selected →

FIGURE F-13: Moving text by dragging it

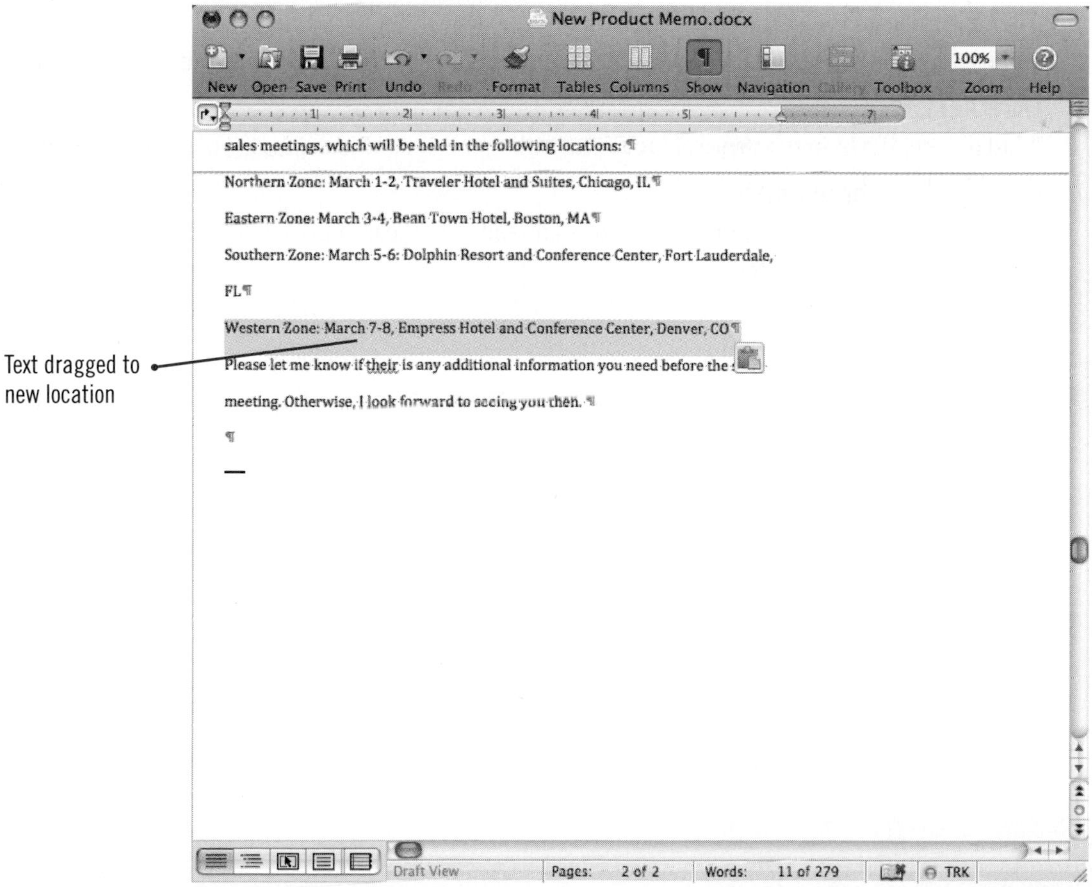

Text dragged to new location →

Finding and Replacing Text

Once in a while you might need to make a global change in a document. For instance, let's say you are writing a novel about a character named Fred. After writing fifty pages of the novel, you decide to change this character's name to Tony. You could manually find and then change each occurrence of Fred to Tony—but fortunately there is a much faster alternative. The **Replace command** helps you quickly and easily substitute a new word or phrase for one or more occurrences of a particular word or phrase in a document. Choosing the Replace command opens the Find and Replace dialog box, which you use to specify the text you want to find and the text with which you want to replace it. You can replace every occurrence of the text in one action or you can review each occurrence and choose to replace or keep the text. █████ George just told you that the title of the new DVD series has been changed from the "You Can Build It" series to the "Yes You Can Build It" series. You decide to use the Replace command to change the titles in the document.

STEPS

TROUBLE

If your keyboard does not have a [home] key, scroll up and click at the beginning of the document.

1. **Press [⌘][home]**

   Pressing [⌘][home] moves the insertion point to the beginning of the document. This ensures that Word starts searching for occurrences of your specified text at the beginning of the document.

2. **Click Edit on the menu bar, then click Replace**

   The Find and Replace dialog box opens, with the Replace tab selected.

QUICK TIP

The page count indicator on the status bar shows you how many pages your document contains. To quickly open the Find and Replace dialog box, click the indicator.

3. **Type You Can in the Find what text box, press [tab], then type Yes You Can in the Replace with text box**

   Compare your screen with Figure F-14.

4. **Click Find Next**

   Word searches the document from the insertion point and highlights the first instance of "You Can." See Figure F-15.

5. **Click Replace**

   Word replaces the first instance of "You Can" with "Yes You Can", then moves to the next instance of "You Can".

QUICK TIP

Click the disclosure triangle to the left of Replace All in the Find and Replace dialog box to expand the dialog box to display additional options, such as matching the case or format of a word or phrase.

6. **Click Replace**

   Word replaces the second instance of "You Can" with "Yes You Can" and finds the next occurrence of it.

7. **Click Replace three times**

   Word replaces the next three instances of "You Can" and finds the next instance of it in a paragraph of text. You do not want to replace this instance.

8. **Click Find Next**

   An alert box opens, indicating that Word has finished searching the document.

9. **Click OK to close the alert box, click Close in the Find and Replace dialog box, then click the Save button 🖫 on the Standard toolbar**

   Your changes are saved.

FIGURE F-14: Find and Replace dialog box

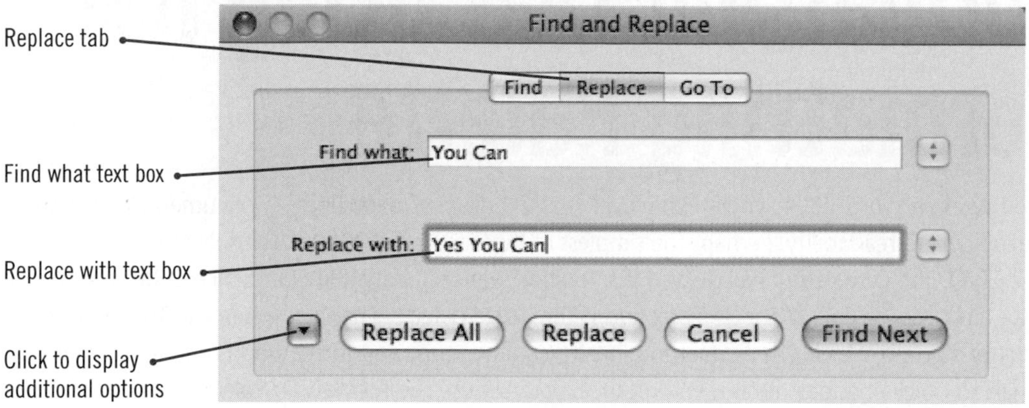

Replace tab

Find what text box

Replace with text box

Click to display
additional options

FIGURE F-15: First occurrence of Find what text

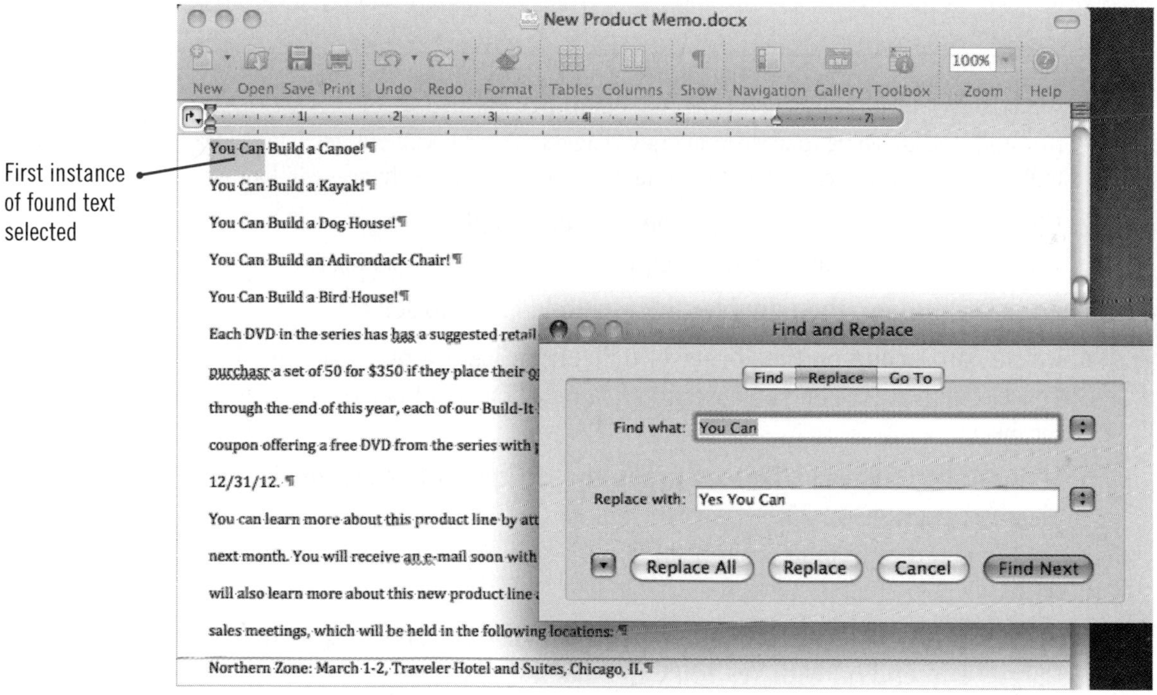

First instance
of found text
selected

Using the Reference Tools in the Toolbox

As you create documents in Word or spreadsheets in Excel, you occasionally might want to look up words and other information on the Internet. Before you go to a search engine or dictionary Web site, you should know that you have a powerful research tool at your fingertips in Office 2008 called Reference Tools. Reference Tools lets you look up information from several data sources provided by Microsoft and a growing number of partners. For instance, if you want to look up the definition of a word, right-click the word, point to Look Up on the shortcut menu, then click Definition. Reference Tools opens in the Toolbox on the right side of your screen and provides access to synonyms for the selected word from the Thesaurus and definitions of the word from the Encarta Encyclopedia and the Dictionary. Other tools available in Reference Tools are the Bilingual Dictionary, Translation, and Web Search. Some of these options can also be opened using the Tools menu. To open Reference Tools manually, click the Reference Tools tab on the Toolbox.

Formatting Text Using the Formatting Palette

As you work in Word 2008, you will discover many tools for **formatting** a document, or enhancing its appearance and readability. Perhaps the simplest of these tools is the Formatting Palette in the Toolbox. In Office 2004, the Formatting Palette and the Toolbox were separate items; in Office 2008, the Formatting Palette has become part of the Toolbox and is the active palette when you open the Toolbox for the first time after starting Word. The Formatting Palette contains common formatting commands, so it's perfect for making quick changes to text. For instance, you can use the Formatting Palette to change the font of selected text. A **font** is the design of a set of characters, such as Arial or Times New Roman. You can also use the Formatting Palette to change the **font style** by applying bold, underline, or italic formatting, or to change the **font size** of selected text so that it is larger or smaller. You can also format selected paragraphs as a bulleted list using the Bullets and Numbering group on the Formatting Palette. You decide to improve the appearance of the memo by changing the font size of the memo header, applying italic font style to the product titles, and formatting the titles and the sales meeting locations as bulleted lists.

STEPS

1. **Click the Print Layout View button 🔲 on the status bar**

   Now that you are going to make formatting changes to your document, it's a good idea to change the view to Print Layout so you can see a more accurate picture of how the changes will look on the page.

TROUBLE

If the Formatting Palette is not the active palette in the Toolbox, click the Formatting Palette tab [AI] at the top of the Toolbox to make it active.

2. **Click the Toolbox button 🔳 on the Standard toolbar**

   The Toolbox opens to the right of the document window. The Formatting Palette is active in the Toolbox.

3. **Press [⌘][home], then double-click Memo in line 1 to select it**

4. **In the Font group on the Formatting Palette, click the Bold button B**

   The selected text "Memo" now appears in a darker and thicker font, to set it apart from the other text in the memo.

5. **Drag the Size slider in the Font group to the right until the font size shown in the Font Size box changes to 20**

   The Memo text grows in size from 12 to 20, as shown in Figure F-16. You measure font size using points. A **point** is $\frac{1}{72}$", so a font size of 12, for example, is $\frac{1}{6}$".

6. **Select the five lines of text containing the DVD titles (starting with Yes You Can Build a Canoe! and ending with Yes You Can Build a Bird House!)**

   The five product titles are now selected.

QUICK TIP

You can open or close a group on the Formatting Palette by clicking the group. The disclosure triangle next to the group's name points to the right when the group is closed and points down when the group is open.

7. **Click the Italic button I on the Formatting Palette**

   The product titles now appear in italic.

8. **Click the Bullets and Numbering group on the Formatting Palette to open it, click the Bullets button 🔲 next to Type, then click outside the selected text**

   Each product title is indented and preceded by a small round dot or **bullet**. The listed titles now stand out much better from the body of the memo text and help create a more organized appearance. See Figure F-17.

9. **Scroll down until you can see the last six lines of text in the document, then select the five lines of text containing the sales meeting locations (starting with Northern Zone: and ending with Denver, CO)**

10. **Click 🔲, click outside the selection, then save your changes**

    Compare your screen to Figure F-18.

FIGURE F-16: Font size of text increased

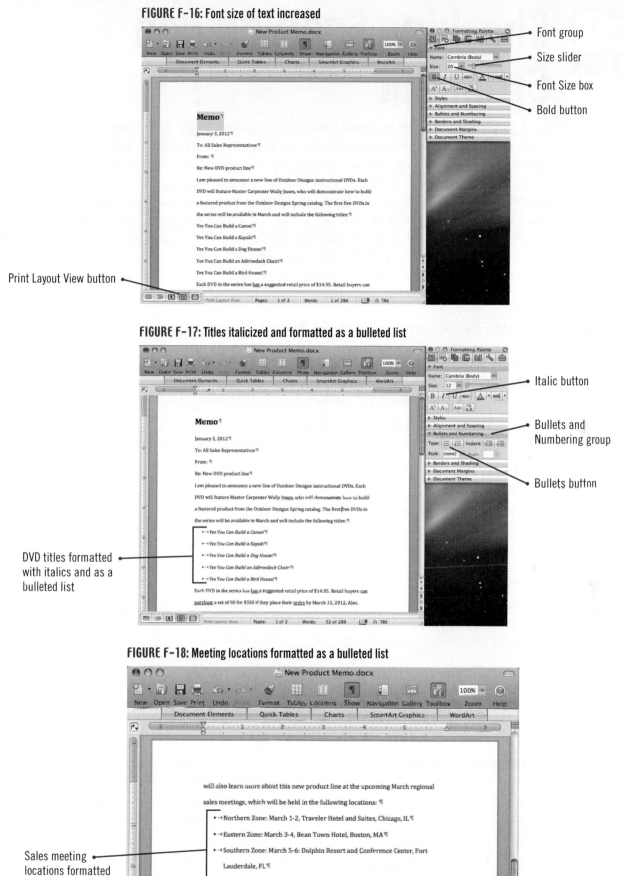

Font group

Size slider

Font Size box

Bold button

Print Layout View button

FIGURE F-17: Titles italicized and formatted as a bulleted list

Italic button

Bullets and Numbering group

Bullets button

DVD titles formatted with italics and as a bulleted list

FIGURE F-18: Meeting locations formatted as a bulleted list

Sales meeting locations formatted as a bulleted list

Checking Spelling and Grammar

Word provides tools to help you make sure that your documents are free of spelling and grammatical errors. Word's AutoCorrect feature corrects your errors as you type them, but Word cannot correct all mistakes in this way. The program identifies possible misspelled words by comparing each word to its built-in dictionary and then underlines with red, wavy lines any words that are not in its dictionary. Word identifies possible grammatical errors, such as passive voice, by underlining them with green, wavy lines. If you right-click a flagged misspelled word or grammatical error, a shortcut menu opens, displaying a list of correctly spelled or phrased alternatives. You can also open the Spelling and Grammar dialog box to check a document for misspelled words and grammatical errors. You decide to use Word's spelling and grammar checking tools to ensure that your memo is free of errors.

STEPS

TROUBLE
If you cannot right-click with your mouse, press and hold [control], then click the word.

1. Right-click the word purchasr in the second long paragraph

A shortcut menu opens, displaying a list of alternatives to the misspelled word. See Figure F-19. Other options you can choose in this menu include Ignore All (if you want Word to stop alerting you to the possible misspelling of this word in the document), Add (if you want Word to add this word as spelled to its built-in dictionary), and AutoCorrect (if you want Word to automatically correct this spelling in the future).

2. Click purchase on the shortcut menu

The shortcut menu closes and the word "purchase" replaces the misspelled word.

3. Press [⌘][Home]

The insertion point moves to the beginning of this document.

4. Click Tools on the menu bar, then click Spelling and Grammar

The Spelling and Grammar dialog box opens. See Figure F-20. The top text box displays text in red that is flagged as a problem, and the bottom text box displays suggestions for fixing it. The dialog box also contains an Ignore button, which you can click if you don't want Word to make a change. Word identifies that the word "has" appears twice in a row.

QUICK TIP
If the Spelling and Grammar dialog box flags a word that is not in fact misspelled, you can prevent Word from flagging the word in the future by clicking Add.

5. Verify that the Check grammar check box contains a check mark, then click Delete

Word deletes the extra occurrence of "has" and moves to the next possible error, which is the misspelled word "ordrs." It suggests changing the spelling to "orders," which is correct.

QUICK TIP
If the correct spelling of the word does not appear in the list, you can type it in the top section of the dialog box, then click Change.

6. Click Change

Word replaces the misspelled word with the suggested word and identifies the next error, an extra space between "Offer" and "expires."

7. Click Change

Word deletes the extra space between "Offer" and "expires." The next error that is identified is a grammatical error. You don't want to change "an e-mail" to "e-mail", so the change isn't necessary.

8. Click Ignore

The next error that is identified is a grammatical error. Even though "their" is not an incorrectly spelled word, Word is able to tell that it is used incorrectly in this context. The correct word should be "there."

9. Click Change

An alert box opens indicating that the spelling and grammar check is complete.

10. Click OK, then save your changes

FIGURE F-19: Spelling shortcut menu

Red, wavy line indicates misspelled word

Correct spelling possibilities

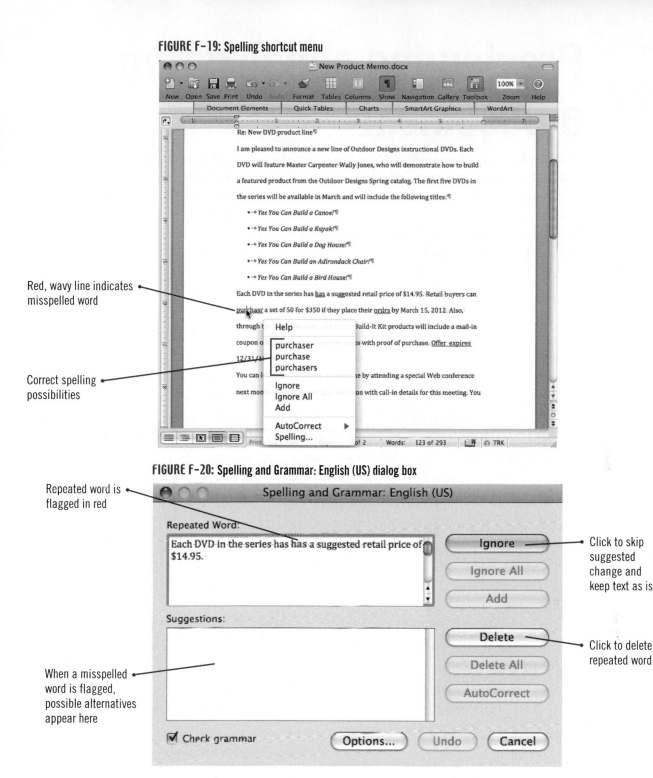

FIGURE F-20: Spelling and Grammar: English (US) dialog box

Repeated word is flagged in red

When a misspelled word is flagged, possible alternatives appear here

Click to skip suggested change and keep text as is

Click to delete repeated word

Translating words or documents into other languages

With Word 2008, you can translate any word in your document, or even an entire document, into any of twelve different languages. To make the translation, click the Reference Tools tab on the Toolbox, then click the Translation group on the Reference Tools tab to open the group. Click the arrows next to From and To in the Translation group to specify which language you want to translate from and which language you want to translate to. Next, select the words or sentences you want to translate, right-click the selected words to open the shortcut menu, then click Translate. The translated text appears in the text box below the selected languages in the Translation group. To translate an entire document from one language to another, click "Translate this document" in the box below the From and To selections. An alert box opens, telling you that the document will be sent over the Internet in unencrypted HTML format. Click Yes to send the document, and seconds later your document appears in your browser window fully translated into the language you specified.

Previewing and Printing a Document

When you finish creating and editing a document, you are ready to print it. Before printing, it's a good idea to view your document in **Print Preview**, which shows the document exactly as it will appear on the printed page. Use Print Preview to check page margins and your document's overall appearance. There are many other ways to view a document in Word. See Table F-3 for a description of these views. Before you print the memo, you want to make sure it looks exactly as you want. Then you can save and close the document and quit Word.

STEPS

1. **Click File on the menu bar, then click Print Preview**

   The Print Preview window opens, showing the memo as it will appear when printed. See Figure F-21. The Print Preview toolbar contains tools for working in the Print Preview window, including changing the magnification level of the document and previewing one page or multiple pages at a time. The Magnifier button on the toolbar is selected by default and the pointer looks like a magnifying glass with a plus sign in it.

2. **Position the Magnifier pointer ⊕ over the top part of the memo, then click**

   The document enlarges to 100% in the Print Preview window, with the top part of the memo displayed, and the pointer changes to ⊖. Notice that 100% appears in the Zoom list box on the Print Preview toolbar.

3. **Click the Magnifier button ⊕ to turn it off, then move the pointer over the document**

   The pointer changes to Ɪ, an I-beam, indicating that you can now edit text in this window.

4. **Click to the right of From: at the top of the document, then type your name**

QUICK TIP

Click the Print button on the Print Preview toolbar to automatically print the document using the default print settings. The Print dialog box does not open.

5. **Click File on the menu bar, then click Print**

   The Print dialog box opens, as shown in Figure F-22. The Print dialog box lets you specify your print settings, such as the range of pages you want to print (if you don't want to print an entire document) and the number of copies you want to print.

6. **Click Print**

   The Print dialog box closes. After a few moments, the memo is printed. Compare your memo to Figure F-23.

7. **Click Close on the Print Preview toolbar**

   The document returns to Print Layout view.

8. **Save your changes, click Word on the menu bar, then click Quit Word**

   The New Product Memo file is saved, and the document, the Toolbox, and Word all close.

TABLE F-3: Available views in Word

view	button	how it displays a document	use for
Draft view	☰	Does not show all page elements	Typing, editing, and simple formatting
Outline view	☰	Shows only the headings in a document	Reviewing the structure of a document
Publishing Layout view	🖼	Shows the document margins as a blue box	Creating a desktop publishing document
Print Layout view	☰	Shows all elements of the printed page	Previewing the layout of printed page
Notebook Layout view	☰	Shows elements as if they were typed on a lined sheet of paper	Taking class or meeting notes
Web Layout view	(only available from View menu)	Shows the document as it would appear as a Web page	Creating a Web page

FIGURE F-21: Document in Print Preview

Print button

Magnifier button

Zoom list box

Print Preview toolbar

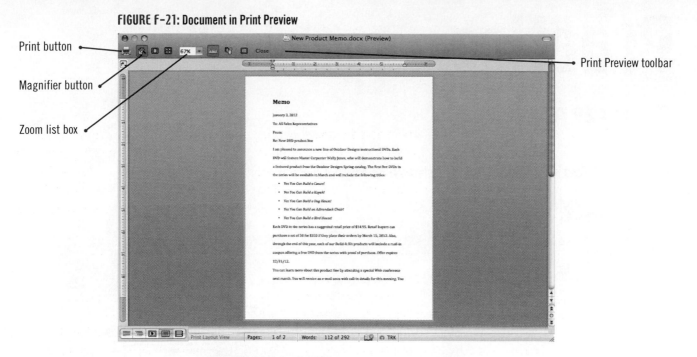

FIGURE F-22: Print dialog box

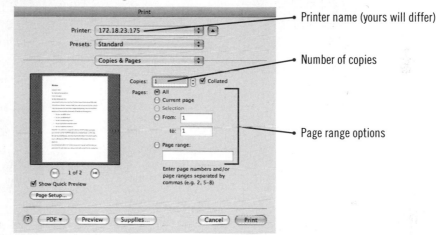

Printer name (yours will differ)

Number of copies

Page range options

FIGURE F-23: Final printed memo

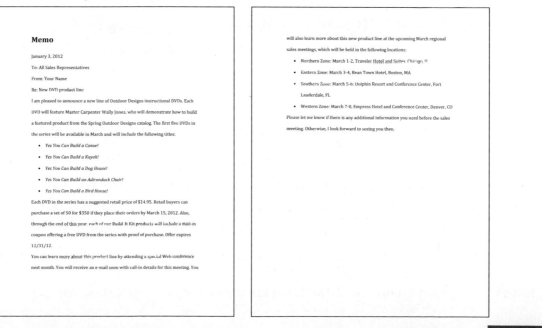

Practice

▼ CONCEPTS REVIEW

Label the Word window elements shown in Figure F-24.

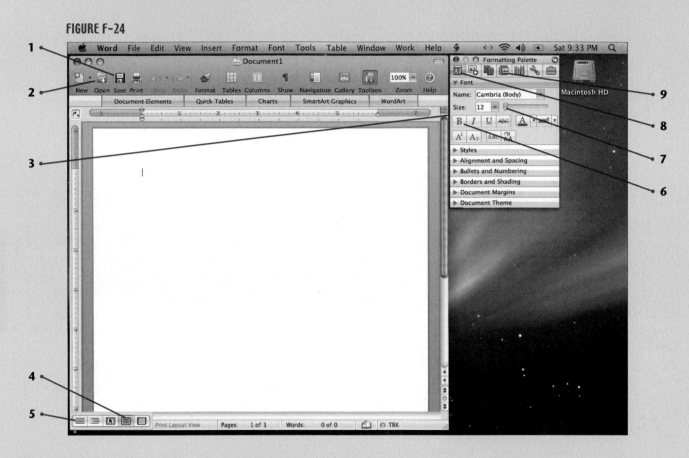

FIGURE F-24

Match each of the toolbar buttons with its function.

10.
11.
12.
13.
14.
15.

a. Reverses one or more previous actions
b. Displays current document in Print Layout view
c. Saves a document to disk
d. Prints a document from Print Preview
e. Displays formatting marks and spaces between words
f. Opens the Toolbox

Select the best answer from the list of choices.

16. **Which of the following statements about the Clipboard is NOT true?**
   a. To activate the Clipboard, click the Clipboard tab on the Toolbox.
   b. The Clipboard stores only one item at a time.
   c. The Clipboard lets you paste only the most recent item that you copied.
   d. To copy and paste text to the Clipboard, you must first select it.

Creating a Document

17. **Which option on the Toolbox gives you access to the Thesaurus and the Dictionary?**
   a. Scrapbook
   b. Reference Tools
   c. Formatting Palette
   d. Object Palette

18. **If you want to edit your document in Print Preview, which of the following actions should you perform first?**
   a. Click the Magnifier button to turn it off.
   b. Click the View Ruler button to turn it off.
   c. Change the view to multiple pages.
   d. Click the One Page button.

19. **Which of the following views is best for seeing exactly what your document will look like when printed?**
   a. Print Layout view
   b. Outline view
   c. Draft view
   d. Print Preview

20. **Which of the following tasks can you complete using the Formatting Palette in the Toolbox?**
   a. Replacing text
   b. Adding bullets to a list
   c. Moving text
   d. Opening a file

▼ SKILLS REVIEW

1. **Create a new document from an existing file.**
   a. Start Word, then open the Open dialog box.
   b. Use the Browse button to navigate to where you store your Data Files, then open the file F-2.docx.
   c. Save the file as **Catering Company Fact Sheet** where you save your Data Files.

2. **Enter text in a document.**
   a. Make sure formatting marks are displayed in the document.
   b. Switch to Draft view.
   c. Move the insertion point to the right of -2100 (the end of the fax number at the end of line four), then press [return] twice.
   d. Type the following text: **About the Company**, then press [return].
   e. Type the following text: **The company was created to serve busy families who have no time to cook and who want to feed their families wholesome and nutritious meals made with the freshest ingredients.**, then press [return].
   f. Move the insertion point to the right of the period after the word up at the end of the paragraph below the heading About Our Chef, press [spacebar], then type **Chef Margaret is also the author of the bestselling cook book Quick Meals for Hungry Families.**
   g. Save your changes.

3. **Select and edit text.**
   a. In the paragraph under the heading About Our Kitchen, replace the text 2500 with **3000**.
   b. In the same paragraph, delete **our own** in the third line and replace it with **all cooking appliances and**.
   c. Scroll down if necessary so you can see the paragraph under the heading Our Menus, then use the [delete] key to delete the words **every day** at the end of that paragraph.
   d. Type **Monday through Friday** so that the last sentence of that paragraph reads "Here are just a few of our best-selling meals, available Monday through Friday:"
   e. Save your changes.

4. **Copy text.**
   a. Select the text **The Hungry Bear Catering Company** in the first line of the document, then copy this text to the operating system Clipboard. (*Note*: Be careful not to select the paragraph mark after the word Company.)
   b. Delete the words **the Company** in the heading About the Company. (*Note*: Be careful not to delete the paragraph mark at the end of the line.)
   c. Paste the copied text where the deleted text used to be. (*Note*: If a blank line was inserted between the heading and paragraph, delete it before proceeding to step d.)
   d. Select the text **Hungry Bear Catering** in the heading About The Hungry Bear Catering Company.

e. Drag a copy of the selected text to the line just below it and to the left of the word company.

f. Edit the c in company that follows the dragged text so that it is capitalized.

g. Save your changes.

5. **Move text.**

a. In the paragraph below the heading Our Hours, select the text **Stop by or call tonight!** and the space following it, then use the Cut command to move this text to the Clipboard.

b. Paste the text you cut after the sentence **Or go straight home and call us: we deliver!** at the end of the paragraph.

c. Add an additional blank line before the heading Our Hours.

d. Scroll down if necessary so that the bottom of the document is visible on your screen.

e. Select the paragraph mark above the heading Our Hours, the heading **Our Hours**, the paragraph below the heading, and the paragraph mark below the paragraph, then drag to move the entire selection down to the end of the document.

f. Save your changes.

6. **Find and replace text.**

a. Move the insertion point to the beginning of the document.

b. Use the Replace command to replace all instances of the word **Broccoli** with **Green Beans**.

c. Close the Find and Replace dialog box.

d. Save your changes.

7. **Format text.**

a. Change the view to Print Layout view, then open the Formatting Palette in the Toolbox.

b. Select **The Hungry Bear Catering Company** in the first line of the document, then use the Formatting Palette to apply bold formatting to this text.

c. With the first line of text still selected, use an option on the Formatting Palette to increase the font size of **The Hungry Bear Catering Company** to 18.

d. Use the Formatting Palette to apply bold formatting to each of the following headings in the document: **About The Hungry Bear Catering Company**, **About Our Chef**, **About Our Kitchen**, **Our Menus**, and **Our Hours**.

e. At the end of the paragraph below the heading About Our Chef, use the Formatting Palette to apply italic formatting to the book title **Quick Meals for Hungry Families**.

f. Scroll down if necessary so that all the text under the heading Our Menus is visible, then select the list of meals starting with **Roast Beef with Roasted Potatoes and Peas** and ending with **Chicken Pot Pie**.

g. Use the Formatting Palette to format the selected text as a bulleted list.

h. Save your changes.

8. **Check spelling and grammar.**

a. In the paragraph below About Our Kitchen, correct the spelling of the misspelled word **kitchn** by right-clicking and choosing the correct spelling from the shortcut menu.

b. Move the insertion point to the beginning of the document.

c. Open the Spelling and Grammar dialog box.

d. Review each spelling and grammar error that Word identifies, and correct or ignore it depending on what seems appropriate for this document.

e. Save your changes.

9. **Preview and print a document.**

a. View the document in Print Preview.

b. Zoom in on the bottom part of the letter using the Magnifier.

c. Deselect the Magnifier so that you can edit text in this window.

d. Type your name in the last blank line of the document.

e. Close Print Preview, then save your changes.

f. Print the document, then compare your printed document with Figure F-25.

g. Close the document, then quit Word.

Creating a Document

FIGURE F-25

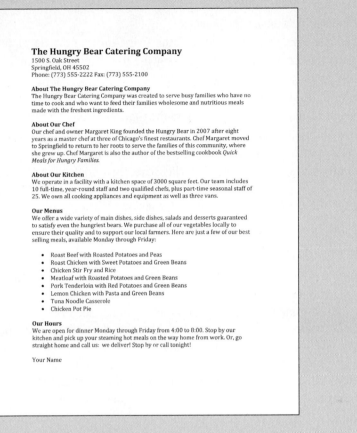

> **The Hungry Bear Catering Company**
> 1500 S. Oak Street
> Springfield, OH 45502
> Phone: (773) 555-2222 Fax: (773) 555-2100
>
> **About The Hungry Bear Catering Company**
> The Hungry Bear Catering Company was created to serve busy families who have no
> time to cook and who want to feed their families wholesome and nutritious meals
> made with the freshest ingredients.
>
> **About Our Chef**
> Our chef and owner Margaret King founded the Hungry Bear in 2007 after eight
> years as a master chef at three of Chicago's finest restaurants. Chef Margaret moved
> to Springfield to return to her roots to serve the families of this community, where
> she grew up. Chef Margaret is also the author of the bestselling cookbook *Quick
> Meals for Hungry Families.*
>
> **About Our Kitchen**
> We operate in a facility with a kitchen space of 3000 square feet. Our team includes
> 10 full-time, year-round staff and two qualified chefs, plus part-time seasonal staff of
> 25. We own all cooking appliances and equipment as well as three vans.
>
> **Our Menus**
> We offer a wide variety of main dishes, side dishes, salads and desserts guaranteed
> to satisfy even the hungriest bears. We purchase all of our vegetables locally to
> ensure their quality and to support our local farmers. Here are just a few of our best
> selling meals, available Monday through Friday:
>
> - Roast Beef with Roasted Potatoes and Peas
> - Roast Chicken with Sweet Potatoes and Green Beans
> - Chicken Stir Fry and Rice
> - Meatloaf with Roasted Potatoes and Green Beans
> - Pork Tenderloin with Red Potatoes and Green Beans
> - Lemon Chicken with Pasta and Green Beans
> - Tuna Noodle Casserole
> - Chicken Pot Pie
>
> **Our Hours**
> We are open for dinner Monday through Friday from 4:00 to 8:00. Stop by our
> kitchen and pick up your steaming hot meals on the way home from work. Or, go
> straight home and call us: we deliver! Stop by or call tonight!
>
> Your Name

▼ INDEPENDENT CHALLENGE 1

As the national sales manager for Fitness Sports, Inc., you are in charge of organizing the company's summer sales conference. You need to prepare a memo inviting the sales managers and field sales representatives to the conference. You previously created a partially completed version of this memo, so now you need to make final edits to finish it.

a. Start Word, open the file F-3.docx from where you store your Data Files, then save it as **Sales Meeting Memo**.

b. In the fourth line of text, replace the text Your Name with your name.

c. At the end of the paragraph under Dates and Location, type the following text: **You should book your flight home any time after 4:00 on June 4.**

d. In the sixth line of text (that begins Our Summer Sales Conference) change the word Conference to **Meeting**.

e. In the first line below the heading Dates and Location, delete **Sales Conference**, then replace it with **4-day meeting**.

f. In the first line of text under the heading Trip Planning, move the text **I look forward to seeing you there!** to the end of the paragraph.

g. Increase the font size of **Memo** in the first line of the document to 22, then apply bold formatting to it.

h. Apply bold formatting to the following headings in the memo: **Dates and Location**, **About the Hotel and Conference Center**, **Meeting Information**, **Planned Activities**, and **Trip Planning**.

i. Under the Planned Activities heading, format the lines that start with **June 2, June 3**, and **June 4** as a bulleted list.

j. You just learned that the Gator Park Hotel will not be able to accommodate the meeting. Fortunately, you are able to make a reservation at the Everglades Golf Resort and Conference Center, also in Orlando. Replace all instances of **Gator Park Hotel** with **Everglades Golf Resort**.

k. After you enter all the text, check the spelling and grammar and correct any spelling or grammar errors as needed. Ignore any proper names that are flagged as misspelled words.

l. Use Print Preview to see how the printed memo will look, then print one copy of the document.

▼ INDEPENDENT CHALLENGE 1 (CONTINUED)

Advanced Challenge Exercise

- (*Note*: These steps require an Internet connection.)
- Click the Reference Tools tab on the Toolbox.
- Open the Translation group if necessary, click the To list arrow in the Translation group, then click German.
- Click "Translate this document" in the box below the To list arrow, then click Yes in the Whole Document Translation dialog box.
- Click File on your browser's menu bar, then click Save As to open a dialog box for saving the Web page as a Web archive. (*Note*: If a dialog box appears that says the page may not save correctly, click Yes to continue.)
- Type **German Memo Translation ACE** in the Export As text box, then click the disclosure triangle to the right of the Export As text box to expand the dialog box if necessary.
- Navigate to where you save your Data Files, click Save, then close your browser window.

m. Save and close the Sales Meeting Memo document, then quit Word.

▼ INDEPENDENT CHALLENGE 2

You own and operate a baking company based in Denver, Colorado that specializes in making cookies. Business is booming, so you would like to expand your product line and offer new types of baked goods. You would also like to have a better understanding of what your customers like about your products. You decide to create a simple customer survey that your customers can fill out in the store for a chance to win a prize. You have started the survey document, and now you need to edit it and improve its appearance before it is ready for distribution.

a. Start Word, open the file F-4.docx from where you store your Data Files, then save it as **Customer Survey**.

b. Replace all instances of the name **Carol** in the survey document with your first name. In the last line of the document, replace the text **Your Name** with your full name.

c. In the third line of text in the document, delete **weekly cookies** and replace it with **a box of cookies each week**.

d. Type **Question 1:** before the first question in the document, then apply bold formatting to **Question 1:**.

e. Type **Question 2:**, **Question 3:**, and **Question 4:** to the left of the remaining three questions in the survey, and apply bold formatting to the new text.

f. Below each of the four questions, format the list of answers as a bulleted list.

g. Reorder the bulleted items under Question 4 so that they are in alphabetical order. Then edit each cookie name in the list so that each word in each name begins with a capital letter.

h. Increase the font size of the text in the first line of the document to 20, then apply bold and italic formatting to it.

i. Check the spelling and grammar and correct all spelling and grammar errors. Ignore flagged words that are spelled correctly.

j. Save your changes.

Advanced Challenge Exercise

- (*Note*: These steps require an Internet connection.)
- Right-click the word **Zesty** under Question 4, then look up the word's definition.
- In the Thesaurus group in the Reference Tools, click the word **fresh** in the Synonyms list, then click the Look Up button.
- Scroll through all the definitions of **fresh** in the Dictionary group, then open the Translation group.
- Specify to translate fresh from English to French, then type the French word one line below your name in the document.
- Save the document as **Customer Survey ACE**.

k. Use Print Preview to see how the printed survey will look. When you're finished, print the survey, close the document, then quit Word.

▼ INDEPENDENT CHALLENGE 3

You are the marketing director for a mail order company that sells educational toys for children. You have contracted with Top Job Recruiters, an executive search firm in Boston, to find candidates to fill the position of marketing manager, reporting to you. The recruiter you hired to locate candidates for the job has requested that you create a document that describes the position and the necessary qualifications that candidates must have.

    a. Start Word, open the file F-5.docx from where you store your Data Files, then save it as **Job Description**.

    b. Place the insertion point at the end of the document, press [return], type **Reporting Structure**, press [return] twice, then type **This position reports to the Vice President of Marketing**.

    c. Delete the words **Vice President** in the line that you typed in step b, then type **Director** in its place.

    d. In the second line of the document, delete **Essential Duties and** as well as the space after it, so that only the word Responsibilities remains in this line.

    e. In the third line of text in the document, move the first sentence that begins **Travel to trade shows** so that it is the last sentence in that paragraph.

    f. Use the Formatting Palette to apply bold formatting to the first line of text in the document, then increase the font size of this text to 26.

    g. Use the Formatting Palette to apply bold formatting to each of the following headings in the document: **Responsibilities**, **Required Skills**, **Work Environment**, **Education and Work Experience**, and **Reporting Structure**.

    h. Move the heading Education and Work Experience and the paragraph below it so it is located below the Responsibilities paragraph.

    i. Check the spelling and grammar in the document and make all appropriate changes. Ignore any occurrences of semi-colon use identified by Word.

    j. Use Print Preview to check the appearance of the document. While in Print Preview, add a blank line below the last line of the document, then type your name.

    k. Print the document, save and close it, then quit Word.

▼ REAL LIFE INDEPENDENT CHALLENGE

Before you apply for a job, it's important that you make a case for why you would be ideally suited for the position for which you are applying. After all, to convince a hiring manager that you are a good fit for the job, you need to be clear in your own mind about why you will be successful. In this Real Life Independent Challenge, you are interested in applying for your dream job at a company for which you would love to work. The job and the company can be in any field you want—it's your choice! You have already submitted your resume to the human resources director at this company, and she has e-mailed you a questionnaire and asked you to fill it out and return it. The answers you provide in the questionnaire will determine whether you will get an interview or not. In the steps below, you will replace the placeholder answers in the questionnaire with your own text that describes why you are especially qualified to get this job.

    a. Start Word, open the file F-6.docx from where you store your Data Files, then save it as **Job Questionnaire**.

    b. If you wish, print a copy of the document so you can refer to it as you complete these steps; the document contains placeholder text to guide you through making your edits.

    c. Add your name after the text Your Name: in the second line of text.

    d. Replace all the text that appears in capital letters with your own information. For example, in the third line of text, delete **REPLACE THIS TEXT WITH YOUR DESIRED JOB TITLE** and type your actual dream job title.

    e. Change the formatting of all the italic text in the document to bold. (*Hint*: To remove italic formatting, select the text, then click the Italic button.)

    f. Increase the font size of the first line in the document to 20 and apply bold formatting to it.

    g. Move the question **Why are you interested in this position?** and its answer so that it is located two lines below the Position for which you are applying... text.

    h. Check the spelling and grammar of the document and make any appropriate changes.

    i. Preview and print the document, save and close the document, then exit Word.

Use the skills you have learned in this unit to create the document shown in Figure F-26. Start Word, then type and format the text as shown. (*Hint*: You can also open a new blank document by clicking File on the menu bar, then clicking New Blank Document.) Save the document as **House For Sale Flyer** where you store your Data Files. Type your name in bold below the last line of the document. Check the spelling and grammar in the entire document, then save and print it. When you are finished, close the document, then quit Word.

FIGURE F-26

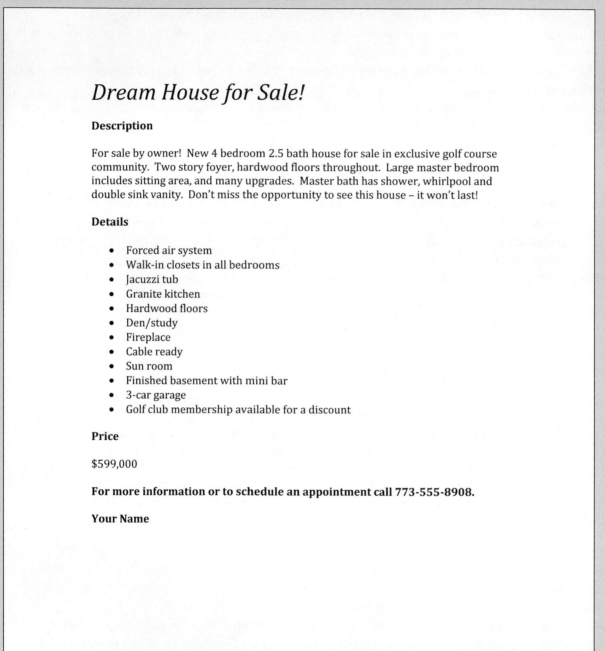

Dream House for Sale!

Description

For sale by owner! New 4 bedroom 2.5 bath house for sale in exclusive golf course community. Two story foyer, hardwood floors throughout. Large master bedroom includes sitting area, and many upgrades. Master bath has shower, whirlpool and double sink vanity. Don't miss the opportunity to see this house – it won't last!

Details

- Forced air system
- Walk-in closets in all bedrooms
- Jacuzzi tub
- Granite kitchen
- Hardwood floors
- Den/study
- Fireplace
- Cable ready
- Sun room
- Finished basement with mini bar
- 3-car garage
- Golf club membership available for a discount

Price

$599,000

For more information or to schedule an appointment call 773-555-8908.

Your Name

Enhancing a Document

Files You Will Need:

G-1.docx
G-2.docx
G-3.docx
G-4.docx
G-5.docx
G-6.docx

Microsoft Word 2008 provides a variety of tools you can use to enhance the appearance of your documents. In this unit, you will learn to change the formatting of characters and paragraphs using tools on the Toolbox. You will also learn how to take advantage of styles, a feature in Microsoft Word that helps you create great looking documents quickly. George Gonzalez, marketing manager for Outdoor Designs, gives you a product information sheet on the Red Cedar Kid's Clubhouse Kit, the company's newest product. Sales representatives will use the sheet as a reference when selling this new product. George asks you to format the information in the sheet so that it is attractive and easy to read.

OBJECTIVES

Change font and font size

Change font color, font style, and font effects

Change alignment and line spacing

Change margin settings

Set tabs

Set indents

Add bulleted and numbered lists

Apply styles

Changing Font and Font Size

Choosing an appropriate font is an important part of formatting a document. The fonts you use help communicate the tone you want to set. For instance, if you are creating a report that discusses the harmful effects of global warming, you should choose a conservative, traditional font such as Times New Roman. On the other hand, if you are creating an invitation to a child's birthday party, you should choose a font that conveys a sense of fun and celebration, such as Lucida Handwriting or Broadway. Table G-1 shows some examples of fonts available in Word. To change the font and font size, you'll use the Font group on the Formatting Palette. You can change the font and font size before you begin typing, or you can select existing text and apply changes to it. 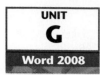 Currently, all the text in the product information sheet is the same font (Cambria) and size (12 point). You decide to increase the title's font size and change the font to something that stands out from the rest of the text in the document. First, however, you will open the document and save it with a new name to keep George's original document intact.

STEPS

1. **Start Word, open the file G-1.docx from where you store your Data Files, then save it as Clubhouse Kit Info Sheet**

   The Clubhouse Kit Info Sheet document is now open in Print Layout view.

2. **Click the Show button ¶ on the Standard toolbar, if necessary, to display formatting marks in the document**

   When formatting, it's helpful to see paragraph marks and spaces while you work.

   > **QUICK TIP**
   > If the Formatting Palette is not the active palette on the Toolbox, click the Formatting Palette tab on the Toolbox.

3. **If the Toolbox is not visible, click the Toolbox button on the Standard toolbar**

   The Toolbox opens with the Formatting Palette active by default.

4. **Place the mouse pointer in the selection bar to the left of Outdoor Designs Product Information Sheet in the first line until it changes to ➤, then click to select the entire line**

   To format existing text, you must first select it.

   > **QUICK TIP**
   > To apply formatting to text as you type, select the formatting options you want and then start typing.

5. **Click the Font Size list arrow in the Font group on the Formatting Palette**

   The Font Size list opens, as shown in Figure G-1. You can click an option on this list to change the font size, or you can change the font size by dragging the Font Size slider located to the right of the Font Size list box.

6. **Click 18 in the Font Size list**

   The Font Size list closes and the selected text changes to 18 point. The first line of text is now much larger than the rest of the text in the document.

7. **Click the Font list arrow in the Font group, move the pointer over the arrow at the bottom of the Font list to scroll down until you see Franklin Gothic Medium, then point to Franklin Gothic Medium**

   A disclosure triangle appears to the right of a font name in the Font list when there are additional options available for that font. As shown in Figure G-2, when you point to the font name, a submenu opens displaying the options for the chosen font.

8. **Click Franklin Gothic Medium in the Font list**

   The selected text changes to the Franklin Gothic Medium font. "Franklin Gothic Medium" appears in the Font list box and will be displayed as long as the insertion point remains in any text with the Franklin Gothic Medium font applied.

9. **Click outside the selected text to deselect it, then click the Save button on the Standard toolbar to save your changes**

Enhancing a Document

FIGURE G-1: Font Size list open in Font group

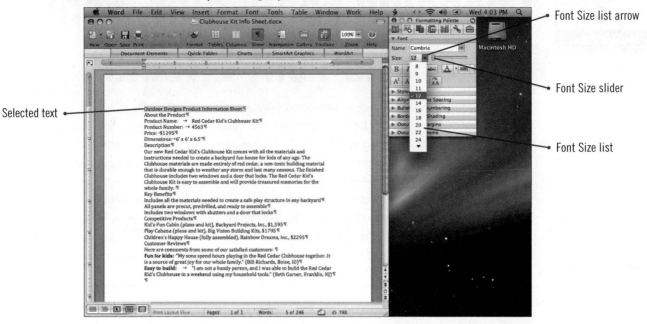

Font Size list arrow

Font Size slider

Selected text

Font Size list

FIGURE G-2: Franklin Gothic Medium font options

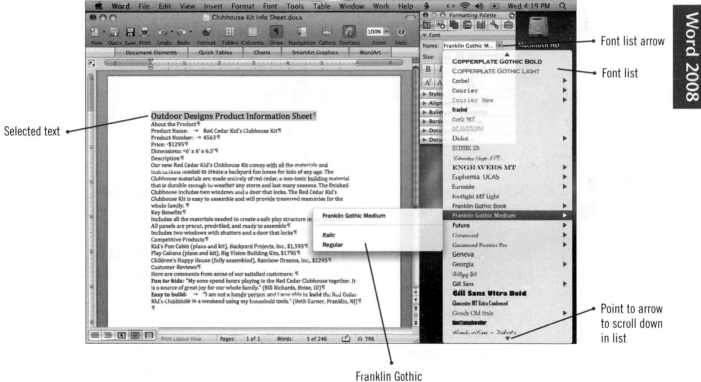

Font list arrow

Font list

Selected text

Point to arrow
to scroll down
in list

Franklin Gothic
Medium submenu

TABLE G-1: Samples of fonts and font sizes

font formats	samples
Font	Times New Roman, *Lucida Handwriting*, **Impact**, ALGERIAN, **Broadway**, Chiller
Size	eight point, twelve point, fourteen point, eighteen point

Changing Font Color, Font Style, and Font Effects

Sometimes you want to emphasize certain words, phrases, or lines of text. To do this, you can use **font styles**, which are font attributes such as **bold** (darker type), *italic* (slanted type), and <u>underline</u>. You can also make certain words stand out by changing their **color**. Or, you can apply font effects to selected text. **Font effects** are special enhancements such as small caps (SMALL CAPS LOOKS LIKE THIS), shadow (shadow looks like this), or strikethrough (strikethrough looks like this) that you can apply to selected text. You can use the Font group on the Formatting Palette to apply formatting changes to selected text. You can apply other font effects using the Font dialog box, which you open by clicking the Font option on the Format menu. To save time, you can use the Format Painter to copy the formatting of selected text to other text. You continue to format the Clubhouse Kit Info Sheet by applying font attributes, colors, and effects to certain words.

STEPS

1. **Select the first line of text, Outdoor Designs Product Information Sheet, then click the Font Color list arrow <u>A</u> ▾ on the Formatting Palette**

   In the color palette that opens, you can choose from Theme Colors, Standard Colors, and More Colors. See Figure G-3. A **theme** is a predesigned set of formatting elements, including colors, that you can use to achieve a coordinated overall look in your document. **Standard colors** are the basic hues of red, orange, and so on.

2. **Click the red color in the top row of Theme Colors (the ScreenTip reads "Accent 2")**

   The first line of the document is now red, and the Font Color button displays a dark red stripe, indicating that this is the color of the text that contains the insertion point. Selecting different text and clicking the Font Color button (not the list arrow) applies the current color (red) to selected text.

> **QUICK TIP**
> You can also open the Font dialog box by right-clicking text, then clicking Font on the shortcut menu.

3. **Click Format on the menu bar, then click Font**

   The Font dialog box opens with the Font tab selected. See Figure G-4. You can use the Font dialog box to change the font, font style, and font size of selected text. In addition, you can apply special font effects that are not available on the Formatting Palette. The Preview box at the bottom of the dialog box shows how the current text will look with the selected formatting attributes.

> **QUICK TIP**
> To underline text, click the Underline button U in the Font group on the Formatting Palette.

4. **Click the Shadow check box in the Effects section of the dialog box, click OK, then click anywhere in the document window to deselect the text**

   The text now appears with a shadow effect that makes it look three dimensional.

5. **Select Product Name: in the third line in the document, click the Bold button B on the Formatting Palette, then click the Italic button I on the Formatting Palette**

   "Product name:" is now formatted in bold and italic, and is still selected.

> **QUICK TIP**
> Click the Format button once when you want to use the Format Painter to apply the selected formatting only once.

6. **Double-click the Format button on the Standard toolbar**

   The Format button activates the Format Painter. Notice that the pointer shape changes to +⌶ when you place it on the document, indicating that the Format Painter is turned on. You can apply the formatting of the selected text (the bold and italic "Product name:") to any text you select next. Because you double-clicked the Format button, you can use the Format Painter to apply the selected formatting multiple times, until you click the Format button again or press [esc].

7. **Select Product Number: in the next line of text**

   The bold and italic formatting is applied to the selected text.

> **QUICK TIP**
> To remove formatting from selected text, click Edit on the menu bar, point to Clear, and click Clear Formatting.

8. **Select Price: in the next line of text, select Dimensions: in the sixth line, press [esc], click outside the selected text, then save your changes**

   Pressing [esc] changes the pointer back to ⌶ and deselects the Format button on the Standard toolbar, indicating that the Format Painter is turned off. See Figure G-5.

FIGURE G-3: Changing the font color of selected text

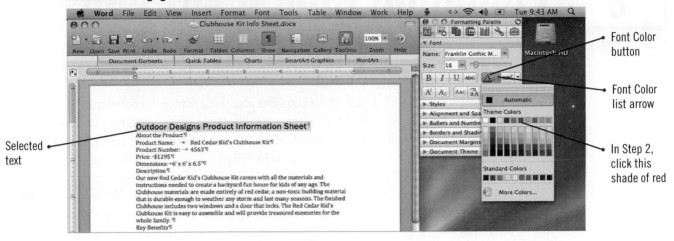

Selected text

Font Color button

Font Color list arrow

In Step 2, click this shade of red

FIGURE G-4: Font tab of Font dialog box

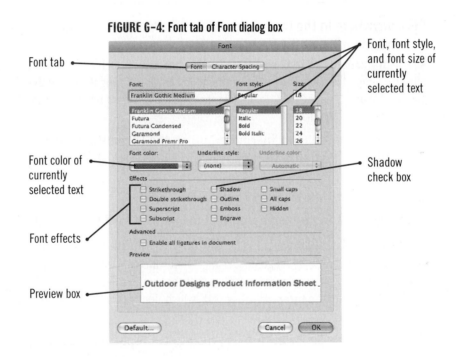

Font tab

Font, font style, and font size of currently selected text

Font color of currently selected text

Shadow check box

Font effects

Preview box

FIGURE G-5: Bold and italic formatting applied to text

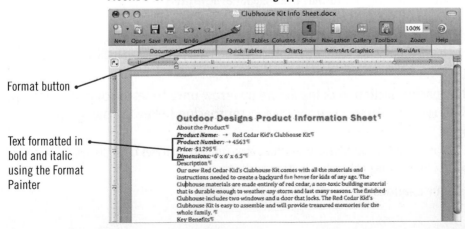

Format button

Text formatted in bold and italic using the Format Painter

Changing Alignment and Line Spacing

The amount of space between the edge of the page and your document text is called the **margin**. You can change the **alignment**, or position of text within a document's margins, using the alignment buttons in the Alignment and Spacing group on the Formatting Palette. For example, titles are often centered, headings are usually left-aligned, and paragraphs are often **justified** (aligned equally between the left and right margins). You can also adjust the line spacing between lines using buttons in the Alignment and Spacing group on the Formatting Palette or using options in the Paragraph dialog box. All of the text in the Clubhouse Kit Info Sheet is aligned along the left margin. You decide to center the title and justify the paragraph below the Description heading. You also want to increase the amount of spacing between the lines in the Description paragraph.

STEPS

1. **Click anywhere in the text** Outdoor Designs Product Information Sheet **in the first line of the document to set the insertion point**

   Although you need to select text to change character formats such as font size or font style, you can change most paragraph formatting, such as alignment, just by positioning the insertion point anywhere in the paragraph. In Word, a **paragraph** is any text that ends with a hard return, so it can be as short as a one-word title or as long as you like.

2. **Click the** Alignment and Spacing group **on the Formatting Palette to open the group, click the** Align Center button ☰ **next to Horizontal, then click anywhere on the document**

   The text is centered between the two margins. See Figure G-6.

3. **Click anywhere in the paragraph text below the word** Description **(in line seven)**

4. **Click the** Justify button ☰ **in the Alignment and Spacing group**

   The Description paragraph's alignment changes to justified. When you select justified alignment, Word adds or reduces the space between each word so that the text is aligned along both the right and left margins. This is different from **center-aligning** text, which does not change the spacing between the words but merely places the text equally between the margins.

5. **Click the** Double Space button ☰ **next to Line spacing in the Alignment and Spacing group**

   The paragraph now has an extra space between each line, making it easier to read. Compare your screen with Figure G-7.

6. **Click** Format **on the menu bar, then click** Paragraph

   The Paragraph dialog box opens with the Indents and Spacing tab selected, as shown in Figure G-8. Alignment is set to Justified and Line spacing is set to Double Space, reflecting the settings you set. This dialog box offers another way to change paragraph settings and provides a Preview section that shows you what the paragraph will look like with the selected settings.

7. **In the Spacing section, click the** Before up arrow **once to set spacing above the paragraph to** 6 pt, **click the** After up arrow **once to set spacing below the paragraph to** 6 pt, **then click** OK

   Notice that the spacing above and below the paragraph text increases to six points. Adding a slight increase in space between paragraphs can enhance readability.

8. **Save your changes**

FIGURE G-6: Modified paragraph alignment

Center aligned text

Align Center button

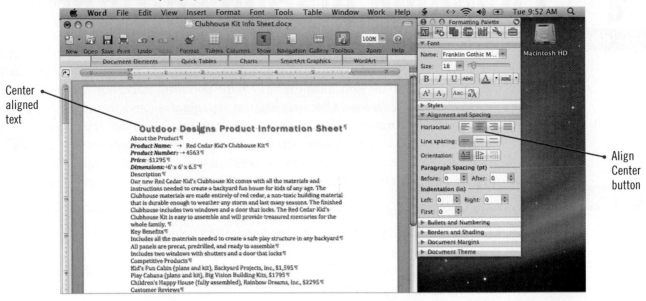

FIGURE G-7: Paragraph with justified alignment and line spacing set to Double Space

Justify button

Double Space button

1.5 Space button

Single Space button

Justified paragraph alignment

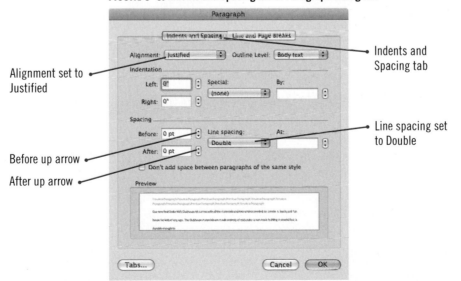

FIGURE G-8: Indents and Spacing tab of Paragraph dialog box

Alignment set to Justified

Indents and Spacing tab

Line spacing set to Double

Before up arrow

After up arrow

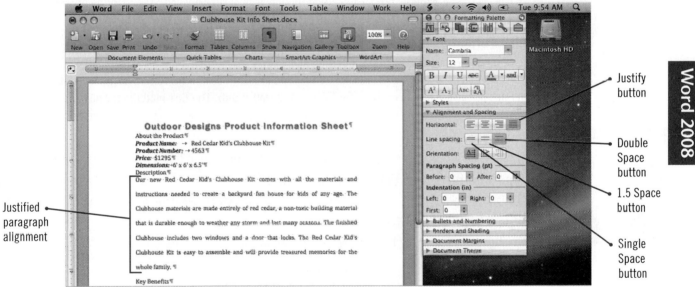

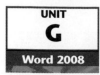

Changing Margin Settings

By default, Word 2008 sets page margins at one inch from the top and bottom of the page and 1.25 inches from the left and right sides of the page. If you'd like to change the margin settings, you can do so with the Document Margins group on the Formatting Palette or in the Document dialog box. When you change the margins, Word automatically adjusts line wrapping and **repaginates** (renumbers the pages of) your document. To evaluate what margin settings to use in a specific document, you should view the document in Print Layout view so you can see and work with the margins as they will appear on the page. The Clubhouse Kit Info Sheet document is currently formatted with the default margins. You decide to explore other margin settings to see whether a different setting would make the document look better.

STEPS

1. **Click the Document Margins group on the Formatting Palette to open it**

   The Document Margins group opens and displays the current margin settings. Currently, the default settings are in use, which specify a 1.25 inch margin for the left and right, and a 1-inch margin for the top and bottom of the page. See Figure G-9.

2. **Click in the Top box in the Document Margins group, type 2, then press [tab]**

   In the document window, the area between the top edge of the paper and the first line of text increases to 2 inches (as you can see on the vertical ruler).

3. **Click Format on the menu bar, then click Document**

   As shown in Figure G-10, the Document dialog box opens with the Margins tab selected. The Margins tab contains margin text boxes, a Preview section, and a Default button (to restore **default settings**, the pre-defined settings that are applied when you first install Word). The first margin text box, Top, is currently selected.

   QUICK TIP
   You can also click a margin text box to select it.

4. **Press [tab] twice**

   The Left text box is selected. Pressing [tab] moves the insertion point from one text box to the next.

5. **Type 1 in the Left text box, then press [tab]**

   The Left text box shows 1, the Preview box shows the new left margin, and the Right text box is selected.

   QUICK TIP
   Most printers require at least a ¼-inch margin around the page.

6. **Type 1 in the Right text box**

   The Right text box shows 1 and the Preview box shows the new right margin.

7. **Click OK**

   The Document dialog box closes, and the left and right margins in the product information sheet change to 1 inch. Compare your screen to Figure G-11.

8. **Save your changes**

FIGURE G-9: Document Margins group on the Formatting Palette

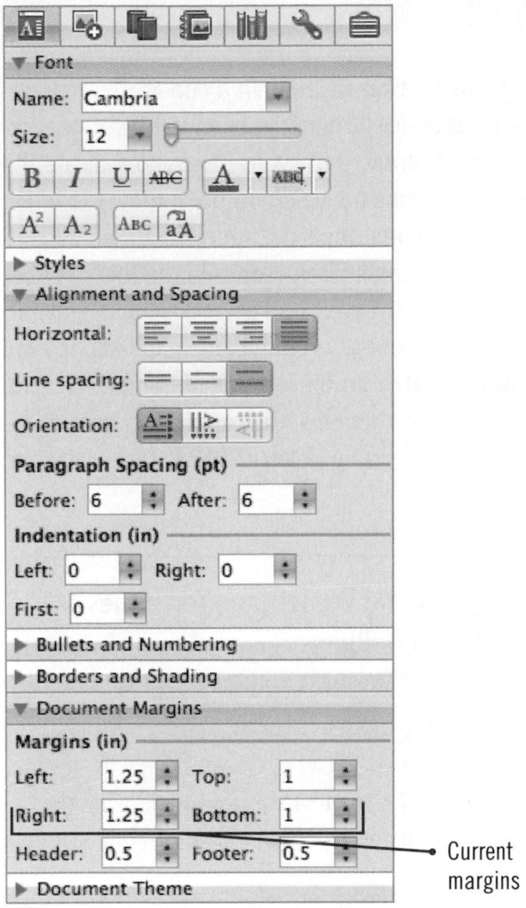

▼ Font

Name: Cambria

Size: 12

B I U ABC A ▾ ABC ▾

A² A₂ ABC aA

▶ Styles

▼ Alignment and Spacing

Horizontal:

Line spacing:

Orientation:

Paragraph Spacing (pt)

Before: 6   After: 6

Indentation (in)

Left: 0   Right: 0

First: 0

▶ Bullets and Numbering

▶ Borders and Shading

▼ Document Margins

Margins (in)

Left: 1.25   Top: 1

Right: 1.25   Bottom: 1

Header: 0.5   Footer: 0.5 ⎯ Current margins

▶ Document Theme

FIGURE G-10: Margins tab of Document dialog box

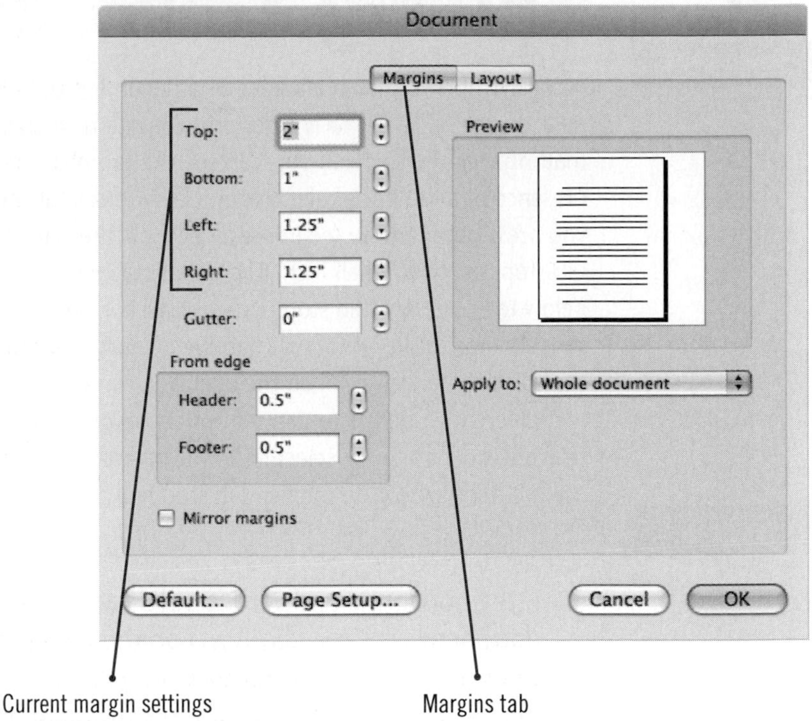

Document

Margins Layout

Top: 2"

Bottom: 1"

Left: 1.25"

Right: 1.25"

Gutter: 0"

From edge

Header: 0.5"

Footer: 0.5"

☐ Mirror margins

Preview

Apply to: Whole document

Default...   Page Setup...   Cancel   OK

Current margin settings   Margins tab

FIGURE G-11: Clubhouse Kit Info Sheet document with new margin settings

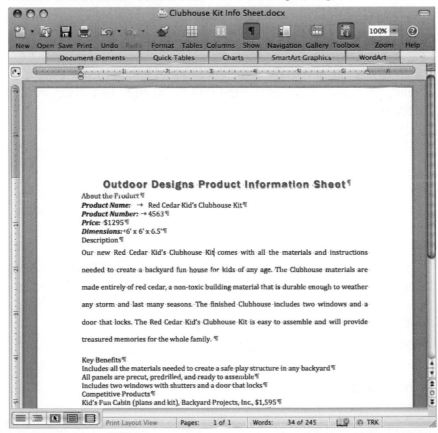

Outdoor Designs Product Information Sheet

About the Product

Product Name: → Red Cedar Kid's Clubhouse Kit

Product Number: → 4563

Price: $1295

Dimensions: 6' x 6' x 6.5'

Description

Our new Red Cedar Kid's Clubhouse Kit comes with all the materials and instructions needed to create a backyard fun house for kids of any age. The Clubhouse materials are made entirely of red cedar, a non-toxic building material that is durable enough to weather any storm and last many seasons. The finished Clubhouse includes two windows and a door that locks. The Red Cedar Kid's Clubhouse Kit is easy to assemble and will provide treasured memories for the whole family.

Key Benefits

Includes all the materials needed to create a safe play structure in any backyard

All panels are precut, predrilled, and ready to assemble

Includes two windows with shutters and a door that locks

Competitive Products

Kid's Fun Cabin (plans and kit), Backyard Projects, Inc., $1,595

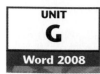
Setting Tabs

You can improve the appearance of a document by using tabs to align text within a line at specific positions on the page. A **tab** is a horizontal position where text is aligned. (When you press [tab] with the formatting marks displayed, you can see the tab character, a right arrow, that Word inserts to indicate the presence of a tab.) The ruler makes it easy to set **tab stops** (locations the insertion point moves to when you press [tab]) and to see immediately how they affect your document. By default, Word sets left-aligned tab stops every one-half inch. The default tab stops are marked as small black slashes in the thin gray bar below the ruler. Any tab stop that you add appears as a tab icon on the ruler and overrides the default tab stop settings to the left of your tab. By default, new tab stops that you set on the ruler are left-aligned tab stops and appear as a ⌐ on the ruler. You can use the **tab indicator** on the left side of the ruler to align text differently, such as to the right or center of a tab stop. When you set tabs, they apply only to text you selected, or, if no text is selected, to the paragraph containing the insertion point. ▓▓▓▓ You decide to use the ruler to change the first tab stop to 1.5 inches.

STEPS

1. **If the horizontal and vertical rulers are not displayed along the left and top edges of the document window, click** View **on the menu bar, then click** Ruler

    To set tabs in the document window using the ruler, you must have the rulers visible on your screen.

2. **Click to the right of** 6' x 6' x 6.5' **in the sixth line of text, press [return], type** Product Weight:, **press [tab], then type** 118 lbs.

    The tab appears as a right-arrow character. As shown in Figure G-12, the text you typed following the tab ("118 lbs.") is aligned at the default 1.5" tab stop. The new text that you typed appears in 12-point Cambria type with no formatting applied.

3. **Select** Dimensions, **click the** Format button 🖌 **on the Standard toolbar, select** Product Weight:, **then click anywhere in the document to deselect the text**

    The text you added now matches the formatting of the previous lines of text. You can see that there is a tab after each colon in the list. The shortest item, Price, aligns with the one-half inch default tab. The longer phrases align with the one inch or 1.5" tab.

QUICK TIP
If you click the wrong place on the ruler, you can click the Undo button 🔄 on the Standard toolbar (or drag the tab marker off the left side of the ruler to remove it), then try again.

4. **Click to the left of** Product Name **in the third line of the document to set the insertion point, press and hold [Shift], then click to the right of** 118 lbs. **in the seventh line of the document**

    The five lines of text below "About the Product" are selected. Any tab stop changes you make will apply to all the selected text.

▶ 5. **Click the** 1.5" **mark on the ruler**

    The left-aligned tab stop ⌐ appears on the ruler at the 1.5" mark. All text that begins at a tab stop moved to the new tab stop location at 1.5". See Figure G-13. All the default tab stops in the thin bar below the ruler no longer appear to the left of the new tab stop. Notice that when you clicked the ruler to add the tab stop, a thin, vertical line appeared briefly, indicating the tab position on the page.

QUICK TIP
To add a tab with a different alignment, click the tab indicator, then click the alignment you want to use on the list: Center ┻, Right ┓, Decimal ┸, or Bar │. Next, click the ruler to insert a tab with the new alignment.

6. **Scroll to the end of the document, then select the last four lines of text in the document beginning with** Fun for kids: **and ending with** (Beth Garner, Franklin, NJ)

    The selected text contains tab stops on two of the lines. Notice that the tabs are not aligned with each other, so that this part of the document looks sloppy.

▶ 7. **Click the** 1.5" **mark on the ruler**

    The two tabs are now aligned at the 1.5" mark on the ruler. Compare your screen to Figure G-14.

8. **Save your changes**

FIGURE G-12: Inserted tab

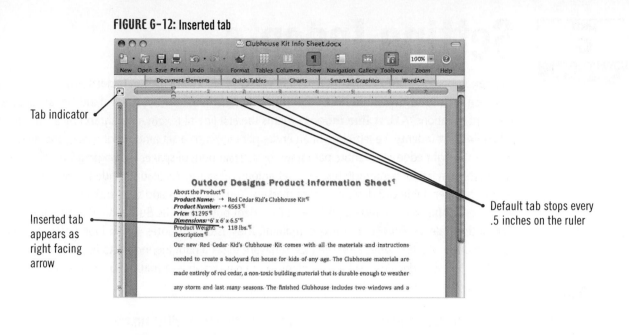

Tab indicator

Default tab stops every .5 inches on the ruler

Inserted tab appears as right facing arrow

FIGURE G-13: Setting a tab stop on the ruler

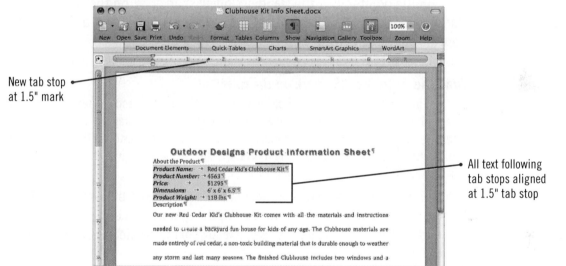

New tab stop at 1.5" mark

All text following tab stops aligned at 1.5" tab stop

FIGURE G-14: Tab stops set at 1.5" for paragraphs

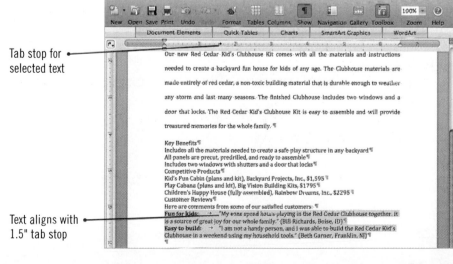

Tab stop for selected text

Text aligns with 1.5" tab stop

Setting Indents

You can improve the appearance of text on a page by setting indents. An **indent** is a set amount of space between the edge of a paragraph and the right or left margin. Different types of indents are appropriate for different situations. A **first line indent** indents the first line of text in a paragraph by a specified amount. A **left indent** indents the left edge of an entire paragraph by a set amount of space, and a **right indent** indents the right edge of an entire paragraph by a set amount of space. A **hanging indent** aligns the text below the first line of paragraph text by a set amount of space. You can set indents using the sliding markers on the ruler. Table G-2 describes these markers. You can set left and right indents at one-half inch increments using the Increase Indent and Decrease Indent buttons in the Bullets and Numbering group on the Formatting Palette. 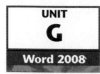 The text containing the customer quotes would look neater if the lines were aligned under the first word after the tab. You want to set a hanging indent to improve the appearance of this text. You also decide to set a left indent to the paragraph text that describes the product.

STEPS

QUICK TIP

Make sure the ScreenTip identifies the marker as Hanging Indent and not First Line Indent or Left Indent.

1. **If necessary, select the four lines of text beginning with** Fun for kids: **and ending with** (Beth Garner, Franklin, NJ)

2. **Position the pointer over the** Hanging Indent marker ⌂ **on the ruler so that the Hanging Indent ScreenTip appears, then click and hold so that a thin vertical line appears on the screen**

   This thin vertical line helps you position the marker in the desired location on the ruler.

QUICK TIP

When you drag an indent marker, make sure the tip of the pointer—and not the body of the pointer—is positioned over the marker; otherwise, you might have difficulty dragging it.

3. **Drag the** ⌂ **to the** 1.5" **mark on the ruler**

   The first line in each of the selected paragraphs remains flush left, and the text below the first line of each paragraph is now aligned at the 1.5" mark on the ruler, where you dragged the hanging indent marker. See Figure G-15. Notice that the hanging indent marker is under the tab stop at the 1.5" mark on the ruler. Tabs and indents often appear together like this on the ruler when you have tabs and indents at the same location in your documents.

4. **Scroll up so that the Description heading and paragraph below it are visible on the screen, then click anywhere in the Description paragraph text**

   The insertion point appears in the paragraph text. Any paragraph formatting changes that you specify apply to the entire paragraph.

5. **Click the** Bullets and Numbering group **on the Formatting Palette to open it, then click the** Increase Indent button ▤ **in the Bullets and Numbering group**

   Clicking the Increase Indent button indents the paragraph by one-half inch, the default amount. This indent is more than you want for this paragraph, so you need to reduce the size of the indent.

QUICK TIP

If the selected text does not move to the correct position, click the Undo button on the Standard toolbar, then move the Left Indent marker to the ¼" mark on the ruler again.

6. **Position the pointer over the** Left Indent marker ⊟ **on the ruler until the Left Indent ScreenTip appears, then drag to the** ¼" **mark on the ruler**

   You reduced the amount of the indent by moving the Left Indent marker to the ¼" position on the ruler. See Figure G-16.

7. **Save your changes**

FIGURE G-15: Setting a hanging indent

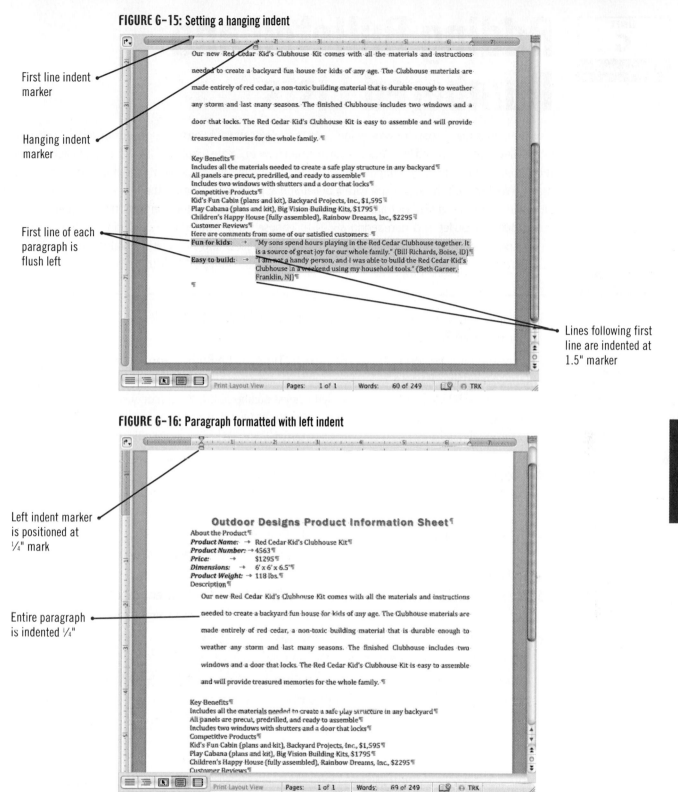

First line indent marker

Hanging indent marker

First line of each paragraph is flush left

Lines following first line are indented at 1.5" marker

FIGURE G-16: Paragraph formatted with left indent

Left indent marker is positioned at ¼" mark

Entire paragraph is indented ¼"

TABLE G-2: Ruler markers used for setting indents

ruler marker name	ruler marker	used for
First Line Indent marker	▽	Indents the first line of a paragraph by a set amount
Hanging Indent marker	△	Indents the lines below the first line of text in a paragraph by a set amount
Left Indent marker	▭	Indents the left edge of an entire paragraph by a set amount
Right Indent marker	△	Indents the right edge of an entire paragraph by a set amount

Word 2008

Adding Bulleted and Numbered Lists

Word provides many tools for organizing your text. You can easily organize groups of related paragraphs into bulleted or numbered lists. You already learned how to create a bulleted list using the Bullets button in the Bullets and Numbering group on the Formatting Palette. When you apply the bullet format to a paragraph, Word sets off the paragraph with a bullet and automatically formats the text with a hanging indent. Numbered lists are similar, but are used when you want to present items in a particular order. There are many different bullet and numbering styles to choose from using the Style option in the Bullets and Numbering group on the Formatting Palette and the Bullets and Numbering dialog box. You decide to add numbered and bulleted lists to the Clubhouse Kit Info Sheet to make it easier to reference.

STEPS

1. **Scroll down if necessary, then select the three lines of text under the heading** Competitive Products

2. **Click the** Numbering button 🔢 **next to Type in the Bullets and Numbering group on the Formatting Palette**

   The text you selected now appears as a left-aligned numbered list. Word indented each number in the list and placed a tab after each number. You can see on the ruler that a hanging indent has been set. If any text in the numbered list wraps to a second line, it will align with the first line of text, not the number. Refer to Figure G-17.

3. **Click** Format **on the menu bar, then click** Bullets and Numbering

   The Bullets and Numbering dialog box opens with the Numbered tab selected. You can use this dialog box to choose from several list formats.

4. **Click the** format **shown in Figure G-18, then click** OK

   The Bullets and Numbering dialog box closes. The numbers in the numbered list now have a single parenthesis after each number.

5. **Click to the right of the third item in the list (after** $2295**), then press** [return]

   The number 4, followed by a parenthesis, appears automatically and takes on the format of the item above it.

6. **Type** Tot House (plans and kit), Handy Kits, Inc., $1995

   The text you typed is now formatted as a fourth item in the numbered list.

7. **Select the three lines of text under the heading** Key Benefits, **then click the** Bullets **button** 📋 **in the Bullets and Numbering group on the Formatting Palette**

   The text you selected now appears as a left-aligned bulleted list with a tab inserted after each bullet.

8. **Click** Format **on the menu bar, click** Bullets and Numbering **to open the Bulleted tab in the Bullets and Numbering dialog box, then click** Customize

   The Customize bulleted list dialog box opens. You use this dialog box to create a custom bullet.

9. **Click** Picture **to open the Choose a Picture dialog box, click** Metallic Orb, **click** Insert, **click** OK, **then click outside the selected text**

   The Key Benefits paragraphs are now formatted as a bulleted list, with each paragraph preceded by a metallic orb bullet, as shown in Figure G-19.

10. **Save your changes**

QUICK TIP

You can also change the numbering or bullet style by clicking the Style list arrow in the Bullets and Numbering group on the Formatting Palette, then clicking a numbering or bullet style on the list. Note that more options are available in the Bullets and Numbering dialog box than on the Style list.

QUICK TIP

If the bullets are not indented one-half inch, move the First Line Indent marker to the ½" mark on the ruler if necessary, then move the Hanging Indent marker to the ¾" mark on the ruler if necessary.

FIGURE G-17: Formatting text as a numbered list

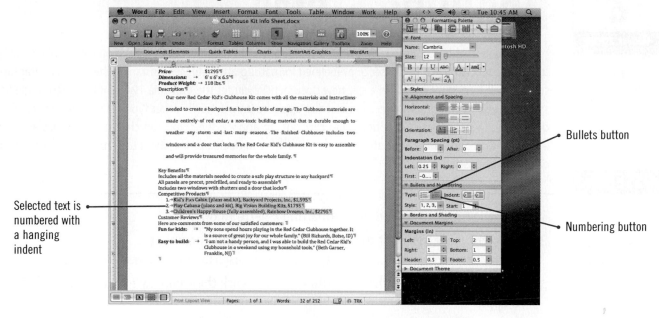

Bullets button

Selected text is numbered with a hanging indent

Numbering button

FIGURE G-18: Numbered tab of the Bullets and Numbering dialog box

In Step 4, click this number style

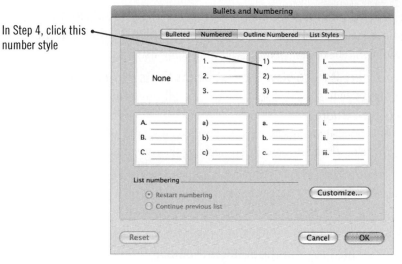

FIGURE G-19: Clubhouse Kit Info Sheet with bulleted and numbered lists

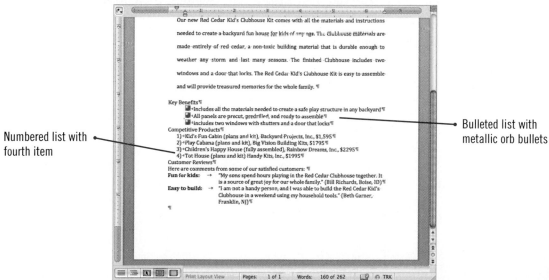

Numbered list with fourth item

Bulleted list with metallic orb bullets

Word 2008

Applying Styles

You can save a lot of formatting time and ensure that your document looks professional by applying styles to your document. A **style** is a set of predefined formatting attributes. For instance, the Normal paragraph style (which is used by default in every new document) includes the Cambria 12-point font with single line spacing. Besides paragraph styles, you can also apply built-in styles for other types of text elements in your document, including headings, titles, and captions. To apply a style, you can choose from styles available in the Styles group on the Formatting Palette. You decide to use styles to complete the formatting of the Clubhouse Kit Info Sheet.

STEPS

1. **Click the Styles group on the Formatting Palette to open it**

2. **Click anywhere in About the Product in line 2 of the document**
   To apply a style to a paragraph, you first click in the paragraph to which you want to apply the style.

3. **In the Styles group on the Formatting Palette, click the Heading 1 style under Pick style to apply**
   See Figure G-20. The About the Product paragraph now has the Heading 1 style applied to it: it is formatted with Cambria 14 point blue font.

4. **Using the process you followed in Steps 2 and 3, apply the Heading 1 style to the following lines: Description, Key Benefits, Competitive Products, and Customer Reviews**
   All of the headings in the document now have the Heading 1 style applied.

QUICK TIP
The default option in the Styles group on the Formatting Palette is to list Available styles. For additional options, click the List styles list arrow at the bottom of the Styles group, then click All styles.

5. **Scroll down if necessary to view the text below Customer Reviews, select the customer quote that starts "My sons spend hours...", scroll down in the list of styles in the Styles group, then click Quote**
   The Quote style is applied to the selected text. When you want to apply a style only to part of a paragraph, you need to first select the desired text before applying the style; otherwise, the style will be applied to the entire paragraph. See Figure G-21.

6. **Select the customer quote that begins "I am not a handy person...", then click Quote in the Styles group**
   The selected text is also formatted with the Quote style.

7. **Click the Show button 🔳 on the Standard toolbar**
   Deselecting the Show button hides all formatting marks.

8. **Press [⌘][end], type your name, save your changes, then print the document**
   Compare your printed document to Figure G-22.

9. **Close the document, then quit Word**

FIGURE G-20: Heading 1 style applied to a paragraph

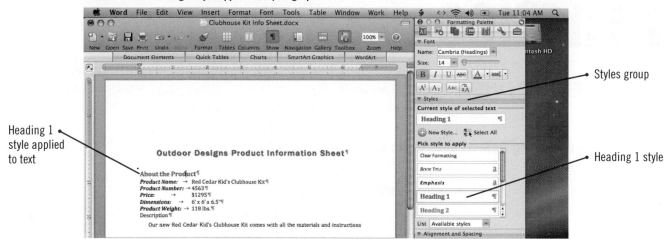

Heading 1 style applied to text

Styles group

Heading 1 style

FIGURE G-21: Quote style applied to selected text

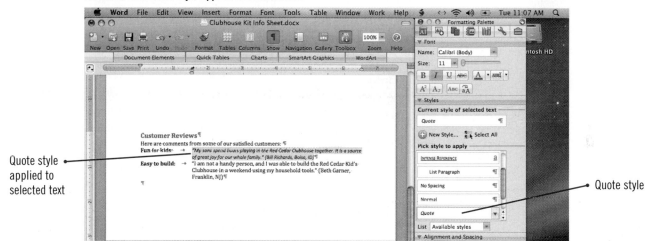

Quote style applied to selected text

Quote style

FIGURE G-22: Completed Clubhouse Kit Info Sheet

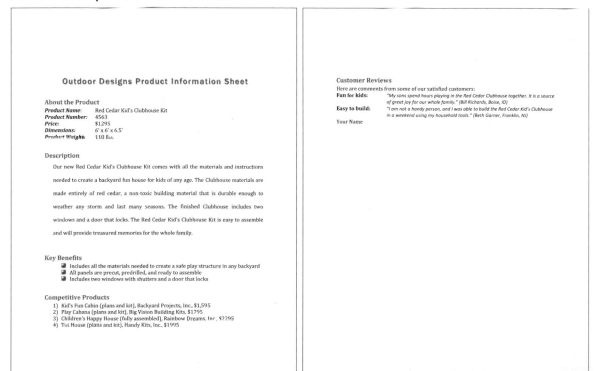

6. **Set indents.**

   a. Select the lines beginning with **Directed by: Suzy Matthews** (in line 15) and ending with **prestigious New York** (in line 17).

   b. Indent the selected paragraphs to the ¼" mark on the ruler. (*Hint*: If the selected paragraphs do not move to the correct position, click the Undo button on the Standard toolbar, then move the Left Indent marker to the ¼" mark on the ruler again.)

   c. Select the lines beginning with **Directed by: Carlos Gomez** (in line 22) and ending with **...1950s, when a** (in line 24).

   d. Indent the selected paragraphs to the ¼" mark on the ruler.

   e. Select the lines containing the Description for The Glass Menagerie (lines 17–19), then set a hanging indent at the 1¼" mark on the ruler.

   f. Select the lines containing the Description for Picnic (lines 24–26), then set a hanging indent at the 1¼" mark on the ruler.

   g. Save your changes.

7. **Add bulleted and numbered lists.**

   a. Format the lines starting with **Encourage all members** and ending **and the audience** (lines 8–10) as a bulleted list, choosing the Green Ball bullet style from the Choose a Picture dialog box. (*Hint*: If the bullets are not indented one-half inch, move the First Line Indent marker to the ½" mark on the ruler if necessary, then move the Hanging Indent marker to the ¾" mark on the ruler if necessary.

   b. Select the three lines of text at the bottom of the document beginning with **Perform a one-minute monologue** and ending with **Sing a song of your choosing**.

   c. Format the selected text as a numbered list, choosing the style 1) 2) 3) (a number followed by a parenthesis).

   d. Save your changes.

8. **Apply styles.**

   a. Apply the Heading 1 style to the text **About Jackson Park Community Theatre** (line 5 in the document).

   b. Apply the Heading 1 style to the following headings: **Announcing Our 2012 Summer Season** and **Auditions for West Side Story**.

   c. Apply the Heading 2 style to the following headings in the document: **The Glass Menagerie** (line 13) and **Picnic** (line 20).

   d. Press [⌘][End], then type your name in the last line of the document.

   e. If necessary, deselect the Show button.

   f. Save your changes.

   g. Preview and print the document, compare your document with Figure G-24, then quit Word.

FIGURE G-24

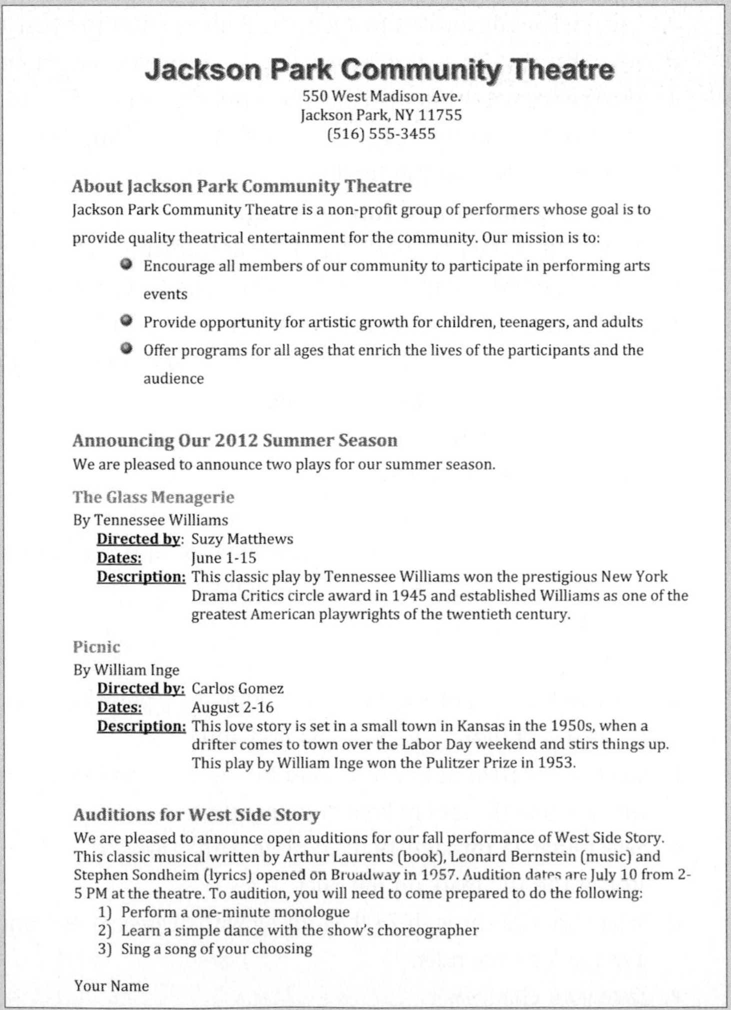

Jackson Park Community Theatre

550 West Madison Ave.
Jackson Park, NY 11755
(516) 555-3455

About Jackson Park Community Theatre

Jackson Park Community Theatre is a non-profit group of performers whose goal is to provide quality theatrical entertainment for the community. Our mission is to:

- Encourage all members of our community to participate in performing arts events
- Provide opportunity for artistic growth for children, teenagers, and adults
- Offer programs for all ages that enrich the lives of the participants and the audience

Announcing Our 2012 Summer Season

We are pleased to announce two plays for our summer season.

The Glass Menagerie

By Tennessee Williams
Directed by: Suzy Matthews
Dates: June 1-15
Description: This classic play by Tennessee Williams won the prestigious New York Drama Critics circle award in 1945 and established Williams as one of the greatest American playwrights of the twentieth century.

Picnic

By William Inge
Directed by: Carlos Gomez
Dates: August 2-16
Description: This love story is set in a small town in Kansas in the 1950s, when a drifter comes to town over the Labor Day weekend and stirs things up. This play by William Inge won the Pulitzer Prize in 1953.

Auditions for West Side Story

We are pleased to announce open auditions for our fall performance of West Side Story. This classic musical written by Arthur Laurents (book), Leonard Bernstein (music) and Stephen Sondheim (lyrics) opened on Broadway in 1957. Audition dates are July 10 from 2-5 PM at the theatre. To audition, you will need to come prepared to do the following:

1) Perform a one-minute monologue
2) Learn a simple dance with the show's choreographer
3) Sing a song of your choosing

Your Name

▼ INDEPENDENT CHALLENGE 1

You work in the marketing department for River's Edge Fitness Center in Cleveland, Ohio. Sofia Price, the marketing manager, needs to create a document that describes the calendar for new programs and events in September. Sofia has already created a draft with all the necessary information; however, she is not happy with its appearance. She has provided you with her unformatted draft and has asked you to format it so that all the information is presented effectively and looks attractive and professional.

- **a.** Start Word, open the file G-3.docx from where your Data Files are stored, then save it as **Health Club Calendar**.
- **b.** Center-align the first four lines of the document.
- **c.** Change the font of **River's Edge Fitness Center** to Gill Sans and increase the font size to 20.
- **d.** Change the font color of **River's Edge Fitness Center** in the first line to dark blue (the ScreenTip reads "Text 2"), apply bold formatting to the text, then apply the Shadow text effect to it.
- **e.** Increase the font size of **Calendar of Events September 2012** (in line 4) to 16 points, then apply underline formatting to it.
- **f.** In the paragraph under "What's New" (lines 6–10), align the paragraph so it is justified, then set the line spacing to 1.5. Increase the space before and after this paragraph to 6 points.
- **g.** Apply the Heading 1 style to the following lines of text: **What's New**, **New Member Orientation**, **Pilates Mat Classes**, **Self Defense Workshop**, and **New Spa Services**.
- **h.** Increase the left indent of all paragraphs under each of the Heading 1 headings to ¼" on the ruler.
- **i.** In the lines of text that contain tabs, set two left tab stops—the first at 2¼" and the second at 5".
- **j.** Format the last four lines in the document as a bulleted list, then change the bullet style to the Metallic Orb picture bullet. (*Hint*: If the bullets are not indented one-half inch, move the First Line Indent marker to the ½" mark on the ruler if necessary, then move the Hanging Indent marker to the ¾" mark on the ruler if necessary.
- **k.** Type your name two lines below the last line of text in the document, then right-align your name.
- **l.** If necessary, deselect the Show button.
- **m.** Compare your document with Figure G-25, save your changes, then print the document.

FIGURE G-25

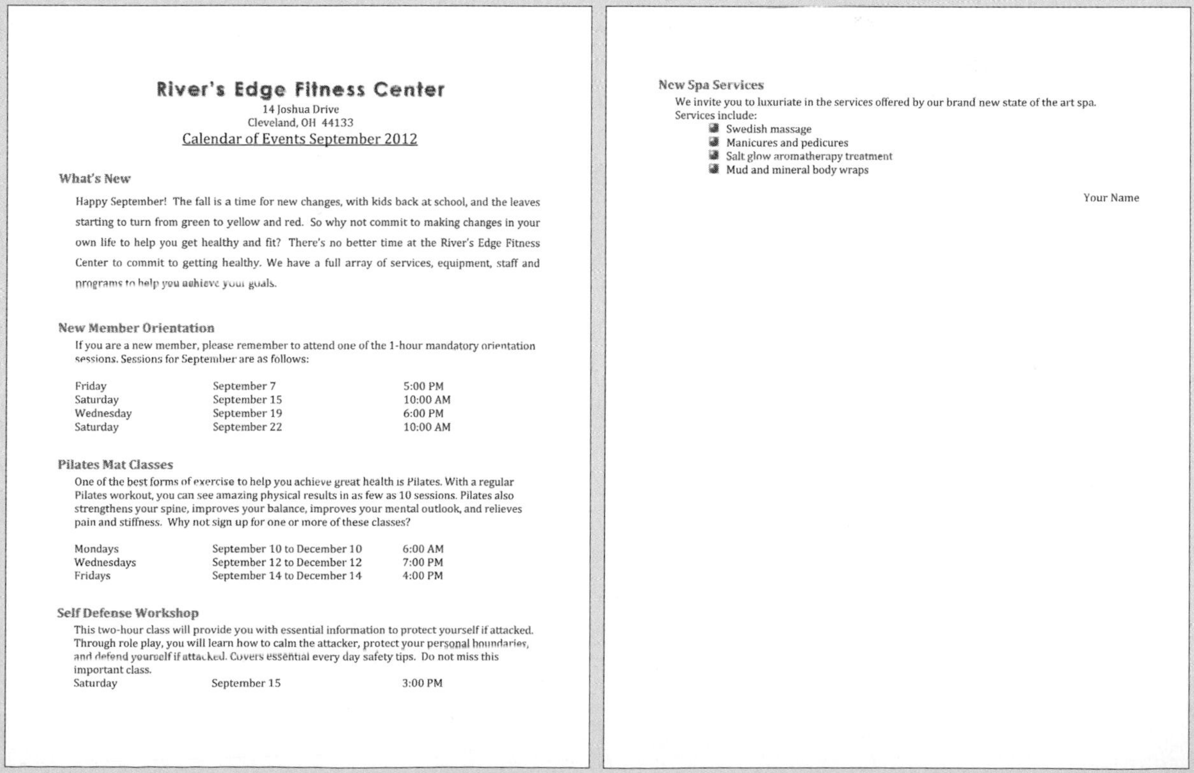

River's Edge Fitness Center
14 Joshua Drive
Cleveland, OH 44133
Calendar of Events September 2012

What's New

Happy September! The fall is a time for new changes, with kids back at school, and the leaves starting to turn from green to yellow and red. So why not commit to making changes in your own life to help you get healthy and fit? There's no better time at the River's Edge Fitness Center to commit to getting healthy. We have a full array of services, equipment, staff and programs to help you achieve your goals.

New Member Orientation

If you are a new member, please remember to attend one of the 1-hour mandatory orientation sessions. Sessions for September are as follows:

Friday	September 7	5:00 PM
Saturday	September 15	10:00 AM
Wednesday	September 19	6:00 PM
Saturday	September 22	10:00 AM

Pilates Mat Classes

One of the best forms of exercise to help you achieve great health is Pilates. With a regular Pilates workout, you can see amazing physical results in as few as 10 sessions. Pilates also strengthens your spine, improves your balance, improves your mental outlook, and relieves pain and stiffness. Why not sign up for one or more of these classes?

Mondays	September 10 to December 10	6:00 AM
Wednesdays	September 12 to December 12	7:00 PM
Fridays	September 14 to December 14	4:00 PM

Self Defense Workshop

This two-hour class will provide you with essential information to protect yourself if attacked. Through role play, you will learn how to calm the attacker, protect your personal boundaries, and defend yourself if attacked. Covers essential every day safety tips. Do not miss this important class.

Saturday	September 15	3:00 PM

New Spa Services

We invite you to luxuriate in the services offered by our brand new state of the art spa.
Services include:

- Swedish massage
- Manicures and pedicures
- Salt glow aromatherapy treatment
- Mud and mineral body wraps

Your Name

Open the file G-6.docx from where your Data Files are stored, then save it as **Sandwich Shop Menu**. Format the document so it appears as shown in Figure G-26. (*Hint*: If you do not have or cannot find the font used in the title, apply the closest match you can find.) Add your name at the bottom of the document, then preview and print the document. Close the document, then quit Word.

FIGURE G-26

Angie's Sandwich Shop
55 Elm Street
Pinewood, WA 96543

Sandwiches

Smoked turkey croissant	**5.75**

Two delicious slices of smoked turkey with lettuce, tomato, and cheddar cheese on a croissant.

Chicken salad	**5.25**

Chicken salad with celery, diced apples, and toasted almonds on a croissant.

Chicken club sandwich	**6.75**

Grilled chicken with lettuce, bacon, tomato, and cheese.

Veggie wrap	**5.75**

Lettuce, tomato, peppers, olives, and cheese in an oversized tortilla wrap.

Roast beef	**6.25**

Roast beef, lettuce and tomatoes on a bulky roll.

Beverages

Lemonade, juices, cola	**1.75**

Desserts

Angie's famous fresh baked pie	**4.25**

Top off your lunch with one of Angie's famous pies (blueberry, apple, or peach) baked fresh daily.

Just for Kids

Any kids meal (includes chips and a drink)	**3.50**

Hot dog	Cheese pizza	Macaroni and cheese
Chicken tenders	Hamburger	Grilled cheese sandwich

Your Name

Adding Special Elements to a Document

Files You Will Need:

H-1.docx
H-2.docx
H-3.docx
H-4.docx
H-5.docx
H-6.docx

Word provides many tools to help you create professional looking documents, such as newsletters, that incorporate graphics and other special elements. For instance, if you need to present detailed information in a row-and-column format, you can insert a table. If you want to add visual interest to your document, Word makes it easy to choose from a wide variety of **clip art**, which are ready-made art objects that you can insert in documents. If your document contains multiple pages, it's a good idea to insert headers and footers, areas at the top and bottom of each page that contain the page number and other information that you want to appear on every page of your document. Word also makes it easy to insert footnotes and citations. Best of all, you can change the entire look of your document in a few clicks by applying a theme to it. ▄▄▄▄ George Gonzalez, marketing manager for Outdoor Designs, has asked you to finish a customer newsletter he's been working on that provides information about the company's newest products.

OBJECTIVES

Create a table

Insert and delete table columns and rows

Format a table

Add clip art

Insert footnotes and citations

Insert a header or footer

Add borders and shading

Work with themes

Creating a Table

Not all information is best presented in a running flow of text. Sometimes, it's more effective to present it within the structure of a table. A **table** is a grid of rows and columns. The intersection of each row and column is called a **cell**. Cells can contain both text and graphics. You can insert a table using the Tables button on the Standard toolbar, the Table option on the menu bar, or the Quick Tables tab in the Elements Gallery. A **Quick Table** is a table with a predefined set of formatting attributes, such as shading, fonts, and border color. Using Quick Tables enables you to quickly create a professionally formatted table that is easily modified to fit your needs. When you insert a Quick Table in a document, the table contains a specific number of rows and columns. You can easily add and delete rows and columns as you modify the table. George gives you a file containing the content for the newsletter. He suggests that you begin by inserting a table on the first page to organize the information about the company's new DVD products.

STEPS

1. **Start Word, open the file H-1.docx from where you store your Data Files, then save it as The Hammer Newsletter**
   The partially completed customer newsletter opens in Print Layout view.

TROUBLE

Depending on your screen resolution and document window size, the number of thumbnails visible in the Elements Gallery may vary from that displayed in Figure H-1.

2. **If formatting marks are not displayed, click the** Show button ¶ **on the Standard toolbar**

3. **Scroll down so that you can see the full paragraph below** Introducing Our New DVD Product Line, **click to the right of** following: **at the end of the paragraph, then press [return] twice**
   This is where you want to insert the table.

4. **Click the** Quick Tables tab **in the Elements Gallery**
   The Quick Tables tab in the Elements Gallery expands, displaying several table styles available in the Basic group.

QUICK TIP

Some Quick Table styles include a differently-formatted first column and/or a total row at the bottom that you can use to add numbers in the table. If your table will contain only text, avoid styles that contain a total row.

5. **On the right side of the Elements Gallery, click the** right scroll arrow ▶ **until the last set of choices is displayed, then click the** Medium Shading 2 Quick Table, **as shown in Figure H-1**
   A table with eight rows and three columns appears below the paragraph, and the insertion point is in the first cell. In the Medium Shading 2 Quick Table, the first row is formatted differently than the remaining rows so that the column headings stand out.

6. **In the first cell of the table, type** Item Number, **then press [tab]**
   Pressing [tab] moves the insertion point to the next cell. The symbol in each cell is an **end-of-cell mark**. Text that you type appears to the left of the end-of-cell mark. The marks to the right of each row are **end-of-row marks**.

7. **Type** DVD Title, **press [tab], type** Price, **then press [tab]**
   Pressing [tab] in the last cell of a row moves the insertion point to the first cell in the next row.

QUICK TIP

You can also move to a different cell by using the arrow keys or by clicking the cell.

8. **Type the following text in the table, pressing [tab] after each entry to move to the next cell, then press [tab] after the last entry**

2204	Yes You Can Build a Kayak!	$14.95
2205	Yes You Can Build a Dog House!	$14.95
2206	Yes You Can Build a Bird House!	$14.95
2207	Yes You Can Build a Clubhouse!	$14.95

9. **Click the** Gallery button ▦ **to deselect it**
   The Elements Gallery closes.

10. **Save your changes, then compare your screen to Figure H-2**
    Notice that when you move the mouse pointer over the table, the table's handle ⊞ appears above the upper-left corner of the table. Clicking the handle selects the entire table.

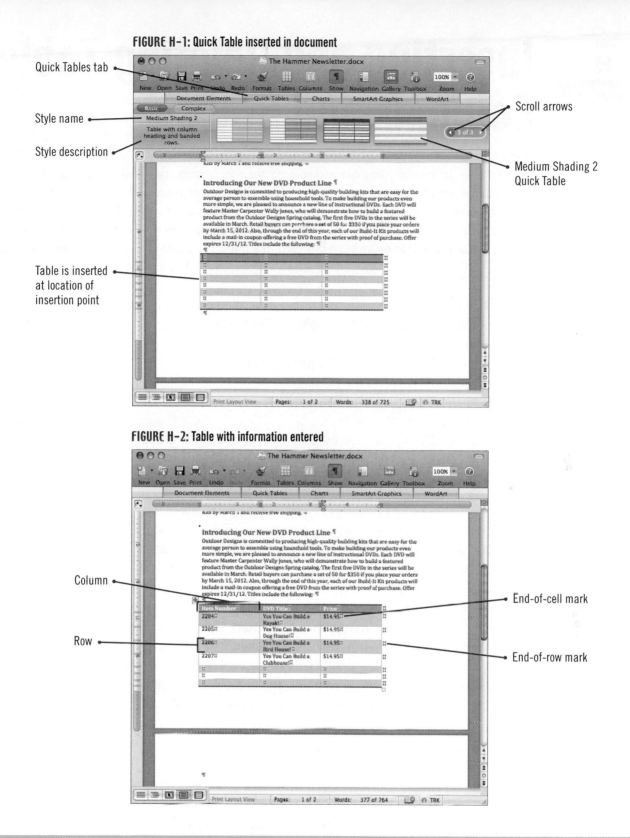

FIGURE H-1: Quick Table inserted in document

Quick Tables tab

Style name — Medium Shading 2

Table with column heading and banded rows.

Style description

Scroll arrows

Medium Shading 2 Quick Table

Table is inserted at location of insertion point

FIGURE H-2: Table with information entered

Column

Row

End-of-cell mark

End-of-row mark

Creating multiple columns

Another way to organize text in a document is to create multiple columns. By default, text you enter in a blank document is formatted in a single column. If you want to increase the amount of text on a page or add white space to improve readability, you can format your text in multiple columns, like a newspaper. To format text in multiple columns, first select the text you want to format in multiple columns, click the Columns button on the Standard toolbar, then click the number of columns that you want in the box that opens under the Columns button. If you want to specify spacing between columns or set individual column widths, click Format on the menu bar, then click Columns to open the Columns dialog box and choose the spacing and width settings you want.

Inserting and Deleting Table Columns and Rows

After you create a table, you might need to add more information or delete existing information. To make room for new information, you can add rows to the top, bottom, or middle of a table. You can add columns anywhere in a table, too. You can use buttons in the Table group on the Formatting Palette to add or delete columns and rows. You need to add a column to the table that indicates the In Stock Date for each DVD title. You'll need to delete rows from the table because it contains empty rows and because one of the DVD titles has been cancelled. You'll also insert a row to include another DVD title.

STEPS

1. **Click any cell in the second row of the table, then click the Toolbox button 🔲 on the Standard toolbar to open the Toolbox, if necessary**

   The Toolbox opens with the Formatting Palette selected by default.

2. **Click the Table group on the Formatting Palette**

   The Table group opens on the Formatting Palette, displaying buttons and other tools for working with tables. The Table group is a **contextual** tool because it appears on the Formatting Palette only when you click inside a table or select a table.

3. **Click the Insert Table button list arrow 🔲 ▾ in the Table group on the Formatting Palette (the ScreenTip reads "Insert or draw table into this document"), then click Insert Rows Above as shown in Figure H-3**

   A new empty row appears above the second row. The Insert Table button list arrow allows you to insert new individual table cells, columns to the left or right of the current cell, rows above or below the current cell, or a table within a table. Once an option is selected, the button next to the list arrow changes to the button for the option last used, such as Insert Rows Above; clicking the button rather than the list arrow repeats the last option selected.

4. **Click the first cell of the new second row, type 2203, press [tab], type Yes You Can Build a Canoe!, press [tab], then type $14.95**

5. **With the insertion point still in the price cell, click the Insert Rows Above button list arrow 🔲 ▾ in the Table group, then click Insert Columns to the Left**

   A new empty column appears between the DVD Title and Price columns. Compare your screen to Figure H-4. Notice that Word narrowed the existing columns to accommodate the new column.

6. **Click the top cell of the new column, type In Stock Date, then press [↓]**

   The insertion point moves down to the second row in the third column.

7. **Type 3/15/12, press [↓], type 4/1/12, press [↓], type 2/15/12, press [↓], type 3/1/12, press [↓], then type 2/8/12**

   You've just learned that the Dog House DVD has been cancelled.

8. **Click any cell in the row that begins with 2205, click the Delete Table button list arrow 🔲 ▾ in the Table group, then click Delete Rows**

   The entire row is deleted, and the other rows move up to close up the space. The icon shown on the Delete button changes to the icon of the last option used.

9. **Click any cell in the first blank row beneath 2207, then click the Delete Rows button 🔲 in the Table group three times**

   The three blank rows at the bottom of the Quick Table are deleted and the insertion point moves outside the table, as shown in Figure H-5. When no part of the table is selected, the Table group disappears from the Formatting Palette.

10. **Save your changes**

Adding Special Elements to a Document

FIGURE H-3: Inserting a new row

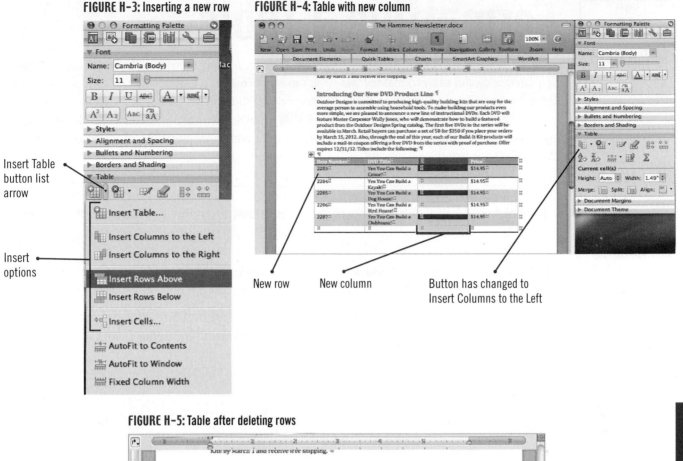

Insert Table button list arrow

Insert options

FIGURE H-4: Table with new column

New row   New column   Button has changed to Insert Columns to the Left

FIGURE H-5: Table after deleting rows

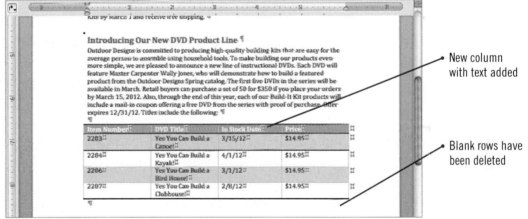

New column with text added

Blank rows have been deleted

Creating a table with the Draw Table command

You can also create a table by drawing on a document using the Draw Table command. To do so, click Table on the menu bar, then click Draw Table. The pointer changes to ✐, which you can drag in a diagonal motion to create the outside borders of the table. To create columns, click and drag vertically from the top border to the bottom border. To create rows, drag horizontally from the left border to the right border. When you're finished drawing the table, press [esc] to turn off the Draw Table feature. You can use commands in the Borders and Shading group on the Formatting Palette or on the Tables and Borders toolbar to change the color, line width,

and style of the table borders before or after you draw them. You can also click the Eraser button 🖉 in the Table group on the Formatting Palette or on the Tables and Borders toolbar and then delete column or row lines by dragging the eraser pointer over existing column or row borders. You can also use the Draw Table command in an existing table by clicking the Draw Table button 🖉 in the Table group on the Formatting Palette. Rows and columns can then be added to the currently selected table by drawing lines from border to border.

Formatting a Table

After you create a table using Quick Tables, the Tables button, the Table menu, or the Draw Table command, you can quickly and easily format the table. You can enhance and customize your table's appearance using the Borders and Shading group on the Formatting Palette. You can also improve the appearance of a table by adjusting row heights and column widths. ▇▇▇ Now that the information in the DVD table is complete, you decide to improve the appearance of the table and adjust the width of the second column so that all DVD title text fits on one line.

STEPS

QUICK TIP

To select an entire column, position the mouse pointer over the top edge of the top cell of a column until it changes to ↓, then click.

1. **Point to the left of the first row of the table so that the pointer changes to ↗, then click**

   The first row of the table is selected. Any formatting settings you choose at this point will be applied to all the cells in the first row. You decide that you want the row of column headings to be shaded a different color.

2. **Click the Borders and Shading group on the Formatting Palette**

   The Borders and Shading group opens, as shown in Figure H-6.

3. **Click the Fill color button list arrow ⬛ in the Borders and Shading group, then click the blue color that is the fifth option in the first row under Theme Colors (the ScreenTip reads "Accent 1")**

   The background fill color of the cells in the first row changes to a blue that matches the Heading 1 font color used in the document.

4. **Select the bottom four rows of the table, click the Border Type button list arrow ⬛ in the Borders and Shading group, then click the All Borders button ⊞**

   A thick border is applied around all cells in the selected rows.

5. **Click the Line Weight list arrow in the Borders and Shading group, then click ½ pt**

   The border of the selected cells becomes thinner.

6. **Click the Border Color button list arrow ⬛, then click the Accent 1 blue color in the first row under Theme Colors**

   The border changes to the same blue used as the background color in the first row of the table.

QUICK TIP

Double-clicking the vertical gridline automatically adjusts the column to the width of its widest entry.

7. **Position the mouse pointer just to the left of DVD Title in the top row of the table until the pointer changes to ↔, drag ↔ to the left until the vertical line that appears aligns with 1¼" on the ruler, then release the mouse button**

   The width of the second column increases and the first column is narrowed.

QUICK TIP

You can also adjust the heights of table rows by dragging the row borders up or down.

8. **Position the mouse pointer just to the left of In Stock Date in the top row of the table until the pointer changes to ↔, drag ↔ to the right until the vertical line that appears aligns with 3¾" on the ruler, then release the mouse button**

   The width of the second column increases again so that all DVD titles now fit on one line instead of two, and the third column is narrower.

9. **Position the mouse pointer just to the left of Price in the top row of the table until the pointer changes to ↔, drag ↔ to the right until the vertical line that appears aligns with 5" on the ruler, then release the mouse button**

   The width of the third column increases so that the title "In Stock Date" now fits on one line instead of two, and the last column is narrower.

10. **Click outside the table, then save your changes**

    The Table group disappears from the Formatting Palette. Compare your screen to Figure H-7.

Adding Special Elements to a Document

FIGURE H-6: Borders and Shading group options

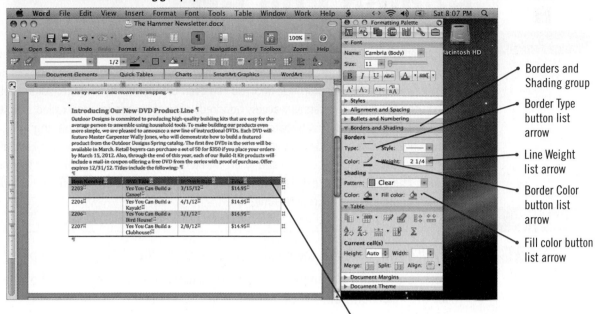

Borders and Shading group

Border Type button list arrow

Line Weight list arrow

Border Color button list arrow

Fill color button list arrow

Selected row

FIGURE H-7: Reformatted table

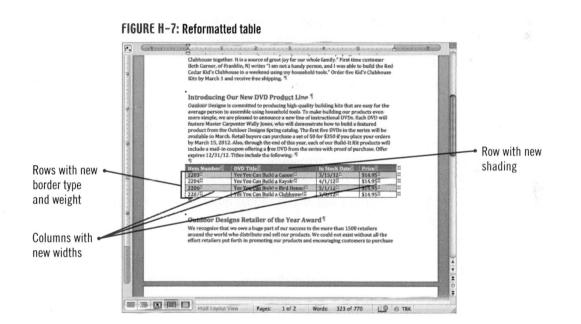

Rows with new border type and weight

Columns with new widths

Row with new shading

Adding SmartArt

Microsoft Office 2008 for Mac offers many tools for adding graphics to your documents to enhance their visual appeal and better communicate your message. **SmartArt** is a new feature that lets you easily create professional looking business diagrams such as organizational charts, process diagrams, and timelines. To create a SmartArt graphic, click the SmartArt Graphics tab in the Elements Gallery. The Elements Gallery opens with the SmartArt Graphics groups and thumbnails visible. Click the SmartArt group from which you want to choose a graphic, then click the SmartArt thumbnail you'd like to insert. The SmartArt Graphic is inserted in your document at the insertion point. Simply edit the placeholder text in the graphic to suit your needs.

Adding Clip Art

You can insert many different types of graphics into your documents to help illustrate a point or to enhance the overall appeal of a document. You can insert images from files stored on disk or downloaded from the Web, you can add SmartArt graphics, and you can even draw your own images using tools on the Object Palette on the Toolbox. You can also access hundreds of ready-made images, called **clip art**, via the **Clip Gallery**. The Clip Gallery lets you search for clip art, animations, videos, and photographs, all called **clips**. Word searches the clip art folders on your hard drive and displays the search results as small pictures called **thumbnails**. Once you select a clip and insert it in a document, you can enhance it by applying Picture Styles to it, change the way text wraps around it, move it, or resize it. You decide to add to the Kayak story an image that represents time.

STEPS

QUICK TIP

To search the Microsoft Clip Art database online, click the Online button at the bottom of the Clip Gallery, then click Yes to launch your default browser.

1. **Scroll down to display the heading** Time to Order Kayak Kits! **and the paragraph below it**

2. **Click to the right of the period following the word** details **at the end of the paragraph to set the insertion point, click** Insert **on the menu bar, point to** Picture, **then click** Clip Art
   The Clip Gallery opens.

3. **In the Search box, type** time, **then press** [return]
   The **Clip Gallery** displays thumbnail previews of all available images that are associated with the word "time." The clip art images available in the Clip Gallery are stored as part of the Microsoft Office program files.

TROUBLE

If the image shown in the figure does not appear in the Search Results area, click a different image.

4. **Click the** image **shown in Figure H-8, then click** Insert
   The image is inserted in the document after the last word of the paragraph.

5. **Click the** image **in the document**
   Round sizing handles on the corners and square sizing handles on the sides of the image indicate that the image is selected. Additional contextual groups appear on the Formatting Palette.

6. **Click the** Wrapping group **on the Formatting Palette to open it**
   The bottom edge of the image you inserted is currently aligned with the paragraph mark at the end of the paragraph because the graphic's **wrapping style**, or the settings for how text flows in relation to the graphic, is set to be inline with the text. An **inline graphic** is a graphic that is part of a line of text.

7. **Click the** Text Wrapping button **to the right of Style in the Wrapping group, then click** Square
   The text now wraps around the image in a square shape. However, the image does not look good in this location; you need to move it.

QUICK TIP

You can move a selected image in small increments by using the arrow keys.

8. **Point to the image so the pointer changes to** ✥, **then drag the** image **so it is positioned in the lower-left corner of the Kayak Kits paragraph, above the last line in the paragraph, as shown in Figure H-9**
   The image's left edge should be left-aligned with the paragraph text. Because you set the wrapping style to square, the image is now a **floating image**, which means you can drag it anywhere on the page.

TROUBLE

To resize an image, click and drag a sizing handle on the corner of the image's frame inward to decrease the image's size or outward to increase the image's size.

9. **In the Quick Styles and Effects group on the Formatting Palette, click the** fourth Quick Style (Drop Shadow Rectangle) **in the first row**
   A drop shadow is added to the image. Compare your screen to Figure H-10.

10. **Click on any text to deselect the image, then save your changes**
    When the image is deselected, the contextual groups disappear from the Formatting Palette.

Adding Special Elements to a Document

FIGURE H-8: Clip Gallery with "time" search results

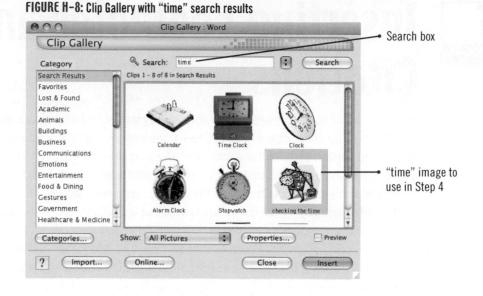

Search box

"time" image to use in Step 4

FIGURE H-9: Clip art repositioned with wrapping style set to Square

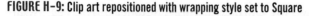
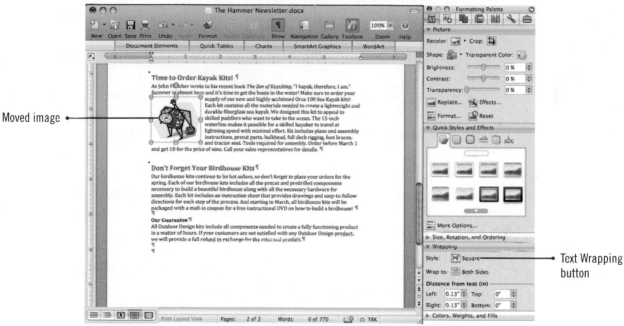

Moved image

Text Wrapping button

FIGURE H-10: Image with Quick Style applied

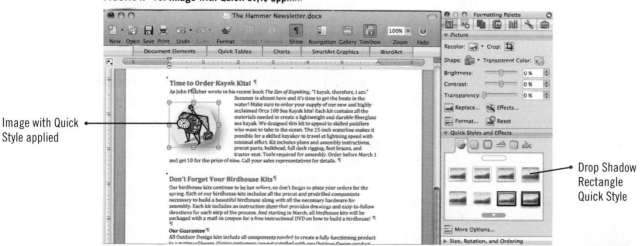

Image with Quick Style applied

Drop Shadow Rectangle Quick Style

Adding Special Elements to a Document

Inserting Footnotes and Citations

If your document contains references to other source material, you might want to add footnotes or endnotes. A **footnote** is a note or citation that appears at the bottom of a document page. An **endnote** is a note or citation that appears at the end of a document. Use an endnote when you don't want to interrupt the flow of text with a footnote. Both footnotes and endnotes contain two linked parts: the **reference mark** (usually a number or symbol) in a document and the corresponding note text. Word 2008 also makes it very easy to create a **bibliography**, which is a list of citations that is usually placed at the end of a document. A bibliography is made up of citations to sources that you add as you are working. Once you have entered all your sources, you can then use the Elements Gallery to insert a bibliography. You need to add a footnote and a citation for a quote to your newsletter, and you plan to insert a bibliography at the bottom of page 2.

STEPS

1. **Scroll up so you can see the Outdoor Designs Retailer of the Year Award heading and the paragraph below it, click to the right of the word details at the end of the paragraph, click Insert on the menu bar, then click Footnote**

   The Footnote and Endnote dialog box opens with the default options selected, as shown in Figure H-11.

QUICK TIP

To delete a footnote from a document, select the footnote reference mark in the body of the text and delete it. Any remaining footnotes are renumbered automatically.

2. **Click OK**

   The insertion point moves to the bottom of the page, in the footnote. The number 1 is inserted at the beginning of the footnote, and a 1 is also added next to the word "details" as the footnote reference mark.

3. **Type Retailers who are family members of Outdoor Designs employees are not eligible to receive this award.**

   This text is added to the footnote at the bottom of the page.

4. **Scroll up so that Time to Order Kayak Kits! and the paragraph below it are visible, click at the end of the sentence "I kayak, therefore I am.", after the closing quote but before the space symbol, then click the Citations tab on the Toolbox**

   The Citations tool opens, as shown in Figure H-12. You want to cite the book where this quote came from.

QUICK TIP

MLA is a popular style used for citations in professional and academic publications.

5. **Click the Citation Style arrows in the Citations tool, click MLA, then click the Create New Source button + at the bottom of the Citations tool**

   The Create New Source dialog box opens. By default, Book is selected in the Type of Source text box.

6. **In the Author text box, type John Fletcher, press [tab], type The Zen of Kayaking in the Title text box, press [tab], type Chicago in the City text box, press [tab], type IL in the State/Province text box, press [tab] twice, type Rapids Press in the Publisher text box, press [tab], type 2008 in the Year text box, compare your screen to Figure H-13, then click OK**

   The Create New Source dialog box closes, the new source appears in the Citations List in the Citations tool, and a reference to the new source is inserted after the quote as (Fletcher).

7. **Press [⌘] [End] to move the insertion point to the end of the document, click the Document Elements tab in the Elements Gallery, then click the Bibliographies group**

8. **Click the right scroll arrow on the right side of the Elements Gallery to move to page 2 if necessary, then click Works Cited**

   Under a new Works Cited heading below the last paragraph in the document, Word inserts the bibliographic information for the source that you added, formatted according to MLA style.

9. **Click the Gallery button, click the Formatting Palette tab on the Toolbox, then save your changes**

   Compare your screen to Figure H-14.

FIGURE H-11: Footnote and Endnote dialog box

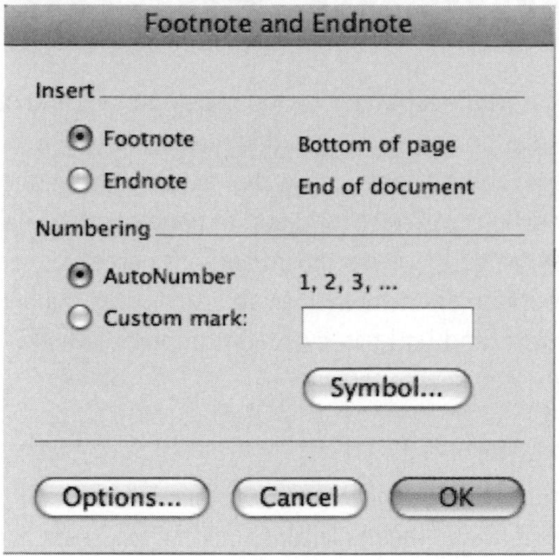

Footnote and Endnote

Insert

○ Footnote   Bottom of page

○ Endnote   End of document

Numbering

● AutoNumber   1, 2, 3, ...

○ Custom mark: [   ]

[Symbol...]

[Options...] [Cancel] [OK]

FIGURE H-12: Citations tool

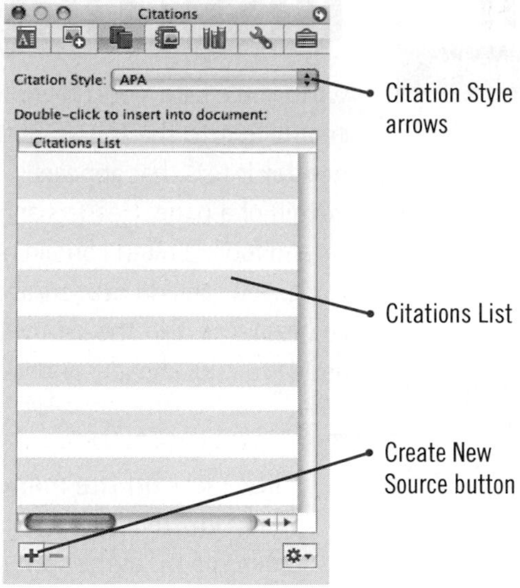

Citations

Citation Style: APA — Citation Style arrows

Double-click to insert into document:

Citations List — Citations List

Create New Source button

FIGURE H-13: Create New Source dialog box with source information entered

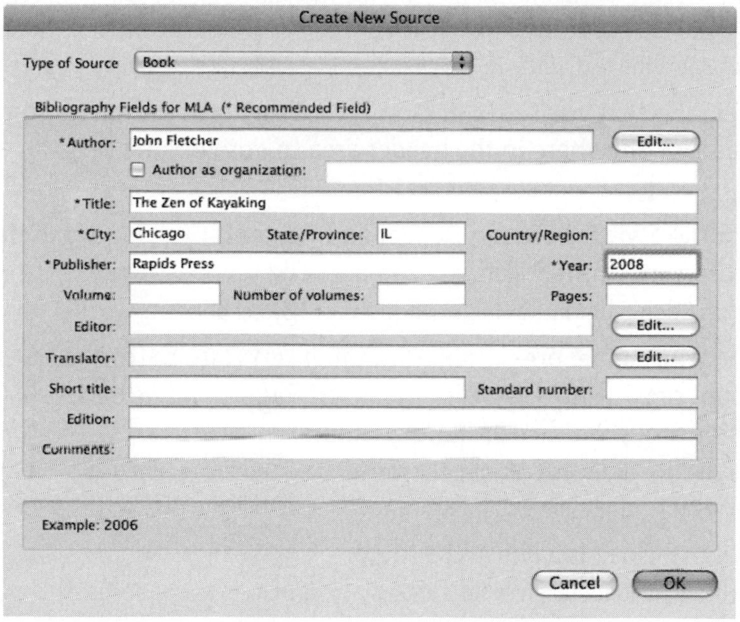

Create New Source

Type of Source   Book

Bibliography Fields for MLA (* Recommended Field)

* Author: John Fletcher   [Edit...]

☐ Author as organization: [   ]

* Title: The Zen of Kayaking

* City: Chicago   State/Province: IL   Country/Region: [   ]

* Publisher: Rapids Press   * Year: 2008

Volume: [   ]   Number of volumes: [   ]   Pages: [   ]

Editor: [   ]   [Edit...]

Translator: [   ]   [Edit...]

Short title: [   ]   Standard number: [   ]

Edition: [   ]

Comments: [   ]

Example: 2006

[Cancel] [OK]

FIGURE H-14: Newsletter with footnote and bibliography added

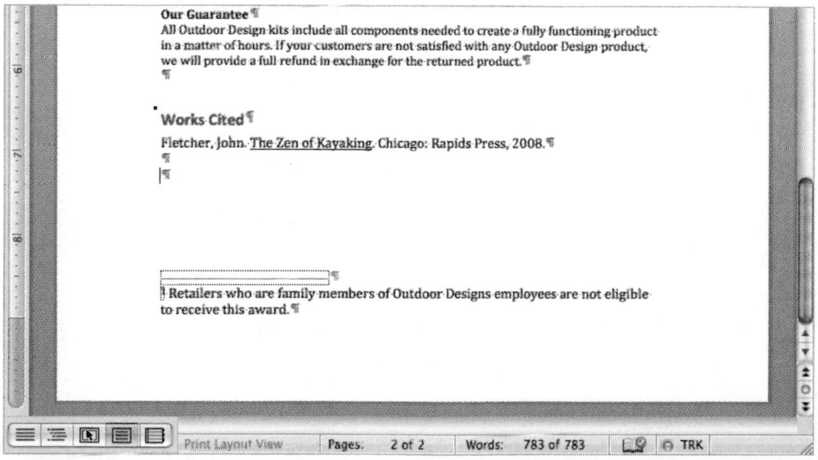

Our Guarantee
All Outdoor Design kits include all components needed to create a fully functioning product
in a matter of hours. If your customers are not satisfied with any Outdoor Design product,
we will provide a full refund in exchange for the returned product.

Works Cited

Fletcher, John. The Zen of Kayaking. Chicago: Rapids Press, 2008.

Retailers who are family members of Outdoor Designs employees are not eligible
to receive this award.

Print Layout View   Pages: 2 of 2   Words: 783 of 783   TRK

Word 2008

Inserting a Header or Footer

When you create a document that contains several pages, you might want to add page numbers and other information to the top or bottom of the pages. You can do this easily by adding headers or footers. A **header** is text that appears in the top margin of a page, and a **footer** is text that appears in the bottom margin of a page. Headers and footers usually appear on every page. In addition to page numbers, headers and footers often contain other information such as the date, the document author's name, or the filename. You can add headers and footers using the View option on the menu bar. You can format the header and footer text in the same way you format regular text, and you can even add graphics. You decide to add a header and footer to the second page of the newsletter.

STEPS

QUICK TIP

You can also open the header or footer by double-clicking in the header or footer area in a document in Print Layout view.

1. **Click** View **on the menu bar, then click** Header and Footer

   The header and footer areas open, the insertion point moves to the header area, and the Header and Footer group appears in the open position on the Formatting Palette.

2. **Type** The Hammer, **press [tab], type** Outdoor Designs Newsletter, **press [tab], then type** Spring 2012

   When you press [tab] the first time, the insertion point moves to a preset center tab that centers the text at 3" on the ruler. When you press [tab] the second time, the insertion point moves to a preset right tab that right-aligns the text at the right margin.

QUICK TIP

When working in a header or footer, the text of the main document appears dimmed, indicating that you cannot edit it.

3. **Select the** text **you typed in Step 2, click the** Italic button *I* **on the Formatting Palette, then click anywhere in the header area to deselect the text**

   The header text is now italicized. See Figure H-15.

4. **Click the** Switch Between Header and Footer button **in the Header and Footer group on the Formatting Palette**

   The insertion point moves to the left side of the footer area.

QUICK TIP

You can see headers and footers only in Print Layout view and Print Preview; you cannot see headers and footers in Draft view or Outline view.

5. **Type** your name, **press [tab], click the** Insert Date button **in the Header and Footer group, press [tab], then click the** Insert Page Number button **in the Header and Footer group on the Formatting Palette**

   Your name is at the left margin, the current date appears centered at 3" on the ruler, and the page number appears at the right margin. Compare your screen to Figure H-16.

6. **Click the** Close tab **above the footer**

   The header and footer areas close and appear dimmed on your document.

TROUBLE

If Print Preview does not display both pages, click the Multiple Pages button on the Print Preview toolbar, then click 1 × 2 Pages.

7. **Click** File **on the menu bar, click** Print Preview, **then compare your screen to Figure H-17**

   The header and footer do not appear on the first page but do appear on the second page.

8. **Click** Close **on the Print Preview toolbar, then save your changes**

Adding Special Elements to a Document

FIGURE H-15: Text entered in header area

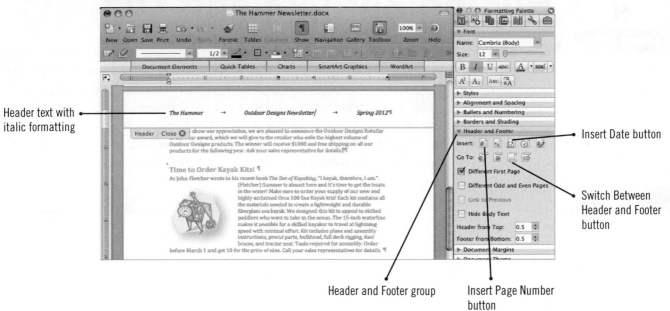

Header text with italic formatting

Insert Date button

Switch Between Header and Footer button

Header and Footer group

Insert Page Number button

FIGURE H-16: Text entered in footer area

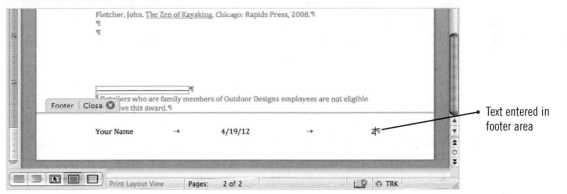

Text entered in footer area

FIGURE H-17: Newsletter in Print Preview showing header and footer on second page

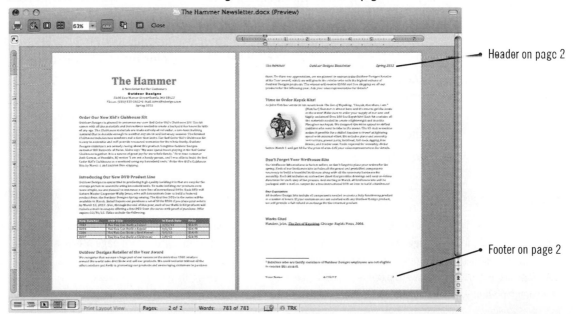

Header on page 2

Footer on page 2

Adding Borders and Shading

You can add borders and background shading to words, paragraphs, graphics, or entire pages to enhance a document. Borders and shading can add visual interest to an entire document and can also help to set a block of text apart from the rest of the page. To add these elements to an entire page, you can use the Borders and Shading dialog box; to add them to selected text, it's easiest to use the Borders and Shading group on the Formatting Palette. You can add borders to the top, bottom, left, or right edges of text or a graphic. You decide to add a border to each page of the newsletter. Also, to set it off from the rest of the newsletter text, you plan to add borders and shading to the "Our Guarantee" paragraph at the bottom of the second page.

STEPS

1. **Press [⌘] [home]**
   The insertion point moves to the top of page one of the document.

2. **Click Format on the menu bar, then click Borders and Shading**
   The Borders and Shading dialog box opens.

3. **Click the Page Border tab in the Borders and Shading dialog box**
   You use the Page Border tab when you want to add a border to each page of a document.

4. **In the Setting section, click Box, then scroll down in the Style list and click the first double line style**
   This will add a box-style double line border to the page. You can also specify a color and thickness for the border.

5. **Click the Color arrows, click the dark blue color in the first row under Theme Colors (the ScreenTip reads "Text 2"), click the Width arrows, click ½ pt if necessary, compare your screen to Figure H-18, then click OK**
   A blue, double-lined border now appears around both pages of the document.

6. **Scroll down so that the last paragraph on page 2 is visible, then select the heading Our Guarantee and the paragraph below it**

7. **Click the Borders and Shading group on the Formatting Palette to open the group if necessary, click the Fill color button list arrow ⬥ ▾ in the Shading area, then click the blue color in the fourth row, fifth column under Theme Colors (the ScreenTip reads "Accent 1, Lighter 60%"), as shown in Figure H-19**
   The Our Guarantee heading and paragraph now have a light blue background.

8. **Click the Border Type button list arrow ⊞ ▾ in the Borders and Shading group, click the Outside Border button ⊡, click the Border Color button list arrow ✎ ▾ in the Borders category, click the darker blue color in the first row of Theme Colors (the ScreenTip reads "Text 2"), then click anywhere in the document**
   The Our Guarantee heading and paragraph now have a dark blue outer border. Compare your screen to Figure H-20.

9. **Save your changes**

Inserting manual page breaks

When you work on a document that is more than one page long, Word automatically inserts a **page break** when you come to the end of a page. Sometimes these automatic page breaks, which are called **soft page breaks**, occur in awkward places—such as in the middle of a paragraph that you'd prefer to keep on one page. Fortunately, you can control where a page ends by inserting a manual page break, also called a **hard page break**, at any point. To do this, click where you want the page to end, click Insert on the menu bar, point to Break, then click Page Break.

FIGURE H-18: Page Border tab of Borders and Shading dialog box

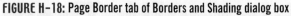

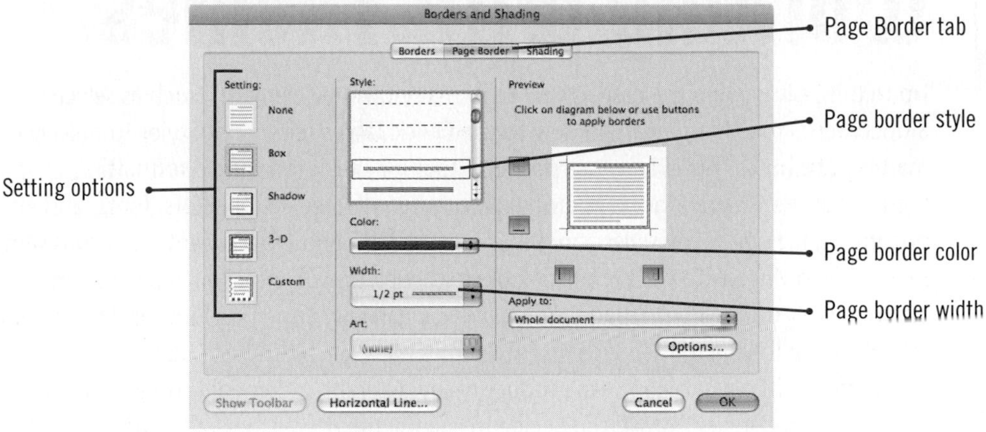

Borders and Shading
Borders
Page Border
Shading
Setting:
None
Box
Shadow
3-D
Custom
Style:
Color:
Width:
1/2 pt
Art:
Preview
Click on diagram below or use buttons to apply borders
Apply to:
Whole document
Options...
Show Toolbar
Horizontal Line...
Cancel
OK
Page Border tab
Page border style
Setting options
Page border color
Page border width

FIGURE H-19: Fill color options for selected paragraphs

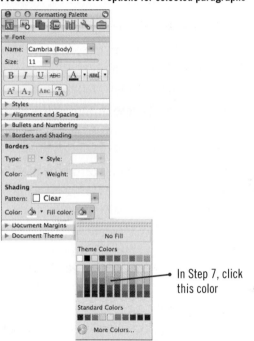

Formatting Palette
Font
Name: Cambria (Body)
Size: 11
Styles
Alignment and Spacing
Bullets and Numbering
Borders and Shading
Borders
Type:
Style:
Color:
Weight:
Shading
Pattern: Clear
Color:
Fill color:
Document Margins
Document Theme
No Fill
Theme Colors
Standard Colors
More Colors...
In Step 7, click this color

FIGURE H-20: Paragraph with border and shading applied

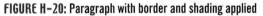

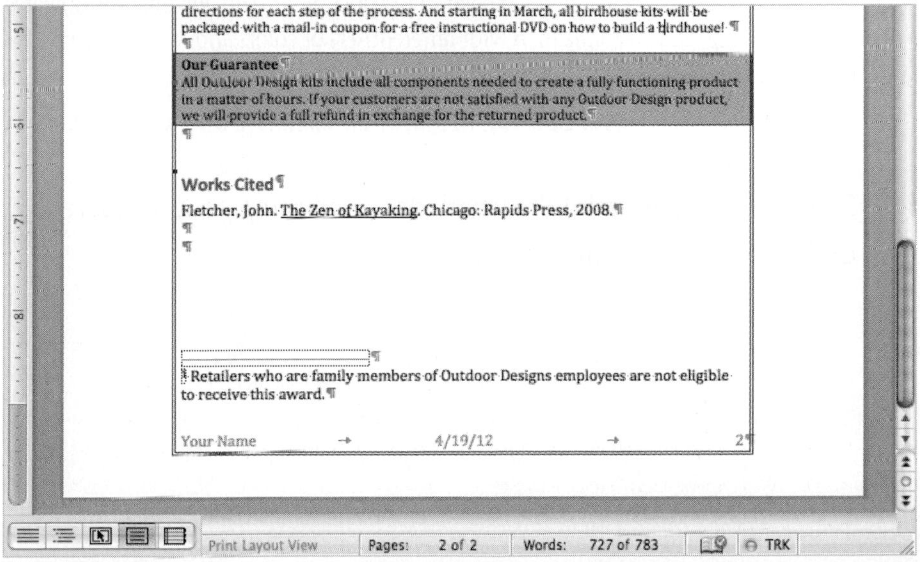

directions for each step of the process. And starting in March, all birdhouse kits will be packaged with a mail-in coupon for a free instructional DVD on how to build a birdhouse!
Our Guarantee
All Outdoor Design kits include all components needed to create a fully functioning product in a matter of hours. If your customers are not satisfied with any Outdoor Design product, we will provide a full refund in exchange for the returned product.
Works Cited
Fletcher, John. The Zen of Kayaking. Chicago: Rapids Press, 2008.
Retailers who are family members of Outdoor Designs employees are not eligible to receive this award.
Your Name
4/19/12
2
Print Layout View
Pages: 2 of 2
Words: 727 of 783
TRK

Working with Themes

Up to this point, you have learned how to format individual elements, such as selected text or an object, in a document. You've also learned how to use Quick Tables and Quick Styles to quickly create or apply formatting attributes. An even more powerful tool for making multiple formatting changes at once is the themes feature. Changing the **theme** applies a coordinated set of colors, fonts, and effects to your entire document, including any styles applied. This ensures that your document has a consistent and professional look, while giving you a wide range of looks from which to choose. You apply a theme using the Document Theme group on the Formatting Palette, and you can vary a theme's fonts and colors by applying different sets of theme fonts and theme colors. All themes are available in Word, Excel, PowerPoint, and Entourage, which means that a company can produce many different documents and ensure that they all have a consistent, branded look. You decide to change the overall look of the newsletter by applying a theme to it. You also want to explore different sets of theme fonts and theme colors to find the perfect combination for this document.

STEPS

1. **Click the Zoom list arrow on the Standard toolbar, then click 50%**
   With the zoom set at 50%, both pages appear side by side in the document window, so you can see at a glance how your changes will affect the whole document.

2. **Click the Document Theme group on the Formatting Palette**
   The Document Theme group opens. As shown in Figure H-21, available themes are displayed as thumbnails. Additional color and font options are also available.

3. **Click the down arrow at the bottom of the Themes gallery seven times, then click the Module theme thumbnail**
   As you point to each thumbnail, a ScreenTip appears with the name of the theme. The Module theme is applied to the newsletter, which, with its different font sizes and spacing, makes the newsletter extend to a third page.

4. **Click the Colors list arrow in the Document Theme group**
   A list opens that displays all the sets of theme colors (color schemes) you can apply to any theme. By default, the Office set is in effect.

5. **Scroll down if necessary, then click Equity, as shown in Figure H-22**

6. **Click the Fonts list arrow in the Document Theme group, point to the arrow at the bottom of the Fonts list to scroll down the list, then click Opulent**
   The Opulent set of theme fonts is applied to the document. The document is now two pages. By applying a different theme and customizing it with different sets of colors and fonts, you have completely transformed the look of the newsletter in just a few clicks.

7. **Change the zoom level back to 100%, then click the Show button ¶ to hide the formatting marks**

8. **Save your changes, print the newsletter, then compare it to Figure H-23**

9. **Close the document, then quit Word**

QUICK TIP

You can create your own customized themes. To do this, change the formatting of any elements you want (such as the font used in headings), click the Save Theme button in the Document Theme group on the Formatting Palette, type a name for the theme, then click Save. The new theme will appear at the top of the Themes gallery and will be available for you to apply to other documents.

Adding Special Elements to a Document

FIGURE H-21: Zoom changed to 50% and Document Theme group open

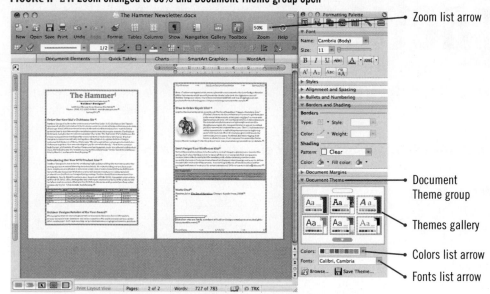

Zoom list arrow

Document Theme group

Themes gallery

Colors list arrow

Fonts list arrow

FIGURE H-22: Equity theme colors applied to document

Module theme and Equity theme colors applied

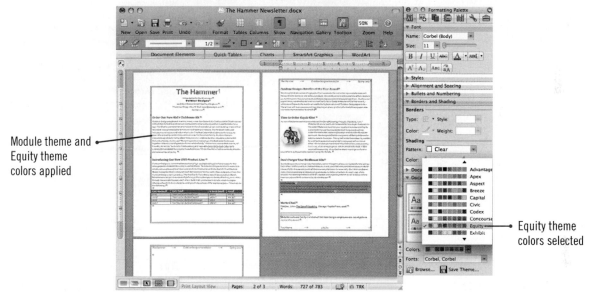

Equity theme colors selected

FIGURE H-23: Finished newsletter with Module theme, Equity theme colors, and Opulent theme fonts applied

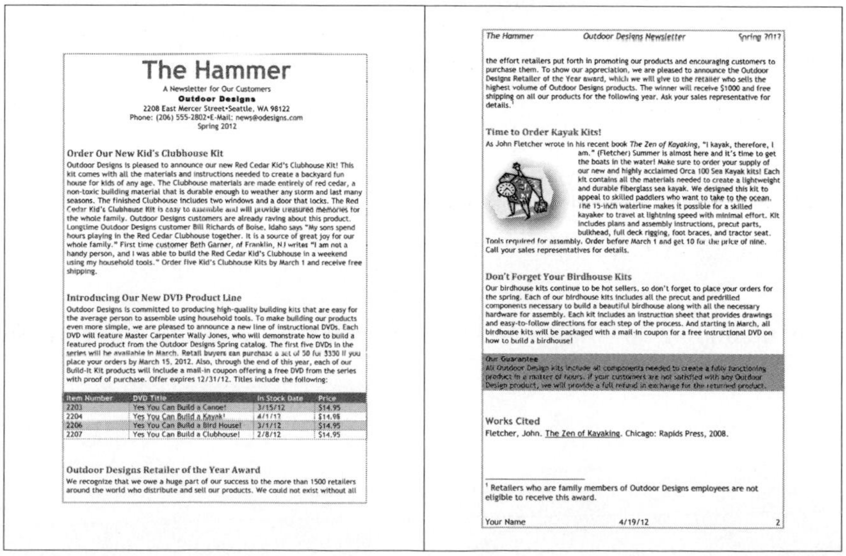

Practice

▼ CONCEPTS REVIEW

Label the Word window and Toolbox elements shown in Figures H-24.

FIGURE H-24

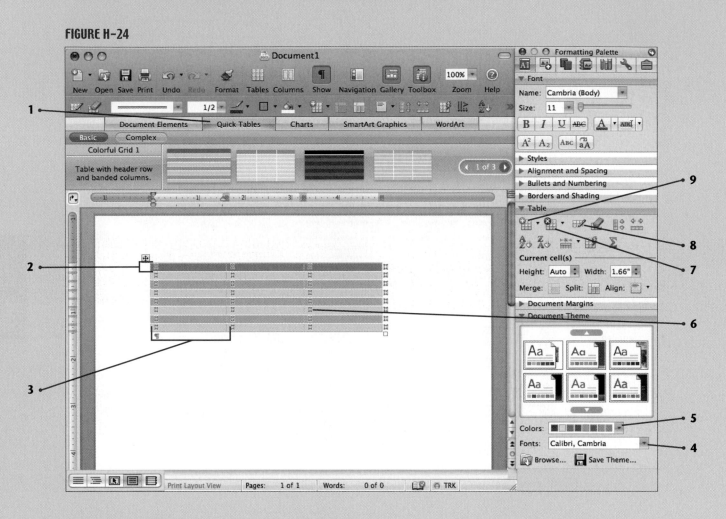

Select the best answer from the list of choices.

10. Clip art is found in the:
   a. Clip Gallery.
   b. Clip Art task pane.
   c. Images folder.
   d. Data files folder.

11. Which option on the menu bar do you use to insert a header or footer in a document?
   a. Edit
   b. View
   c. Insert
   d. Format

12. Borders can be applied to:

   a. document pages.

   b. selected text.

   c. selected paragraphs.

   d. all of the above.

13. In Office 2008 for Mac, a theme is:

   a. a coordinated set of colors, fonts, and effects that can be applied to a document.

   b. available only in Word.

   c. a distinctive font.

   d. a characteristic of a font effect.

14. Which of the following is NOT true about applying a theme?

   a. Themes are applied across an entire document.

   b. Themes are applied only to text that you select in a document.

   c. You can choose from several theme font sets and theme color sets to customize a theme.

   d. Themes ensure that your documents have a consistent, professional look.

▼ SKILLS REVIEW

1. Create a table.

   a. Start Microsoft Word, open the file H-2.docx from where you store your Data Files, then save the new document as **Walking Adventures Newsletter**.

   b. Place the insertion point at the end of the second paragraph on the first page, to the right of the colon following the word "trips", then press [return] twice.

   c. Insert the Colorful Grid 1 Quick Table.

   d. Enter the information shown in the table below into the table you created.

Tour Name	Start Date	Destinations
Great Northwest Walking Adventure	9/15/12	Seattle and Victoria, BC
Vermont Leaves Walking Adventure	10/1/12	Burlington, VT
Canyon Walking Adventure	10/15/12	Bryce, UT
Canyon Walking Adventure II	11/1/12	Bryce, UT

   e. Format the title of the document, Classic Walking Adventures News, in bold.

   f. Save your changes to the document.

2. Insert and delete table columns and rows.

   a. Insert a new row below the row that contains the column headings, then insert the following in the new cells:
   Great Northwest Walking Adventure   9/1/12   Seattle and Victoria, BC

   b. Delete the row that contains the September 15 Great Northwest Walking Adventure.

   c. Insert two new columns to the right of the Destinations column.

   d. Insert the information from the table at right into the new columns.

   e. Delete the last 3 blank rows of the table.

   f. Save your changes.

End Date	Price
9/5/12	$1795
10/5/12	$1495
10/21/12	$1895
11/6/12	$2095

3. Format a table.

   a. Decrease the width of the fifth column so that it starts at 5½" on the ruler.

   b. Decrease the width of the fourth column so that it starts at 4½" on the ruler.

   c. Decrease the width of the third column so that it starts at 3½" on the ruler.

   d. Decrease the width of the second column so that it starts at 2½" on the ruler.

   e. Select the bottom four rows of the table, apply the All Borders border type to the rows, then, if necessary, change the border color to the dark blue color in the first row under Theme Colors (Text 2) and the border weight to ½ pt.

   f. Save your changes.

4. Add clip art.

  a. Scroll to the second page of the newsletter, then set the insertion point before the word "If" in the paragraph text below the heading Don't Miss Our Literary Walking Adventure.

  b. Open the Clip Gallery, then search for an image of a **book**.

  c. Insert the image shown in Figure H-25, or a similar one.

  d. Set the wrapping style of the image to Square.

  e. Drag the image as necessary so that its top edge is positioned just below the first line of paragraph text and its left edge is aligned with the left margin.

  f. Save your changes.

FIGURE H-25

5. Insert footnotes and citations.

  a. Scroll up so that the paragraph above the table is visible.

  b. Set the insertion point to the right of the word "prices" in the next to last line of paragraph text above the table.

  c. Insert a footnote.

  d. Type the following text as footnote text: **Prices do not include transportation costs to the destination city.**

  e. Scroll to page two so that the heading Don't Miss Our Literary Walking Adventure! and the paragraph below it are visible.

  f. Set the insertion point after the closing quotation mark that follows the word "trail" near the end of the paragraph, then use the Citations tool to add a new source.

  g. Enter the following information in the Create New Source dialog box:
Author: **Ralph Waldo Emerson**
Title: **The Essential Writings of Ralph Waldo Emerson**
City: **New York**
State: **NY**
Publisher: **Modern Library**
Year: **2000**

  h. Close the Create New Source dialog box and scroll to the last blank line of the document.

  i. At the end of the document, use the Document Elements tab in the Elements Gallery to insert a Works Cited list. (Don't worry if this action creates a third page; you will fix this in a later step.)

  j. Save your changes.

6. Insert a header or footer.

  a. Click to place the insertion point on page two in the document, if necessary.

  b. Insert a header.

  c. Type **Classic Walking Adventures News** in the header area, press [tab] twice, then type **Fall 2012**.

  d. Format the header text in italic.

  e. Switch to the footer.

  f. Type your name at the left margin, press [tab], insert today's date, press [tab], then insert the page number.

  g. Format the footer text in italic.

  h. In the Header and Footer group on the Formatting Palette, click the check box for Different First Page. Selecting this option puts the header and footer on all pages except page one.

  i. Close the footer area, then save your changes.

7. Add borders and shading.

  a. Use the Borders and Shading dialog box to apply a page border with blue (Text 2), single-line, ½ pt width Box style page border to all pages.

  b. Select the heading About Classic Walking Adventures, Inc. and the paragraph below it at the bottom of page two, then apply a blue (Text 2), outside border around it.

Adding Special Elements to a Document

c. Apply light blue fill color to the selected text using Blue (Text 2, Lighter 40%).

d. Save your changes.

8. Work with themes.

a. Set the zoom level of the document to 50% so that you can see all three pages of the newsletter.

b. Apply the Solstice theme to the document.

c. Apply the Flow theme colors set to the document.

d. Apply the Inkwell theme fonts set to the document.

e. If necessary, delete any extra blank lines at the end of the document so that the document fits on two pages.

f. Change the zoom level back to 100%.

g. Save your changes, print the document and compare your printout to Figure H-26, then close the document and quit Word.

FIGURE H-26

Classic Walking Adventures News
55 Hawkins Road
Oakland, CA 94601
Phone (510) 555-9865
www.classicwalkingadventures.com
Fall 2012

Autumn is Here!

Hello! We hope you had a carefree, relaxing summer. After all that lounging around the pool or the beach, it's time to get out the walking shoes and sign up for another Classic Walking Adventure! Whether you've experienced one of our walking adventures before or whether you are considering trekking out with us for the first time, we have a walking adventure that is just right for you. We offer cultural tours to more than ten destinations around the United States. Visit us on the Web for a complete listing of our exciting trips. Happy adventures!

New Fall Walking Adventures

We are pleased to announce three exciting new tours for the Fall of 2012. First, if you like the Pacific Northwest, you will want to sign up for our **Great Northwest Walking Adventure**. This 6-day trip begins in Seattle, where we will explore the city sights by foot and Puget Sound by sea kayaks. We will then take a ferry to Victoria, British Columbia and spend two nights there walking and enjoying the beauty of Canada. Second, if you enjoy the historic and picturesque atmosphere of New England, you should consider signing up for our **Vermont Leaves Walking Adventure**. During this 4-day trip we will stay in a lovely bed and breakfast in Burlington, Vermont and take daily walks to enjoy all that Burlington has to offer. Finally, if you are in the mood for canyons, consider joining us for one of our **Canyon Walking Adventures**. In this 6-day adventure, we will explore the spectacular scenery in Bryce, Grand Canyon, and Zion. Two are scheduled for this fall! See the table below for information on start and end dates and prices[1] for all three trips:

Tour Name	Start Date	Destinations	End Date	Price
Great Northwest Walking Adventure	9/1/12	Seattle and Victoria, BC	9/5/12	$1795
Vermont Leaves Walking Adventure	10/1/12	Burlington, VT	10/5/12	$1495
Canyon Walking Adventure	10/15/12	Bryce, UT	10/21/12	$1895
Canyon Walking Adventure II	11/1/12	Bryce, UT	11/6/12	$2095

[1] Prices do not include transportation costs to the destination city.

Classic Walking Adventures News   *Fall 2012*

Introducing Culinary Walking Adventures

We are pleased to announce plans to introduce Culinary Walking Adventures in the Summer of 2013! Our first Culinary Walking Adventure will take us to the culinary region of Tuscany, where we will enjoy walks in the Italian countryside by day and experience the flavors of the region as we go. You will experience the legendary food of the region by visiting hotel kitchen, and getting group cooking lessons from a series of local chefs. Don't miss this first special culinary adventure! It is sure to be a mouth watering experience!

Walking on the Maine Coast

If you like salt air, mountains, lush natural settings, and picturesque New England beaches with lighthouses, then you will love our Maine Coast Tour. This seven day tour is ideal for those who are new to walking adventures and want to start out with a relaxed, fun experience. We will start our trip in Boothbay Harbor and venture to Camden. We will enjoy days of kayaking and exploring the many coves and inlets along the rocky Maine coast. We will spend one night aboard a schooner singing songs of the sea and listening to tales of old sea captains. We will also enjoy an old fashioned clambake on Monhegan Island, where we will watch seals playing along the beach. To sign up for this trip or to find out more information about it, visit our Web site at classicwalkingadventures.com.

Don't Miss Our Literary Walking Adventure!

If you like literature and reading the great works of the Transcendentalists, then sign up soon for our first ever Literary Walking Adventure in Concord, Massachusetts. In this adventure, we will visit Orchard House, the home of Louisa May Alcott, author of the classic American novel *Little Women*. We will also visit Walden Pond and discuss the writings of Thoreau and Emerson, and take in many historic sites in the area. As Ralph Waldo Emerson once wrote "Do not go where the path may lead, go instead where there is no path and leave a trail." (Emerson) So why not sign up today! This adventure starts October 15 and ends October 18.

About Classic Walking Adventures, Inc.

Classic Walking Adventure Tours was founded in 2001, when Vivian and Alex Simpson decided to turn their love of exploring the world on foot into a tour business. Since then more than 1000 people have participated in a Classic Walking Adventure Tour in the United States, Europe, China, New Zealand, and Australia.

Works Cited

Emerson, Ralph Waldo. The Essential Writings of Ralph Waldo Emerson. New York: Modern Library, 2000.

Your Name   2/1/13   2

▼ INDEPENDENT CHALLENGE 1

You are the new marketing manager at Fiesta Dance Studios, a small studio in Massachusetts that offers dance instruction. You need to create a one-page information sheet for prospective customers. You have a partially completed document that you need to finish. You will add a table containing the class schedule and a bibliography that lists titles of books that key instructors have written.

a. Open the file H-3.docx from where you store your Data Files, then save it as **Dance Studio Info Sheet**.

b. Insert a new line below the heading Class Schedule, then insert the Dark Blue List Quick Table.

c. Add two additional columns to the right side of the table, then enter the information shown in the table below into your table.

Monday	Tuesday	Wednesday	Thursday	Friday
Tap	Jazz Toddlers	Tap	Jazz Toddlers	Tap
Ballet	Hip Hop Moms	Ballet	Hip Hop Moms	Ballet
African Dance	Ballet	African Dance	Ballet	African Dance
Jazz Kids	Brazilian	Jazz Kids	Brazilian	Jazz Kids
Irish Step	Belly Dance	Irish Step	Belly Dance	Irish Step

d. Add a column to the left of the Monday column, then enter the information in the table at right into the new column.

e. Delete the two blank rows at the bottom of the table.

f. Insert a page border of your choosing that looks good with the rest of the document.

g. Search for clip art images using the word **girl**. Insert a clip art image of a young girl jumping, then position it to the right of the paragraph about Ivana Yashenko. Apply the Square text wrapping to it.

Time
9:00
11:00
3:00
5:00
7:00

h. Insert a footer, type your name at the left margin, press [tab], then insert today's date.

i. In the About Our Instructors section, at the end of the paragraph about Ivana Yashenko, add a new citation source in the MLA style about the book that Ivana Yashenko wrote. Enter the following information:
Author: **Ivana Yashenko**
Title: **Easy Dance Steps for Kids**
City: **Chicago**
State: **IL**
Publisher: **Dance Press**
Year: **2003**

j. In the same section, add a new citation source in the MLA style about the book that Calvin Caspar wrote at the end of the paragraph about him. Enter the following information:
Author: **Calvin Caspar**
Title: **Dancing For Life**
City: **Los Angeles**
State: **CA**
Publisher: **Valiant Press**
Year: **2005**

k. Set the insertion point in the last line of the document, then type **Read These Books by Our Instructors**. Use the Format Painter to copy the formatting from the About Our Instructors heading to this new text.

l. On the following line, insert the bibliography for the titles you entered. (*Hint*: Click Document Elements in the Elements Gallery, click the Bibliographies group, then click Bibliography.)

m. Delete the word Bibliography but not the paragraph mark next to it.

n. Close the Elements Gallery.

o. Apply the Trek theme to the document, then apply the Median theme fonts to the document.

p. Apply the Technic theme colors to the document.

q. If necessary, delete any extra blank lines at the end of the document so that the document fits on one page.

r. Save your changes.

Advanced Challenge Exercise

- Move the clip art above the table so that its bottom edge is positioned ½" above the last column in the table. Resize the clip art so the telephone number in the heading does not wrap around the clip art.
- Select the two paragraphs below the heading About Our Instructors.

- Click the Columns button on the Standard toolbar, then click the second column icon in the box under the Columns button.
- Delete the blank line above Calvin Caspar so the columns start on the same line.

s. Save your changes, then close the document.

▼ INDEPENDENT CHALLENGE 2

You are the human resources manager at Paramount Pens, a company located in Los Angeles, California that manufactures high quality writing instruments. A candidate named Hilary Lynch is coming to interview for the position of marketing director. You need to create an interview schedule for Hilary that shows the times of each interview, the names of the interviewers, and the location of each interview.

a. Open the file H-4.docx from where you store your Data Files, then save it as **Interview Schedule**.

Start Time	Interviewer	Job Title	Location
9:30	Sam Jordan	Human Resources Director	#200
10:45	Denny Chow	Vice President, Sales	#417
12:00	Ann Brown	President, CEO	#300
1:30	Lisa Bronson	Marketing Manager	#100

b. Two lines below the first full paragraph, insert a Quick Table with a style of your choosing. (*Hint*: Choose a style that does not have a total row or a differently-formatted first column.)

c. Add an additional column.

d. Enter the information shown in the table above into the new Quick Table.

e. Below the 1:30 row, type another row of information that you make up. Adjust the column widths so that the text fits on one line in each cell.

f. Delete any blank rows at the bottom of the table.

g. At the bottom of the page, add a border around the Paramount Pens, Inc. hiring statement heading and the paragraph below it, and add a background fill color to this text. Format all text using fonts, formatting, alignment, and font styles to make it look attractive.

h. Insert an appropriate piece of clip art somewhere in the document. Resize the clip art as necessary and set a wrapping style to make it attractive and professional.

i. Insert a footnote next to Lisa Bronson's name in the table. The footnote should read **Lisa will take you to lunch at the Goldfish Café.**

j. Insert a footer that contains your name at the left margin.

k. Apply a theme fonts set to the document that you think looks good and is appropriate for this type of document.

l. Save your changes.

Advanced Challenge Exercise

- Click anywhere in the table, then click the Table group on the Formatting Palette to open it if necessary.
- Increase the row height of the 10:45 row to approximately 1".
- Click the Draw Table button in the Table group on the Formatting Palette, then use the pencil pointer to create a new row below the 10:45 row. (*Hint*: Drag from the middle of the left edge of the 10:45 cell all the way to the right edge of the cell containing #417.) When you're finished, click the Draw Table button again to turn off the pencil pointer.
- Adjust the border formatting if necessary so the borders in your new row match the rest of the table.
- Enter the following information in the new row: **11:30**; **Quinn Hartman**; **Vice President, Marketing**; **#415**.
- Adjust the row height of the 10:45 row and the 11:30 row to be the same as all others.
- Adjust the column widths if necessary so the contents of each cell fit on one line.

m. Save, print, and close the document.

▼ INDEPENDENT CHALLENGE 3

Felicia Johnson in the Human Resources Department at Bluebell Organic Products, Inc. has asked you to create a one-page flyer for the annual executive family clambake on August 1, 2012. The clambake will take place at Stinson Beach north of San Francisco from 10:00 a.m. until 5:00 p.m. Lunch will include lobster and clams for adults, hot dogs and hamburgers for children, and build-your-own ice cream sundaes for all. Attendees can spend the day swimming, playing volleyball, and competing in the sandcastle contest. Other activities include a scavenger hunt and children's relay races.

a. Open the file H-5.docx from where you store your Data Files, then save it as **Clambake Flyer**.

b. Format the text in this document so that it reflects the casual, festive nature of the event. Choose fonts, font sizes, and formatting attributes that make the key information stand out. Apply a shaded box around the paragraph text using a fill color and border style you like.

c. Apply a page border around the entire document, choosing a line style, width, and color that make the flyer look professional.

d. Under the paragraph text, insert a Quick Table style of your choosing. (*Hint*: Choose a style that does not have a total row or a differently-formatted first column.)

e. Enter the information shown at right into the new table.

f. Delete any empty rows from the table.

g. Center the table between the left and right margins. (*Hint*: Click Table on the menu bar, click Table Properties, click Center under Alignment in the Table Properties dialog box, then click OK.)

h. Insert an appropriate piece of clip art for the occasion.

i. Insert a footer that contains the text **Bluebell Organics, Inc.** at the left margin, press [tab] twice, then type your name at the right margin.

Activity	Time	Coordinator
Lunch	12:00	Alice Wells
Scavenger hunt	2:00	Lacey Wilkins
Volleyball tournament	3:00	Fred Smith
Softball game	4:00	Ernesto Gonzalez
Sandcastle contest	4:30	Ginny Owens

j. Apply a theme and a theme colors set of your choosing to the document. If necessary, adjust the table's column widths so the contents of each cell fit on one line. Figure H-27 shows one possible solution; yours will vary depending on the formatting choices you made.

k. Save your changes, print the flyer, close the document, then quit Word.

FIGURE H-27

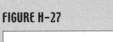

Please come to the

Executive Family Clambake!

Where: Stinson Beach

When: August 1, 2012

Don't miss the annual executive family clambake at Stinson Beach on August 1, 2012! Enjoy a delicious lunch of lobster and clams on the beach and enjoy quality time with your family and colleagues. Compete in a beach volleyball game or sandcastle contest. Or simply enjoy a quiet conversation in a beach chair and enjoy the spectacular setting! See below for a listing of activities!

Activity	Time	Coordinator
Lunch	12:00	Alice Wells
Scavenger hunt	2:00	Lacey Wilkins
Volleyball tournament	3:00	Fred Smith
Softball game	4:00	Ernesto Gonzalez
Sandcastle contest	4:30	Ginny Owens

Bluebell Organics, Inc.   Your Name

▼ REAL LIFE INDEPENDENT CHALLENGE

You and your friends have decided to take a trip to a city somewhere in the world. (You can pick any city you want for this exercise—it's up to you!) You are in charge of identifying five attractions in your chosen city that you want the group to visit while there. You decide to do some research on the Internet. Once you've completed your research, you then need to create an information sheet about your findings that you can give to your friends.

a. Log on to the Internet, then go to a search engine of your choice. Enter keywords appropriate for finding information about tourist attractions for your city (for instance, **London tourist attractions**). Browse the various sites that you find and print out the sites that contain the best information. Circle five attractions on your printouts that you want to recommend to the group.

b. Start Word, then save a new, blank document as **Travel Research** where you store your Data Files.

c. In the first line of the document, type **Tourist Attractions in [your city]**. Format this text in a way that is appropriate for a title, using a font, font size, and alignment that make it look good.

d. Below the document title, insert a Quick Table style of your choosing. (*Hint*: Choose a style that does not have a total row.) In the heading row of the table, type **Attraction** in the first cell and **Description** in the second cell. Complete the table with the information from your research; enter your five attractions in the first column and brief descriptions of the attractions in the cells in the second column.

e. Delete any extra columns or rows.

f. Insert a piece of clip art that relates to your chosen city between the document title and the table. Center-align the clip art. (*Hint*: Click next to the image, then click the Align Center button in the Alignment and Spacing group on the Formatting Palette.) Resize the image if necessary so that it looks good.

g. For any two attractions in your table, add a citation to the Web site where you found the information. In the Create New Source dialog box, choose Web site as your Type of Source. Complete the citations with as much information as you can find; you may need to visit the Web site again to locate information such as the author, and all information may not be available.

h. Two lines below the table, insert a bibliography. Delete the word Bibliography and type **Selected Research Sources** in its place. Format the heading with shading of your choice.

i. Apply a theme to the document that you think looks good.

j. Make sure all of the information fits on one page. Resize the clip art or choose a different theme if necessary to make it all fit.

k. Insert a footer that contains your name at the left margin.

l. Save the document, print it, then close the file.

Open the file H-6.docx from where you store your Data Files, then save it as **Seaside Villa Flyer**. Use the skills you learned in this unit to create the flyer shown in Figure H-28. (*Hint*: Use Trebuchet MS for the headings and Calibri for the body text and table text. Use the Gray Shading 1 Quick Table style. Select a different clip art image if the one shown in the figure is not available to you. Set the wrapping style to Square for the image and apply the Simple Frame, Black Quick Style to it.) Type your name somewhere on the flyer, save your changes, then print the flyer.

FIGURE H-28

Seaside Villa for Rent!

Escape your stress and take in the breathtaking view of Lake Windermere from this English villa. Enjoy water skiing and boating on one of the most popular lakes in England. The exquisite villa features hardwood floors throughout, high-end appliances, and three spacious bedrooms. The living room and master bedroom feature a wood-burning fireplace. A backyard hot tub contains water from hot springs. Water sports, fine dining, and entertainment are within walking distance.

Property Details

Feature	Description
Location	Lake Windermere, Cumbria, England
Weekly rate	$2,000 US
Bedrooms	3
Bathrooms	2.5
Pool	No
Hot tub	Yes

For more details, contact:

Lake Windermere Rentals, Inc.
Lake Road
Windermere
Cumbria, LA23 2JF
Phone: +44 (0) 15394-42622

Your Name

Creating and Enhancing a Worksheet

Files You Will Need:

No files needed.

In this unit, you learn how to create and work with an Excel worksheet. A **worksheet** is an electronic grid that performs numeric calculations. You can use a worksheet for many purposes, such as analyzing sales data, calculating a loan payment, organizing inventory information, and displaying your results in a chart. Using Excel, you create a file called a **workbook**, which can contain one or more worksheets. People sometimes refer to a worksheet or a workbook as a **spreadsheet**, which is a general term for this type of data analysis tool. You can enhance the look of a worksheet so it looks more attractive and the information is easier to read. To help the sales representatives track their product orders, Paulette Chen, the sales director for Outdoor Designs, asks you to create a worksheet that records individual product orders as they arrive from the sales reps. You will create the worksheet, enter information for one order, modify the worksheet so it is attractive and easy to read, and print it for Paulette's review.

OBJECTIVES

Navigate a workbook

Enter values and labels

Change column width and row height

Use formulas

Edit a worksheet

Change alignment and number format

Change fonts, borders, and shading

Add headers and footers

Print a worksheet

Navigating a Workbook

Every new Excel workbook contains one worksheet. You can add more worksheets to the workbook if you need to use more than one worksheet to help organize your information. An Excel worksheet consists of a grid of rows and columns. Similar to a Word table, the intersection of a row and a column is called a **cell**. ▰▰▰ Before working on the product order worksheet, you need to start Excel, familiarize yourself with the workbook window, and save a blank workbook.

STEPS

TROUBLE

If the Excel icon is not visible on the dock, click the Finder icon on the dock, click Applications in the Finder window, locate and click Microsoft Office 2008, then double-click Microsoft Excel.

1. **Click the Microsoft Excel icon 🖳 on the dock**

   Excel starts and a blank workbook opens, as shown in Figure I-1. Excel contains elements that are in every Microsoft Office program, including the menu bar, the title bar, the Standard toolbar, the Elements Gallery, the document window, scroll bars, the status bar, and View buttons. By default, the Toolbox opens when you start Excel and the Formatting Palette is displayed. The cell with the blue border in the upper-left corner of this worksheet (called Sheet1) is the **active** (or **selected**) cell. Data that you enter appears in the active cell. When you first start Excel or open a workbook, the cell in the upper-left corner of Sheet1 is always the active cell. You can refer to a cell by its **cell address**, a column letter followed by a row number. The currently selected cell is cell A1, the cell where column A and row 1 intersect.

2. **Click the Normal View button 🖳 on the status bar**

   The worksheet appears in Normal view, and the margins around the spreadsheet area disappear. By default, worksheets open in Page Layout view, where the worksheet grid is divided into pages and you can see how your data will appear when printed.

TROUBLE

If the formula bar covers the Formatting Palette, click and drag the Formatting Palette to an open section of the screen. To hide the formula bar, click View on the menu bar, then click Formula Bar to deselect it.

3. **Click View on the menu bar, click Formula Bar to select it if necessary, then click cell B1**

   Cell B1 becomes the active cell. Clicking a cell selects it and makes it active. Table I-1 lists several methods for selecting cells with the mouse or keyboard. You can see that the mouse pointer changes to ✚ when you move it over any cells in the workbook. Notice that the column and row headings of the active cell (column B and row 1) appear in a contrasting color to make it easy for you to identify the cell. The **formula bar** appears as a floating element below the menu bar and shows the contents of the selected cell (it is currently empty). The **name box** appears to the left of the formula bar and displays the address of the active cell. You can resize the formula bar by dragging its lower-right corner.

4. **Press [→]**

   Cell C1 is now the active cell. You can move to and select a cell by clicking it, by using the arrow keys, by pressing [tab] (to move one cell to the right) or [shift][tab] (to move one cell to the left), or by pressing [return] (to move one cell down).

QUICK TIP

To navigate quickly to a specific cell, press [control][G] to open the Go To dialog box, type the cell address you want to navigate to in the Reference text box, then click OK.

5. **Press [return] three times to move to cell C4**

6. **Scroll down if necessary until you see row 41, and then click cell F41**

7. **Click the Insert Sheet button ➕**

   A new sheet, named Sheet2, becomes the active sheet, as shown in Figure I-2. To work with different sheets in a workbook, you click the sheet tab of the sheet you want to see. A blank worksheet can contain up to 1,048,576 rows and 16,384 columns.

QUICK TIP

To rename a worksheet, click Format on the menu bar, point to Sheet, then click Rename.

8. **Click the Sheet1 sheet tab, then click cell A1**

   Clicking the sheet tab returns you to Sheet1.

9. **Click the Save button 🖫 on the Standard toolbar, navigate to where you store your Data Files, then save the file as Outdoor Designs Product Order**

Creating and Enhancing a Worksheet

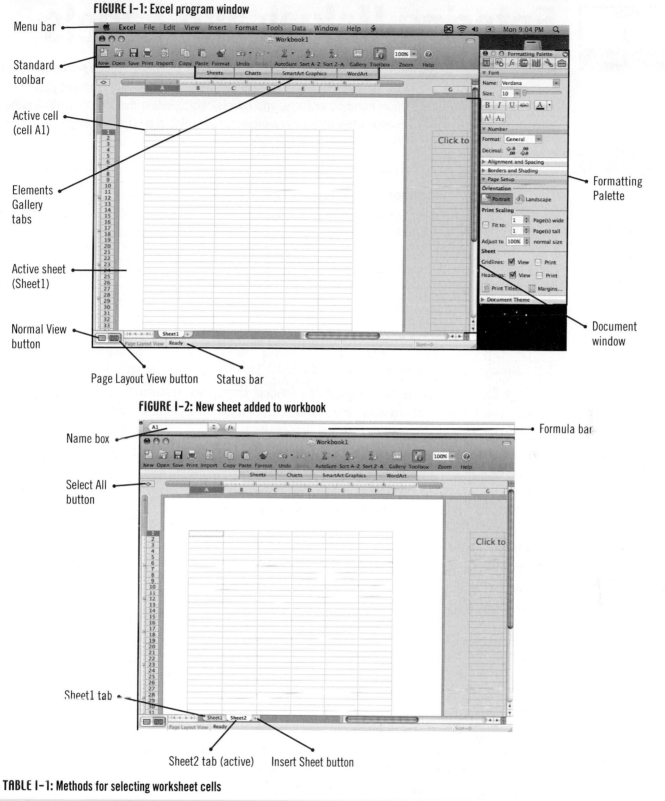

FIGURE I-1: Excel program window

Menu bar

Standard toolbar

Active cell (cell A1)

Elements Gallery tabs

Active sheet (Sheet1)

Normal View button

Page Layout View button   Status bar

Click to

Formatting Palette

Document window

FIGURE I-2: New sheet added to workbook

Name box

Select All button

Sheet1 tab

Sheet2 tab (active)   Insert Sheet button

Formula bar

Click to

TABLE I-1: Methods for selecting worksheet cells

to select	with the mouse	with the keyboard
A cell	Click the cell	Use arrow keys
A row	Click the row heading	Select a cell in the row, then press [shift][spacebar]
A column	Click the column heading	Select a cell in the column, then press [control][spacebar]
A group of cells	Drag across the cells	Press [shift], then use arrow keys
A worksheet	Click the Select All button to the left of the A column heading	Press [⌘][A]

Entering Values and Labels

Before you can enter data in a cell, the cell must be active. Entering data in a worksheet is similar to typing in Word, but requires an extra step: first you type data into the active cell, then you must accept your entry. Data can include **values**, such as numbers or dates, and **labels**, which is text that describes data rather than calculating it. Paulette asks you to enter a product order placed by Open Air Depot, a store in Augusta, Maine.

STEPS

1. **In cell A1, type Outdoor Designs Product Order**

   As you type, the text appears in cell A1 and in the formula bar, as shown in Figure I-3. The text you typed is a label that describes the worksheet contents.

2. **Press [return]**

   Pressing [return] accepts your entry and activates the next cell in the column, cell A2. Labels can extend into neighboring cells that don't contain data, so the text "Outdoor Designs Product Order" extends into cells B1 and C1, but it is contained only in cell A1.

3. **Press [▼]**

   Cell A3 is selected and "A3" appears in the name box, identifying your current location. You can use the arrow keys to accept an entry and move to the next cell in the direction of the arrow key.

   > **QUICK TIP**
   > Pressing [tab] is the same as pressing [→] in the worksheet. You might find that using [tab] is more convenient for entering multiple columns of data.

4. **Type Sales rep:, press [tab], type Philip Roscoe, then press [return]**

   A4 is now the active cell. Pressing [return] at the end of a row of data you have just typed activates the first cell in the next row down, rather than activating the next cell in the current column.

5. **Type Store:, press [tab], type Open Air Depot, Augusta, ME, press [return], type Date:, press [tab], type March 1, 2012, then press [control][return]**

   Pressing [control][return] accepts the cell contents, but unlike when you use the [return] key alone, the active cell does not change. Excel recognized that you typed a date in cell B5 and applied the date format 1-Mar-12 to it after you accepted the entry.

6. **Click cell A7, then type the following text in columns A through D of rows 7 and 8, pressing [tab] to move to the next cell in a row, and pressing [return] at the end of each row**

Item Number	Item Name	Price	Quantity
4563	Red Cedar Kid's Clubhouse Kit	1295	2

   Notice that some cells do not display their entire contents because the text is too long to fit. When text is wider than a cell, it spills into the adjacent cell, unless that cell has data in it. (The data hasn't been deleted; it is just not visible.) You'll widen the necessary cells later to display all the data.

7. **Beginning with cell A9, continue typing the following data in the worksheet; remember to press [tab] to move one cell to the right and [return] to move to the beginning of the next row**

2207	Yes You Can Build a Clubhouse	14.95	5
5698	Canoe Kit	129.95	5
2203	Yes You Can Build a Canoe	14.95	5
2901	Bird Bungalow Kit	49.95	3

   The text is entered in the worksheet, as shown in Figure I-4.

8. **Click the Save button 🖫 on the Standard toolbar**

FIGURE I-3: Worksheet text in active cell and formula bar

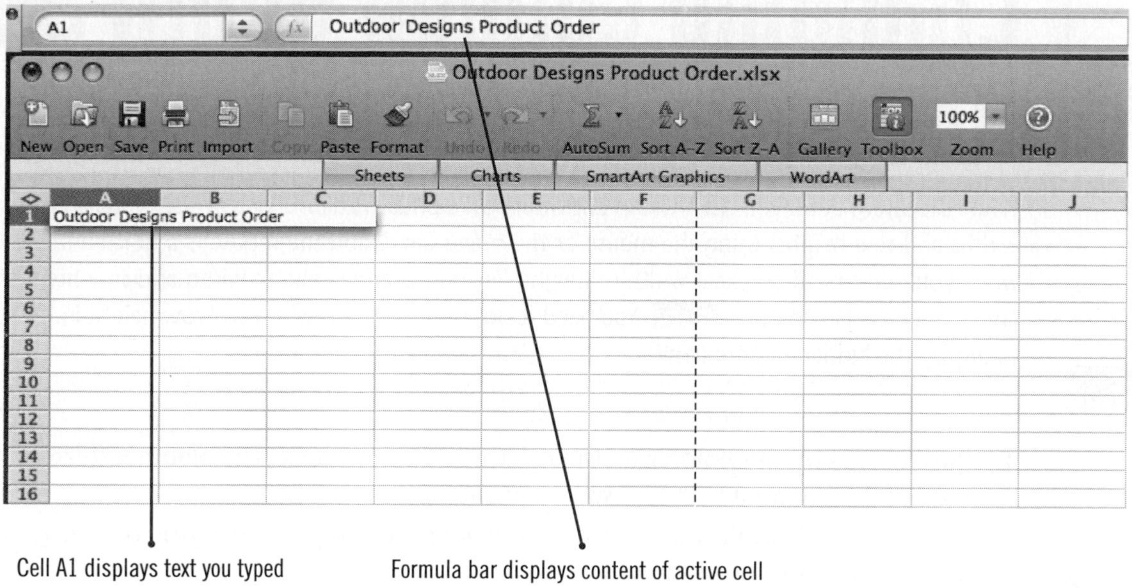

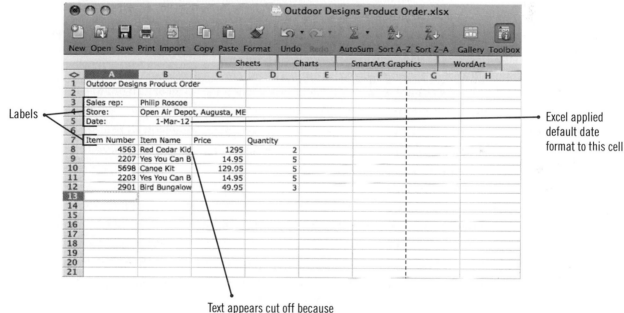

Cell A1 displays text you typed

Formula bar displays content of active cell

FIGURE I-4: Worksheet after entering product order data

Labels

Excel applied default date format to this cell

Text appears cut off because contents are too long to fit in column

Using data entry keys

As you enter data in your worksheets, you can use the keyboard to save time. Press [caps lock] to enter text labels as all uppercase characters. If you need to enter many numbers in a worksheet, the numeric keypad on your keyboard can speed the process significantly. On keyboards without a numeric keypad, pressing [num lock] changes the keyboard to a keypad, by allowing the J K L and U I O keys to function as 1 2 3 and 4 5 6 (7 8 9 remain the same), and making the other keys inactive.

Changing Column Width and Row Height

When the information you enter doesn't fit within the standard column or row size, you can adjust column widths and row heights using the mouse or the menu bar. Using the mouse is a quick and easy method when you don't need an exact width or height. You can change column width and row height before or after you enter data in cells. You need to adjust the column width and row height in the worksheet to display the hidden information.

STEPS

1. **Position the mouse pointer on the column separator between column letters B and C so the pointer changes to ↔, as shown in Figure I-5**

   The boxes containing the letters B and C are **column headings**, and the boxes containing numbers in front of each row are **row headings**.

2. **Double-click the column separator**

   Double-clicking a column separator automatically widens or narrows the column to the left of the separator to fit the longest entry in that column; this feature is called **AutoFit**. The item names in cells B8 through B12 are now fully visible; the column is wide enough to display all the text in these cells.

3. **Point to the separator between columns A and B, then drag to the right so the dotted line is on top of the second s in the word Designs in row 1**

   Column A is now wider. When you drag a separator, a dotted line appears to help you position it right where you want it, and a ScreenTip displays the width of the column in the number of characters and in inches.

4. **Point to the separator between rows 6 and 7**

   The pointer changes to ↨. Excel automatically adjusts the height of each row to accommodate the largest font in the row, so you need to change the row height only if you want to create extra space.

5. **Click the separator, hold down the mouse button, slowly drag the pointer down until the ScreenTip reads Height: 21.00 (0.29 inches), as shown in Figure I-6, then release the mouse button**

   The height of row 6 changes from 13 to 21 points (0.29 inches). The extra space creates a visual separation between the sales rep information and the product listing. Using the dragging method is not the only way to increase or decrease row height or column width. You can also click Format on the menu bar if you know the precise measurement you want.

6. **Click cell A6, click Format on the menu bar, point to Row, then click Height**

   The Row Height dialog box opens. See Figure I-7. The Row height text box displays the selected value 0.29", because this is the height you specified in Step 5.

7. **Type 0.5, then click OK**

   The height of row 6 increases to 0.5 inches.

8. **Click the Save button 🖫 on the Standard toolbar**

FIGURE I-5: Changing column width in the worksheet

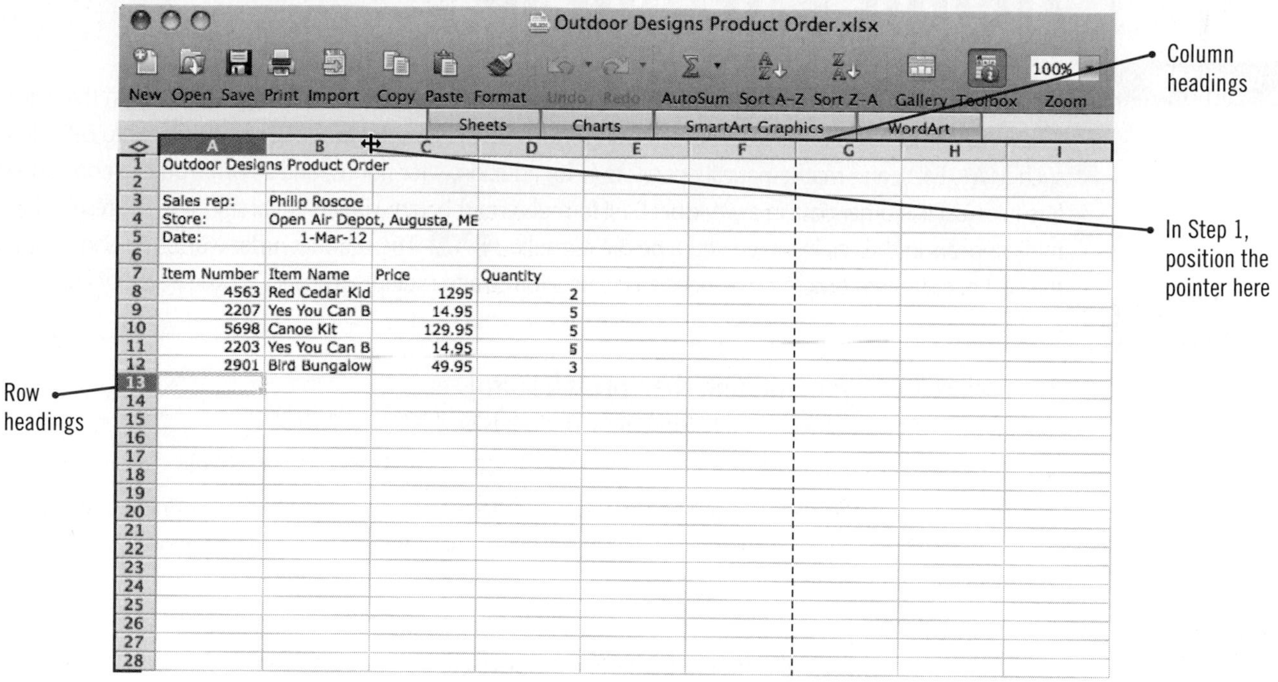

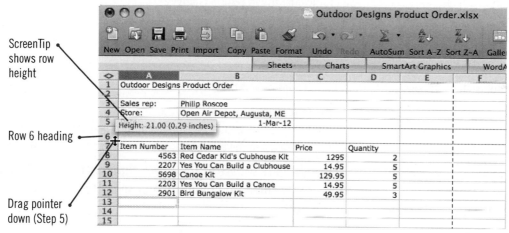

Column headings

In Step 1, position the pointer here

Row headings

FIGURE I-6: Changing row height in the worksheet

ScreenTip shows row height

Row 6 heading

Drag pointer down (Step 5)

FIGURE I-7: Row Height dialog box

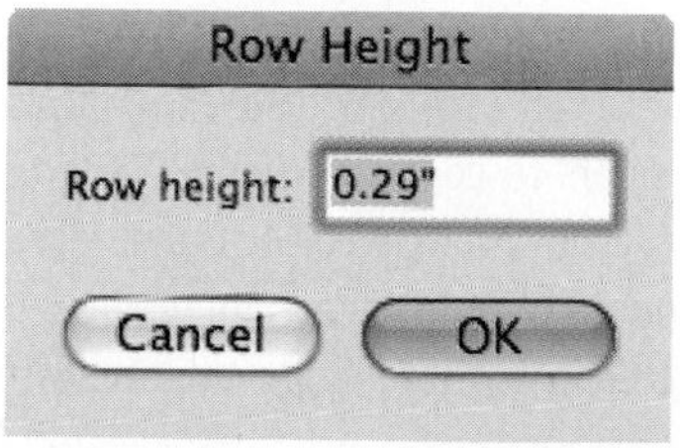

Row Height

Row height: 0.29"

Cancel   OK

Excel 2008

Using Formulas

To perform a calculation in a worksheet, you enter a formula in a cell. A **formula** is an equation that calculates a new value from existing values. Formulas can contain numbers, **cell references** (references to cell addresses, such as A1, E42), and mathematical operators (+ for addition, – for minus, and so on). You can copy and move formulas just like other data in a worksheet. All formulas must begin with an equal sign (=). The result of the formula appears in the cell in which you type the formula. ▰▰▰▰ The product order worksheet should calculate the cost of each item ordered. You need to create a formula to multiply the price by the quantity for each item.

STEPS

1. **Click cell E7, type Amount, then press [return]**
    Amount is now a label in cell E7, and the active cell is now E8.

2. **Type =**
    The equal sign (=) indicates that you're about to enter a formula in cell E8. Everything you enter in a cell after the equal sign, including any numbers, mathematical operators, cell references, or functions, is included in the formula.

3. **Click cell C8**
    Cell C8, the first cell reference in the formula, is selected, meaning that Excel will use the value in cell C8 when it calculates the formula. As you enter formulas in a cell, they appear in both the formula bar and in the cell containing the formula.

4. **Type * (an asterisk), then click cell D8**
    See Figure I-8. In Excel, the asterisk symbol is the operator for multiplication. When Excel calculates the formula, it will multiply the product price in cell C8 (which for this product is $1295) by the quantity in cell D8 (which in this case is 2). Entering a cell reference instead of a number, like 2, means that the formula will always be accurate even if the quantity in cell D8 changes.

5. **Press [return]**
    The result of the formula (2590) appears in cell E8 and the active cell is now E9.

6. **Press [↑]**
    Notice that although the formula's result appears in cell E8, the formula =C8*D8 appears in the formula bar.

7. **Press [↓], type =C9*D9, then press [return]**
    As you typed, the formula appeared in the formula bar. After you pressed [return], the result (74.75) appeared in cell E9. Instead of manually entering a formula in the cells below, you decide to copy this formula.

8. **Click cell E9, point to the small light blue square in the lower-right corner of cell E9 so that the pointer changes to ✛, press and hold down the mouse button, drag down to cell E12, then release the mouse button**
    Excel copies the formula in cell E9 into cells E10 through E12, and the amount for each product appears in the respective cells, as shown in Figure I-9. The small square that you pointed to is called the **fill handle**. Dragging a cell's fill handle is a fast way to copy the contents of the cell to adjacent cells. The icon that appears after you release the mouse button is the Auto Fill Options button, which you can click to choose additional options when copying cells.

9. **Click cell E10, then save your changes**
    The formula bar shows the formula =C10*D10. Notice that this copied formula uses different cell references than those used in the original formula. The original formula contains references to cells C9 and D9. When Excel copied the formula to cell E10, it adjusted the original cell references to match the new formula location. The formula now refers to cells C10 (which is two cells to the left of the copied formula) and D10 (which is one cell to the left of the copied formula). When you copy a formula using the fill handle or the Copy and Paste commands, Excel automatically replaces the original cell references with cell references that are in the *same relative position* as those in the original formula. This is called **relative cell referencing**.

Creating and Enhancing a Worksheet

FIGURE I-8: Entering a formula

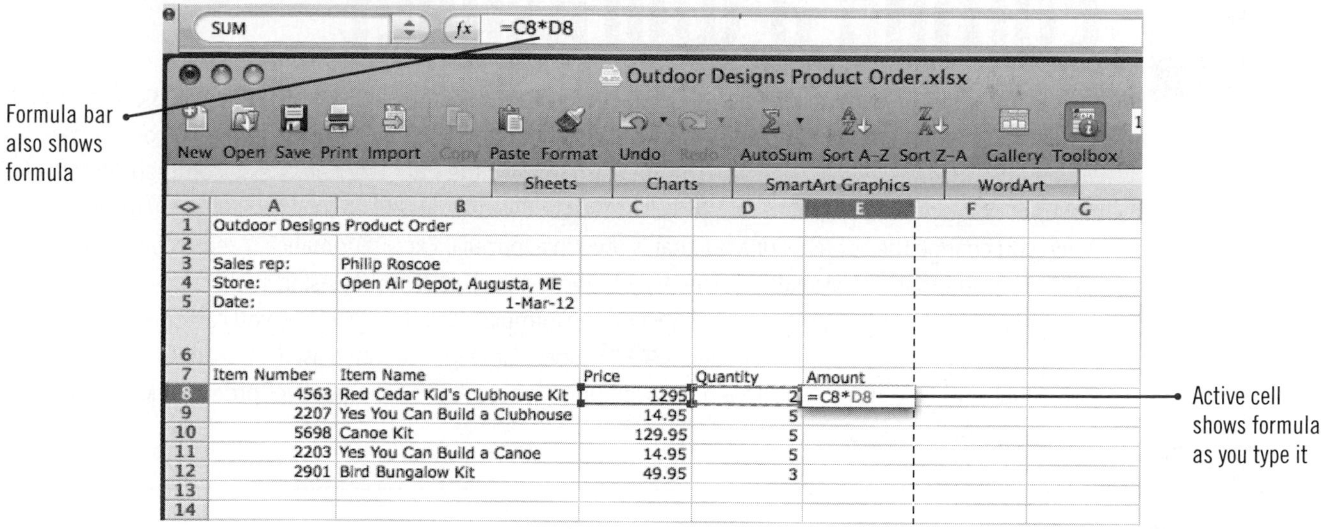

Formula bar also shows formula

SUM | fx | =C8*D8

Outdoor Designs Product Order.xlsx

New Open Save Print Import Copy Paste Format Undo Redo AutoSum Sort A-Z Sort Z-A Gallery Toolbox

Sheets | Charts | SmartArt Graphics | WordArt

	A	B	C	D	E	F	G
1	Outdoor Designs Product Order						
2							
3	Sales rep:	Philip Roscoe					
4	Store:	Open Air Depot, Augusta, ME					
5	Date:	1-Mar-12					
6							
7	Item Number	Item Name	Price	Quantity	Amount		
8	4563	Red Cedar Kid's Clubhouse Kit	1295	2	=C8*D8		
9	2207	Yes You Can Build a Clubhouse	14.95	5			
10	5698	Canoe Kit	129.95	5			
11	2203	Yes You Can Build a Canoe	14.95	5			
12	2901	Bird Bungalow Kit	49.95	3			
13							
14							

Active cell shows formula as you type it

FIGURE I-9: Worksheet after using fill handle to copy formulas

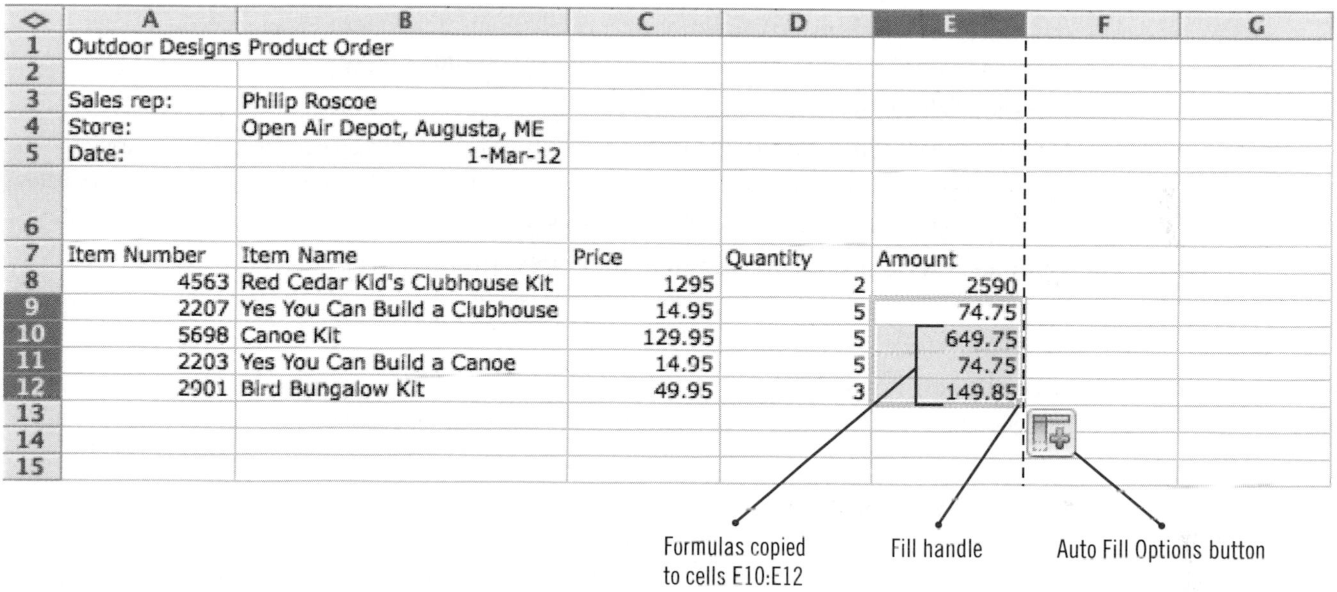

	A	B	C	D	E	F	G
1	Outdoor Designs Product Order						
2							
3	Sales rep:	Philip Roscoe					
4	Store:	Open Air Depot, Augusta, ME					
5	Date:	1-Mar-12					
6							
7	Item Number	Item Name	Price	Quantity	Amount		
8	4563	Red Cedar Kid's Clubhouse Kit	1295	2	2590		
9	2207	Yes You Can Build a Clubhouse	14.95	5	74.75		
10	5698	Canoe Kit	129.95	5	649.75		
11	2203	Yes You Can Build a Canoe	14.95	5	74.75		
12	2901	Bird Bungalow Kit	49.95	3	149.85		
13							
14							
15							

Formulas copied to cells E10:E12   Fill handle   Auto Fill Options button

Using absolute cell references

When you copy a formula, Excel automatically adjusts the cell references in the copied formula to reflect the new formula location. For example, a formula in cell D5 that reads "=B5*C5" changes to "=B6*C6" when you copy the formula down one row. This is the default in Excel because you usually use **relative cell references** when entering a formula. However, there may be times when you want a cell reference to always refer to a specific cell, no matter where you move or copy the formula. In this case, you use an **absolute cell reference** in the formula, so that when you move or copy the formula, the cell reference remains constant. For example, see Figure I-10. The formulas in cells B7:B13 calculate the cost of producing a birdhouse kit for quantities of 100, 150, and so on. Cell B4 contains the cost of producing one kit ($4.25). Each formula in column B multiplies the quantity in column A by the constant value in cell B4. Each formula in cells B7:B13 contains both a relative reference (to the cell to its left, containing the quantity) and an absolute reference (to cell B4, the cell containing the production

cost). To indicate an absolute cell reference, you type a dollar sign ($) before the part of the address you want to remain constant.

FIGURE I-10: Using an absolute cell reference

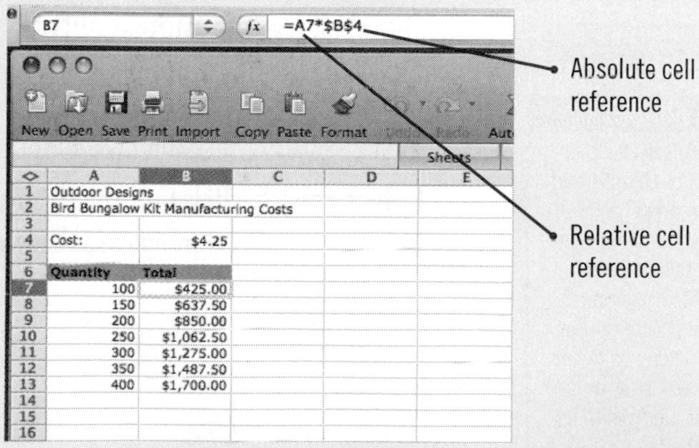

B7 | fx | =A7*$B$4

New Open Save Print Import Copy Paste Format Auto

Sheets

	A	B	C	D	E
1	Outdoor Designs				
2	Bird Bungalow Kit Manufacturing Costs				
3					
4	Cost:	$4.25			
5					
6	Quantity	Total			
7	100	$425.00			
8	150	$637.50			
9	200	$850.00			
10	250	$1,062.50			
11	300	$1,275.00			
12	350	$1,487.50			
13	400	$1,700.00			
14					
15					
16					

Absolute cell reference

Relative cell reference

Creating and Enhancing a Worksheet

Editing a Worksheet

You can edit worksheet cells in several ways. You can revise the contents of a cell by editing its contents in the formula bar or by double-clicking and typing directly in the cell. To copy or move cells, rows, or columns, you can use the Copy and Paste buttons on the Standard toolbar; the Cut, Copy, and Paste commands on the Edit menu; or dragging and dropping. You can also insert or delete rows and columns anywhere in the worksheet. When you change the contents of a cell that is used in a formula, Excel automatically recalculates the formula result. This automatic recalculation is one way to perform **what-if analysis**, in which you can change the values in a formula and instantly see the effect on the formula result. For example, you can change a price and see its effect on a calculated sales figure. Open Air Depot has increased its order for the Red Cedar Kid's Clubhouse and has moved to a new location. You need to edit the product order worksheet to reflect these and other changes.

STEPS

TROUBLE

If you realize you made a mistake after pressing [return], press [⌘][Z] and then try again.

1. **Click cell D8, type 7, then press [return]**

   If you type in a cell that contains data without first selecting any data in the cell, the entire contents of the cell are replaced by what you type. The number in cell D8 changes from 2 to 7, and the formula in cell E8 is recalculated when you press [return], so the subtotal changes from 2590 to 9065.

2. **Double-click cell B4**

   Cell B4 is now in Edit mode. Double-clicking a cell lets you make edits directly in the cell instead of in the formula bar. You can tell that the cell is in Edit mode because the cell pops forward with a shadow below, and it expands to display the entire contents of the cell.

3. **Double-click Augusta, type Camden, then press [return]**

   The updated label appears in the worksheet in cell B4. Similar to Word, when you select text in the formula bar, new text replaces the selected text as you type.

4. **Click the row heading for row 6**

   All cells in row 6 are selected. Clicking a row heading selects the entire row. When you insert a new row into the worksheet, it is inserted above the selected row.

QUICK TIP

You can also insert a row or column by right-clicking a row or column heading, then clicking Insert on the shortcut menu. If you cannot right-click with your mouse, press and hold [control], then click the row or column heading.

5. **Click Insert on the menu bar, then click Rows**

   A new row is added to the worksheet, and the rows below it are renumbered. By default, inserted rows are formatted like the row above, so the new row is the same height as row 5. You can choose a different formatting option by clicking the Insert Options button, which appears next to the new row.

6. **Click the Insert Options button [image], then click Format Same As Below, as shown in Figure I-11**

   The new row 6 is now formatted like row 7, with a taller row height than the other rows.

7. **Select row 3, position the pointer over the right border of the row heading so it changes to ↔, drag row 3 down until row 6 is selected and the ScreenTip reads 6:6, then release the mouse button**

   The contents of row 3 move to row 6, leaving row 3 empty. Notice that row 6 is no longer extra tall, like row 7; it is now the same height as rows 4 and 5. This is because the contents of row 3, with its formatting intact, replaced the contents and formatting of row 6.

QUICK TIP

If you select a cell, row, or column and then press [delete], only the contents of the selection are deleted. You must click Delete on the Edit menu to delete the cell, row, or column along with its contents.

8. **Select row 3, click Edit on the menu bar, click Delete, then save your changes**

   The empty row is eliminated, as shown in Figure I-12, and your changes to the workbook are saved.

FIGURE I-11: Changing the formatting of the new row

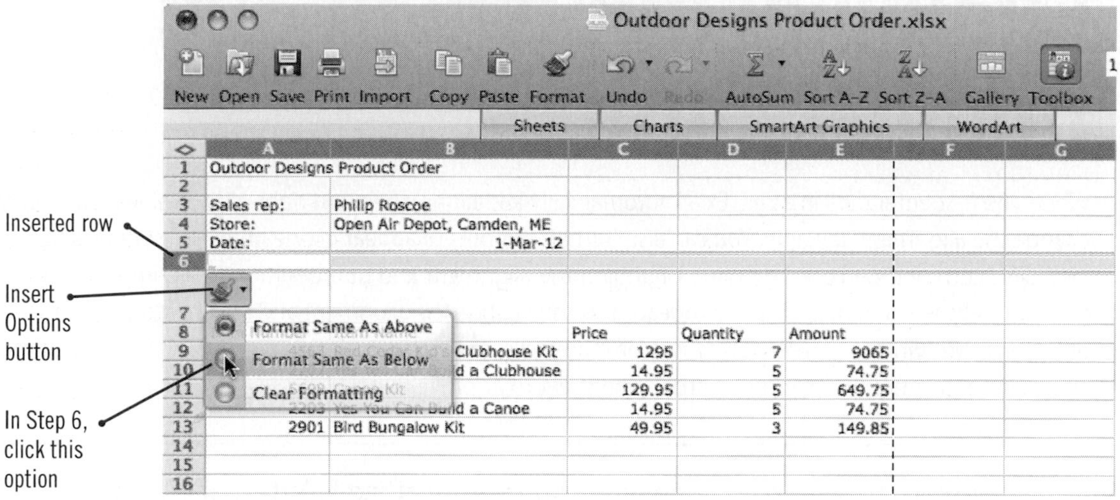

Inserted row

Insert Options button

In Step 6, click this option

FIGURE I-12: Worksheet after making edits

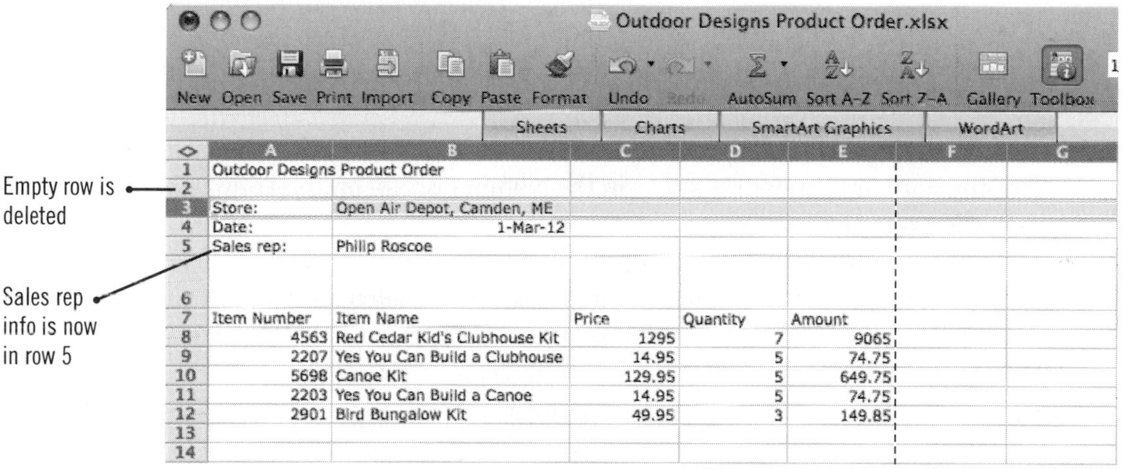

Empty row is deleted

Sales rep info is now in row 5

Copying, moving, and pasting cells

Just like in Word, you can use the Clipboard to copy or move cells from one location to another. To copy cells, select the cells you want to copy, click the Copy button on the Standard toolbar, click the cell where you want the first cell of the copied cells to appear, then click the Paste button. If you know you want to copy or move only the resulting value in a cell containing a formula (and not the formula itself) click Edit on the menu bar, click Paste Special to open the Paste Special dialog box, then click Values under the Paste heading. You can use the Paste Special dialog box to specify other paste options, such as pasting only the formatting of a cell.

Changing Alignment and Number Format

When you first enter data in a cell, Excel automatically left-aligns labels and right-aligns values, but you can change the alignment any time. You can also format numbers to appear in one of several standard formats, including currency, percent, and date. Changing the alignment and number format can improve the look of your worksheet and make it easier to read. You can change the alignment and number format of one cell or of a **range**, which is a selection of two or more cells. You decide to apply different alignment and number formats to the product order worksheet to improve its appearance.

STEPS

TROUBLE

If the Toolbox is not open, click the Toolbox button on the Standard toolbar.

QUICK TIP

The Formatting toolbar contains frequently used formatting buttons. To display the Formatting toolbar, click View on the menu bar, point to Toolbars, then click Formatting.

QUICK TIP

To increase the number of digits following a decimal point in a number, click the Increase Decimal button in the Number group on the Formatting Palette; to decrease the number, click the Decrease Decimal button.

QUICK TIP

If you want text in a cell to appear in multiple lines so that long text can be viewed in a narrow column, select the cell, then click the Wrap text check box in the Alignment and Spacing group on the Formatting Palette.

1. **Click the Alignment and Spacing group on the Formatting Palette in the Toolbox**
   The Alignment and Spacing group expands to show its contents.

2. **Select row 7, then click the Align Center button in the Alignment and Spacing group**
   Each label in row 7 becomes centered in its cell. The Alignment and Spacing group also has buttons to align text vertically with the top, center, or bottom of a cell. The Orientation buttons let you position cell contents to be read from bottom to top, at a 45-degree angle, or vertically. You can use other options in this group to wrap text in a cell, shrink text to fit in a cell, indent cell contents, or merge selected cells.

3. **Click cell D8, press and hold the mouse button, drag down to cell D12, release the mouse button, then click**
   You selected and formatted the range D8 through D12.

4. **Select the range A8 through A12, then click**
   The contents of the range A8 through A12 are centered.

5. **Select the range C8 through C12, press and hold [⌘], select the range E8 through E12, click the Format Number list arrow in the Number group on the Formatting Palette, then click Accounting**
   Pressing and holding [⌘] when you select cells allows you to select groups of noncontiguous cells. The five cells in the Price column and the five cells in the Amount column now are formatted in the Accounting number format and they contain dollar signs.

6. **Select cell B4, click Format on the menu bar, then click Cells**
   The Format Cells dialog box opens. You can use the Format Cells dialog box to change cell appearance in a variety of ways. For example, you can format the cell contents using the Number tab; you can change the way text is aligned in cells using the Alignment tab; you can change font type, size, and other font attributes using the Font tab; and you can add borders, patterns, and shading to cells using the Border and Patterns tabs. You can also use the Protection tab to protect a worksheet so users cannot make inadvertent changes. The selected cell contains data that was automatically formatted as a date and right-aligned. You want to choose a different date format.

7. **Click the Number tab if necessary, click Date in the Category list if necessary, scroll to the top of the Type list, then click the second option in the Type list as shown in Figure I-13**

8. **Click the Alignment tab, click the Horizontal arrows, click Left (Indent), then click OK**
   The date in cell B4 now appears as 3/1/12 and is left-aligned. It looks better because it is aligned with the data in the cells above and below it.

9. **Select the range A1 through E1, click the Merge cells check box in the Alignment and Spacing group on the Formatting Palette, click , then save your changes**
   The worksheet title is centered across the five selected cells, which have merged into one cell. (Note that the cell reference of the title is still A1, however.) See Figure I-14.

Creating and Enhancing a Worksheet

FIGURE I-13: Number tab of the Format Cells dialog box

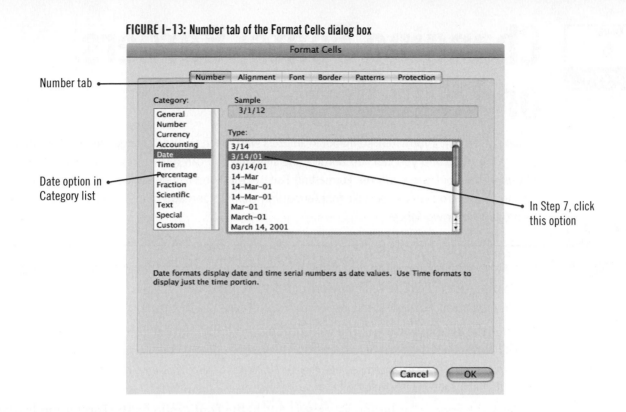

Number tab •

Date option in Category list •

In Step 7, click this option

FIGURE I-14: Formatted information in worksheet cells

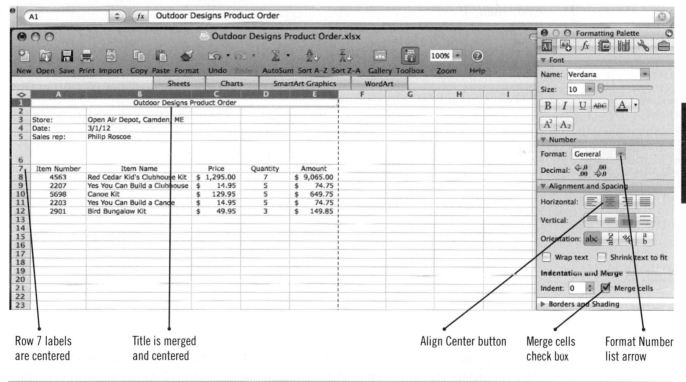

Row 7 labels are centered

Title is merged and centered

Align Center button

Merge cells check box

Format Number list arrow

Changing the number format

You can format numbers using the Format Number list or the Formatting toolbar. The Formatting toolbar has buttons for common number formats such as the Accounting Number Format button, the Percent Style button, and the Comma Style button. The Number Format list in the Number group on the Formatting Palette contains other useful number formats including Time, which formats numbers in various time formats; Fraction, which formats numbers as fractions; and Scientific, which formats numbers in scientific notation. To change the number format in cells, select the cell(s) to change, then click the appropriate button on the Formatting toolbar or click a format in the Format Number list on the Formatting Palette.

Changing Fonts, Borders, and Shading

To make important information stand out in an Excel worksheet, you can change the font, font style, and font color of text, and you can add borders and shading. You can format individual cells or a range of cells using the Font group on the Formatting Palette, the Format Cells dialog box, or the Formatting toolbar. ▨▨▨ You decide to make font formatting changes and add borders and shading to enhance the product order worksheet.

QUICK TIP

You can also press [⌘][B] to apply bold formatting to a selected cell or range and press [⌘][I] to apply italic formatting.

1. **Select cell A1 if necessary, click the Bold button ☐B☐ in the Font group on the Formatting Palette, then click the Italic button ☐I☐ in the Font group**

   The formatting of the title "Outdoor Designs Product Order" changes to bold and italic.

2. **Click the Font list arrow in the Font group on the Formatting Palette, scroll down, click Gill Sans, click the Font Size list arrow in the Font group, then click 20**

   The size and font of the worksheet title changes to 20-point Gill Sans. Notice how the row height increases to accommodate the new font.

QUICK TIP

The Draw Border button ☐ in the Borders and Shading group on the Formatting Palette lets you drag a pencil pointer around the cells to which you want to add borders.

3. **Click the Font Color button list arrow ☐A▾☐ in the Font group on the Formatting Palette, then click the blue color located in the sixth column in the second row (the ScreenTip reads "Blue")**

   The color of the worksheet title changes to blue.

4. **Select row 7 in the worksheet, then click ☐B☐ in the Font group**

   The formatting of all the cells in the row changes to bold.

5. **Drag to select the range A3 through B5**

   The range of cells from A3 to B5 is selected. You can also represent a range by using a colon between the cell references, such as "A3:B5", which refers to cell A3, cell B5, and all the cells in between.

QUICK TIP

If you want to create a colored border, first select the desired border type, click the Border Color button list arrow ☐▾☐, then select the desired border color.

6. **Click the Borders and Shading group on the Formatting Palette**

   The Borders and Shading group opens. You can use the commands in the Borders section to add or change borders, line styles, and color formatting options.

7. **Click the Border Type button list arrow ☐▾☐ in the Borders and Shading group, click the Outside Borders button ☐, then click the Border Style list arrow and click the double-line style (the seventh style in the list)**

   A double-line border appears around the range A3:B5. As you choose the border type and style, the worksheet changes to reflect your selections.

8. **Select the range A7:E12, click ☐▾☐, then click the All Borders button ☐**

   A single line border appears around each cell in the selection, as shown in Figure I-15.

9. **Select the range A7:E7, click the Fill Color button list arrow ☐▾☐ in the Borders and Shading group, click the light blue color located in the sixth column in the fifth row (the ScreenTip reads "Pale Blue"), click cell A1, click ☐▾☐, click the Pale Blue color, then save your changes**

   Light blue shading is applied to the range A7:E7 and to cell A1. See Figure I-16.

FIGURE I-15: Worksheet with borders added and formatting applied

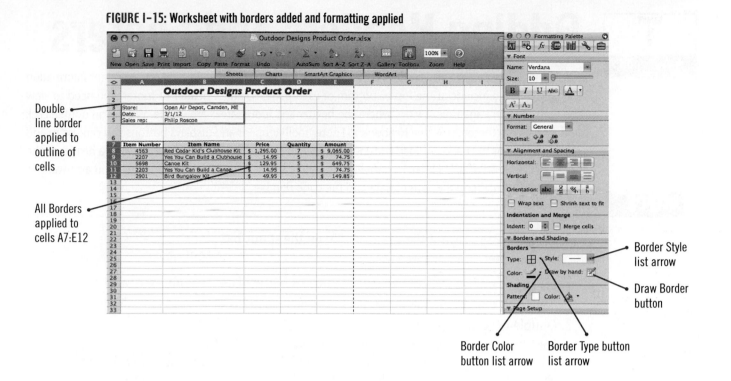

Double line border applied to outline of cells

All Borders applied to cells A7:E12

Border Style list arrow

Draw Border button

Border Color button list arrow

Border Type button list arrow

FIGURE I-16: Shading applied to cells

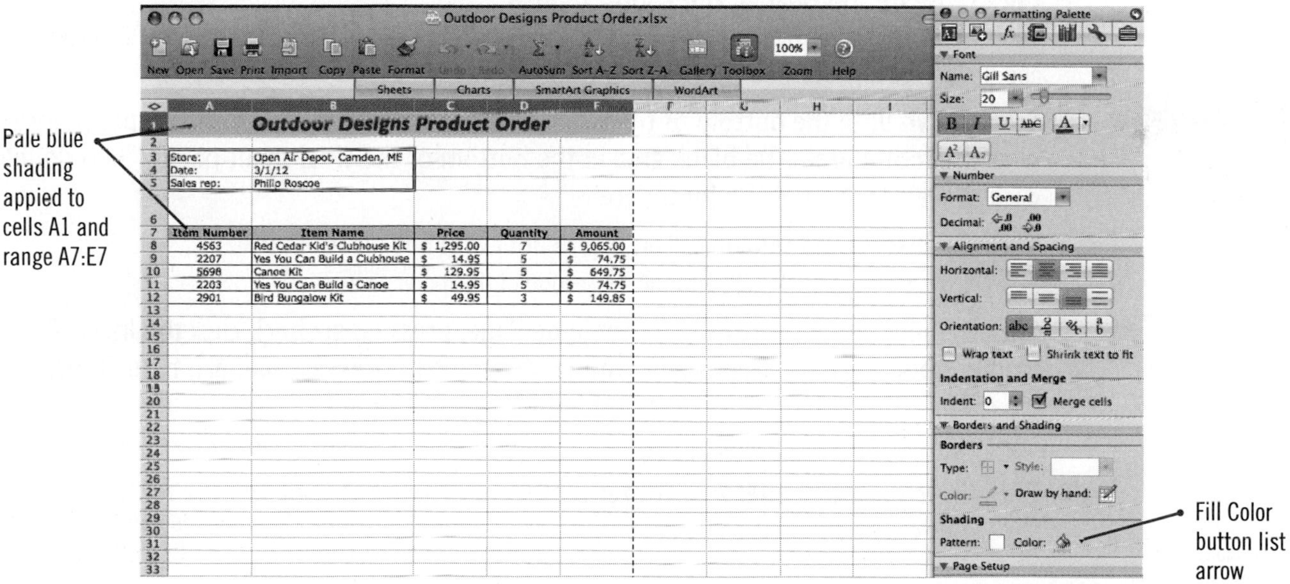

Pale blue shading appied to cells A1 and range A7:E7

Fill Color button list arrow

Adding Headers and Footers

Just like in Word, you can add headers and footers in an Excel worksheet containing important information that you want to include at the top or bottom of each page. To add a header or footer, you need to view the worksheet in Page Layout view, where the header and footer areas are visible. When you double-click in the header or footer areas, the Header and Footer toolbar opens and displays buttons you can use to add elements such as the page number, current date, and file name. ▰▰▰▰▰ You decide to add a header to the Outdoor Designs Product Order worksheet that contains your name and the file name. You also want to add a footer containing the current date and the page number.

STEPS

1. **Click the Page Layout View button 🖩 on the status bar**

   The worksheet appears in Page Layout view.

2. **Move the mouse pointer over the header area (the blank area above row 1)**

   A dimmed outline of the header area appears containing the text "Double-click to add header".

3. **Double-click the left section of the header area**

   The left third of the header pops out, indicating it is active, and the Header and Footer toolbar appears. This is an example of a contextual toolbar; it is open because you clicked in the header area. If the toolbar obscures the header area, click the handle of the toolbar and drag it to a different location.

4. **Type your name**

   Your name appears left-aligned in the left section of the header area.

QUICK TIP

You can also press [tab] to move to the next section.

5. **Click the middle section of the header, then click the Insert File Name button 🗐 on the Header and Footer toolbar**

   The text "&[File]" appears in the middle section of the header area. This is the code that Excel uses to display the name of the file. See Figure I-17.

6. **Click Close on the Header and Footer toolbar**

   The Header and Footer toolbar closes, and the name of the file Outdoor Designs Product Order.xlsx now appears in the middle section of the header area.

TROUBLE

You may need to move the Formatting Palette in order to see the scroll bar.

7. **Scroll down until the bottom of the worksheet page is visible, move the mouse pointer over the footer area (the blank area at the bottom of the worksheet page), then double-click the left section of the footer area**

8. **Click the Insert Date button 🗓 on the Header and Footer toolbar**

   Excel inserts the code "&[Date]" into the left section of the footer area.

QUICK TIP

You can insert a preset header or footer, which contains a selected combination of text and codes, by clicking View on the menu bar, clicking Header and Footer, then clicking a selection in the Header list or Footer list in the Page Setup dialog box; Excel replaces any existing text with the preset.

9. **Click the middle section of the footer, type Page, press [spacebar], click the Insert Page Number button 🗔 on the Header and Footer toolbar, press [spacebar], type of, press [spacebar], then click the Insert Number of Pages button 🗟**

   Excel inserts the code "Page &[Page] of &[Pages]" in the middle section of the footer area. See Figure I-18.

10. **Click Close on the Header and Footer toolbar, notice the changes to the footer, then save your changes**

FIGURE I-17: Header with text and file name added

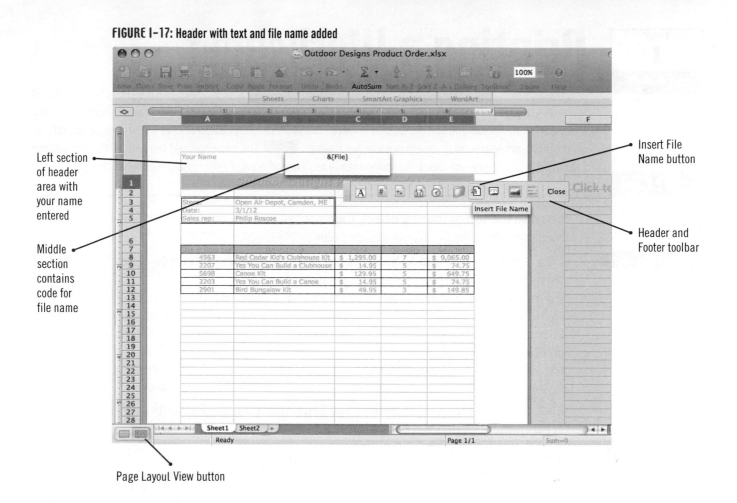

Left section of header area with your name entered

Middle section contains code for file name

Insert File Name button

Header and Footer toolbar

Page Layout View button

FIGURE I-18: Footer with current date and page number added

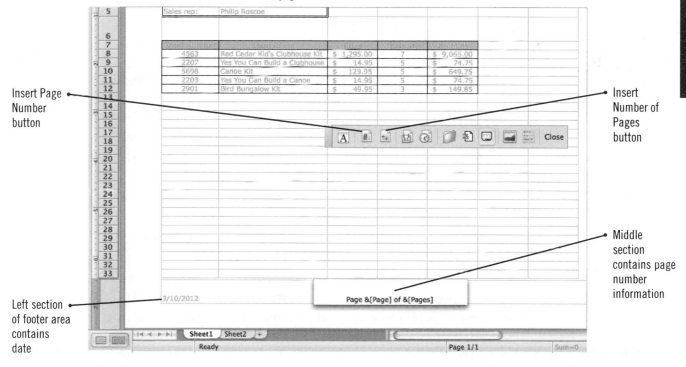

Insert Page Number button

Insert Number of Pages button

Middle section contains page number information

Left section of footer area contains date

Printing a Worksheet

When you finish creating and formatting a worksheet and have saved your work, you are ready to print it. It is important to review the page setup before printing, especially when working with large worksheets, to ensure that your data prints as you intend. Be sure to save your work before printing so that if you experience technical problems while printing, you do not lose your work. ▰▰▰▰ You have finished working with the Outdoor Designs Product Order workbook, so you are ready to review the page setup and print the worksheet.

STEPS

1. **Scroll to the top of the worksheet, then save your changes**
   It's always a good idea to save your changes before printing.

TROUBLE
If the Page Setup group is not open, click the Page Setup group to open it.

2. **Click the Alignment and Spacing group on the Formatting Palette to close the group, then click the Borders and Shading group to close it**
   The Alignment and Spacing and Borders and Shading groups close, and the Page Setup group is now visible on the Formatting Palette, as shown in Figure I-19. Here you can change the orientation of the worksheet from portrait to landscape. You can scale the worksheet to fit on a desired number of pages and choose to print gridlines or headings. The Print Titles button opens the Sheet tab of the Page Setup dialog box, where you can specify whether row or column headers will print on subsequent pages, while the Margins button opens the Margins tab of the Page Setup dialog box, where you can set the page margins.

3. **Click the Landscape button in the Page Setup group on the Formatting Palette**
   The orientation of the worksheet changes to landscape. Given the format of the worksheet, you see that portrait orientation is more appropriate.

4. **Click the Portrait button in the Page Setup group**
   The orientation of the worksheet changes back to portrait. You want to see what the worksheet will look like without gridlines, because the gridlines are not currently set to print.

5. **Click the View Gridlines check box in the Page Setup group to deselect it**
   The gridlines no longer appear onscreen, and you can see how the worksheet will look when printed.

QUICK TIP
If you want to print one copy of the worksheet without changing any settings from the last time you printed something, click the Print button 🖨 on the Standard toolbar.

6. **Click File on the menu bar, then click Print**
   The Print dialog box opens, as shown in Figure I-20. You use this dialog box to specify the printer you want to use, the range to print (the selected cells, the active worksheet, specific pages in the worksheet, or the whole workbook), and the number of copies you want to print. Verify that the Show Quick Preview check box is checked, so that in the Preview box you can review thumbnail images of your document as it will appear when printed. The current settings specify to print one copy of the active worksheet, which is what you want.

7. **Verify that your printer is on and connected to your computer, and that the correct printer appears in the Printer text box, then click Print**
   The Print dialog box closes and the worksheet prints. Compare your printed worksheet to Figure I-21.

8. **Click Excel on the menu bar, then click Quit Excel**
   The Outdoor Designs Product Order workbook and the Excel program both close.

Alternatives to printing

The Print dialog box offers two alternatives to printing your worksheet or document. Click the Preview button to open Preview, a Mac OS X program for displaying images and Portable Document Format (PDF) documents. Using Preview, you can zoom in on sections of your document, add or remove pages, or annotate the content by adding notes. Preview also can be separately opened from the Applications folder in the Finder window.

Click the PDF button in the Print dialog box to open a list of specialized commands for saving your document in different formats; the first option is to save as PDF. Other commands on the list may differ, depending on what programs you have installed on your computer. Saving an Excel workbook as a PDF document can be helpful when you need to email it or post it to the Web, or if you don't know whether the recipient has access to Excel.

FIGURE I-19: Page Setup group on the Formatting Palette

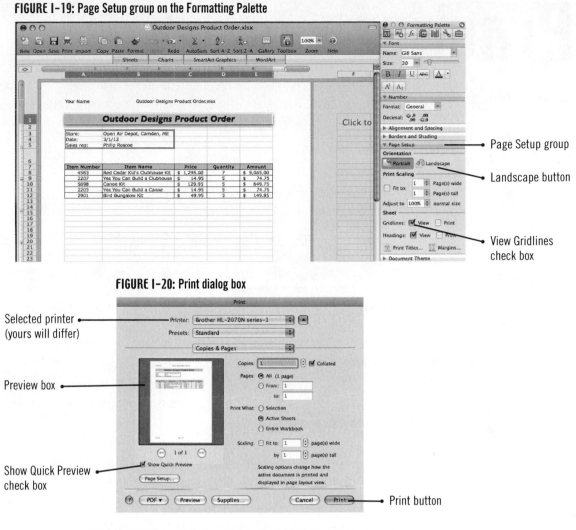

Page Setup group

Landscape button

View Gridlines check box

FIGURE I-20: Print dialog box

Selected printer (yours will differ)

Preview box

Show Quick Preview check box

Print button

FIGURE I-21: Printed Outdoor Designs Product Order worksheet

Practice

▼ CONCEPTS REVIEW

Label each item shown in Figure I-22.

FIGURE I-22

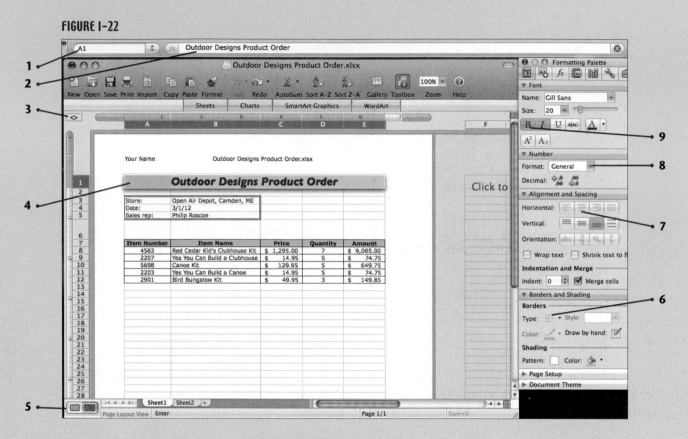

Match each pointer or button to its appropriate description.

10. ✛
11. ⊞
12. ✚
13. ✛
14. ◇ ▾
15. ✋

a. Pointer shape when it is placed over a worksheet cell
b. Button used to return to Normal view
c. Button used to apply shading to selected cells
d. Pointer shape when it is positioned over a fill handle
e. Pointer shape used to change the width of a column
f. Pointer shape used to move a row to a new location

Select the best answer from the list of choices.

16. The name of the cell located at the intersection of column F and row 223 is:
    a. 223F
    b. F223
    c. F222
    d. 22F3

17. Which of the following operators do you use to begin typing a formula in a cell?
    a. =
    b. +
    c. -
    d. *

18. Cell C1 contains the formula =A1+B1. If you copy the formula in C1 to cell C2, which of the following formulas will appear in cell C2?
    a. =A1+B1
    b. =C1+C2
    c. =A2+B2
    d. =B2+B3

19. Which view do you need to work in to add a header?
    a. Normal view
    b. Page Layout view
    c. Header/Footer view
    d. Page Setup view

20. For which of the following tasks would you use the fill handle?
    a. To apply shading to selected cells
    b. To apply a border to selected cells
    c. To copy a formula from cell A2 to cell F7
    d. To copy a formula from cell A2 to cell A3

▼ SKILLS REVIEW

1. **Navigate a workbook.**
   a. Start Microsoft Excel.
   b. Identify the program window elements without referring to the lesson material.
   c. Switch to Normal view, if necessary.
   d. Click cell E7, then click cell Y75.
   e. Hide the formula bar, then show it again.
   f. Insert a second sheet in the workbook, then make Sheet1 the active worksheet.

2. **Enter values and labels.**
   a. Save the new workbook with the name **Furniture Invoice** in the drive and folder where you store your Data Files.
   b. Use the table to the right to enter information in the worksheet in the specified cells.
   c. Use the information provided in the table below to enter the order information in the worksheet.

in cell	enter
A1	The Rustic Cabinet
A3	Bill to:
A4	Furniture Mart
A5	47 Beekman Road
A6	Indianapolis, IN 46201
A7	April 1, 2012

in cell	enter	in cell	enter	in cell	enter	in cell	enter
A9	Product Number	B9	Product Name	C9	Quantity	D9	Net Price
A10	16502	B10	Dining Table	C10	4	D10	800
A11	15667	B11	Armchair	C11	8	D11	125
A12	14557	B12	Side Chair	C12	16	D12	100
A13	17892	B13	Armoire	C13	4	D13	750
A14	18754	B14	Bedside Table	C14	5	D14	250

Excel 2008

3. **Change column width and row height.**
   a. Increase the size of column A by dragging the appropriate column boundary so that the Product Number column heading is visible in cell A9.
   b. Increase the width of column B by double-clicking the appropriate column boundary.
   c. Increase the height of row 8 to 34.00 (0.47 inches).
   d. Save your changes.

4. **Use formulas.**
   a. Enter the label **Total** in cell E9.
   b. Type a formula in cell E10 that multiplies the value of cell C10 and the value of cell D10. When you create the formula, insert the cell references in the formula by clicking the cells.
   c. Type a formula in cell E11 that multiplies the value of cell C11 and the value of D11.
   d. Use the fill handle to copy the formula you entered in cell E11 to cells E12 through E14.
   e. Save your changes.

5. **Edit a worksheet.**
   a. Use the formula bar to change the text in cell A5 to 47 **East** Beekman Road.
   b. Use the formula bar to change the contents of cell D12 to **125**.
   c. Select row 3, then insert a new row above this row.
   d. Insert another new row above the new row you just created.
   e. Select row 9 (the row that contains the date), then drag the contents of this row up to row 3.
   f. Delete row 4 (the row below the date) and row 9 (the row below Indianapolis, IN 46201).
   g. Save your changes.

6. **Change alignment and number format.**
   a. Select row 9, then center the data in the row.
   b. Merge and center cells A1 through E1.
   c. Center the text in the range A10:A14 and in the range C10:C14.
   d. Left-align the date in cell A3, then change the number format of the date so that it appears as April 1, 2012.
   e. Change the number format of the data in the Net Price and Total columns to Accounting.
   f. Save your changes.

7. **Change fonts, borders, and shading.**
   a. Apply bold formatting to cell A5.
   b. Select cell A1, format it with bold formatting, then change the font to Franklin Gothic Medium (or a font of your choice if this font is not available) and the font size to 20 point.
   c. Change the font color of cell A1 to orange using the orange color in the second column in the second row (the ScreenTip reads "Orange").
   d. With cell A1 still selected, use the Border Type button list arrow in the Borders and Shading group on the Formatting Palette to apply the Thick Box Border around this cell.
   e. Select the range A9:E9, then apply bold formatting to these cells. Adjust column widths as necessary to make each heading fully visible within its cell.
   f. Select the range A9:E14, then use the Border Type button list arrow to apply All Borders around these selected cells.
   g. Apply shading to cell A1 using the light yellow color in the third column in the fifth row (the ScreenTip reads "Light Yellow").
   h. Apply the same light yellow shading you applied in Step g to the range A9:E9.
   i. Save your changes.

8. **Add headers and footers.**
   a. Change to Page Layout view.
   b. Type your name in the left section of the header.
   c. Insert a code for the file name in the middle section of the header.
   d. Scroll to the footer area, then add a code for the current date in the left section of the footer.
   e. Add a code for the page number to the middle section of the footer.
   f. Save your changes.

9. **Print a worksheet.**
   a. Scroll to the top of the document, apply landscape orientation to the worksheet, then re-apply Portrait orientation.
   b. Change the page setup so that gridlines are not visible onscreen.
   c. Print the invoice. Compare your printed invoice to Figure I-23.
   d. Close the workbook, then exit Excel.

FIGURE I-23

Your Name   Furniture Invoice.xlsx

The Rustic Cabinet

April 1, 2012
Bill to:
Furniture Mart
47 East Beekman Road
Indianapolis, IN 46201

Product Number	Product Name	Quantity	Net Price	Total
16502	Dining Table	4	$ 800.00	$ 3,200.00
15667	Armchair	8	$ 125.00	$ 1,000.00
14557	Side Chair	16	$ 125.00	$ 2,000.00
17892	Armoire	4	$ 750.00	$ 3,000.00
18754	Bedside Table	5	$ 250.00	$ 1,250.00

3/1/2011   1

▼ INDEPENDENT CHALLENGE 1

At Pink Tiger Teas, Inc., a tea company based in Vancouver, British Columbia, you provide administrative help to Felicity Waters, the vice president of sales. Felicity has asked you to create a worksheet for the Sales and Marketing Department that shows a summary of monthly orders. The summary needs to include the order number, account name, order date, order total, and payments received. The worksheet also needs to show the monthly sales total and the outstanding balance due.

a. Open a new workbook, then save it as **September Order Summary** in the drive and folder where you store your Data Files.

b. Switch to Normal view if necessary, then enter the title **September Order Summary** in cell A1.

c. Enter the information shown in the table below, starting in cell A3.

Order Number	Account Name	Date	Total	Paid
2346	Aunt Myrna's Coffee	9/2/2012	678	0
2347	Queen's Grocers	9/5/2012	326	246
2348	Fannie's Coffee	9/6/2012	567	478
2349	Blue Fox Beverages	9/7/2012	1254	954
2350	Sip and Soothe	9/7/2012	2468	2468

d. Widen or narrow each column as necessary so that all the labels and data are visible.

e. Add the label **Balance Due** in cell F3. Apply bold formatting to the range A3:F3.

f. Enter a formula in cell F4 that subtracts cell E4 from cell D4, then use the fill handle to copy the formula to cells F5:F8.

g. Enter a formula in cell D9 that adds the figures in the Total column. (*Hint*: The correct formula should appear as =D4+D5+D6+D7+D8.) Then change the amount in cell D4 from 678 to 1248.

h. Use the fill handle to copy the formula in cell D9 to cells E9 and F9.

i. Drag row 9 down to row 10, then enter the label **September Totals** in cell B10.

j. Center the order numbers in cells A4 through A8, then center row 3.

k. Format the figures in the Total, Paid, and Balance Due columns (including the totals) as Currency.

l. Merge and center the title in cell A1 across columns A through F. Change the font to 20-point Arial Narrow, then apply bold formatting to it. Change the font color of the title text to the dark blue color located in the seventh column in the first row (the ScreenTip reads "Indigo").

m. Change the font in cells B10:F10 and in cells A3:F3 to Arial Narrow. Apply bold formatting to cells B10:F10.

n. Apply shading to the range B10:F10, choosing the lightest shade of red (first column, fifth row; the ScreenTip reads "Rose"). Apply this same shading to cell A1.

o. Apply All Borders to the range A3:F8, then apply a Thick Box Border around the range A3:F8.

p. Change to Page Layout view, then enter your name in the left section of the header. Enter the current date in the left section of the footer.

Advanced Challenge Exercise

- Format the numbers in cells D4 through F10 so that there are no decimals.
- Use the Draw Border pointer to draw a thin, dark red border around the range B10:F10.
- Add the same type of red border around cell A1.

q. Save the workbook, then print it.

r. Close the workbook, then exit Excel.

▼ INDEPENDENT CHALLENGE 2

You are the national sales manager for Geared Up To Go, Inc., a travel supplies company. You need to create a worksheet that analyzes first quarter sales by region. Your worksheet needs to compare first quarter sales for the current year (2012) to the previous year (2011). You also want to show how first quarter actual sales compare to the forecast. Each region was forecast to meet a sales increase of 15% over the prior year.

a. Create a new workbook, then save it as **Q1 Sales** in the drive and folder where you store your Data Files.

b. In Normal view, enter the company name **Geared Up To Go, Inc.** in cell A1, then enter **Q1 2012 Sales Analysis** in cell A2.

c. Enter the information shown in the table at the right in the worksheet, starting with the Region label in cell A4. Do not type the commas, decimal points, and dollar signs in the cells; instead, format the amounts using Currency format.

Region	Q1 2012	Q1 2011
North	$85,667.00	$76,423.00
South	$48,779.00	$33,098.00
East	$89,765.00	$77,654.00
West	$98,345.00	$67,542.00

d. Enter **Increase** in cell D4, then enter a formula in cell D5 that calculates the North region's increase in sales in Q1 2012 over Q1 2011. (*Hint*: The formula should subtract cell C5 from cell B5.)

e. Copy the formula in cell D5 to cells D6 through D8.

f. Enter **Forecast** in cell E4, then enter a formula in cell E5 that multiplies the North Region's Q1 2011 sales by 1.15. (*Hint*: The formula should use the * operator to multiply cell C5 by 1.15.) Copy this formula to cells E6 through E8.

g. Enter the label **Actual vs. Forecast** in cell F4, then enter a formula in cell F5 that subtracts the amount in cell E5 from the amount in cell B5. Copy this formula to cells F6 through F8, then widen the column as necessary.

h. Enter **Totals** in cell A9, then enter a formula in cell B9 that calculates the total of cells B5 through B8. (*Hint*: Your formula should use the + operator to add B5, B6, B7, and B8.) Copy this formula to cells C9 through F9, then widen the columns as necessary so all the totals are visible.

i. Format the worksheet using fonts, font styles, font colors, borders, shading, and alignments so that the worksheet looks attractive and is easy to understand. Increase column widths as necessary so that all labels and data are visible in each cell.

j. Insert your name in the left section of the header.

k. Change the worksheet to landscape orientation.

Advanced Challenge Exercise

ACE

- Select cell F4, then click the Wrap text check box in the Alignment and Spacing group to wrap text in this cell.
- Resize the width of column F if necessary, so that the column is just slightly wider than the longest dollar amount in cells F5 through F9. Make sure the label in cell F4 now wraps to two lines in the cell.
- Select all the cells containing dollar amounts in the worksheet. Use the Decrease Decimal button in the Number group on the Formatting Palette so that the dollar amounts show no decimal points. (Cell B5 should appear as $85,667.)

l. Save and print the worksheet, then close the workbook and exit Excel.

▼ INDEPENDENT CHALLENGE 3

You are an entrepreneur who owns an antiques business called Prairie Sue's Antiques. You purchase early American antiques at flea markets and yard sales and then resell these items on Internet auction sites for a profit. You decide to create a spreadsheet to track your profits for items you have sold so far this year.

a. Create a new workbook and save it as **YTD Profits** in the drive and folder where you store your Data Files.

b. Enter the company name **Prairie Sue's Antiques** in a cell somewhere at the top of the worksheet. Enter **YTD Profits** in a cell one row below the company name.

c. Enter the labels and data shown in the table below in an appropriate place in the worksheet. Use Accounting formatting for the Purchase Price and Sale Price columns, rather than typing a dollar sign.

Item	Date Purchased	Purchase Price	Date Sold	Sale Price
High Chair	1/17/11	$135.00	3/3/12	$270.00
Weather Vane	2/2/11	$125.00	4/15/12	$225.00
Oak Chest	3/2/11	$185.00	6/1/12	$475.00
Grandfather Clock	4/7/11	$250.00	7/10/12	$750.00
Folk Art Portrait	5/20/11	$145.00	7/1/12	$325.00

d. Adjust the width of the columns, as necessary, so that all the data in each cell is visible.

e. Enter **Profit** in the cell to the right of the Sale Price label, then enter a formula in the cell below the Profit label that calculates the difference between the sale price value and the purchase price value of the High Chair. Copy this formula to the other cells in the Profit column.

f. Select the cell below the cell that contains the value $145.00. Enter a formula in this cell that calculates the sum of the values in the Purchase Price column. Select the cell below the cell that contains the value $180.00. Enter a formula in this cell that calculates the sum of the values in the Profit column. Add the label **Total** in an appropriate cell.

g. Change the number format of the Date Purchased and Date Sold values. Choose the format type that makes the High Chair date purchased value appear as 17-Jan-11.

h. Format the titles, labels, and values in the worksheet using any fonts, alignments, borders, colors, and other formatting attributes you learned about in this unit so that the worksheet is easy to understand and looks professional. Figure I-24 shows the printed completed worksheet with possible formatting options applied.

i. Enter your name somewhere in the worksheet header, then save and print the worksheet.

j. Close the YTD Profits workbook, then exit Excel.

FIGURE I-24

Your Name

Prairie Sue's Antiques
YTD Profits

Item	Date Purchased	Purchase Price	Date Sold	Sale Price	Profit
High Chair	17-Jan-11	$ 135.00	3-Mar-12	$ 270.00	$ 135.00
Weather Vane	2-Feb-11	$ 125.00	15-Apr-12	$ 225.00	$ 100.00
Oak Chest	2-Mar-11	$ 185.00	1-Jun-12	$ 475.00	$ 290.00
Grandfather Clock	7-Apr-11	$ 250.00	10-Jul-12	$ 750.00	$ 500.00
Folk Art Portrait	20-May-11	$ 145.00	1-Jul-12	$ 325.00	$ 180.00
Total		$ 840.00			$ 1,205.00

Creating and Enhancing a Worksheet

▼ REAL LIFE INDEPENDENT CHALLENGE

You have just been hired for a summer internship working for your dream company in a location of your choosing. The internship will pay you a total stipend of $2400 for working from June 1 through August 31, which works out to be $800 per month. You need to create a budget spreadsheet to allocate your monthly expenses for the three months you are working there. You also have an additional $1000 in savings that you can use to pay for your expenses during this time. You need to find out whether your income and savings will cover your expenses during this time. If there is a variance between your available funds and your expenses, you may be able to request an increase in the stipend.

a. Start Excel, then save a new workbook as **Summer Budget** where you store your Data Files.

b. Type **Summer Budget** in cell A1, then enter the following labels in cells A3:E3: **Expense**, **June**, **July**, **August**, **Total**.

c. Enter the following labels in cells A4 through A12: **Rent**, **Food**, **Transportation/Gas**, **Moving Costs**, **Utilities**, **Cable**, **Phone**, **Entertainment**, **Total Expenses**.

d. Enter data into cells B4:D11 that you think is appropriate, considering the location that you have chosen for your dream city and the type of lifestyle you want to lead while there. Format all the cells in this range as currency. (*Hint:* You may want to enter all the data for June, and then copy the cells to the July and August columns, omitting moving expenses in July.)

e. Enter a formula in cell E4 that calculates the total Rent cost for June, July, and August.

f. Use the fill handle to copy the formula in cell E4 to cells E5:E11.

g. Enter a formula in cell B12 that calculates the monthly expenses for June. Use the fill handle to copy this formula to cells C12:E12, then format these cells as Currency if necessary.

h. Type the following labels in cells A14:A16: **Internship Stipend**, **Savings**, and **Total Funds**. Type the amount of money you will be paid for the internship (**2400**) in cell B14, then type the amount of your savings (**1000**) in cell B15. Enter a formula in cell B16 that adds cells B14 and B15. Format cells B14:B16 as currency.

i. Type the label **Variance** in cell A18. Enter a formula in cell B18 that calculates the difference between your total funds available and your total expenses. (*Hint:* This formula should subtract cell E12 from B16.)

j. Format the worksheet using fonts, borders, shading, and alignment so that it is attractive and easy to read. Make sure to use formatting to emphasize the key cells in the worksheet, such as the labels, the totals, and the variance information.

k. Insert a header that contains your name centered and the current date left-aligned.

l. Save the worksheet, print it, then exit Excel.

▼ VISUAL WORKSHOP

Create the worksheet shown in Figure I-25 using the commands, formulas, and formatting skills you learned in this unit. Use formulas for all subtotals and totals. Save the workbook as **Holiday Sales Analysis** in the drive and folder where you store your Data Files, enter your name in the center section of the footer, then print a copy.

FIGURE I-25

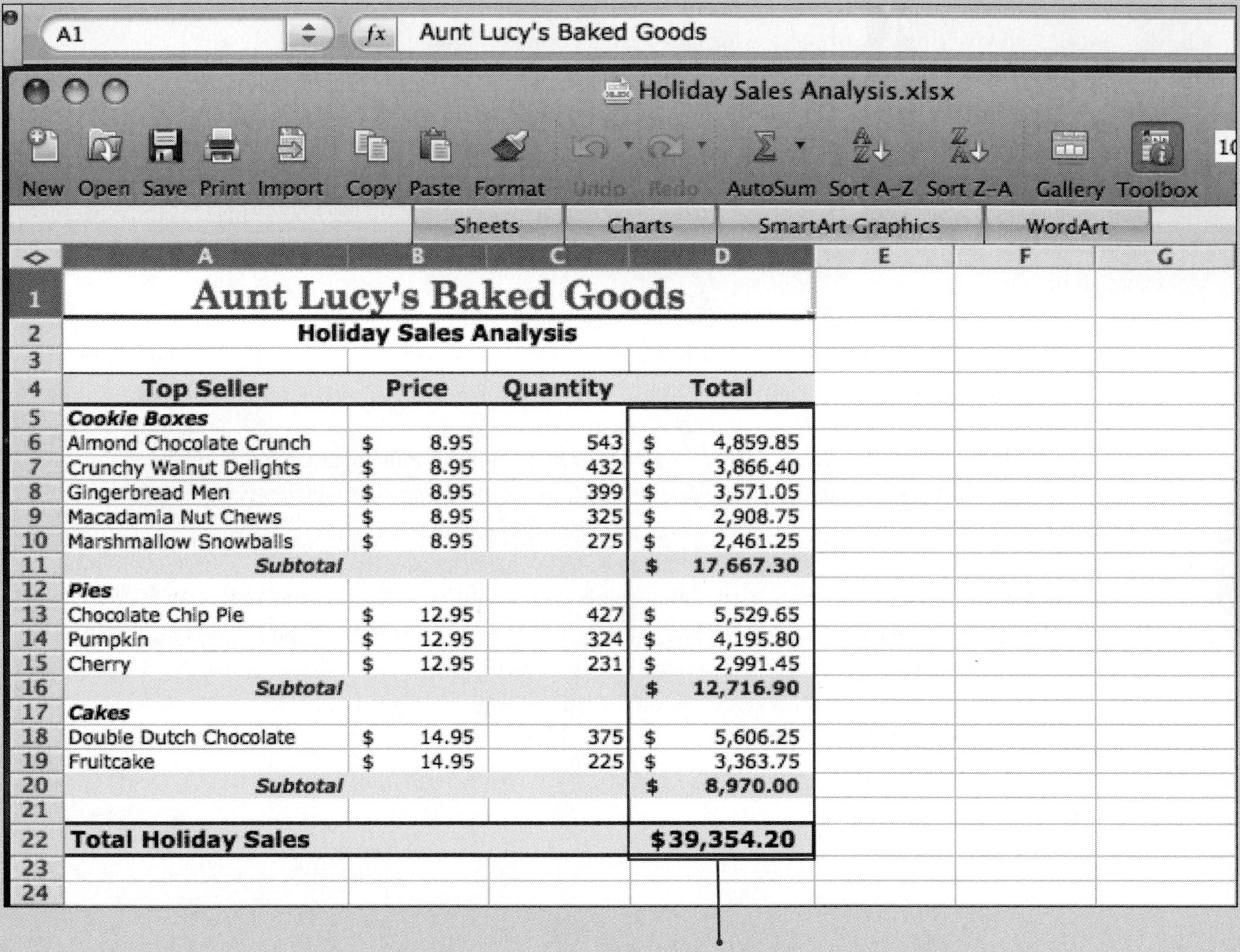

	A	B	C	D	E	F	G
1	**Aunt Lucy's Baked Goods**						
2	**Holiday Sales Analysis**						
3							
4	**Top Seller**	**Price**	**Quantity**	**Total**			
5	*Cookie Boxes*						
6	Almond Chocolate Crunch	$ 8.95	543	$ 4,859.85			
7	Crunchy Walnut Delights	$ 8.95	432	$ 3,866.40			
8	Gingerbread Men	$ 8.95	399	$ 3,571.05			
9	Macadamia Nut Chews	$ 8.95	325	$ 2,908.75			
10	Marshmallow Snowballs	$ 8.95	275	$ 2,461.25			
11	*Subtotal*			$ 17,667.30			
12	*Pies*						
13	Chocolate Chip Pie	$ 12.95	427	$ 5,529.65			
14	Pumpkin	$ 12.95	324	$ 4,195.80			
15	Cherry	$ 12.95	231	$ 2,991.45			
16	*Subtotal*			$ 12,716.90			
17	*Cakes*						
18	Double Dutch Chocolate	$ 14.95	375	$ 5,606.25			
19	Fruitcake	$ 14.95	225	$ 3,363.75			
20	*Subtotal*			$ 8,970.00			
21							
22	**Total Holiday Sales**			**$39,354.20**			
23							
24							

Cell reference box: A1 — fx — Aunt Lucy's Baked Goods

Holiday Sales Analysis.xlsx

Toolbar: New Open Save Print Import Copy Paste Format Undo Redo AutoSum Sort A-Z Sort Z-A Gallery Toolbox

Tabs: Sheets Charts SmartArt Graphics WordArt

Enter formulas (not values) in these cells

Using Complex Formulas and Functions

In addition to the simple, single-operator formulas you learned about in the previous unit, Excel includes powerful data analysis tools. These tools include **complex formulas**, which perform more than one calculation at a time, and **functions**, which are prewritten formulas, many containing multiple operators, that you can use instead of typing all the formula parts. To analyze Excel data, you can automatically **sort** the information to change its order and **filter** it to display only the type of data you specify. You can also make certain data stand out in your worksheets by applying conditional formatting. Paulette Chen, director of sales for Outdoor Designs, has given you a worksheet that shows year-to-date sales for the company's western sales region. She has asked you to perform some calculations on the data, organize it so its easier to read, and highlight important information.

OBJECTIVES

Create complex formulas

Understand functions

Use AutoSum

Use date and time functions

Use statistical functions

Apply conditional formatting

Sort rows in a worksheet

Filter data

UNIT
J
Excel 2008

Creating Complex Formulas

When you create worksheets that contain many calculations, you often need to create formulas that contain more than one mathematical operator. For instance, to calculate profits for a particular product, a formula would first need to calculate product sales (product price multiplied by number of products sold) and then subtract costs from that result. Formulas that contain more than one operator are called **complex formulas**. When a formula contains multiple operators, Excel uses standard algebraic rules to determine which calculation to perform first. Calculations in parentheses are always evaluated first. Next, exponential calculations are performed, then multiplication and division calculations, and finally addition and subtraction calculations. If there are multiple calculations within the parentheses, they are performed according to this same order. Table J-1 lists the common mathematical operators and the order in which Excel evaluates them in a formula. Paulette provides you with a worksheet showing year-to-date sales for the western region and asks you to calculate the sales commission due for each customer sales amount.

STEPS

1. **Start Excel, open the file J-1.xlsx from where you store your Data Files, then save it as Western Region YTD Sales**

   A copy of Paulette's partially completed worksheet is open and saved with a new name.

QUICK TIP

If you see a list open when you begin typing the formula, ignore it and continue typing; this is the AutoComplete list, which is covered in the next lesson.

2. **Click cell G4**

   The Commission Due formula for the order placed by Kayaks and More first needs to add the January amount in cell D4 and the February amount in cell E4. Then it should multiply this total by the Commission rate of 5% (or .05) to calculate the Commission Due amount.

3. **Type =(D4+E4)*F4**

   The formula bar displays the formula =(D4+E4)*F4 and the cells referenced in the formula are highlighted.

QUICK TIP

Even if you had entered the formula =F4*(D4+E4), Excel would perform the calculation in the parentheses first, because it always evaluates formulas according to standard algebraic rules.

4. **Press [control][return]**

   See Figure J-1. The result of the formula you typed, $702.50, appears in cell G4. Excel performed the calculation in the parentheses first, which added the contents of cell D4 (the January sales amount for Kayaks and More) to the contents of cell E4 (the February order amount from Kayaks and More). Excel then multiplied this result by the commission rate in cell F4 (5% or .05). In effect, Excel calculated (8376+5674)*.05. This cell already has Accounting formatting applied to it, so the value appears as a dollar amount.

5. **Drag the cell G4 fill handle down through cell G22 to copy the formula to the range G5:G22**

   The results of the copied formula appear in cells G5 through G22. Compare your screen to Figure J-2.

6. **Click the Save button ▣ on the Standard toolbar**

   Excel saves your changes to the workbook.

FIGURE J-1: Complex formula and its returned value

Calculation in parentheses is performed first

Complex formula has two mathematical operators

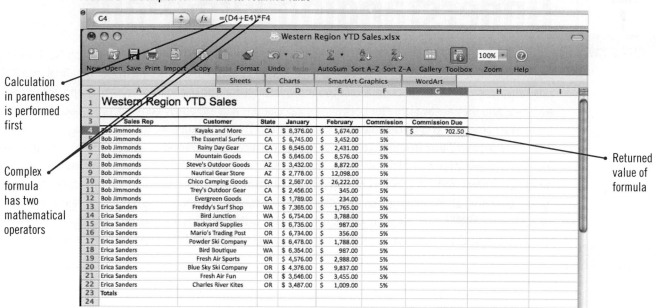

Returned value of formula

FIGURE J-2: Formula copied to a range of cells

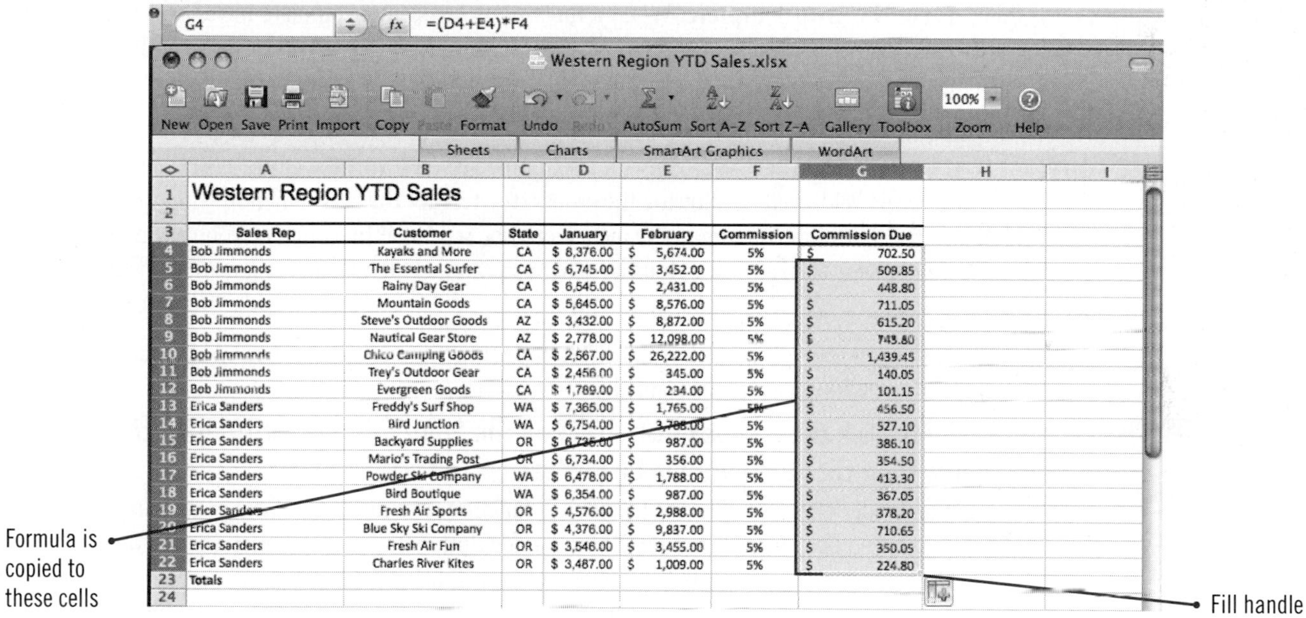

Formula is copied to these cells

Fill handle

TABLE J-1: Useful mathematical operators (listed in order of evaluation)

operator	description	example	result
( )	Parentheses	(4+7)*3	33
^	Exponent	9^2	81
*	Multiplication	7*5	35
/	Division	20/4	5
+	Addition	5+5	10
−	Subtraction	12–8	4

Understanding Functions

Functions are prewritten formulas that come with Excel. Instead of figuring out which calculations you need to achieve a particular result—and what order in which to type them so the final result is accurate—you can use a function to compose the formula for you. Functions save time and help ensure accuracy, and they are available for both simple calculations and extremely complex ones. Each Excel function has a name that you usually see in all capital letters. The SUM function, for example, adds values; the AVERAGE function calculates the average value of a specified range of cells or values; and so on. There are four parts to every function: an equal sign, the function name, a set of parentheses, and arguments separated by commas and enclosed in the parentheses. **Arguments** are information a function needs to perform a task and can be values (such as 100 or .02), cell references (such as B3), or range references (such as A9:G16). ▰▰▰▰ You want to familiarize yourself with functions so that you can use them in the Western Region YTD Sales worksheet. You decide to experiment with functions in a blank worksheet.

1. **Click the** Insert Sheet button +

   The Sheet2 worksheet opens; it is blank and offers a perfect place to practice using functions.

2. **Click the** Normal View button 🖿 **, click cell A5, type =, then type s**

   See Figure J-3. A list of functions beginning with the letter S appears by cell A5. Anytime you type an equal sign followed by a letter, a list of valid functions and names beginning with that letter appears. This feature is called **Formula AutoComplete**. When a function is used, AutoComplete includes it under the Most Recently Used category heading at the top of the list (your Most Recently Used list may differ). Once you select a function, a ScreenTip appears to guide you through inserting appropriate arguments.

   > **QUICK TIP**
   >
   > When using Formula AutoComplete to enter a function, you can type either capital or lower-case letters; the feature is not case sensitive. You can also shorten the list by typing additional letters in the function name.

3. **Click** SUM **in the list of functions**

   Now SUM is entered into cell A5 along with a set of parentheses with the cursor positioned in-between. A ScreenTip appears below cell A5 showing the proper structure for the SUM function. The placeholders number1 and number2 indicate arguments, which should be separated by commas; you can insert values, cell references, or ranges. The ellipsis (...) indicates that you can include as many arguments as you wish.

4. **Type** 5,6,7 **, press [return], then click cell A5**

   Cell A5 displays the value 18, which is the result of the function. Clicking on cell A5 displays the function =SUM(5,6,7) in the formula bar. See Figure J-4.

   > **QUICK TIP**
   >
   > You can display a list of all of the functions by category by opening the "List of all functions by category" topic in Excel Help.

5. **Click cell A6, click the** Toolbox button 📷 **on the Standard toolbar to open the Toolbox if necessary, then click the** Formula Builder tab fx **on the Toolbox**

   The Formula Builder offers several ways to choose a function. You can scroll through the function list to see functions organized by category. (See Table J-2 for a description of common function categories.) The Most Recently Used category appears at the top, followed by an alphabetical list of categories. You can also use the Search for a function box. The Search for a function box is great if you've forgotten the name of a function or aren't sure which one to use. You can type a function name, business problem, or related word. If Excel recognizes part of the phrase you entered, it lists the related functions in the function list.

6. **Type** calculate loan payments **in the Search for a function box on the Formula Builder**

   As you type, Excel displays a list of functions related to calculating a loan payment.

   > **QUICK TIP**
   >
   > Clicking a function in the function list displays a description of what the function does.

7. **Scroll to locate the PMT function in the function list if necessary, then double-click** PMT

   The Arguments list opens at the bottom of the Formula Builder and displays the arguments required by the PMT function. To enter an argument in an argument box, click the relevant cell in the worksheet or type directly into the argument box in the Arguments list. When the insertion point is in an argument box, a description of the selected argument is provided in the Description box above. See Figure J-5.

8. **Press [esc], click the** Sheet1 tab **, then save your changes**

   Pressing [esc] cancels the PMT function, and the Sheet1 worksheet containing the Western Region YTD Sales information is now open on your screen.

FIGURE J-3: Entering a formula using Formula AutoComplete

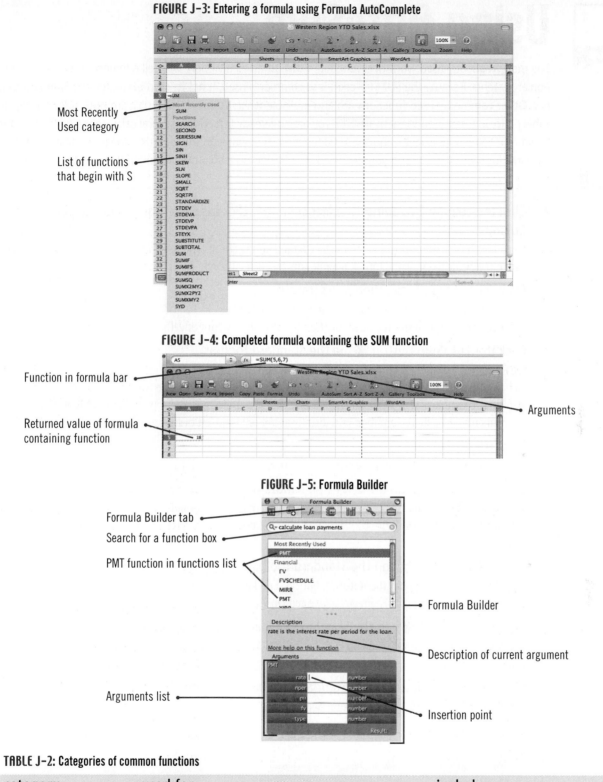

Most Recently Used category

List of functions that begin with S

FIGURE J-4: Completed formula containing the SUM function

Function in formula bar

Arguments

Returned value of formula containing function

FIGURE J-5: Formula Builder

Formula Builder tab

Search for a function box

PMT function in functions list

Formula Builder

Description of current argument

Arguments list

Insertion point

TABLE J-2: Categories of common functions

category	used for	includes
Date and Time	Calculations involving dates and times	NOW, TODAY, WEEKDAY
Financial	Loan payments, appreciation, and depreciation	PMT, FV, DB, SLN
Logical	Calculations that display a value if a condition is met	IF, AND, NOT
Lookup and Reference	Finding values in lists or finding cell references	ADDRESS, ROW, HYPERLINK
Math and Trigonometry	Simple and complex mathematical calculations	ABS, ASIN, COS
Text	Comparing, converting, and reformatting text strings in cells	FIND, REPLACE

Using AutoSum

The most frequently used worksheet function, **SUM**, totals all numbers and cell references included as function arguments. Because the SUM function is so commonly used, it has its own button on the Standard toolbar. Other commonly used functions are also available when you click the AutoSum button list arrow; see Table J-3 for a description of each. You are now ready to perform several calculations on the Western Region YTD Sales worksheet using the SUM function. First you want to total the January and February sales amounts for each customer, so you decide to start by adding a column to contain these totals.

STEPS

1. **Click the column F heading to select column F, click Insert on the menu bar, then click Columns**

    You added a new column to the left of the Commission heading. The new column is now column F. This is where you want to enter the total sales amounts for each customer for January and February.

2. **Click cell F3, type Total, then press [return]**

    The label Total appears in cell F3 and is formatted exactly like cells E3 and G3. The active cell is now F4; this is where you want to enter the SUM function to calculate the sum of cells D4 and E4.

3. **Click the AutoSum button Σ on the Standard toolbar**

    See Figure J-6. The proposed function =SUM(D4:E4) appears in cell F4 and on the formula bar, ready for you to edit or accept. Cells D4 and E4 are highlighted, indicating that these are the two cells that Excel assumes you want to add together. When you use the AutoSum button, Excel "guesses" what range of cells you want to use as arguments—usually the group of cells directly above or to the left of the cell containing the function.

4. **Press [return]**

    Excel accepts the formula, and the result, $14,050.00, appears in cell F4.

5. **Click cell F4, then drag the cell F4 fill handle down to cell F23**

    You copied the formula from F4 to all the cells in the range F5 through F23. Notice that cell F23 contains no value; this is because cells D23 and E23 contain no values. Therefore, the sum of these two cells is currently zero.

6. **Click cell D23, click Σ on the Standard toolbar, then press [return]**

    This time when you clicked the AutoSum button, Excel guessed (correctly) that you wanted to calculate the sum of cells D4:D22, the cells directly above cell D23.

7. **Click cell E23, click Σ on the Standard toolbar, then press [return]**

    The result of the formula, $94,864.00, appears in cell E23. The sum of cells D23 and E23, $191,602.00, now appears in cell F23.

8. **Click cell H23, click Σ on the Standard toolbar, then press [return]**

    Cell H23 now shows $9,580.10, the sum of cells H4:H22. Compare your screen to Figure J-7.

9. **Save your changes**

Using ledger sheets

A new feature in Excel 2008 is ledger sheets. **Ledger sheets** are preformatted Excel worksheets designed to help you with common financial tasks. For example, you can use ledger sheets to record checkbook entries, to create an expense report, to track your stocks, or even to create a list of addresses. Each ledger sheet contains all of the appropriate formulas and columns; you just enter your data. To access ledger sheets, click the Sheets tab in the Elements Gallery, click the group you want (such as Budgets), then click the desired ledger sheet. The ledger sheet opens in a new worksheet in the current workbook, ready for you to begin entering data. Ledger sheets make it easy to manage your finances by preventing errors (for example, ledger sheets do not allow a date in a column formatted for currency), and by allowing you to sort and filter the columns easily. When working in a ledger sheet, you can use the Ledger Sheet group on the Formatting Palette to customize the sheet as desired.

FIGURE J-6: SUM function inserted in cell F4

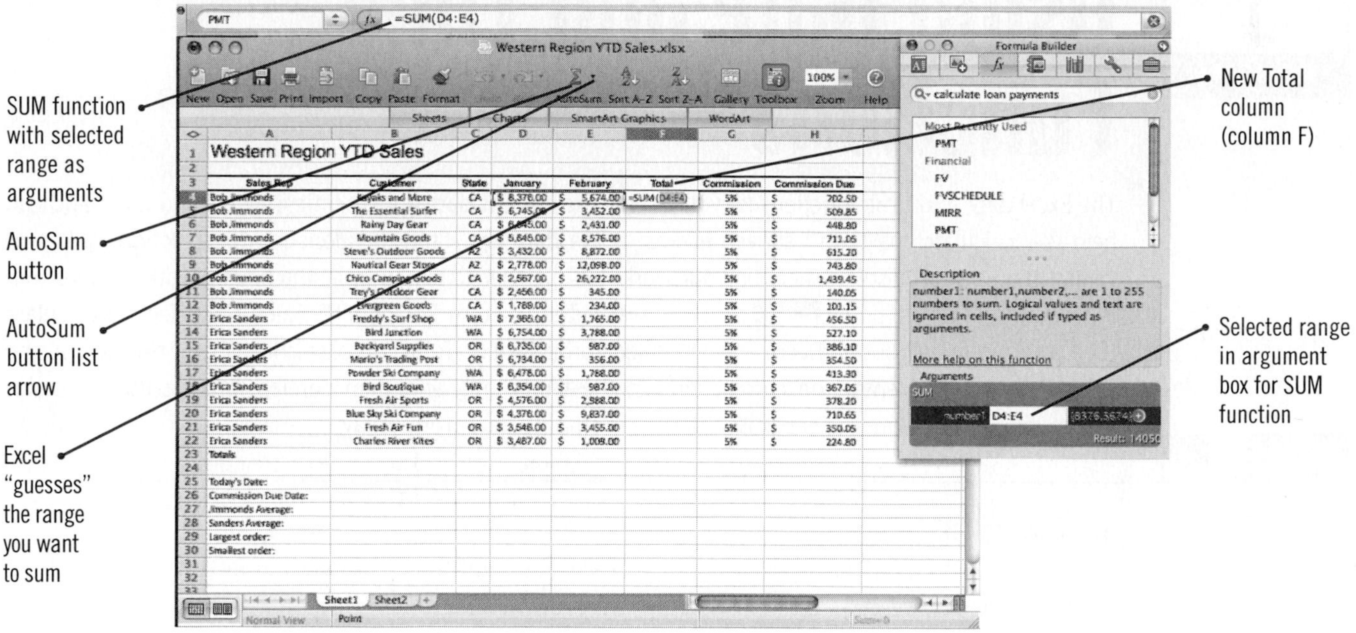

SUM function with selected range as arguments

AutoSum button

AutoSum button list arrow

Excel "guesses" the range you want to sum

New Total column (column F)

Selected range in argument box for SUM function

FIGURE J-7: Worksheet with all totals calculated using the SUM function

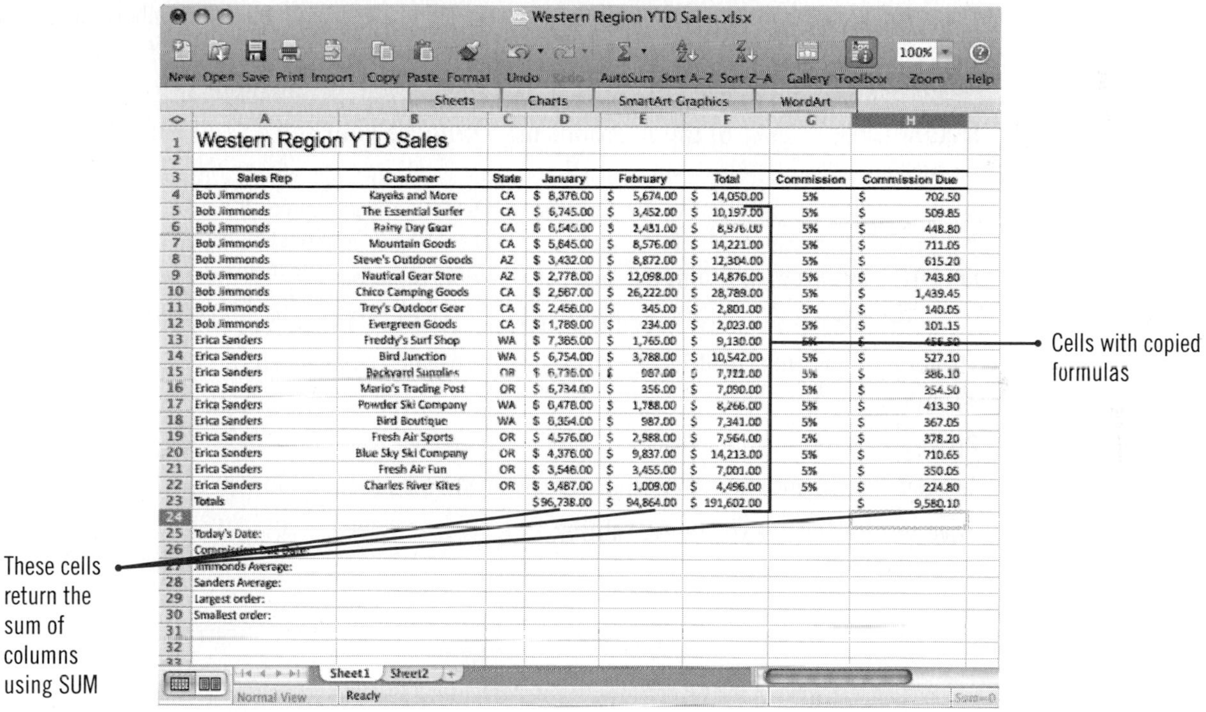

Cells with copied formulas

These cells return the sum of columns using SUM

TABLE J-3: Commonly used functions available through the AutoSum button list arrow

function	description
SUM	Calculates the sum of the arguments
AVERAGE	Calculates the average value of the arguments
COUNT NUMBERS	Calculates the number of values in the list of arguments
MAX	Calculates the largest value in the list of arguments
MIN	Calculates the smallest value in the list of arguments
More Functions	Inserts an equal sign in the selected cell, ready for you to type a function name or click a cell

Using Date and Time Functions

The Excel date and time functions let you display the current date and/or time in your worksheet and can help you calculate the time between events. Some date and time functions produce recognizable text values that you can display "as is" in your worksheets. Other date and time functions produce values that require special formatting. ██████ Paulette wants the Western Region YTD Sales worksheet to calculate the date that commission checks are scheduled to be issued. To accomplish this, you decide to use the TODAY function to enter the current date in the worksheet, and then enter a formula that uses this information to calculate the check issue date, which is 30 days from today.

1. **Click cell B25**

   This cell is to the right of the label Today's Date. You want to enter a function in this cell that returns today's date.

2. **Type today in the Search for a function box on the Formula Builder, then click TODAY in the functions list**

   The description of this function explains that the TODAY function returns a number that represents the current date. The syntax shows empty parentheses, meaning that the TODAY function requires no arguments, so you don't need to add values between the parentheses in the formula.

   > **QUICK TIP**
   > The TODAY function uses your computer's internal clock to return current date information, and recalculates this result as needed.

3. **Double-click TODAY in the functions list, compare your screen to Figure J-8, then press [return]**

   When you double-click TODAY, the function, =TODAY(), appears in cell B25 and in the formula bar. After you press [return], the result of this function, the current date, appears in cell B25. You next want to enter a formula in cell B26 that returns the date that is 30 days from today.

4. **With the insertion point in cell B26, type =, press [↑] to select cell B25, then type +30**

   The formula you entered, =B25+30, calculates the day when commission checks should be issued, which is 30 days after today's date.

5. **Press [return]**

   The commission due date now appears as a date in cell B26, as shown in Figure J-9.

6. **Save your changes to the workbook**

FIGURE J-8: Inserting the TODAY function

Function
bar calcu
average
D4:E12

Formula
bar also
shows
function

AutoSum
list arrow

Average
for Bob Ji

Function in
cell B25

TODAY
function in
functions
list

Description
of TODAY
function

Function
syntax

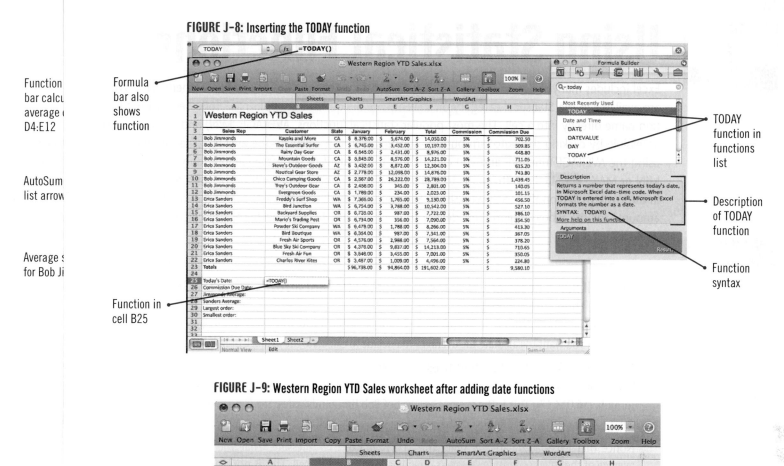

FIGURE J-9: Western Region YTD Sales worksheet after adding date functions

Result of
TODAY
function
(your date
will differ)

Result of
=B25+30
(your date
will differ)

Understanding how dates are calculated using serial values

When you enter a date in a worksheet cell, the date is actually stored as a serial value, regardless of whether it appears in a familiar format (such as August 11, 2012). A **serial value** is a number in a sequential series of numbers. Date serial values represent the number of days since January 1, 1900. Dates are stored as serial values so they can be used in calculations. For example, in this lesson you added 30 days to the current date. To Excel, the formula in cell B26 in

Figure J-9 is really =40973+30. This is useful to know if you remove the formatting from a cell previously formatted as a date, or apply the General format to a cell containing a date. Instead of displaying the date, Excel displays the serial value that represents that date. To make the cell contents recognizable again, click the cell, click the Format Number list arrow on the Formatting Palette, then click Date.

Sorting Rows in a Worksheet

Excel lets you analyze worksheet data by sorting and filtering that data. When you **sort** data, you change the order of your data using the column you specify. In a customer worksheet, you might sort by the Last Name column or the Zip Code column. When you sort or filter data, Excel keeps the information from each row together. Paulette wants the data in the Western Region YTD Sales worksheet sorted by state, in alphabetical order, and then within each state by order amount from largest to smallest.

STEPS

QUICK TIP

To undo the results of a sort immediately after performing it, click the Undo button on the Standard toolbar.

1. **Select cell C4, then click the Sort A-Z button on the Standard toolbar**

   As shown in Figure J-16, the items in the table are now sorted by state in alphabetical order, with the Arizona customers at the top and the Washington customers at the bottom. Paulette also wants the list to be sorted by totals within each state, from largest to smallest.

2. **Select cell F4, click Data on the menu bar, then click Sort**

   The Sort dialog box opens. Because you already performed one sort on this data, your sort criteria is listed in the dialog box. You can use this dialog box to sort your data based on up to three criteria.

3. **Click the Then by arrows, click Total, then click the Descending option button to the right of the Then by arrows**

   Compare your screen to Figure J-17.

QUICK TIP

If numbers have the Text cell format applied, they appear left-aligned instead of right-aligned and are sorted as text rather than as numbers. For example, if numbers formatted as text are sorted in ascending order, the number 12 will appear before the number 8 because the first characters are compared first, and 1 comes before 8.

4. **Click OK**

   The list is now sorted first by the State column in alphabetical order. Within each State listing, the customers with the highest value in the Total column are listed first. See Figure J-18.

5. **Type your name in cell A32, then save your changes to the workbook**

Adding subtotals and grand totals to a worksheet

Excel can automatically calculate subtotal and grand total values in a list. For example, you could calculate subtotals for each sales rep, along with the grand total for all units. First you need to sort the data by the columns for which you want to generate subtotals, such as by Sales Rep. Once the data is sorted, click Data on the menu bar, then click Subtotals to open the Subtotal dialog box. In the At each change in list, click Sales Rep. In the Use function list, click Sum. Click the check box next to the column in the Add subtotal to list that you want to be totaled, such as Commission Due. Click OK to close the dialog box and add the subtotals to the worksheet, as shown in Figure J-19. Once subtotals are calculated, click the outline symbols to the left of the row numbers to display or hide the summary details. To remove subtotals, click Data, click Subtotals, then click the Remove All button.

FIGURE J-19: Subtotals added to worksheet

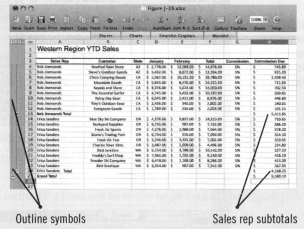

Outline symbols   Sales rep subtotals

FIGURE J-16: List sorted by state from A to Z

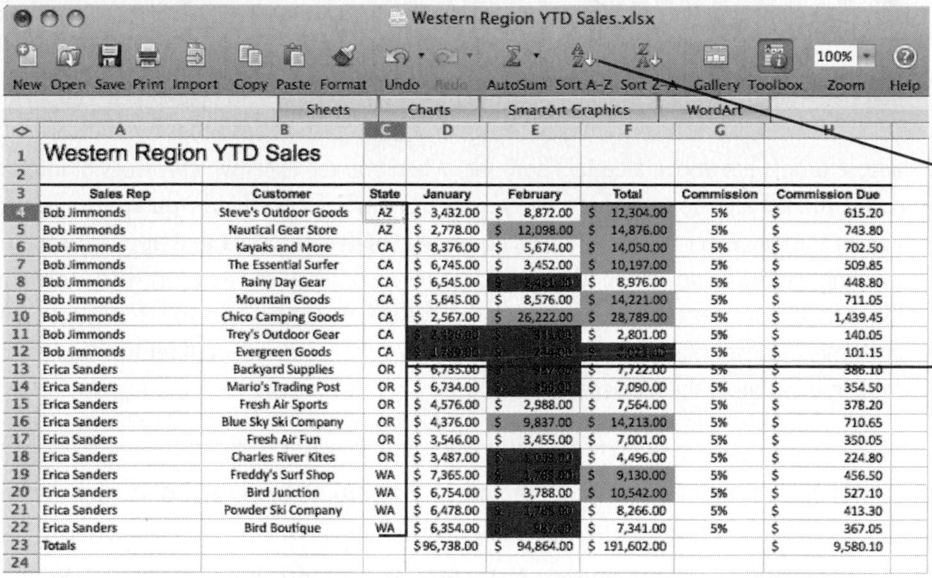

- Sort A-Z button
- States sorted in alphabetical order

FIGURE J-17: Sort dialog box

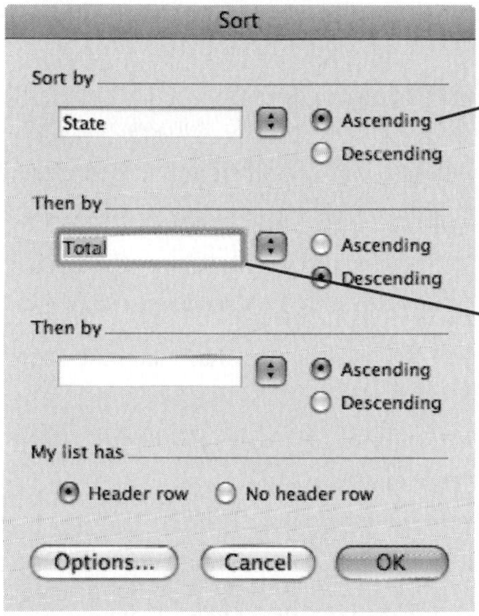

- Sort applied using Sort A-Z button
- Secondary sort on Total column with largest values appearing at top of list

FIGURE J-18: Data sorted by two sort criteria

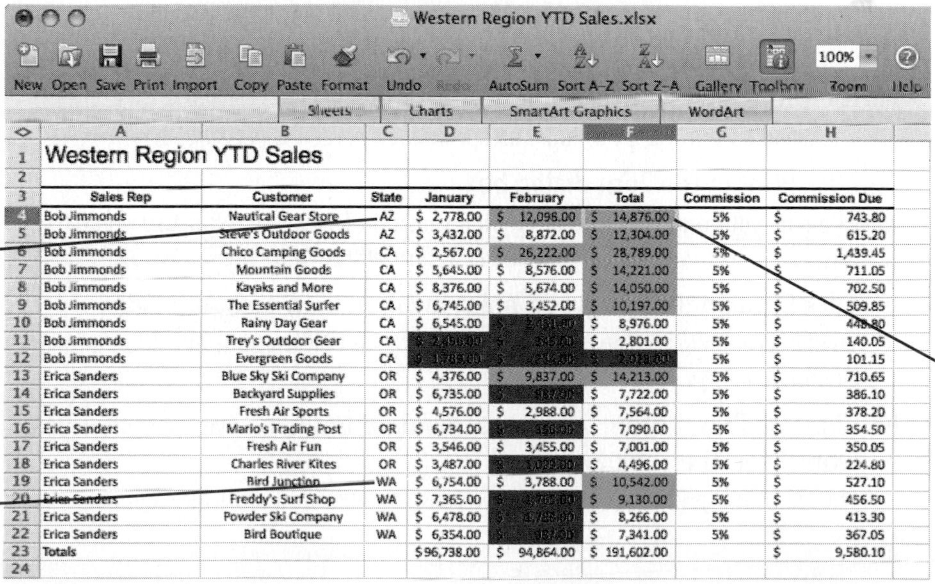

- Arizona customers are listed first
- Washington customers are listed last
- Within each state grouping, orders are listed from largest to smallest in Total column

Excel 2008

Filtering Data

If your Excel worksheet contains a large amount of data, you might want to **filter** it to display only the data that you specify by entering certain information, such as customers with a particular zip code, or those whose orders are above a certain amount. When you tell Excel which pieces of information (such as a zip code) you want to see, you are specifying the **criteria** for the filter. You apply a filter to a list by first turning on the AutoFilter feature, then using the **AutoFilter arrows** that appear to the right of each column heading. Unlike a sort, a filter does not change the order of the items in your table; instead, it temporarily hides data that does not meet your criteria. **▨▨▨** Paulette wants to see a list of orders for Erica Sanders' customers whose total orders are greater than $7500. You decide to filter the data so only the desired information is visible in the worksheet.

STEPS

1. Click cell A4, click Data on the menu bar, point to Filter, then click AutoFilter

Notice that each cell in the header row now has AutoFilter arrows on its right side.

QUICK TIP

You can also sort data in a column by selecting the column's AutoFilter arrows, then clicking Sort Ascending or Sort Descending.

2. Click the Sales Rep column AutoFilter arrows in cell A3, then click Erica Sanders

The AutoFilter drop-down list displays the list of available filters for this column. Excel creates filters for each of the values in the column, plus filters to automatically select all values, custom values, or specified text or numeric values. By selecting Erica Sanders on the drop-down list, you have applied a filter that shows only the rows that contain the value Erica Sanders in the Sales Rep column. See Figure J-20. You can tell that worksheet data is filtered because the AutoFilter arrows in the column header change color. You can also see that the row numbers have breaks in their numeric sequence and have changed color too.

3. Click the Total column AutoFilter arrows, then click (Custom Filter...)

The Custom AutoFilter dialog box opens. You use this dialog box to specify one or more criteria for a filter.

4. Click the arrows to the right of "equals", then click is greater than

The box below Total displays "is greater than," and the insertion point blinks in the box where you need to specify an amount.

5. Type 7500, compare your screen to Figure J-21, then click OK

The table is filtered to show all the customers of Erica Sanders whose total orders were greater than $7500. Now the table displays only six items. By using the AutoFilter arrows in succession like this, you can apply more than one criterion to the same data in your worksheet.

6. Click File on the menu bar, then click Print

The Print dialog box opens and displays a preview of the worksheet in the Preview box. You can see that the worksheet is page 1 of 2 and is currently set to print in portrait orientation.

7. Click the Page Setup button in the Print dialog box, click the Page tab if necessary, click the Landscape option button, then click OK

The document now appears in landscape orientation and is page 1 of 1.

8. Click Print in the Print dialog box

Compare your printed document to that shown in Figure J-22. Now that you have printed the information filtered the way you want it, you decide to turn off the AutoFilter.

QUICK TIP

You can also remove an applied filter by clicking Data on the menu bar, pointing to Filter, then clicking Show All.

9. Click Data on the menu bar, point to Filter, then click AutoFilter

The filters are removed and all the rows of data are visible again. AutoFilter arrows no longer appear in the column headings.

10. Click the Print button 🖶 on the Standard toolbar, save your changes, close the worksheet, then exit Excel

The worksheet prints, your changes are saved, and both the worksheet and Excel close.

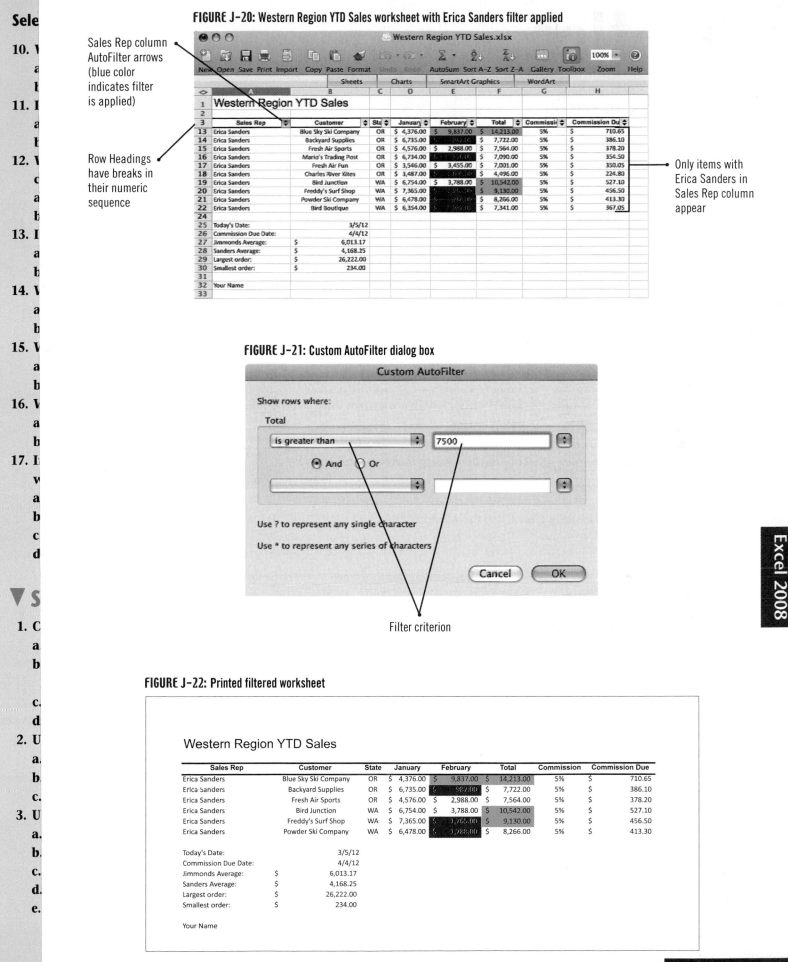

FIGURE J-20: Western Region YTD Sales worksheet with Erica Sanders filter applied

Sales Rep column AutoFilter arrows (blue color indicates filter is applied)

Row Headings have breaks in their numeric sequence

Only items with Erica Sanders in Sales Rep column appear

FIGURE J-21: Custom AutoFilter dialog box

Filter criterion

FIGURE J-22: Printed filtered worksheet

Excel 2008

Moving and Resizing a Chart and Chart Objects

If your chart is not the exact size you want it to be, or if it is in an inconvenient place on the worksheet, you can easily move or resize it. You can also move or resize many of the **chart objects**, which are the individual components of a chart such as the plot area or the legend. To move a chart object, you select it and drag it to a new location. To resize a chart object, drag one of its sizing handles. Note that some chart objects (such as the chart axis) cannot be moved and that others (such as the chart title) cannot be resized by dragging. In these cases, you'll need to be content with the location or size of the object.  To improve the overall appearance of the worksheet, you decide to move the chart below the worksheet data and make it bigger. You also decide to move the legend so that it is aligned with the top edge of the chart.

1. If the chart is not selected, click the chart border to select it

2. Point to the top edge of the chart so that the pointer changes to ✥, drag the chart so that its upper-left corner is aligned with the upper-left corner of cell A10, then release the mouse button

   The chart is now directly below the worksheet data. As you dragged the chart, a dimmed outline of the chart moved with the pointer.

3. Position the pointer over the chart's lower-right sizing handle so the pointer changes to ↘, click and drag the sizing handle down so the chart's lower-right corner is aligned with the lower-right corner of cell F28, then release the mouse button

   The chart enlarges to the new dimensions, as shown in Figure K-4. If you drag a corner sizing handle, you increase or decrease a chart's height and width simultaneously. To increase or decrease only the height or width of a chart, drag one of the side sizing handles.

4. Click the chart legend

   Sizing handles appear around the edge of the legend, indicating it is selected. Note that the sizing handles on the legend—and on all chart objects—are circular at the corners and square on the midpoints. This is different from the sizing handles on the chart itself, where the sizing handles are groups of dots.

5. Point to any border of the legend (but not to a sizing handle) until the pointer changes to ✥, then drag the legend up to the position shown in Figure K-5

   The legend is now positioned in the upper-right corner of the chart.

6. Click a blank area of the chart, then click the Save button 🖫 on the Standard toolbar

> **QUICK TIP**
> To move a chart, click and drag an edge and not a sizing handle; to resize a chart, click and drag a sizing handle and not an edge. If you make a mistake when moving or resizing a chart or chart object, click the Undo button on the Standard toolbar, then try again.

> **QUICK TIP**
> To delete a chart or chart object, select it, then press [delete].

FIGURE K-4: Resized chart

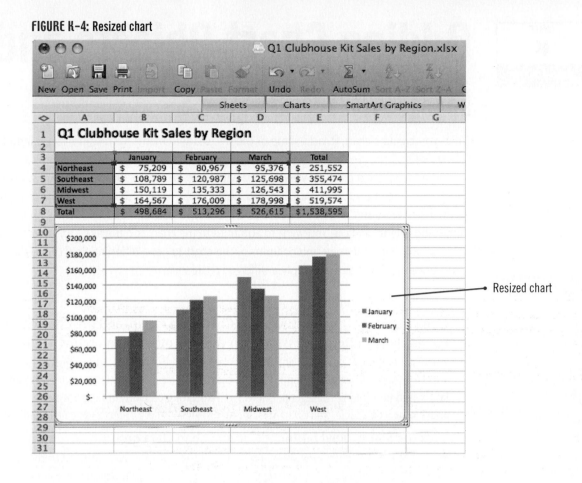

Resized chart

FIGURE K-5: Moving the legend

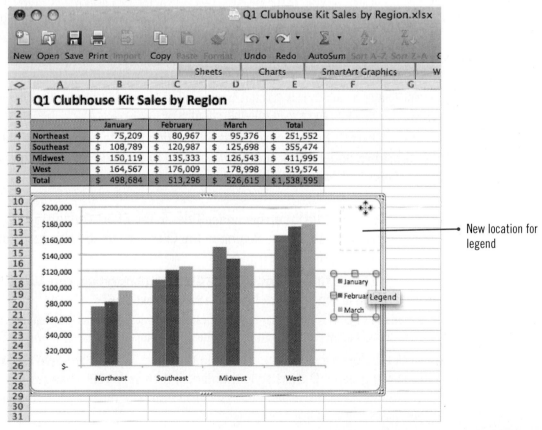

New location for legend

UNIT
K
Excel 2008

Adding Chart Objects and Applying Styles

When you create a chart, it lacks some of the necessary elements for full understanding of the information shown. For instance, you might want to add chart objects to the chart such as the chart title and axis titles. You can also explore a different view of your data by reversing the rows and columns. An additional way to change how the information in a chart is presented is by using a chart style. A **chart style** is a predefined set of chart colors and fills. You can select a chart style from the gallery in the Chart Style group on the Formatting Palette. ▰▰▰▰ You want to add titles to the chart and the axes, and you also decide to experiment by switching the rows and columns of the chart to get a different view of the data. To improve the appearance of your chart, you apply a different chart style.

STEPS

> **QUICK TIP**
> Depending on the size of your screen, you may find it helpful to open and close groups on the Formatting Palette as you need them.

1. **Open the Chart Options group, the Chart Data group, and the Chart Style group on the Formatting Palette if necessary, then click any other open groups to close them**

   The Chart Options, Chart Data, and Chart Styles groups are contextual; they are available only when a chart is selected. The Chart Options group contains commands for adding titles, showing axes and gridlines, adding labels, and positioning the legend. The Chart Data group contains options for switching rows and columns and adding a data table. The Chart Style group displays a gallery of predesigned chart fills and textures.

2. **Click the Sort by Row button ▦ in the Chart Data group**

   See Figure K-6. The chart now shows only three clusters of data series (instead of the original four), one for each month. Each data series now represents the revenue for each region (instead of each month), so there are four data points for each cluster instead of three. The horizontal axis labels now list the three months of the first quarter (instead of the regions). This view of the data does not as clearly illustrate the trend that three of the regions increased their sales in February and March, or that the Midwest region experienced a decline in sales in February and March. The original view of the data is better for your purposes.

3. **Click the Sort by Column button ▦ in the Chart Data group**

   The chart reverts back to the original structure, with four clusters of three data series and each data series representing a month. This structure is more effective at communicating the sales trends for each region. Next you decide to add a chart title and axis titles.

4. **In the Chart Options group on the Formatting Palette, verify that Chart Title appears in the list box under Titles, click the Click here to add title text box, then type Q1 Clubhouse Kit Sales by Region**

   The title "Q1 Clubhouse Kit Sales by Region" appears above the chart.

5. **Click the Chart Title list arrow under Titles in the Chart Options group, click Horizontal (Category) Axis, then type Region in the Click here to add title text box**

   A horizontal axis label is added to the chart.

6. **Click the Chart Title list arrow in the Chart Options group, click Vertical (Value) Axis, then type Sales in the Click here to add title text box**

   A vertical axis label is added, clarifying that each data series represents sales figures. The chart and axis titles make it easier to interpret the meaning of the chart. Compare your screen to Figure K-7.

7. **Click the down scroll arrow ▭▾▭ in the Chart Style gallery five times, click the blue-red-green 3-D chart style thumbnail, then save your changes**

   The new style is applied to the chart, as shown in Figure K-8. This style has a three-dimensional appearance and makes your chart look more professional.

Working with Charts

FIGURE K-6: Chart with rows and columns switched

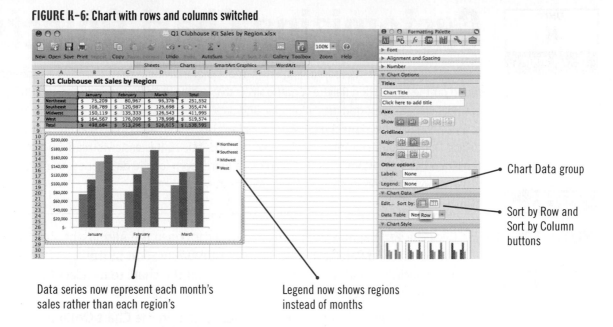

Data series now represent each month's sales rather than each region's

Legend now shows regions instead of months

Chart Data group

Sort by Row and Sort by Column buttons

FIGURE K-7: Chart with title and axis titles added

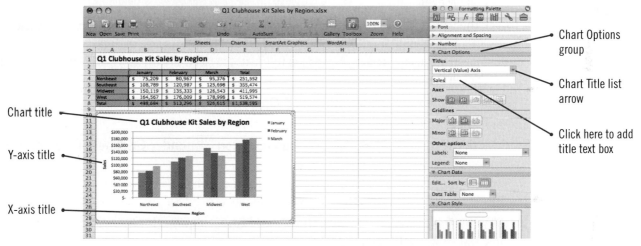

Chart title

Y-axis title

X-axis title

Chart Options group

Chart Title list arrow

Click here to add title text box

FIGURE K-8: New chart style applied to chart

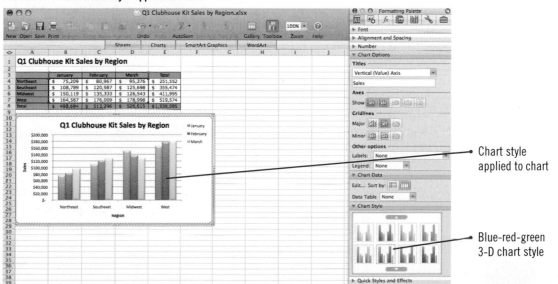

Chart style applied to chart

Blue-red-green 3-D chart style

Customizing Chart Objects

You can easily change the positioning and attributes of individual chart objects by choosing from options found on the Formatting Palette. Chart objects that can be modified include the chart title, axis titles, legend, data labels, axes, gridlines, plot area, and data table. A **data table** in a chart is a grid containing the chart's underlying worksheet data, which is added below the x-axis in certain types of charts. You decide to change the orientation of the vertical-axis title so it is easier to read, and you want to position the legend at the bottom of the chart to make more room for the data series. You also decide to explore other options to improve the chart's effectiveness.

STEPS

1. **Click the vertical-axis title (Sales) on the chart, open the Alignment and Spacing group on the Formatting Palette, click the Horizontal Orientation button ⊞ in the Alignment and Spacing group, then click a blank area on the chart to deselect the axis title**
   The y-axis title changes from a vertical to a horizontal position.

2. **Click the Legend list arrow under Other options in the Chart Options group on the Formatting Palette, then click Bottom**
   As shown in Figure K-9, the legend now appears below the chart, and the chart expands to fill the empty space on the right.

3. **Click the Labels list arrow under Other options in the Chart Options group, then click Value**
   Labels for each worksheet value in cells B4 through D7 now appear above each data marker on the chart. Unfortunately, the values are too big to fit in the chart. The labels also overlap, making them look cluttered and difficult to read.

4. **Click the Labels list arrow in the Chart Options group, then click None**
   The data labels are removed.

5. **Click the Vertical Gridlines for Major units button ⊞ under Gridlines in the Chart Options group**
   Vertical gridlines now appear in the chart, enclosing the monthly sales for each region. This effect helps to visually separate each region's monthly sales.

6. **Click the Data Table list arrow in the Chart Data group on the Formatting Palette, then click Data Table with Legend Keys**
   See Figure K-10. A data table is inserted, with a legend in the first column that identifies the data series in each row. Data tables are helpful when you want to show both the chart and the underlying worksheet data. Because this worksheet already contains the data for the chart, you don't need the data table here; it makes the worksheet look cluttered.

7. **Click the Data Table list arrow in the Chart Data group, then click None**
   The data table is removed from the chart.

8. **Close the Alignment and Spacing group, the Chart Options group, the Chart Data group, and the Chart Style group on the Formatting Palette, then save your changes**
   You are finished selecting and arranging the chart objects, so you closed the open groups on the Formatting Palette.

FIGURE K-9: Chart with rotated vertical axis title and legend moved to bottom

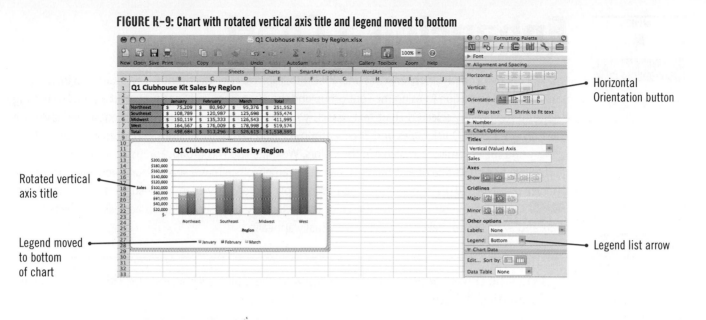

Rotated vertical
axis title

Legend moved
to bottom
of chart

Horizontal
Orientation button

Legend list arrow

FIGURE K-10: Data table in chart

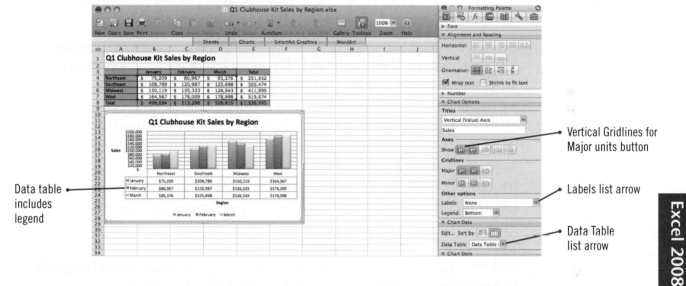

Data table
includes
legend

Vertical Gridlines for
Major units button

Labels list arrow

Data Table
list arrow

Fine-tune your formatting

A Format dialog box is available for every chart object; it offers many options beyond the presets available on the Formatting Palette. Each Format dialog box contains a list of formatting categories on the left side of the dialog box. Each category contains tabs, and each tab contains a variety of options to enhance and change the appearance of the selected chart object. The categories in the Format dialog box are contextual; they differ depending upon the chart object selected. For example, in the Format Chart Area dialog box, which allows you to format the chart background, the Fill category contains tabs with options for formatting the chart area fill by using a solid color, by applying a gradient to a color, by using a picture, or by applying a texture. Figure K-11 shows the Format Chart Area dialog box with a linear gradient selected for the fill. To open the Format dialog box for any chart object, right-click the chart object and then click Format [name of object], or click Format on the menu bar and then click [name of object].

FIGURE K-11: Format Chart Area dialog box

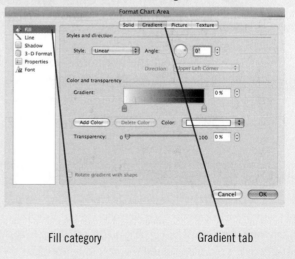

Fill category

Gradient tab

Enhancing a Chart

You can choose from a variety of styles and effects to improve the effectiveness of a chart and increase its visual appeal. In addition to using the Font group and the Alignment and Spacing group on the Formatting Palette to modify any selected chart text object, you can choose from a variety of predesigned styles for chart objects in the Quick Styles and Effects group. Or you can make custom enhancements and adjustments using the commands available in the Colors, Weights, and Fills group. For instance, you can apply a Quick Style to a chart title or axis title, you can apply an effect such as a shadow, and you can change the fill color of a selected chart object. You can even apply WordArt styles to any text to make it stand out. George asks you to change the color of the January data series and to add visual effects to the chart and axis titles to make the chart more visually appealing.

STEPS

1. **Open the** Quick Styles and Effects group **and the** Colors, Weights, and Fills group **on the Formatting Palette**

> **QUICK TIP**
> To select a single data marker, click the data marker twice.

2. **Click** one of the January data markers **(any blue bar) in the chart**
   Sizing handles and a border surround all the data markers in the January data series. Clicking a single data marker selects all the data markers in the series. You decide to change the selected data series color to orange.

3. **Click the** Fill Color button list arrow **in the Colors, Weights, and Fills group on the Formatting Palette, then, as shown in Figure K-12, click the** orange color **in the first row under Theme Colors (the ScreenTip reads "Accent 6")**
   The January data series color is now orange in the chart.

4. **Select the chart title,** Q1 Clubhouse Kit Sales by Region, **verify that the** Quick Styles tab ☑ **in the Quick Styles and Effects group is selected, then click the** down scroll arrow ▼ **four times**
   The Quick Styles gallery includes a variety of styles that you can apply to the selected chart title.

5. **Click the** Intense Effect – Accent 2 style **in the Quick Styles gallery, as shown in Figure K-13**
   The chart title is now formatted with a three-dimensional red background and white font. You decide to add a shadow special effect to the title.

> **TROUBLE**
> To undo all the changes you have made to a chart object, right-click the object, then click Reset to Match Style.

6. **Click the** Shadows tab ☐ **in the Quick Styles and Effects group, then click the** Outside Bottom Right style **(first row, first column) in the Shadows gallery**
   The chart title now has a shadow along its bottom and right edges, enhancing the impression that it is three-dimensional.

> **QUICK TIP**
> You can also use Quick Styles to change the background fill of a chart.

7. **Click** ☑ **in the Quick Styles and Effects group, click the** vertical-axis title **(Sales), then click the** Subtle Effect – Accent 2 style **(first row, second column) in the Quick Styles gallery**

8. **Select the** horizontal-axis title **(Region), then click the** Subtle Effect – Accent 2 style **in the Quick Styles gallery**
   Compare your screen to Figure K-14.

9. **Type your name in cell** A2, **then save your changes**

Using WordArt in a chart

You can use the WordArt feature in Excel to create stylized text in your charts. WordArt provides a selection of preset text styles that you can apply to make text look exciting and eye-catching. To apply a WordArt style, select the chart text you want to enhance, click the

WordArt tab in the Elements Gallery to open it, then click the WordArt style you want. You can use the commands on the Formatting Palette to further enhance the selected WordArt text.

FIGURE K-12: Selecting a new fill color

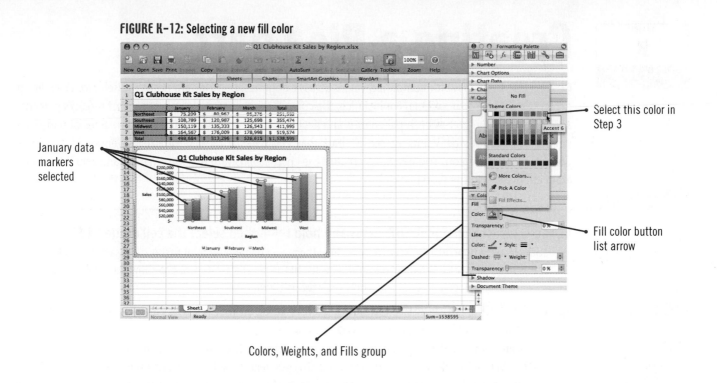

January data markers selected

Select this color in Step 3

Fill color button list arrow

Colors, Weights, and Fills group

FIGURE K-13: Applying a Quick Style to a chart object

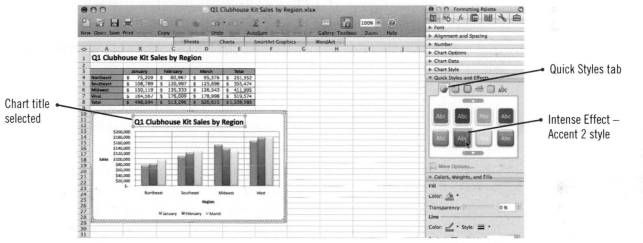

Chart title selected

Quick Styles tab

Intense Effect – Accent 2 style

FIGURE K-14: Completed chart with new formatting

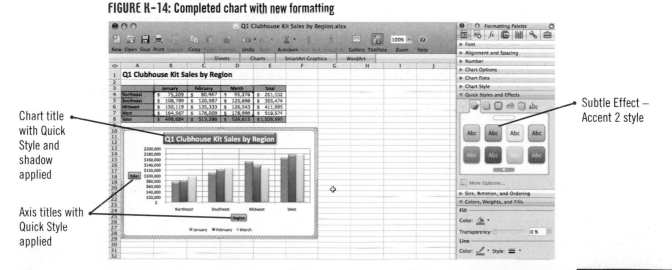

Chart title with Quick Style and shadow applied

Axis titles with Quick Style applied

Subtle Effect – Accent 2 style

Creating a Pie Chart

Column charts are great for comparing values across categories, but they are not very useful for comparing percentages or parts to a whole. For instance, the column chart does not convey the West region's percentage of total first quarter sales. A pie chart is an effective tool for comparing the relative values of parts to a whole. George wants to see a chart that compares total first quarter revenues of the Kid's Clubhouse Kit by region. You decide to create a pie chart to illustrate this information and add it to a separate chart sheet in the workbook.

STEPS

1. **Select the cell range A4:A7, press and hold [⌘], then select the cell range E4:E7**
   You selected a noncontiguous range to include the region names and total first quarter sales for each region; this is the only worksheet data you want reflected in the pie chart. You want to show the total sales for each region and what percentage of the whole each region produced.

2. **Click the Charts tab in the Elements Gallery to open it, click the Pie group on the Charts tab, then click the 3-D Pie chart type**
   See Figure K-15. A 3-D style pie chart now appears in the worksheet and covers part of the column chart. You can see that the purple pie wedge (representing the West region) is the largest and the blue pie wedge (representing the Northeast region) is the smallest. You need to move the pie chart to a new chart sheet in the workbook.

3. **Close the Elements Gallery, click Chart on the menu bar, then click Move Chart**
   The Move Chart dialog box opens.

4. **Click the New sheet option button, type Q1 Clubhouse Sales % in the New sheet text box as shown in Figure K-16, then click OK**
   The pie chart moves to a new chart sheet. The chart sheet tab reads "Q1 Clubhouse Sales %," reflecting the text you typed in the dialog box.

5. **Open the Chart Options group on the Formatting Palette if necessary, click the Legend list arrow in the Chart Options group, then click None**

6. **Click the Labels list arrow in the Chart Options group, then click Category Name and Percent**
   Each data marker (pie slice) in the chart now shows its region and region percentage.

7. **Type Q1 Clubhouse Kit Sales by Region in the Click here to add title text box in the Chart Options group**

8. **Select the chart title on the chart, click the down scroll arrow ▬▬▬ twice in the Quick Styles gallery in the Quick Styles and Effects group, then click the Colored Fill – Accent 1 style**
   The chart title, Q1 Clubhouse Kit Sales by Region, is now formatted with a dark blue border, a blue background, and white text.

9. **Click West on the purple data marker, notice that the labels on all the slices are now selected, open the Font group on the Formatting Palette if necessary, click the Font Size list arrow, click 20, close the Font group, click a blank area of the chart, then save your changes**
   Compare your screen to Figure K-17.

FIGURE K-15: Creating a pie chart

3-D Pie
chart type

Each pie slice
represents the
percentage of the
total sales

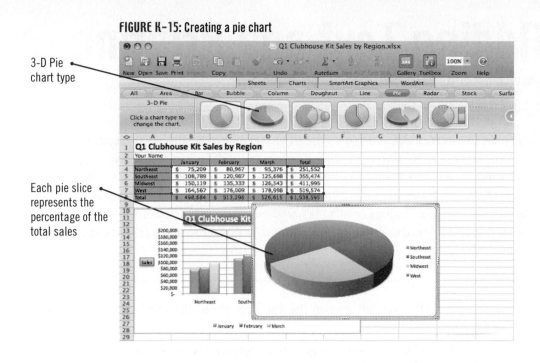

FIGURE K-16: Move Chart dialog box

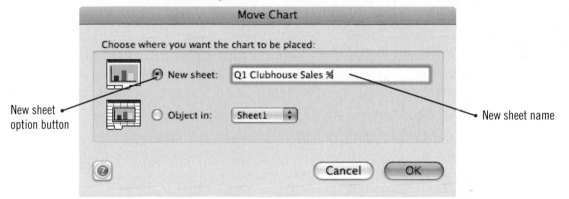

New sheet
option button

New sheet name

FIGURE K-17: Completed pie chart in chart sheet

Formatted
chart title

Data labels show
region name and
percentage of
total sales

New sheet

Selected data labels

Colored Fill –
Accent 1 style

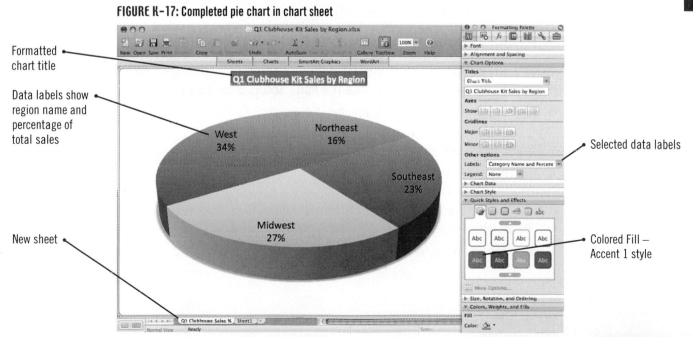

Adding Text and Printing Charts

Before printing a chart sheet, you might want to add some text to explain a particular point. You can add text to a header or footer, or you can add text by inserting a shape and typing text into it. Text boxes can be useful for adding explanation or commentary to key data points on a chart and for simply adding your name or other identifying information. When you finish formatting your chart, you can preview and print it. You can print the chart by itself or with the worksheet data. You're almost ready to preview and print the two charts you created for George. But first, you want to add a text box to the pie chart that indicates the total sales.

STEPS

1. **Click the Object Palette tab 🗔 on the Toolbox, then click the Rectangle shape**

2. **Click just below Q1 in the chart title, drag down and to the right to create a rectangle the height and width of the chart title, then release the mouse button**

   A blue rectangle appears under the chart title. Compare your screen to Figure K-18.

> **QUICK TIP**
> To reduce the size of the rectangle to fit the text, click the Shrink to fit text check box in the Alignment and Spacing group.

3. **Type Total Q1 Clubhouse Sales: $1,538,595**

   The text you typed appears in the shape. It is very small and hard to read; to make it readable, you need to increase its size. You also want to change the appearance of the text box.

4. **Select the blue Rectangle 1 shape if necessary, click the Formatting Palette tab 🔳 on the Toolbox, click the up scroll arrow ▭▭▭ once in the Quick Styles gallery in the Quick Styles and Effects group, then click the Colored Outline – Accent 1 style (second row, first column)**

   The rectangle is now formatted with a blue outline and black text.

> **QUICK TIP**
> To select all text in a text box, click in the text box, then triple-click.

5. **Select the text Total Q1 Clubhouse Sales: $1,538,595, open the Font group on the Formatting Palette if necessary, click the Font Size list arrow in the Font group, click 14, then close the Font group**

> **TROUBLE**
> Use the top Alignment and Spacing group because it offers more ways of aligning and spacing text within a shape.

6. **Open the top Alignment and Spacing group on the Formatting Palette if necessary, then click the Horizontal Center button 🗐**

   The text is now larger and centered in the text box. See Figure K-19.

7. **Click View on the menu bar, click Header and Footer, click Customize Footer under Footer, type your name in the left section of the footer, click OK to close the Footer dialog box, then click OK to close the Page Setup Dialog box**

8. **Click File on the menu bar, then click Print**

   The Print dialog box opens, and the chart sheet appears in the Preview box. You can faintly see the footer you just added below the chart in the Preview box.

> **QUICK TIP**
> If you plan to print a chart using a black-and-white printer, make sure you have chosen appropriate contrasting colors that appear in different shades of gray when printed. Many colors, such as red and green, look the same when printed by a black-and-white printer.

9. **Click the Entire Workbook option button, then click the Print button**

   When you selected the Entire Workbook option, the Preview box caption changed to "1 of 2", indicating that a quick preview was available for both worksheets. Both the chart sheet and the worksheet print. Compare your printed worksheets to Figure K-20.

10. **Save your changes, close the workbook, then exit Excel**

FIGURE K-18: Rectangle added to chart

Rectangle added to chart

Object Palette tab

Formatting Palette tab

Rectangle shape

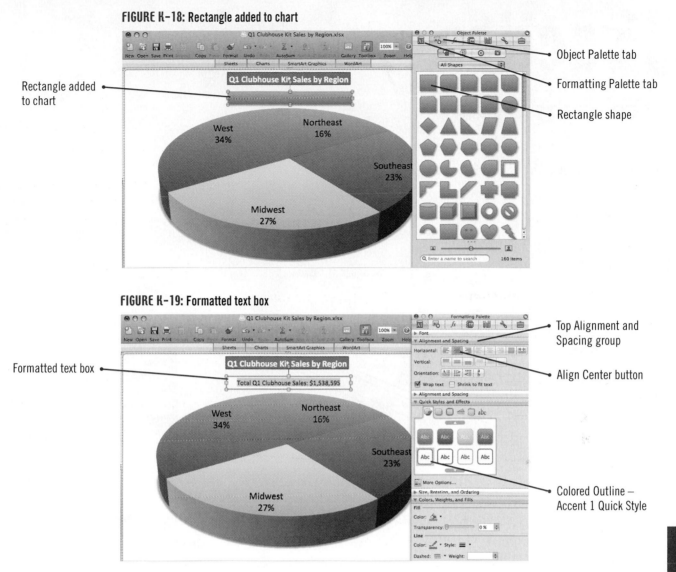

FIGURE K-19: Formatted text box

Formatted text box

Top Alignment and Spacing group

Align Center button

Colored Outline – Accent 1 Quick Style

FIGURE K-20: Completed worksheets

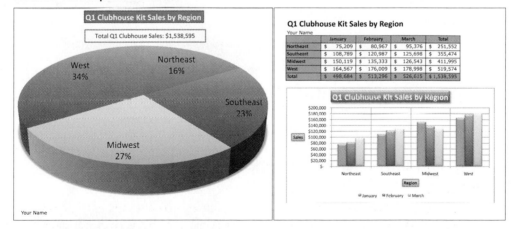

Guidelines for enhancing a chart

You can change a chart's appearance in many ways to make your chart more effective and visually appealing, but don't overdo it. A chart with too many colors or visual effects distracts your audience from the information you are trying to present. Use consistent theme colors to ensure that all colors complement each other. Remember, your primary goal when using charts is to communicate worksheet information effectively. In a business setting, you also want your documents to look professional.

Practice

▼ CONCEPTS REVIEW

Label each item shown in Figure K-21.

FIGURE K-21

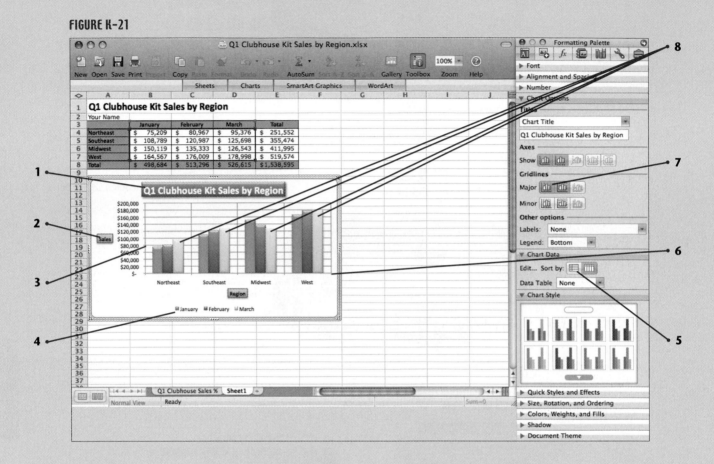

Match each chart type with its description.

9. **Line chart**	**a.** Shows relative importance of values over a period of time
10. **Pie chart**	**b.** Describes the relationship of parts to a whole
11. **Area chart**	**c.** Shows trends by category over time
12. **Column chart**	**d.** Compares values across categories

Working with Charts

Select the best answer from the list of choices.

13. A chart symbol that represents a single data point on a chart is called a(n):
    a. Data bar.
    b. Data marker.
    c. Data series.
    d. Axis.

14. Which of the following chart objects identifies what the colors or patterns in a chart represent?
    a. The data marker
    b. The category axis
    c. The legend
    d. The plot area

15. Which definition best describes the x-axis in an Excel chart?
    a. The vertical gridline that shows measurements or values
    b. The horizontal gridline that shows measured categories
    c. A line in a chart that indicates the direction or trend of the chart data
    d. A box that explains what the labels, colors, and patterns in the chart represent

16. Which definition best describes a data table in an Excel chart?
    a. A predefined set of chart colors and fills
    b. A sequence of related numbers that shows a trend
    c. A chart that compares values among individual items
    d. A grid containing the chart's underlying worksheet data

17. Which of the following groups on the Formatting Palette do you use to apply gridlines to a chart?
    a. Chart Data
    b. Quick Styles and Effects
    c. Chart Options
    d. Chart Style

18. Which of the following groups on the Formatting Palette do you use to apply a data table to a chart?
    a. Chart Data
    b. Quick Styles and Effects
    c. Chart Options
    d. Chart Style

▼ SKILLS REVIEW

1. **Understand and plan a chart.**
    a. Open the file K-2.xlsx from where you store your Data Files, then save it as **Walking Tours Revenue Chart**.
    b. Examine the worksheet data, then consider what Excel chart types would best present this type of information.
    c. Is the worksheet designed in such a way that it will be easy to create a chart? Would you recommend any modifications to the worksheet?

2. **Create a chart.**
    a. Select cells A4 through C10.
    b. Open the Charts tab in the Elements Gallery.
    c. Insert a 3-D Clustered Column chart.
    d. Examine the chart on the worksheet. What meaning does the chart convey? What trends do you see in the data?
    e. Save your changes to the workbook.

3. **Move and resize a chart and chart objects.**
    a. Drag the chart so that the upper-left corner of the chart is aligned with the upper-left corner of cell A13.
    b. Use the lower-right corner sizing handle to align the lower-right corner of the chart with the lower-right corner of cell G33.
    c. Move the legend so that its top edge aligns with the top of the tallest data marker in the chart.
    d. Save your changes.

4. Apply chart objects and styles.

   a. Use a button in the Chart Data group to reverse the columns and rows and get a different view of the data. Examine the chart and identify what new meaning this new structure conveys.

   b. Switch the rows and columns again so that the chart is structured like it was when you first inserted it.

   c. Enter Tour Revenue, 2011-2012 as the chart title.

   d. Enter Tours as the horizontal-axis title on the chart.

   e. Enter Revenue as the vertical-axis title.

   f. Scroll to the top of the Chart Style gallery if necessary, then apply the chart style in the first row, third column to the chart.

   g. Save your changes.

5. Customize chart objects.

   a. Rotate the vertical axis title so that it reads from left to right.

   b. Change the location of the legend so that it is at the top of the chart.

   c. Add major gridlines for the vertical axis.

   d. Add a data table with legend keys to the chart.

   e. Display the data labels as values. Compare the methods of displaying and identifying the chart data.

   f. Remove the data table and the data labels.

   g. Save your changes.

6. Enhance a chart.

   a. Make sure the Quick Styles and Effects group and the Colors, Weights, and Fills group are open and visible on the Formatting Palette.

   b. Select one of the 2012 data markers in the chart.

   c. Click the Fill color list arrow, then click the green color in the first row under Theme Colors (the ScreenTip reads "Accent 3").

   d. Select the chart title, then apply the Colored Fill – Accent 4 style.

   e. Apply an Inside Bottom Right shadow effect to the title. (*Hint*: Scroll down in the Shadows gallery to locate the Inside Bottom Right shadow effect.)

   f. Apply the Moderate Effect – Accent 4 style to the vertical-axis title and the horizontal-axis title.

   g. Save your changes.

7. Create a pie chart.

   a. Select cells A5:A10, then press and hold [⌘] while selecting cells D5:D10.

   b. Insert a pie chart, choosing the 3D Exploded Pie chart type.

   c. Move the pie chart to a new sheet in the workbook. Name the sheet Revenue by Tour.

   d. Enter Revenue by Tour as the chart title.

   e. Remove the legend and change the data labels to Category Name and Percent.

   f. Increase the font size of the data labels to 14.

   g. Save your changes.

8. Add text and print charts.

   a. Insert a rectangle just below the chart title whose left side is above the word Ireland and whose right side is above the word Maine. Apply the Subtle Effect – Accent 3 style to the rectangle.

   b. Type the text Total Tour Revenue: $841,200 in the rectangle.

   c. Select the text, then increase the size of the text to 16. Center the text in the text box. Drag the text box so it is centered above the chart and below the title.

   d. Insert a footer with your name located in the right section.

   e. Open Sheet1, then type your name in cell A3.

   f. Open the Print dialog box and select the option to print the entire workbook.

g. View both sheets in the workbook in the Preview box in the Print dialog box, then print the sheets. Compare your printed sheets to Figure K-22.

h. Save your changes.

i. Close the workbook, then exit Excel.

FIGURE K-22

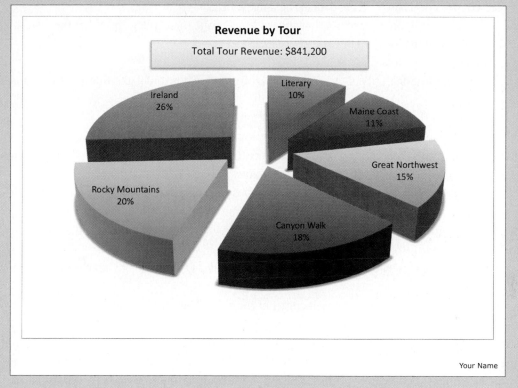

Revenue by Tour

Total Tour Revenue: $841,200

Ireland 26%
Literary 10%
Maine Coast 11%
Great Northwest 15%
Rocky Mountains 20%
Canyon Walk 18%

Your Name

Classic Walking Adventures
Tours Revenue, 2011-2012
Your Name

	2011	2012	Totals
Literary	$ 23,122.00	$ 25,344.00	$ 48,466.00
Maine Coast	$ 24,567.00	$ 28,654.00	$ 53,221.00
Great Northwest	$ 35,466.00	$ 36,344.00	$ 71,810.00
Canyon Walk	$ 40,680.00	$ 42,375.00	$ 83,055.00
Rocky Mountains	$ 45,766.00	$ 46,746.00	$ 92,512.00
Ireland	$ 55,344.00	$ 65,344.00	$ 120,688.00
Totals	$ 369,855.00	$ 471,345.00	$ 841,200.00

Tour Revenue, 2011-2012

■ 2011 ■ 2012

▼ INDEPENDENT CHALLENGE 1

You are an entrepreneur who owns a collectibles business called Prairie Sue's Antiques. You purchase Early American antiques at flea markets and yard sales and then resell them on Internet auction sites for a profit. You have created a spreadsheet that contains quarterly sales results for the five categories of products that you sell. You decide to chart this worksheet data to show the results for each quarter.

   a. Open the file K-3.xlsx from where you store your Data Files, then save it as **Annual Antique Sales**.

   b. Create a Stacked Area chart based on the data in the range A3:E8.

   c. Move the chart so it is positioned directly below the worksheet data, then enlarge it so that the lower-right corner of the chart is aligned with the lower-right corner of cell E27.

   d. Apply a chart style of your choice.

   e. Enter **Annual Sales** as the chart title. Enter **Product Groups** as the horizontal-axis title and **Revenue** as the vertical-axis title.

   f. Change the location of the legend so that it is at the bottom of the chart.

   g. Apply a Quick Style that you like to the chart title, then apply a shadow effect of your choosing.

   h. Change the chart area color to a solid color of your choice. (*Hint*: Select the chart area by clicking a blank area of the chart, then choose the fill color of your choice in the Colors, Weights, and Fills group.)

   i. Create an Exploded Pie chart by selecting the noncontiguous cell ranges A4:A8 and E4:E8. Move the pie chart to a separate chart sheet named **Sales by Product Group**. Apply the chart style of your choice.

   j. Remove the legend. Add data labels that display the category name and percent. Increase the font size of the data labels to 20.

   k. Add the chart title **Sales by Product Group** to the chart. Apply a Quick Style of your choice and increase the font size to 20.

   l. Insert a rounded rectangle in the bottom-right corner of the chart sheet, apply a Quick Style of your choice, then type your name in it.

   m. Open Sheet1, then type your name in cell A30. Format the worksheet data and worksheet title using fonts, font sizes, borders, alignments, and shading to make the worksheet look professional and easy to understand. Choose formatting options that are complementary to the colors and style of the chart. Figure K-23 shows one possible way to format the worksheet data; your worksheet and chart will look different depending on the options you choose.

Advanced Challenge Exercise

   ■ Open the Sales by Product Group chart sheet.

   ■ Click one of the data labels on the pie chart (such as Pottery 18%) to select all the data labels.

   ■ Click the WordArt tab in the Elements Gallery, then click the WordArt Style 9. (*Hint*: You may have to click the right scroll arrow to see additional WordArt styles.)

   n. Save your changes, preview the Sheet1 worksheet and chart, print the worksheet and chart, close the workbook, then exit Excel.

FIGURE K-23

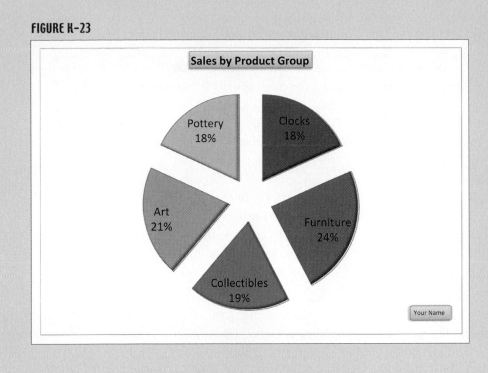

Prairie Sue's Antiques
Annual Sales

	Q1	Q2	Q3	Q4
Clocks	$1,876.00	$2,635.00	$4,787.00	$7,567.00
Furniture	$4,358.00	$1,342.00	$5,478.00	$9,867.00
Collectibles	$1,556.00	$2,765.00	$5,784.00	$7,863.00
Art	$1,678.00	$1,854.00	$6,476.00	$8,467.00
Pottery	$1,768.00	$2,756.00	$5,489.00	$7,465.00
Quarter Totals:	**$11,236.00**	**$11,352.00**	**$28,014.00**	**$41,229.00**

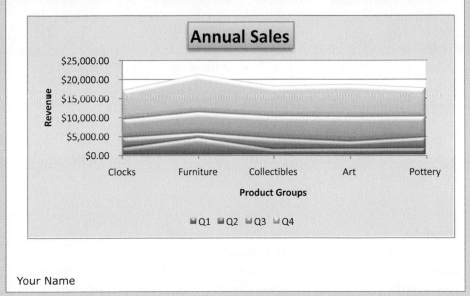

▼ INDEPENDENT CHALLENGE 2

You work for Fiona Johnson, the owner of a gift basket online retailer called The Gift Basket Outpost. Fiona has created an Excel worksheet showing the number of gift baskets sold in March and the revenue generated by each gift basket type. She has asked you to create a chart in the worksheet that shows the percentage of total sales each category represents.

a. Open the file K-4.xlsx from where your Data Files are located, then save it as **First Quarter Gift Basket Sales**.

b. Create a pie chart of the data in the range A4:B9. Choose the 3-D Pie chart option.

c. Move the chart below the worksheet data.

d. Resize the chart so that its lower-right corner is aligned with the lower-right corner of cell E28.

e. Change the value in cell B9 (the number of Happy Birthday Basket units sold) to **502**. Observe the change in the chart.

f. Apply a chart style of your choice.

g. Remove the legend and add data labels that display the category names.

h. Change the chart title to **Gift Baskets Sold** and increase the font size of the title.

i. Make any other formatting enhancements to the chart and to the worksheet data to make it attractive and more professional looking. Enter your name in cell A30 in the worksheet.

Advanced Challenge Exercise

- Select the data labels, then apply a Quick Style of your choice.
- Apply a Quick Style and a glow effect to the chart title. (*Hint*: Click the Glows tab to the right of the Shadows tab in the Quick Styles and Effects group to view the glow effects gallery.)
- Double-click the chart area to open the Format Chart Area dialog box. Verify that the Fill category is selected on the left side of the dialog box, click the Color arrows, then select a color of your choice. Click the Gradient tab, click the Style arrows, then click the Linear gradient style. Use the Transparency slider to adjust the fill transparency to a level that you think looks good. Experiment by choosing different settings, then click OK when you are satisfied with how the chart area looks.

j. Save your changes, preview the worksheet with the chart, print it, close the file, then exit Excel.

▼ INDEPENDENT CHALLENGE 3

You work for Alex Barton, the general manager of a natural history museum in Newfoundland, Nova Scotia. In September, the museum opened an exhibit of newly discovered dinosaur fossils. Museum attendance increased dramatically in that month due to the high public interest in the exhibit and a strong marketing campaign. Alex is preparing to meet with the museum's board of directors to discuss the increased attendance. He has asked you to create a chart that shows the number of people who visited the museum from June through October. He also needs the chart to show a breakdown of adults, seniors, and children who attended. The data you need to create the chart has already been put into a worksheet.

a. Open the file K-5.xlsx from where you store your Data Files, then save it as **Museum Visitors Chart**.

b. Create a Marked Line chart of all three customer categories during the months June through October.

c. Move the chart to a new chart sheet in the workbook. Name the chart sheet **Museum Attendance June – Oct**.

d. Apply a chart style that you think looks good. Enter the chart title **Museum Attendance, June – October**.

e. Add minor vertical gridlines to the chart. Add an appropriate vertical-axis title that is rotated, then add an appropriate horizontal-axis title.

f. Apply a solid color fill to the plot area, choosing a color you think looks good. (*Hint*: Select the plot area, then open the Colors, Weights, and Fills group to specify a color.)

g. Apply Quick Styles of your choosing to the chart title and axis titles.

h. Insert a shape, apply a Quick Style, and type the following text in it: **Dinosaur exhibit opened on September 1**. Resize the shape if necessary to fit the text, then position the shape in the upper-left of the chart's plot area.

i. Add another shape to the lower-left corner of the chart, apply a Quick Style, then type your name in it. Figure K-24 shows one possible example of the completed chart.

FIGURE K-24

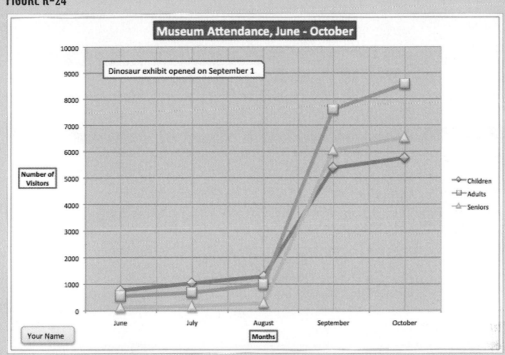

j. Switch to the Sheet1 worksheet that contains the chart data, then type your name in cell A9.

k. Save your changes, preview the worksheet and chart, print both pages, close the file, then exit Excel.

▼ REAL LIFE INDEPENDENT CHALLENGE

Creating a personal budget is a great way to keep your finances in order. In this challenge, you will create a personal budget for monthly expenses. For the purposes of this exercise, imagine that you earn $2000 per month. Your budget needs to include categories of expenses and the amounts for each expense. The total expenses in the worksheet must add up to $2000. Once you enter all your monthly expenses in the worksheet, you will then create a pie chart that shows the percentage of each individual expense.

a. Start a blank Excel workbook, and save it as **Personal Budget** where you store your Data Files.

b. Enter an appropriate title for your budget in cell A1. Format the title so that it stands out.

c. Create a two-column worksheet starting in cell A3 that contains your budget. Enter the label **Expense** in the first column heading and enter the label **Amount** in the second column heading.

d. Enter at least 8 labels for the expenses in the cells below the Expense heading. Enter appropriate amounts for each expense in the cells below the Amount heading.

e. When you have entered all your expenses in the worksheet, enter the label **Total** below the first cell of the last row of expenses. Enter a formula below the second cell of the last row that totals all the dollar amounts in the Amount column. If the returned value in the formula cell does not add up to $2000, then adjust the numbers in your budget so that the total adds up to $2000.

f. Insert a pie chart based on the data in your chart. (*Hint:* Remember not to include the Total row when you select the data; select only the heading row, the labels, and expense amounts.) Choose any pie chart option that you like. Move the chart so it is located below the worksheet data.

g. Apply a chart style to the chart that you think looks good. Add and format a chart title.

h. Remove the legend and add category name data labels.

i. Enter your name in a cell below the chart.

j. Save your changes, preview the worksheet with the chart, print the worksheet, close the file, then exit Excel.

▼ VISUAL WORKSHOP

Create the worksheet and chart shown in Figure K-25 using the commands and techniques you learned in this unit and previous units. Save the workbook as **Day Spa Annual Sales** where you store your Data Files. Save your changes, preview the worksheet and chart, print it, close the file, then exit Excel.

FIGURE K-25

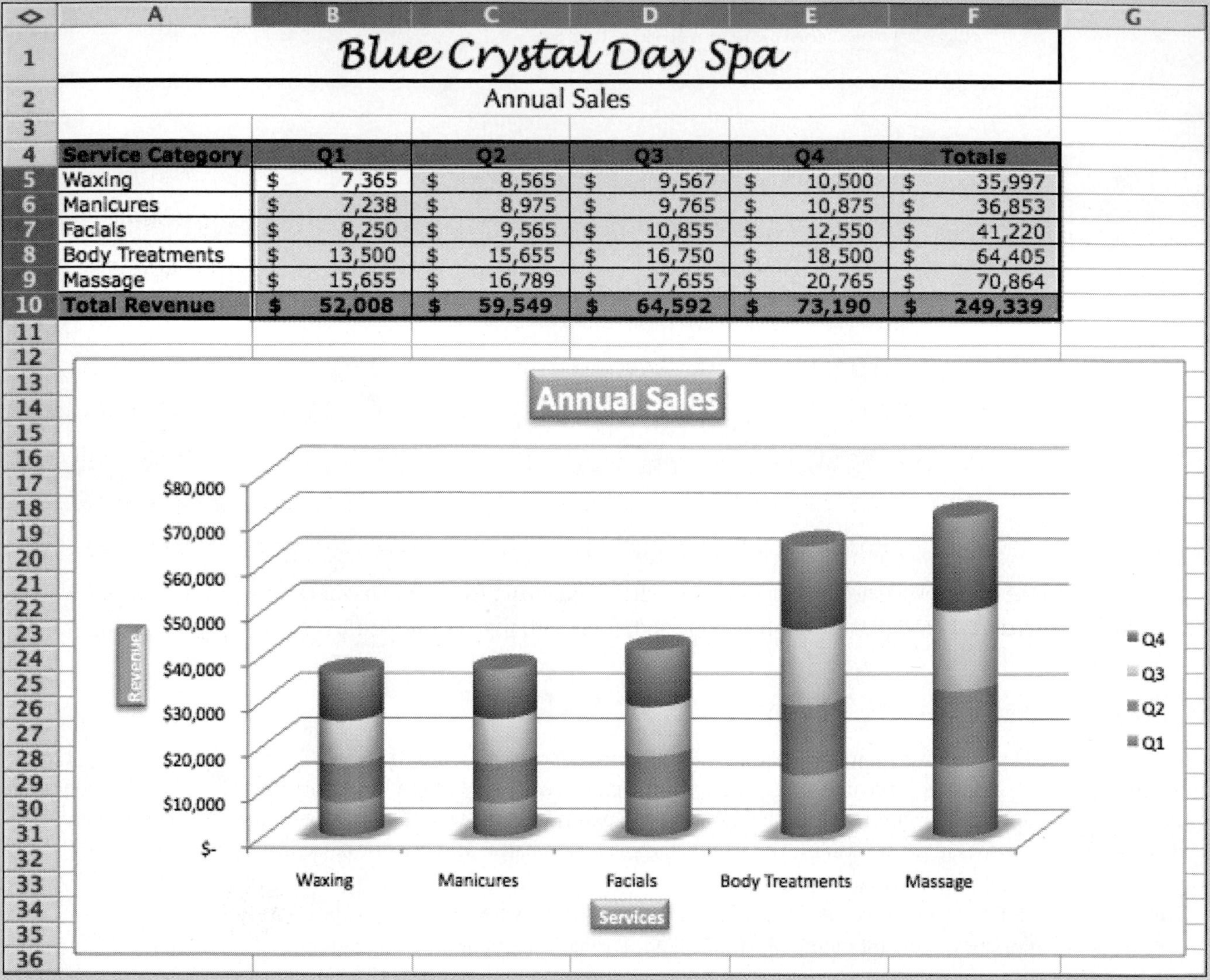

	A	B	C	D	E	F	G
1			Blue Crystal Day Spa				
2			Annual Sales				
3							
4	Service Category	Q1	Q2	Q3	Q4	Totals	
5	Waxing	$ 7,365	$ 8,565	$ 9,567	$ 10,500	$ 35,997	
6	Manicures	$ 7,238	$ 8,975	$ 9,765	$ 10,875	$ 36,853	
7	Facials	$ 8,250	$ 9,565	$ 10,855	$ 12,550	$ 41,220	
8	Body Treatments	$ 13,500	$ 15,655	$ 16,750	$ 18,500	$ 64,405	
9	Massage	$ 15,655	$ 16,789	$ 17,655	$ 20,765	$ 70,864	
10	Total Revenue	$ 52,008	$ 59,549	$ 64,592	$ 73,190	$ 249,339	

Creating a Presentation

PowerPoint is a **presentation authoring program** that allows you to create dynamic **slides**, which are onscreen pages for use in a slide show. When creating a presentation, you can select from an array of templates and themes and add media such as photographs, clip art, sound, and video. PowerPoint also contains graphics features that convert ordinary text into stunning graphics. You can create handouts, notes, and outlines to augment the presentation and ensure its success with an audience. Once your presentation is complete, you can show it on a computer or video projector, convert it to a PDF (portable document format) file for distribution to others, or publish it to a Web page. George Gonzalez, marketing manager for Outdoor Designs, asks you to create a presentation to educate the sales reps so they have strong talking points when presenting this year's product line. The presentation will name each product line to better brand it to customers.

OBJECTIVES

View a presentation

Use a theme

Enter text on a slide

Format text

Add a text box

Create SmartArt

Add a header and footer

Print handouts

Viewing a Presentation

PowerPoint includes several different ways to view a presentation. When you start PowerPoint, the workspace opens by default in **Normal view** and is divided into three areas that allow you to concentrate on specific information. The largest area, the Slide pane, shows the full layout of the selected slide. On the left side of the window, the **Slides tab** and **Outline tab** show slide thumbnails and text-only hierarchical versions of the slides, respectively. These tabs are useful for navigating through the presentation. The **Notes pane** at the bottom of the window is used to input text relevant to a specific slide; you can use these notes as part of your audience handout or as reference notes during your presentation. You can also switch between views to make certain tasks easier. **Slide Sorter view** uses the entire window to show thumbnails of the presentation slides and is very useful for reordering and deleting slides. To preview a presentation as your audience will see it, you can switch to **Slide Show view**. PowerPoint also includes a dedicated Notes Page view, Presenter Tools view for practicing and delivering presentations, and three Master views for working with recurring elements within a presentation, such as headers and footers. 🖙 Before you get started in PowerPoint, you view a presentation from an installed template to become familiar with the workspace.

STEPS

1. **Click the Microsoft PowerPoint icon** 🅟 **on the dock**

   The PowerPoint program window opens in Normal view with a new, untitled presentation.

2. **Click File on the menu bar, click Project Gallery, then click the New tab in the Project Gallery if necessary**

   As shown in Figure L-1, the New tab in the Project Gallery gives you access to a variety of useful templates.

3. **Click Presentations in the Category list, click Introducing PowerPoint 2008 in the right pane of the Project Gallery, then click Open**

   The presentation opens in a new window in Normal view and is titled Presentation2.pptx. (The number in the presentation title may differ for you.) See Figure L-2. Scroll bars in each pane allow you to move within the sections of the workspace. The status bar includes buttons for switching among the three most commonly used views: Normal view, Slide Sorter view, and Slide Show view. The Notes pane lets you add notes to remind you of important points about the slide for use when presenting a slide show.

4. **Click the Next Slide button** ⊻ **in the Slide pane**

   Slide 2 becomes the active slide. You can move to the next or previous slide by clicking the Next Slide button ⊻ or Previous Slide button ⊼, or by pressing [▼] or [▲], respectively, on the keyboard.

5. **Click the Outline tab** ☰ **, then click anywhere in the text for Slide 4**

   You can also move to a slide by clicking it in the Slides tab or in the Outline tab. The text outline form of the presentation appears in the Outline tab. Viewing a presentation in this form makes it easy to read and move text.

6. **Click the Slide Sorter View button** ▦ **on the status bar**

   The view changes to Slide Sorter view, as shown in Figure L-3. The slides are arranged in rows across the window. The currently selected slide, Slide 4, is highlighted in blue. To move a slide, click and hold the pointer on the selected slide, then drag it to its new location.

7. **Click Slide 1, then click the Slide Show button** 🖵 **on the status bar**

   The currently selected slide fills the screen.

8. **Press [return] until you reach the end of the presentation**

   The slide show advances. The last time you press [return], the view returns to the last view selected. In this example, it's Slide Sorter view.

9. **Click File on the menu bar, then click Close**

   The Presentation2.pptx file closes.

FIGURE L-1: New tab in Project Gallery

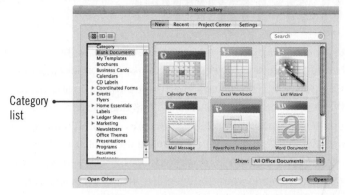

Category list

FIGURE L-2: Presentation open in Normal view

Outline tab

Slides tab

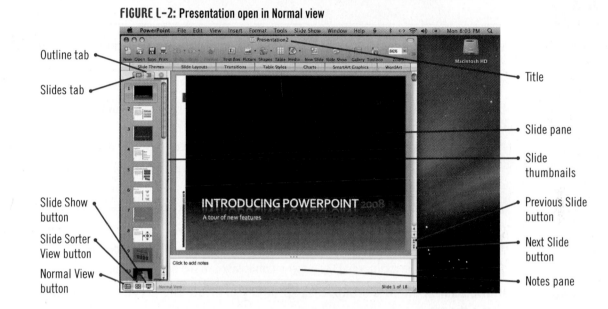

Title

Slide pane

Slide thumbnails

Slide Show button

Slide Sorter View button

Normal View button

Previous Slide button

Next Slide button

Notes pane

FIGURE L-3: Viewing a presentation in Slide Sorter view

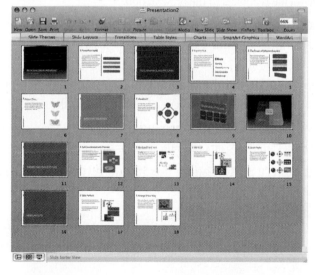

Moving among slides in a slide show

When you're in Slide Show view, you can advance to the next slide in a slide show by pressing [return], clicking the screen, or by pressing [page down], [spacebar], [↓], [→], or [n]. To go to the previous slide in the slide show, press [↑], [←], or [p]. To move to a specific slide during a slide show, right-click the screen, point to Go to Slide, then click the slide you want to see. To exit the slide show and return to the previous view at any time during the presentation, press [esc].

PowerPoint 2008

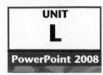

Using a Theme

When you create a new presentation, you need to consider how the slide show will communicate your content. Even the most interesting subject matter can be lost on an audience if the visual presentation is monotonous or overpowering. Fortunately, PowerPoint provides a wide variety of themes that apply a distinctive look to the text, bullets, background colors, and graphics in a presentation. Using a theme is a big time-saver and immediately adds a professional touch to any presentation. You can apply a theme when you create a new presentation, and you can change the theme after creating a presentation. You can apply a theme to all slides in a presentation or to selected slides. It's also easy to customize themes, so you have great flexibility while developing your presentation.   You are ready to create the presentation George requested, and you begin by selecting a theme and changing its background style.

STEPS

QUICK TIP

To create a new, blank presentation, click File on the menu bar, then click New Presentation.

1. **With a blank presentation open in the document window, click the Gallery button 🖼 on the Standard toolbar**

   The Slide Themes tab in the Elements Gallery slides open and the Built-in Themes group is displayed.

2. **Click the right scroll arrow ▶ on the right side of the Elements Gallery, then locate the Concourse theme**

   As you point to each slide theme thumbnail in the Elements Gallery, the name of the theme is displayed on the left side of the Slide Themes tab.

3. **Click the Concourse theme**

   The Concourse theme is applied to the new presentation, as shown in Figure L-4.

4. **Click File on the menu bar, click Save As, type Reinforced Product Branding in the Save As text box, navigate to where you store your Data Files, then click Save**

   The Save As dialog box closes and the presentation is saved to the designated location.

QUICK TIP

To apply a theme to two or more slides but not the entire presentation, select the slides in Normal view or Slide Sorter view, then click the theme in the Elements Gallery. However, keep in mind that too many themes in a single presentation can be visually overwhelming and diminish its effectiveness.

5. **In the Built-in Themes group, click ▶ until you locate the Verve theme, then click the Verve theme**

   The Verve theme is applied to the presentation.

6. **Click the Toolbox button 🖼 to open the Toolbox if necessary**

   The Toolbox opens with the Formatting Palette selected. Notice the different groups on the Formatting Palette.

7. **In the Slide Background group on the Formatting Palette, point to each thumbnail**

   As you point to each thumbnail, a ScreenTip appears with the name of the slide background style.

8. **Click Style 8 in the Slide Background group**

   The Style 8 background is applied to the slide, as shown in Figure L-5.

9. **Click the Gallery button 🖼 on the Standard toolbar to close the Elements Gallery, then save your changes**

FIGURE L-4: Concourse theme applied to presentation

Slide
Themes tab

Theme name

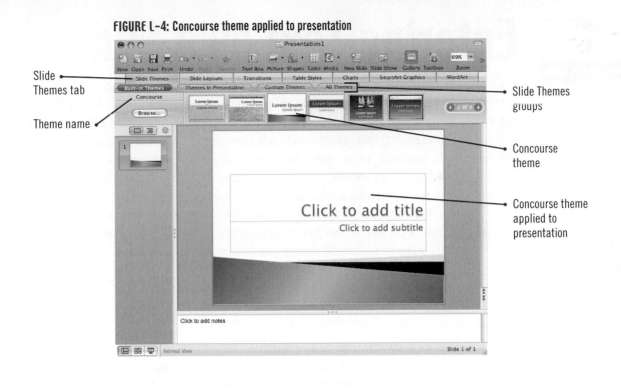

Slide Themes
groups

Concourse
theme

Concourse theme
applied to
presentation

FIGURE L-5: Style 8 background applied

Verve theme

Style 8
background
applied to
presentation

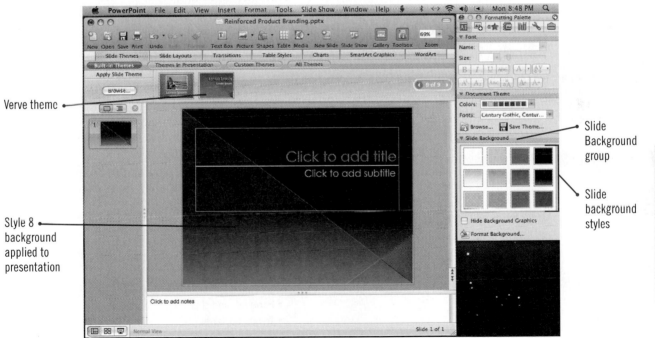

Slide
Background
group

Slide
background
styles

Entering Text on a Slide

You can add text to a slide in the Slide pane or in the Outline tab. Working in the Slide pane shows you exactly how the text will look on the slide, while Outline view can be useful when you have a lot of text to edit and rearrange. When you create a new presentation, the first slide is a **title slide**. It contains two placeholders: a title placeholder that reads "Click to add title" and a subtitle placeholder that reads "Click to add subtitle." When you add a new slide, the default placeholders adjust to new content. By default, subsequently added slides are title and content slides; they have a title placeholder and a content placeholder that supports bulleted text and graphic elements. Once you fill in a placeholder of any type—text, table, graphics, or any combination thereof—the placeholder becomes an editable **object** in the slide.  You begin your presentation by adding text to the title slide. You fill in the substance of the presentation by adding three content slides and adding text to them.

STEPS

1. **Position the mouse pointer over the** "Click to add title" **placeholder in the Slide pane**
   The pointer changes to Ι, indicating that it is positioned in a text placeholder.

2. **Click the** "Click to add title" **placeholder**
   A light blue **selection box** surrounds the title placeholder, the placeholder text is hidden, and a blinking vertical insertion point indicates where the new text will be entered. See Figure L-6.

3. **Type Creating Product Champions**
   The title text appears in the title font and style, and it automatically wraps in the title placeholder.

4. **Click the** "Click to add subtitle" **placeholder, then type Sales and Success With Names**
   The subtitle text appears in the subtitle font and style.

5. **Click the New Slide button 🗐 on the Standard toolbar**
   A new slide with Title and Content layout appears in the Slide pane. A **layout** is an arrangement of placeholders and formatting configured to support a particular type of content.

6. **Click the** "Click to add title" **placeholder, type Bird House: Meet the Peeps, then click the** "Click to add text" **content placeholder**

   > **QUICK TIP**
   > The default formatting for text in a content placeholder is a bulleted list.

7. **Type Kestrel, press [return], type Great Crested Flycatcher, press [return], then type Chickadee**
   Each time you press [return], the insertion point moves to a new bulleted line. See Figure L-7.

   > **QUICK TIP**
   > Except for when you are on a title slide, each time you click 🗐, PowerPoint inserts a new slide with the same slide layout as the slide before it.

8. **Click 🗐, then enter the text shown in the following table**

title:	bullets:
Kayak: Reading the Water	• Rising Trident
	• Sailfish Racer
	• Loch Ness

9. **Click 🗐, enter the text shown in the following table, then save your changes**

title:	bullets:
Adirondack Chair: Form & Function	• Lap of luxury
	• Hang out and chill
	• Tranquility base

   Each completed slide thumbnail appears in the Slides tab, as shown in Figure L-8. The presentation has four slides total.

Creating a Presentation

FIGURE L-6: Entering text in a placeholder

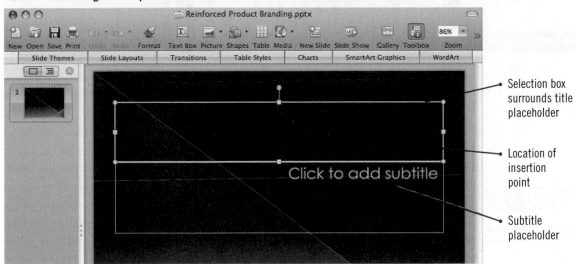

Selection box surrounds title placeholder

Location of insertion point

Subtitle placeholder

FIGURE L-7: Entering bulleted text

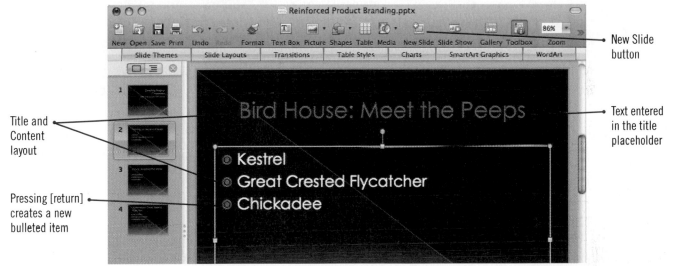

New Slide button

Title and Content layout

Pressing [return] creates a new bulleted item

Text entered in the title placeholder

FIGURE L-8: Completed slides

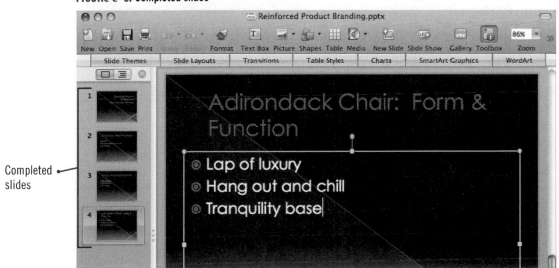

Completed slides

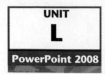
Formatting Text

You can format text in your presentation to emphasize specific words or phrases or to improve the way text appears on the slide. For example, in a bulleted list, you might want to enhance one bullet point by changing its color or by increasing its font size. Formatting text in a slide is similar to formatting text in other Office programs, particularly Microsoft Word. You can use commands on the Formatting Palette to alter the font type, size, and color. You can also adjust the theme fonts using the Formatting Palette. ▓▓▓▓ Some of the product names have been submitted by a marketing intern. George wants you to format this text differently so it is easily identifiable in the presentation and has given you a list of the names to change. You also want to experiment with changing the theme fonts in the presentation.

QUICK TIP
To select a single word, double-click the word.

1. **Click Slide 1 in the Slides tab, then triple-click the word Creating in the title**
   The phrase "Creating Product Champions" is selected.

2. **Click the Bold button B in the Font group on the Formatting Palette, then click a blank area of the slide**
   The text is bold and deselected.

3. **Click Slide 2 in the Slides tab, click just before the word Meet in the title, then press [return]**
   The phrase "Meet the Peeps" now appears on its own line beneath the words "Bird House."

4. **Select the text Meet the Peeps, click the Font Color button list arrow A · in the Font group, then click the top pink color in the sixth column under Theme Colors (the ScreenTip reads "Accent 2"), as shown in Figure L-9**
   The text changes to a darker shade of pink.

TROUBLE
If the Font size does not increase to 48 pt the first time you click 48, click the Font Size list arrow, then click 48 again.

5. **Select Bird House:, click the Font Size list arrow in the Font group, scroll down in the Font Size list, then click 48**
   The text increases in size from 42 pt to 48 pt.

6. **Double-click Kestrel in the bulleted list, then click the Italic button I in the Font group**
   The text changes to italicized text, as shown in Figure L-10.

QUICK TIP
If the Font Color button displays the color you want, you can simply click the button instead of the list arrow to apply the color to a selection.

7. **Move to Slide 3, click just before the word Reading, press [return], format the text Reading the Water in the pink color used in Step 4, increase the size of the text Kayak: to 48 pt, then italicize the bulleted text Sailfish Racer**

8. **Move to Slide 4, click just before the word Form, press [return], format the text Form & Function in the pink color used in Step 4, increase the size of the text Adirondack Chair: to 48 pt, then italicize the bulleted text Tranquility base**

9. **Click the Document Theme group on the Formatting Palette to open it, click the Fonts list arrow in the Document Theme group, click Apex, click in a blank area of the current placeholder, then compare your screen to Figure L-11**
   The bulleted text is now smaller and looks better on the slide. Changing the theme fonts instantly changes all the text in a presentation that is formatted with those fonts.

10. **Save your changes, click Slide 1 in the Slides tab, click the Slide Show button ⬚ on the status bar, view the presentation, then return to Normal view**

FIGURE L-9: New font color applied to text

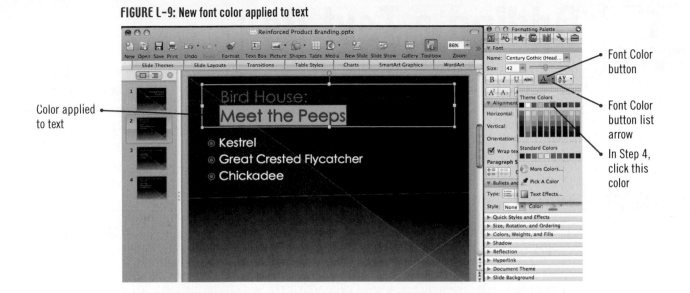

Color applied to text

Font Color button

Font Color button list arrow

In Step 4, click this color

FIGURE L-10: Italicized text

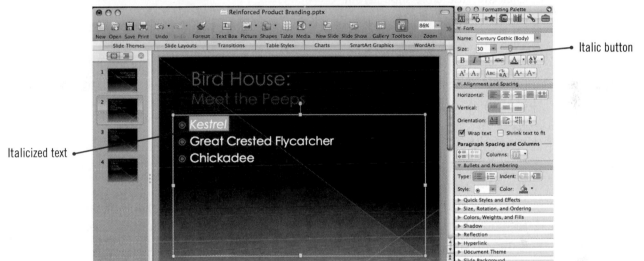

Italicized text

Italic button

FIGURE L-11: New theme fonts applied to presentation

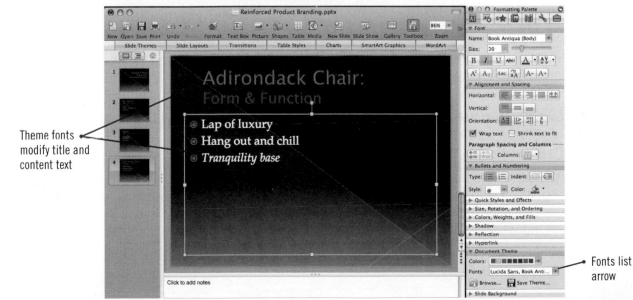

Theme fonts modify title and content text

Fonts list arrow

Adding a Text Box

There may be times when you want to add new text to a slide but you want to locate it outside the confines of a text placeholder, such as in a label or as part of a graphic. To do this, you can add a text box, apply a style to it, and place it anywhere on the slide. You can format the text in a text box using the Formatting Palette. As with any object, you can modify a text box by moving, resizing, and realigning it. Like Microsoft Word, PowerPoint includes text box Quick Styles that you can use to apply multiple formatting attributes at once. 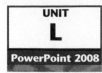 George wants you to add a slide about the Outdoor Designs' Retailer of the Year Award and create a colorful text box that reminds sales reps to play up the award with their clients.

1. **Move to** Slide 4 **if necessary, click the** Slide Layouts tab **in the Elements Gallery, then click the** Insert new slide option button **as shown in Figure L-12**

   The Slide Layouts tab in the Elements Gallery contains various slide layout options. When you click the Insert new slide option button, a green circle with a plus appears in the upper left corner of each slide layout; clicking a layout then adds a new slide with that layout to the presentation.

2. **Click the** Title Only slide layout

   A new slide is added with only a title text placeholder at the top.

3. **Click the** "Click to add title" **placeholder, type** Retailer of the Year Award, **then click outside this text box**

4. **Click the** Text Box button ☐ **on the Standard toolbar, then click the approximate** center **of the slide**

   A blank text box is inserted on the slide.

5. **Type** Obtain local news contacts, **press [return], then type** Send winner video of awards ceremony

   The text appears in the new text box, as shown in Figure L-13.

6. **Select the** text **in the text box, click the** Bold button ☐B☐ **in the Font group on the Formatting Palette, then click the** Align Center button ☐ **in the Alignment and Spacing group on the Formatting Palette**

   The text now appears more vibrant and is centered in the text box.

7. **Click the** Font Size list arrow **in the Font group, then click** 28

   The text increases in size to 28 pt.

8. **In the** Quick Styles and Effects group **on the Formatting Palette, click the** down scroll arrow ☐▼☐ **in the Quick Styles gallery until you reach the bottom of the gallery, then click the** Quick Style **second from the left in the bottom row (the ScreenTip reads "Intense Effect – Accent 5")**

   This Quick Style is applied to the text box.

9. **Open the** Size, Rotation, and Ordering group **on the Formatting Palette, click the** Align button list arrow ☐·, **then click** Align Center

   The text box is center-aligned beneath the title object.

10. **In the** Size, Rotation, and Ordering group, **click the** Distribute button list arrow ☐·, **click** Distribute Vertically, **click a blank area in the slide away from the text box, then save your changes**

    The object is centered vertically on the slide, as shown in Figure L-14.

FIGURE L-12: Slide layouts

Slide Layouts tab

Insert new slide option button

Indicates a new slide will be inserted with this layout when clicked

Title Only slide layout

FIGURE L-13: Creating a text box

Text Box button

Text box (your location may differ)

FIGURE L-14: Completed text box

Quick Style and alignment applied

Creating a custom theme

In addition to applying a predefined theme to a presentation, you can create a unique document theme using an existing theme, theme colors, and theme fonts. To create a custom theme, apply the theme, theme colors, and theme fonts as desired to the current presentation. Next, click the Save Theme option in the Document Theme group, type a unique name in the Save As text box, then click Save. The new theme appears in the Custom Themes group on the Slide Themes tab in the Elements Gallery.

Creating SmartArt

Although regular or bulleted text can be effective in capturing a viewer's attention, there may be times when you need a more striking visual. You can convert text to **SmartArt** and instantly create visually rich and professional-looking diagrams. SmartArt includes dozens of layouts, organized by type: List, Process, Cycle, Hierarchy, Relationship, Matrix, and Pyramid. Table L-1 describes these types in greater detail. For example, you can show proportional or hierarchical relationships, various processes, and directional flows. Once you create a SmartArt graphic, you can modify its style as you can with any object. 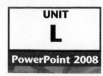 You want to create another slide about the Retailer of the Year award and decide to use SmartArt to create a diagram for the text. You also want to convert some existing text to SmartArt.

STEPS

TROUBLE

To select a text box rather than the text inside it, make sure that your mouse pointer is a 4-headed arrow and not $\mathcal{I}$ when you click the text box.

1. **Click** Insert **on the menu bar, click** Duplicate Slide, **select the** text box **in the Slide pane, then press** [Delete]

   A duplicate of Slide 5 is inserted and the text box is deleted. Duplicating a slide is a quick way to reuse selected information. You want to use the title text but not the content text box.

2. **Click the** SmartArt Graphics tab **in the Elements Gallery**

   As shown in Figure L-15, the SmartArt Graphics tab in the Elements Gallery opens, displaying options for SmartArt Graphics.

TROUBLE

If the text pane is not open when you insert a SmartArt graphic, click the text pane button to open it. To close the text pane, click the Close button in its upper-left corner.

3. **Click the** Cycle group, **click the** right scroll arrow **if necessary until you locate the Multidirectional Cycle layout, then click the** Multidirectional Cycle layout

   A blank SmartArt object with the Multidirectional Cycle layout appears on the slide using the current slide theme colors, and the SmartArt Graphic Styles group appears on the Formatting Palette. Each SmartArt graphic element has placeholders where text can be added. The top text box in the current graphic is selected, ready for you to add text. The SmartArt object also contains a text pane you can use to enter text for the graphic, as shown in Figure L-16.

4. **In the selected text box, type** Increased Market Share

   The text automatically wraps and resizes to fit the text box. Notice that the text in the other placeholders is resized as well.

5. **Click the** bottom left text box, **type** Spotlight Marketing, **click the** bottom right text box, **type** Vendor Retail Sales, **then click away from the SmartArt object**

   The SmartArt object is complete.

6. **Click** Slide 4, **click anywhere in the bulleted text, then click the** Process group **on the SmartArt Graphics tab in the Elements Gallery**

   The SmartArt options change to include those used to illustrate a process.

QUICK TIP

You do not have to first select all the bulleted text you want to convert to SmartArt; you only need to click in the bulleted text object you want to convert.

7. **Click** **until you locate the Chevron List layout, then click the** Chevron List layout

   The Chevron List layout is applied to the bulleted list, and the SmartArt Graphic Styles group opens on the Formatting Palette.

8. **In the SmartArt Graphic Styles group on the Formatting Palette, point to each style in the Styles gallery until you see** Polished, **click the** Polished style, **click away from the SmartArt graphic, then compare your screen to Figure L-17**

   The objects appear three-dimensional with a slick texture.

9. **Click the** Gallery button **on the Standard toolbar to close the Elements Gallery, then save your changes**

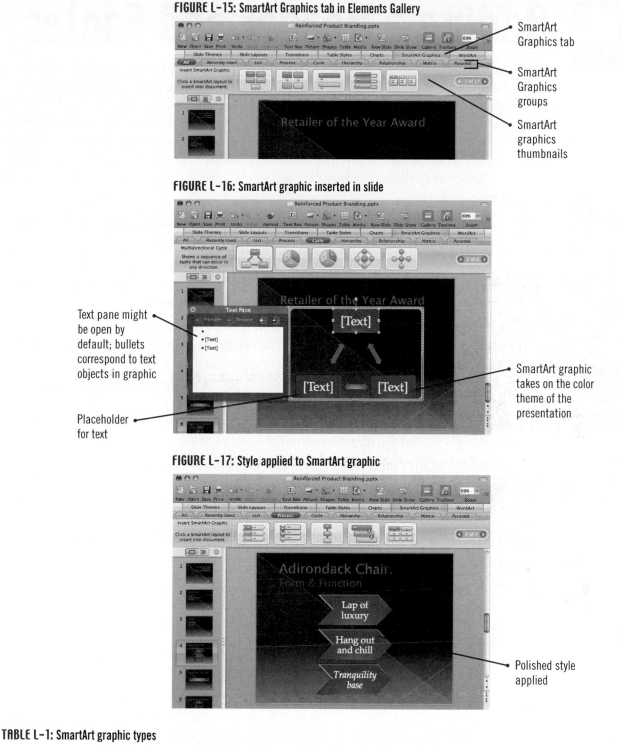

FIGURE L-15: SmartArt Graphics tab in Elements Gallery

SmartArt Graphics tab

SmartArt Graphics groups

SmartArt graphics thumbnails

FIGURE L-16: SmartArt graphic inserted in slide

Text pane might be open by default; bullets correspond to text objects in graphic

Placeholder for text

SmartArt graphic takes on the color theme of the presentation

FIGURE L-17: Style applied to SmartArt graphic

Polished style applied

TABLE L-1: SmartArt graphic types

type	use
List	Non-sequential information
Process	Directional flow and connections between parts of a process
Cycle	Repeating or circular processes
Hierarchical	Decision tree, chain of command, and organizational chart
Relationship	Connections between two or more sets of information
Matrix	Complex relationships relating to a whole
Pyramid	Proportional or hierarchical relationship

Adding a Header and Footer

A slide show can easily contain several slides. You can add a footer to a presentation if you want certain information, such as the current slide number, presentation date or location, or presenter's name, to appear on each slide. Because the text in footers repeats on every slide, it can help the audience (and presenter) keep track of and focus on the presentation. Footers appear on each slide during the presentation and when you print notes, outlines, or handouts. You can add a header to notes and handouts, but unlike footers, headers do not appear on the slides themselves. 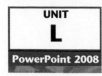 The meeting will include several slide shows, and George wants everyone to know this information is not yet finalized. You decide to add a footer to the presentation to include this and other useful information.

STEPS

QUICK TIP

The Notes and Handouts tab of the Header and Footer dialog box allows you to add headers and footers to all printed output (handouts, notes pages, and outlines).

1. **Click View on the menu bar, then click Header and Footer**

   The Header and Footer dialog box opens with the Slide tab active. You use this tab to specify the information you want visible in the slide's footer. The Preview box shows the location of the footer information. As you select each item, the appropriate text box will be bold in the Preview box.

2. **Click the Date and time check box to select it, click the Update automatically arrows, click the fourth entry (Month Day, Year), then compare your dialog box to Figure L-18**

   The date will appear in a formal date style. The Update automatically selection means that the date on the slide will always update to the date the presentation file is opened. To select a date that never changes, select the Fixed option button and type the date you want shown on the slide.

QUICK TIP

You can add footers and headers to the presentation from any slide.

3. **Click the Slide number check box, click the Footer check box, then in the Footer text box type DRAFT – Do not distribute**

4. **Verify that the Don't show on title slide check box is not selected, click Apply to All, then compare your screen to Figure L-19**

   The dialog box closes and the footer information is applied to each slide. Because you did not select the Don't show on title slide check box, the footer information appears on the title slide. Usually, the title slide is not paginated. You decide to customize the footer for the title slide and remove the page number.

QUICK TIP

To modify the footer text for an individual slide, select the footer text you want to edit, then make changes as desired.

5. **Click Slide 1 in the Slides tab, click View on the menu bar, then click Header and Footer**

6. **Click the Slide number check box and the Footer check box to deselect them, then click Apply**

   Only the date appears in the title slide. Because you clicked Apply instead of Apply to All, the change affects only the title slide. See Figure L-20.

7. **Save your changes**

Editing the slide master

Themes and templates come with default settings. However, there may be times when you want to make a design change to every slide, change the alignment or font size of text, or add a logo or other graphic to every slide. Instead of making the change manually on each slide, you can modify the slide master. Every PowerPoint presentation contains a slide master. The **slide master** contains the layouts, design elements, and other formatting attributes for a presentation. After you apply a theme or a template, you can customize the slide master and save it for future use. To modify the slide master, click View on the menu bar, point to Master, then click Slide

Master. In Slide Master view, the template for each layout is displayed in the left pane and the Title and Content layout is displayed in the right pane. You can select additional slide masters, insert placeholders, apply multiple themes, and change backgrounds and layouts. To create a new slide master, right-click the Title and Content Layout slide thumbnail, click New Master, then customize the slide master as desired. To save the new layout with a unique name, right-click the thumbnail, click Rename Layout, type a name, then click the Rename button.

FIGURE L-18: Header and Footer dialog box

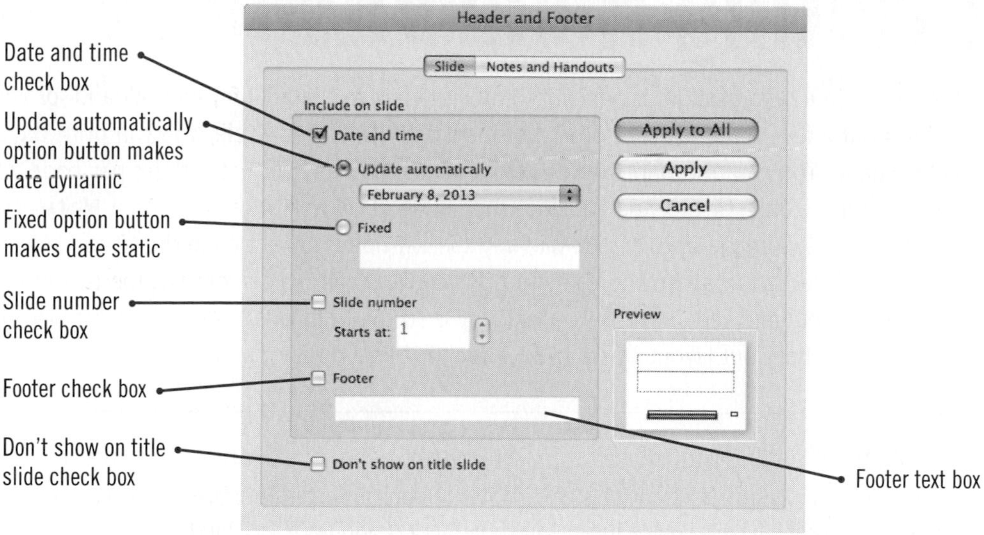

Header and Footer
Slide
Notes and Handouts
Include on slide
Date and time
Update automatically
February 8, 2013
Fixed
Slide number
Starts at: 1
Footer
Don't show on title slide
Apply to All
Apply
Cancel
Preview
Date and time check box
Update automatically option button makes date dynamic
Fixed option button makes date static
Slide number check box
Footer check box
Don't show on title slide check box
Footer text box

FIGURE L-19: Footer text applied to slides

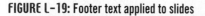

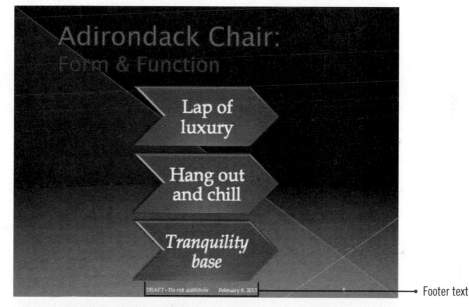

Adirondack Chair:
Form & Function
Lap of luxury
Hang out and chill
Tranquility base
Footer text

FIGURE L-20: Modified footer applied to title slide only

Creating Product Champions
Sales and Success With Names
February 8, 2013
Only the date appears in the footer

PowerPoint 2008

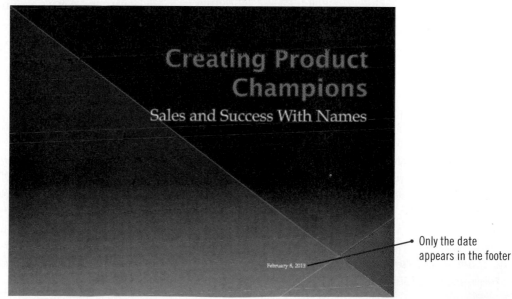

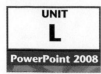

Printing Handouts

When you give a presentation, it's helpful to provide printed material for yourself and for your audience. You can print a few different types of supporting materials. For example, you can print the actual slides, one to a page. You can also print **handouts**, which contain one or more slides per page. One handout option includes blank lines for the audience member to take notes. You can print **Notes pages**, which contain a miniature image of each slide plus any speaker notes you added in the Notes pane as well as any header and footer information. You can also print an **Outline**, which contains the text of your presentation, similar to outline view. 🖼 You've completed the draft of the slide show for George. Now, you want to select a handout layout, add a header, and print out a handout for him to review.

STEPS

1. **Click** View **on the menu bar, point to** Master, **then click** Handout Master

   The view changes to Handout Master view, where you can determine how the handouts will appear on a page and what information to include in the header or footer. The default layout for handouts appears in the window, and the Handout Master View toolbar becomes active just below the Standard toolbar, as shown in Figure L-21. You can quickly change the number of slides per page and the handout headers and footers using this toolbar. By default, only the page number and date print; footer information you enter for slides does not carry over to handouts.

2. **Click the** Header placeholder, **then type** George's Review 1

3. **Click the** Footer placeholder, **type** Your Name, **then click the** Close Master **button on the Handout Master View toolbar**

   The Handout Master layout closes.

4. **Click** File **on the menu bar, then click** Print

   The Print dialog box opens as shown in Figure L-22.

   > **QUICK TIP**
   > To see a full screen preview, click the Preview button at the bottom of the Print dialog box.

5. **Click the** Print What arrows **in the Page Setup group, then click** Handouts (6 slides per page)

   The Preview box shows how this presentation will look printed with six slides per page.

   > **QUICK TIP**
   > The Print dialog box also gives you options for printing multiple copies or a range of slides.

6. **Click the** Print What arrows, **then click** Handouts (3 slides per page)

   The Preview box now shows how this presentation will look printed with three slides per page. This handout option is the only one that includes note lines.

7. **Click the** Output arrows, **click** Grayscale, **then click** Print

   Your presentation is printed as handouts with 3 slides per page in grayscale. Compare your printed copy to Figure L-23.

8. **Save your changes to the presentation, close it, then quit PowerPoint**

Converting a presentation to a PDF file

PowerPoint presentations can easily become large files, making them difficult to e-mail or upload to a server. You can convert the file to a PDF (portable document format), a file type that is easily read on most computers. This file type does not require PowerPoint to open it; it requires only Acrobat Reader, a free program that is installed on most computers. Converting to a PDF file allows any user to be able to view your presentation in a static form. However, any sound or video files, transitions, and animations will not convert and will no longer be part of your presentation. The advantages for converting to a PDF file are: the recipient can view your presentation, but cannot change it; you don't need Microsoft Office to open the file; the file size is much smaller, so it will be easier to share via e-mail or upload to a server; and you can control how many slides per page are viewable. To convert your presentation to a PDF file, click File on the menu bar and click Print. Click the PDF button in the Print dialog box, click Save as PDF, navigate to where you store your Data Files, then click Save. If your computer is set to display the file extension, delete the file extension from the file name, then click Save. The file will be saved with the same file name as your PowerPoint file, but with the file extension .pdf.

Select the best

15. Which view
   a. Normal view
   b. Slide Sorter

16. What does Sr
   a. Transforms
   b. Formats text

17. Which of the
   a. You can pri
   b. You can pri
   c. You can save
   d. You can pri

▼ **SKILLS R**

1. View a presen
   a. Start Microso
     Book templa
   b. Move to Slid
   c. Make the Ou
   d. View the pre
   e. View the pre
   f. Return to No
   g. Close the pre

2. Use a theme.
   a. If necessary,
   b. Open the Slid
   c. Save the pres
   d. Change the si
   e. Apply the Sty
   f. Save your cha

3. Enter text on
   a. Type **Telecor**
   b. Type **Hold th**
   c. Use a button
   d. Type **19th Ce**
   e. Type **Telegra**
   f. Add Slides 3 a
   g. Save your cha

4. Format text.
   a. Move to Slide
     the title text, t
     the text italic.
   b. Move to Slide
     the text **19th,**
     change the for
     to 48.
   c. Use a button o
     Formatting Pal

FIGURE L-21: Viewing the Handout Master layout

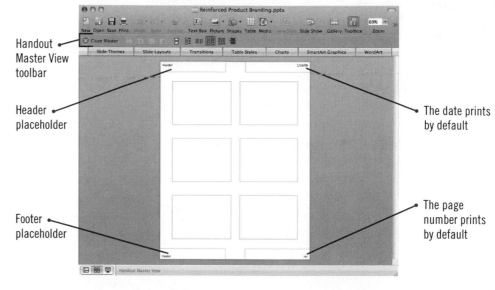

Handout Master View toolbar

Header placeholder

The date prints by default

Footer placeholder

The page number prints by default

FIGURE L-22: Print dialog box

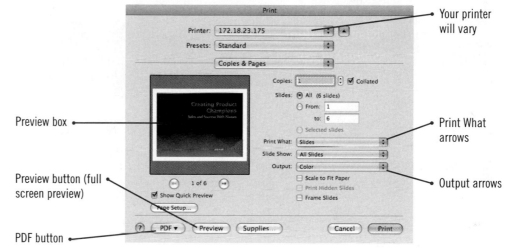

Your printer will vary

Preview box

Print What arrows

Preview button (full screen preview)

Output arrows

PDF button

FIGURE L-23: Printed PowerPoint presentation

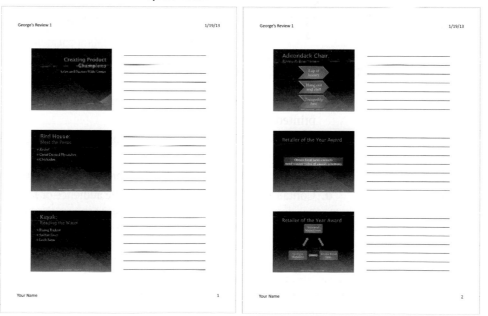

PowerPoint 2008

Creating a Presentation   **PowerPoint 301**

Label the

1

2

Match each

10. Slide Sort
11. Placehold
12. Notes pan
13. Slide The
14. Handout

3

▼ VISUAL WORKSHOP

Using the skills you learned in this unit, create and format the presentation shown in Figure L-28. The Outline tab shows the text to include in the slides. (*Hint*: Apply the Simple Fill style to the SmartArt diagram on Slide 4.) Add today's date and the slide number on each slide. Add your name in the handout footer. Save the presentation as **Airport Runway** to the drive and folder where you store your Data Files. Print the slides of your presentation. Save your changes, close the presentation, then quit PowerPoint.

FIGURE L-28

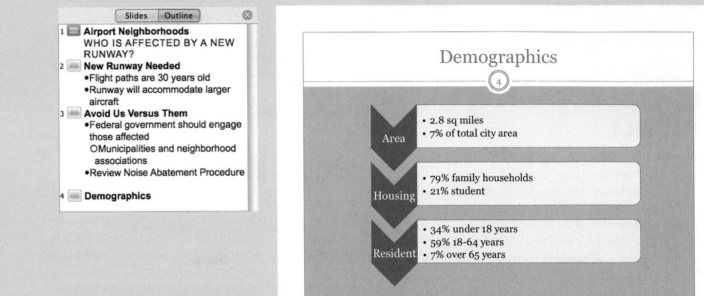

Polishing and Running a Presentation

Files You Will Need:

M-1.pptx
birdhouse.jpg
M-2.pptx
sisal.jpg
M-3.pptx
M-4.pptx
M-5.pptx
cubicles.jpg

You can enhance a PowerPoint presentation by adding media such as shapes, clip art, photographs, sounds, and video. You can add graphics, such as images and photographs, to your slides to illustrate information. You can embed sound effects and movie clips to narrate or add excitement. You can also customize the way slides appear on the screen by creating effects between slides or text elements, so that information progresses in a more interesting way when you run your presentation. Paulette Chen, director of sales, is preparing detailed background information about each kit. She knows that the sales representatives can better sell kits to vendors if they are familiar with the finer points of each kit. To kick off the training, she asks you to create a distinctive, attention-getting presentation. You begin with the one for the bird house kit.

OBJECTIVES

Add a shape

Add clip art

Work with pictures

Add video and sound

Customize a slide show

Set slide timing and transitions

Animate slide objects

Create speaker notes

Adding a Shape

PowerPoint has dozens of built-in shapes you can use to present, highlight, or connect information, or to simply add visual interest to a slide show. Shapes have the same formatting properties as other Office objects: you can alter various attributes such as style, fill, and so on. You can also instantly add text to a shape. Among the many ways you can align an object on a slide is to use rulers; the precise measurements allow you to insert a shape in the same location on multiple slides. You want to add a shape to a slide in the bird house kit presentation to reinforce the impact of bulleted text. In order to increase the shape's impact, you also change its style and fill it with a texture.

STEPS

1. **Start PowerPoint, open the file M-1.pptx from where you store your Data Files, then save it as Bird House**

2. **Click Slide 6 in the Slides tab, click View on the menu bar, then click Ruler to put a check mark next to it, if necessary**
   Slide 6 is active and the horizontal and vertical rulers appear above and to the left of the slide.

3. **Click the Object Palette tab 🖼 on the Toolbox, scroll down to locate the Quad Arrow shape, as shown in Figure M-1, then click the Quad Arrow shape**
   On the Shapes tab on the Object Palette, you can select from a variety of shape styles, including Rectangles, Basic Shapes, Lines and Connectors, Block Arrows, Equation Shapes, Flowcharts, Stars and Banners, Callouts, and Action Buttons. After you click the shape you want, the pointer changes to + so that you can draw the shape on the slide.

> **QUICK TIP**
> Another way to insert a shape is to click the shape on the Object Palette, then click and drag anywhere on the slide to draw the shape to any size you prefer.

4. **Click to the right of the bulleted text on the slide**
   The shape is inserted in the slide. If you click once on a slide to add a shape, the shape is added at a default size.

5. **Position ✥ on the left edge of the shape's selection box, drag it so that the left edge aligns with the 1" mark on the right side of the horizontal ruler, position ✥ on the top edge of the shape's selection box, then drag it so that the top edge aligns with the 2" mark at the top of the vertical ruler**
   The shape is positioned on the slide so the shape's left edge aligns with the 1" mark on the horizontal ruler and its top edge aligns with the 2" mark on the vertical ruler.

6. **Click the Formatting Palette tab 🄰 on the Toolbox, click the down scroll arrow ◥▼ until you reach the bottom of the Quick Styles gallery in the Quick Styles and Effects group, then click the style in the fourth column of the last row (the ScreenTip reads "Intense Effect – Accent 6")**
   The style is applied to the shape.

7. **Click the Colors, Weights, and Fills group on the Formatting Palette, click the Fill Color button list arrow 🄰 ▾, then click Fill Effects**
   The Format Shape dialog box opens with the Solid tab selected.

8. **Click the Texture tab in the Format Shape dialog box, scroll down to the bottom of the texture gallery, click the texture in the first column of the last row ("Cork"), as shown in Figure M-2, then click OK**
   The dialog box closes and the texture is applied to the shape.

9. **Type QA, select the text on the shape, click Format on the menu bar, click Font, click the Font style arrows on the Font tab in the Format Text dialog box, click Bold, then click OK**
   You can enter text in a shape whenever the shape is selected. The text appears centered and bold on the shape.

10. **Click away from the shape, compare your screen to Figure M-3, then save your changes**

FIGURE M-1: Selecting a shape

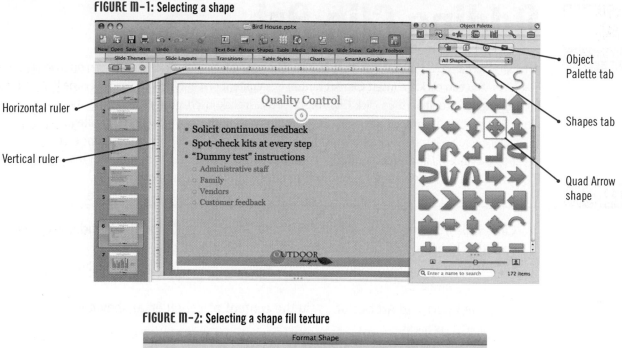

Horizontal ruler

Vertical ruler

Object Palette tab

Shapes tab

Quad Arrow shape

FIGURE M-2: Selecting a shape fill texture

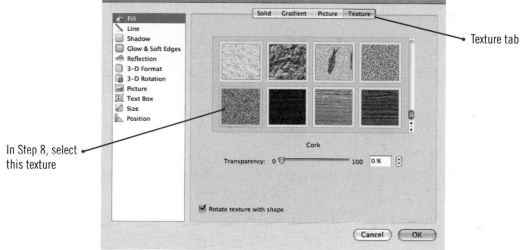

Texture tab

In Step 8, select this texture

FIGURE M-3: Style, texture, and text added to shape

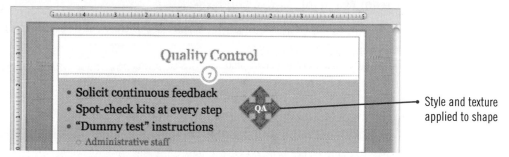

Style and texture applied to shape

Resizing and modifying images

You can modify shapes, clip art, illustrations, and other images using the Picture group on the Formatting Palette; this contextual group opens whenever a graphic is selected. To resize an image, drag the sizing handles of the graphic in the slide. To resize a graphic proportionately, drag a corner (circle) sizing handle inward or outward. To resize only the height or width, drag a side (square) sizing handle. You can also adjust an image's size numerically using the Height and Width controls in the Size, Rotation, and Ordering group on the Formatting Palette.

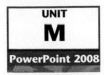

Adding Clip Art

You can insert a clip art image anywhere in a slide using the Clip Gallery, which you can open in any of several ways. You can click the Insert Clip Art button in a content placeholder; you can click the Picture button on the Standard toolbar, then click Clip Art; or you can click Insert on the menu bar, then click Clip Art. Once it's open, you can search the Clip Gallery using keywords or by selecting the category you want to view. Once you've inserted a piece of clip art into your presentation, you can resize or crop it, or add an effect to enhance its appearance. You decide to add clip art to a new slide in the presentation to tie in with the bird house motif. You also format the clip art to make it stand out.

STEPS

1. **Click Slide 1 in the Slides tab, click the New Slide button on the Standard toolbar, click the "Click to add title" placeholder, then type We Know Birds**
   The Title and Content layout is applied to the new slide by default. The content placeholder contains icons for inserting media.

2. **Click the Insert Clip Art button in the content placeholder, as shown in Figure M-4**
   The Clip Gallery opens.

   > **QUICK TIP**
   > To add clip art to a slide from the Object Palette on the Toolbox, click the Clip Art tab on the Object Palette. Click and drag a clip art image from the Object Palette onto the slide to insert it in its default size. Note that if you drag the image to a content placeholder, then it will fill the content placeholder.

3. **Type bird in the Search text box, then click Search**
   Thumbnail previews of bird clip art appear in the task pane.

4. **Click the duck clip art shown in Figure M-5, then click Insert**
   The clip art is inserted on the slide and the size is constrained within the content placeholder.

5. **Click the clip art image on the slide to select it, then click the Shadows tab in the Quick Styles and Effects group on the Formatting Palette**
   The Shadows effects gallery is displayed.

6. **Click the down scroll arrow four times to scroll down to the seventh row in the Shadow effects gallery, then click the effect in the middle of the seventh row (the ScreenTip reads "Perspective Upper Right"), as shown in Figure M-6**
   The selected shadow effect is applied to the image.

7. **Click outside the content placeholder, then save your changes**

Downloading clip art from Microsoft Office Online

You can download additional clip art into your Clip Gallery from the Microsoft Office Web site. Open the Clip Gallery, then click the Online button. Click Yes to launch your default Internet browser and open the Microsoft Office Online Clip Art page, as shown in Figure M-7. In the Clip Art search box, type in a keyword or words describing the clip art you want, then click the Search button. When your search results are returned, click the check box below the clip art you want. Under "Selection Basket" in the left task pane, click Download 1 item, review and accept the Microsoft Service Agreement if necessary, then click the Download Now button. The Downloads window will open, confirming the image was downloaded and placed in the Downloads folder on your dock. Close the Downloads window and your browser, click the Downloads folder on the dock, then click the clip art image in the Downloads folder stack. The image will be added to the Clip Gallery in the Favorites category so that you can use it from any Office program.

FIGURE M-7: Microsoft Office Online Clip Art page

FIGURE M-4: Inserting media using the content placeholder

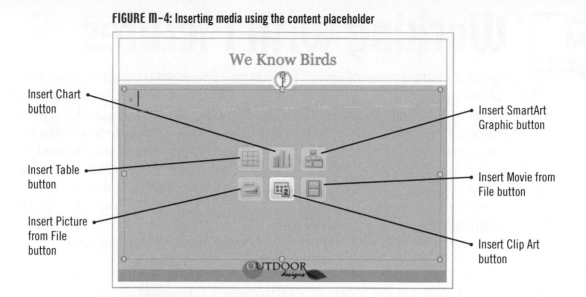

Insert Chart button

Insert Table button

Insert Picture from File button

Insert SmartArt Graphic button

Insert Movie from File button

Insert Clip Art button

FIGURE M-5: Duck clip art image

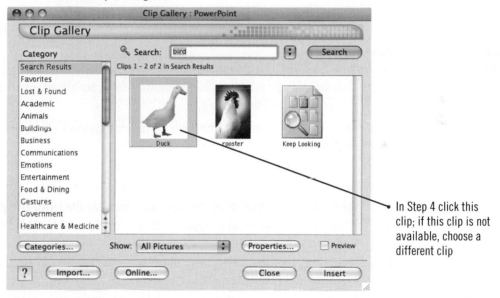

In Step 4 click this clip; if this clip is not available, choose a different clip

FIGURE M-6: Shadow effect applied to clip

In Step 6 click this shadow effect

Shadow effect applied to clip

Working with Pictures

You can insert many different kinds of pictures into a PowerPoint presentation. While you may think of "picture" to mean a piece of clip art or a photograph, in presentation graphics a picture can be an image created and saved in any number of file formats. Different file formats support images differently. For example, most photographs are saved in **Joint Photographic Experts Group (JPEG)** because the format utilizes and compresses color so well, whereas the **Graphic Interchange Format (GIF)** format is best suited for line art such as clip art. Images created using Preview, a Mac OS X program for creating and displaying images, are created in **Portable Network Graphics (PNG)** format. You can modify a picture in any format by resizing and aligning it on the slide. You can also trim away portions of a picture (called **cropping**) and adjust its color.  You decide to insert a photograph in a slide and modify it using several drawing features so that it appears transparent against the slide background.

STEPS

QUICK TIP
To insert a picture using a content placeholder, click the Insert Picture from File button on the content placeholder, navigate to the picture's location in the Choose a Picture dialog box, select the picture, then click Insert.

1. **Click Slide 5 in the Slides tab, click the Picture button on the Standard toolbar, then click Insert Picture**

   The Choose a Picture dialog box opens.

2. **Navigate if necessary to where you store your Data Files, click birdhouse.jpg, then click Insert**

   A photograph of a bird house is inserted on the slide on top of the bulleted text, and contextual groups become available for the picture on the Formatting Palette. Because the photograph obscures a considerable amount of text, you need to modify it.

3. **Click the picture to select it, then click the Crop button in the Picture group on the Formatting Palette**

   Crop handles replace the sizing handles surrounding the photo, as shown in Figure M-8. You want to crop out the post.

4. **Move the mouse pointer over the bottom crop handle until the pointer changes to T, then drag the bottom crop handle up to the bottom of the bird house in the photo**

   By default, when you crop an image, you delete those pixels from the file, which not only makes the picture fit better, but it also reduces the file size of the picture and therefore the presentation as well. A **pixel** is the smallest element in a digital image: a single square.

TROUBLE
If by mistake you click on a non-white part of the birdhouse with the Set Transparent Color button selected, the pixels of that color in the birdhouse image will become transparent. Simply click the Undo button on the Standard toolbar and repeat this step.

5. **Click the Set Transparent Color button in the Picture group, then click in a white section of the photo**

   When you click a white area of the image, all white pixels are deleted from the image, making the areas surrounding the bird house transparent.

6. **Click the Recolor button list arrow in the Picture group, then click Washout in the Color Modes section, as shown in Figure M-9**

   The Washout option adjusts the **opacity** of the image, which is the opaqueness or transparency of an image. Other color variations in the Recolor gallery add a tint to an image. With its new opacity, the photo is perfect to use as a faded background image, but first you want to align it on the slide.

7. **Click the Distribute button list arrow in the Size, Rotation, and Ordering group of the Formatting Palette, then click Distribute Vertically**

   The photo is distributed, or centered, vertically on the slide.

8. **Click the Arrange button list arrow in the Size, Rotation, and Ordering group, then click Send to Back**

   The photo is in back of the bulleted items, visible but not obscuring other parts of the slide.

9. **Click away from the photo; compare your screen to Figure M-10, then save your changes**

FIGURE M-8: Picture inserted in slide

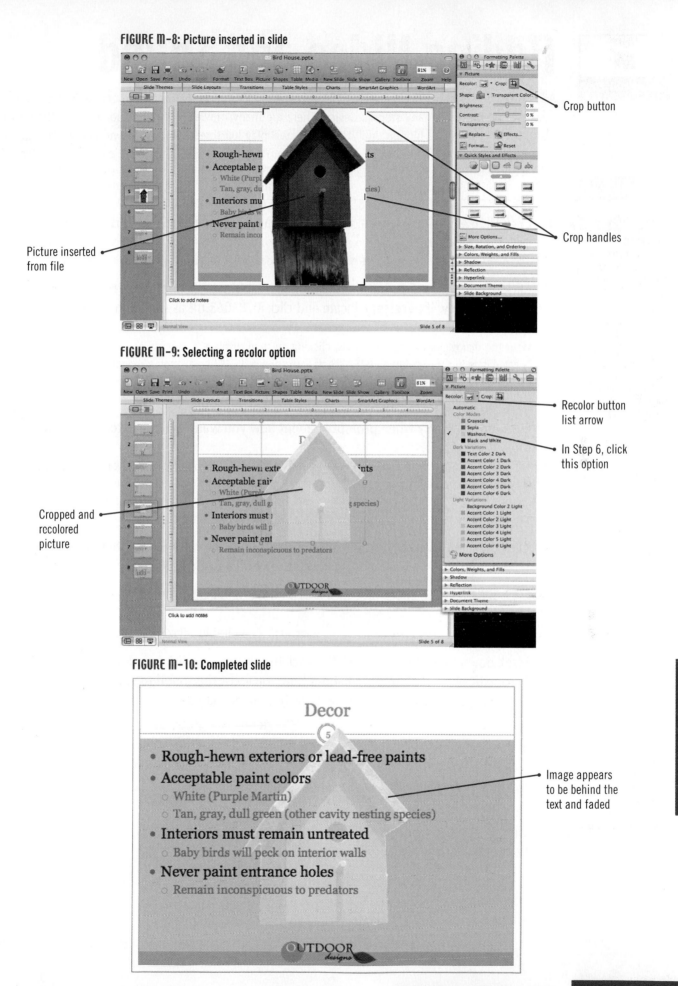

Picture inserted from file

Crop button

Crop handles

FIGURE M-9: Selecting a recolor option

Recolor button list arrow

In Step 6, click this option

Cropped and recolored picture

FIGURE M-10: Completed slide

Image appears to be behind the text and faded

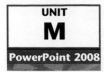
Adding Video and Sound

Adding video and sound to a presentation can make it more effective and memorable. You can insert movies and sound from any storage device. There are many movie settings, including when the movie plays, whether it will be hidden until it is played, will play full screen, and will rewind after playing. For sounds, you can direct PowerPoint to play a song from a CD and even record your own narration for the slide show. You decide to add an animated GIF file as a video and a sound effect to a slide.

STEPS

1. Click Slide 4 in the Slides tab, click the Media button 📷 **on the Standard toolbar, then click Insert Movie**

The Insert Movie dialog box opens with the animated GIF files installed in Office 2008 displayed.

2. Click the Columns View button ▥ **in the Insert Movie dialog box to change the dialog box view if necessary, locate and click j0283063.gif as shown in Figure M-11, then click Choose**

With the dialog box in columns view, clicking an item displays a preview and file information for the selected item in a new column. J0283063.gif is an animated GIF file. A "movie" literally means a sequence of images that give the illusion of movement. Hence, a movie can be a motion picture, an animation (such as an animated GIF), or any digital video file.

3. Click Automatically when prompted about how you want the movie to start in the slide show

The movie is inserted in the center of the slide, as shown in Figure M-12. By clicking Automatically, you choose for the movie to play immediately when the slide appears on the screen during a slide show. The option "When Clicked" allows you to click on the movie to start it after the slide appears in the slide show. You want to preview the movie in the slide show, so you need to switch to Slide Show view.

4. Click the Slide Show button 🖥 **on the status bar, watch the movie, then press [esc]**

The movie plays once. GIF files do not include an audio track, so the movie is silent.

5. Click Slide 2 in the Slides tab, click 📷 **on the Standard toolbar, then click Insert Sound and Music**

The Insert Sound dialog box opens with the sound files installed in Office 2008 displayed.

6. Scroll down to locate the Quack file, click the Quack file, click Insert, then click Automatically when prompted about how you want the sound to start

The sound is inserted in the slide on top of the Duck image and a Sound group becomes available on the Formatting Palette.

7. In the Sound group on the Formatting Palette, click the Hide During Show check box, click the Loop Until Stopped check box, then compare your screen to Figure M-13

You want the sound to play as long as the slide is onscreen during the slide show, and you don't want the icon for the sound to appear during the slide show.

8. Click 🖥 **on the status bar, view the slide, press [esc], then save your changes**

The sound clip plays continuously while the slide is open in Slide Show view and then stops when you return to Normal view.

FIGURE M-11: Inserting a movie in a slide

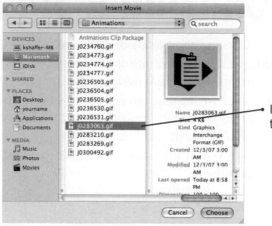

In Step 2, click this clip

FIGURE M-12: Slide with inserted movie

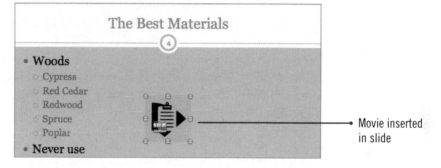

Movie inserted in slide

FIGURE M-13: Modified sound settings

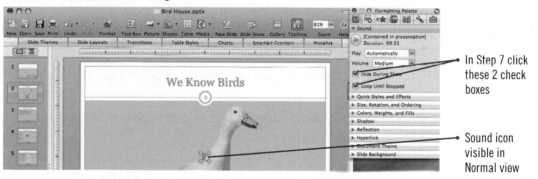

In Step 7 click these 2 check boxes

Sound icon visible in Normal view

Inserting media files

When inserting sounds or video files into a presentation, consider that not all audio and video file formats are supported by Macs. See Table M-1 for Mac-supported audio and video file formats. Also, consider the media file size. Files larger than 100 KB will be linked and not embedded in your presentation file. **Embedded** files are actually part of a presentation; but **linked** files are not; they must be located in the same folder as your PowerPoint file and travel with it if it's moved to a different folder, storage device, or computer.

TABLE M-1: Audio and video file formats supported by Macs

file type	formats supported
Audio	.aif, .aiff, .aifc, .mov, .moov, .sfil, .rsrc, .alaw, .auu, .snd, .ulaw, .wave, .wav, .mp3, .aac, .mpeg, .midi, .mid, .kar
Video	.mov, .mpeg, .avi

Customizing a Slide Show

Once you've created and modified your slide show, you're ready to present it. During a presentation, you may want to mark up a slide to emphasize or add information, move to a specific slide, or show or hide the pointer. You can accomplish these tasks using the Slide Show Menu button. This button is hidden during a presentation until you move the onscreen pointer. When you click the Slide Show Menu button, a menu opens that you can use to navigate through the presentation or activate tools that allow you to draw directly on a slide. ████ Paulette will play the presentation to various groups of sales reps and wants to be able to emphasize certain information as needed on each slide. You experiment with some of PowerPoint's pointer options.

STEPS

1. **Click** Slide 6 **in the Slides tab, then click the** Slide Show button 🖥 **on the status bar**

   The slide show begins with Slide 6. Outdoor Designs considers hardware quality to be a key point, so you highlight these issues in the slide.

2. **Move the mouse until the mouse pointer is visible on the screen and the** Slide Show Menu button 🔲▲ **appears in the lower-left corner of the screen, as shown in Figure M-14**

   The Slide Show Menu button is translucent and appears only when the mouse pointer is active onscreen. If you don't move the mouse pointer for several seconds, both the mouse pointer and the Slide Show Menu button disappear.

> **QUICK TIP**
>
> You can also access Slide Show Menu options by right-clicking a slide.

3. **Click the** Slide Show Menu button 🔲▲

   A pop-up menu opens that displays all available options.

4. **Point to** Pointer Options, **then click** Pen

   The onscreen pointer changes to a pen.

> **QUICK TIP**
>
> To change the ink color of the Pen pointer, click the Slide Show Menu button, point to Pointer Options, point to Pen Color, then click an ink color.

5. **Drag** 𝄃 **on the slide to underline both lines of bulleted text**

   The slide text is underlined, as shown in Figure M-15.

6. **Click** 🔲▲, **point to** Screen, **then click** Erase Pen

   All marks or lines on the slide drawn by the pen pointer are erased.

7. **Click** 🔲▲, **point to** Go to Slide, **then click** 8 Competition Comparison

   Slide 8 fills the screen.

8. **Drag** 𝄃 **to draw a circle around the top of the Outdoor Designs data in the Quality column, as shown in Figure M-16**

   Drawing on a slide lets you make more precise marks to call attention to certain information.

9. **Click** 🔲▲, **point to** Pointer Options, **then click** Automatic

   The pointer changes back to ▲.

10. **Press [esc] to return to Normal view, then save your changes**

    The circle you drew on the slide is deleted in Normal view. Any drawings or marks on your slide show are temporary—used only during a presentation—and are erased as soon as you return to Normal view.

FIGURE M-14: Viewing the Slide Show Menu button

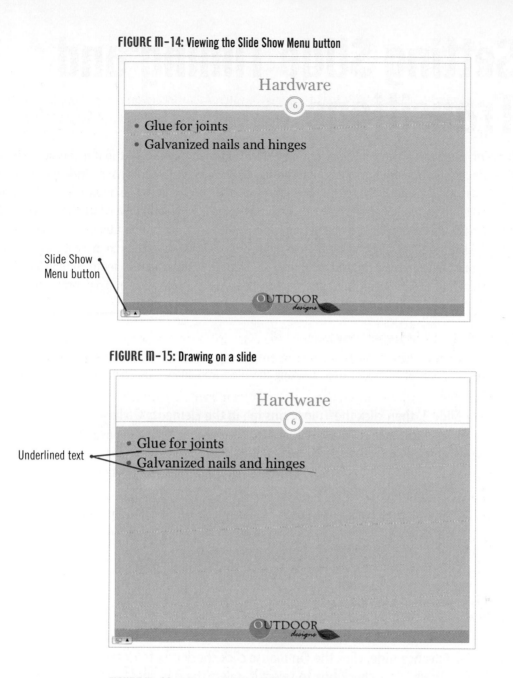

Slide Show
Menu button

FIGURE M-15: Drawing on a slide

Underlined text

Hardware

Glue for joints
Galvanized nails and hinges

FIGURE M-16: Noting important information in a slide

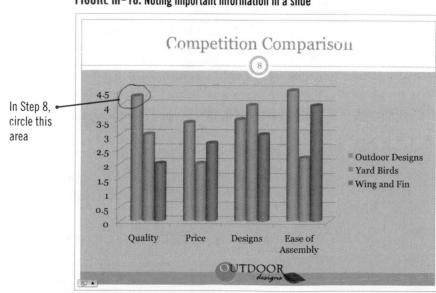

In Step 8,
circle this
area

Setting Slide Timing and Transitions

There may be times when you want to run a presentation automatically, without manually controlling the slide progression. To accomplish this, you can set slide timings in PowerPoint. A **timing** is the number of seconds a slide remains on the screen before advancing to the next one. You might also want to customize how slides are shown in a slide show. To do this, you choose a **transition**, which is a special effect that determines how a slide appears as it enters or leaves the screen. You can adjust timing and transition settings for individual slides or apply one setting to multiple slides. You want to make it easy for Paulette to concentrate on her message instead of running the slide show. You decide to set the timing for each slide in the presentation to 12 seconds, add a consistent slide transition, and add an audio transition to the last slide.

STEPS

1. **Click the Slide Sorter View button**

   The view is changed to Slider Sorter view. The effect icon appears under any slide that has an effect (sound or animation) added to it. Clicking the effect icon allows you to preview the effect on the slide thumbnail.

2. **Click Slide 1, then click the Transitions tab in the Elements Gallery**

   The Transitions tab in the Elements Gallery slides open with the All Transitions group displayed. When you point to a transition, the name of the transition appears on the left side of the Elements Gallery.

> **QUICK TIP**
> To remove a transition from the current slide, click the No Transition thumbnail in the Elements Gallery.

3. **Click the Wipes group on the Transitions tab, then click the Wipe Down transition as shown in Figure M-17**

   The Wipe Down transition is applied to Slide 1. A transition icon now appears beneath the slide in Slide Sorter view, indicating that a transition is applied to Slide 1. Clicking the transition icon lets you view the transition applied to that slide.

4. **Click the Options button in the Elements Gallery**

   The Transition Options dialog box opens as shown in Figure M-18.

> **QUICK TIP**
> During a presentation, you can manually override slide timings by using any slide progression method on the keyboard, such as by pressing [spacebar] or [return].

5. **Next to the Preview box, click the Slow option button**

   The Preview box displays the Wipe Down transition playing at a slow rate.

6. **Under Advance slide, click the On mouse click check box to deselect it, click the Automatically after check box to select it, select the 0 in the Automatically after text box, then type 12**

   Each slide will remain on the screen for 12 seconds before automatically advancing to the next slide.

> **QUICK TIP**
> To adjust the options for a single slide, select the slide, adjust the settings in the Transition Options dialog box, then click Apply.

7. **Click the Apply to All button**

   The Transition Options dialog box closes, and the transition and speed you applied to Slide 1 are now applied to all slides in the presentation.

> **TROUBLE**
> Be aware that you can overwhelm or distract the audience if you apply several transitions or effects to a presentation.

8. **Click Slide 8, click the Options button in the Elements Gallery, click the arrows next to [No Sound], scroll down and click Drum Roll, then click Apply**

   The Drum Roll sound is added to the transition to Slide 8. Compare your screen to Figure M-19.

9. **Click the transition icon below slide 8 to preview the transition with its sound effect, click the Gallery button on the Standard toolbar to close the Elements Gallery, then click the Normal View button**

10. **Click Slide 1, click the Slide Show button on the status bar and view the slide show, then save your changes**

    The slide transitions, timing, animation, and sounds play in the slide show.

Polishing and Running a Presentation

FIGURE M-17: Transitions tab in the Elements Gallery

Transitions tab

Wipes group

Name of highlighted transition

Options button

In Step 3, click this transition

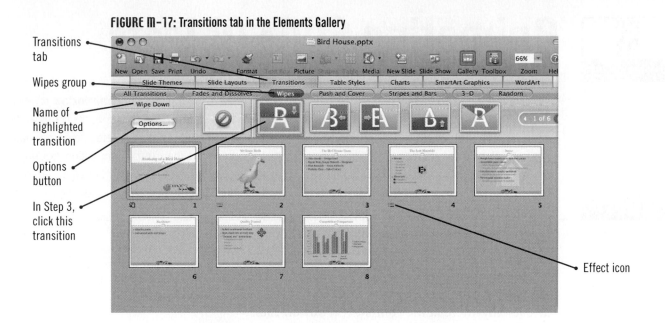

Effect icon

FIGURE M-18: Transition Options dialog box

Preview box

Sound effect options that can be added to the transition

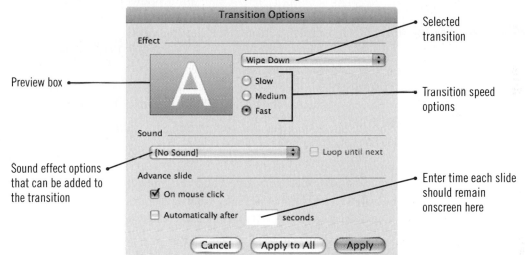

Selected transition

Transition speed options

Enter time each slide should remain onscreen here

FIGURE M-19: Transitions applied to slides

Transition icon

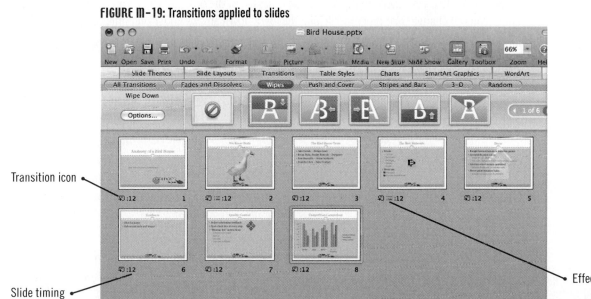

Effect icon

Slide timing

PowerPoint 2008

Animating Slide Objects

While transitions animate the way slides advance onscreen during a slide show, you can also animate individual objects in a slide such as text, clip art, illustrations, and charts. You can apply a preset **animation scheme**, such as Appear, Fade, Fly In, Peek In, or Rise Up, or create a **custom animation** from dozens of choices. For example, you can apply an animation to individual lines of bulleted text, so that each bulleted item is animated at certain intervals. You select and adjust custom animation effects on the Custom Animation tab on the Toolbox, where you can adjust how and when the animation effect plays in three areas: Entrance, Emphasis, and Exit. You decide to animate the bulleted text on Slide 5 and the duck clip on Slide 2.

STEPS

1. **Click Slide 5 in the Slides tab**

2. **Click the Custom Animation tab on the Toolbox**
   The Custom Animation tool opens on the Toolbox.

3. **Click anywhere in the content text box on Slide 5**
   The content text box is selected and three of the four Add Effect buttons become active on the Custom Animation tool, as shown in Figure M-20. The fourth button, the Add Media Actions button, is used only with media files and is not active.

QUICK TIP
Click the disclosure triangle next to an animation in the Animation order list to view all of the items (such as bullets in a content text box) associated with that animation.

4. **Click the Add Entrance Effect button, then click Fade**
   The context text box is added to the Animation order list as Content Placeholder 2, and each major bullet on the slide fades in one by one with its sub-bullets. Using the Custom Animation tool, you can choose from three effects: **Entrance** changes the way text or objects move onto a slide; **Emphasis** adds an effect to an object already visible on a slide; and **Exit** changes the way text or an object leaves the slide.

5. **Click Slide 2 in the Slides tab, click the duck clip in the slide, click, then click More Effects**
   The Animation Effects dialog box opens with the Entrance tab selected, as shown in Figure M-21. The Animation Effects dialog box contains an Entrance tab, an Emphasis tab, and an Exit tab. These tabs contain all the animation effects available in PowerPoint 2008. The effects on each tab are organized by category; for example, the Entrance tab effects are organized into Basic, Subtle, Moderate, and Exciting categories.

TROUBLE
The number after "Content Placeholder" in your Animation order list may differ from that shown in the figure.

6. **Scroll down to the Exciting category, click Swish, then click OK**
   You can preview the Swish effect when you click the animation name in the dialog box, but you do not apply this effect until you click OK. The effect is then listed as "Content Placeholder 4" in the Animation order list under Quack. Effects are added to the Animation order list in the order in which you add them to the presentation; you can change their order by clicking the up or down arrows under the Animation order list.

QUICK TIP
To delete a selected effect, click ✖ under the Animation order list on the Custom Animation tool.

7. **With Content Placeholder 4 selected in the Animation order list, click the up arrow under the Animation order list**
   The Content Placeholder 4 effect is now listed first in the Animation order list. By default, the Content Placeholder 4 effect is set to start On Click, which means you have to click or otherwise use your slide show navigation tools to start the animation during a slide show. You want the Content Placeholder 4 effect to animate immediately during the slide show without having to click.

8. **Click the Start arrows in the Custom Animation tool, then click With Previous**
   The new Start setting triggers the animation to start automatically after the slide transition is complete. The Quack sound will then play after the duck clip enters the slide. Compare your Custom Animation tool to Figure M-22.

9. **Click the Play button at the top of the Custom Animation tool**
   The slide transition and all effects applied to this slide are played in the slide pane in Normal view.

10. **Navigate to Slide 1, view the slide show from the beginning, then save your changes**
    The animations play with the settings you applied to them.

FIGURE M-20: Custom Animation tool

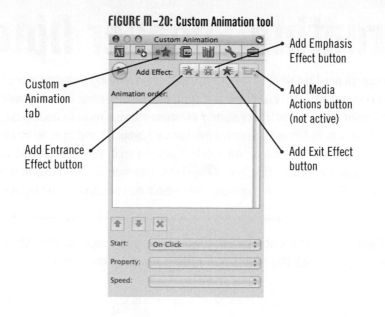

Custom Animation tab

Add Entrance Effect button

Add Emphasis Effect button

Add Media Actions button (not active)

Add Exit Effect button

FIGURE M-21: Animation Effects dialog box

Entrance tab

Basic category

List of all available Entrance effects

FIGURE M-22: Re-ordered animations

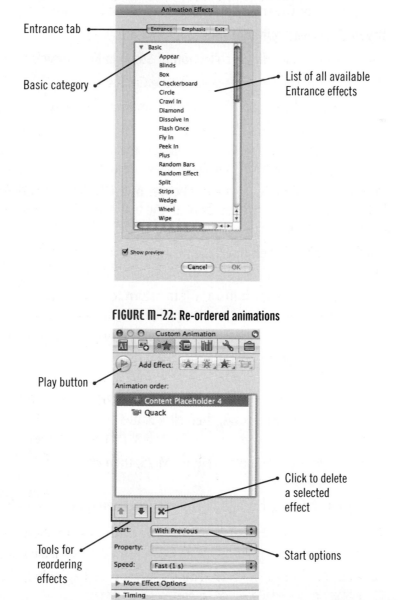

Play button

Tools for reordering effects

Click to delete a selected effect

Start options

Creating Speaker Notes

Even experienced speakers can feel nervous or anxious giving a presentation. Having notes on hand can be very helpful, even if you just glance at them from time to time. **Speaker notes** contain information such as key points you can reference during the presentation. You can add speaker notes in the Notes area in Normal view or in Notes Page view. You can add graphics and images to your notes in Notes Page view. When you print speaker notes, each slide is printed on its own page, and the notes you added, including graphics, appear beneath the slide.  Paulette has asked you to add some speaker notes to a couple of slides in the presentation to ensure she doesn't miss important information.

STEPS

1. **Click the** Formatting Palette tab 🖼 **on the Toolbox, click** Slide 1 **in the Slides tab if necessary, click the** Notes pane, **then type** We know our kits are great. Now we're going to learn why.

   The text appears in the Notes pane. Paulette has sent you personal notes she wants you to add on the team slide.

> **QUICK TIP**
> For longer sentences, the text wraps automatically in the Notes pane, as when typing text in a Word document.

2. **Click** Slide 3 **in the Slides tab, click the** Notes pane, **type** Jake: Won 3rd place at the Fiery Food Show for Green Chili Stew, **then type the following text, each on its own line:**

   Bryan: Plays lead guitar in his band Cap Com

   Sanjay: Has a first edition collection of Stephen King novels

   Pam: Keynote speaker at Festival of the Cranes

   Me: Dropped the cake at the company anniversary party

   Sales Reps: Your Name

   The default space allotted to the Notes pane is not sufficient for the note text and cuts off the first lines of text. You can resize the Notes pane so you can see all the text.

3. **Position the pointer over the** top border **of the Notes pane until the pointer changes to** [↕], **then drag the** border **up until all the text is visible, as shown in Figure M-23**

   All the text is visible in the Notes pane.

> **TROUBLE**
> The status bar does not contain a button for Notes Page view; this view is accessible only by using the View menu.

4. **Click** View **on the menu bar, then click** Notes Page

   The slide opens in Notes Page view, as shown in Figure M-24. You want to print only the pages that have notes.

5. **Click the** Normal View button 🖼 **to return to Normal view, click** Slide 1 **in the Slides tab, press and hold** [⌘], **then click** Slide 3 **in the Slides tab**

   Pressing [⌘] while clicking a second slide allows you to add another slide to the selection.

6. **Click** File **on the menu bar, then click** Print

   The Print dialog box opens.

7. **Click the** Selected slides option button **in the Print range section of the Print dialog box, click the** Print What arrows, **then click** Notes

   The text under the Preview box changes from "1 of 8" to "1 of 2," and the Preview box shows Slide 1 with notes.

8. **Compare your dialog box to Figure M-25, then click** Print

   Notes pages 1 and 3 print.

9. **Save your changes, close the presentation, then quit PowerPoint**

FIGURE M-23: Resized Notes pane

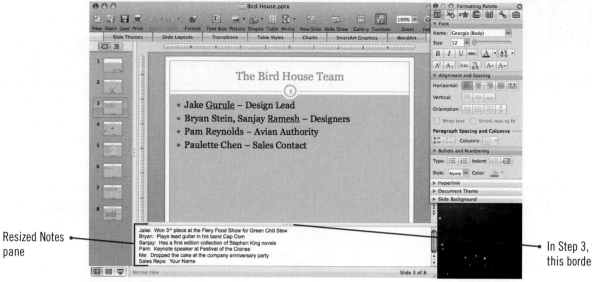

Resized Notes pane

In Step 3, drag this border

FIGURE M-24: Viewing a slide and notes in Notes Page view

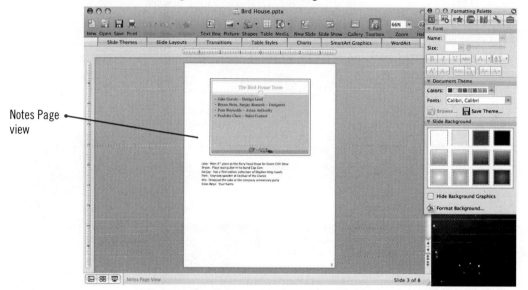

Notes Page view

FIGURE M-25: Printing Notes

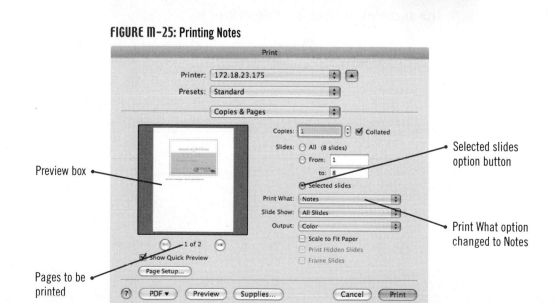

Preview box

Selected slides option button

Print What option changed to Notes

Pages to be printed

Practice

▼ CONCEPTS REVIEW

Label the PowerPoint window elements shown in Figure M-26.

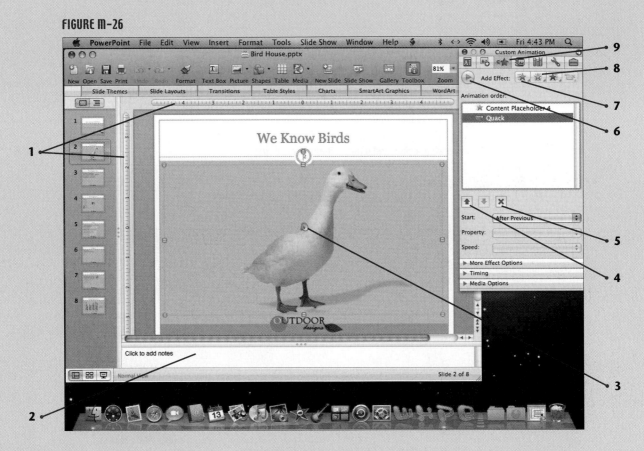

FIGURE M-26

Match each term with the statement that best describes it.

10. Pen
11. Transition
12. Animation
13. Crop
14. Transition sound

a. A tool that deletes pixels from an image file when you trim it
b. A slide markup tool you can use to draw on a slide during a presentation
c. A special effect that determines how a slide advances on the screen
d. A sound effect that plays as one slide advances to the next slide in a presentation
e. An effect that triggers movement of a specific element in a slide

Select the best answer from the list of choices.

15. Which of the following about transitions is *not* correct?

    a. They are animation-like effects.

    b. You can add only one to a presentation.

    c. You can control the speed at which they play.

    d. You can add sound effects to them.

16. Which of the following is *not* a custom animation category?

    a. Transition   **c.** Emphasis

    b. Exit   **d.** Entrance

17. Which of the following views *does not* have a view icon on the status bar?

    a. Slide Sorter view   **c.** Notes Page view

    b. Slide Show view   **d.** Normal view

18. Which of the following tools lets you play the effects that have been added to the selected slide?

    a. ⬆   **c.** 🖼

    b. ▷   **d.** ⭐

▼ SKILLS REVIEW

1. Add a shape.

    a. Start Microsoft PowerPoint, open the file M-2.pptx from where you store your Data Files, then save it as **Natural Fiber Rugs Sales**.

    b. Move to Slide 6.

    c. Make sure that the rulers are visible; if necessary, use a tool on the View menu to display them.

    d. Insert the Down Ribbon shape in this slide so that its left selection box border is aligned with the 2" mark on the right side of the horizontal ruler and its top border is aligned with the 3 ½" mark at the top of the vertical ruler. (*Hint*: This shape is located in the Stars and Banners section on the Shapes tab in the Object Palette. Once you've selected the shape, click the slide to insert the shape.)

    e. Open the Formatting Palette, then apply the Colored Fill — Accent 2 style to the shape from the Quick Styles and Effects group.

    f. Open the Colors, Weights, and Fills group on the Formatting Palette if necessary, click the Fill Color button list arrow, then click Fill Effects. Click the Texture tab, then apply the Woven mat texture to the shape.

    g. Type **Banner Year** in the shape.

    h. Drag the bottom-right sizing handle down and to the right until the text fits in the shape, one word per line. See Figure M-27.

    i. Save your changes.

FIGURE M-27

2. Add clip art.

    a. Move to Slide 7, then insert a new title and content slide.

    b. Click the Click to add title placeholder, then type **To the Future**....

    c. Click the Insert Clip Art button in the content placeholder.

    d. Search all collections in the Clip Gallery for **time** clip art, then insert the clip shown in Figure M-28.

    e. Select the image on the slide, then locate and apply the Soft Edge Rectangle style to the clip.

    f. Save your changes.

FIGURE M-28

time flies

3. Work with pictures.

    a. Move to Slide 2, then use a button on the Standard toolbar to open the Insert Picture dialog box.

    b. Insert the file sisal.jpg from the drive and folder where you store your Data Files.

    c. Use a command in the Size, Rotation, and Ordering group on the Formatting Palette to send the object to the back of the slide.

    d. Use a command in the Picture group to crop the left border of the image to the start of the bulleted text.

    e. Recolor the photo to Accent Color 4 Light.

    f. Save your changes.

4. Add video and sound.

    a. Move to Slide 3, then use a button on the Standard toolbar to open the Insert Movie dialog box.

    b. In the Insert Movie dialog box, search for the animated GIF file shown in Figure M-29, and have the movie start automatically in the slide show. (*Hint*: When searching, change the view in the Insert Movie dialog box to columns view if necessary in order to view a thumbnail of each selected animated GIF in a new column to the right.)

FIGURE M-29

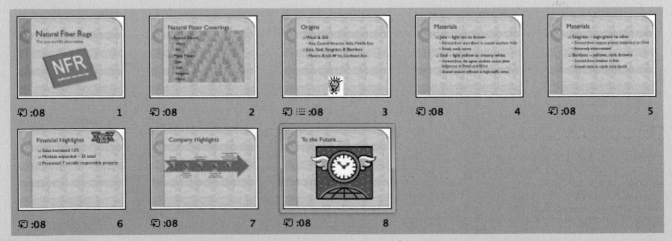

    c. Select the movie in the slide, then use a command in the Size, Rotation, and Ordering group on the Formatting Palette to align the clip to the bottom center of the slide.

    d. Preview the slide in Slide Show view, then return to Normal view.

    e. Use a button on the Standard toolbar to open the Insert Sound dialog box.

    f. In the Insert Sound dialog box, scroll down and insert the Vibro Up file to play automatically. Set the sound to loop until stopped and to be hidden during the slide show.

    g. View the slide in Slide Show view, then save your changes.

5. Customize a slide show.

    a. Move to Slide 7, then view the slide in Slide Show view.

    b. Activate the Slide Show Menu button, then select the black pen color from the Pointer Options submenu. (*Hint*: Move the pointer on screen to make the Slide Show Menu button visible.)

    c. In the 1993 text, cross out 300, then write 210.

    d. Use a command on the Slide Show Menu to go to Slide 5.

    e. Draw on the slide to underline the text **Smooth texture repels most liquids**.

    f. Return to Normal view.

    g. Save your changes.

6. Set slide timing and transitions.

    a. Change the view to Slide Sorter view.

    b. Open the Transitions tab in the Elements Gallery, select the Diamond transition in the Wipes group, then change the transition speed to Medium.

    c. Apply the transition to all the slides.

    d. Change the slide timing to 8 seconds and apply it to all the slides.

    e. Move to Slide 8, then add the Yeehaw sound effect to the slide transition for this slide only.

    f. Close the Elements Gallery, view the slide show from the beginning, then return to Slide Sorter view. See Figure M-30.

    g. Save your changes.

FIGURE M-30

7. Animate slide objects.

  a. Switch to Normal view, move to Slide 6, then click the content text box.

  b. Apply a Fly In animation to the list. (*Hint*: This effect is located in the Entrance category.)

  c. Move to Slide 2, then select the title text box.

  d. Add a Wave Emphasis effect to the title text.

  e. For the Wave Emphasis effect, change the Start setting to After Previous, click the Speed arrows below the Start and Property settings on the Custom Animation tool, then click Fast (1 s).

  f. Preview the slide using a command in the Custom Animation tool, then view the entire slide show.

  g. Save your changes.

8. Create speaker notes.

  a. Move to Slide 2, then type in the Notes pane **Weaving started in Egypt at least 8,000 years ago**.

  b. Move to Slide 6, then type in the Notes pane the following text on separate lines:

    Sales figure is for wholesale — exact retail still pending

    Markets are growing beyond flooring stores into lifestyle stores

    Third year we paid for staff to participate in giving-back projects

  c. Increase the size of the Notes pane to accommodate the notes text, if necessary.

  d. View the slides in Notes Page view.

  e. Return to Normal view.

  f. Open the Header and Footer dialog box, then add your name to the slide footer on all slides except the title slide.

  g. Select slides 2 and 6, then open the Print dialog box.

  h. Print slides 2 and 6 as Notes, save your changes, close the presentation, then quit PowerPoint.

▼ INDEPENDENT CHALLENGE 1

You work at *A Fine Ruse*, a local, independent weekly newspaper. To boost readership, you've decided to host an Annual Best of Ruse contest, honoring a host of different categories. Readers will send in the winning entries, and the paper will devote an issue to the contest. Your job is to come up with categories that are distinctive, interesting, and sure to elicit a response. You want to present your ideas to your colleagues for feedback and fine tuning.

  a. Start PowerPoint, open the file M-3.pptx from where you store your Data Files, then save it as **Best of Ruse**.

  b. Insert a shape on Slide 1 and type **And the winner is...** in the shape. (*Hint*: Resize the shape and modify the shape fill and style as desired.)

  c. Add a shadow effect of your choice to the shape.

  d. Insert clip art from the Clip Gallery to Slides 3, 5, 6, 7, and 9, choosing clips that pertain to each topic. (*Hint*: When searching, use keywords that are relevant to the slide title.) Adjust the size and location of the images to give the slides a balanced and attractive look.

  e. Insert the Paper Cup clip art shown in Figure M-31 on Slide 4. Recolor the image using Sepia. Enlarge the image, center it on the slide, and send it to the back.

  f. Insert the j0300492.gif (swimming fish) animation on Slide 8. In the Movie group on the Formatting Palette, click the Loop Until Stopped check box so that the movie will play continuously during a slide show. Adjust the size and location of the animation on the slide for a balanced look.

  g. Insert sounds in Slides 6 and 9, choosing sounds that pertain to each topic. Hide both sounds during the show.

  h. Apply the Checkerboard Down slide transition to all slides, and set the timing to 7 seconds for all slides in the presentation. (*Hint*: Look in the Stripes and Bars group for the transition.)

  i. Add the Cash Register sound effect to the transition to Slide 2.

  j. Animate the title text box on Slide 2 with the Light Speed Entrance effect that starts With Previous.

FIGURE M-31

Paper Cup

▼ INDEPENDENT CHALLENGE 1 (CONTINUED)

k. Animate the SmartArt graphic on Slide 2 with the Compress Entrance effect that starts After Previous.

l. On Slide 1, animate the subtitle text box with the Wipe Entrance effect.

m. Add the following notes to Slide 2:

Allow readers to submit their own categories

Include side pieces from local personalities listing their favorites

n. Add your name to the slide footer on all slides except the title slide, switch to Slide Sorter view, then compare your presentation to Figure M-32. (*Note*: The shape and the clip art you used on the slides may differ from those shown in the figure.)

FIGURE M-32

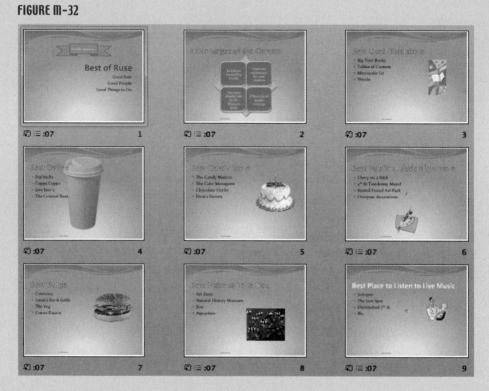

Advanced Challenge Exercise

- Add a sound to at least one additional slide. (*Hint*: You can experiment by adding multiple sounds to the same slide.)
- Add an additional movie to at least one of the other slides in the presentation.

o. Save your changes.

p. Print Slide 2 as Notes, then print the entire presentation as handouts, 9 slides per page.

q. Close the presentation, then quit PowerPoint.

▼ INDEPENDENT CHALLENGE 2

Your graphics and Web design company, Grafik Traffic, just merged with another large graphics business, Pipeline Design. As you've begun to work on joint projects, you have realized that members of the Pipeline Design staff are not well-versed in copyright law. You create a PowerPoint presentation for in-house training on the basics of copyright law.

a. Start PowerPoint, open the file M-4.pptx from where you store your Data Files, then save it as **Copyright 101**.

b. Search for a clip art image using the keyword **law**, then insert it in Slide 1. Adjust the image as desired so it complements the look of the slide.

c. Search for a clip art image using the keyword **dragon**, then insert it in Slide 2. Adjust the image as desired so it complements the look of the slide.

d. Add clip art to at least one other slide in the presentation. (*Hint*: For media searches, use words from the slide as keywords. Also, consider using the Object Palette to look for clip art instead of using keyword searches.)

e. On Slide 6, use the keyword **book** to search the Clip Gallery for a piece of clip art for this slide. Adjust the size of the image to fit on the right half of the slide using the sizing handles. Use a command from the Size, Rotation, and Ordering group on the Formatting Palette to send the image to the back. Recolor the image so the text on top of the image is clear and readable. Refer to Figure M-33.

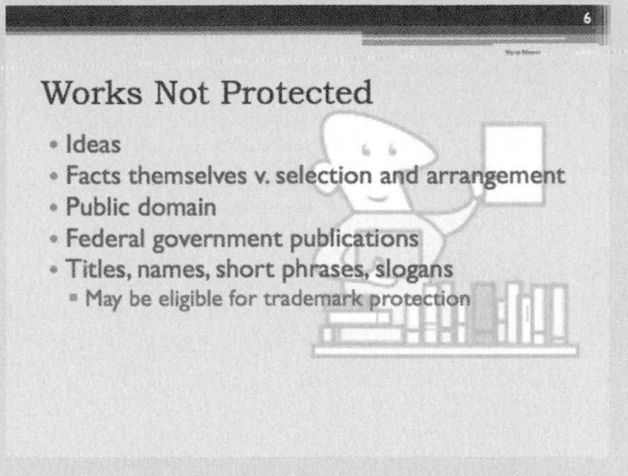

f. On Slide 11, animate the bulleted text with the Change Font Color Emphasis effect. (*Hint*: After adding the effect, click the Property arrows under the Animation order list, then click the red color.) Next, change the Start time to After Previous.

g. To Slide 1, add a "bubbles" sound to start automatically and to be hidden during the show.

h. Animate the bulleted text on at least five slides with the animation effects of your choice.

i. Apply a slide transition to all slides and adjust the slide timing to be 8 seconds.

j. Add a photo from the Clip Gallery to at least one additional slide in the presentation. If necessary, recolor the picture and send it to the back.

k. Add a movie to one slide in the presentation.

l. Add the following notes to Slide 5:
Copyright holder has rights over work: reproduce, prepare derivative works, distribute copies, perform, and display the work

m. Add your name to the slide footer on all slides, switch to Slide Sorter view, then compare your presentation to Figure M-34. (*Note*: The movies and the clip art you used on the slides may differ from those shown in the figure.)

FIGURE M-33

Works Not Protected

- Ideas
- Facts themselves v. selection and arrangement
- Public domain
- Federal government publications
- Titles, names, short phrases, slogans
  - May be eligible for trademark protection

FIGURE M-34

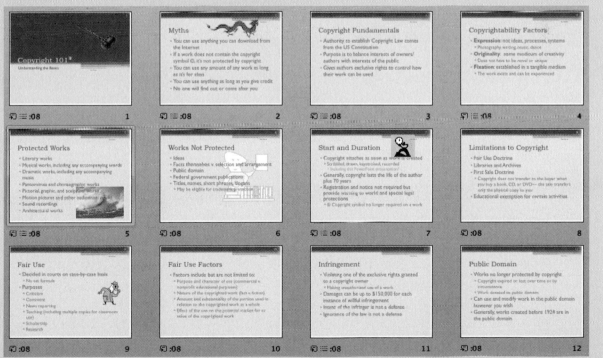

▼ INDEPENDENT CHALLENGE 2 (CONTINUED)

Advanced Challenge Exercise

- Add a movie of your choosing to a slide in the presentation that does not currently include a movie.
- Add a transition sound to a slide in the presentation.

n. Save your changes.

o. Print Slide 5 as Notes, then print the entire presentation as Handouts, 6 slides per page.

p. Close the presentation, then quit PowerPoint.

▼ INDEPENDENT CHALLENGE 3

You are a business consultant specializing in customer relations. You've been hired to do a workshop for a small business that has a great product, but their internal processes need some improvement. You create a PowerPoint presentation that emphasizes customer relationships.

a. Start PowerPoint, open the file M-5.pptx from where you store your Data Files, then save it as **Customer Trust**.

b. On Slide 1, animate the subtitle with the Whip Entrance effect that starts With Previous.

c. Move to Slide 4, then insert a clip art image from the Business category of the Clip Gallery. (*Hint*: Click Business in the Category list.) Recolor the image if necessary, or adjust its Brightness or Contrast, then send to back of the bulleted text. Resize as necessary. Refer to Figure M-35. (Your clip art image may differ from that in the figure.)

FIGURE M-35

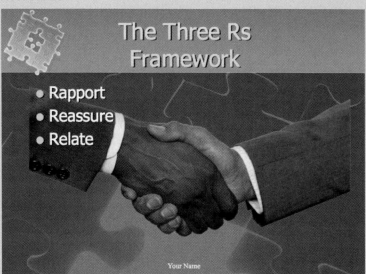

d. Move to Slide 5, insert the image file cubicles.jpg from where you store your Data Files, then crop the image as desired. Move and resize the image so it looks attractive on the slide.

e. Add one clip art image to Slide 7 and one to the slide of your choice.

f. Add at least one movie and one sound to slides of your choice.

g. Add at least one shape to a slide of your choice. Modify the shape fill and style as desired.

h. Add a transition to all of the slides and adjust slide timing as desired.

i. Add a transition sound to Slide 7.

j. Animate at least one text object or image on a slide.

k. Animate each slide title in Slides 2-7 with an Entrance effect, then add an Emphasis effect to at least two titles in the presentation, each set to start After Previous.

l. Add notes to at least two slides that don't already have them.

▼ INDEPENDENT CHALLENGE 3 (CONTINUED)

m. Add your name to the footer to all slides except the title slide, switch to Slide Sorter view, then compare your presentation to Figure M-36. (The shapes, movies, and clip art you used may differ from those in the figure.)

n. Save your changes, close the presentation, then quit PowerPoint.

FIGURE M-36

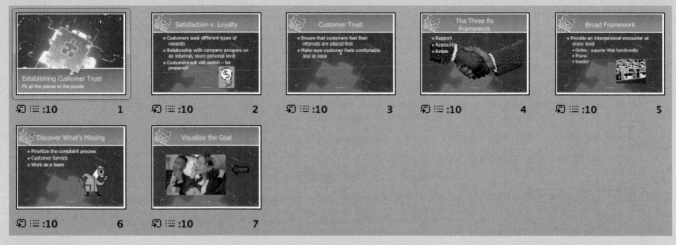

▼ REAL LIFE INDEPENDENT CHALLENGE

Take advantage of your new skills in PowerPoint to create a presentation for friends, family, or co-workers. Create a slide show about your favorite hobby or topic of interest, and intersperse the slides with related facts or stories.

a. Start PowerPoint; create a new file, apply a theme, then save the file as **My Personal Favorite** where you store your Data Files.

b. Insert photos of your topic, either from your computer or from the Clip Gallery. (*Hint*: Apply various styles to the photos.)

c. Create slides describing the item, person, or creature, or about something in the photo, then insert relevant clip art, movies, and sounds to at least three slides.

d. Apply slide transitions, sounds, and slide timings to the presentation.

e. Add at least one shape to the presentation.

f. Add notes on at least two slides.

g. Animate objects as desired.

h. Add your name to the slide footer on all slides except the title slide.

i. Save your changes, then print the Notes pages.

j. Close the presentation, then quit PowerPoint.

Create a slide that resembles Figure M-37. Save the presentation as **Password Tips** where you store your Data Files. Use default settings for each element. (*Hints*: Start with a blank presentation; after you apply the design theme, add a title and content slide. For the image, search on the keyword **lock** and apply an Entrance effect from the Basic section.) Add your name to the slide footer, then print the slide. Save your changes, close the presentation, then quit PowerPoint.

FIGURE M-37

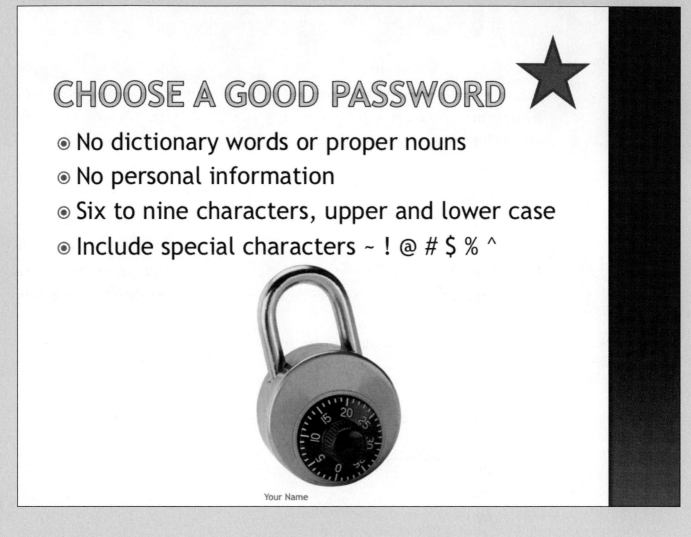

Integrating Office 2008 Programs

Files You Will Need:

N-1.pptx
N-2.docx
N-3.docx
N-4.docx
N-5.xlsx
N-6.xlsx
N-7.pptx
N-8.docx
N-9.docx
N-10.docx
N-11.xlsx
N-12.xlsx
N-13.pptx
N-14.docx
N-15.docx
N-16.docx
N-17.xlsx
N-18.xlsx
N-19.rtf
N-20.xlsx
N-21.rtf

So far you've created many documents, worksheets, and presentations using individual Office programs. Sometimes, however, you might want to create files that combine information from different Office programs, such as a newsletter you create with Word that also contains a table of data created with Excel. You also can save any Office document as a Web page for use on the Internet or an intranet. Paulette Chen, director of sales for Outdoor Designs, needs you to insert an Excel chart in a presentation she created, create slides from a Word outline, and then publish the presentation to the Web. She also has a letter for the shareholders; she needs you to add text and data to the letter and then send it out as a mail merge form letter. You will use several Office programs to accomplish these tasks.

OBJECTIVES

Insert an Excel chart onto a PowerPoint slide

Create PowerPoint slides from a Word document

Save a PowerPoint presentation for the Web

Insert text from a Word file into an open document

Link Excel data to a Word document

Update linked Excel data in a Word document

Insert placeholders in a Word document

Perform a mail merge

Inserting an Excel Chart onto a PowerPoint Slide

Because an Excel chart is an excellent tool for communicating numerical data in a visual way, you might want to create an Excel chart on a PowerPoint slide to convey financial results or trends to an audience. When you create a chart in PowerPoint, you **embed** data in the presentation that is editable in Excel. When you save your presentation, the chart data is saved with it; you do not save the data separately in Excel. ▓▓▓▓ Paulette has given you a presentation she created for the quarterly sales meeting and a hard copy of sales figures. You need to insert a chart comparing sales, so you decide to create the chart directly in PowerPoint.

STEPS

1. **Start PowerPoint, open the file N-1.pptx from where you store your Data Files, then save it as Sales Comparisons.pptx**

2. **Click Slide 2 in the Slides tab, then click the Insert Chart button 📊 in the content placeholder**
   The Charts tab in the Elements Gallery opens.

3. **Click the Column group on the Charts tab, then click the Clustered Column chart type as shown in Figure N-1**
   Excel opens with sample data in a new spreadsheet, as shown in Figure N-2.

4. **Click the PowerPoint icon 📇 on the dock to switch to PowerPoint**
   In the PowerPoint window, a chart based on the sample data appears in the slide, and the Chart Styles, Chart Options, and Chart Data groups are available on the Formatting Palette. You plan to replace the sample data in Excel with figures from Paulette's hard copy report.

5. **Click the Excel icon 📊 on the dock to switch to Excel, then replace the data in the worksheet with the data in the following table:**

Cell	Data	Cell	Data	Cell	Data	Cell	Data
		B1	Q1 2010	C1	Q1 2011	D1	Projected Q1 2012
A2	Northeast	B2	55000	C2	67000	D2	73000
A3	Midwest	B3	69500	C3	72500	D3	80000
A4	South	B4	86000	C4	106000	D4	116000
A5	West	B5	106000	C5	138000	D5	152000

6. **Click Excel on the menu bar, then click Quit Excel**
   The Excel window closes, displaying the PowerPoint window. As you entered the report data in the Excel spreadsheet, the chart in the slide was updated, as shown in Figure N-3. It is not necessary to save the spreadsheet in Excel; if you later edit the chart data from PowerPoint, the data will open in a new spreadsheet.

7. **Close the Elements Gallery, then save your changes to the document**

FIGURE N-1: Choosing the Clustered Column chart type on the Charts tab

Column group

Clustered Column chart type

In Step 2, click this button

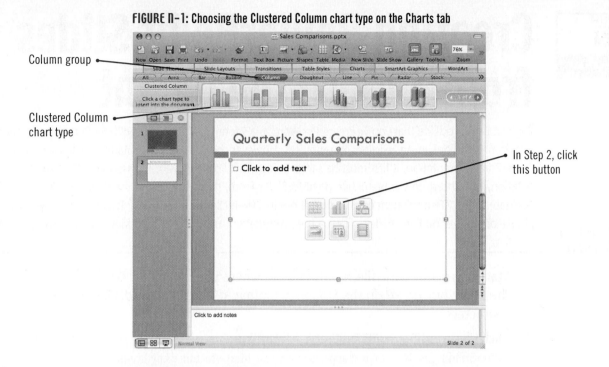

FIGURE N-2: Sample chart data in Excel

Spreadsheet opened in Excel

Sample data

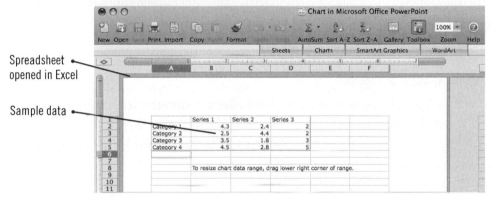

FIGURE N-3: Updated chart

Chart updated with data entered in Excel

Edit in Excel button

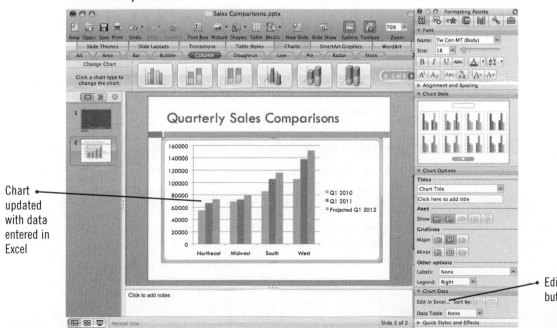

Integration

Creating PowerPoint Slides from a Word Document

You can use an outline that you've created in Word as a starting point for a new PowerPoint presentation, or as additional slides in an existing presentation. However, before a Word outline can be inserted into a PowerPoint presentation, it first must be saved in Rich Text Format (RTF). To insert an RTF outline in a presentation, click Insert on the menu bar, point to Slides From, then click File. In the Choose a File dialog box, navigate to the RTF document containing the outline, then click Insert. Paulette wants you to incorporate one of her outlines as new slides in the presentation. First, you want to view the document in Word.

1. **Start Word, open the file N-2.docx from where you store your Data Files, then click the Show button ¶ on the Standard toolbar, if necessary, to display the nonprinting characters**

2. **Click View on the menu bar, then click Outline**

   As shown in Figure N-4, the text appears in a hierarchical structure using headings and subheadings, which structures it perfectly for a PowerPoint presentation. You can use Outline view in Word any time you need to organize topics or restructure a document. You can adjust the outlining structure by clicking the Promote, Demote, Move Up, and Move Down buttons on the Outlining toolbar. You can change the level of headings and subheadings that are displayed by clicking the Expand or Collapse buttons.

3. **Click File on the menu bar, then click Save As**

   The Save As dialog box opens.

4. **Navigate if necessary to where your Data Files are stored, click the Format arrows in the Save As dialog box, click Rich Text Format (.rtf), then click Save**

   Word saves the file as a Rich Text Format document with the filename N-2.rtf.

5. **Click Word on the menu bar, then click Quit Word**

   The Word document and the Word program close.

QUICK TIP

You can also insert material from a PowerPoint presentation into a Word document, including slide notes, blank lines, or just an outline. To send a presentation to Word, click File, point to Send To, then click Microsoft Word.

6. **In PowerPoint, click Insert on the menu bar, point to Slides From, then click Outline File**

   The Choose a File dialog box opens.

7. **Navigate to where your Data Files are stored, click N-2.rtf as shown in Figure N-5, then click Insert**

   Three new slides are inserted in the presentation, as shown in Figure N-6. Each Level 1 line of the outline appears as the slide title, and lower level text appears as bulleted text. The new slides display the theme that was applied to the original Word document; in this instance, the theme applied to the outline and the theme applied to the presentation are the same. When the theme of the original Word document differs from the theme of the presentation into which its outline is inserted, you may need to use Format Painter to change the font formats on the inserted slides so that they match the font formats on existing slides.

8. **Add your name to the slide footer, click Apply to All, then save your changes**

Creating an outline in Word for use in a PowerPoint presentation

If you want to create an outline in Word that you can use as the basis for a PowerPoint presentation, it's best to create or structure a document that is formatted for this purpose. Start a new document in Word, click View on the menu bar, then click Outline. As you type your outline text, use the Promote and Demote buttons on the Outlining toolbar to apply an outline level for each line. Word applies the Heading 1 style for slide titles, Heading 2 for the first level of indented text, and so on. It's important to use the built-in heading styles in Word when you create your outline, because the heading tags determine the structure of the outline when it is saved as an RTF document and then inserted into PowerPoint.

FIGURE N-4: Word document in Outline view

Promote button

Demote button

Demote to Body Text button

Expand and Collapse buttons

Move Up and Move Down buttons

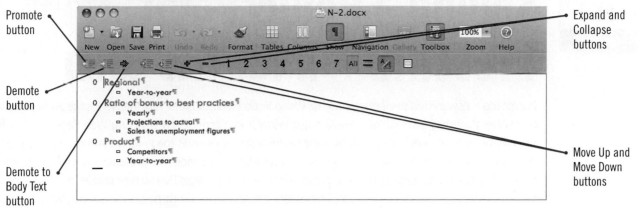

FIGURE N-5: Choose a File dialog box

New Rich Text Format file

Insert button

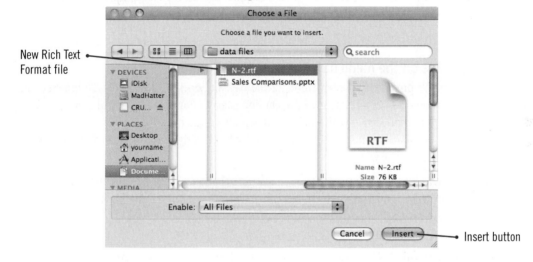

FIGURE N-6: PowerPoint slides created from outline text

Slides added from outline

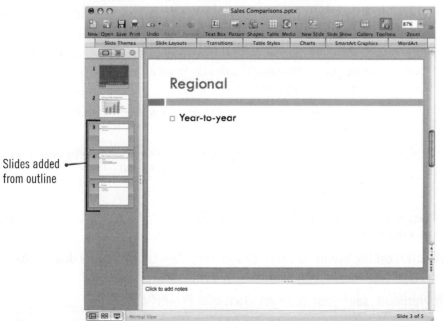

Integration

Saving a PowerPoint Presentation for the Web

Publishing a PowerPoint presentation to the World Wide Web is a great way to give a large audience access to it. After finalizing a presentation, you can preview it in a browser by selecting Web Page Preview from the File menu. If you are happy with how the presentation appears in the browser, you can save it as a Web page by selecting the Save as Web Page command and then saving the presentation in Web file format (.htm). During the process of saving a presentation as a Web page, PowerPoint creates a folder that contains the images, style sheets, links, and other files needed for the Web page. The Save as Web Page command is also available in Word and Excel, so you can save your documents and worksheets as Web pages too. Note that in order to publish Web pages to the Web so that anyone with Internet access can visit them, the computer from which you publish the Web pages must be a **Web server**, which is a computer directly linked to the Web that has software capable of hosting Web pages. Paulette wants to put the sales comparison presentation on the company intranet, and so she asks you save it as a Web page.

STEPS

QUICK TIP
When viewing the presentation in Full Screen Slide Show view, click to advance the presentation.

1. **Click File on the menu bar, then click Web Page Preview**

   PowerPoint prepares the presentation for the Web and opens it in your default browser. The Web page contains an outline frame, similar to the Outline pane in PowerPoint Normal view, and a navigation frame, which you can use to move through the presentation. You can also show or hide and expand or collapse the outline, or view the slide show at full screen size by clicking the Full Screen Slide Show button in the lower-right corner of the window. See Figure N-7.

2. **Click the Next Slide button ⟫ at the bottom of the screen four times to view the entire presentation, click Safari on the menu bar, then click Quit Safari**

   The browser closes. Now that you know how the presentation will appear in the browser, it's time to save the file as a Web page.

3. **Click File on the PowerPoint menu bar, then click Save as Web Page**

   The Save As dialog box opens. The Web Page (.htm) format is already selected and the dialog box displays the location where the new Web page (and any supporting folder and files) will be saved.

4. **Click Web Options in the Save As dialog box, click the Encoding tab in the Web Options dialog box, click the Always save Web pages in the default encoding check box to select it if necessary, as shown in Figure N-8, then click OK**

   By saving Web pages using the default encoding, you maximize the Web page's compatibility with multiple browsers. If you have problems opening the Web page in some browsers, verify that this setting is checked and then save the presentation as a Web page.

5. **In the Save As dialog box, navigate if necessary to where your Data Files are stored, then click Save**

6. **Start Safari, click File on the menu bar, click Open File, navigate to where your Data Files are stored, click Sales Comparisons.htm, then click Open**

   The Sales Comparisons Web page opens in Safari.

7. **Click ⟫ at the bottom of the screen four times to view the entire presentation**

   Figure N-9 shows the second slide of the presentation displayed in Safari.

8. **Click Safari on the menu bar, click Quit Safari, then click Quit if a dialog box opens asking if you want to close 2 Safari windows**

9. **In PowerPoint, save your changes, then quit PowerPoint**

FIGURE N-7: Previewing the presentation as a Web page in a browser

Your path will differ

Outline frame with
slide numbers

Expand/Collapse
Outline button

Show/Hide Outline
button

Full Screen Slide
Show button

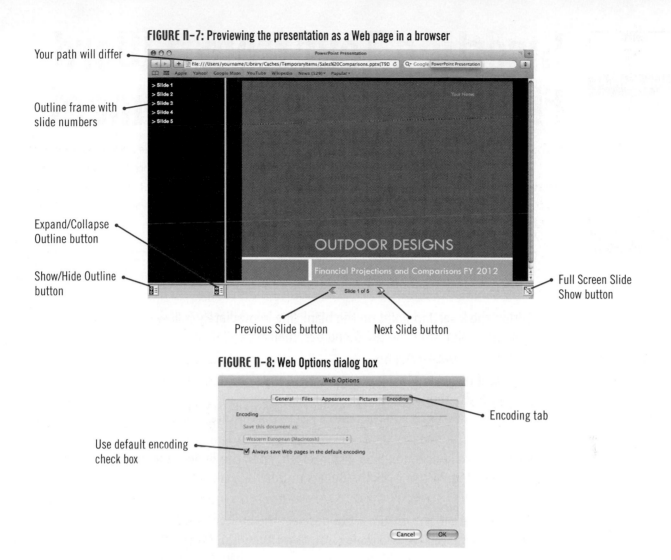

Previous Slide button   Next Slide button

FIGURE N-8: Web Options dialog box

Encoding tab

Use default encoding
check box

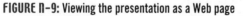

FIGURE N-9: Viewing the presentation as a Web page

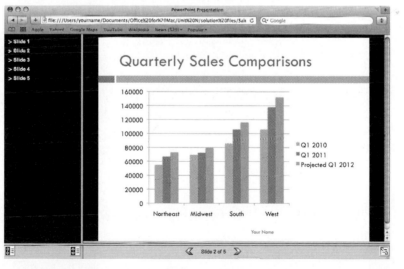

Customizing the presentation for the Web

You can set Web-specific options for your presentation by using the tabs in the Web Options dialog box before saving the presentation. For example, the General tab contains text boxes where you can enter a title and keywords for the Web page. The Appearance tab allows you to position the navigation buttons on the top of the screen, or in a floating window, instead of at the bottom. Be aware that not all browsers will support these modifications.

Inserting Text from a Word File into an Open Document

As you work, you might want to combine two Word files into one, or insert one document into another one. Although you can easily copy and paste information between two or more open documents, it is sometimes easier to insert the contents from a file without having to open it first. Paulette wants you to include sales highlights from a Word document she created in a letter to shareholders that you've already started.

STEPS

1. **Start Word, open the file** N-3.docx **from where you store your Data Files, then save it as** Shareholder letter.docx

2. **Position the insertion point on the blank line immediately following the text** Strategic highlights:, **click** Insert **on the menu bar, then click** File

   The Insert File dialog box opens.

3. **Navigate if necessary to where you store your Data Files, click the file** N-4.docx **as shown in Figure N-10, then click** Insert

   The contents of the file, consisting of five lines of text, are inserted at the bottom of the letter, as shown in Figure N-11.

4. **Select the five lines of text you just inserted, open the** Bullets and Numbering group **on the Formatting Palette, click the** Bullets button ☰, **click the** Style list arrow, **then click the** arrow bullet style

5. **Click** anywhere in the document **to deselect the bulleted text**

   The strategic highlights text is formatted as a bulleted list with arrows as bullets, as shown in Figure N-12.

6. **Save your changes to the document**

FIGURE N-10: Insert File dialog box

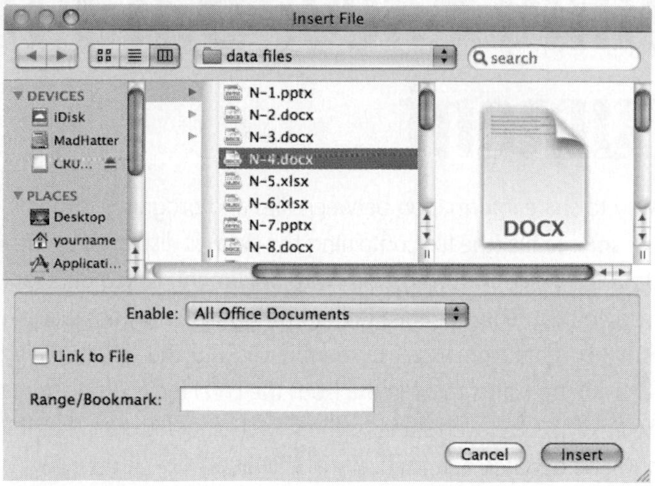

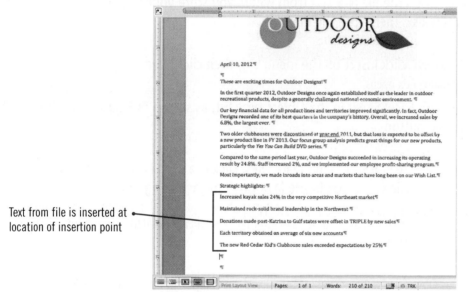

FIGURE N-11: File inserted in letter

Text from file is inserted at location of insertion point

FIGURE N-12: Bulleted text

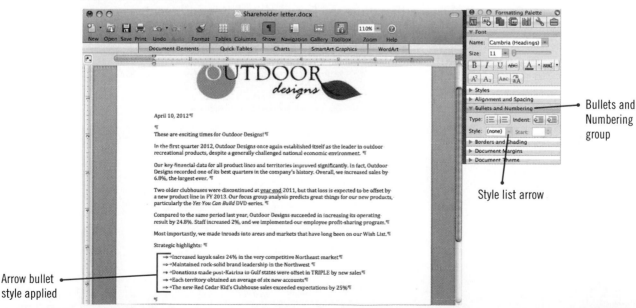

Bullets and Numbering group

Style list arrow

Arrow bullet style applied

Integration

Linking Excel Data to a Word Document

A powerful way to share information between files and programs is to link data. When you **link** files, information from a **source** file (the file containing the data) is displayed in the **destination** file (the location to which that data is copied or moved). In a Word document, linked data looks just like inserted or embedded data. However, you can edit the linked data in its native program just by double-clicking it. For example, you can edit linked data from Excel by double-clicking the table in Word and making the changes you want. Paulette wants to add data from the DVD focus group spreadsheet to the shareholder letter. You decide to link the Excel worksheet to the shareholder letter so that if Paulette updates any of the data, the changes will be updated automatically in the letter.

STEPS

1. **Start Excel, open the file N-5.xlsx from where you store your Data Files, save it as DVD Focus Group.xlsx, then close the file**
   The worksheet contains a table of data.

2. **Switch to Word, click Insert on the menu bar, then click Object**
   The Object dialog box opens.

3. **Click Microsoft Excel Sheet in the Object type list, as shown in Figure N-13, then click the From File button**
   The Insert as Object dialog box opens.

4. **Navigate to where you store your Data Files, click the DVD Focus Group.xlsx file, then click the Link to File check box in the lower half of the dialog box**
   Inserting the content of the file as a linked object permits automatic updating from Word or in Excel, which is useful if you want to insert the same data in multiple files and not have to worry about updating each file every time the data changes.

5. **Click Insert**
   The Insert as Object dialog box closes and the Excel cells appear in the Shareholder letter document as a linked worksheet object, as shown in Figure N-14. When an Excel workbook is linked as a Microsoft Excel Sheet object, only the active sheet in the linked workbook is displayed.

6. **Save your changes, then close the Shareholder letter document**

FIGURE N-13: Object dialog box

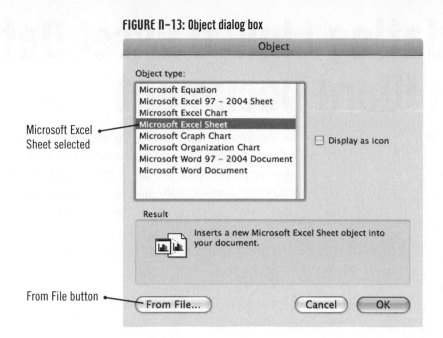

Microsoft Excel Sheet selected

From File button

FIGURE N-14: Excel cells inserted as a linked object in Word

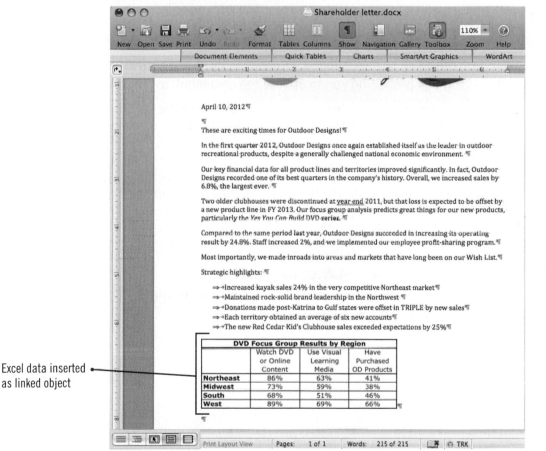

Excel data inserted as linked object

The differences between embedding and linking data

When you embed data, such as an Excel chart embedded in a PowerPoint presentation, the data becomes part of the document and does not exist as a separate file. If you distribute the file to others, all the embedded data travels within the file. When you link data, however, it's different. In order to view the linked data, you need access to both the document containing the link and the file containing the data. Sharing a linked document with others, therefore, is a bit more complicated, because you have to keep the linked files together. Moving one file can break the link with other documents.

Updating Linked Excel Data in a Word Document

The beauty of working with linked files is that you can make changes to the source file and every linked object in a destination file is updated with the changes. The update can occur automatically (every time you open the linked file, for example), or you can update a linked object manually by selecting the linked object, clicking Edit on the menu bar, clicking Links, selecting the link, then clicking Update Now. Paulette just received updates to the focus group data for the South region. You make the changes in Excel and view the results in the linked Word document.

STEPS

1. **Switch to Excel, then open the** DVD Focus Group.xlsx **file**

2. **Edit the data in the DVD Focus Group workbook, as shown in the following table:**

Cell	Data
B5	72
C5	56
D5	71

3. **Save your changes, then close the workbook**

4. **Switch to Word, open the file** Shareholder letter.docx **you created earlier, then click** Yes **in the dialog box prompting you to update the document, as shown in Figure N-15**

5. **Scroll down to view the updated table, then double-click the** linked worksheet object
   The table is updated in the Shareholder letter, as shown in Figure N-16.

6. **Double-click the** linked worksheet object
   The DVD Focus Group workbook opens in Excel.

7. **Select the range** A1:D6, **open the** Borders and Shading group **on the Formatting Palette, click the** Fill Color button list arrow , **then click the** blue color **in the fifth row, sixth column (ScreenTip reads "Pale Blue")**
   The cells are shaded in blue.

8. **Save your changes to the worksheet, then quit Excel**
   In the Shareholder letter document, the cell color of the linked data has been updated, as shown in Figure N-17.

9. **Save your changes to the Word document**

FIGURE N-15: Updating data in a linked object

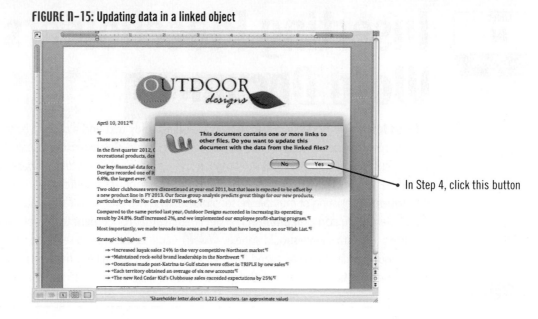

In Step 4, click this button

FIGURE N-16: Updated data in Word

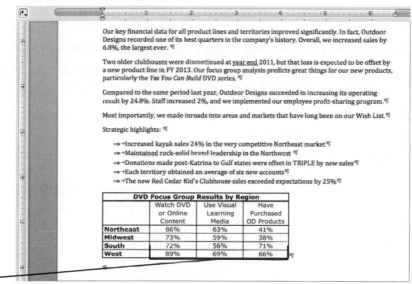

Updated data in table

FIGURE N-17: Table color updated in Word

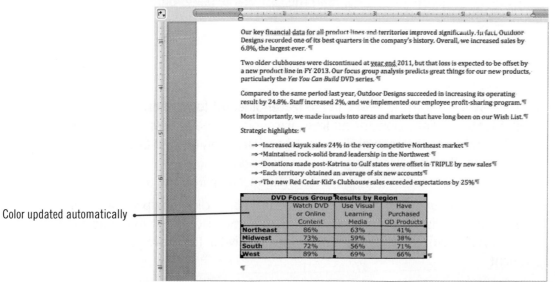

Color updated automatically

Inserting Placeholders in a Word Document

A **form letter** is a document that contains standard body text and a custom heading containing the name and address for one of many recipients. The letter, or **main document**, is usually created in Word; the data for the custom headings is usually compiled in a table, worksheet, or database, also known as the **data source**. From these two files, the main document and the data source, you create a third file, a **merged document**, consisting of multiple personalized letters. This process is called **mail merge**. Before performing a mail merge you add **placeholders**, or fields, to the main document to indicate where the custom information from the data source should appear. Paulette asks you to send the shareholder letter to the company's four principal investors, and gives you an Excel file containing their names and addresses. Before you merge the shareholder letter with the spreadsheet file, you need to insert placeholders in the main document.

STEPS

1. **Scroll to the top of the document, click Tools on the menu bar, then click Mail Merge Manager**

   The Mail Merge Manager opens and displays the Select Document Type group, as shown in Figure N-18.

2. **Click the Create New button in the Select Document Type group, then click Form Letters**

   In the Select Document Type group, Shareholder letter.docx is now listed as the main document, while the merge type is listed as Form Letters. The second group, Select Recipients List, is now open in the Mail Merge Manager.

3. **Click the Get List button in the Select Recipients List group, then click Open Data Source**

   The Choose a File dialog box opens.

4. **Navigate if necessary to where you store your Data Files, click N-6.xlsx, click Open, click OK when asked to use the Excel Workbook text converter, verify that Office_Address_List appears in the Open Document in Workbook field and Entire Worksheet appears in the Cell Range field in the Open Workbook dialog box, then click OK**

   The Open Workbook dialog box closes and the Excel file is designated as the data source, although it is not visible on your screen. In the Mail Merge Manager, the Insert Placeholders group opens, which allows you to create the address block by dragging the placeholders (fields) to the document.

5. **Drag the Title placeholder from the Insert Placeholders group to the line below the date in the Shareholder letter document, press [spacebar], drag the First_Name placeholder to the document, press [spacebar], drag the Last_Name placeholder to the document, then press [return]**

   The first line of the address block is in place in the document, as shown in Figure N-19.

6. **Drag the Address_Line_1 placeholder to the line below the title and name placeholders, then press [return]**

7. **Click the down scroll arrow ▼ in the placeholder list four times, drag the City placeholder to the line below the address placeholder, type ,, press [spacebar], drag the State placeholder to the document, press [spacebar], drag the ZIP_Code placeholder to the document, then press [return]**

   The last line of the address block is in place in the document. Now you will add the greeting.

8. **Press [return] a second time, type Dear, press [spacebar], click the up scroll arrow ▲ in the placeholder list three times, drag the First_Name placeholder to the document, type ,, press [return], compare your screen to Figure N-20, then save your changes to the document**

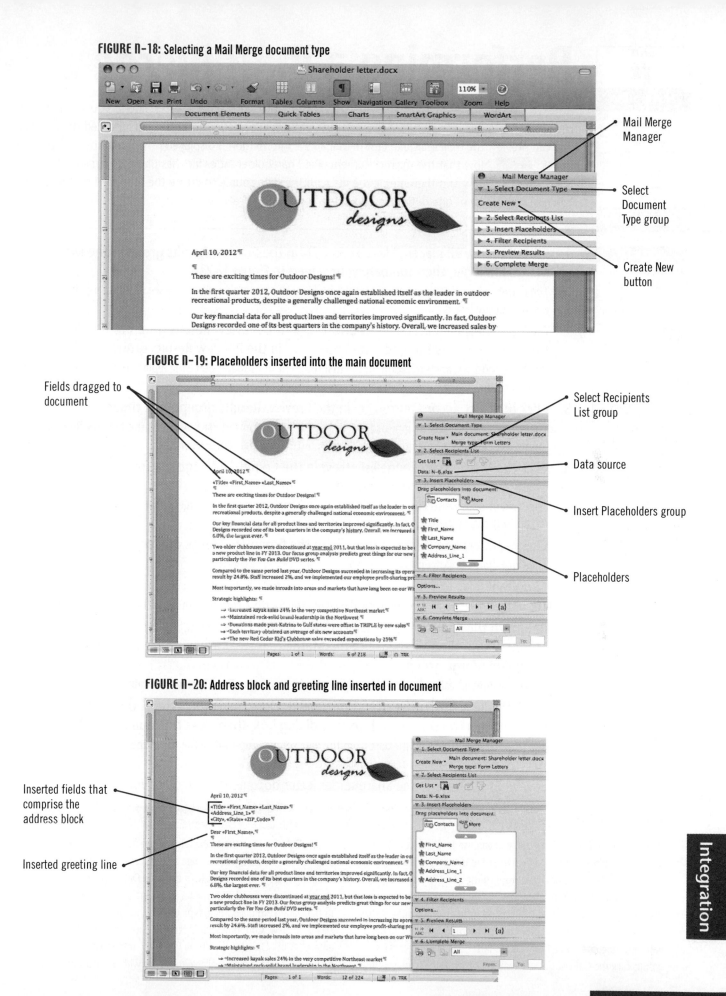

FIGURE N-18: Selecting a Mail Merge document type

Mail Merge Manager

Select Document Type group

Create New button

FIGURE N-19: Placeholders inserted into the main document

Fields dragged to document

Select Recipients List group

Data source

Insert Placeholders group

Placeholders

FIGURE N-20: Address block and greeting line inserted in document

Inserted fields that comprise the address block

Inserted greeting line

Integration

Performing a Mail Merge

After you set up a main document, specify a data source, and insert placeholders, you are ready to **merge**, or combine, the standard text with the custom information to create personalized documents. You can preview the mail merge to ensure that all the information is displayed properly in the final printed pages. ▰▰▰▰ Now that the main document, the Shareholder letter file, has placeholders inserted, you are ready to preview and then merge the file with the data source to create the final mail merge letters. You also want to print one of the merged letters for Paulette's review.

STEPS

1. **Click the View all placeholders button {a} in the Preview Results group in the Mail Merge Manager, then compare your screen to Figure N-21**

   The placeholder fields are enclosed by a {MERGEFIELDS} tag, making it easy to see where merged data will be inserted in the letter.

2. **Click the View all placeholders button {a} in the Preview Results group to deselect it, then click the View Merged Data button «»ABC in the Preview Results group**

   The name, address, and salutation for the first recipient in the data source file replace the placeholders in the document. See Figure N-22.

3. **Click the Next Record button ▶ in the Preview Results group three times**

   The data from each record appears in its respective letter. You can use buttons in the Preview Results group to move backward or forward through records, or to find a particular record.

4. **Click the Merge Data Range list arrow in the Complete Merge group in the Mail Merge Manager, then click Current Record**

   The current document, containing the text of the main document merged with the data from the fourth record in the data source, is selected in the Complete Merge group.

5. **Click the Merge to Printer button 🖨 in the Complete Merge group**

   The Print dialog box opens.

6. **Click Print**

   The merged document containing the data from the fourth record is printed, as shown in Figure N-23.

7. **Return to the Shareholder letter, click the Merge Data Range list arrow in the Complete Merge group, click All, then click the Merge to New Document button 📄 in the Complete Merge group**

   A Word document called Form Letters1 opens in a new window. Form Letters1 contains all the merged letters.

8. **Scroll through the Form Letters1 document, close the Form Letters1 document, click Don't Save in the Do you wish to save dialog box, then close the Mail Merge Manager**

   You want to be certain that the data from the data source is up-to-date the next time you open this letter, so you do not need to save the merged documents.

9. **Save your changes to the Shareholder letter document, then quit Word**

Using Word to create a data source

When you perform a mail merge, you can use an Excel worksheet, the Office Address Book, or a FileMaker Pro database as a data source. But what if the data you want to use is not in any of those formats? You can easily create a new data source in Word. Starting from a blank document that you can delete later, or from the document you want to merge, open the Mail Merge Manager and designate your document as a Form Letter. In the Select Recipients List group, click the Get List button, then click New Data Source. In the Create Data Source dialog box, remove the field names that you don't want to include in your data source from the Field names in header row box, then click OK. In the Save Data Source dialog box, choose a location and filename for your data source, then click Save. In the Data Form dialog box, type the data for your first record, then click Add New. Continue adding records until all your data has been entered. Click OK when you have finished entering your data. Your new data source is now available to merge with any document.

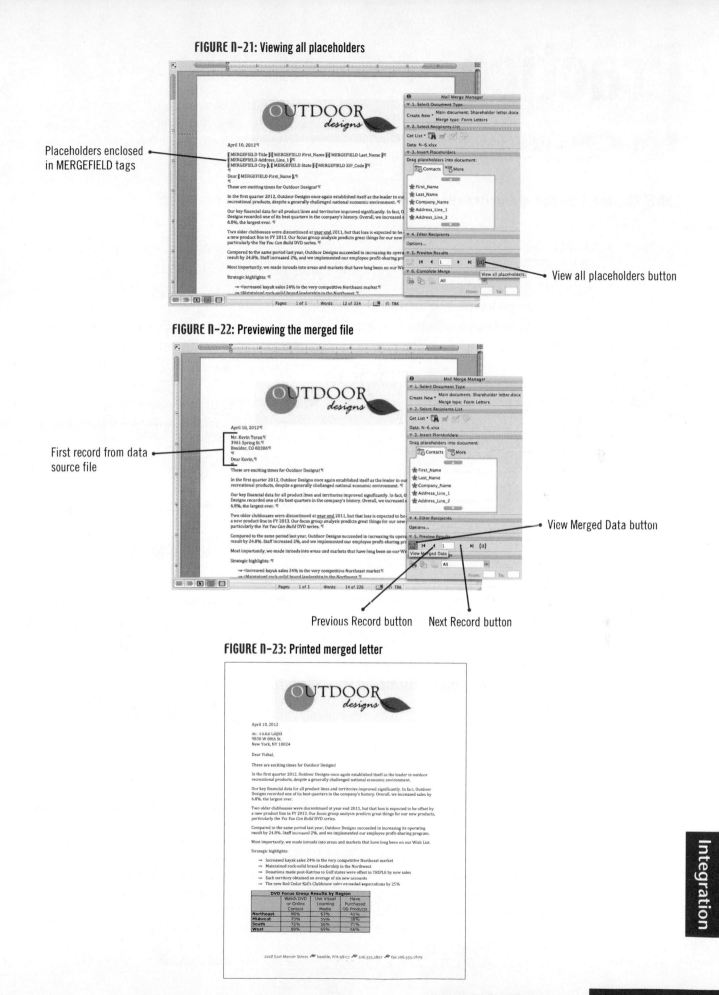

FIGURE N-21: Viewing all placeholders

Placeholders enclosed in MERGEFIELD tags

View all placeholders button

FIGURE N-22: Previewing the merged file

First record from data source file

View Merged Data button

Previous Record button　　Next Record button

FIGURE N-23: Printed merged letter

Integration

Practice

▼ CONCEPTS REVIEW

Label the mail merge elements shown in Figure N-24.

FIGURE N-24

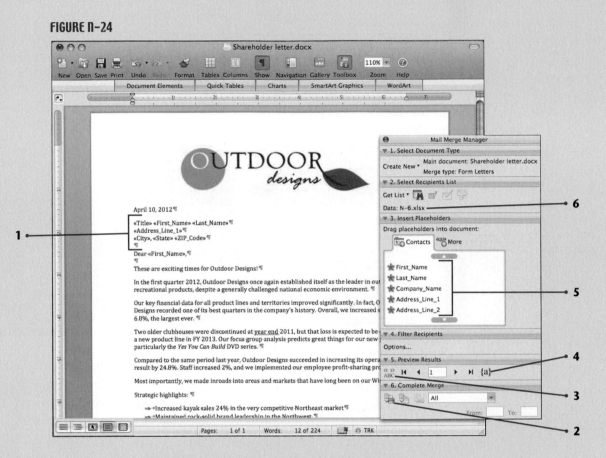

Match each term with the statement that best describes it.

7. **Linked object**
8. **Placeholders**
9. **Web server**
10. **Outline view**
11. **Mail merge**

a. Updates data automatically in a destination file when source file is updated
b. Presents text in a hierarchical structure in Word and automatically formats headings and subheadings
c. The process of combining a main document and a data source file
d. A computer directly linked to the Web that is capable of hosting Web pages
e. Fields that indicate where custom information from a data source should appear

Select the best answer from the list of choices.

12. Which of the following can *not* be produced by performing a mail merge?

    a. Envelopes   c. Form Letters

    b. Labels   d. Bookmarks

13. Receiving a prompt to update data in a document indicates that:

    a. The document has been published to the Web.

    b. The document has an embedded object.

    c. The document contains a linked object.

    d. The document is a mail merge document.

14. What does the View all placeholders button do?

    a. Displays the merge fields in a main document

    b. Inserts fields into a main document

    c. Excludes or filters records in a merged document

    d. Verifies the data in a merge file

▼ SKILLS REVIEW

1. **Insert an Excel chart into a PowerPoint slide.**

    a. Start PowerPoint, open the file N-7.pptx from where you store your Data Files, then save it as **LL Sales.pptx**.

    b. Move to Slide 2, then use the content placeholder to insert a 3-D Pie chart.

    c. In Excel, enter the following data:

Cell	Data	Cell	Data
		B1	Percent of Sales
A2	Garden	B2	5.8
A3	Deck	B3	8.4
A4	Path	B4	9.3
A5	Water	B5	3.5

    d. Quit Excel.

    e. In PowerPoint, close the Elements Gallery, then save your changes.

2. **Create PowerPoint slides from a Word document.**

    a. Start Word, then open the file N-8.docx from where you store your Data Files.

    b. View the document in Outline view.

    c. Save the document as a Rich Text Format (.rtf) file, then quit Word.

    d. In PowerPoint, insert the file N-8.rtf after Slide 2 using the Slides From Outline File command. (*Hint:* Use the Format Painter to change the title font format on Slides 3-6 to match the title font format on Slide 2.)

    e. Add your name to the slide footer for all slides, then save your changes.

3. **Save a PowerPoint presentation for the Web.**

    a. View the presentation using Web Page Preview, then quit Safari.

    b. In PowerPoint, use the Save as Web Page command to open the Save As dialog box, open the Web Options dialog box and verify that the Always save Web pages in the default encoding check box is selected, then save the presentation as a Web page where you save your Data Files.

    c. Start Safari, then open the file LL Sales.htm.

    d. View each page of the presentation, print the first page, then quit the browser.

    e. In PowerPoint, save your changes, close the presentation, then quit PowerPoint.

4. **Insert text from a Word file into an open document.**

    a. Start Word, open the file N-9.docx from where you store your Data Files, then save it as **LL Events.docx**.

    b. Position the insertion point at the beginning of the line that starts "As marketing managers," then insert the file N-10.docx. (*Hint:* Click Insert on the menu bar.)

   c. Select the text you just inserted from the file, then format it as a bulleted list using the arrow bullet style.

   d. Save your changes.

5. Link Excel data to a Word document.

   a. Start Excel, open the file N-11.xlsx, save it as **LL Event Analysis.xlsx**, then quit Excel.

   b. In Word, position the insertion point in the last line of the LL Events.docx document, open the Object dialog box, select Microsoft Excel Sheet, click the From File button, click the Link to File check box, then insert the file LL Event Analysis.xlsx.

   c. Save your changes, then close the document.

6. Update linked Excel data in a Word document.

   a. Start Excel, then open the LL Events Analysis.xlsx file.

   b. Change cell B3 to 86 and cell B4 to 73, save your changes, then close the workbook.

   c. Switch to Word, open the LL Events document, then update the document with data from the linked file.

   d. Double-click the linked table in the Word document, then in Excel, remove the shading from the table. (*Hint:* Select the shaded cells, click the Fill Color button list arrow, then click No Fill.)

   e. Save your changes, close the worksheet, then quit Excel.

   f. View the updated table in Word, then save your changes.

7. Insert data source placeholders in a Word document.

   a. Scroll to the top of the document if necessary, insert two blank lines below the date, then place the insertion point on the second blank line.

   b. Create a new form letter using the Mail Merge Manager.

   c. Open the file N-12.xlsx as the data source in the Select Recipients List group. (*Hint:* Click OK to use the Excel Workbook text converter.)

   d. Create an address block by dragging the first name, last name, address, city, state, and zip code fields to appropriate locations in the document, then insert two blank lines below the address block.

   e. Create a greeting line that uses just the first name.

   f. Save your changes.

8. Perform a mail merge.

   a. Use a button on the Mail Merge Manager to view all the placeholders, then deselect the button.

   b. Preview your results, reviewing each record in the mail merge, add your name to the footer of the document, then compare your screen to Figure N-25.

   c. Select All from the Merge Data Range list if necessary, then print the merged letters.

   d. Save your changes to LL Events.docx, close the document, then quit Word.

FIGURE N-25

Landscape Lightning
outdoor lighting specialists
408 Cumberland Ave Portland, Oregon 97211   800-111-0090

November 2, 2012

Lilly Wang
8436 6th Ave
Santa Monica, CA 90405

Lilly,
Landscape Lightning has great products and an unbeatable combination:
1. An effective broad-based advertising and marketing strategy.
2. You and your sales team.

That's why we want to keep you and your teams well-versed in our most successful marketing events: the home and garden, home builders, and landscape conferences, trade shows, and events.

This letter illustrates the importance of using the same criteria when evaluating the techniques that will best reinforce Landscape Lightning to the customer:
⇒ ALWAYS consider our target audience
⇒ Who is a potential buyer?
⇒ Who is the most qualified buyer?

As marketing managers, you are responsible for assessing the likelihood a visitor will become a customer. The high-end gifts we give away during events have been part of that success.

Event Sales Conversion Analysis

	Current Customer	Potential Customer	Qualified Customer
Yes--Survey & Gift	86%	32%	66%
No--Survey & Gift	73%	19%	45%

Your Name

▼ INDEPENDENT CHALLENGE 1

You are the new intern assigned to Nikkie Kay, the manager of customer service at Luggage Xpress. Luggage Xpress delivers lost luggage to airline customers staying at hotels and they handle luggage pick-up for travelers. The company is beginning to franchise operations to other cities, and Nikkie needs your help in preparing a PowerPoint presentation and publishing it to the Web. She also needs you to send out a personalized form letter to clients who had lost luggage.

a. Start PowerPoint, open the file N-13.pptx from where you store your Data Files, then save it as **Luggage Xpress Franchise.pptx** where you store your Data Files.
b. In Slide 2, insert a 3-D Pie chart.
c. In Excel, enter the following data, change column widths as necessary so that all newly entered data is visible, select only newly entered data to display in the chart, then quit Excel. (*Hint*: To select only the newly entered data for display, drag the lower-right corner of the originally selected range to the lower-right corner of cell B3.)

Cell	Data	Cell	Data
		B1	**Luggage Statistics**
A2	**3 Million Bags Lost**	B2	**3,000,000**
A3	**Over 1/2 Million Bags Lost Forever**	B3	**530,000**

▼ INDEPENDENT CHALLENGE 1 (CONTINUED)

d. Start Word, open the file N-14.docx, view the file in Outline view, save the file as **N-14.rtf**, then quit Word.

e. Following Slide 2 in PowerPoint, insert slides from an outline using the file N-14.rtf.

f. Add your name to all slides in the footer, then save your changes.

g. Preview the presentation as a Web Page.

h. Save the presentation as a Web Page. Before clicking Save, click the Web Options button, click the General tab if necessary, then change the Web page title to **Luggage Xpress Franchise**.

i. Start your browser, then open the Luggage Xpress Franchise.htm Web page. Close the browser, close the presentation in PowerPoint, then quit PowerPoint.

j. Start Word, open the file N-15.docx from where you store your Data Files, then save it as **Luggage Xpress Feedback Letter.docx**.

k. Go to the end of the page, click Insert on the menu bar, point to Break, click Page Break, then insert the file N-16.docx at the top of the new second page.

l. On the first page of the letter, position the insertion point three lines below the "Manager, Customer Service" line.

m. Start Excel, open the file N-17.xlsx from where you store your Data Files, save it as **Luggage Xpress Feedback Table.xlsx**, then close the workbook.

n. Switch to Word, open the Object dialog box, select Microsoft Excel Sheet in the Object type list, click From File, verify that the Link to File check box is selected, then insert the Luggage Xpress Feedback Table.xlsx file.

o. Save and close Luggage Xpress Feedback Letter.docx.

p. Switch to Excel, open Luggage Xpress Feedback Table.xlsx, change the value in cell B3 to **42**, save your changes to the workbook, then quit Excel.

q. Switch to Word, open the file Luggage Xpress Feedback Letter.docx, updating the linked table during the process.

r. Add your name to the footer of the letter.

s. Move to the top of the first page of the document, place the insertion point on the blank line beneath the date, then create a Form Letter mail merge that uses the file N-18.xlsx as the data source file. Add the appropriate fields to create an Address Block and greeting line. (*Hint:* Do not use Address_Line_2 or any of the placeholders below ZIP_Code in the placeholders list.) Insert spaces, punctuation, and blank lines as appropriate.

t. Preview your results, then complete the merge by merging to the printer.

u. Save and close any open files, then quit all open programs.

▼ INDEPENDENT CHALLENGE 2

You and your business partner, chef Stacy Nakano, are planning to start a new restaurant in Ann Arbor, Michigan. You need to apply for a start-up loan to get the business going. Your first task is to write a cover letter that will accompany your loan package. You need to send this to several banks. You also prepare a PowerPoint presentation of a few menu items that potential lenders can view on your Web site.

a. Start Word, then write a letter that you can send to banks along with the loan package. You'll add recipient information in a future step; for now, write the body of the letter, including the name and location of your new restaurant, why you are applying for the loan, why the business will be successful, and how much you would like to borrow.

b. Save the letter as **Restaurant loan letter.docx** where you store your Data Files.

c. Position the insertion point below the content of the letter, and then create a clustered column chart in the document using the following data in the Excel data range:

Cell	Data	Cell	Data	Cell	Data
		B1	Projected	C1	Actual
A2	The Chicken Bowl	B2	148,000	C2	163,000
A3	Yum Teriyaki	B3	210,000	C3	249,000
A4	Asian Delight	B4	171,000	C4	186,000

Integration 356   Integrating Office 2008 Programs

Leopard operating syste...
change the features and...
first turn on a new M...
ck location, and the s...
nufacturer (Apple). Th...
ge the system preferen...
eeds. ▰▰▰ This appe...
d operating system, su...
tion, sleep settings, an...
e to back up your com...
ound options.

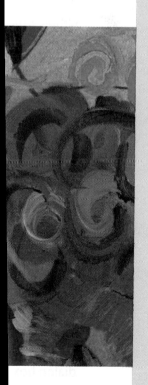

▼ REAL LIFE INDEPENDENT CHALLENGE

Creating a form letter is a great way to manage your correspondence with efficiency and style. You can use the mail merge features in Word to personalize thank you notes, e-mail messages, and invitations. Think of an event where you'd like to use personalized form letters to save time yet still include a personal touch. It could be a thank you note to recipients of a recent party or special event, a party invitation, or perhaps a change of address notice. Then create a personalized form letter you can send to at least four recipients.

a. Start Word, then save a new document as **My event.docx** where you store your Data Files.

b. Write a brief letter containing the text of the thank you, invitation, or other notice. Add clip art or photographs as desired.

c. Include a sentence asking the recipient to confirm his or her e-mail address.

d. Add your name as the signatory to the document.

e. Open Excel, then open N-20.xlsx and use it to create a data source that has at least four records and includes first name, last name, street, city, state, postal code, and e-mail. Save the file as **My event list.xlsx** where you store your Data Files.

f. Create a form letter mail merge, select the My event list.xlsx file as the data source, then at the top of the document, insert placeholders to create an address block and greeting line. Insert spaces, punctuation, and blank lines as needed.

g. After the sentence asking to confirm their e-mail address, insert the E-mail placeholder.

h. Complete the mail merge by merging to a Word document. Print the merged records from record 3 to record 4.

Advanced Challenge Exercise

- Remove all the merge fields in the document and restore the document to a normal Word document. (*Hint*: In the Select Document Type group in the Mail Merge Manager, click the Create New button, then click Restore to Normal Word Document.)
- Replace the Greeting Line with **Hi Friends,**.
- Replace the line of text requesting confirmation of e-mail information with the text **Send me your e-mail address!**.
- Preview the document as a Web Page, then return to Word and adjust spacing and formatting as needed. Save the document as a Web page named **My Event Web Page**; when saving, change the Web page title in the Web Options dialog box to **My Event**.
- Start your browser, open the My Event Web Page file, print the page, then close your browser.

i. Save and close any open files, then quit Word.

▼ INDEPENDENT CHALLENGE 2 (CONTINUED)

d. Apply a new chart style to use different colors for the data series if desired, then save your changes to the document.

e. Start a letters mail merge, then create a new data source with at least four entries. To create the list, click the Get List button in the Select Recipients List group, then click New Data Source. Remove the fields that you do not want in your data source. Save the file where you store your Data Files as **Restaurant bank loan list.docx**. Enter names and addresses in the Data Form dialog box, clicking Add New as needed. When the list is complete, click OK.

f. At the top of the Word document, insert the placeholders to create the address block and formal greeting line. Insert spaces, punctuation, and blank lines as appropriate.

g. Add your name to the footer.

h. Preview the mail merge, print the first record, close the document, then click Save to save the new data source if necessary. An example printout is shown in Figure N-26.

i. Start PowerPoint, create a presentation that contains a title slide with the name and a slogan for your restaurant. Add four slides that highlight menu items, then save the file as **Restaurant menu.pptx** where you store your Data Files.

j. Apply a theme and insert clip art and photographs as desired, then add your name to the footer or header.

k. Preview the presentation as a Web page, then save it as a Web Page. Using the Web Options button, change the title of the Web page to the name of your restaurant.

l. View the slide show in your browser, print the first page from the browser, then quit the browser.

m. Save and close any open files, then quit any open programs.

FIGURE N-26

Kyoto Teriyaki   8397 Washington Avenue Royal Oak, MI 48067 www.kyototeriyaki.com

May 9, 2012

Ms. Barbara Smyth
Enterprise Bank and Trust
1230 Main Street
Ann Arbor, MI 48103

Dear Ms. Smyth,
I am currently seeking an investor for my new restaurant, Kyoto Teriyaki, which serves chicken, beef, or tofu with steamed vegetables over rice. You were referred to us by Jody Chu, Executive Chef at Five Luck Palace, Detroit's only five-star Chinese restaurant.

Based on your interest in revitalizing Michigan's economy, I believe that our business plan may be of interest to you, and have enclosed a copy. I have also included a chart illustrating the success of teriyaki bowl establishments from similar markets in the midwest.

Kyoto Teriyaki is poised to become a fixture as a student eatery around colleges and universities in mid and southeast Michigan. We have targeted student areas first in the Ann Arbor, and then in greater Detroit area and East Lansing for our restaurants because our menu is affordable, healthy, and of interest. Our competitive advantage stems from our uniqueness; there are no other restaurants like ours around. We have a versatile menu, yet one based on the same core ingredients. We also have a strong management base; both partners have a solid financial background.

We are seeking $50,000, all of which will be used for start up and renovation costs for our first restaurant.

Thank you for your consideration and interest in Kyoto Teriyaki. Please contact me with any questions you have, and I will be pleased to provide any additional information you require. If, upon completing your review, you would like to discuss this matter further, please do not hesitate to contact me, by telephone at 248-837-4477 by e-mail at lilly@kyototeriyaki.com.

Yours truly,

Stacy Nakano
Owner

Your Name

Comparison of Actual to Projected Sales in Chicago Market

Your Name

▼ INDEPENDENT CHALLENGE 3

The Open Lake Bass Fishing Challenge is organizing for its annual Memorial Day weekend event, which features the region's largest bass fishing contest and a fish-off that benefits local charities. The organization's president, Duane Roberts, has asked you to create a PowerPoint presentation that includes information about bass fishing and financial information for potential sponsors and participants. He also wants you to save it for the Web.

a. Start PowerPoint, create a new, blank presentation using any theme you like, change the color scheme if desired, then save it as **Fishing Event.pptx** where you store your Data Files.

b. Create at least two slides, including a title slide, then add your name to the footer.

c. Insert the file N-19.rtf after Slide 2 in the presentation.

d. Use the Format Painter to adjust the text formatting on the newly added slides to match the text formatting on the pre-existing slides. Insert clip art and photographs as desired.

e. At the end of the presentation, add a new slide titled **Donations to Charity**, then create a column chart in the style of your choice showing how much money has been donated to charity over the past three years. Assume the amount of money has increased each year. Apply styles to the chart and modify it as desired. (*Hint*: Enter years in cells A2:A4 and donation amounts in cells B2:B4; you do not need to use the rest of the data sheet.)

f. In PowerPoint, add a new slide titled **We Got Bass**, then insert a chart in the style of your choice that shows the largest fish caught over each of the past five years. (*Hint*: In Excel, enter the years in row 1 and bass weights in row 2. An acceptable weight range for this category is 7-12 pounds.)

g. Preview the presentation as a Web Page.

h. Save the presentation as a Web Page, and change the title of the Web page to **Open Lake Bass Fishing Challenge**.

i. View the Web page in your browser, then print the title slide. Quit your browser and the Web page file.

Advanced Challenge Exercise

- Start Word, then compose an informal confirmation letter for the event. Include text confirming the recipient is registered for the event. Add your name to the bottom of the letter. Save the letter as **Fishing Confirmation.docx** where you store your Data Files.
- Start a mail merge using the Fishing Confirmation document as the main document.
- Using the New Data Source command on the Get List menu in the Mail Merge Manager, create a data source in Word that includes first name, last name, one address line, city, state, and postal code, and has at least four records. Save the file as **Fishing Registration.docx** where you store your Data Files.
- At the top of the Fishing Confirmation document, insert placeholders and any necessary punctuation to create an address block and an informal greeting line, preview the mail merge, then print the first merged letter.

j. Close any open files, then quit all programs.

▼ VISUAL WORKSHOP

Using the skills you learned in this unit, create the Web page shown in Figure N-27. To get started, start Pow... new blank presentation using the Urban theme, then insert the file N-21.rtf to create Slides 2 and 3. Create your own and add your name to the footer to appear on all slides. (*Hint*: For the chart on Slide 4, use the fo... fuel mileage values: 1908: **20**; 1998: **23**; Present & beyond: **26**.) Save the presentation as **Fuel Economy &... Cars.pptx** where you store your Data Files, then save this presentation as a Web Page. Print the last slide o... from your Web browser. Save your changes, close any open files, then quit all programs.

FIGURE N-27

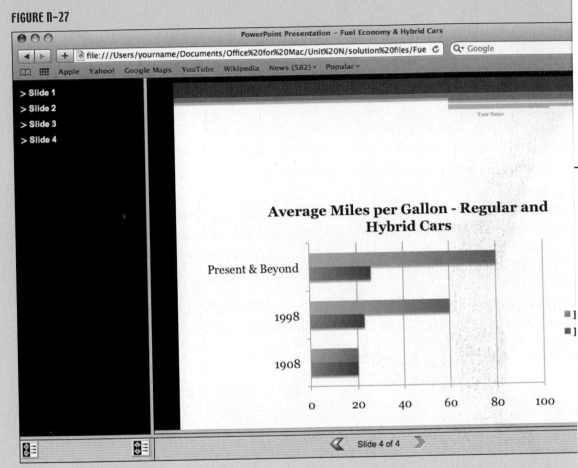

Ch
Re

Your Ma... monitor... display t... is the n... pixels in... smaller... comput... the Disp... ambien... options...

STEPS

1. Cl... Ha...
   Th... the... res...

   TROUBLE
   If the 1280 × 800 resolution setting is not available, click the setting on the Resolutions list that is closest to 1280 × 800.

2. Cl... If... im... se... Se...

3. C... Yo... re...

4. C...

5. U... A... t...

6. N...

7. C...

Setting System Preferences

Files You Will Need:

No files needed.

One of the many appealing features of the Mac OS X Leopard operating system is that it is user-friendly. You don't need to be a computer expert to change the features and functionality of your Mac or to customize its appearance. When you first turn on a new Mac, the system preferences—such as the desktop background, the dock location, and the source for the system date and time—have been preset by the manufacturer (Apple). These are called **default settings**, or simply defaults. Most people change the system preferences in one way or another to customize their Macs to better fit their needs. This appendix explains how to change the settings for the interface of the Leopard operating system, such as the desktop background image, screen saver, dock, screen resolution, sleep settings, and system date and time. You'll also learn how to use the Time Machine to back up your computer, how to update your software, and how to modify your system's sound options.

OBJECTIVES

Change the desktop background
and screen saver
Change the dock
Change the screen resolution
Change the sleep settings
Change the date and time
Use Time Machine
Update your software
Change sound options

Changing the Desktop Background and Screen Saver

When you start your Mac, Leopard displays the Aurora image as the background image on the desktop by default. You can select a different image to appear as the background, either by choosing from several built-in background images provided with Leopard or by using an image of your own. You can change the desktop background image using the Desktop & Screen Saver dialog box. Another setting you can change in this dialog box is the **screen saver**, which appears when you leave your computer idle for several minutes; it is an image that moves around the screen to prevent damage to your monitor. Without the screen saver, the crystals in an LCD monitor can be damaged and will continue to display an image faintly even after the on-screen image has changed. This is known as **image persistence**. You can select from several different screen saver options provided with Leopard. You decide to change the desktop background and screen saver to give your Mac a more personalized look.

STEPS

QUICK TIP

You can also open the System Preferences dialog box by clicking the Apple icon on the menu bar, then clicking System Preferences.

1. **Click the System Preferences icon on the dock**

   As shown in Figure A-1, the System Preferences dialog box opens. It is divided into 4 or 5 categories: Personal, Hardware, Internet & Network, System, and Other. Depending on how your Mac is configured, your screen may differ. Some icons and the Other category may not appear in your dialog box.

2. **In the Personal category, click the Desktop & Screen Saver icon**

   The Desktop & Screen Saver dialog box opens with the Desktop tab selected, as shown in Figure A-2. At the top of the Desktop tab, a preview of the current background image appears (Aurora). On the left side of the tab is a list of folders containing images that can be used as the background image. You can access the standard Apple choices or use an image stored in one of your iPhoto albums. When a folder is selected on the left, the sample box on the right displays thumbnails of the images available in the selected folder.

3. **In the list of image folders, click a folder of your choice, then click any image in the sample box**

   The desktop background changes to the image you selected. The preview at the top of the Desktop tab now shows the selected image.

4. **Click the Screen Saver tab**

   The options on the Screen Saver tab become available, as shown in Figure A-3. On the left side of the Screen Saver tab is the Screen Savers list, which includes several built-in Apple choices as well as stock pictures. You can even select an image or photo you created if it's stored in the Pictures folder in your home folder. When a static image is selected, the screen saver changes the screen display over time by increasing and decreasing the dimensions of the photo. On the right side of the Screen Saver tab is a Preview box, which shows how the currently selected screen saver appears when activated.

5. **Click an option in the Screen Savers list, watch the preview in the Preview box, then continue clicking options in the Screen Savers list until you select the screen saver you would like to use**

   The Preview box displays the selected screen saver.

QUICK TIP

To return to the System Preferences dialog box from the Desktop & Screen Saver dialog box, click Show All or click the Back button in the upper-left corner of the dialog box.

6. **Drag the Start screen saver slider to 15**

   The slider below the Preview box lets you select when the screen saver should be activated. With the slider set at 15, the screen saver will start after 15 minutes of no activity on your screen.

7. **Click the Desktop tab, then click the Close button in the Desktop & Screen Saver dialog box**

   The desktop background image and screen saver options you just selected are now active.

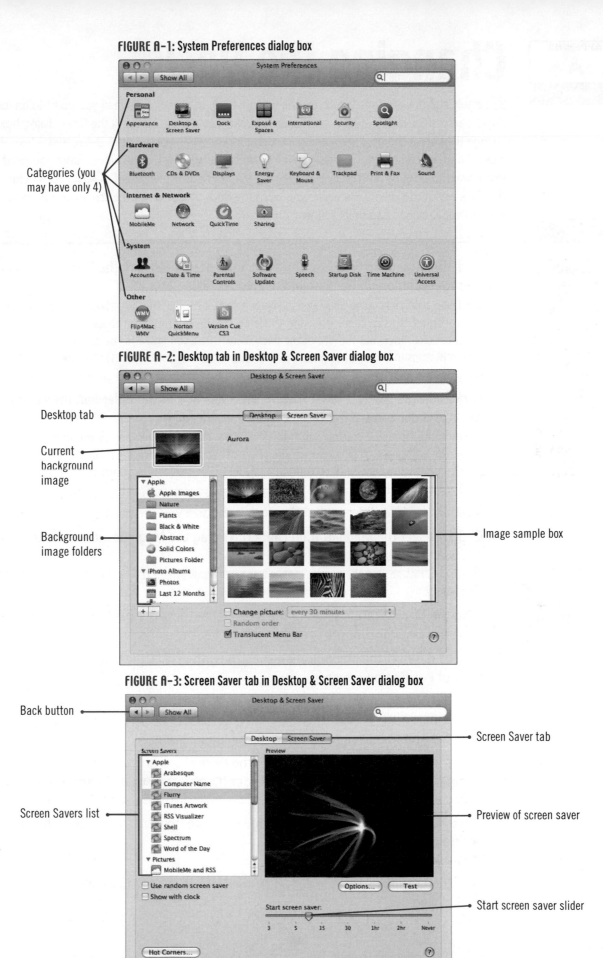

FIGURE A-1: System Preferences dialog box

FIGURE A-2: Desktop tab in Desktop & Screen Saver dialog box

FIGURE A-3: Screen Saver tab in Desktop & Screen Saver dialog box

Changing the Dock

By default, the dock is displayed across the bottom of your screen, and when you point to an item on the dock, a ScreenTip with the name of the item appears above its icon. Using the Dock dialog box, you can change the size of the dock, how the dock icons appear when you point to them, and where the dock is located on the screen. For instance, you might prefer for the dock to be hidden until you need it, or you might want to position it vertically along the left or right edge of the screen. ▰▰▰▰ You decide to explore the dock options to determine where you want the dock to appear on the screen and how you want the icons to appear when you point to them.

STEPS

QUICK TIP

You can also open the Dock dialog box by clicking the Apple icon on the menu bar, pointing to Dock, then clicking Dock Preferences.

1. **Click the System Preferences icon ▨ on the dock, then click the Dock icon ▦ in the Personal category in the System Preferences dialog box**

   The Dock dialog box opens, as shown in Figure A-4. At the top of the dialog box is the Size slider, which you use to control the size of the dock and its elements. The Magnification check box (below the Size slider), when selected, increases the size of the dock icons when you point to them. Use the Position on screen option buttons to change the position of the dock to the left, bottom, or right of the screen. The Minimize using options allow you to choose the effect used to animate items as they are minimized to the dock.

2. **Click and drag the Size slider toward the Small end of the slider bar, then click and drag the Size slider toward the Large end of the slider bar**

   As you move the slider towards Small, the size of the dock decreases, and as you move the slider towards Large, the size of the dock increases. The effect of the Size slider depends on the size of your computer screen, because the dock size is proportional to your screen size. The larger your screen, the more of an effect the Size slider will have.

3. **Position the Size slider so that the dock is the size you prefer**

QUICK TIP

You can also turn Magnification on or off by clicking ▨ on the menu bar, pointing to Dock, then clicking Turn Magnification On or Turn Magnification Off.

4. **Click to select the Magnification check box, drag the Magnification slider to Max if necessary, then point to any icon on the dock**

   The dock icons around the icon to which you point grow larger; the icon to which you point directly is the largest.

5. **Drag the Magnification slider to the location on the slider bar that magnifies the dock icons the amount that you prefer**

QUICK TIP

You can also reposition the dock by clicking ▨ on the menu bar, pointing to Dock, then clicking Position on Left, Position on Bottom, or Position on Right.

6. **Click to deselect the Magnification check box, then click the Left option button to the right of Position on screen**

   The dock moves to the left side of the screen in a vertical position, as shown in Figure A-5. If you click the Right option button, the dock appears vertically on the right edge of your screen.

7. **Click the option button for the dock position you prefer**

QUICK TIP

You can also show or hide the dock by clicking ▨ on the menu bar, pointing to Dock, then clicking Turn Hiding On or Turn Hiding Off.

8. **Click the Automatically hide and show the Dock check box to select it**

   As shown in Figure A-6, the dock is hidden, maximizing the space of the work area on your desktop. If you prefer to have the dock open and visible at all times, make sure to deselect this check box.

9. **Move the on-screen pointer to the edge of the computer screen where the dock was last positioned**

   The dock slides into view and is available for use.

10. **Click the Automatically hide and show the Dock check box to deselect it, then close the Dock dialog box**

FIGURE A-4: Dock dialog box

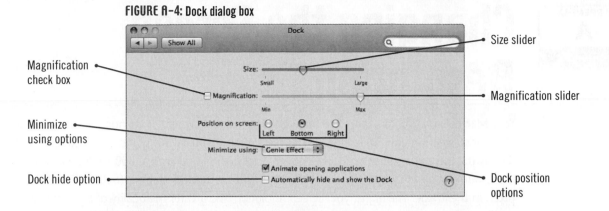

Magnification
check box

Size slider

Magnification slider

Minimize
using options

Dock hide option

Dock position
options

FIGURE A-5: Left dock position

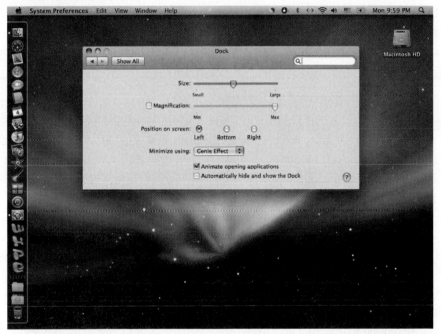

FIGURE A-6: Screen with dock hidden

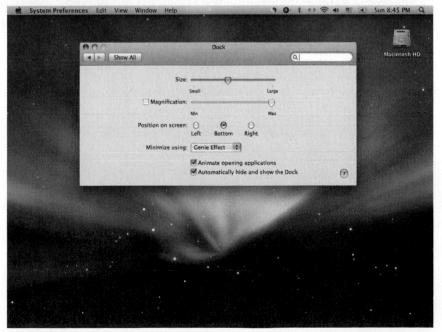

Changing the Screen Resolution

Your Mac has many different options to choose from that allow you to change the size and quality of your monitor's screen image. Your monitor's **screen resolution** is the number of pixels, or dots, used to display the computer screen image. In a screen resolution setting such as 800 × 600, the first number (800) is the number of horizontal pixels in the image, and the second number (600) is the number of vertical pixels in the image. The higher your screen resolution, the greater the quality of the screen image and the smaller the components within the image (such as icons) appear. To adjust the screen resolution for your computer, you use the Display tab of the Color LCD (or Apple Studio Display) dialog box. You can also use the Display tab to change the brightness of your screen to an appropriate level based on the amount of ambient lighting in the room where your Mac is located. ▟▛▙▟ You decide to investigate the display options for your screen to determine the resolution and brightness you prefer as you work.

STEPS

1. **Click the System Preferences icon ▧ on the dock, then click the Displays icon ▩ in the Hardware category in the System Preferences dialog box**
   The Color LCD dialog box opens with the Display tab selected, as shown in Figure A-7. On the left side of the Display tab is the Resolutions list, containing several resolution options. In Figure A-7, the current resolution setting is 1024 × 768, but the resolution setting of your computer may differ.

> **TROUBLE**
> If the 1280 × 800 resolution setting is not available, click the setting on the Resolutions list that is closest to 1280 × 800.

2. **Click 1280 × 800 in the Resolutions list**
   If your computer was previously at a lower resolution setting than 1280 × 800, then more of the background image is visible now and the dialog box appears smaller. If your computer was previously at a higher resolution setting than 1280 × 800, then less of the background image is visible now and the dialog box appears larger. See Figure A-8.

3. **Click 800 × 600 in the Resolutions list**
   Your computer screen displays a larger dialog box and less of the background image than at the 1280 × 800 resolution setting. Your dock icons may appear less clear when you use this resolution.

4. **Click the setting in the Resolutions list that you prefer**

5. **Under the Resolutions list, drag the Brightness or Contrast slider to the left and right**
   As you drag the slider to the left, the brightness of your screen decreases. As you drag the slider to the right, the brightness of your computer screen increases.

6. **Move the Brightness or Contrast slider to the location you prefer**

7. **Close the Color LCD (or Apple Studio Display) dialog box**

FIGURE A-7: Display tab in Color LCD dialog box

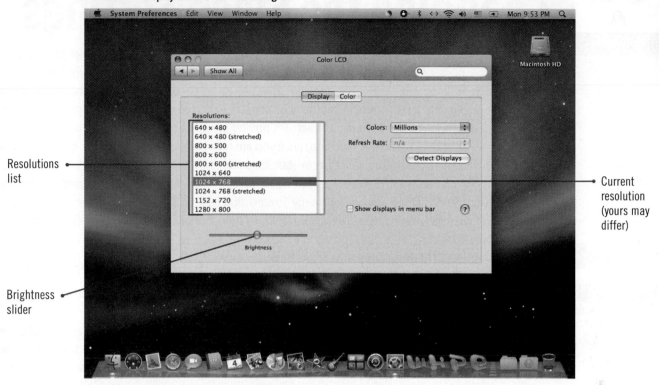

Resolutions
list

Brightness
slider

Current
resolution
(yours may
differ)

FIGURE A-8: 1280 × 800 screen resolution

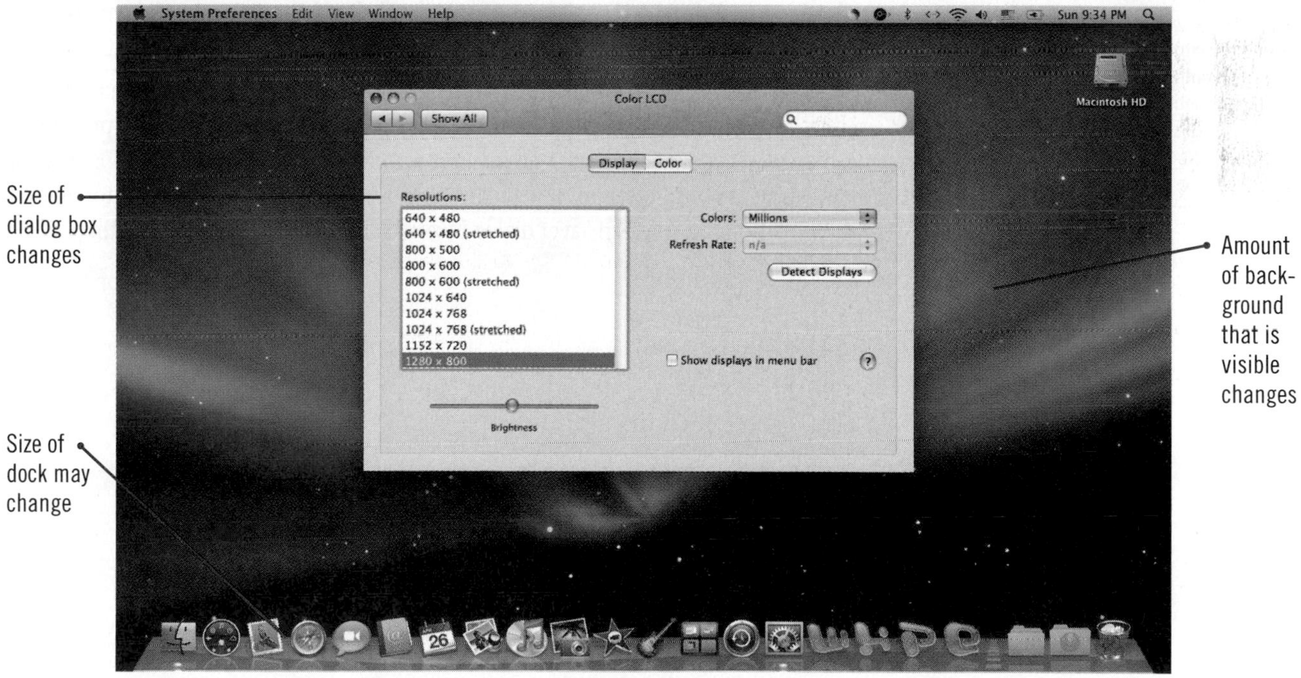

Size of
dialog box
changes

Size of
dock may
change

Amount
of back-
ground
that is
visible
changes

Changing the Sleep Settings

Your Mac "goes to sleep" after you haven't used your computer for a period of time, which means that it goes into a low power mode but does not shut off. There are separate sleep settings for your monitor display and for your computer. When your display is about to go to sleep, it dims. When the display or the computer is asleep, the screen is black and the Mac appears to be turned off. To wake up your Mac, you press any key on the keyboard or move the on-screen pointer in any direction. When asleep, your Mac uses much less energy to keep running. In addition, once you are ready to use your Mac again, it takes less time to wake your Mac up from sleep than it does to start it up after being shut down. You can work more efficiently and optimize the energy needed to power your computer by adjusting the sleep settings for your Mac. The sleep settings are located in the Energy Saver dialog box. ▄▄▅▅▅ You'd like to conserve energy that your Mac uses and plan to adjust the sleep settings so that your computer goes to sleep after it is inactive for a brief time.

STEPS

TROUBLE

Click Show Details to expand the Energy Saver dialog box, if necessary.

1. **Click the System Preferences icon** ▦ **on the dock, then click the Energy Saver icon** ▨ **in the Hardware category in the System Preferences dialog box**

    The Energy Saver dialog box opens, as shown in Figure A-9 (your dialog box and settings may differ). By default, the Sleep tab is active. Below the tab are 2 sliders: one to put your computer to sleep, and one to put your display to sleep. The two sliders can have the same or different times selected. Putting the display to sleep before the computer can be beneficial if you use a program that requires a long time to process data. Putting the display to sleep earlier reduces power to the display but keeps full power to the computer, enabling active programs to continue running.

2. **Click and drag the upper slider to the 15 min location on the slider bar**

    After 15 minutes of inactivity, all components of your Mac will go to sleep and the computer will use less energy.

QUICK TIP

As you drag either slider, the number of minutes currently selected appears above the right end of the slider bar.

3. **Click and drag the lower slider to the tick mark to the left of the 15 min tick mark on the slider bar**

    After 10 minutes of inactivity, only your display will go to sleep and draw less power. Note that the settings for when your screen saver is activated and when your display goes to sleep can differ. Both prevent image persistence, but sleep draws less power than a screen saver. A warning may appear in the dialog box stating that the display will sleep before your screen saver activates. You can click the Screen Saver button to open to the Screen Saver tab of the Desktop & Screen Saver dialog box and change the screen saver settings.

4. **Close the Energy Saver dialog box**

Setting System Preferences

FIGURE A-9: Energy Saver dialog box

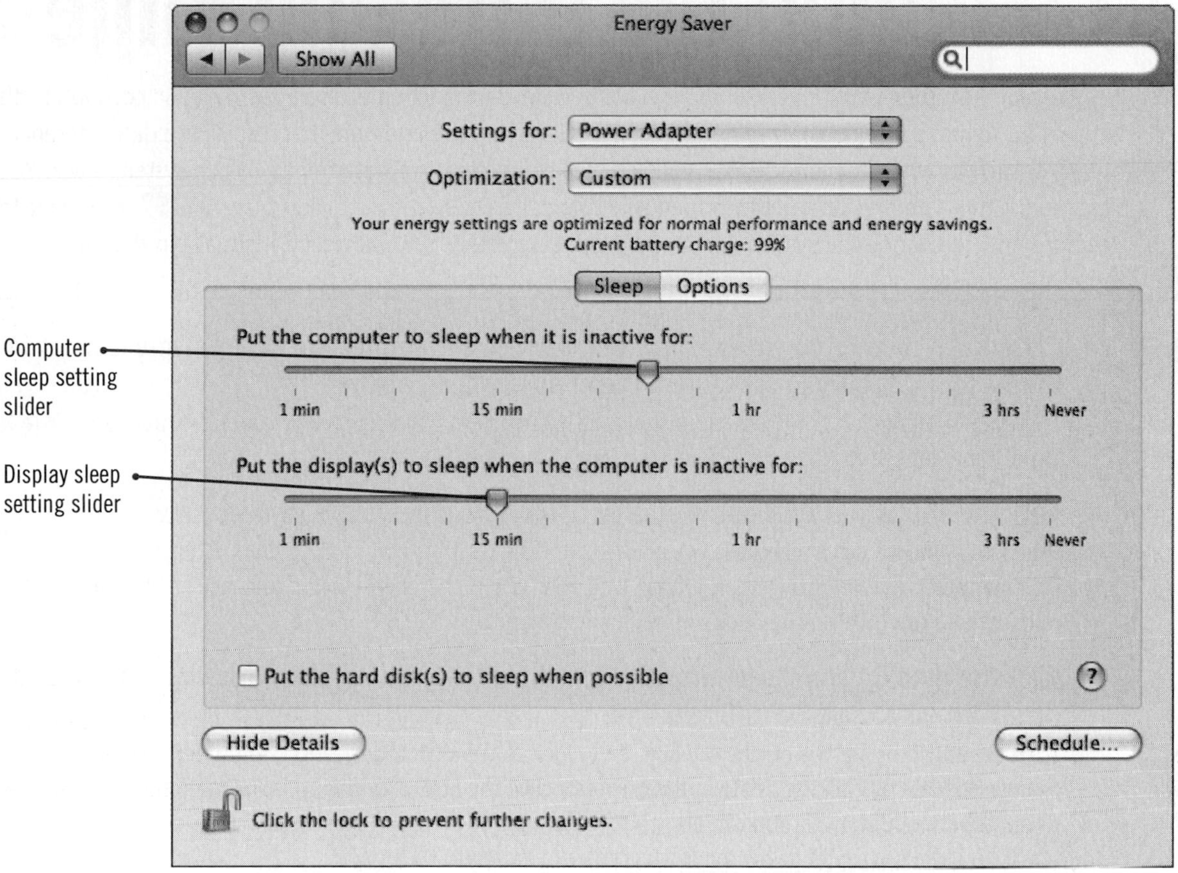

Computer sleep setting slider

Display sleep setting slider

Changing the Date and Time

There may be times you'll need to change the system date and time displayed by your computer. It's important to make sure your computer displays the accurate date and time, because all the date references for files, such as when they are saved, modified, or last opened, are determined by the system clock. You can adjust the date and time settings manually using the Date & Time dialog box. ▰▰▰▰ You want to explore how to change the system date and time in case you need to correct it manually in the future.

STEPS

QUICK TIP

You can also open the Date & Time dialog box by clicking the day and time on the right end of the menu bar, then clicking Open Date & Time.

1. Click the System Preferences icon ▧ on the dock, then click the Date & Time icon ▨ in the System category in the System Preferences dialog box

The Date & Time dialog box opens, as shown in Figure A-10. This dialog box contains three tabs: Date & Time, Time Zone, and Clock. By default, the Date & Time tab is active.

2. Click the Set date & time automatically check box to deselect it, if necessary

When this check box is checked, your computer displays the current time automatically based on the information it receives from Apple's time Web site. When the check box is unchecked, the date on the calendar and the time on the clock can be changed manually.

3. Click the date up and down arrows to select a different date, then click the time up and down arrows to select a different time

The date and time shown on the calendar and clock in the dialog box reflect your changes. You can also change the date by clicking a date in the calendar; click the arrows in the upper-left corner of the calendar to move between months. You can also change the time by dragging the hands on the clock to new locations; click the AM or PM below the clock's center to switch to PM or AM.

QUICK TIP

To set the date and time automatically from Apple's Asia or Europe time Web sites, click the list arrow next to Apple Americas/U.S., then click Apple Asia or Apple Europe.

4. Click the Set date & time automatically check box to select it

The date and time displayed on the calendar and clock return to the current date and time, updated automatically from Apple's time Web site.

5. Click the Time Zone tab

Options for changing the time zone appear in the dialog box, as shown in Figure A-11. Click the Closest City list arrow to see a list of major cities in your time zone. You can also click a section of the map to locate a major city near your home and change the time zone if necessary. Once you have selected a major city in your time zone, the date and time on the Date & Time tab are updated accordingly.

6. Click the Clock tab

The options available for changing the appearance of the clock on your menu bar appear on the Clock tab, as shown in Figure A-12. You can change how the date and time are displayed on the menu bar, and you can choose to have the computer announce the time out loud by clicking the Announce the time check box and choosing the timing of the announcement. By default, the date and time are displayed digitally on the right end of the menu bar.

7. Click the Analog option button to the right of View as

The digital clock on the menu bar changes to a clock icon showing the current time.

8. Click the Show date and time in menu bar check box to deselect it

The menu bar no longer displays the clock icon.

9. Click the Show date and time in menu bar check box to select it, then click the Digital option button to the right of View as

The menu bar displays the date and time in digital format on the menu bar again. Additional check boxes under the Digital and Analog option buttons enable you to further adjust the display of the date and time.

10. Click the Date & Time tab, then close the Date & Time dialog box

Setting System Preferences

FIGURE A-10: Date & Time tab in Date & Time dialog box

Date up and down arrows

Time up and down arrows

Set date & time automatically check box

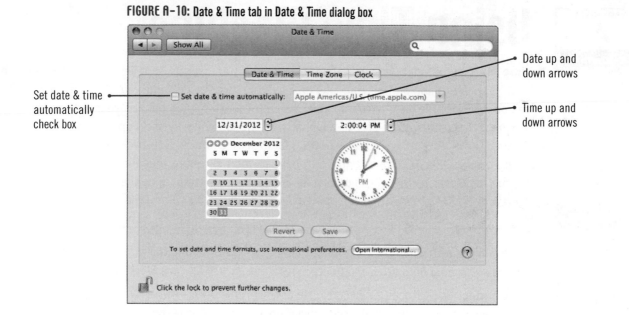

FIGURE A-11: Time Zone tab in Date & Time dialog box

Closest City list arrow

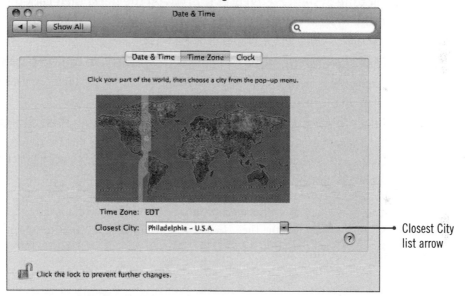

FIGURE A-12: Clock tab in Date & Time dialog box

Clock on menu bar

Show date and time in menu bar check box

Announce the time check box

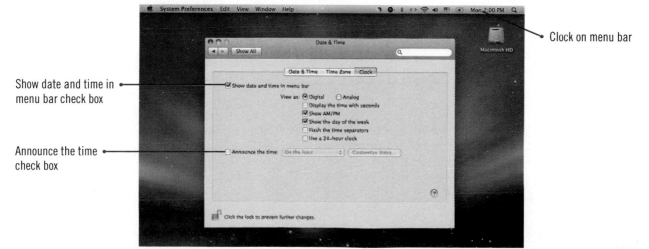

Using Time Machine

Time Machine is a new feature in Leopard that helps you maintain your files, folders, and programs by backing up everything on your computer on a regular basis. The first time you use Time Machine, it backs up not only all of the files, folders, and programs on your computer, but also your system files, accounts, and preferences. After the initial backup, Time Machine subsequently backs up only those items that have changed. Time Machine keeps hourly backups for the past 24 hours, daily backups for the past month, and weekly backups. Backups are catalogued by date, so you can restore your entire system from any backup, or you can recover individual files or folders. You want to back up the contents of your computer to prevent the loss of data if something were to go wrong, so you set up Time Machine for your computer.

STEPS

The following instructions require a storage device capable of storing the entire contents of your computer, such as an external hard drive. This device should be dedicated for Time Machine use only.

TROUBLE

If the Time Machine icon does not appear in the System Preferences dialog box, click the Show All button.

1. **Connect your storage device to the appropriate port**

   Depending on the make and model of your storage device, it may connect to a USB port or to a FireWire port. Please read the manufacturer's instructions for set up of the storage device before proceeding.

2. **Click the System Preferences icon on the dock, then click the Time Machine icon in the System category in the System Preferences dialog box**

   The Time Machine dialog box opens, as shown in Figure A-13.

QUICK TIP

After you set up Time Machine to make automatic backups, you can turn off Time Machine at any time by clicking and dragging the On switch to the Off position. Backups will no longer be made.

3. **Click and drag the Time Machine Off/On switch to the On position**

   This activates Time Machine and opens a window listing the drives available for making your backups, as shown in Figure A-14.

4. **Select the storage device you want to use as backup, then click Use for Backup**

   If the storage device is not blank, you may receive a message that the device needs to be erased to continue. Click OK to continue. The backup starts. This process may take several minutes the first time you run it. While the files are being copied, you will see progress bars. When complete, the dialog box will change to that shown in Figure A-15. In order for Time Machine to continue to automatically make backups, the storage device must remain attached to your computer. Should you need to restore a file, folder, or program from the Time Machine device, click the Time Machine icon on the dock to access the catalogued backups.

QUICK TIP

Once Time Machine is set up and you'd like only to make a backup of certain files or devices, click Options in the Time Machine dialog box, then click + to select items you would like to exclude from future backups.

5. **Close the Time Machine dialog box**

FIGURE A-13: Time Machine dialog box

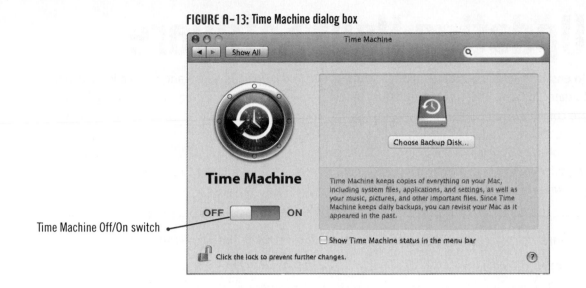

Time Machine Off/On switch

FIGURE A-14: List of backup drives

Available backup drives (yours will differ)

FIGURE A-15: Backup complete

Backup drive

Time Machine icon on dock

Setting System Preferences

Updating Your Software

To ensure that your computer runs efficiently, you should keep your system and application software up-to-date. Software updates are provided by the software manufacturer as improvements are made and bugs are corrected. You can use the Software Update dialog box to set your Mac to search for and download Apple software updates on a daily, weekly, or monthly basis. You can also click the Check Now button in the Software Update dialog box to activate a search for updates yourself. You want to ensure that the software on your Mac is kept up-to-date, so you set up your computer to search for updates and alert you when they are ready to be installed.

STEPS

An Internet connection is required to successfully complete the following steps.

1. **Click the System Preferences icon** 📷 **on the dock, then click the Software Update icon** 🔄 **in the System category in the System Preferences dialog box**

   The Software Update dialog box opens with the Scheduled Check tab selected, as shown in Figure A-16.

2. **Click to select the Check for updates check box, if necessary**

   When this check box is selected, your Mac will check for software updates on a regular basis. Depending on the settings for the Mac you are using, this check box may already be selected.

3. **Click the arrows to the right of Check for Updates, then select Weekly if necessary**

   The options for how frequently your computer will search for software updates are Daily, Weekly, and Monthly. Your Mac will notify you when updates are available for software on your computer.

4. **Click the Download important updates automatically check box to select it, if necessary**

   When this check box is checked, your Mac will automatically download critical software updates as soon as they are available and will alert you when they are ready to be installed.

5. **Click the Check Now button**

   A new dialog box opens and a progress bar appears as your Mac checks for updates, as shown in Figure A-17. If there are any available updates, your Mac will provide you with a list of available updates and you can select the updates you'd like to install. If your Mac is up-to-date, you'll receive a message notifying you that your software is up-to-date.

6. **If any updates are listed, click the Install button**

   Your Mac will install the available updates.

7. **Close the Software Update dialog box**

FIGURE A-16: Software Update dialog box

Scheduled
Check tab

Check for
updates
check box

Download
important
updates
automatically
check box

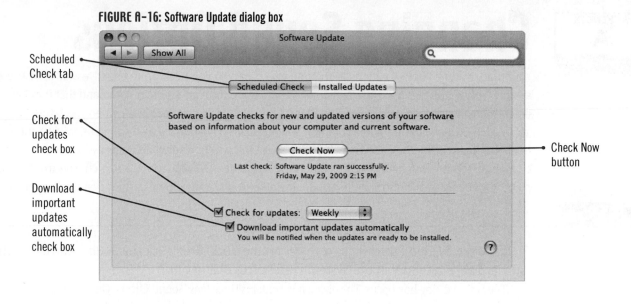

Check Now
button

FIGURE A-17: Checking fo updates

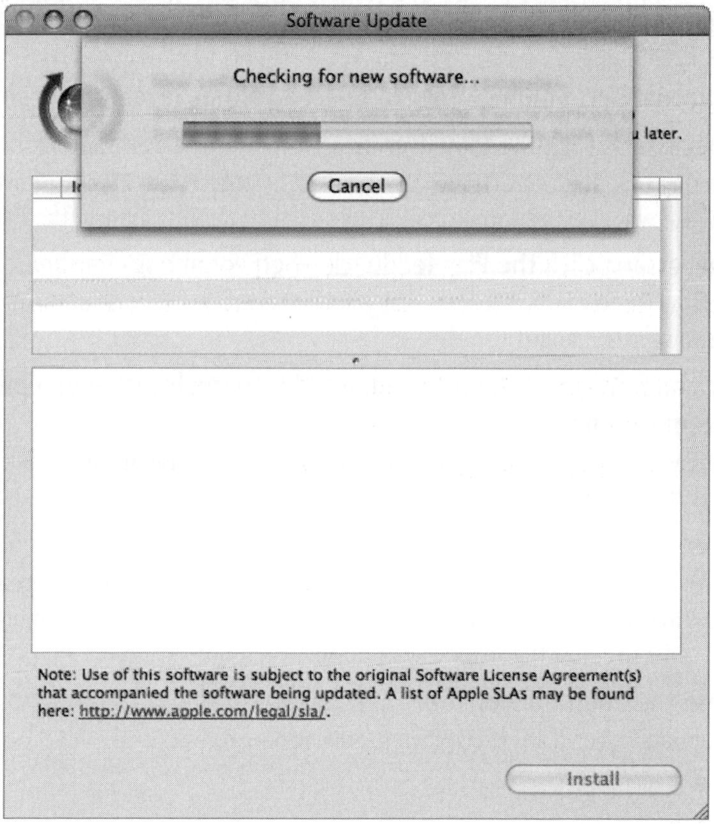

Changing Sound Options

Your Mac comes equipped with built-in sound effects to help you become an effective Mac user. The **alert sound** feature provides a sound effect when you try to perform an action or command that is not available or when an alert dialog box appears. The alert sound is also played as **feedback** when you adjust the system volume to let you hear the volume at its new setting. You can change the alert sound using the Sound dialog box. The Sound dialog box also enables you to adjust the system volume and select whether or not you can change the system volume using an icon on the menu bar. You want to change the alert sound played by your Mac and also want to explore the other sound and volume options available for your system.

STEPS

1. **Click the** System Preferences icon 🔘 **on the dock, then click the** Sound icon 🔊 **in the Hardware category in the System Preferences dialog box**
   The Sound dialog box opens. The dialog box contains three tabs: Sound Effects, Output, and Input.

2. **If necessary, click the** Sound Effects tab
   The Sound Effects tab displays a list of options for the alert sound and several check boxes for turning sound options on and off. By default, Funk is selected as the alert sound.

3. **In the Choose an alert sound list, click** Bottle
   The Bottle alert sound is played.

4. **Click additional alert sound options to listen to them, and then click the** alert sound **that you prefer**

5. **Drag the** Alert volume slider **to select a volume level for the alert sound that you prefer**

6. **If necessary, click the** Play user interface sound effects check box
   Selecting this check box ensures that you will hear **user interface sound effects**, which are the sounds you hear when you perform Finder actions such as dragging a file to the Trash and emptying the Trash.

7. **If necessary, click the** Play feedback when volume is changed check box
   Selecting this check box ensures that you will hear an alert sound at the new volume setting when the system volume is changed.

8. **Click and drag the** Output volume slider **to the location you prefer to adjust the system volume**
   When you drag the slider to a new location and then release the mouse button, the alert sound plays at the new volume setting.

9. **If necessary, click the** Show volume in menu bar check box
   Selecting this check box places the speaker icon near the right end of the menu bar and allows you quick access to it without opening a dialog box. You can click the speaker icon on the menu bar to access the vertical slider to adjust the volume up or down.

10. **Close the Sound dialog box**
    All options selected are saved when the dialog box closes.

Glossary

Absolute cell reference In Excel, a cell reference that does not change when the formula is copied and pasted to a new location; for example, the formula "=$B$5*$C$5" in cell D5 does not change to "=$B$6*$C$6" when copied to cell D6. *See also* Relative cell reference.

Action button A button on the Finder toolbar that provides access to file management commands such as creating a folder, opening a file, or copying a file or folder.

Active Currently available.

Active cell In an Excel worksheet, the current location of the cell pointer.

Active window The window that is currently in use.

Add a bookmark button A button found on the Safari toolbar that enables users to name a bookmark and add it to the bookmarks bar or to the Bookmarks menu.

Address field A text field on the Safari toolbar that displays the address of the Web page that is open in the active tab.

Alert sound A sound that occurs when you try to perform an action or command that is not available, when an alert dialog box appears, or when you change the system volume.

Alias A link that provides quick access to a file, folder, or program located on the hard disk; for example, each icon on the dock is an alias for a program, folder, or file stored elsewhere on the computer.

Alignment In Word, the position of text in a document relative to the margins; in Excel, the position of text in a cell relative to the cell edges, such as left, center, or right.

American Standard Code for Information Interchange *See* ASCII.

Analog signal A continuous wave signal (sound wave) that can traverse ordinary phone lines.

Animation scheme A set of special transition effects and graphics effects that control the way individual PowerPoint slide elements appear on the screen.

Anti-spyware software Software that detects and removes spyware.

Antivirus software Software that searches executable files for the sequences of characters that may cause harm and disinfects the files by erasing or disabling those commands. Also called virus protection software.

Application Software that can be used to perform a task, such as creating a document, analyzing data, or creating a presentation. Also called a program.

Application software Software that enables users to perform specific computer tasks, such as document production, spreadsheet calculations, database management, and presentation preparation.

Architecture The design and construction of a computer. Also called configuration.

Area chart A chart that shows the relative importance of values over a period of time.

Argument A value, cell reference, or text used in an Excel function. Commas or a colon separate arguments and parentheses enclose them; for example, AVERAGE(A1,10,5) or SUM(A1:A5).

ASCII (American Standard Code for Information Interchange) The number system that personal computers use to represent character data.

Attributes Styling characteristics such as bold, italics, and underlining that users can apply to change the way text and numbers look in a worksheet or chart.

AutoCorrect A feature that automatically detects and corrects typing errors, minor spelling errors, and capitalization, and inserts certain typographical symbols as a user types.

AutoFilter arrows In Excel, arrows to the right of each column heading that appear when AutoFilter is selected for a list; click the arrows to open a menu containing options for filtering and sorting the list data.

AutoFit A feature that automatically adjusts the width of a column or the height of a row to accommodate its widest or tallest entry.

Automatic page break A page break that is inserted automatically at the bottom of a page. Also called a soft page break.

AVERAGE function Calculates the average value of the arguments in a list.

Axis titles Labels in a chart that identify the information represented by each axis.

Back button A button commonly found at the top of a window that, when clicked, displays the previous Web page, file, folder, or drive in the window.

Background The area behind the text and graphics on a slide.

Backup A copy of a file stored in another location.

Bar chart A chart that compares values among individual items, with minimal emphasis on time.

Bibliography A list of citations from works referenced in a document that is usually placed at the end of the document.

BIOS (Basic Input/Output System) Instructions that initialize the motherboard, recognize peripheral devices, and start the boot process.

Binary digit (bit) The representation of data as a 1 or 0.

Bit *See* Binary digit.

Bits per second (bps) The unit of measurement for the speed of data transmission.

Bluetooth A wireless technology standard that allows electronic devices to use short range radio waves to communicate with one another or connect to the Internet; the radio waves can be transmitted around corners and through walls.

Bold A font style that makes text appear in darker type; used to emphasize text in a document, spreadsheet, or presentation.

Bold command On a menu, a command or operation that can be executed.

Bookmark To add a favorite Web page to the bookmarks bar or Bookmarks menu, where the page can be easily accessed in the future by clicking instead of entering the Web address in the address field.

Bookmarks bar A feature of Safari that contains buttons users can click to go directly to bookmarked Web pages, to the bookmarks library, to a page showing Top Sites, or to several popular Web sites whose bookmarks are built into the bookmarks bar.

Bookmarks library In Safari, a list of bookmark collections that can be used to view, organize, add, and delete bookmarks and bookmark folders.

Boot process The set of events that occurs between the moment the computer is turned on and the moment you begin to use the computer.

Booting The process that Leopard steps through to get the computer up and running.

Border A line that can be added above, below, or to the sides of a paragraph, text, or table cell; a line that divides the columns and rows of a table.

bps *See* Bits per second.

Browser A software program, such as Safari, used to access the Internet and display Web pages.

Browser window The rectangular area on the computer screen where the current Web page appears.

Bullet A small graphic symbol used to identify items in a list.

Byte One character of storage space on disk or in RAM; comprised of a series of eight bits.

Cable Plastic-enclosed wires that attach a peripheral device to a computer port.

Cache memory Special high-speed memory chips on the motherboard or CPU that store frequently-accessed and recently-accessed data and commands. Also called RAM cache or CPU cache.

Card A removable circuit board that is inserted into a slot in the motherboard to expand the capabilities of the motherboard.

Category axis The horizontal line at the base of a chart. Also called the x-axis.

Cathode ray tube monitor *See* CRT monitor.

CD (compact disc) An optical storage device that can store approximately 700 MB of data.

CD-R (compact disc recordable) A CD on which users can record data with a laser that changes the reflectivity of a dye layer on the blank disk, creating dark spots on the disk's surface that represent the data; once the data is recorded, it cannot be erased or modified.

CD-ROM (compact disc read-only memory) A CD that contains software or music when you purchase it, but you cannot record additional data on it.

CD-RW (compact disc rewritable) A CD on which you can record data as on a CD-R, and then delete or re-record data on it as needed.

Cell The intersection of a row and a column in an Excel worksheet or a Word table.

Cell address In Excel, a column letter followed by a row number that specifies the location of a cell.

Cell reference The address of a cell in an Excel worksheet that defines its location in the worksheet by column letter and row number (for example, A1), and that can be used in formulas and functions.

Center alignment In Word, the centering of an item between the margins. In Excel, the centering of a cell's contents within the cell.

Central processing unit (CPU) *See* Microprocessor.

Channel The medium, such as a telephone line or coaxial cable, over which a message is sent in data communications.

Chart A visual representation of selected worksheet data.

Chart area A chart object that contains all of the chart objects.

Chart object Individual component of a chart, such as the chart background or legend, that can be moved or resized independently.

Chart sheet A worksheet in an Excel workbook that contains a chart.

Chart style A predefined set of chart colors and fills that can be applied to any chart.

Check box A box that turns an option on when checked or off when unchecked.

Chip An integrated circuit embedded in semiconductor material.

Circuit A path along which an electric current travels.

Circuit board A rigid piece of insulating material with circuits on it that control specific functions.

Citations A tab on the Word Toolbox that enables users to insert citations and build a bibliography.

Click To quickly press and release the left button on a pointing device. Also called single-click.

Click and Type A feature that allows users to begin typing in almost any blank area of a Word document by double-clicking in the desired location.

Client A computer connected to a network that is dependent on a server.

Client/server network A network with a server and computers dependent on the server.

Clip A media file, such as a graphic, photograph, sound, movie, or animation, that can be inserted into an Office document.

Clip art Simple art objects that are included as collections with many software packages.

Clip Gallery A library of clip art, animations, videos, and photographs that all Office programs share.

Clipboard A temporary storage area in the computer's memory containing an item that was cut or copied from a file and is available for pasting. *See also* System Clipboard.

Clock speed The pulse of the processor measured in megahertz or gigahertz.

Close button Window control button that closes and removes a window from the desktop.

CMOS *See* Complementary metal oxide semiconductor memory.

Collapse button A button that shrinks a portion of a dialog box to hide some settings.

Column chart A chart that compares values across categories over time.

Column headings In Excel, the boxes containing letters that appear above every column.

Columns view A view of items in a window that displays the contents of a device or folder in a multicolumn format.

Command An instruction to perform a task.

Command button A button that completes or cancels an operation.

Compact disc *See* CD.

Compact disc read-only memory *See* CD-ROM.

Compact disc recordable *See* CD-R.

Compact disk rewritable *See* CD-RW.

Compatibility The capability of different programs to work together and exchange data.

Compatibility Report A tab on the Office Toolbox that enables users to check for compatibility issues with earlier versions of the Office suite, including both Windows and Mac versions.

Complementary metal oxide semiconductor (CMOS) memory A chip installed on the motherboard powered by a battery whose content changes every time you add or remove hardware on your computer system and that is activated during the boot process so it can identify where essential software is stored. Also called semipermanent memory.

Complex formula A formula in Excel that contains more than one mathematical operator (for example, +, –, *, or /) and performs more than one calculation at a time.

Computer An electronic device that accepts input, processes data, displays output, and stores data for retrieval later.

Computer network The hardware and software that makes it possible for two or more computers to share information and resources.

Computer system A computer, its peripheral devices, and software.

Conditional formatting In Excel, formatting that is applied to cells in a spreadsheet when specified criteria are met.

Configuration *See* Architecture.

Content placeholder In PowerPoint, a slide area that is used to enter text or objects such as clip art, charts, or pictures.

Context-sensitive Help Onscreen guidance tools that display topics and instructions geared to the specific task the user is performing.

Contextual tool Tool that appears on the Toolbox in an Office program only when a certain type of item is selected, such as a table or a chart.

[control]-click To press and hold [control] while clicking the mouse button once; functions as a right-click for a single-button pointing device.

Controller card A card that plugs into a slot on the motherboard and connects to a port to provide an electrical connection to a peripheral device. Also called expansion card or interface card.

Copy To create a duplicate of a file in new location, while the original file stays in its current location.

COUNT function Counts the number of values in the list of arguments.

Cover Flow A view of items in a window that provides a preview of the first page of the files and a detailed list of the files in the currently selected location.

CPU *See* Microprocessor.

CPU cache *See* Cache memory.

Create a new tab button A button at the right side of the tab bar in Safari that, when clicked, opens a new Web page tab in the browser window.

Criteria In Excel, conditions or qualifications that determine whether data is chosen for a filter.

Crop To trim part of an image so that it is no longer visible. Cropping does not delete any part of an image; you can restore the trimmed parts at any time.

CRT (cathode ray tube) monitor A monitor that uses gun-like devices to direct beams of electrons toward the screen to activate dots of color to form an image.

Custom Animation A tab on the PowerPoint Toolbox that enables users to create animations, or to add special effect to individual slide elements in a slide show.

Cut To remove data from a file and place it on the system Clipboard, usually to be pasted into another location or file.

Data The words, numbers, figures, sounds, and graphics that describe people, events, things, and ideas.

Data bus The path between the microprocessor, RAM, and the peripherals along which communication travels.

Data communications The transmission of data from one computer to another or to a peripheral device via a channel using a protocol.

Data file A file created by a user, usually with software, such as a report written with a word processing program.

Data label Text in a chart that describes or names a data series value, a data series, or a category.

Data marker A bar, area, dot, slice, or other symbol in a chart that represents a single data point or value that originates from a worksheet cell.

Data series In a chart, a sequence of related numbers that show a trend, such as sales amounts of various months, quarters, or years.

Data source The file that stores the variable information for a form letter or other mail merge document.

Data table A grid in a chart that contains the chart's underlying worksheet data, and that is usually placed below the x-axis.

Database A collection of information stored on one or more computers organized in a uniform format of records and fields.

Database management software Software used to collect and manage data.

Default setting A setting preset by the manufacturer of an operating system or program.

Delete To permanently remove an item from a document. (Office)

Delete To place a file or folder in the Trash, where you can either remove it from the disk permanently or restore it. (Leopard)

Depth axis In a chart, a third axis that compares data equally across categories and series. Also called the Z-axis.

Desktop The graphical user interface (GUI) displayed on screen after you start Leopard that you use to interact with Leopard and other software on your computer.

Desktop computer A personal computer designed to sit compactly on a desk.

Destination file When linking and embedding data between documents, the target file or program.

Device *See* Storage device.

Device driver System software that handles the transmission protocol between a computer and its peripheral devices. Also called a driver.

Devices Group in the sidebar in the Finder window that provides quick access to all of the storage devices available to your Mac, such as the hard disk and any external drives.

Dialog box A window that opens to enable users to select options or provide the information needed to complete an operation.

Digital signal A stop-start signal that your computer outputs.

Digital subscriber line *See* DSL.

Dimmed command On a menu, a command or operation that is not currently available.

Disclosure triangle A small triangle that indicates a command or group has additional options or categories available.

DNS server A computer responsible for directing Internet traffic.

Dock A glossy ribbon at the bottom of the computer screen that contains icons for frequently used programs, folders and files, and the Trash.

Document An electronic file that you create using a program such as Word.

Document Elements A tab in the Elements Gallery in Word that enables users to insert elements used in professional documents such as cover pages, headers, and bibliographies.

Document production software Software, such as word processing software, desktop publishing software, e-mail editors, and Web authoring software, that assists users in writing and formatting documents, including changing the font and checking the spelling.

Document window The main work area within the program window that displays all or part of an open document.

Domain name The name of a Web site that appears after *www* in a Web address; for example, in *www.apple.com*, *apple* is the domain name.

Dot matrix printer A printer that transfers ink to paper by striking a ribbon with pins.

Dot pitch (dp) The distance between pixels on a monitor.

Double-click To press and release the left mouse button twice quickly, opening a window or program.

dp *See* Dot pitch.

Draft view In Word, a view that shows a document without margins, headers and footers, or graphics.

Drag To point to an object, press and hold the left button on the pointing device, move the object to a new location, and then release the left button.

Drag and drop The action of moving or copying an entire file or selected text in a document by dragging it with the mouse and placing it at a new location.

Drive A physical location for storing files. Also called a storage device.

Driver *See* Device driver.

DSL (digital subscriber line) A high-speed connection over phone lines.

Dual-core processor A CPU that has two processors on the chip.

DVD An optical storage device that can store up to 15.9 GB of data; was originally an acronym for *digital video disc* and later *digital versatile disc*.

Edit To change the content or format of an existing file.

Elements Gallery A new feature for Office 2008 for Mac made up of tabs below the Standard toolbar in each Office program window that provide quick, easy access to commonly used, preformatted elements.

Ellipsis (...) On a menu, indicates that the command opens a dialog box containing additional options.

Embed To insert a separate copy of a file in a different program that can be edited using the tools of the program in which it was created.

Emphasis effect In PowerPoint, an animation category that adds an effect to an object already visible on a slide.

End-of-cell mark In a Word table, the formatting mark in each cell that appears to the right of typed text.

End-of-row mark In a Word table, the formatting mark that appears to the right of each row.

Endnote A note or citation that corresponds to a number or symbol in a document and appears at the end of the document. *See also* Footnote.

Enter To type information in a document or dialog box.

Entrance effect In PowerPoint, a category of animation effect that specifies the way text or objects move onto a slide.

Ergonomic Designed to fit the natural placement of the body to reduce the risk of repetitive-motion injuries.

Ethernet port A port used to connect computers in a LAN or sometimes directly to the Internet; it allows for high-speed data transmission.

Executable file A file that contains the instructions that tell a computer how to perform a specific task, such as the files that are used during the boot process.

Exit effect In PowerPoint, an animation category that specifies the way text or an object leaves the slide.

Expand button A button that expands a dialog box to display additional settings.

Expansion card *See* Controller card.

Expansion slot An electrical connector on the motherboard into which a card is plugged. Also called a slot.

Feedback The playing of an alert sound when the system volume is adjusted.

Field One piece of information in a database record.

File A collection of stored electronic data, such as text, a picture, video, or music, that has a unique name, distinguishing it from other files.

File extension Additional characters assigned by a program to the end of a filename to identify the type of file.

File hierarchy A logical structure for folders and files that mimics how you would organize files and folders in a filing cabinet.

File management A strategy for organizing files and folders so you can find your data quickly and easily.

Filename A unique, descriptive name for a file that identifies the file's content.

Fill handle In Excel, a small square that appears on the lower-right corner of a selected worksheet cell that users can drag to the right or down to copy the cell's contents into adjacent cells.

Filter A command that displays only the data that you want to see in an Excel worksheet based on criteria you set.

Find command Search option available on the Finder File menu that performs the same operation as Finder's Search field.

Finder Part of the Mac operating system (Leopard) that provides access to files and programs.

Firewall Hardware or software that prevents other computers on the Internet from accessing a computer or prevents a program on a computer from accessing the Internet.

First line indent In Word, a paragraph indent in which the first line of a paragraph is indented more than subsequent lines.

Flash drive *See* USB flash storage device.

Flash memory Memory that is similar to ROM except that it can be written to more than once.

Flash memory card A small, portable card encased in hard plastic to which data can be written and rewritten.

Flash storage device A removable storage device that is plugged into a USB port to which data can be written and rewritten. Also called a USB drive or a flash drive.

Flat panel monitor A lightweight monitor that takes up very little room on the desktop and uses LCD technology to create the image on the screen.

Floating graphic A graphic to which text wrapping has been applied, making the graphic independent of text and able to be moved anywhere on a page.

Floppy disk A flat circle of magnetic oxide-coated plastic enclosed in a hard plastic case that can store 1.44 MB of data. Also called a 3½" disk.

Folder A container for a group of related files.

Folder name A unique, descriptive name for a folder that identifies what you store in that folder.

Font The design of a set of characters; for example, Arial or Times New Roman.

Font effects Special enhancements to fonts such as small caps, shadow, and superscript, that you can apply to selected text in a document, spreadsheet, or presentation.

Font size The size of text characters, measured in units called points (pts); a point is equal to 1/72 inch.

Font style Attribute that changes the appearance of text when applied; bold, italic, and underline are common font styles.

Footer Information, such as text, a page number, or a graphic, that appears in the bottom margin of a page in a document.

Footnote A note or citation that corresponds to a number or symbol in a document and that is placed at the bottom of the document page.

Form letter A mail merge document that contains standard body text and a custom header for each recipient.

Format To enhance the appearance of text in a document, spreadsheet, or presentation without changing the content.

Format Painter A feature used to copy the format settings applied to selected text to other text you want to format the same way.

Formatting marks Nonprinting characters that appear onscreen to indicate the ends of paragraphs, tabs, and other formatting elements.

Formatting Palette A tab on the Office Toolbox that provides the most commonly used formatting options.

Formula An equation that calculates a new value from existing values. Formulas can contain numbers, mathematical operators, cell references, and built-in equations called functions.

Formula AutoComplete In Excel, a feature that helps you enter a formula in a cell by suggesting a listing of functions as you type letters and providing syntax information to help you write the formula correctly.

Formula bar A floating element below the menu bar in which users enter, edit, or display a formula or data in the selected cell.

Formula Builder A tab on the Excel Toolbox that helps users create mathematical calculations.

Forward button A button commonly found at the top of a window that, when clicked, displays the next Web page, file, or folder.

Function A prewritten formula you can use instead of typing a formula from scratch. Each function includes the function name, a set of parentheses, and function arguments separated by commas and enclosed in parentheses. *See also* Formula.

GB *See* Gigabyte.

GHz *See* Gigahertz.

Gigabyte (G or GB) 1,073,741,824 bytes, or about one billion bytes.

Gigahertz (GHz) One billion cycles per second.

Graphic Interchange Format (GIF) File format for graphics that is often used for line art and clip art images.

Graphical user interface (GUI) A computer environment in which the user manipulates graphics, icons, and dialog boxes to execute commands.

Graphics card The card installed on the motherboard that controls the signals the computer sends to the monitor. Also called a video display adapter or video card.

Graphics display A monitor that is capable of displaying graphics by dividing the screen into a matrix of pixels.

Graphics software Software that allows you to create illustrations, diagrams, graphs, and charts.

Gridlines Horizontal and vertical lines connecting to the X-axis and Y-axis in a chart that make it easier to identify the value of each data series.

Group A collection of related commands in a section of the Toolbox.

GUI *See* Graphical user interface.

Hand-held computer A small computer designed to fit in the palm of your hand and that generally has fewer capabilities than personal computers.

Handles Small squares that appear around the perimeter of a selected object and are used to resize it.

Handouts In PowerPoint, hard copies of a presentation that are printed for distribution to an audience, showing one or more slides per page.

Hanging indent In Word, a paragraph indent in which the second and subsequent lines of text in a paragraph are indented further than the first line by a set amount of space.

Hard copy A printed, paper copy of computer output.

Hard disk A magnetic storage device that contains several magnetic oxide-covered metal platters that are usually sealed in a case inside the computer, providing built-in, high-capacity, high-speed storage for all the software, folders, and files on a computer. Also called a hard drive.

Hard drive *See* hard disk.

Hard page break A page break inserted manually in a Word document to cause the text following the page break to begin at the top of a subsequent page. Also called a manual page break.

Hardware The physical components of a computer system.

Header Information, such as text, a page number, or a graphic, that appears in the top margin of a page in a document.

Highlight To shade an icon or text differently, indicating it is selected. *See also* Select.

Hits The items in a list of search results that include your keyword(s) or that meet the search criteria. *See also* Search results.

Home folder A folder provided by Leopard for each user that contains several subfolders in which you can save your files on the hard drive.

Home page The first Web page that opens every time you start Safari; also, the main page of a Web site.

Horizontal ruler An onscreen ruler at the top of the document window in Word that helps you place objects in a precise location.

Horizontal scroll bar *See* Scroll bar.

Hyperlink Words, phrases, or graphics that, when clicked, open a new location on the current document or page, open a file or a new Web page, or play audio or video. Also called a link.

I-beam pointer The pointer used to move the insertion point and select text.

Icon A small image on the desktop or in a window that represents a program, tool, folder, or file.

Icon view A view of items in a window that displays the contents of a selected device or folder as icons.

Image A nontextual piece of information such as a picture, piece of clip art, drawn object, or graph.

Image persistence Damage to the crystals in an LCD computer monitor that occurs when an image stays too long onscreen without changing; the crystals continue to display the image faintly even after the onscreen image has changed.

Inactive window An open window you are not currently using.

Indent A set amount of space between the edge of a paragraph and the right or left margin.

Indent marker A marker on the horizontal ruler that shows the indent settings for the active paragraph.

Information management software Software that keeps track of schedules, appointments, contacts, and "to-do" lists.

Infrared technology A wireless technology in which devices communicate with one another using infrared light waves; the devices must be positioned so that the infrared ports are pointed directly at one another.

Inkjet printer A printer that sprays ink onto paper and produces output whose quality is comparable to that of a laser printer.

Inline graphic A graphic that is part of a line of text.

Input The data or instructions you type into the computer.

Input and output (I/O) The flow of data from the microprocessor to memory to peripherals and back again.

Input device An instrument, such as a keyboard or a mouse, that you use to enter data and issue commands to the computer.

Insertion point A flashing vertical line that indicates where the next character will appear when the user types.

Integration The act of inserting and linking information among applications. *See also* Object Linking and Embedding.

Interface The look and feel of a program; for example, the appearance of commands and the way they are organized in the program window.

Interface card *See* Controller card.

Internet A network of connected computers and computer networks located around the world.

Intranet A computer network that connects computers in a local area only, such as computers in a company's office.

I/O *See* Input and output.

Italic Formatting applied to text to make the characters slant to the right.

Joint Expert Photographic Experts Group (JPEG) File format that is often used for photographs because it uses and compresses color so well.

Justified text Text aligned equally between the right and left margins.

KB *See* Kilobyte.

Keyboard An input device that consists of three major parts: the main keyboard, the numeric keypad, and the function keys.

Keyboard shortcut A combination of keyboard keys that you press to perform a command.

Keyword A descriptive word or phrase you enter to obtain a list of results that includes that word or phrase.

Kilobyte (KB or K) 1,024 bytes, or approximately one thousand bytes.

Label Descriptive text used to identify worksheet data in Excel.

LAN *See* Local area network.

Landscape Layout orientation for a document that specifies to print the page so it is wider than it is long.

Laptop computer *See* Notebook computer.

Laser printer A printer that produces high-quality output quickly and efficiently by transferring a temporary laser image onto paper with toner.

Launch To open or start a program on your computer.

Layout *See* Slide layout.

LCD (liquid crystal display) A display technology that creates images by manipulating light within a layer of liquid crystal.

Ledger sheet Preformatted Excel worksheet designed to help you with common financial tasks.

Left alignment Alignment in which the item is flush with the left margin.

Left indent In Word, a set amount of space between the left margin and the left edge of an entire paragraph.

Legend Area in a chart that explains what the labels, colors, and patterns of the chart represent.

Leopard The Mac OS X v10.5 operating system.

Line chart A graph of data mapped by a series of lines. Because line charts show changes in data or categories of data over time, they are often used to document trends.

Line spacing The amount of space between lines of text.

Link *See* Hyperlink. (Internet)

Link A shortcut for opening a Help topic or a Web site. (Leopard)

Link A connection created between a source file and a destination file. When an object created in a source file is linked to a destination file, any changes made to the object in the source file also appear in the object contained in the destination file. (Office)

Liquid crystal display *See* LCD.

List arrow An arrow that, when clicked, displays a list of options from which you can choose.

List box A box containing a list of items. To choose an item, click the list arrow and then click the desired item.

List view A view of items in a window that displays the contents of the selected storage device or folder as an alphabetic list with additional details about each file and folder such as Name, Date Modified, Size, and Kind.

Local area network (LAN) A network in which the computers and peripheral devices are located relatively close to each other, generally in the same building, and are usually connected with cables.

Log in To sign in with a user name and password before being able to use a computer.

Log Out An option for ending a Leopard session in which all open files and programs are closed, all drives are disengaged and memory is cleared, and then the current user's session ends but the Mac continues running so the next user can log in and begin using the computer immediately, without waiting for the computer to boot up.

Mac OS X Mac operating system, version 10.

Macintosh HD icon The only icon that appears on the Leopard desktop by default; provides quick access to all items stored on the computer.

Magnetic storage device A storage device that stores data as magnetized particles on mylar, a plastic, which is then coated on both sides with magnetic oxide.

Mail merge The process of combining a Word document that contains placeholders with data from a data source to create a third document that contains multiple personalized letters or labels.

Main document A document that stores the standard body text for a form letter or other mail merge document.

Mainframe computer A computer used by larger business and government agencies that provides centralized storage, processing, and management for large amounts of data.

Malware A broad term that describes any program that is intended to cause harm or convey information to others without the owner's permission; short for malicious software.

Manual page break A page break inserted to force the text following the break to begin at the top of the next page. Also called a hard page break.

Margin In a document, the amount of space between the edge of the page and the text in your document.

MAX function Calculates the largest value in the list of arguments.

MB *See* Megabyte.

Megabyte (MB) 1,048,576 bytes, or about one million bytes.

Megahertz (MHz) One million cycles per second.

Memory A set of storage locations on the main circuit board that store instructions and data.

Memory capacity The amount of data that a device can handle at any given time. Also called storage capacity.

Menu A list of commands in a program (for example, the File menu) that you can use to accomplish a task.

Menu bar A bar at the top of a program window or the desktop that provides access to most of a program's features through categories of related commands.

Merge To combine information from a data source, such as an Excel spreadsheet, with standard text contained in a Word document to create personalized form letters or other mail merge documents. *See also* Mail merge.

Merged document A file or printout that contains all the personalized letters or labels in a mail merge document.

MHz *See* Megahertz.

Microprocessor A silicon chip, located on the motherboard, that is responsible for executing instructions to process data; *also called* processor or central processing unit (CPU).

Microsoft Entourage An e-mail program and information manager created by Microsoft Corporation that comes with Office 2008 for Mac that you use to send and receive e-mail, schedule appointments, maintain task lists, and store names, addresses, and other contact information.

Microsoft Excel A spreadsheet program created by Microsoft Corporation you can use to manipulate, analyze, and chart quantitative data, as well as to calculate financial information.

Microsoft PowerPoint A presentation graphics program created by Microsoft Corporation you can use to develop materials for presentations, including electronic slide shows, computer-based presentations, speaker notes, and audience handouts.

Microsoft Word A word processing program created by Microsoft Corporation you can use to create text-based documents such as letters, memos and newsletters.

MIDI (musical instrument digital interface) card A sound card used to record and play back musical data.

MIN function Calculates the smallest value in a list of arguments.

Minimize button Window control button that collapses a window to an icon on the dock.

Minimized window A window that has collapsed to an icon on the right side of the dock.

Modem Stands for *mo*dulate-*dem*odulate; a device that converts the digital signals from your computer into analog signals that can traverse ordinary phone lines, and then converts analog signals back into digital signals at the receiving computer.

Modifier key A keyboard key that is used in conjunction with another keyboard key to execute a keyboard shortcut.

Monitor The TV-like peripheral device that displays the output from the computer.

Motherboard The main circuit board of the computer on which processing tasks occur.

Mouse A pointing device that contains buttons for clicking commands; you control the movement of the pointer by moving the entire mouse around on your desk.

Mouse pointer The typically arrow-shaped object on the screen that follows the movement of the mouse. The shape of the mouse pointer changes depending on the program and the task being executed. *See also* Mouse.

Move To change the location of a file or a selection in a document by physically placing it in another location different from its original location.

MP3 player A hand-held computer that is used primarily to play and store music, but that can also be used to watch digital movies and television shows.

Multimedia authoring software Software that allows you to record digital sound files, video files, and animations that can be included in presentations and other documents.

Multitasking Working with more than one window or program at a time.

Musical instrument digital interface card *See* MIDI card.

Name box In Excel, displays the name or address of the currently selected cell in the worksheet.

Network Two or more computers that share data and resources and which are connected to each other and to peripheral devices.

Network interface card (NIC) The card in a computer on a network that creates a communications channel between the computer and the network.

Network software Software that establishes the communications protocols that will be observed on the network and controls the "traffic flow" as data travels throughout the network.

NIC *See* Network interface card.

Node Any device connected to a network.

Nonvolatile memory *See* Read-only memory.

Normal view A view in PowerPoint that divides the presentation window into three sections: Slides or Outline tab, Slide pane, and Notes pane.

Notebook computer A small, lightweight computer designed for portability. Also called a laptop computer.

Notebook Layout view A view option in Word that displays the contents of a document as if they were typed on a lined sheet of paper.

Notes pages Hard copy of a PowerPoint presentation that contains a miniature version of each slide plus the text added in the Notes pane.

Notes pane In PowerPoint, the area in Normal view located below the slide that is used to input text relevant to the current slide; can be used as an audience handout or reference notes during a presentation.

Object A graphic or other item or set of items that can be moved and resized as a single unit. In Word, any item that is embedded or linked to the document is called an object. In Excel, the components of a chart are called objects. In PowerPoint, each graphic or text element is an object.

Object Linking and Embedding (OLE) The ability to use data created in one application in a document created by another application. Linking creates a "live" connection between an object in a source file and a linked version in a destination file; embedding places an unconnected copy in the destination file.

Object Palette A tab on the Office toolbox that contains objects such as shapes, images, symbols, and photos, which can be inserted into a document.

OLE *See* Object Linking and Embedding.

On-screen presentation A PowerPoint slide show run from a computer.

Opacity The opaqueness or transparency of an image.

Open To start a program; to display a window that was previously closed or that is currently running but isn't displayed in an active window; or to load an existing file into an Office program.

Operating environment An operating system that provides a graphical user interface that acts as a liaison between the user and all of the computer's hardware and software, such as Microsoft Windows and the MAC OS.

Operating system A computer program that manages the complete operation of your computer and keeps all the hardware and software working together properly. The operating system allocates system resources, manages storage space, maintains security, detects equipment failure, and controls basic input and output. Examples of the operating system for Mac are Mac OS X Leopard and Mac OS X Tiger.

Optical storage device A polycarbonate disk coated with a reflective metal on which data is recorded using laser technology as a trail of tiny pits or dark spots in the surface of the disk; the data that these pits or spots represent can then be "read" with a beam of laser light.

Option button A small circle in a dialog box to select only one of two or more related options.

Orientation *See* Page orientation.

Outline In PowerPoint, a print option that prints the text of a presentation in outline form.

Outline tab In PowerPoint, the section in Normal view that displays your presentation text in the form of an outline, without graphics.

Outline view In Word, a view that shows the headings of a document organized as an outline.

Output The result of the computer processing input.

Output device Any peripheral device that receives and/or displays output from a computer.

Page break The point at which text in a document flows to the top of a new page.

Page orientation Printing or viewing a page of data in either a portrait (8.5 inches wide by 11 inches tall) or landscape (11 inches wide by 8.5 inches tall) direction.

PAN *See* Personal area network.

Paragraph In Word, any text that ends with a hard return.

Parallel port A port that transmits data eight bits at a time.

Password A string of characters used to verify the identity of the user.

Paste To insert items stored on the Clipboard or Scrapbook into a document at the insertion point.

PC card *See* Portable computer card.

PDA (personal digital assistant) A hand-held computer that is generally used to maintain an electronic appointment book, address book, calculator, and notepad.

Peer-to-peer network A network in which all the computers are considered equal, and programs and data are distributed among them.

Peripheral device The components of a computer that accomplish its input, output, and storage functions.

Permanent memory *See* Read-only memory.

Personal area network (PAN) A network that allows two or more devices located close to each other communicate or to connect a device to the Internet.

Personal computer A computer typically used by a single user in the home or office for general computing tasks such as word processing, working with photographs or graphics, e-mail, and Internet access.

Personal digital assistant *See* PDA.

Pharm To break into a DNS server and redirect any attempts to access a particular Web site to a spoofed site.

Phish To send e-mails to customers or potential customers of a legitimate Web site asking them to click a link in the e-mail and then verify their personal information, which may then be used for illegal purposes; the link leads to a spoofed site.

Photo editing software Software that allows you to manipulate digital photos.

Picture A digital photograph, or a piece of line art or clip art that is created in another program and can be inserted into an Office program.

Pie chart A chart that describes the relationship of parts to the whole.

Pixel One of the small dots in a matrix into which a graphics display is divided.

Placeholder A container for text or graphics on a slide used to reserve space for text or graphics the user will insert in its place. (PowerPoint)

Placeholder A field name from a specified data source that is inserted in a main document to indicate where the custom information from the data source should appear. (Word)

Places A group in the sidebar in the Finder window that provides quick access to the user's Desktop folder, Applications folder, home folder, and Documents folder.

Plot area In a chart, the area that contains the data markers.

Point A unit of measurement for font size; a point equals 1/72 of an inch.

Pointer A small arrow or other symbol on the screen controlled by a pointing device.

Pointing Positioning the pointer over an item and hovering on it.

Pointing device A device, such as a mouse or trackpad, that controls the on-screen pointer.

Pointing stick A small, eraser-like device embedded among the typing keys on a notebook computer that you push up, left, right, or down to move the on-screen pointer; buttons for clicking commands are located in front of the spacebar.

Pop-up menu A menu that opens when you click a set of pop-up menu arrows.

Pop-up menu arrows Arrows that, when clicked, display a pop-up menu of options from which you can choose.

Port The interface between a cable and a controller card.

Portable computer card (PC card) A credit-card–sized card that plugs directly into a slot in a notebook computer and that can contain additional RAM, a fax modem, or a hard disk drive (similar to a flash storage device).

Portable Network Graphics (PNG) A graphics file format used primarily by Macs and the default file type created when the Preview program generates an image.

Portrait orientation A print setting that positions the document on the page so the page is taller than it is wide.

Presentation authoring program *See* Presentation graphics program.

Presentation graphics program Software designed to develop materials for presentations including slide shows, computer-based presentations, speaker notes, and audience handouts.

Presentation software A software program used to create illustrations, diagrams, graphs, and charts that can be projected before a group, printed out for quick reference, or transmitted to remote computers.

Preview The built-in PDF viewer for Mac OS X.

Print Layout view A view in Word that displays layout, graphics, and footnotes exactly as they will appear when printed.

Print Preview In Word, a view that displays how a document will appear when printed.

Printer The peripheral computer component that produces a hard copy of the text or graphics processed by the computer.

Process To modify data in a computer.

Processor *See* Microprocessor.

Program Software you can use to perform a task, such as create a document, analyze data, or create a presentation. Also called an application.

Programming language A language used to write computer instructions that are translated into electrical signals that the computer can manipulate and process.

Project Gallery A collection of the templates and wizards used with the Office programs.

Projects A tab on the Entourage Toolbox that enables users to group different elements, including Office documents, e-mail, and calendar events, into projects.

Protocol The set of rules that establishes the orderly transfer of data between the sender and the receiver in data communications.

Publishing Layout view In Word, a view that enables users to work with the contents of a document as a desktop publishing document.

Quick Look A tool in Finder that displays the contents of a selected file as a large preview without actually opening the file.

Quick Style A preset format that can be applied to Smart Art, shapes, charts, or text.

Quick Table A table with a predefined set of formatting attributes, such as shading, fonts, and border color, that can easily be inserted into a document via the Elements Gallery.

RAM *See* Random access memory.

RAM cache *See* Cache memory.

Random access memory (RAM) A temporary storage place for data and instructions (software) while being used by the CPU.

Range A selected area of adjacent cells in an Excel worksheet.

Range reference The cell references denoting a group of contiguous worksheet cells, for example, C5:E15, that is used in a formula or function.

Read-only memory (ROM) A chip on the motherboard that is prerecorded with and permanently stores the set of instructions that the computer uses when you turn it on; *also called* nonvolatile memory or permanent memory.

Receiver The computer or peripheral at the message's destination in data communications.

Record A collection of related fields that contains all information for an entry in a database such as a customer, item, or business.

Reference mark The mark next to a word in a document that indicates a footnote or endnote is associated with the word.

Reference Tools A tab on the Office Toolbox that contains dictionary, thesaurus, and translation tools.

Relative cell reference In Excel, a cell reference that changes when copied to refer to cells relative to the new location. For example, the formula "=B5*C5" in cell D5 changes to "=B6*C6" when you copy the formula to cell D6. *See also* Absolute cell reference.

Removable storage Storage media that you can easily transfer from one computer to another, such as DVDs, CDs, or flash drives.

Repaginate To renumber the pages in a document; Office programs automatically repaginate files as necessary when you add or delete information.

Replace command A command on the Edit menu in Office programs that enables users to search for a word or format in a document, spreadsheet, or presentation and insert another word or format in its place.

Report Bugs to Apple button A button on the Safari toolbar that opens a dialog box to be used to notify Apple of problems encountered while using Safari to browse the Web.

Resolution The number of pixels used to display the screen image on a computer monitor. Also called screen resolution.

Restart To shut down your computer, then start it again.

Restore To move a file from the Trash to a new location on the computer.

Right alignment Alignment in which an item is flush with the right margin.

Right-click To press and release the right mouse button once, opening a shortcut menu on the screen.

Right indent In Word, a paragraph indent in which the right edge of a paragraph is moved in from the right margin by a set amount of space.

ROM *See* Read-only memory.

Rotation tool A green circular handle at the top of a selected object that you can drag to rotate the object.

Router A device that controls traffic between network components and usually has a built-in firewall.

Row headings In Excel, the boxes containing numbers that appear in front of each row.

Safari A popular browser made by Apple that comes installed on the Mac.

Save To store a file permanently on a disk or to overwrite the copy of a file that is stored on a disk with the changes made to the file.

Save As A command used to save a file for the first time or to create a new file with a different filename or location, leaving the original file intact.

Scale To change the size of a graphic to a specific percentage of its original size.

Scanner A device that transfers the content on a piece of paper into memory; you place a piece of paper on the glass, a beam of light moves across the glass, similar to a photocopier, and stores the image or words on the piece of paper as digital information.

Scrapbook A tab on the Office Toolbox that enables users to copy and paste multiple items to and from documents.

Screen resolution *See* Resolution.

Screen saver Moving image that appears on the computer screen after the computer is idle for several minutes; prevents image persistence.

Screen size The diagonal measurement from one corner of the computer screen to the other.

ScreenTip A label that appears on the screen when you point to an item, providing the name of the item.

Scroll To use the scroll bars or the arrow keys to display different parts of a document in the document window.

Scroll arrow The arrow at the bottom or right end of a scroll bar that is clicked to scroll a document one line at a time or to scroll a document left and right in the document window.

Scroll bar A bar on the right edge (vertical scroll bar) or bottom edge (horizontal scroll bar) of a document window that allows you to move around in a document that is too large to fit on the screen all at once.

Scroll box A rounded rectangle located within the vertical and horizontal scroll bars that indicates your relative position in a file and that you can drag to view other parts of the document or page in the window. *See also* Scroll bar.

Scroll wheel A wheel on a mouse that you roll to scroll vertically on the page.

SCSI (small computer system interface) port A port that provides an interface for one or more peripheral devices at the same port.

Search box A text box accessible from the Help menu where you type keywords to search the built-in help files.

Search criteria One or more pieces of information that helps Leopard identify the program, folder, or file you want to locate.

Search engine A special Web site that searches the Internet for Web sites based on words or phrases that you enter.

Search field A text box on the Finder toolbar that the user can use to search for files by filename or file content. (Leopard)

Search field A text box on the Safari toolbar that uses the Google search engine to help users search the Internet for Web sites about a particular topic. (Safari)

Search For A group in the sidebar in the Finder window that helps locate a file quickly by viewing files used recently or by viewing only a certain type of file.

Search results A list of items or links produced by entering keywords or specific criteria in a search field.

Security The steps a computer owner takes to prevent unauthorized use of or damage to the computer.

Select To highlight an item in order to perform some action on it. *See also* Highlighting.

Selection bar In Word, the area to the left of the left margin that users click to select entire lines of text.

Selection box A dashed border that appears around a text object or placeholder, indicating that it is ready to accept text.

Semipermanent memory *See* Complementary metal oxide semiconductor memory.

Sender The computer that originates the message in data communications.

Serial port A port that transmits data one bit at a time.

Serial value A number used in an Excel worksheet that represents a date or time used in calculations; a date that is formatted in General format will appear as a serial value.

Server A computer on a network that acts as the central storage location for programs and provides mass storage for most of the data used on the network.

Shading A background color or pattern that can be applied to text, tables, or graphics.

Shared Group in the sidebar in the Finder window that is shown only when your Mac is connected to a network; lists all shared computers and servers that the user has access to.

Sheet tab In Excel, displays the names of a worksheet in a workbook; click to make the worksheet active in the window.

Shortcut menu A menu that appears when you right-click an object, listing common commands for the object.

Shut down An option for ending a Leopard session in which all open files and programs are closed, all drives are disengaged and memory is cleared, and then the Mac safely turns itself off.

Sidebar The left section of a window (such as the Finder window) or a dialog box (such as the Open or Save As dialog boxes) that provides quick access to many frequently-used resources.

Single-click *See* Click.

Single-core processor A CPU with one processor on the chip.

Size control The lower-right corner of a window that enables the user to resize the window by clicking and dragging.

Sizing handles Small squares or circles that appear when an object is selected that you can drag to change the size of the object.

Sleep A partial shut-down option that puts the Mac in a low power state to conserve energy while not in use.

Slide Onscreen page for use in a PowerPoint slide show.

Slide layout This determines how all of the elements on a slide are arranged, including text and content placeholders.

Slide master A feature of PowerPoint that contains the layouts, design elements, and other formatting attributes for a presentation; enables users to make design changes to multiple slides at once.

Slide pane The section of Normal view that contains the current slide.

Slide Show toolbar The toolbar that appears in PowerPoint Slide Show view that lets you navigate to different slides or change the pointer to a pen or arrow to identify key slide points.

Slide Show view A view in PowerPoint that displays presentation slides full-screen as the audience will see them.

Slide Sorter view A view in PowerPoint that displays a thumbnail of all slides in the order in which they appear in your presentation; used to rearrange and delete slides.

Slide thumbnail A reduced view of a PowerPoint slide, displayed on the Slides tab in Normal view, and in Slide Sorter view.

Slide timing The number of seconds a slide remains onscreen before advancing to the next slide during a slide show.

Slide transition The special effect that determines how a slide appears as it enters or leaves the screen during a slide show.

Slider An item in a dialog box that you drag to set the degree to which an option is in effect.

Slides tab In Normal view in PowerPoint, the area to the left of the Slide pane that displays thumbnails of every slide in a presentation.

Slot *See* Expansion slot.

Small computer system interface port *See* SCSI port.

SmartArt A new Office 2008 for Mac feature for creating professional quality diagrams such as organizational charts, process diagrams, and timelines.

SmartArt Style A preset combination of formatting options that follows the design theme that you can apply to a SmartArt graphic.

Soft page break Page breaks that are automatically inserted by Word at the bottom of a page. Also called an automatic page break.

Software The intangible components of a computer system, particularly the programs or instructions that the computer needs to perform a specific task.

Sort A command that organizes columns in an Excel spreadsheet or a Word table numerically or alphabetically, and in ascending or descending order.

Source file When linking and embedding data between documents, the file from which information is copied or used. An Excel file inserted into a Word report is a source file. *See also* Destination file.

Speaker notes In PowerPoint, notes that accompany slides; used to help the speaker remember important information that should not appear on the slides themselves.

Specifications The technical details about a hardware component.

Spell check The feature in document production software that helps you avoid typographical and grammatical errors.

Spin box A text box with up and down arrows; you can type a setting in the text box or click the arrows to increase or decrease a setting.

Spoofed site A Web site set up to look exactly like another Web site, such as a bank's Web site, but which does not actually belong to the organization portrayed in the site.

Spotlight search field A search option accessible in all programs by clicking the magnifying glass on the right side of the menu bar.

Spreadsheet Another word for a workbook or worksheet.

Spreadsheet software Software that you can use to manipulate, analyze, and chart quantitative data, as well as to calculate financial information.

Spring-loaded folder A folder in the Finder window that springs open when a file is dragged on top of it, displaying its contents in the right pane of the Finder window and enabling the user to drag and drop files between different locations without having to open additional Finder windows.

Spyware Programs that track a computer user's Internet usage and send this data back to the company or person that created it, most often without the computer user's permission or knowledge.

Stack A method of displaying the contents of a folder on the dock; when the user clicks a folder on the dock, the folder springs open in an arc or a grid to reveal its contents.

Standalone computer A personal computer that is not connected to a network.

Standard colors A group of ten colors that appear below the Theme Colors in any Office color palette and that contain basic hues such as red, orange, green, and blue.

Standard toolbar A bar below the title bar in all Office program windows that contains buttons to perform the most common tasks in a program.

Status bar The bar at the bottom of the Finder window that lists the number of items in the selected device or folder and the available space on a device. (Leopard)

Status bar The bar at the bottom of an Office program window that displays information such as the current page and word count. (Office)

Status bar The bar at the bottom of the Safari window that displays information about the Web page that is loading and that displays the Web address of a link when you point to it. (Safari)

Storage capacity The amount of data a device can handle at any given time.

Storage device A physical location for storing files. Also called a drive.

Strong password A string of at least eight characters of upper and lowercase letters and numbers.

Style A setting that controls how text and paragraphs are formatted using predefined formatting attributes.

Subfolder A folder within another folder for organizing sets of related files into smaller groups.

Subscript A font effect in which text is formatted in a smaller font size and placed below the line of text.

Subtitle text placeholder A box on a PowerPoint title slide reserved for subpoint text.

Suite A collection of programs that share a common user interface and are distributed together. Microsoft Office 2008 for Mac is a software suite.

SUM function In Excel, the function used to calculate the total of the arguments.

Supercomputer The largest and fastest type of computer used by large corporations and government agencies for processing a tremendous volume of data.

Superscript A font effect in which text is formatted in a smaller font size and placed above the line of text.

Synchronous dynamic RAM (SDRAM) RAM that is synchronized with the CPU to allow faster access to its contents.

System Clipboard A clipboard that stores only the last item cut or copied from a document. *See also* Clipboard.

System resource Any part of the computer system, including memory, storage devices, and the microprocessor, that can be used by a computer program.

System software A collection of programs and data that helps the computer carry out its basic operating tasks.

Tab A clickable item near the top of a dialog box or the Toolbox that switches to a different set of options or tools. (Leopard)

Tab A horizontal position where text is aligned. (Word)

Tab bar A bar at the top of the Safari window that contains the name of the Web pages currently open in tabs in the Web browser.

Tab indicator In Word, a tool that enables users to align text differently where tab stops are set.

Tab stop A location on the horizontal ruler to which the insertion point moves when [tab] is pressed.

Tabbed browsing Web browsing that enables you to open more than one Web page at a time on individual tabs in a browser window.

Table A grid made up of rows and columns of cells that you can fill with text and graphics.

Table style A predefined set of formatting attributes such as shading, fonts, and border color, that specifies how a table looks.

Tablet PC A computer designed for portability that includes the capability of recognizing ordinary handwriting on the screen.

Tape A magnetic storage media that provides inexpensive archival storage for large quantities of data.

TB *See* Terabyte.

Telecommunications The transmission of data over a comparatively long distance using a phone line or some other conduit.

Template A special file that contains predesigned formatting, text, and other tools for creating common business documents such as letters, business presentations, and invoices.

Temporary memory *See* Random access memory.

Terabyte (TB) 1,024 GB, or approximately one trillion bytes.

Terminal A computer connected to a network that uses mainframes as a server; it has a keyboard for input and a monitor for output, but processes little or no data on its own.

Terminal emulator A personal computer, workstation, or server that uses special software to imitate a terminal so that it can communicate with a mainframe or supercomputer for complex data processing.

Text box A box in which you type text.

Text placeholder A designated area on a PowerPoint slide for entering text, such as titles, subtitles, and body text.

Theme A predesigned set of formatting elements, including colors, that you can apply to an Office 2008 for Mac document to achieve a coordinated overall look throughout the document.

Thumbnails A miniature version of an image or slide.

Time Machine A new feature in Leopard that enables users to maintain files, folders, and programs by backing up everything on the computer on a regular basis.

Timing *See* slide timing.

Title In PowerPoint, the title or first line of text in a slide.

Title bar The area across the top of a window that displays the program name, document name, or the name of the currently selected file, folder, or device.

Title placeholder A box on a slide reserved for the title of a presentation or slide.

Title slide The first slide in a PowerPoint presentation.

Toner A powdery substance used by laser printers to transfer a laser image onto paper.

Toolbar A customizable set of buttons that allows you to activate commands using one click.

Toolbar control A feature in the Finder window that hides or unhides the toolbar and sidebar when clicked.

Toolbox An updated feature in Office 2008 for Mac that provides quick access to several tabs of tools you can use as you work within an Office program.

Top-level domain The part of a Web site address that identifies the type of site you are visiting; examples of top-level domains are com (for commercial site), edu (for educational institutions), and org (for organizations).

Top Sites A feature of Safari that displays your most frequently visited Web sites as thumbnail images on a page in the browser window.

Trackball A pointing device with a rolling ball on the top side and buttons for clicking commands; you control the movement of the on-screen pointer by moving the ball.

Trackpad A touch-sensitive device on a laptop computer that you drag your finger over to control the on-screen pointer.

Transition *See* Slide transition.

Trash A storage area on your computer's hard disk for deleted files, which remain in the Trash until you empty it.

Triple-click To press and release the left mouse button three times quickly. In some programs, including Word, this action causes an entire line to be selected.

Underline A font style that underlines text; used to emphasize text in a document.

Uniform Resource Locator (URL) The address of a Web page.

Universal Serial Bus port *See* USB port.

URL (Uniform Resource Locator) The address of a Web page.

USB connector A small, rectangular plug attached to a peripheral device and that you connect to a USB port.

USB drive *See* USB flash storage device.

USB flash storage device A popular, removable storage device for folders and files that provides ease of use and portability. Also called a USB drive or flash drive.

USB (Universal Serial Bus) port A high-speed port to which you can connect a device with a USB connector to have the computer recognize the device and allow you to use it immediately.

User interface A term for the way commands and features users interact with are organized on screen in a software program.

User interface sound effect A sound effect that occurs when you perform certain Finder actions such as dragging a file to the Trash.

Utility A type of system software that augments the operating system by taking over some of its responsibility for allocating hardware resources.

Value In Excel, data entered into a cell, such as a number or a date.

Value axis The vertical line that defines the left edge of a chart and usually measures values. Also called the y-axis.

Vertical scroll bar *See* Scroll bar.

Video card *See* Graphics card.

Video display adapter *See* Graphics card.

View A way of displaying files and folders in the Finder window. (Leopard)

View A preset configuration that determines which elements of a file are visible on-screen in an Office program; does not affect the actual content of the document. (Office)

View buttons Buttons that change the arrangement and view of the contents of a window.

Virtual memory Space on the computer's storage devices that simulates additional RAM.

Virus A harmful program that instructs a computer to perform destructive activities, such as erasing a disk drive.

Virus protection software *See* Antivirus software.

Volatile memory *See* Random access memory.

WAN *See* Wide area network.

Web browser *See* Browser.

Web Layout view In Word, a view that shows a document as it will look when viewed with a Web browser.

Web page A document located on another computer that you can view over the Internet and that often contains words, phrases, and graphics that link to other documents.

Web server A computer directly linked to the Web that has software capable of hosting Web pages.

Web site A group of Web pages focused on a particular subject.

Web site creation and management software Software that allows you to create and manage Web sites and to see what the Web pages will look like as you create them.

What-if analysis Type of analysis you can perform in Excel where you can change the formula input numbers and instantly see the effect on the formula result.

Where pop-up menu In the Open dialog box and Save As dialog box, displays the currently selected folder or drive.

Wi-Fi *See* Wireless fidelity.

Wide area network (WAN) A network that covers a large geographic area and usually connects one or more LANs.

WiMAX (Worldwide Interoperability for Microwave Access) A standard of wireless communication defined by the IEEE that allows computers to communicate wirelessly over many miles; signals are transmitted from WiMAX towers to a WiMAX receiver in a device.

Window A rectangular work area on a screen that can contain a program, the contents of a file, and/or other usable data.

Window control buttons Buttons located in the upper-left corner of most windows and some dialog boxes that allow you to close, minimize, or increase the size of the window or dialog box.

Wireless fidelity The term created by the nonprofit Wi-Fi Alliance to describe networks connected using a standard radio frequency established by the Institute of Electrical and Electronics Engineers (IEEE); frequently referred to as *Wi-Fi*.

Wireless local area network (WLAN) A LAN connected using high frequency radio waves rather than cables.

Wizard A series of dialog boxes that guides you step-by-step through the process of creating a document or accomplishing a task.

WLAN *See* Wireless local area network.

Word processing program A program used to create and manipulate text-based documents, such as memos, newsletters, or term papers.

Word size The amount of data that is processed by a microprocessor at one time.

Word wrap In Word, a feature that automatically pushes text to the next line when the insertion point meets the right margin.

WordArt Stylized text object created in Word, Excel, or PowerPoint with special text formatting features.

Workbook A collection of related worksheets saved in a single Excel file.

Worksheet An Excel spreadsheet comprised of rows and columns of information that is used for performing numeric calculations, displaying business data, presenting information on the Web, and other purposes.

Workstation A computer that is connected to the network.

World Wide Web The part of the Internet that contains Web pages that are linked together. *See also* Internet.

Worldwide Interoperability for Microwave Access *See* WiMAX.

Wrap *See* Word wrap.

Wrapping style The setting for how text flows in relation to a graphic.

X-axis The horizontal line at the base of a chart that contains a series of related values from the worksheet data. Also called the category axis.

XML format An acronym that stands for eXtensible Markup Language, which is a language used to structure, store, and send information and is the file format used for all files created in Office 2008 for Mac.

Y-axis The vertical line in a chart that contains a series of related values from the worksheet data. Also called the value axis.

Z-axis In a chart, a third axis that compares data equally across categories and series. Also called the depth axis.

Zoom To change the magnification level of the screen.

Zoom button Window control button that maximizes the size of a window or dialog box.

Index

Note: Page numbers in boldface indicate key terms.

SPECIAL CHARACTERS
* (asterisk), 214
, (comma), 238
= (equal sign), 214
() (parentheses), 238

►A

ABS function, 239
Add a bookmark button, 84–85
Address Book, 350
address field, **84–85**, 86, 88, 90
ADDRESS function, 239
alert sound, 16
aliases, **58**
alignment. *See also* tabs
   of cells, 218–219
   described, **162**
   of labels, 218–219
   of text, 162–163
analog signals, **10**
AND function, 239
animation, 320–323
Animation Effects dialog box, 322–323
ANSI (American National Standards Institute), **10**
anti-spyware software, **20**
antivirus software, **20**, 21
Apache Web server, 61
application(s)
   described, **106**
   software, 24–25
architecture, **4**
archive files, 96
area charts, 261
arguments, **244–245**
ARPANET (Advanced Research Projects Agency Network), 82
ascending sort order, 250
ASCII (American Standard Code for Information Interchange), **10**, 11
ASIN function, 239
asterisk (*), 214
audio. *See* sound
audio ports, 17
AutoComplete, 236, **238**
AutoCorrect, **135**
AutoFill, 86–87
AutoFilter arrows, **250**
AutoFit, 212–213
AutoSum, 240–241
AVERAGE function, **238**, 241, 244–245

►B

Back button, 60, 84–86, 88, 94, 132
backups, **68–69**, APP-12–13

bar charts, 261
bibliographies, 190–191
binary digits (bits), **10**, 11, 117
BIOS (basic input/output system), 12
Bilingual Dictionary tool, 143
Bluetooth, **18**
Blu-ray Discs, 14
boldface text, 160–161, 292–294
bookmark(s)
   creating, 90–91
   described, **82**, 84–85, 90
   library, **86–87**
   organizing, 91
   tabbed browsing and, 88
bookmarks bar, 84–85
boot process, **12**, 34
border(s)
   color, 185, 186–187, 194–195, 220–221, 272
   drawing, 220
   tables and, 185–187
Borders and Shading dialog box, 194–195
bps (bits per second), **10**
browser(s). *See also* Safari browser (Apple)
   exploring, 84–85
   home page settings, 87
   history of, 82
   previewing presentations with, 340–341
   printing Web pages with, 92–93
   starting, 84–85
   tabbed browsing, 84–85, 88–89
   translation tools and, 147
   understanding, 82–83
   Web searches and, 94–95
   window, **84–85**
Bryce Canyon National Park, 90–91
bubble charts, 261
bulleted lists, **144–145**, 170–171, 290–291, 342–343
bullets, **144**
Bullets and Numbering dialog box, 170–171

►C

cache memory, 12
cards, **4**
category axis. *See* x-axis
CD-R format, 15
CD-ROM format, 15
CD-RW format, 15
CDs (compact discs), 14
cell(s). *See also* cell references
   active/selected, **208**, 211
   addresses, **208**
   alignment, 218–219
   conditional formatting and, 246–247
   copying, 217
   described, **182**
   entering data in, 182–183, 210–211
   formatting, 186–187
   merging, 218

   moving, 217
   pasting, 217
   selecting, 209, 218
cell references. *See also* cells
   absolute, **215**
   described, **214**
   entering, 214–215
   relative, **214–215**
center-aligned text, 162
channels, 16
chart(s)
   3-D (three-dimensional), 272–273
   adding text to, 274–275
   creating, 262–263
   described, **259**
   enhancing, 270–271
   guidelines, 274–275
   inserting, into slides, 336–337
   legends, **260**, 264–265, 268–269
   moving, 264–265
   objects, **264–269**
   opening, 336
   parts of, 260–261
   planning, 260–261
   printing, 274–275
   resizing, 264–265
   saving, 264
   styles, **266–267**
   types, choosing, 260
   understanding, 260–261
   working with, 259–284
   worksheet design and, 260
Charts tab, 114, 336
check boxes, **44–45**
chips, **4**
circuit(s)
   board, **4**
   described, **4**
citations, 190–191
Citations Palette, 112
Click and Type, 136
clicking, **37**
client/server networks, **18**
clip art. *See also* Clip Gallery; graphics
   databases, 188
   described, **24**, 181
   downloading, 312
   PowerPoint and, 312–313
   resizing, 188
   tables and, 188–189
   Word and, 181, 188–189
Clip Gallery, **188–189**, 312–313. *See also* clip art
Clipboard
   copying text and, 138–139
   described, **138**
   moving text and, 140
   Safari and, 92
clips, **188**
clock speed, **5**

Close button, 41, 42, 96, 108–109
CMOS (complementary metal oxide semiconductor) memory, 12
Collapse button, 64, 92
Collapse/Expand button, 44–45
color
    background, 186–187
    border, 185, 186–187, 194–195, 220, 272
    charts and, 270–271
    fill, 194–195, 220, 270–271
    text, 292–293
    theme, 196–197, 270–271, 295
    transparent, 314–315
column(s)
    creating multiple, 183
    deleting, 184–185
    described, 261, 262–263, 335–336
    headings, 216
    inserting, 184–185
    selecting, 209
    totals, 248–249
    width, 209, 212–213, 216, 248–249, 261–263
columns view, 62–63
comma (,), 238
Command button, 44
commands, 4, 36
computer(s)
    concepts, understanding essential, 1–32
    described, 2
    investigating types of, 2–3
    systems, 4–5
conditional formatting, 246–247
configuration, 4
Congress (United States), 82
contextual tools, 184
[control]-clicking, 37
controller cards, 16
copy-and-paste, 24, 138–139, 217
COS function, 239
COUNT NUMBERS function, 241
Cover Flow view, 62–63
CPU (central processing unit) cache, 12
Create New Source dialog box, 190–191
CRTs (cathode ray tubes) monitors, 8–9. See also screens
Custom Animation Palette, 112
Custom Animation tool, 322–323
cut-and-paste, 24
cylinder charts, 261

▶D

data
    bus, 16
    communications, 16–17
    embedding, 336
    entry keys, 211
    files, 10–11
    linked, 345, 346–347
    markers, 260
    sorting, 235, 248, 250, 350
    sources, 348, 350
    tables, in charts, 268–269
    use of the term, 4
databases, 24, 188, 350
date(s)
    Excel and, 222–223, 242–243
    functions, 229, 242–243
    serial values, 243
    system, changing, APP-10–11

DB function, 239
default settings. See also system preferences
    column width, 212
    described, 164, APP-1
    Excel and, 212
    margin, 164
depth axis, 260
descending sort order, 250
desktop
    background settings, APP-2–3
    described, 33, 108–109
    starting Leopard and, 34–35
Desktop folder, 60, 61, 72–73
device drivers, 16
Devices group, 60
dialog boxes, 44–45, 110–111
Dictionary, 143
digital signals, 10
disabled individuals, input devices for, 6
disclosure triangle, 112, 118
disk reading utilities, 73
DNS servers, 20
dock(s)
    default settings, APP-4–5
    described, 38–39
    hiding/displaying, 38, 109
    stacks and, 71
    starting programs not found on, 39
document(s). See also files
    creating, 64–65
    main, 348
    merged, 348
    production software, 24
    saving, 64–65
    window, 108–109
Documents folder, 58–59, 64, 66, 71
domain(s)
    names, 85
    top-level, 85
dot matrix printers, 8
dot pitch (dp), 8
double-clicking, 37
doughnut charts, 261
Downloads folder, 61, 71, 312
Draft view, 134–135, 148
drag and drop, 68–69, 138–139
dragging, 37
drivers, 16
drives, 57
DSL (digital subscriber line), 10
dual-core processors, 5
DVDs (digital video discs), 14, 15

▶E

Edit menu
    Clear command, 160
    Cut command, 140
    Delete command, 216
    Paste command, 140
Elements Gallery, 120, 262, 270
    described, 108–109, 114
    PowerPoint and, 288, 295, 296–297, 320–321
    Word and, 182, 187, 190
e-mail. See also Entourage (Microsoft)
    sending Web pages via, 82, 96
    software, 24
embedded files, 317
embedding data, 24, 345

Encarta Encyclopedia, 143
endnotes, 190–191
energy saving. See sleep settings
Entourage (Microsoft), 24–25, 106. See also e-mail
equal sign (=), 214
Ethernet ports, 16
Excel (Microsoft). See also charts; workbooks; worksheets
    borders and, 220–221
    conditional formatting and, 246–247
    creating/enhancing worksheets with, 207–234
    described, 106–107
    fonts and, 220–221
    formatting numbers with, 218–219
    linked data with, 344–346
    number formats, 243
    Reference Tools and, 143
    shading effects and, 220–221
expansion cards. See controller cards

▶F

fields, 24
file(s). See also documents; filenames; Finder
    copying, 68–69
    closing, 116–117
    deleting, 58, 72–73
    formats, 117, 312, 317
    hierarchy, 58–59
    linked, 317, 344–345
    management, 57–80
    moving, 58, 68–69
    naming, 68–69
    renaming, 58
    restoring, 58, 72–73
    saving, 96, 116–117, 132
    use of the term, 10, 33, 57
File menu
    New Presentation command, 288
    Open Recent command, 120
    Print command, 300
    Print Preview command, 148
    Save As command, 96, 116, 132
    Send To command, 338
    Web Page Preview command, 340
FileMaker Pro, 350
filename(s)
    choosing, 64
    extensions, 64, 116
    saving files and, 116
fill(s)
    handles, 214–215
    textures, 309–310
filtering
    criteria, 250
    described, 235, 250–251
financial functions, 229
Find and Replace dialog box, 142–143
Find command, 70
FIND function, 239
Finder
    changing views with, 62–63
    delete/restore operations, 72–73
    described, 33, 39, 57
    file searches, 70–71
    help and, 46
    opening, 60–61, 66–67
firewalls, 20, 21
FireWire ports, 17

flash drives, **14–15**, 61, 64, 68–69
flash memory
    cards, **14**
    described, **14**
floppy disks, 14
folder(s)
    creating, 58
    default, 59
    deleting, 58
    described, **33**, 57–58
    hierarchy, 58–59
    home, **58**
    locating, 58
    names, **58**
    restoring, 58
    spring-loaded, 68–69
    stacks and, 71
    sub-, **58**
font(s). *See also* text
    charts and, 268, 272
    color, 160–161
    described, **144**, 160–161, 172–173
    effects, 160–161
    Excel and, 220–221
    PowerPoint and, 310
    size, **144–145**, 158–159, 292
    styles, **144–145**
    themes and, 196–197
    Word and, 144–145, 158–161, 172–173, 196–197
footnotes, 190–191
form letters, 348–349
Format Painter, 160, 246–247
Formatting Palette, 112–113, 188
    described, **144–145**
    Excel and, 208, 218–220, 222–223, 266, 268, 274–275
    fonts and, 158–159
    indents and, 168–169
    lists and, 170–171
    margins and, 164–165
    PowerPoint and, 288, 292–295, 310, 316–317, 324
    styles and, 172–173
    tables and, 184–187
    themes and, 196–197
    Word and, 144–145, 158–159, 164–165, 168–171, 184–188
formula(s)
    cell references and, 214–215
    complex, **235–237**
    creating, 236–237
    described, **214–215**
    displaying, 214
Formula AutoComplete, 238–239
formula bar, **208**
Formula Builder, 112, 238–239, 244–245
function(s)
    categories of, 239
    complex, **235**
    described, **235**
    understanding, 238–239
FV function, 239

▶ **G**

GIF (Graphics Interchange Format), **312**
gigahertz (GHz), **5**
Google, 94–95
grammar checking, 146–147

graphic(s). *See also* clip art; images; SmartArt
    borders, 194–195
    card, **8**
    display, for monitors, 8
    shading, 194–195
    software, 24
gridlines, 186, 224, 260, 268–269

▶ **H**

handheld computers
    described, **2**
    information management software and, 24–25
handout(s)
    described, **300**
    presentations and, 298, 300–301
    printing, 300–301
hard copy, **8**, 66
hard disks, **14**, 57
hardware. *See also* specific devices
    described, **4–5**
    specifications, 4
HD-DVD discs, 14
headers and footers, 93, 192–193, 222–223, 298–299, 338
help, 120–121, 238
    described, **46–47**
    opening, 46
    Safari and, 96–97
hits, 94
home folder, 61
home pages, setting, 87. *See also* Web pages
horizontal scroll bar, 84–85
HTML (HyperText Markup Language), 147
HTTP (HyperText Transfer Protocol), 85, 86
HYPERLINK function, 239
hyperlinks. *See* links

▶ **I**

iCal, 38–46
iChat, 62
icon view, 62–63
IF function, 239
iMac (Apple)
    monitor, 9
    ports, 17
image(s). *See also* clip art; graphics
    borders, 194–195
    formats, 312
    shading, 194–195
    sizing/positioning, 311, 314–315
indent(s)
    described, **168**
    first line, **168–169**
    hanging, **168–169**, 170
    right, **168–169**
information management software, 24, 25
infrared technology, 18
inkjet printers, 8–9
input. *See also* I/O (input/output)
    described, 4, 22–23
    devices, 4, 6–7
insertion point, 108–109
integration, 24
Internet, use of the term, **82**
Internet Explorer browser (Microsoft), 82. *See also* browsers
intranets, 82

I/O (input/output), **22–23**. *See also* input; output
iPhone (Apple), 2–3
italic text, 160–161, 292–293

▶ **J**

JPEG (Joint Photographics Expert Group) format, 312

▶ **K**

keyboard(s). *See also* keyboard shortcuts
    described, **6–7**
    ergonomic, 6–7
    ports, 17
keyboard shortcuts
    described, **43**
    copying text with, 138
    entering data with, 211
    formatting cells with, 220
    moving text with, 140
    selecting cells with, 209
keywords
    described, **46**
    help and, 46, 47
kilobytes (KB), **10**

▶ **L**

label(s)
    alignment, 218–219
    charts and, 268
    described, 210–211
landscape orientation, 92, 93, 224
LANs (local area networks), 16, 18
laptop computers. *See* notebook computers
laser printers, 8–9
launching programs, 109–110
LCDs (liquid crystal displays), 8–9. *See also* screens
ledger sheets, **240**
legend, **260**, 264–265, 268–269
Leopard (Mac OS X v10.5.6)
    file management and, 57–80
    launching programs with, 38–39
    sessions, ending, 48–49
    starting, 22–23, 34–35
Library of Congress Web site, 86–87
line(s)
    grid-, 186, 224, 260, 268–269
    spacing, 162–163
    width, 185
line charts, 261, 262–263
link(s). *See also* linked data; linked files; URLs (Uniform Resource Locators)
    described, **82**
    navigating the Web with, 82–83, 86–87
    OLE and, **24**
linked data
    described, **345**
    updating, 346–347
linked files, 317, 344–345
linked objects, 24, 345–346
list(s)
    bulleted, **144–145**, 170–171, 290–291, 342–343
    numbered, 170–171
    view, 62–63
logging in, 21
logging out, 48–49
logical functions, 229
lookup functions, 229

►M

MacBook, 2–3
Macintosh HD icon, 34–36
magnetic storage devices, 14–15
mail merge, **348**, 349–351
Mail Merge manager, 348
mainframe computers, 2
malware, 20
margin(s)
    described, **162**
    Excel and, 224
    printing and, 224
    Word and, 162–165
mathematical
    functions, 229
    operators, 236–237
MAX function, 241, 244–245
megabytes (MB), 10
megahertz (MHz), 5
memory
    capacity (storage capacity), 12
    described, **12–13**
    scanners and, 6
    shut down operations and, 48
    types of, 12–13
menu(s). *See also* menu bar
    customizing, 110–111
    described, **42–43**
    shortcut, **36**, 37
menu bar. *See also* menus
    described, **42–43**, 84–85, 108
    help and, 46
    Safari and, 84–85
microphone(s)
    described, 6
    ports, 17
microprocessor(s)
    described, **4–5**
    speeds, 5
    system resources and, 22
Microsoft Excel. *See* Excel (Microsoft)
Microsoft Office Web site, 312
Microsoft PowerPoint. *See* PowerPoint (Microsoft)
Microsoft Windows. *See* Windows (Microsoft)
Microsoft Word. *See* Word (Microsoft)
MIDI (Musical Instrument Digital Interface) cards, 16
Mighty Mouse, 36–37
MIN function, 241, 244–245
Minimize button, 40, 108–109
MLA (Modern Language Association) style, 190
modem(s)
    conversion of data by, 19
    described, **10**
    Ethernet ports and, 16
modifier keys, 43
monitor(s). *See also* screens
    described, **8–9**
    ports, 17
    resolution, **6–8**, 182, APP-6
    starting Leopard and, 34
Mosaic browser, 82. *See also* browsers
motherboard, **4**, 17
mouse, 6–7
movies, previewing, 316
MP3 players, 2–3
multimedia authoring software, 24
multitasking, 40

►N

name box, 208
National Science Foundation, 82
Netscape Navigator browser, 82. *See also* browsers
network(s)
    described, **18**, 82
    overview, 18–19
    software, **18**
NFSNET, 82
NICs (network interface cards), 18
Normal view, 286–287, 318, 322–323
NOT function, 239
notebook computers
    described, **2**
    pointing devices for, 6–7
Notebook Layout view, 136, **148**
notes. *See* speaker notes
Notes pane, **286–287**, 324–325
Notes pages, 300
NOW function, 239
numbered lists, 170–171
numeric keypad, 7, 211

►O

object(s)
    adding, 310–311
    aligning/positioning, 294–295
    animating, 322–323
    linked, 24, 345–346
Object Palette, 112–113, 310, 312
OLE (object linking and embedding), 24
operating environment, 22
operating systems, 22–23, 33. *See also* Leopard (Mac OS X v10.5)
optical storage devices, 14
Option button, 44
Outline tab, 286–287
Outline view, **148**, 338, 339
outlines
    creating, 338
    described, **300**
    printing, 300
output, **4**. *See also* I/O (input/output); output devices
output devices
    described, **4**
    examining, 8–9

►P

page break(s)
    described, **194**
    hard, **194**
    soft, **194**
page numbers, 164–165, 222–223
PANs (personal area networks), 18
paragraph(s)
    described, **162**
    fill color options, 194–195
    formatting, 162–163
    indents and, 168–169
    tabs and, 166–167
parentheses, 238
passwords, 21, 22, 34
PC Cards, 16
PCs (personal computers), 2
PDF (Portable Document Format), 93, 224, 300–301
peer-to-peer networks, 18

peripheral devices, 4
pharming, 20
phishing, **20**
photo editing software, 24
pie charts
    creating, 272–273
    described, **261**
pixels, 8
placeholders, 348–349
Places group, 60
plot areas, 260
PMT function, 238, 239
PNG (Portable Network Graphics), 312
pointer(s)
    described, **6**, 36
    shapes, list of, 36
pointing, use of the term, **37**
pointing devices
    described, **6–7**
    using, 36–36
pointing stick, 6–7
pop-up(s)
    described, 94
    menu arrows, **44–45**
port(s)
    described, **16**, 17
    parallel, **16**
portrait orientation, 93, 250
Power button, 34
PowerPoint (Microsoft). *See also* presentations; slides
    described, **106–107**, 285
    launching, 286
    overview, 285–308
    speaker notes, **324–325**
presentation(s). *See also* PowerPoint (Microsoft); slide shows
    converting, to PDF format, 300–301
    creating new, 288–289
    customizing, 318–319, 341
    polishing, 309–334
    printing, 300–301
    running, 309–334
    saving, for the Web, 340–341
    software, 24, 106–107, 285
    speaker notes, **324–325**
    timing settings, 320–321
    transition settings, 320–321
    viewing, 286–287
Print dialog box, 92–93, 148–149, 224–225, 300–301, 324
Print Layout view, 136, 192–193
    described, **148**
    formatting text in, 144–145
Print Preview, 92, 148–149, 224
printer(s). *See also* Print Preview; printing
    described, **8–9**
    ports, 17
printing. *See also* Print Preview; printers
    charts, 274–275
    filtering data and, 250–251
    headers/footers and, 192–193
    mail merge and, 350
    margins and, 164
    merged letters, 351
    notes, 324
    orientation, 92, 93, 224
    previewing, 66–67
    Web pages, 92–93

processing
  described, **4**
  investigating, 10–11
program(s). *See also* software
  described, **4**, 106
  opening help for, 46
  starting, 38–39, 108–109
programming languages, 22
Project Gallery, **118–119**, 286–287
protocols, 16, 85, 86
Publishing Layout view, 120, **148**

►Q

Quick Look view, 62–63
Quick Styles, 270–271, 294–295, 310. *See also* styles
Quick Tables, 114–115, **182–187**. *See also* tables

►R

radar charts, **261**
RAM (random access memory), 15, 64, 116
  cache, 12
  cards, 13
  described, **12–13**
  upgrades, 13
ranges, of cells, **218–219**, 236–237
receivers, **16**
record(s)
  use of the term, **24**
  viewing, in data sources, 348
reference
  functions, 229
  marks, **190–191**
Reference Tools, 112, 143, 147
REPLACE function, 239
Restart option, **48–49**
right-clicking, **36**, 37
ROM (read-only memory), **12**
routers, **20**
row(s)
  borders, 186
  deleting, 184–185
  formatting, 216–217
  headings, 216
  height, 212–213
  inserting, 184–185
  selecting, 209
  sorting, 248–249
ROW function, 239
RTF (Rich Text Format), 338
rulers, 168, 170

►S

Safari browser (Apple), 81–104, 340–341. *See also* browsers
  described, **82–83**
  exploring, 84–85
  help, 96–97
  home page settings, 87
  printing Web pages with, 92–93
  quitting, 88, 96–97
  starting, 84–85
  viewing Web pages with, 86–87
  Web searches and, 94–95
Save As dialog box, 64–65, 116–119, 132–133, 340
scanners, **6**
Scrapbook, 112, 138–139

screen(s). *See also* monitors
  resolution, **6–8**, 182, APP-6
  saver settings, **APP-2–3**
  size, **8**
  starting, **22–23**
ScreenTips, 86, 110, 120–121
Scroll
  box, **84–85**
  wheel, **6–7**
SCSI (small computer system interface) ports, **16**
SDRAM (synchronous dynamic random access memory), **12**
search engines, **82–83**, 94–95
Search field, 70–71, 84–85, 94
Search For group, 60
security
  firewalls, **20**, 21
  overview, 20–21
  passwords, **21**, 22, 34
  pop-ups and, 95
  viruses, **20**, 22
sender, use of the term, **16**
serial values, 243
servers
  described, **18–19**
  DNS, **20**
  as terminal emulators, 2
service agreements, 312
sessions, ending, 48–49
shading effects, 194–195, 220–221
shadow effects, 160, 270–271, 312–313
shapes, adding, 309–311. *See also* objects
Shared group, 60
shortcut menus, 36, 37
Shut Down option, 48–49
sidebar, 132
single-core processors, **5**
size control, 60
sleep settings, **48–49**, APP-8–9
slide(s). *See also* slide shows
  adding text to, 290–291
  created from Word documents, 338–339
  described, **285**
  drawing on, 318–319
  inserting charts in, 336–337
  moving between, 287
  printing, 300–301
  timing settings, 320–321
  titles, **290–291**
slide master, 298
Slide Show view, **286–287**
slide shows. *See also* presentations; slides
  customizing, 318–319
  headers and footers for, 298–299
  navigating, 287
  text boxes in, 293–294
Slide Sorter view, **286–287**
Slides tab, **286–287**, 310
SLN function, 239
small caps, 160
SmartArt, 114, 120, 187, 296–297
software. *See also* programs; *specific software*
  described, **4–5**
  updates, checking for, APP-14–15
sort criteria, 248–249
Sort dialog box, 248–249
sorting data, **235**, 248, 250, 350

sound. *See also* speakers
  adding, to presentations, 316–317
  alert, **APP-16**
  options, **APP-16**
source files, 24, 344
speaker(s). *See also* sound
  described, **8**
  ports, 17
speaker notes, 324–325
spell checking, 24, 25, 146–147
spin box, 44–45
spoofed sites, 20
spreadsheet(s). *See also* Excel (Microsoft)
  described, **207**
  programs, 24, 106–107
  virtual memory and, 13
spyware, **20**
stacks, 71
standalone computers, 18
Standard toolbar, **108–112**, 120
starting screen, **22–23**
statistical functions, 244–245
status bar
  described, **60**, 84–85, 108, 142
  hiding/displaying, 84–85
stock charts, **261**
storage devices, 57
storage media, **13–14**
SUM function, 238, 239, 240–241
supercomputers, 2–3
surface charts, **261**
system
  preferences, setting, APP-1–16
  resources, 22
  software, use of the term, **22–23**

►T

tab(s). *See also* tabbed browsing
  bar, **84–85**
  described, **44**, 166–167
  indicators, 166
  stops, **166–167**
tabbed browsing, 84–85, 88–89
table(s). *See also* columns; QuickTables; rows
  borders, 185, 186
  clip art and, 188–189
  creating, 182–183
  described, **182**
  drawing, with the Draw Table command, 185
  formatting, 186–187
  resizing, 186
tablet PCs, **2**
tape storage, **14**
templates, 10, 118–119, 298
terabytes (TB), **10**
terminal(s)
  described, **2**
  emulators, **2**
text. *See also* fonts; paragraphs; text boxes
  adding, to shapes, 309–310
  copying, **138–139**
  deleting, 136
  editing, **136–137**
  entering, 134–135
  finding and replacing, 142–143
  formatting, **66–67**, 144–145, 292–293
  inserting, into open documents, 342–343
  justified, 162–163

moving, **140–141**
selecting, **136–137**, 216
shading, 194–195
text boxes, 44–45, 293–294, 296–297
theme(s), 288–289, 338
working with, 196–197
colors, 270–271
custom, 295
described, **196–197**
fonts and, 292–293
slide master and, 298
thumbnails, **188–189**, 320
time
functions, 229, 242–243
system, changing, APP-10–11
Time Machine, **12–13**
timing settings, 320–321
title bar
described, **60–61**, 108–109
minimizing windows and, 40
TODAY function, 239, 242–243
toolbar(s)
control, **60–61**
customizing, 110–111
described, **60–61**, 84–85, 108–109
Toolbox
activating palettes in, 144
described, **112–113**
top-level domains, **85**
totals, 248–249
trackball, **6–7**
trackpad, **6–7**, 37
transition settings, 320–321
Translate tool, 147
Trash
described, **72–73**
emptying, 72–73

▶U

underlined text, 160–161
Undo feature, 136, 166, 168, 248, 264
University of Illinois, 82
updates, checking for, APP-14–15
URLs (Uniform Resource Locators). *See also* links
described, **84–85**
home page settings and, 87
parts of, 85
spoofing and, 20
U.S. Government Web site, 88–89
USB (Universal Serial Bus)
connectors, 16, **17**
flash drives, **14–15**, 61, 64, 68–69
ports, 16
utilities, **22**

▶V

value(s)
charts and, 261
complex formulas and, 236–237

described, **210**
entering, 210–211
value axis. *See* y-axis
vertical scroll bar, **84–85**
video(s)
adding, 316–317
cards, **8**
display adapters, **8**
view(s)
buttons, **132**
changing, 62–63
described, **62**
presentations and, 286–287
switching, 286
virtual memory, **12–13**
viruses, 20, 22

▶W

WANs (wide-area networks), **18**
Web Archive files, 96
Web browsers. *See* browsers; Safari browser (Apple)
Web Layout view, 136, **148**
Web page(s). *See also* Web sites
copying information from, 92
described, **82–83**
navigating, 86–87
printing, 92–93
saving, 96
viewing, 86–87
Web site(s). *See also* Web pages
creation software, **24**
described, 82–83
management software, 24
WEEKDAY function, 239
what-if analysis, **216–217**
White House Web site, 82–83
Wi-Fi (wireless fidelity), **18**
WiMAX (Worldwide Interoperability for Microwave Access), **18**
window(s)
control buttons, 40
described, **33**
inactive, **40**
moving, 40–41
resizing, 40–41
Windows (Microsoft), **22**
WLANs (wireless local area network), **18**
word
count, 134
size, **5**
wrap, 218, 324
Word (Microsoft)
adding special elements with, 181–206
creating/saving documents with, 64–65, 131–156
data sources and, 348, 350
described, **106–107**
documents, creating slides from, 338–339
editing text with, 136–137
enhancing documents with, 157–180

entering text with, 134–135
file searches and, 70–71
finding and replacing text with, 142–143
formatting text with, 144–145
help, 46
inserting text from, 342–343
linked data and, 344–346
menus, 110–111
outlines, 338
previewing documents with, 148–149
printing documents with, 148–149
selecting text with, 136–137
starting, 108–109
styles and, 172–173
tabs and, 166–167
toolbars, 110–111
WordArt, 114, 270
word-processing programs, 106–107
workbook(s). *See also* worksheets
conditional formatting and, 246–247
described, **207**
exporting, as PDF documents, 224
navigating, 208–209
printing, 274–275
saving, 224
worksheets. *See also* workbooks
adding, to workbooks, 208–209
conditional formatting and, 246–247
described, **24**, 25, 207
editing, 216–217
entering values in, 210–211
labels and, 210–211
overview, 207–234
printing, 224–225
protecting, 218
selecting, 209
sorting rows in, 248–249
workstation(s)
described, **18–19**
as terminal emulators, 2
World Wide Web. *See also* browsers; Web pages; Web sites
described, **82–83**
saving presentations for, 340–341

▶X

X Y (scatter) charts, 261
x-axis, **260**, 262
XML (Extensible Markup Language), 117

▶Y

y-axis, **260**

▶Z

Zoom button, 40, 108–109